Exam 70-647: Pro: Windows Server 2008, Enterprise Administrator

OBJECTIVE	CHAPTER	LESSON
PLANNING NETWORK AND APPLICATION SERVICES (23 PERCENT)		
Plan for name resolution and IP addressing.	Chapter 1	Lesson 1, 2
Design for network access.	Chapter 5	Lesson 1, 2
Plan for application delivery.	Chapter 7	Lesson 2
Plan for Remote Desktop Services.	Chapter 7	Lesson 1
DESIGNING CORE IDENTITY AND ACCESS MANAGEMENT COMPONENTS (25 PERCENT)		
Design Active Directory forests and domains.	Chapter 2	Lesson 1
Design the Active Directory physical topology.	Chapter 2	Lesson 2
Design the Active Directory administrative model.	Chapter 4	Lesson 1
Design the enterprise-level group policy strategy.	Chapter 4	Lesson 2
DESIGNING SUPPORT IDENTITY AND ACCESS MANAGEMENT COMPONENTS (29 PERCENT)		
Plan for domain or forest migration, upgrade, and restructuring.	Chapter 3	Lesson 1
Design the branch office deployment.	Chapter 6	Lesson 1, 2
Design and implement public key infrastructure.	Chapter 10	Lesson 1, 2
Plan for interoperability.	Chapter 3	Lesson 2
DESIGNING FOR BUSINESS CONTINUITY AND DATA AVAILABILITY (23 PERCENT)		
Plan for business continuity.	Chapter 9	Lesson 3
Design for software updates and compliance management.	Chapter 11	Lesson 1, 2
Design the operating system virtualization strategy.	Chapter 8	Lesson 1, 2
Design for data management and data access.	Chapter 2, 4	Lesson 1, 1

Exam Objectives   The exam objectives listed here are current as of this book's publication date. Exam objectives are subject to change at any time without prior notice and at Microsoft's sole discretion. Please visit the Microsoft Learning website for the most current listing of exam objectives: http://www.microsoft.com/learning/en/us/Exam .aspx?ID=70-647.

Microsoft

MCITP Self-Paced Training Kit (Exam 70-647): Windows Server® 2008 Enterprise Administrator (2nd Edition)

David R. Miller
Paul Mancuso
John Policelli
Orin Thomas
Ian McLean
J.C. Mackin
with GrandMasters

PUBLISHED BY
Microsoft Press
A Division of Microsoft Corporation
One Microsoft Way
Redmond, Washington 98052-6399

Library of Congress Control Number: 2011924627
ISBN: 978-0-7356-5665-9

Printed and bound in the United States of America.

First Printing

Microsoft Press books are available through booksellers and distributors worldwide. If you need support related to this book, email Microsoft Press Book Support at mspinput@microsoft.com. Please tell us what you think of this book at http://www.microsoft.com/learning/booksurvey.

Acquisitions Editor: Jeff Koch
Developmental Editor: Karen Szall
Project Editor: Carol Dillingham
Editorial Production: nSight, Inc.
Technical Reviewer: Bob Hogan; Technical Review services provided by Content Master, a member of CM Group, Ltd.
Copyeditor: Teresa Horton
Indexer: Lucie Haskins
Cover: Twist Creative • Seattle

I dedicate this, and each of my books, to my daughter, Veronica, and my son, Ross. With all my love, appreciation, and admiration.

—DAVID R. MILLER

I would like to dedicate my contribution to this book to my loving wife, Yaneth, and wonderfully musical son, Anthony. Thank you both for all of your love and support.

—PAUL MANCUSO

This book is dedicated to my beautiful wife, Maria. Your continued love and support means the world to me, and I wouldn't be where I am today without you.

—JOHN POLICELLI

Contents at a Glance

Contents

What do you think of this book? We want to hear from you!

Microsoft is interested in hearing your feedback so we can continually improve our
books and learning resources for you. To participate in a brief online survey, please visit:

www.microsoft.com/learning/booksurvey/

Chapter 10 Planning and Designing a Public Key Infrastructure   451

Chapter 11 Designing Software Update Infrastructure and Managing Compliance   491

What do you think of this book? We want to hear from you!

Microsoft is interested in hearing your feedback so we can continually improve our
books and learning resources for you. To participate in a brief online survey, please visit:

www.microsoft.com/learning/booksurvey/

Introduction

This training kit is designed for enterprise administrators who have several years' experience managing the overall IT environment and architecture of medium to large organizations and who plan to take the Microsoft Certified Information Technology Professional (MCITP) 70-647 exam. As an enterprise administrator, you likely are responsible for translating business goals into technology decisions and designs and for developing mid-range and long-term strategies. You are responsible for making key decisions and recommendations about network infrastructure, directory services, identity management, security policies, business continuity, IT administrative structure, best practices, standards, and Service Level Agreements (SLAs). Your job role involves 20 percent operations, 60 percent engineering, and 20 percent support tasks. The Preparation Guide for Exam 70-647 is available at *http://www.microsoft.com/learning/en/us/exam.aspx?ID=70-647*.

By using this training kit, you learn how to do the following:

- Plan network and application services.
- Design core identity and access management components.
- Design support identity and access management components.
- Design for business continuity and data availability.

Refer to the objective mapping page in the front of the book to see where in the book each exam objective is covered.

Lab Setup Instructions

The exercises in this training kit require a minimum of two computers or virtual machines:

- One server running Windows Server 2008 R2 Enterprise configured as a domain controller.
- One computer running Windows Vista (Enterprise, Business, or Ultimate). (Windows 7 Pro, Enterprise, or Ultimate may be used; however, dialogs may be slightly different than described or shown.)

You can obtain an evaluation version of Windows Server 2008 R2 Enterprise from the Microsoft download center at *http://www.microsoft.com/downloads/en/default.aspx*.

All computers in these lab exercises must be connected to the same network. It is recommended that you use an isolated network that is not part of your production network to do the practice exercises in this book. To minimize the time and expense of configuring physical computers, using virtual machines is recommended. To run computers as virtual machines within Windows, you can use Virtual PC 2007, Virtual Server 2005 R2, Hyper-V, or third-party virtual machine software. To download any of these virtual platforms, visit the Microsoft Download Center at *http://www.microsoft.com/downloads/en/default.aspx*.

Hardware Requirements

You can complete almost all practice exercises in this book by using virtual machines rather than real server hardware. The minimum and recommended hardware requirements for Windows Server 2008 and Windows Server 2008 R2 are listed in the following tables:

TABLE I-1 Windows Server 2008 Minimum Hardware Requirements

HARDWARE COMPONENT	MINIMUM REQUIREMENTS	RECOMMENDED
Processor	1GHz (x86), 1.4GHz (x64)	2GHz or faster
RAM	512 MB	2 GB
Disk Space	15 GB	40 GB

TABLE I-2 Windows Server 2008 R2 Minimum Hardware Requirements

HARDWARE COMPONENT	MINIMUM REQUIREMENTS	RECOMMENDED
Processor	1.4GHz (x64) or 1.3GHz (x64 Dual Core)	2GHz or faster
RAM	512 MB	2 GB
Disk Space	32 GB	80 GB

If you intend to implement several virtual machines on the same computer (recommended), a higher specification will enhance your user experience. In particular, a computer with 4 GB of RAM and 100 GB of free disk space can host all the virtual machines specified for all the practice exercises in this book.

Preparing the Computer Running Windows Server 2008 R2 Enterprise

Detailed instructions for preparing for Windows Server 2008 R2 installation and installing and configuring the Windows Server 2008 R2 Enterprise domain controller are given in Chapter 1, "Planning Name Resolution and Internet Protocol Addressing." The required server roles are added in the practice exercises in subsequent chapters.

Preparing the Computer Running Windows Vista or Windows 7

Perform the following steps to prepare your computer running Windows Vista or Windows 7 for the exercises in this training kit.

Check Operating System Version Requirements

In System Control Panel (found in the System And Maintenance category), verify that the operating system version is Windows Vista or Windows 7 (Enterprise, Business, Professional, or Ultimate). If necessary, choose the option to upgrade to one of these versions.

Name the Computer

In System Control Panel, specify the computer name as **Melbourne**.

Configure Networking

To configure networking, carry out the following tasks:

1. In Control Panel, click Set Up File Sharing.
2. In Network And Sharing Center, verify that the network is configured as a Private network and that File Sharing is enabled.
3. In Network And Sharing Center, click Manage Network Connections.
4. In Network Connections, open the properties of the Local Area Connection. Specify a static IPv4 address that is on the same subnet as the domain controller.

   For example, the setup instructions for the domain controller specify an IPv4 address 10.0.0.11. If you use this address, you can configure the client computer with an IP address of 10.0.0.21. The subnet mask is 225.225.225.0, and the Domain Name System (DNS) address is the IPv4 address of the domain controller. You do not require a default gateway. You can choose other network addresses if you want to, provided that the client and server are on the same subnet.

Using the CD

The companion CD included with this training kit contains the following:

- **Practice tests**   You can reinforce your understanding of how to configure Windows Vista and Windows 7 by using electronic practice tests you customize to meet your needs from the pool of Lesson Review questions in this book, or you can practice for the 70-647 certification exam by using tests created from a pool of 200 realistic exam questions to ensure that you are prepared.

- **An eBook** An electronic version of this book is included for when you do not want to carry the printed book with you. The eBook is available in two formats: Portable Document Format (PDF), which can be viewed by using Adobe Acrobat or Adobe Reader, and XML Paper Specification (XPS).

How to Install the Practice Tests

To install the practice test software from the companion CD to your hard disk, do the following:

1. Insert the companion CD into your CD drive and accept the license agreement. A CD menu appears.

> **NOTE** IF THE CD MENU DOES NOT APPEAR
>
> If the CD menu or the license agreement does not appear, AutoRun might be disabled on your computer. Refer to the Readme.txt file on the CD-ROM for alternative installation instructions.

2. Click Practice Tests and follow the instructions on the screen.

How to Use the Practice Tests

To start the practice test software, follow these steps:

1. Click Start, click All Programs, and then select Microsoft Press Training Kit Exam Prep.

   A window appears that shows all the Microsoft Press training kit exam prep suites installed on your computer.

2. Double-click the lesson review or practice test you want to use.

> **NOTE** LESSON REVIEWS VS. PRACTICE TESTS
>
> Select the (70-647) Windows Server 2008 Enterprise Administrator (2nd Edition) lesson review to use the questions from the "Lesson Review" sections of this book. Select the (70-647) Windows Server 2008 Enterprise Administrator (2nd Edition) practice test to use a pool of 200 questions similar to those that appear on the 70-647 certification exam.

Lesson Review Options

When you start a lesson review, the Custom Mode dialog box appears so that you can configure your test. You can click OK to accept the default settings, or you can customize the number of questions you want, how the practice test software works, the exam objectives to which you want the questions to relate, and whether you want your lesson review to be timed. If you are retaking a test, you can select whether you want to see all the questions again or only the questions you missed or did not answer.

After you click OK, your lesson review starts.

- To take the test, answer the questions and use the *Next* and *Previous* buttons to move from question to question.

- After you answer an individual question, if you want to see which answers are correct—along with an explanation of each answer—click Explanation.

- If you prefer to wait until the end of the test to see how you did, answer all the questions, and then click Score Test. You will see a summary of the exam objectives you chose and the percentage of questions you got right overall and per objective. You can print a copy of your test, review your answers, or retake the test.

Practice Test Options

When you start a practice test, you choose whether to take the test in Certification Mode, Study Mode, or Custom Mode.

- **Certification Mode** Closely resembles the experience of taking a certification exam. The test has a set number of questions. It is timed, and you cannot pause and restart the timer.

- **Study Mode** Creates an untimed test during which you can review the correct answers and the explanations after you answer each question.

- **Custom Mode** Gives you full control over the test options so that you can customize them as you like.

In all modes, the user interface when you are taking the test is basically the same, but has different options enabled or disabled, depending on the mode. The main options are discussed in the previous section, "Lesson Review Options."

When you review your answer to an individual practice test question, a "References" section is provided that lists where in the training kit you can find the information that relates to that question and provides links to other sources of information. After you click Test Results to score your entire practice test, you can click the Learning Plan tab to see a list of references for every objective.

How to Uninstall the Practice Tests

To uninstall the practice test software for a training kit, use the Programs And Features option in Windows Control Panel.

Acknowledgments

David Miller would like to acknowledge his coauthors, Paul Mancuso and John Policelli. Great job, guys. I am proud to be working with you. Thank you both.

All the authors would like to acknowledge and thank the talented teams from GrandMasters, LLC, and Microsoft Press for their tireless pursuit of accuracy, precision, and clarity. Thank you for your assistance, your support, and your skillful efforts.

Lastly, the authors would like to acknowledge and thank you, the reader, for your desire for self-improvement and your faith in us to produce a resource worthy of your time and consumption. We've done our best to make this book a powerful asset in your efforts to be a better IT professional. We hope you find it so. Thank you.

Support & Feedback

The following sections provide information on errata, book support, feedback, and contact information.

Errata

We've made every effort to ensure the accuracy of this book and its companion content. Any errors that have been reported since this book was published are listed on our Microsoft Press site at oreilly.com:

http://go.microsoft.com/FWLink/?Linkid=219405

If you find an error that is not already listed, you can report it to us through the same page.

If you need additional support, please email Microsoft Press Book Support at *mspinput@microsoft.com*.

Please note that product support for Microsoft software is not offered through the addresses above.

We Want to Hear from You

At Microsoft Press, your satisfaction is our top priority, and your feedback our most valuable asset. Please tell us what you think of this book at *http://www.microsoft.com/learning /booksurvey*.

The survey is short, and we read *every one* of your comments and ideas. Thanks in advance for your input!

Stay in Touch

Let's keep the conversation going! We're on Twitter: *http://twitter.com/MicrosoftPress*.

Preparing for the Exam

Microsoft certification exams are a great way to build your resume and let the world know about your level of expertise. Certification exams validate your on-the-job experience and product knowledge. Although there is no substitute for on-the-job experience, preparation through study and hands-on practice can help you prepare for the exam. We recommend that you augment your exam preparation plan by using a combination of available study materials and courses. For example, you might use the Training Kit and another study guide for your "at home" preparation, and take a Microsoft Official Curriculum course for the classroom experience. Choose the combination that you think works best for you.

Microsoft
C E R T I F I E D
IT Professional

CHAPTER 1

Planning Name Resolution and Internet Protocol Addressing

As an enterprise administrator, you will be responsible for the overall IT environment and architecture within your organization. Enterprise administrators translate business goals into technology decisions; design midrange to long-term strategies; and make key decisions and recommendations about, for example, network infrastructure, directory services, security policies, business continuity, administrative structure, best practices, standards, and service-level agreements (SLAs).

IMPORTANT

Have you read page xxii?

It contains valuable information regarding the skills you need to pass the exam.

The enterprise administrator is responsible for infrastructure design and global configuration changes. If you intend to extend your career and become an enterprise administrator, or if you already carry out enterprise administrator tasks and want to acquire a certification that matches your experience, you will already be an experienced network and server administrator with typically two or more years' experience administering corporate networks. The 70-647 exam is not designed for beginners, nor is this training kit. Only 20 percent of the 70-647 exam focuses on your skills in performing tasks; it is primarily focused on strategic planning and designing Microsoft Windows Server 2008 R2 technologies to satisfy the information technology needs of the business.

As an experienced administrator, you will almost certainly be familiar with name resolution and Internet Protocol version 4 (IPv4) addressing. You will probably have come across Internet Protocol version 6 (IPv6) addresses but might not be familiar with them. This chapter does not attempt to cover old ground but, rather, looks at the new features and approaches implemented in Windows Server 2008 R2.

Exam objectives in this chapter:

- Plan for name resolution and IP addressing.

Lessons in this chapter:

Before You Begin

To complete the lessons in this chapter, you must have done the following:

- Installed Windows Server 2008 R2 Enterprise on a server configured as a domain controller in the *contoso.internal* domain. Active Directory–integrated Domain Name System (DNS) is installed by default on the first domain controller in a domain. The computer name is Glasgow. Configure a static IPv4 address of 10.0.0.11 with a subnet mask 255.255.255.0. The IPv4 address of the DNS server is 10.0.0.11. Other than IPv4 configuration and the computer name, accept all the default installation settings. You can obtain an evaluation version of the Windows Server 2008 R2 Enterprise software from the Microsoft Download Center at *http://technet.microsoft.com/en-us/evalcenter /default.aspx*.

- Installed Windows 7 Business, Enterprise, or Ultimate on a client computer joined to the *contoso.internal* domain. The computer name is Melbourne. Initially, this computer should have a static IPv4 address of 10.0.0.21 with a subnet mask 255.255.255.0. The IPv4 address of the DNS server is 10.0.0.11. You can obtain evaluation software that enables you to implement the Windows 7 Enterprise 30-day evaluation edition at *http://technet.microsoft.com/en-us/evalcenter/default.aspx*.

- Created a user account with the username Kim_Akers and password P@ssw0rd. Add this account to the Domain Admins, Enterprise Admins, and Schema Admins groups.

- It's recommended that you use an isolated network that is not part of your production network to do the practice exercises in this book. Internet access is not required for the exercises, and you do not need to configure a default gateway. To minimize the time and expense of configuring physical computers, it's recommended that you use virtual machines. To run computers as virtual machines within Windows, you can use Virtual PC 2007, Virtual Server 2005 R2, Hyper-V Server 2008 R2, or third-party virtual machine software. To download Virtual PC 2007, visit *http://www.microsoft.com/downloads/en/details.aspx?FamilyId=04D26402-3199 -48A3-AFA2-2DC0B40A73B6&displaylang=en.*

■ To download Virtual Server 2005 R2 or Hyper-V Server 2008 R2, visit *http://www .microsoft.com/windowsserversystem/virtualserver/downloads.aspx.*

REAL WORLD

David R. Miller

As a consultant for many years, I have been approached by many companies having unexpected networking problems. Very often, one of the main causes of the issues has been the faulty or incomplete implementation of name resolution services. The variety of peculiarities reported by users of the network is a laundry list of seemingly unrelated phenomena. From missing icons and applications on a user's desktop, to printing failures, to failed logins, and more.

Even if you run only the latest versions of the Microsoft operating systems, it is quite likely that there are NetBIOS-based applications running on the network that will periodically fail without a proper implementation of Windows Internet Name Service (WINS).

The DNS Server role in Windows Server 2008 R2 complies with all request for comments (RFCs) that define and standardize the DNS protocol. Although Microsoft's implementation of DNS should be interoperable with third-party DNS servers and appliances, very often, when DNS is causing a wrinkle in the organization, it is just this subtle difference that can mean smooth sailing for name resolution and network service location services. Often I've seen that, as the third-party DNS servers and DNS appliances are phased out, the variety of networking problems become problems of the past.

If your environment has more than a few Windows servers, you probably should be running WINS, and you should carefully plan the DNS implementation, with a preference toward using Microsoft's DNS services, which are finely tuned to support Active Directory.

Lesson 1: Planning Name Resolution

As an experienced administrator, you will have worked with DNS and with Microsoft dynamic DNS. You should also be familiar with Network Basic Input Output System (NetBIOS) names, the NetBIOS Extended User Interface (NetBEUI), and WINS. It is not, therefore, the purpose of this lesson to explain the basic operation of these features, but rather to look at Windows Server 2008 R2 enhancements, particularly to DNS, and to discuss the planning of a name resolution infrastructure across an enterprise network.

One of the first planning decisions you need to make is whether to use WINS to resolve NetBIOS names. Microsoft describes WINS as approaching obsolescence and introduced the GlobalNames DNS zone to provide single-label name resolution for large enterprise networks that might not want to deploy WINS. This was seen as a replacement for WINS, but NetBIOS name resolution is still required by many applications and legacy operating systems. For most environments, WINS is still a requirement and is, fortunately, fully supported in Windows Server 2008 R2.

When planning a DNS infrastructure, you must decide when to use Active Directory–integrated, standard primary, secondary, stub, reverse lookup, and GlobalNames DNS zones. You need to plan DNS forwarding and when to use conditional forwarding, which is especially relevant to the enterprise environment in which you can have multiple Active Directory Domain Services (AD DS) forests work in the same intranet. Windows Server 2008 R2 (and Windows Vista and Windows 7) supports IPv6 by default, and you need to understand and use the IPv6 records in DNS. The security of the DNS system has been enhanced in the release of Windows Server 2008 R2, with the addition of DNSSEC, DNS Cache Locking, and the use of nonintuitive source ports from the DNS Socket Pool.

After this lesson, you will be able to:

- Identify the role of WINS in your IT environment.
- Consider Windows Server 2008 R2 DNS features when planning your name resolution infrastructure.
- Identify Windows Server 2008 R2 enhancements to DNS and use these in your planning process.
- Determine the need for DNSSEC to provide reliable name resolution information.
- Administer DNS using the Microsoft Management Console (MMC) snap-in and command-line tools.

Estimated lesson time: 45 minutes

Planning Domain Name System Using Windows Server 2008 R2

DNS resolves hostnames to IP addresses and can also resolve IP addresses to hostnames in reverse lookup DNS zones. The Windows Server 2008 R2 DNS server role retains the features introduced by Windows Server 2003 and Windows Server 2008 DNS, including dynamic configuration and incremental zone transfer, and introduces several new features and security enhancements. Windows Server 2008 R2 provides support for IPv4, as well as for IPv6, and is nearly essential for the support of Microsoft Active Directory directory service. This section covers the enhancements to DNS introduced in Windows Server 2008 R2 and how DNS deals with IPv6 addresses.

Microsoft recommends that you use the Windows Server 2008 R2 DNS Server service to support AD DS, although other types of DNS servers can support the AD DS deployment. A feature introduced in Windows Server 2003 DNS that can take advantage of the Directory Replication Services (DRS) of AD DS is the application directory partition for replication. A partition is a data container in AD DS that holds data for replication. You can store application data in the application directory partitions of AD DS, and then you can specify which domain controllers should receive a copy of the partition using DRS.

Configuring Windows Server 2008 R2 DNS

Close integration with other Windows services, including AD DS, WINS (if enabled), and Dynamic Host Configuration Protocol (DHCP and DHCPv6) ensures that Windows Server 2008 R2 dynamic DNS requires little or no manual configuration. Computers that run the DNS Client service register their hostnames and IPv4 and IPv6 addresses (although not link-local IPv6 addresses) dynamically. You can configure the DNS Server and DNS Client services to perform secure dynamic updates. This ensures that only authenticated, domain member computers with the appropriate rights can update resource records on the DNS server.

> **MORE INFO** **DYNAMIC UPDATE PROTOCOL**
>
> For more information about the dynamic update protocol, see *http://www.ietf.org/rfc /rfc2136.txt* and *http://www.ietf.org/rfc/rfc3007.*

> **NOTE** **SECURE DYNAMIC UPDATES**
>
> Secure dynamic updates are available only for zones that are integrated with AD DS.

Using Stub Zones

A *stub zone*, supported in Windows Server 2008 R2 DNS, is a zone copy that contains only the resource records necessary to identify the authoritative DNS servers for that zone. This includes the SOA and NS records for a namespace or zone. A stub zone also holds the A resource records for the name servers, but not for all hosts registered in the zone. Stub zones ensure that DNS servers hosting parent zones can determine authoritative DNS servers for child zones, thus helping maintain efficient DNS name resolution. Figure 1-1 shows a stub zone specified in the New Zone Wizard.

You can use stub zones when name servers in the target zone are in transition, such as if part or all of the company network is undergoing IP address transition and accurate resolution of names is problematic. For example, Contoso, Ltd., recently acquired the sales organization Litware, Inc. Contoso and Litware have Windows Server 2008 R2 domains. The Litware DNS servers have a complex configuration with many resource records within many zones and subzones. Litware uses security controls in place to securely manage its DNS namespaces, so these DNS systems must remain intact. Also, you don't want to have to reproduce these numerous zones and controls on your DNS servers. You would configure stub zones on your DNS servers so they always know how to find the Litware DNS servers for accurate name and service resolution, even if the IP addresses of the Litware DNS servers change.

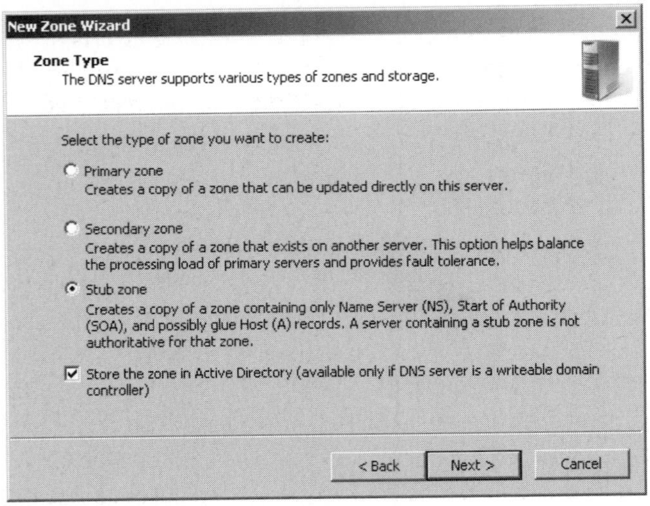

FIGURE 1-1 Creating a stub zone

In this case, your plan would include a stub zone on the Contoso DNS servers that contains resource records that identify the authoritative DNS servers for the *litware.com* domain. As the names and IP addresses of the *litware.com* DNS servers change, the stub zone on the Contoso DNS servers will be automatically updated with the changes through small zone transfers.

Stub zones are useful when child domains exist (Active Directory or namespace only). Delegation records are created in a zone for the child domain on the parent domain's DNS server. Delegation records (actually an NS and an A record for each child domain DNS server of interest) are often called *glue records* because they glue the child namespace to the parent namespace for resolution. For example, the name server for the *contoso.com* zone can delegate authority for the *sales.contoso.com* zone to a DNS server in that child domain. Then you use stub zones in child domains to hold the records for DNS servers for parent domains. You use delegation records to get resolution for names and services in child domains (delegate down), and you can use stub zones on the child domain DNS servers to perform resolutions and services in parent domains (stub up).

> **NOTE STUB ZONES REQUIRE ADMINISTRATIVE COOPERATION ON THE TARGET DNS SERVERS**
>
> The stub zone only holds a few records from the target zone. This keeps the amount of DNS zone transfer traffic to a minimum. However, the stub zone acquires those few records through zone transfers. When done securely, zone transfers must be specifically approved and configured on the source DNS server. This means that you must be able to get administrative cooperation from the source if you hope to pull a stub zone to your DNS server.

DNS Forwarding

If a DNS server does not have a zone in its database for the target host specified in a client request, it can query another (preconfigured) DNS server. When a DNS server forwards a name resolution request on behalf of a client, the upstream DNS server that hopefully can assist with the resolution is known as a *forwarder*. This process takes place recursively until either the client computer receives the IP address or the DNS server and forwarder system establishes that the queried name cannot be resolved.

The Windows 2008 R2 DNS Server service uses *conditional forwarders* to extend the standard forwarder configuration. A conditional forwarder is a DNS server that forwards DNS queries according to the DNS domain name in the query. For example, you can configure a DNS server to forward all the queries that it receives for names ending with *adatum.com* to the IP address of one or more specified DNS servers that are authoritative for the *adatum.com* domain. This feature is particularly useful on enterprise extranets, where several organizations and domains access the same private internetwork. When a Windows Server 2008 R2 DNS server receives a query for an unknown namespace, the DNS server first checks to see if the query matches conditional forwarders. If it does not, then the DNS server will recursively query the forwarder. If there is no matching conditional forwarder, and the forwarder is unable to resolve the name, if configured, the DNS server will use its root hints in its attempt to resolve the name.

When the DNS server is installed on a domain controller, it is generally recommended to remove the *root hints* from the server so the DNS server (which is also a domain controller) does not attempt to perform iterative name resolution on the Internet. These DNS servers should be configured with a forwarder, often a caching-only DNS server, to perform the iterative queries with the public root server system.

> **NOTE REPLICATING ADDITIONAL FORWARDERS**
>
> In Windows Server 2008 R2, conditional forwarding entries can be stored in AD DS and configured to replicate to all DNS servers in the forest, all DNS servers in the domain, or all domain controllers in the domain.

Figure 1-2 shows the dialog box used to create a conditional forwarder. You cannot actually configure this on your test network because you have only one DNS server.

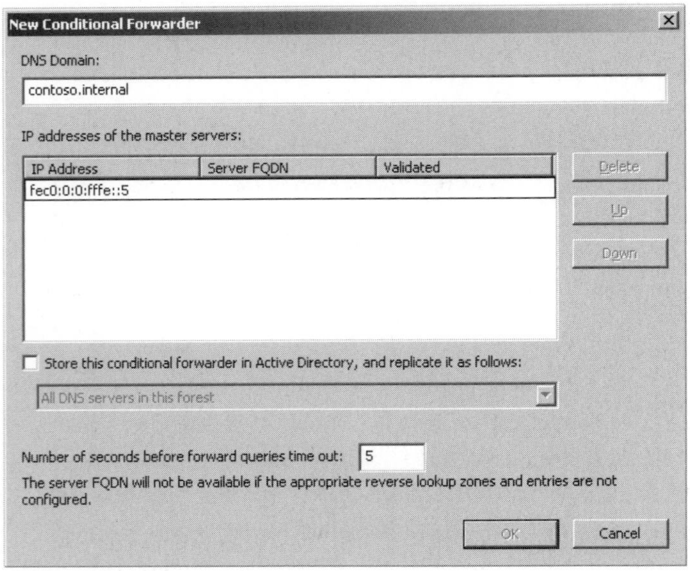

FIGURE 1-2 Specifying a conditional forwarder

Zone Transfers and Replication

Windows Server 2008 R2 DNS zones can be transferred or replicated between DNS servers for redundancy and to improve DNS name resolution efficiency. Zones are replicated to DNS servers when the zone is Active Directory–integrated and both DNS servers exist on domain controllers. Otherwise, the zone is transferred between a master and a secondary or slave DNS server. If you add a new DNS server to the network and configure it as a secondary DNS server for an existing zone, it performs a full *zone transfer* to obtain a read-only copy of all resource records in the zone. Any further changes to the authoritative zone are transferred to the secondary zone on subsequent zone refreshes. Windows Server 2003 introduced the incremental zone transfer that updates only the changes to the authoritative zone, and Windows Server 2008 R2 supports this functionality. Prior to Windows Server 2003, a full zone transfer was required, which updated all records in the authoritative DNS zone to the secondary DNS server, even if the records had not changed.

You must configure zone transfers to any DNS server, to specified DNS servers only, and to DNS servers listed on the Name Servers tab (any server that has registered an NS record). Figure 1-3 shows a DNS zone configured to allow zone transfers only to DNS servers listed on the Name Servers tab.

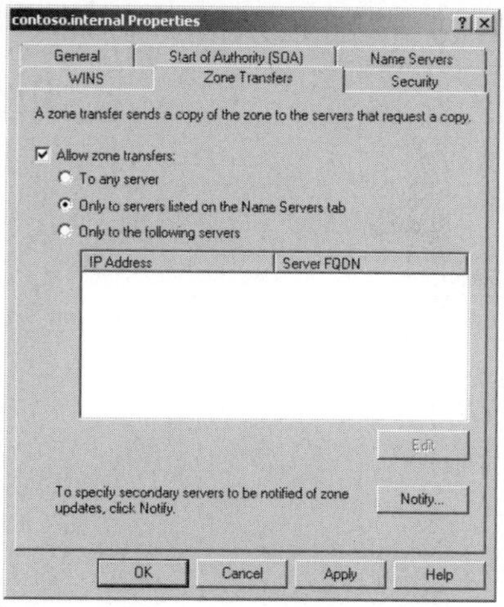

FIGURE 1-3 Configuring zone transfers

DNS Records

As a network professional, you should be familiar with standard DNS record types such as IPv4 host (A), Start of Authority (SOA), Pointer (PTR), canonical name or alias (CNAME), name server (NS), Mail Exchanger (MX), Service Location (SRV), and so on. You might use other DNS record types, such as Andrew File System Database (AFSDB) and Asynchronous Transfer Mode (ATM) address, if you are configuring compatibility with non-Windows DNS systems. If you need to create an IPv6 record for a client that cannot register itself with Active Directory, you need to create an AAAA record manually.

Administering DNS

You can use the DNS Manager MMC snap-in graphical user interface (GUI) to manage and configure the DNS Server service. Windows Server 2008 R2 also provides configuration wizards for performing common server administration tasks. Figure 1-4 shows the DNS Manager tool as well as IPv4 and IPv6 host records dynamically registered in DNS. Note that if you access this tool at this point in the lesson, IPv6 records will not be displayed because you have not yet configured IPv6 addresses. You do this in the practice session later in this lesson and in Lesson 2 of this chapter.

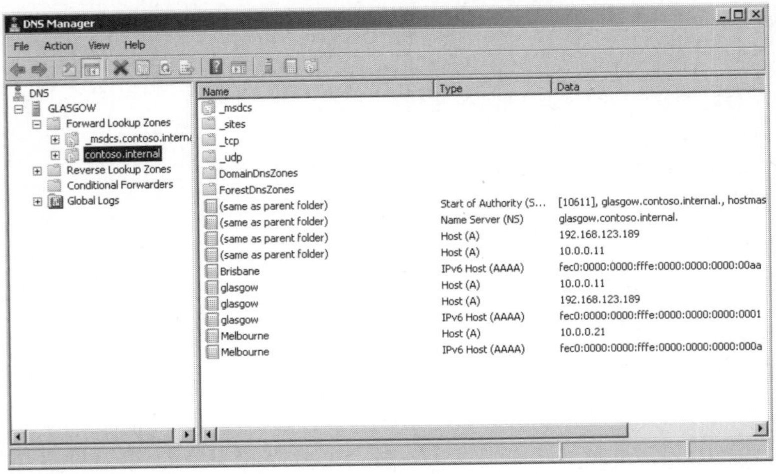

FIGURE 1-4 DNS Manager

Windows Server 2008 R2 provides command-line tools that help you better manage and support DNS servers and clients on your network. The following tools will prove helpful in configuring and administering your DNS environment. Remember to view the help on each of these commands for a list of their switches and detailed functions:

- **dnscmd**   To configure and administer the DNS service. You can manage both IPv4 and IPv6 records, create forward and reverse lookup zones, and manage application directory partitions for replication.

- **ipconfig**   To view network adapter IP configurations. You can release and renew the DHCP IPv4 and IPv6 leases bound to a network adapter. Don't forget the command *ipconfig /all* to view IP configuration.

- **nslookup**   To test the DNS service and query for record information. This command provides its own command prompt and can be used to retrieve all records for a zone by using the command *ls -d <domain name>*.

> **NOTE   NSLOOKUPLS -D <DOMAIN NAME>**
>
> This command is essentially requesting a zone transfer. For security purposes, by default, zone transfers are disabled. To make this command work correctly, you must allow zone transfers to the computer making the *nslookup* request.

- **netsh**   A diverse and powerful tool to manage network interfaces. This command also provides its own command prompt. The *netshinterface ipv6 show dnsservers* command displays IPv6 DNS configurations and indicates which DNS server addresses are statically configured.

Using New DNS Features and Enhancements

The DNS Server role in Windows Server 2008 R2 provides the following new or enhanced features:

■ The Windows Server 2008 R2 DNS Server role provides primary *read-only zones* on read-only domain controllers (RODCs). A DNS zone on an RODC is authoritative but is not dynamically updated whenever a new network entity (client, server, network printer, or network projector) is added to the domain. If a network entity is added on the same site as an RODC, the RODC can pull its corresponding DNS records from a writable domain controller, provided the writable domain controller is configured to allow this. This enables name resolution to be performed locally on a site rather than over a wide area network (WAN).

> **MORE INFO** **RODCS**
>
> For more information about RODCs, go to *http://technet2.microsoft.com /windowsserver2008/en/library/ea8d253e-0646-490c-93d3-b78c5e1d9db71033 .mspx?mfr=true.*

■ *DNS Security Extensions (DNSSEC)* uses digital certificates and digital signatures to add an element of verification and trust to the name resolution system.

■ DNS Cache Locking can be used to secure entries in the DNS server cache from being overwritten. DNS poisoning attacks can hijack client connections by overwriting entries in the DNS cache with entries pointing to IP addresses of malicious servers.

■ DNS Socket Pool uses a randomized pool of source ports selected at service startup instead of using a predictable source port. This further reduces the attack surface of the DNS cache and helps to protect against DNS poisoning.

- DNS Devolution provides hostname resolution for systems that exist in parent domains by first appending the domain namespace for the home domain to the hostname and querying, and then appending the domain namespace for each parent domain to the hostname and querying.

- Loading DNS zone data is a background operation in Windows Server 2008 R2. If you need to restart a DNS server that hosts one or more large DNS zones that are stored in AD DS, the server is able to respond to client queries more quickly because it does not need to wait until all zone data is loaded.

- The *GlobalNames DNS zone* provides single-label name resolution for large enterprise networks that do not deploy WINS. This zone is used when it is impractical to use DNS name suffixes to provide single-label name resolution.

- The Windows Server 2008 R2 DNS Server role fully supports IPv6 addresses. It implements AAAA and IPv6 records and supports IPv6 reverse lookup zones.

Supporting RODCs

An RODC provides a shadow copy of a domain controller and cannot be directly configured. This makes it less vulnerable to attack. Microsoft advises using RODCs in locations where you cannot guarantee the physical security of a domain controller. You can delegate RODC configuration to nonadministrative accounts and do not need to have domain or enterprise administrators working at branch offices.

Windows Server 2008 R2 DNS supports primary read-only authoritative zones (sometimes called branch office zones). When a Windows Server 2008 R2 server is configured as an RODC, it replicates a read-only copy of all Active Directory partitions that DNS uses, including the domain partition, ForestDNSZones, and DomainDNSZones. A user with the appropriate permissions can view the contents of a primary read-only zone but cannot change its contents. The contents of a read-only zone in an RODC change only when the DNS zone on the master domain controller changes and the master domain controller is configured to allow the RODC to pull these changes.

DNS Security Extensions

Historically, the DNS system has remained unprotected with few, if any, security protections. However, the risks to the DNS system within an organization and on the Internet are numerous. Imagine what attackers could accomplish if they could reconfigure the DNS servers on the Internet. They could hijack all the web sessions they desire and redirect connections to spoofed sites or man-in-the-middle sites that pilfer data, inject malicious code, and infect and compromise client computers around the world. DNSSEC is targeted as a key solution to these types of vulnerabilities.

Based on RFCs, Windows Server 2008 R2 DNSSEC uses digital certificates and signatures to provide origin authority, data integrity, and authenticated denial of existence. Zone signatures are verified using a trusted public key, called a trust anchor. Clients are configured for

DNSSEC using settings in a new Name Resolution Policy Table (NRPT), which can be deployed by Group Policy object (GPO) for domain members, or through registry settings for non-domain members. Communications between DNS clients and DNS servers are authenticated and secured using IPsec. Further DNSSEC uses Next Secure (NSEC or NSEC3) to prohibit "zone walking" by attackers to retrieve all records in a zone.

> **NOTE** DNSSEC INTEROPERABILITY
>
> Implementations of DNSSEC on Windows Server 2003 and Windows Server 2008 are not interoperable with the DNSSEC implementation on Windows Server 2008 R2 due to the deprecation of earlier DNSSEC-related RFCs.

DNS Cache Locking

Cache locking provides enhanced security against cache poisoning. A common and relatively easy attack has been DNS cache poisoning, where an attacker sends the DNS server a DNS response (usually unsolicited) to write or overwrite an entry in the server's DNS cache of previously resolved name-to-IP-address mappings. This bogus mapping is used to redirect clients to malicious websites or other malicious web services. New in Windows Server 2008 R2 is the ability to control whether or not these cached mappings can be overwritten before their Time-to-Live (TTL) expires naturally.

DNS Socket Pool

Another feature to protect against DNS cache poisoning is the *DNS Socket Pool*. This feature is new in Windows Server 2008 R2 and allows you to specify a randomly selected source port for the DNS server to use when issuing DNS queries. Instead of always using a predictable, single, and easily attacked port, you can configure your DNS server to randomly select a source port to use for its DNS queries from a range of 1 to 10,000 different ports. The larger the pool, the more difficult it is for the attacker to correctly guess. Exclusions can be configured for reserved ports and ranges. The DNS Socket Pool defaults to using a pool size of 2,500, with the specific port selected from within that range at service startup.

DNS Devolution Control

DNS Devolution is the process of appending a local domain suffix to a queried hostname and, if not resolved, removing one name from the structure (the parent domain name), building the fully qualified domain name (FQDN), and then querying again. If there is no resolution, repeat the process until you reach some default limits in the namespace. Windows Server 2008 R2 adjusts the default behavior to produce more successful resolutions and adds the ability to adjust the depth of the namespace to build FQDNs. For example, to have the queries stop at *corp.contoso.com*, you would set a devolution level of 3, because the domain namespace has three labels: corp, contoso, and com.

Background Zone Loading

In a large organization with large Windows Server 2003 (or earlier) zones that store DNS data in AD DS, restarting a DNS server can take considerable time. The DNS server needs to retrieve zone data from AD DS and is unavailable to service client requests while this is happening.

Windows Server 2008 R2 DNS addresses this situation through background zone loading. A Windows Server 2008 R2 DNS server loads zone data from AD DS in the background and can respond almost immediately to client requests when it restarts, instead of waiting until its zones are fully loaded. Also, because zone data is stored in AD DS rather than in a file, that data can be accessed asynchronously and immediately when a query is received. File-based zone data can be accessed only through a sequential file read and takes longer to access than data in AD DS.

When the DNS server starts, it identifies all zones to be loaded, loads root hints from files or AD DS storage, loads any file-backed zones, and starts to respond to queries and remote procedure calls (RPCs) while using background processes (additional processor threads) to load zones that are stored in AD DS. The effect of background loading in this situation is that a rebooted DNS server comes online more quickly to share the load of satisfying client requests.

✔ **Quick Check**
- Which DNS record enables a hostname to be resolved to an IPv6 address?

Quick Check Answer
- AAAA

Using the GlobalNames DNS Zone for Legacy Support

WINS uses NetBT, which Microsoft describes as approaching obsolescence. Nevertheless, it provides static, global records with single-label names and is still widely used. Windows Server 2008 R2 DNS introduces the GlobalNames zone to hold single-label names and provide legacy support for networks that previously used WINS for NetBIOS name resolution. Typically, the replication scope of this zone is the entire forest, which ensures that the zone can provide single-label names forest wide. This does, however, require that the globalname for a host is unique throughout the forest. The GlobalNames zone also supports single-label name resolution throughout an organization that contains multiple forests—provided that you use Service Location (SRV) resource records to publish the GlobalNames zone location. This potentially enables organizations to disable WINS and NetBT. As you've probably heard over the last ten years or so, WINS and NetBT will probably not be supported in future Windows Server releases. You need to keep this in mind when planning changes in your name resolution structure and deciding whether to retain WINS. Disabling NetBT reduces the attack surface of your servers and makes them less vulnerable to malicious users, but might introduce some problems for some NetBIOS-based applications.

The GlobalNames zone provides single-label name resolution for a limited set of hostnames, usually centrally managed corporate servers and websites, and is not used for peer-to-peer name resolution. Client workstation name resolution and dynamic updates are not supported. Instead, the GlobalNames zone holds CNAME resource records to map a single-label name to an FQDN. In networks that are currently using WINS, the GlobalNames zone usually contains resource records for centrally managed names that are already statically configured on the WINS server.

Microsoft recommends that you integrate the GlobalNames zone with AD DS and that you configure each authoritative DNS server with a local copy of the GlobalNames zone. This provides maximum performance and scalability. AD DS integration of the GlobalNames zone is required to support deployment of the GlobalNames zone across multiple forests.

> **NOTE** **ENABLING A DNS SERVER TO SUPPORT GLOBALNAMES ZONES**
>
> The */config* switch in the *dnscmd* command-line tool enables a DNS server to support GlobalNames zones.

> **NOTE** **REGISTERING GLOBALNAMES**
>
> Unlike WINS, GlobalNames zone functionality does not permit hostname entries to be registered dynamically. All hostname entries in the GlobalNames zone must be created manually.

Planning WINS Replication for Legacy Support

As an enterprise administrator, you need to support earlier networks, for example, Windows NT 4.0 domains. Although we've heard that WINS is nearly obsolete, you need to know how to support it and include it in your planning and design process. Questions about WINS are likely to appear on the 70-647 exam. The major planning and design decisions you need to make when planning WINS services will be about which WINS replication topology to use. You might not have looked at WINS for some time and, therefore, this section includes some basic information for the purpose of review.

WINS database replication occurs whenever the WINS database changes on any WINS server, for example, when a NetBIOS name is released. WINS replication enables a WINS server to resolve NetBIOS names of hosts registered with other WINS servers. To replicate database entries, each WINS server must be configured as either a pull or a push partner with at least one other WINS server.

A push partner sends a message to its pull partners, notifying them when its WINS database has changed. When a WINS server's pull partners respond to the message with a replication request, the WINS server pushes a copy of its new database entries to its pull partners.

A pull partner is a WINS server that requests new database entries from its push partners by requesting entries with a higher version number than the entries it received during the last replication.

Push replication occurs when a specified number of updates to the WINS database have occurred and works best when you have fast links between your WINS servers that can support a high bandwidth. You can configure pull replication to occur at specific intervals, and you can control the replication traffic by adjusting the bandwidth. Pull replication is used between sites connected by slow WAN links. To replicate database entries in both directions, configure each server to be both a push and a pull partner. Every WINS server must be both a push partner and a pull partner (but not necessarily with each other) for the replication to complete.

> **NOTE WINS REPLICATION**
> Push replication occurs when a specified number of updated WINS database entries is reached. Pull replication can be configured to occur at specific intervals.

How you plan your WINS replication topology primarily depends on the network topology and disaster recovery requirements in your organization. The following WINS replication topologies are available:

- **Centralized WINS topology** This topology uses a single, centralized, high-availability WINS server or WINS server cluster. Centralized WINS topology simplifies deployment and maintenance. No server-to-server replication overhead exists, and all clients are configured with the same WINS server address. Fault tolerance can be achieved by using clustering. If, however, the shared cluster database is corrupted, it needs to be restored from backup. No WINS replication occurs in this topology. Centralized WINS topology does not provide WINS database fault tolerance.

- **Full mesh WINS topology** This topology is a distributed WINS design with multiple WINS servers or clusters deployed across the enterprise. You need to plan WINS replication to ensure synchronization of the WINS database among all WINS servers. All WINS servers replicate with all other WINS servers. You can configure replication manually or by using the WINS autodiscovery (automatic partner configuration) feature. In a full mesh WINS topology, some clients can be configured to use one WINS server as their primary, and the remaining clients can use another WINS server, which enables you to implement load balancing. Full mesh WINS topology is typically used when the network topology consists of multiple data centers and remote offices. Each WINS server replicates with every other WINS server in this topology, which causes a significant amount of network traffic. This topology can introduce security risks and requires more management and support than other technologies. The full mesh WINS topology is illustrated in Figure 1-5.

- **Ring WINS topology** This topology is a distributed WINS design in which each WINS server replicates with a specific neighboring partner, forming a circle. This topology needs to be created manually because relationships between each server pair must be determined and configured by a WINS administrator. A ring WINS topology is easier to maintain than a full mesh WINS topology, and you can provision for load balancing by distributing your clients across WINS servers. However, troubleshooting is more difficult in a ring WINS topology, and the *convergence time*, which is the time it takes for a database change to replicate to all WINS servers, is longer because updates are passed sequentially from server to server. The ring WINS topology is illustrated in Figure 1-5.

- **Hub and spoke WINS topology**   This is a distributed WINS design in which a central WINS server is designated as the hub, and additional WINS servers replicate only with the hub in the site where they are located. A hub and spoke WINS topology provides efficient convergence, simple management, and convenient provisioning for load balancing. It is typically used when the network topology consists of a central data center and multiple remote offices or branch offices. The central data center usually provides name resolution for the majority of the computers on the network, and the branch offices provide name resolution for local computers. The hub and spoke WINS topology is illustrated in Figure 1-5.

When you have planned your WINS replication topology, you can determine the number of WINS servers required. This depends on the number of clients that need WINS name resolution services, the available bandwidth for client name queries and registrations, and server-to-server replication between sites. As a guideline, there should be one WINS server for every 10,000 clients, with a minimum of two WINS servers to provide redundancy in sites that require highly available WINS services.

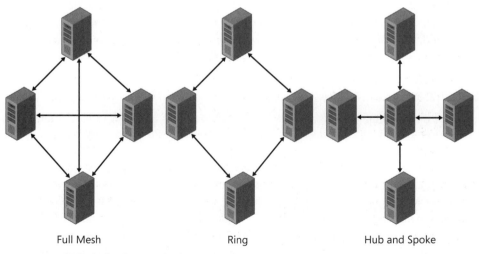

Full Mesh   Ring   Hub and Spoke

FIGURE 1-5 WINS replication topologies

Supporting IPv6 Addresses

Windows Server 2008 R2 DNS supports IPv6 addresses as fully as it supports IPv4 addresses. IPv6 addresses register dynamically, and you can create an AAAA host record for any computer on the network with an operating system that does not support dynamic registration. You can also create IPv6 reverse lookup zones. You configure an AAAA record and create an IPv6 reverse lookup zone in the practice session later in this lesson.

> **MORE INFO   IPV6 REVERSE LOOKUP ZONES**
>
> For more information about IPv6 reverse lookup zones and additional information about a wide range of IPv6 topics, see *http://www.microsoft.com/technet/network/ipv6/ipv6faq .mspx*.

The *dnscmd* command-line tool accepts addresses in both IPv4 and IPv6 format. Windows Server 2008 R2 DNS servers can send recursive queries to IPv6-only servers, and a DNS server forwarder list can contain both IPv4 and IPv6 addresses. DHCP clients can register IPv6 addresses in addition to (or instead of) IPv4 addresses. Windows Server 2008 R2 DNS servers support the *ip6.arpa* domain namespace for reverse lookups.

> ✔ **Quick Check**
> - What feature does Windows Server 2008 R2 DNS introduce that will help organizations phase out WINS and NetBT?
>
> **Quick Check Answer**
> - The GlobalNames zone

Planning a DNS Infrastructure

As a network professional, you will almost certainly know that, in a dynamic DNS system, most hosts and servers register their host (A) records automatically, and you can configure DHCP to create DNS records when it allocates leases. In comparison with former static DNS, in which records needed to be added manually (unless DNS was integrated with WINS), dynamic DNS requires very little manual configuration.

As you advance in your chosen profession, you will discover that planning takes up much of your time, and the exam guide mentions planning tasks carried out and decisions made by enterprise administrators; therefore, you need to consider the process of planning a DNS infrastructure.

Planning a DNS Namespace

Planning and defining a DNS namespace is typically a task for the enterprise administrator. You need to know the options available so that you can plan and implement enterprise-level decisions more efficiently.

If you use a DNS namespace for internal purposes only, the name does not need to conform to the standard defined in RFC 1123, "Requirements for Internet Hosts—Application and Support"; RFC 2181, "Clarifications to the DNS Specification"; and the character set specified in RFC 2044, "UTF-8, a Transformation Format of Unicode and ISO 10646." The *contoso.internal* namespace you configured in your test network is an example of this type of namespace.

However, when you specify a corporate namespace to be used on the Internet, it needs to be registered with the appropriate authority and conform to the relevant RFC standards. Examples of corporate namespaces are *treyresearch.net* and *tailspintoys.com*. Most organizations have both a private and a public network. You can implement the DNS namespace infrastructure by using one of the following schemes:

- Use different (also called broken or discontiguous) namespaces for your external and internal namespaces, such as *contoso.lan* and *contoso.com*. This improves security by isolating the two namespaces from each other and preventing internal resources from being exposed directly to the Internet.

  A DNS design worthy of consideration uses this discontiguous namespace to represent the internal network and Active Directory environment and the public-facing web resources. Use something like *contoso.lan* and *contoso.com,* respectively. On the corporate local area network (LAN), build a DNS server on a domain controller to support the private enterprise. Add the *Active Directory integrated zone* for *contoso.lan,* and configure it using all the latest and greatest features, like secure, dynamic updates and replication to appropriate internal DNS servers for load balancing, geographic distribution, and redundancy. Configure your Active Directory/DNS clients to use a nearby DNS server that hosts the Active Directory integrated zone for *contoso.lan* as its Preferred DNS server, and point to a different, same-site, or next-site DNS server that hosts *contoso.lan* as the alternate.

  On this same internal DNS server, build a primary DNS zone for the resources that live in the public *contoso.com* namespace. In this *contoso.com* zone, you should disallow dynamic updates, and you'll need to manually add resource records for each public host you want the public world to find.

  Build a stand-alone (not a member of the *contoso.lan* Active Directory domain), file-based DNS server that is connected to the perimeter network (also known as the DMZ or demilitarized zone). Add a secondary zone for *contoso.com*, using the internal *contoso.com* zone and server as its master. This allows you to administer the public namespace on your internal DNS server, and makes the exposed, perimeter network copy of the zone a read-only zone, hardening the public zone against attacks. You will, of course, need to allow and configure zone transfers from the master to the secondary, configure the Notify function for fast updates, and make a point-to-point allow rule in the internal perimeter network firewall to pass the port 53 zone transfers.

Now the public can access only your intended, public resources, and your internal Active Directory clients can access all of the Active Directory namespace as well as the corporation's public resources.

- Use the same corporate namespace for both the internal and external (public-facing) portions of your network. This configuration is called *split-horizon DNS* and can provide secure name resolution to resources on both internal and external networks. However, you need to ensure that the appropriate zone types and records are being stored on the internal and external DNS servers and that the security of your internal network is protected.

  Use Active Directory integrated zones on internal DNS servers to support Active Directory. Use a Primary (file-based) zone on the external, stand-alone DNS server to support only the public-facing resources. Disallow dynamic updates on the public DNS zone. Manually add resource records for the public resources to both the internal, Active Directory–integrated zone and the public zone.

  The public DNS server only holds public records. The internal zone holds all Active Directory records plus the manually added public records. These servers never share DNS data.

  NOTE **INTERNAL USERS REQUIRE ACCESS TO EXTERNAL RESOURCES**

  Using a single corporate namespace presents a challenge when internal users require name resolution for publicly accessible resources, because the external DNS zone is not configured to resolve internal resources. This challenge can be overcome by manually duplicating the external resource records on internal DNS servers for internal clients to resolve the corporation's public-facing resources. You can also configure split DNS, which is described later in this lesson.

- Use delegated namespaces to identify your organization's internal network. For example, Trey Research could have the public namespace *treyresearch.net* and the private namespace *intranet.treyresearch.net*. This fits neatly with Active Directory structure and is easily implemented if you use Active Directory–integrated DNS. You need to ensure that internal clients can resolve external namespace addresses but that external clients cannot resolve internal namespace addresses. All internal domain data is isolated in the domain tree and requires its own DNS server infrastructure. An internal DNS server will forward requests for an external namespace address to an external DNS server. The disadvantage of namespace delegation is that FQDNs can become quite long. The maximum length of an FQDN is 255 bytes. FQDNs for domain controllers are limited to 155 bytes.

The Active Directory–integrated zone provides several advantages. Not least of these is that DNS zone information is automatically replicated with other AD DS information through distributed file system replication (DFSR). You can implement RODCs that hold authoritative read-only DNS zones and provide secure local name resolution in branch offices where the physical security of servers cannot be guaranteed. You can implement secondary DNS zones on Windows DNS or *BIND servers* that need not be part of the Active Directory structure. For example, DNS servers on peripheral zones are frequently stand-alone servers.

How you implement Active Directory on your network plays a critical role in determining how domains should be created and nested within each other. Your zone structure typically mirrors your Active Directory domain structure, although this is not compulsory. You can easily create delegated zones. For example, you could use *engineering.tailspintoys.com* rather than *tailspintoys.com/engineering*.

You can partition your DNS namespace by geographical location, by department, or both. For example, if Tailspin Toys has several locations but only a single human resources department located at the central office, you could use the namespace *hr.tailspintoys.com*. If Contoso, Ltd., has a main office in Denver and manufacturing facilities in Boston and Dallas, you could configure the namespaces *denver.contoso.com*, *boston.contoso.com*, and *dallas.contoso.com*.

Planning DNS Forwarding

A forwarder is an upstream DNS server that typically has access to additional namespaces for resolution. DNS clients, called *resolvers*, are configured with the IP address of their preferred DNS server. Resolvers submit name resolution queries to their preferred DNS server. If the DNS server cannot perform the resolution itself and is configured with the IP address of a forwarder, the DNS server will forward the resolution query to the forwarder.

Windows Server 2003 introduced conditional forwarding, described earlier in this lesson, and this can be used in Windows Server 2008 R2. Because conditional forwarders are mapped to specific namespaces, a queried namespace is checked against the conditional forwarder listings before the (standard) forwarder is queried. You should plan to use conditional forwarders when you need name resolution for namespaces for which the DNS server is not authoritative and when you know the IP address of a DNS server that is authoritative for that namespace. This is common in large, geographically dispersed or politically dispersed forests with many Active Directory domains.

EXAM TIP

Forwarding DNS requests requires the DNS server to be capable of making recursive queries. Exam answers that suggest that you should configure forwarding and disable recursion can be discarded as incorrect.

A typical DNS forwarding scenario could specify a DNS server that is permitted to forward queries to DNS servers outside the corporate firewall, like to the Internet service provider's (ISP's) public DNS server. This implementation enables the firewall to be configured to allow DNS traffic only from this specific internal DNS server and to allow only valid replies back to the DNS server to enter the protected network. By using this approach, all other DNS traffic—both inbound and outbound—can be dropped at the firewall. This improves the overall security of the network and the DNS service.

Planning the Zone Type

Active Directory networks typically use DNS servers installed on domain controllers and use Active Directory–integrated zones for internal name resolution. In this case, DNS zone information is held on writable domain controllers in the domain (usually all the writable domain controllers). This gives the advantages of DFSR, failover, and data redundancy if one domain controller goes down and increased ability to accept updates through its multimaster arrangement. Standard primary zones installed on Windows stand-alone servers can be used where a writable DNS server is required, but access to the Active Directory database is seen as a security risk; for example, in peripheral zones like the perimeter network. RODCs can be used when you want the advantages of Active Directory–integrated DNS but cannot guarantee the physical security of your servers, such as in branch offices.

Active Directory–integrated, standard *primary*, and standard *secondary zones* can provide zone information to standard secondary DNS zones. In Windows Server 2008 R2 networks, secondary DNS zones can be implemented on domain controllers, member servers, stand-alone servers, and RODCs. Installing a secondary DNS server at a remote location can significantly improve the reliability and speed of name resolution at that location. Secondary zone servers increase redundancy by providing name resolution even if the primary zone server is unresponsive, and, when resolvers are configured correctly, reduce the load on primary servers by distributing name resolution requests among more DNS servers. A secondary zone server does not need to be part of the Active Directory domain (except in the case of domain controllers and RODCs), and you can install secondary zones on non-Windows servers. You can also configure secondary zone servers on virtual machines.

✔ **Quick Check**

- Which is the name of the record that connects a parent namespace to its child namespace? (This record type actually contains two resource records, an NS record and an A record.)

Quick Check Answer

- A glue record

As a network professional, you have probably configured the aging and scavenging settings for DNS records, configured dynamic updates, specified zone replication scopes, and configured zone transfers. However, it is one thing to know how to configure these settings. It is quite another to plan your zones and decide what the optimum settings are for your name resolution structure. This is a job for the enterprise administrator.

If a large number of stale resource records remain in zones, they take up server disk space and cause unnecessarily long zone transfers. DNS servers that load zones containing stale resource records risk using outdated information to answer client queries, potentially causing name resolution problems. DNS servers and zones can be configured to scavenge stale resource records within a period of time. In environments in which resource records can become stale, you need to ensure that you enable the scavenging of these records.

The design of aging and scavenging settings is dependent on your name resolution traffic and on how often your network changes. A network that is reasonably stable, with few stations being added or removed, can probably be configured with long aging settings and less-frequent scavenging cycles than can a more dynamic environment. Frequent scavenging and short aging periods can increase your network traffic.

DNS zones can also be configured to allow or disallow dynamic updates, although it is unusual for dynamic updates to be disallowed in modern networks. Active Directory–integrated zones can also be configured to allow secure dynamic updates only. Secure dynamic updates, discussed earlier in this lesson, are strongly recommended because they ensure that only authorized changes are made to DNS data.

NOTE **SECURE DYNAMIC UPDATES**

Only Active Directory–integrated zones support secure dynamic updates.

When you plan the replication scope of Active Directory–integrated zones, you need to decide whether the zone should be replicated to all DNS servers in the forest, all DNS servers in the domain (the default), or all domain controllers in the domain. If you need to broaden the replication scope, you can configure the zone to replicate to all DNS servers in the forest. Replicating to all domain controllers in the domain is recommended only if you have Windows 2000 Server domain controllers in your environment.

You can configure the primary name server, the refresh interval, and the minimum default TTL values for zone resource records in the zone's SOA record. The TTL controls the minimum amount of time clients, including other DNS servers, cache resource records for the zone. If your environment is dynamic, with frequent IP address changes, plan to configure the minimum TTL to a low value, such as one day.

When planning DNS zones, you need to specify whether zone transfers are permitted, and, if so, to which servers. You can configure zone transfers to any server, to the name servers listed on the Name Servers tab or the zone, or to a specific list of name servers.

Planning Root Hints

When you install a Windows Server 2008 R2 DNS server that has access to the Internet, the server is automatically configured with a list of root servers. If a DNS server receives a query for a DNS zone for which it is not authoritative, the server will send a query to one of the root servers that initiates a series of iterative queries until the name is resolved. You can use root hints to prepare servers that are authoritative for nonroot zones so that they can discover authoritative servers that manage domains at a higher level or in other subtrees of the DNS domain namespace.

Root hints are essential for servers that are authoritative at lower levels of the namespace when locating and finding other servers. By default, the DNS Server service implements root hints by using a file named *Cache.dns* that normally contains the NS and A resource records for the Internet root servers. If, however, you are using the DNS Server service on a private network, you should plan to remove this file to disable your DNS server from querying Internet name servers, or edit or replace this file with similar records that point to your own internal root DNS servers.

Planning to Integrate AD DS with an Existing DNS Infrastructure

Many enterprise-level organizations already use one or more Berkeley Internet Name Domain (BIND) servers. BIND provides name resolution for UNIX systems or Internet name resolution for internal users. In this case, Active Directory–integrated DNS needs to interoperate with the BIND DNS infrastructure.

Two options are available within the Windows Server 2008 R2 DNS infrastructure:

- You can use the existing DNS infrastructure to host the DNS zone for AD DS. Potentially, this can reduce hardware requirements and administrative effort. However, this option can also mean that the DNS infrastructure is supported by a different team than that which supports AD DS. As an enterprise administrator, one of your tasks is to rationalize your support organization, and you, or your line manager, might find this option unacceptable.

- You can deploy Windows Server 2008 R2 DNS to take advantage of the many fine features like Active Directory integrated zones, zone replication, and secure dynamic updates. Use forwarders and stub zones to integrate both DNS infrastructures. This can give you more flexibility for DNS infrastructure design, DNS namespace design, and DNS administration model. Windows Server 2008 R2 DNS servers can forward any DNS queries for records hosted on the existing DNS infrastructure to the existing DNS servers.

Figure 1-6 depicts the forwarding of DNS queries between a Windows Server 2008 R2 DNS infrastructure and a BIND DNS infrastructure.

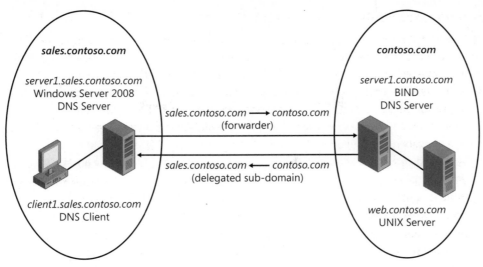

FIGURE 1-6 Forwarding DNS queries

For example, Contoso, Ltd., has an existing BIND-based DNS infrastructure with a DNS domain name of *contoso.com*. Contoso plans to deploy a new Windows Server 2008 R2 DNS infrastructure for AD DS with a DNS domain name of *sales.contoso.com*. A conditional forwarding entry for *contoso.com* has been created on the Windows Server 2008 R2 DNS server in the *sales.contoso.com* domain. Delegation records (or glue records) for *sales.contoso.com* have been created on a BIND-based DNS server in the *contoso.com* domain.

When a client in the *sales.contoso.com* namespace needs to access a UNIX Web server in the *contoso.com* namespace, it queries its preferred DNS server in the *sales.contoso.com* namespace. This DNS server is not authoritative for the *contoso.com* zone, but it does have a conditional forwarding entry for the *contoso.com* zone. Through the conditional forwarding entry on the DNS server in the *sales.contoso.com* namespace, the Windows DNS server contacts the BIND-based DNS server for the *contoso.com* namespace to retrieve the requested name resolution for *web.contoso.com* for the resolver.

Planning the GlobalNames Zone

Historically, DNS resolved only FQDNs. These FQDNs needed a hostname with a domain component, like *webserver1.contoso.com*. GlobalNames allows resolution of a hostname only, much like WINS does in the NetBIOS world, because, by default, hostnames and NetBIOS names are the same. To plan your GlobalNames zone design, you need to understand the deployment scenarios in which a GlobalNames zone can be configured. You can deploy a GlobalNames zone in a single-forest environment or a multiple-forest environment. A single-forest deployment of a GlobalNames zone allows single-label or hostname resolution through DNS, using a single Active Directory–integrated GlobalNames zone. A multiple-forest deployment of a GlobalNames zone allows single-label hostname resolution through DNS, using an Active Directory–integrated GlobalNames zone for each forest within the multiple-forest environment.

You can adapt a single-forest GlobalNames zone deployment to meet an assortment of single-label hostname resolution requirements in the following ways:

- **All domains and client computers in a forest** Microsoft recommends this scenario for organizations that have a single forest and a small number of domains. Single-label name resolution is provided to all domain-joined client computers in the forest. In this scenario, you need to ensure that all authoritative DNS servers in the forest are Windows Server 2008 domain controllers. You then need to create an AD DS–integrated GlobalNames zone on one DNS server in the forest and replicate this to all domain controllers in the forest that are DNS servers. You then add CNAME records for single-label names pointing to the FQDNs of the resource servers.

- **A multiple-forest GlobalNames zone** This deployment scenario is recommended for companies that have multiple domains and multiple forests. You can customize a multiple-forest DNS server to meet diverse single-label name resolution requirements for all domains and client computers in all forests by ensuring that all authoritative DNS servers in the forest are Windows Server 2008 domain controller DNS servers. You also need to ensure that GlobalNames zone functionality has been enabled on each DNS server in the forest. You create an AD DS-integrated GlobalNames zone on one DNS server in a forest and replicate the GlobalNames zone to all domain controllers in the forest that are DNS servers. You then add CNAME records for single-label names pointing to the FQDN of the resource servers. In each of the other forests, you add *SRV resource records* pointing to each remote domain controller DNS server that hosts a local copy of the GlobalNames zone to the forest-wide *_msdcs* zone.

- **A selected set of DNS servers host the GlobalNames zone** Microsoft recommends this deployment scenario for companies that have multiple domains and multiple forests but want to limit the GlobalNames zone to a selected set of DNS servers. This deployment scenario provides single-label name resolution to all client computers in the forests.

- **Selected domains across multiple forests** Microsoft recommends this deployment when you want to deploy a GlobalNames zone in a multiple-forest environment in a set of selected domains as a pilot program.

PRACTICE Configuring DNS

In this practice, you configure a static IPv6 configuration on the Glasgow domain controller. You then configure a static AAAA record and an IPv6 reverse lookup zone. Finally, you create a pointer (PTR) record in the reverse lookup zone for the Glasgow computer.

EXERCISE 1 Configure IPv6 on the Glasgow Computer

In this exercise, you configure IPv6 on the Glasgow computer (the domain controller). You need to do this because you create a reverse lookup IPv6 zone and a PTR record for the Glasgow computer in subsequent exercises. The exercise asks you to log on interactively to the domain controller. If you want to make this more realistic, you can log on to the Melbourne client instead and connect to the domain controller through Remote Desktop.

1. Log on at the Glasgow domain controller with the Kim_Akers account.
2. From Control Panel, start Network And Sharing Center. Click Change Adapter Settings.
3. Right-click the network connection to your private network and choose Properties.
4. If a Universal Access Control (UAC) dialog box appears, click Continue to close it.
5. Select Internet Protocol Version 6 (TCP/IPv6) and click Properties.
6. Configure the static site-local IPv6 address **fec0:0:0:fffe::1**.
7. Configure the preferred DNS server address **fec0:0:0:fffe::1**. The Properties dialog box should look similar to Figure 1-7.

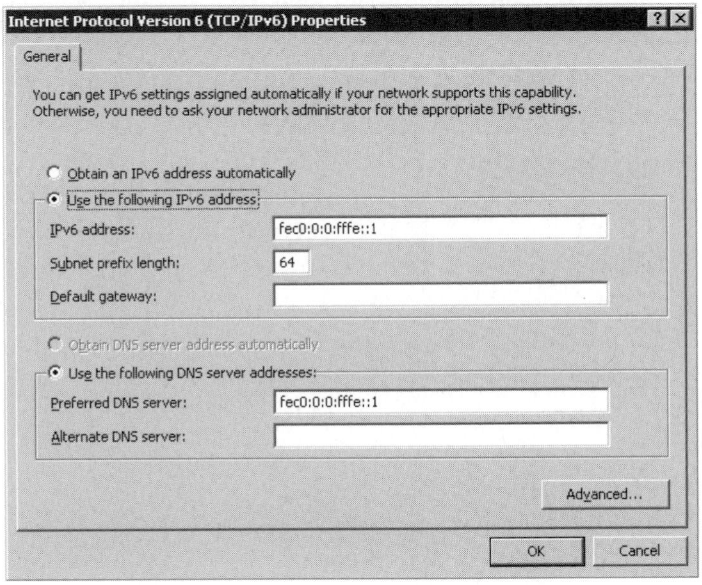

FIGURE 1-7 IPv6 configuration on the domain controller

8. Click OK. Close the Local Area Connections Properties dialog box.
9. Close the Network Connections window.
10. Close Network And Sharing Center.

> **NOTE VIRTUAL MACHINES**
>
> If you are using a virtual machine to implement your server and client on the same computer, it is a good idea to close your virtual machine and restart your computer after configuring interfaces.

EXERCISE 2 Configure an AAAA Record

The stand-alone server Brisbane has an operating system that cannot register in Windows Server 2008 R2 DNS. Therefore, you need to create a manual AAAA record for this server. Its IPv6 address is fec0:0:0:fffe::aa. Note that you can create an AAAA record for this server even though it does not currently exist on your network.

1. If necessary, log on to the Glasgow domain controller with the Kim_Akers account.
2. In Administrative Tools, open DNS Manager.
3. If a UAC dialog box appears, click Continue.
4. In DNS Manager, expand Forward Lookup Zones. Right-click *contoso.internal* and choose New Host (A or AAAA).
5. Enter the server name and IPv6 address as shown in Figure 1-8. Ensure that the Create associated pointer (PTR) Record check box is not selected.

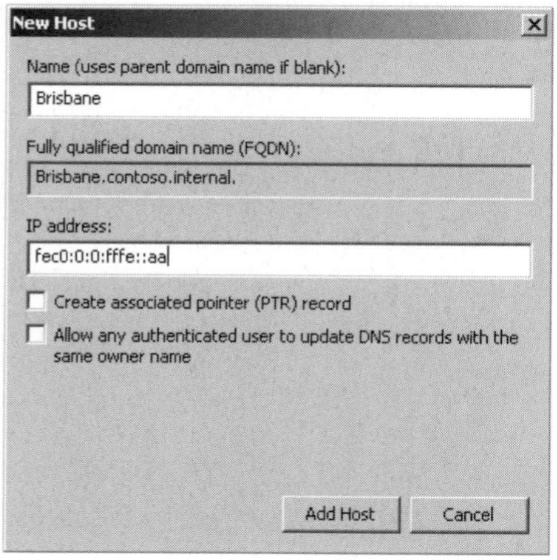

FIGURE 1-8 Specifying a DNS host record

6. Click Add Host. Click OK to clear the DNS message box.
7. Click Done. Ensure that the new record exists in DNS Manager.
8. Close DNS Manager.

EXERCISE 3 Configure a Reverse Lookup IPv6 Zone

In this exercise, you create an IPv6 reverse lookup zone for all site-local IPv6 addresses—that is, addresses starting with fec0. You will then create a PTR record in the zone. Note that in IPv6, reverse lookup zone addresses are entered as reverse-order 4-bit nibbles, so fec0 becomes 0.c.e.f.

1. If necessary, log on to the domain controller with the Kim_Akers account.

2. Click Start, right-click Command Prompt, and choose Run As Administrator.

3. If a UAC dialog box appears, click Continue.

4. Enter **dnscmdglasgow /ZoneAdd 0.c.e.f.ip6.arpa /DsPrimary**. Close the command console.

5. In Administrative Tools, open DNS Manager. If a UAC dialog box appears, click Continue.

6. Expand Forward Lookup Zones. Select *contoso.internal*.

7. Right-click the AAAA record for Glasgow, and then choose Properties.

8. Select the Update Associated Pointer (PTR) Record check box. Click OK.

9. Expand Reverse Lookup Zones and select 0.c.e.f.ip6.arpa. Ensure that the PTR record for Glasgow exists, as shown in Figure 1-9.

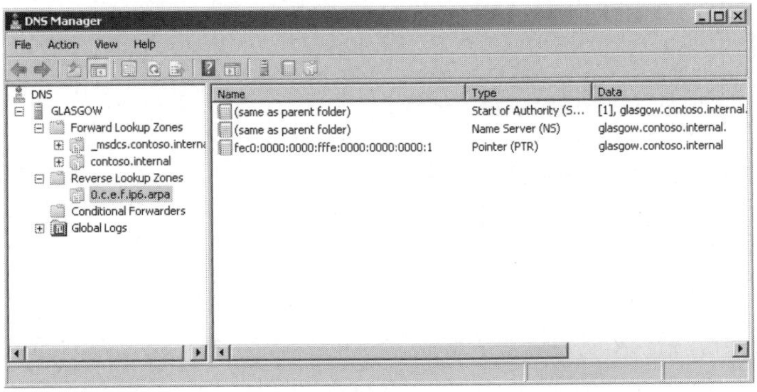

FIGURE 1-9 The PTR record for Glasgow

10. Log off from the domain controller.

Lesson Summary

- The DNS Server role in Windows Server 2008 R2 complies with all current standards and can work successfully with most other DNS server implementations.

- Windows Server 2008 R2 DNS is dynamic and typically requires very little static configuration. You can use the DNS Manager GUI or command-line tools such as *dnscmd*, *nslookup*, *ipconfig*, and *netsh* to configure and manage DNS.

- New Windows Server 2008 R2 DNS functions include background zone loading, support for RODCs, and the GlobalNames DNS zone. Windows Server 2008 R2 DNS fully supports IPv6 forward lookup and reverse lookup zones.
- WINS resolves NetBIOS names to IP addresses. Windows Server 2008 R2 supports WINS to provide support for previous networks. The GlobalNames DNS zone provides single-label name resolution for large enterprise networks that do not deploy WINS.

Lesson Review

Use the following questions to test your knowledge of the information in Lesson 1, "Planning Name Resolution." The questions are also available on the companion CD if you prefer to review them in electronic form.

> **NOTE ANSWERS**
>
> Answers to these questions and explanations of why each answer choice is correct or incorrect are located in the "Answers" section at the end of the book.

1. Which WINS topology uses a distributed WINS design with multiple WINS servers or clusters deployed across the enterprise, with each server or cluster replicating with every other WINS server or cluster?

    A. Centralized WINS topology

    B. Full mesh WINS topology

    C. Ring WINS topology

    D. Hub and spoke WINS topology

2. Which DNS record enables you to specify refresh interval and TTL settings?

    A. SOA

    B. NS

    C. SRV

    D. CNAME

3. Which command enables a DNS server to support GlobalNames zones?

    A. *dnscmd /createdirectorypartition*

    B. *dnscmd /enlistdirectorypartition*

    C. *dnscmd /config*

    D. *dnscmd /createbuiltindirectorypartitions*

4. You want to list all the DNS records in the *adatum.internal* domain. You connect to the *Edinburgh.adatum.internal* DNS server by using Remote Desktop and open the command console. You type **nslookup**. At the nslookup> prompt, you type **ls –d adatum.internal**. An error message tells you that zone data cannot be loaded to

that computer. You know all the DNS records in the domain exist on Edinburgh. Why weren't they displayed?

  A. You have not configured the *adatum.internal* forward lookup zone to allow zone transfers.

  B. You need to run the command console as an administrator to use *nslookup*.

  C. You should have typed **nslookupls –d adatum.internal** directly from the command prompt. You cannot use the *ls* function from the nslookup> prompt.

  D. You need to log on to the DNS server interactively to use *nslookup*. You cannot use it over a Remote Desktop connection.

5. A user tries to access the company internal website from a client computer but cannot do so because of a network problem. You fix the network problem, but the user still cannot reach the website, although she can reach other websites. Users on other client computers have no problem reaching the internal website. How can you quickly resolve the situation?

  A. Create a static host record for your local web server in DNS.

  B. Run *ipconfig /flushdns* on the primary DNS server.

  C. Run *ipconfig /registerdns* on the user's computer.

  D. Run *ipconfig /flushdns* on the user's computer.

6. You are planning the deployment of DNSSEC in your Active Directory environment. You plan to control the DNS client's behavior with respect to DNSSEC using the Name Resolution Policy Table (NRPT). What utility do you use to configure the NRPT?

  A. Notepad.exe to create an .inifile

  B. Group Policy object editor

  C. *netsh* commands in logon scripts

  D. *ipconfig* commands in startup scripts

Lesson 2: Planning Internet Protocol Addressing

As an experienced network professional, you are familiar with IPv4 addresses. You know that the private IP address ranges are 10.0.0.0/8, 172.16.0.0/12, and 192.168.0.0/16 and that the Automatic Private IP Addressing (APIPA) range is 169.254.0.0/16. You are aware that *Network Address Translation* (NAT) typically enables you to use relatively few public IP addresses to enable Internet access to many internal clients with private IP addresses. You are able to identify Class A, B, and C networks, but you are also aware that most modern network design uses Classless Interdomain Routing (CIDR). You know that Class D addresses (224.0.0.0/4) are used for multicasting.

You know that DHCP can allocate IPv4 addresses, subnet masks, default gateways, DNS and WINS servers, and many other settings and that APIPA can automatically configure IPv4 addresses for use in an isolated private network. You are aware that three DHCP infrastructure models exist: the centralized DHCP infrastructure model, the decentralized DHCP infrastructure model, and the combined DHCP infrastructure model. You know that DHCP works with DNS so that host and (if appropriate) PTR records are added to DNS zones when DHCP allocates IP addresses.

You might be less familiar with the IPv6 infrastructure, the advantages of IPv6, the types of IPv6 addresses, the operation of DHCPv6 and how to set up a DHCPv6 scope, and how to install the Windows Server 2008 R2 DHCP server role. Several new services in Windows Server 2008 R2 rely on IPv6, like HomeGroup or DirectAccess, and you can plan on more to follow. As IPv6 usage increases, you need to be aware of IPv4-to-IPv6 transition strategies and IPv4 and IPv6 interoperability, particularly the use of Teredo addresses. This lesson looks at IPv6, DHCPv6, transition strategy, and interoperability. Note that the objectives of the 70-646 and 70-647 exams are very similar for this topic. If you studied IPv6 for the 70-646 exam, please treat this lesson as review.

After this lesson, you will be able to:

- Identify the various types of IPv6 addresses and explain their uses.
- Describe the advantages of IPv6 and how these are achieved.
- Identify IPv6 addresses that can be routed on the IPv4 Internet.
- Recommend an appropriate IPv4-to-IPv6 transition strategy.
- Implement IPv4 and IPv6 interoperability.
- Use IPv6 tools.
- Configure DHCPv6 scopes.

Estimated lesson time: 55 minutes

Sometimes I wonder whether NAT and CIDR did us any good in the long run.

They solved a problem. IPv4 address space exhaustion was suddenly no longer an issue. (It will be again.) We were granted breathing space to transition to IPv6. There was and still is a huge amount of money invested in the IPv4 intranet, and there would have been severe problems had we suddenly found that no addresses were left. Many of us sighed with relief.

However, the other problems haven't gone away. Backbone routers still host huge route tables. Quality of service remains problematic when traffic is encrypted. End-to-end security is not ensured.

Had we seen NAT and CIDR for the temporary fixes they are and implemented a controlled but steady IPv6 transition, things would all have been well. Alas, it is only now, years after the crisis loomed, that operating systems such as Windows Server 2008 R2, Windows 7, and Windows Vista that support IPv6 by default are being released. The acronym WYKIWYL (what you know is what you like) reigned supreme. We were happy with IPv4. Why worry about that nasty IPv6 thing? Some even grew to love NAT, seeing it as a security enhancement. (That's an argument I won't go into.)

IPv6 is coming, and we can't afford to ignore it. We need it too much. Sometimes I'm reminded of the argument that the airplane would never catch on. It frightened the horses.

Analyzing the IPv6 Address Structure

IPv4 and IPv6 addresses can be readily distinguished. An IPv4 address uses 32 bits, resulting in an address space of just over 4 billion. An IPv6 address uses 128 bits, resulting in an address space of 2^{128}, or 340,282,366,920,938,463,463,374,607,431,768,211,456—a number too large to comprehend. This represents 6.5×2^{23} or 54,525,952 addresses for every square meter of the earth's surface. In practice, the IPv6 address space allows for multiple levels of subnetting and address allocation between the Internet backbone and individual subnets within an organization. The vastly increased address space available enables users to allocate not one but several unique IPv6 addresses to a network entity, with each address being used for a different purpose. This section describes the IPv6 address syntax and the various classes of IPv6 address.

IPv6 Address Syntax

The IPv6 128-bit address is divided at 16-bit boundaries, and each 16-bit block is converted to a four-digit hexadecimal number. Colons are used as separators. This representation is called *colon-hexadecimal.*

Global unicast IPv6 addresses are equivalent to IPv4 public unicast addresses. To illustrate IPv6 address syntax, consider the following IPv6 global unicast address:

21cd:0053:0000:0000:03ad:003f:af37:8d62

IPv6 representation can be simplified by removing the leading zeros within each 16-bit block. However, each block must have at least a single digit. With leading zero suppression, the address representation becomes:

21cd:53:0:0:3ad:3f:af37:8d62

A contiguous sequence of 16-bit blocks set to 0 in the colon-hexadecimal format can be compressed to ::. Thus, the previous example address could be written:

21cd:53::3ad:3f:af37:8d62

Some types of addresses contain long sequences of zeros and thus provide good examples of when to use this notation. For example, the multicast address ff05:0:0:0:0:0:0:2 can be compressed to ff05::2.

IPv6 Address Prefixes

The prefix is the part of the address that indicates either the bits that have fixed values or the network identifier bits. IPv6 prefixes are expressed in the same way as CIDR IPv4 notation, or *slash notation.* For example, 21cd:53::/64 is the subnet on which the address 21cd:53::23ad:3f:af37:8d62 is located. In this case, the first 64 bits of the address are the network prefix. An IPv6 subnet prefix (or subnet ID) is assigned to a single link. Multiple subnet IDs can be assigned to the same link. This technique is called *multinetting.*

NOTE **IPV6 DOES NOT USE DOTTED DECIMAL NOTATION IN SUBNET MASKS**

Only prefix-length notation is supported in IPv6. IPv4 dotted decimal subnet mask representation (such as 255.255.255.0) has no direct equivalent in IPv6.

IPv6 Address Types

The three types of IPv6 address are unicast, multicast, and anycast.

- **Unicast**   Identifies a single interface within the scope of the unicast address type. Packets addressed to a unicast address are delivered to a single interface. RFC 2373 allows multiple interfaces to use the same address, provided that these interfaces appear as a single interface to the IPv6 implementation on the host. This accommodates load balancing and fault tolerance on systems.

- **Multicast**   Identifies multiple interfaces. Packets addressed to a multicast address are delivered to all interfaces that are identified by the address.

- **Anycast**   Identifies multiple interfaces. Packets addressed to an anycast address are delivered to the nearest interface identified by the address. The nearest interface is the closest in terms of routing distance, or number of hops. An anycast address is used for one-to-one-of-many communication, with delivery to a single interface. Anycast addresses are used to provide high availability for services that provide access to replicated data, like DNS.

> **MORE INFO**   **IPV6 ADDRESSING ARCHITECTURE**
>
> For more information about IPv6 address structure and architecture, see RFC 2373 at *http://www.ietf.org/rfc/rfc2373.txt*.

> **NOTE**   **INTERFACES AND NODES**
>
> IPv6 addresses identify interfaces rather than nodes. A node is identified by any unicast address that is assigned to one of its interfaces.

IPv6 Unicast Addresses

IPv6 supports the following types of unicast address:

- Global
- Link-local
- Site-local/unique-local
- Special
- Network Service Access Point (NSAP) and Internetwork Packet Exchange (IPX) mapped addresses

Global Unicast Addresses

Global unicast addresses are the IPv6 equivalent of IPv4 public addresses and are globally routable and reachable on the Internet. These addresses can be aggregated to produce an efficient routing infrastructure and are, therefore, sometimes known as aggregatable global unicast addresses. An aggregatable global unicast address is unique across the entire Internet. (The region over which an IP address is unique is called the *scope* of the address.)

The Format Prefix (FP) of a global unicast address is held in the three most significant bits, which are always 001. The next 13 bits are allocated by the Internet Assigned Numbers Authority (IANA) and are known as the top-level aggregator (TLA). IANA allocates TLAs to local Internet registries, which, in turn, allocate individual TLAs to large ISPs. The next 8 bits of the address are reserved for future expansion. This represents the first 24 bits of the IPv6 address.

The next 24 bits of the address contain the next-level aggregator (NLA). This identifies a specific customer site. The NLA enables an ISP to create multiple levels of addressing hierarchy within a network. The next 16 bits contain the site-level aggregator, which is used to organize addressing and routing for downstream ISPs and to identify sites or subnets within a site. The first half, or 64 bits of the IPv6 address, is now spoken for.

The next 64 bits identify the interface within a subnet. This is the 64-bit Extended Unique Identifier (EUI-64) address, as defined by the Institute of Electrical and Electronics Engineers (IEEE). EUI-64 addresses are either assigned directly to network adapter cards or derived from the 48-bit Media Access Control (MAC) address of a network adapter, as defined by the IEEE 802 standard. Put simply, the interface identity is provided by the network adapter hardware.

Privacy Extensions for Stateless Address Autoconfiguration in IPv6

Concerns have been expressed that deriving an interface identity (ID) directly from computer hardware could enable the itinerary of a laptop and, hence, that of its owner to be tracked. This raises privacy issues, and future systems might allocate interface IDs differently.

RFC 3041 and RFC 4941 address this problem. For more information, see *http://www.ietf.org/rfc/rfc3041.txt* and *http://www.ietf.org/rfc/rfc4191.txt*.

To summarize, the FP, TLA, reserved bits, and NLA identify the public topology; the site-level aggregator identifies the site topology; and the ID identifies the interface. Figure 1-10 illustrates the structure of an aggregatable global unicast address.

3 bits (FP)	13 bits	8 bits	24 bits	16 bits	64 bits
001	TLAID	Res	NLAID	SLAID	Interface ID

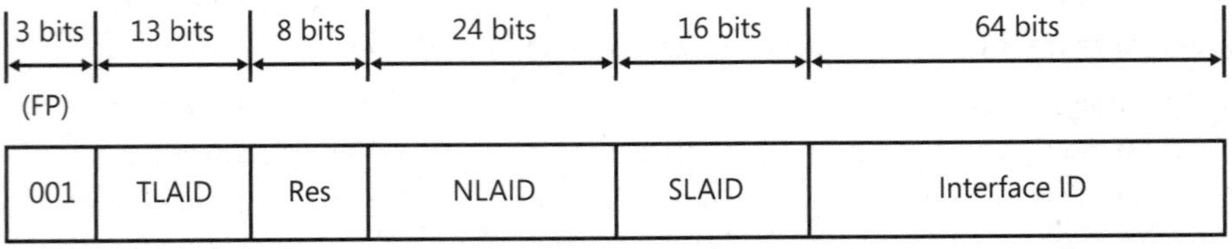

FIGURE 1-10 Global unicast address structure

LINK-LOCAL ADDRESSES

Link-local IPv6 addresses are equivalent to IPv4 addresses that are autoconfigured through APIPA and use the 169.254.0.0/16 prefix. You can identify a link-local address by an FP of 1111 1110 1000, which is followed by 52 zeros. (Link-local addresses always begin with fe80.) Nodes use link-local addresses when communicating with neighboring nodes on the same link. The scope of a link-local address is the local link. A link-local address is required for Neighbor Discovery (ND) and is always automatically configured, even if no other unicast address is allocated.

SITE-LOCAL/UNIQUE-LOCAL ADDRESSES

Site-local IPv6 addresses are equivalent to the IPv4 private address space (10.0.0.0/8, 172.16.0.0/12, and 192.168.0.0/16). Private intranets that do not have a direct, routed connection to the Internet can use site-local addresses without conflicting with aggregatable global unicast addresses. The scope of a site-local address is the site (or organization internetwork).

Site-local addresses can be allocated by using stateful address configuration, such as from a DHCPv6 scope. A host uses stateful address configuration when it receives router advertisement messages that do not include address prefixes. A host will also use a stateful address configuration protocol when no routers are present on the local link.

Site-local addresses can also be configured through stateless address configuration. This is based on router advertisement messages that include stateless address prefixes and require that hosts do not use a stateful address configuration protocol.

Alternatively, address configuration can use a combination of stateless and stateful configuration. This occurs when router advertisement messages include stateless address prefixes but require that hosts use a stateful address configuration protocol.

> **MORE INFO   IPV6 ADDRESS AUTOCONFIGURATION**
>
> For more information about how IPv6 addresses are configured, see *http://technet* *.microsoft.com/en-us/magazine/2007.08.cableguy.aspx*. Although the article is titled "IPv6 Autoconfiguration in Windows Vista," it also covers Windows Server 2008 autoconfiguration and describes the differences between autoconfiguration on a client and on a server operating system.

Site-local addresses begin with fec0 followed by 32 zeros and then by a 16-bit subnet identifier that you can use to create subnets within your organization. The *64-bit Interface ID* field identifies a specific interface on a subnet.

The command *ipconfig /all* shows link-local and site-local addresses (for DNS servers) configured on interfaces on the Windows Server 2008 domain controller Glasgow. No global addresses exist in the configuration because domain controllers should never be exposed directly to the Internet. The IPv6 addresses on your test computer will probably be different. The Glasgow domain controller has a virtual interface to the virtual machine that hosts the Melbourne client.

Link-Local and Site-Local/Unique-Local Addresses

You can implement IPv6 connectivity between hosts on an isolated subnet by using link-local (fe80::) addresses. However, you cannot assign link-local addresses to router interfaces (default gateways), and you cannot route from one subnet to another if only link-local addresses are used. DNS servers cannot use only link-local addresses. If you use link-local addresses, you need to specify their interface IDs—that is, the number after the % symbol at the end of the address. Link-local addresses are not dynamically registered in Windows Server 2008 DNS.

For these reasons, site-local (fec0::) or unique-local (fc00::) addresses are typically used on the subnets of a private network to implement IPv6 connectivity over the network. If every device on the network has its own global address (a stated aim of IPv6 implementation), global addresses can route between internal subnets, to peripheral zones, and to the Internet.

SPECIAL ADDRESSES

Two special IPv6 addresses exist—the *unspecified address* and the *loopback address*. The unspecified address 0:0:0:0:0:0:0:0 (or ::) indicates the absence of an address and is equivalent to the IPv4 unspecified address 0.0.0.0. It is typically used as a source address for packets attempting to verify whether a tentative address is unique. It is never assigned to an interface or used as a destination address. The loopback address 0:0:0:0:0:0:0:1 (or ::1) identifies a loopback interface and is equivalent to the IPv4 loopback address 127.0.0.1.

NSAP AND IPX ADDRESSES

NSAP addresses are identifying labels for network endpoints used in Open Systems Interconnection (OSI) networking. They are used to specify a piece of equipment connected to an Asynchronous Transfer Mode (ATM) network. IPX is no longer widely used because modern Novell Netware networks support TCP/IP. IPv6 addresses with an FP of 0000001 map to NSAP addresses. IPv6 addresses with an FP of 0000010 map to IPX addresses.

EXAM TIP

The 70-647 exam is unlikely to include questions about NSAP or IPX mapping.

IPv6 Multicast Addresses

IPv6 multicast addresses enable an IPv6 packet to be sent to a number of hosts, all of which have the same multicast address. They have an FP of 11111111. (They always start with ff.) Subsequent fields specify flags, scope, and group ID, as shown in Figure 1-11.

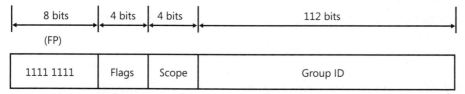

FIGURE 1-11 Multicast address structure

The *flags* field holds the flag settings. Initially, the only flag defined is the *Transient* (T) flag that uses the low-order field bit (bit number 12). If this flag is set to 0, the multicast address is well known—in other words, it is permanently assigned and has been allocated by IANA. If the flag is set to 1, the multicast address is transient.

Additionally, two new flags are available: the R flag and the P flag (bits number 10 and 11, respectively). When the R flag = 1, this signals a multicast address that embeds the address on the rendezvous point (Embedded RP). The P flag, when set to 1, signals that the multicast source's unicast prefix is included in the multicast group address. This defines a globally unique Group Address. If the R flag is set to 1, then the P and T flags must be set to 1 as well; for example, 1111 1111 0111. With R = 1, the P or T flags set to zero are undefined.

✔ **Quick Check**

- Which type of address is fc00:0:0:eadf::1ff?

Quick Check Answer

- Unicast unique-local

The *scope* field indicates the scope of the IPv6 internetwork for which the multicast traffic is intended. Routers use the multicast scope, together with information provided by multicast routing protocols, to determine whether multicast traffic can be forwarded. For example, traffic with the multicast address ff02::2 has a link-local scope and is never forwarded beyond the local link. Table 1-1 lists the assigned *scope* field values.

TABLE 1-1 *Scope* Field Values

0	Reserved
1	Node-local scope
2	Link-local scope
5	Site-local scope
8	Organization-local scope
E	Global scope
F	Reserved

The group ID represents the multicast group and is unique within the scope. Permanently assigned group IDs are independent of the scope. Transient group IDs are relevant only to a specific scope. Multicast addresses from ff01:: through ff0f:: are reserved, well-known addresses.

In theory, 2^{112} group IDs are available. In practice, because of the way that IPv6 multicast addresses are mapped to Ethernet multicast MAC addresses, RFC 2373, "IP Version 6 Addressing Architecture," recommends assigning the group ID from the low-order 32 bits of the IPv6 multicast address and setting the remaining original group ID bits to zero. In this way, each group ID maps to a unique Ethernet multicast MAC address.

THE SOLICITED-NODE MULTICAST ADDRESS

The solicited-node multicast address facilitates the querying of network nodes during address resolution. IPv6 uses the ND message to resolve a link-local IPv6 address to a node MAC address. Rather than use the local-link scope all-nodes multicast address (which would be processed by all nodes on the local link) as the neighbor solicitation message destination, IPv6 uses the solicited-node multicast address. This address comprises the prefix ff02::1:ff00:0/104 and the last 24 bits of the IPv6 address that is being resolved.

For example, if a node has the link-local address fe80::6b:28c:16d2:c97, the corresponding solicited-node address is ff02::1:ffd2:c97.

The result of using the solicited-node multicast address is that address resolution uses a mechanism that is not processed by all network nodes. Because of the relationship between the MAC address, the Interface ID, and the solicited-node address, the solicited-node address acts as a pseudo-unicast address for efficient address resolution.

IPv6 Anycast Addresses

An anycast address is assigned to interfaces on multiple hosts on the network. Packets sent to an anycast address are forwarded by the routing infrastructure to the nearest of these interfaces. The routing infrastructure must be aware of the interfaces that are assigned anycast addresses and their distance in terms of routing metrics. Currently, anycast addresses are used only as destination addresses and are assigned only to routers and several of the Internet's DNS root servers. Anycast addresses are assigned from the unicast address space, and the scope of an anycast address is the scope of the unicast address type from which the anycast address is assigned.

The objective of anycast addresses (although not yet fully implemented) is that an anycast address gets assigned to interfaces on different servers that provide the same service. These servers can reside on different subnets. When a client needs a service, the client sends its request for service to the anycast address for that service. The anycast packet gets routed to the nearest server with that anycast address. Any of the servers with the same anycast address could have responded, but IPv6 tunes itself in this manner to optimize efficiency.

THE SUBNET-ROUTER ANYCAST ADDRESS

The subnet-router anycast address is created from the subnet prefix for a given interface. In a subnet-router anycast address, the bits in the subnet prefix retain their current values and the remaining bits are set to zero.

All router interfaces attached to a subnet are assigned the subnet-router anycast address for that subnet. The subnet-router anycast address is used for communication with one of multiple routers that are attached to a remote subnet.

Investigating the Advantages of IPv6

IPv6 was designed to overcome the limitations of IPv4. This section lists the advantages that IPv6 has over its predecessor.

Increased Address Space

In retrospect, the 32-bit structure that IPv4 uses was not sufficient for an addressing structure. IPv6 offers 128 bits. This gives enough addresses for every device that requires one to have a unique public IPv6 address. In addition, the 64-bit host portion (interface ID) of an IPv6 ad-dress can be automatically generated from the network adapter hardware.

Automatic Address Configuration

Typically, IPv4 is configured either manually or by using DHCP. Automatic configuration (auto-configuration) through APIPA is available for isolated subnets that are not routed to other networks. IPv6 deals with the need for simpler and more automatic address configuration by supporting both stateful and stateless address configuration. Stateful configuration uses DHCPv6. If stateless address configuration is used, hosts on a link automatically configure themselves with IPv6 addresses for the link and (optionally) with addresses that are derived from prefixes advertised by local routers. You can also configure a stateless DHCPv6 configu-ration that does not assign addresses to hosts but can assign settings to (for example) DNS servers, the domain names of which are not included in the router advertisements.

Network-Level Security

Private communication over the Internet requires encryption to protect data from being viewed or modified in transit. IPsec provides this facility, but its use is optional in IPv4. IPv6 makes IPsec mandatory. This provides a standards-based solution for network security needs and improves interoperability among different IPv6 implementations.

Real-Time Data Delivery

Quality of service (QoS) exists in IPv4, and bandwidth can be guaranteed for real-time traffic (such as video and audio transmissions) over a network. However, IPv4 real-time traffic support relies on the *Type of Service* (*ToS*) field and the identification of the payload, typically using a User Datagram Protocol (UDP) or Transmission Control Protocol (TCP) port.

The *IPv4 ToS* field has limited functionality, and payload identification using a TCP port and a UDP port is not possible when an IPv4 packet payload is encrypted. Payload identification is included in the *Flow Label* field of the IPv6 header, so payload encryption does not affect QoS operation.

> ✔ **Quick Check**
>
> 1. How many bits are in an IPv4 address?
>
> 2. How many bits are in an IPv6 address?
>
> **Quick Check Answers**
>
> 1. 32
>
> 2. 128

Routing Table Size

The IPv6 global addresses used on the Internet are designed to create an efficient, hierarchical, and summarizable routing infrastructure based on the common occurrence of multiple levels of ISPs. On the Internet, backbone routers have greatly reduced routing tables that use route aggregation and correspond to the routing infrastructure of top-level aggregators.

Route Aggregation

Route aggregation provides for routing of traffic for networks with smaller prefixes to networks with larger prefixes. In other words, it permits a number of contiguous address blocks to be combined and summarized as a larger address block. Route aggregation reduces the number of advertised routes on large networks. When an ISP breaks its network into smaller subnets to provide service to smaller providers, it needs to advertise the route only to its main supernet for traffic to be sent to smaller providers.

Route aggregation is used when a large ISP has a contiguous range of IP addresses to manage. IP addresses (IPv4 or IPv6) that are capable of summarization are termed *aggregatable addresses*.

Header Size and Extension Headers

IPv4 and IPv6 headers are not compatible, and a host or router must use both IPv4 and IPv6 implementations to recognize and process both header formats. Therefore, the IPv6 header was designed to be as small as was practical. Nonessential and optional fields are moved to extension headers placed after the IPv6 header. As a result, the IPv6 header is only twice as large as the IPv4 header, and the size of IPv6 extension headers is constrained only by the size of the IPv6 packet.

Removal of Broadcast Traffic

IPv4 relies on Address Resolution Protocol (ARP) broadcasts to resolve IP addresses to the MAC addresses of network interface cards (NICs). Broadcasts increase network traffic and are inefficient because every host processes them.

The ND protocol for IPv6 uses a series of Internet Control Message Protocol for IPv6 (IC-MPv6) messages that manage the interaction of nodes on the same link (neighboring nodes). ND replaces ARP broadcasts, ICMPv4 router discovery, and ICMPv4 Redirect messages with efficient multicast and unicast ND messages.

Implementing IPv4-to-IPv6 Compatibility

In addition to the various types of addresses described earlier in this lesson, IPv6 provides the following types of compatibility addresses to aid migration from IPv4 to IPv6 and to implement transition technologies.

IPv4-Compatible Address

The IPv4-compatible address 0:0:0:0:0:0:w.x.y.z (or ::w.x.y.z) is used by dual-stack nodes that are communicating with IPv6 over an IPv4 infrastructure. The last four octets (w.x.y.z) represent the dotted decimal representation of an IPv4 address. Dual-stack nodes are nodes with both IPv4 and IPv6 protocols. When the IPv4-compatible address is used as an IPv6 destination, the IPv6 traffic is automatically encapsulated with an IPv4 header and sent to the destination using the IPv4 infrastructure.

IPv4-Mapped Address

The IPv4-mapped address 0:0:0:0:0:ffff:w.x.y.z (or ::ffff:w.x.y.z) is used to represent an IPv4-only node to an IPv6 node and, hence, to map IPv4 devices that are not compatible with IPv6 into the IPv6 address space. The IPv4-mapped address is never used as the source or destination address of an IPv6 packet.

Teredo Address

Teredo is an IPv6-within-IPv4 tunneling protocol. It is intended to tunnel the IPv6 packets within IPv4 to allow IPv6 systems to communicate with other IPv6 systems through a NAT server. In Windows Server 2008 R2 and Windows 7, the Teredo client is enabled but inactive by default and must be configured for proper functionality.

> **MORE INFO**   **TEREDO IMPLEMENTATION**
>
> For more information about implementing Teredo on Windows Server 2008 R2 and on Windows 7, see *http://technet.microsoft.com/en-us/library/ee126159(WS.10).aspx*.

A Teredo address consists of a 32-bit Teredo prefix. In Windows Server 2008 R2 (as well as Windows Vista and Windows 7), this is 2001::/32. The prefix is followed by the IPv4 (32-bit) public address of the Teredo server that assisted in the configuration of the address. The next 16 bits are reserved for Teredo flags. Currently, only the highest-ordered flag bit is defined. This is the *cone* flag and is set when the NAT device connected to the Internet is a cone NAT. A cone NAT stores the mapping between an internal address and port number and the public address and port number.

> **NOTE**   **WINDOWS XP AND WINDOWS SERVER 2003**
>
> In Windows XP and Windows Server 2003, the Teredo prefix was originally 3ffe:831f::/32. Computers running Windows XP and Windows Server 2003 use the 2001::/32 Teredo prefix when updated with Microsoft Security Bulletin MS06-064.

The next 16 bits store an obscured version of the external UDP port that corresponds to all Teredo traffic for the Teredo client interface. When a Teredo client sends its initial packet to a Teredo server, NAT maps the source UDP port of the packet to a different, external UDP port. All Teredo traffic for the host interface uses the same external, mapped UDP port. The value representing this external port is masked or obscured by XORing it with 0xffff. Obscuring the external port prevents NATs from translating it within the payload of packets that are being forwarded.

The final 32 bits store an obscured version of the external IPv4 address that corresponds to all Teredo traffic for the Teredo client interface. The external address is obscured by XORing the external address with 0xffffffff. As with the UDP port, this prevents NAT devices from translating the external IPv4 address within the payload of packets that are being forwarded. For example, the obscured version of the public IPv4 address 131.107.0.1 in colon-hexadecimal format is 7c94:fffe. (131.107.0.1 equals 0x836b0001 in hexadecimal, and 0x836b0001 XOR 0xffffffff equals 0x7c94fffe.) Obscuring the external address prevents NAT devices from translating it within the payload of the packets that are being forwarded. You can perform this operation using Windows Calculator in Scientific view.

As a further example, Northwind Traders currently implements the following IPv4 private networks at its headquarters and branch offices:

- Headquarters: 10.0.100.0 /24
- Branch1: 10.0.0.0 /24
- Branch2: 10.0.10.0 /24
- Branch3: 10.0.20.0 /24

The company wants to establish IPv6 communication among Teredo clients and between Teredo clients and IPv6-only hosts. The presence of Teredo servers on the IPv4 Internet enables this communication to take place. A Teredo server is an IPv6/IPv4 node connected to both the IPv4 Internet and the IPv6 Internet that supports a Teredo tunneling interface. The Teredo addresses of the Northwind Traders networks depend on a number of factors, such as the port and type of NAT server used, but they could, for example, be the following:

- Headquarters: 2001::ce49:7601:e866:efff:f5ff:9bfe through 2001::0a0a:64fe:e866:efff:f5ff:9b01
- Branch 1: 2001:: ce49:7601:e866:efff:f5ff:fffe through 2001::0a0a:0afe:e866:efff:f5ff:ff01
- Branch 2: 2001:: ce49:7601:e866:efff:f5ff:f5fe through 2001::0a0a:14fe:e866:efff:f5ff:f501
- Branch 3: 2001:: ce49:7601:e866:efff:f5ff:ebfe through 2001::0a0a:1efe:e866:efff:f5ff:ebfe

Note that, for example, 10.0.100.1 is the equivalent of 0a00:6401, and 0a00:6401 XORed with ffff:ffff is f5ff:9bfe.

EXAM TIP

The 70-647 exam objectives specifically mention Teredo addresses, which are supported by Microsoft. However, the exam is unlikely to ask you to generate a Teredo address. You might, however, be asked to identify such an address and work out its included IPv4 address. Fortunately, you have access to a scientific calculator during the exam.

Cone NATs

Cone NATs can be full cone, restricted cone, or port-restricted cone. In a full cone NAT, all requests from the same internal IP address and port are mapped to the same external IP address and port, and any external host can send a packet to the internal host by sending a packet to the mapped external address.

In a restricted cone NAT, all requests from the same internal IP address and port are mapped to the same external IP address and port, but an external host can send a packet to the internal host if the internal host had previously sent a packet to the external host.

In a port-restricted cone NAT, the restriction includes port numbers. An external host with a specified IP address and source port can send a packet to an internal host only if the internal host had previously sent a packet to that IP address and port.

Intra-Site Automatic Tunneling Addressing Protocol Addresses

IPv6 can use an *Intra-Site Automatic Tunnel Addressing Protocol* (ISATAP) address to communicate between two nodes over an IPv4 intranet. An ISATAP address starts with a 64-bit unicast link-local, site-local, global, or 6to4 global prefix. The next 32 bits are the ISATAP identifier 0:5efe. The final 32 bits hold the IPv4 address in either dotted decimal or hexadecimal notation. An ISATAP address can incorporate either a public or a private IPv4 address.

For example, the ISATAP fe80::5efe:w.x.y.z address has a link-local prefix; the fec0::1111:0:5efe:w.x.y.z address has a site-local prefix; the 3ffe:1a05:510:1111:0:5efe:w.x.y.z address has a global prefix; and the 2002:9d36:1:2:0:5efe:w.x.y.z address has a 6to4 global prefix. In all cases, w.x.y.z represents an IPv4 address.

By default, Windows Server 2008 automatically configures the ISATAP address fe80::5efe:w.x.y.z for each IPv4 address that is assigned to a node. This link-local ISATAP address enables two hosts to communicate over an IPv4 network by using each other's ISATAP address.

You can implement IPv6-to-IPv4 configuration by using the *netsh interface ipv6 6to4*, *netsh interface ipv6 isatap*, and *netsh interface ipv6 add v6v4tunnel* IPv6 commands. For example, to create an IPv6-in-IPv4 tunnel between the local address 10.0.0.11 and the remote address 192.168.123.116 on an interface named *Remote*, you would type **netsh interface ipv6 add v6v4tunnel "Remote" 10.0.0.11 192.168.123.116**.

You can also configure the appropriate compatibility addresses manually by using the *netsh interface ipv6 set address* command or the Internet Protocol Version 6 (TCP/IPv6) GUI as described in the next section of this lesson.

NOTE **6TO4CFG**

Windows Server 2008 does not support the 6to4cfg tool.

Planning an IPv4-to-IPv6 Transition Strategy

No specific timeframe is mandated for IPv4-to-IPv6 transition. As an enterprise administrator, one of your decisions is whether to be an early adopter and take advantage of IPv6 enhancements, such as addressing and stronger security, or wait and take advantage of the experience of others. Both are valid strategies.

However, you do need to find out whether your upstream ISPs support IPv6 and whether the networking hardware in your organization (or the several organizations in your enterprise) also supports the protocol. The most straightforward transition method, *dual stack*, requires that both IPv4 and IPv6 be supported. By the same token, do not delay the decision to transition to IPv6 for too long. If you wait until the IPv4 address space is fully depleted, dual stack will no longer be available, and you (and the users you support) will find the transition process much more challenging.

Currently, the underlying assumption in transition planning is that an existing IPv4 infrastructure is available and that your most immediate requirement is to transport IPv6 packets over existing IPv4 networks so that isolated IPv6 network islands do not occur. As more networks make the transition, the requirement will change to transporting IPv4 packets over IPv6 infrastructures to support earlier IPv4 applications and avoid isolated IPv4 islands.

Several transition strategies and technologies exist because no single strategy fits all. RFC 4213, "Basic Transition Mechanisms for Hosts and Routers," describes the key elements of these transition technologies, such as dual-stack and configured tunneling. The RFC also defines a number of node types based on their protocol support, including previous systems that support only IPv4, future systems that will support only IPv6, and the dual node that implements both IPv6 and IPv4.

> **MORE INFO** **IPV4-TO-IPV6 TRANSITION**
>
> For more information about basic transition mechanisms, see *http://www.ietf.org/rfc /rfc4213.txt,* and download the white paper, "IPv6 Transition Technologies," from *http://technet.microsoft.com/en-us/library/bb726951.aspx.*

Dual-Stack Transition

Dual stack (also known as a dual IP layer) is arguably the most straightforward approach to transition. It assumes that hosts and routers provide support for both protocols and can send and receive both IPv4 and IPv6 packets. Thus, a dual-stack node can interoperate with an IPv4 device by using IPv4 packets and interoperate with an IPv6 device by using IPv6 packets. It can also operate in one of the following three modes:

- Only the IPv4 stack enabled
- Only the IPv6 stack enabled
- Both IPv4 and IPv6 stacks enabled

Because a dual-stack node supports both protocols, you can configure it with both IPv4 32-bit addresses and IPv6 128-bit addresses. It can use, for example, DHCP to acquire its IPv4 addresses and stateless autoconfiguration or DHCPv6 to acquire its IPv6 addresses. Current IPv6 implementations are typically dual stack. An IPv6-only product would have very few communication partners.

Configured Tunneling Transition

If a configured tunneling transition strategy is employed, the existing IPv4 routing infrastructure remains functional but also carries IPv6 traffic while the IPv6 routing infrastructure is under development. A tunnel is a bidirectional, point-to-point link between two network endpoints. Data passes through a tunnel using encapsulation, in which the IPv6 packet is carried inside an IPv4 packet. The encapsulating IPv4 header is created at the tunnel entry point and removed at the tunnel exit point. The tunnel endpoint addresses are determined from configuration information that is stored at the encapsulating endpoint.

Configured tunnels are also called *explicit tunnels*. You can configure them as router-to-router, host-to-router, host-to-host, or router-to-host, but they are most likely to be used in a router-to-router configuration. The configured tunnel can be managed by a *tunnel broker*, a dedicated server that manages tunnel requests coming from end users, as described in RFC 3053, "IPv6 Tunnel Broker."

> **MORE INFO TUNNEL BROKER**
>
> For more information about tunnel brokers, see *http://www.ietf.org/rfc/rfc3053.txt*.

Automatic Tunneling

RFC 2893, "Transition Mechanisms for IPv6 Hosts and Routers" (replaced by RFC 4213), describes automatic tunneling. This enables IPv4/IPv6 nodes to communicate over an IPv4 routing infrastructure without using preconfigured tunnels. The nodes that perform automatic tunneling are assigned a special type of address called an IPv4-compatible address, which carries the 32-bit IPv4 address within a 128-bit IPv6 address format. The IPv4address can be automatically extracted from the IPv6 address.

> **MORE INFO AUTOMATIC TUNNELING**
>
> For more information about automatic tunneling, see *http://www.ietf.org/rfc/rfc2893.txt*. Be aware, however, that the status of this document is obsolete; RFC 4213 is the current standard.

6to4

RFC 3056, "Connection of IPv6 Domains via IPv4 Clouds," describes the 6to4 tunneling scheme, which enables IPv6 sites to communicate with each other via an IPv4 network without using explicit tunnels and to communicate with native IPv6 domains by relay routers. This strategy treats the IPv4 Internet as a single data link.

> **MORE INFO   6TO4 TUNNELING**
>
> For more information about 6to4 tunneling, see *http://www.ietf.org/rfc/rfc3056.txt*.

Teredo

RFC 4380, "Teredo: Tunneling IPv6 over UDP through Network Address Translations (NATs)," describes Teredo, which is an enhancement to the 6to4 method and is supported by Windows Server 2008 R2. Teredo enables nodes that are located behind an IPv4 NAT device to obtain IPv6 connectivity by using UDP to tunnel packets. Teredo requires the use of server and relay elements to assist with path connectivity. Teredo address structure was discussed earlier in this lesson.

> **MORE INFO   TEREDO**
>
> For more information about Teredo, see *http://www.ietf.org/rfc/rfc4380.txt* and *http://technet.microsoft.com/en-us/network/cc917486.aspx*.

ISATAP

RFC 4214, "Intra-Site Automatic Tunnel Addressing Protocol (ISATAP)," defines ISATAP, which connects IPv6 hosts and routers over an IPv4 network, using a process that views the IPv4 network as a link layer for IPv6, and other nodes on the network as potential IPv6 hosts or routers. This creates a host-to-host, host-to-router, or router-to-host automatic tunnel.

> **MORE INFO   ISATAP**
>
> For more information about ISATAP, see *http://www.ietf.org/rfc/rfc4214.txt* and download the "Manageable Transition to IPv6 Using ISATAP" white paper from *http://www.microsoft.com/downloads/details.aspx?FamilyId=B8F50E07-17BF-4B5C -A1F9-5A09E2AF698B&displaylang=en*.

Using IPv6 Tools

Windows Server 2008 R2 provides tools with which you can configure IPv6 interfaces and check IPv6 connectivity and routing. Tools also exist that implement and check IPv4 to IPv6 compatibility.

In Windows Server 2008 R2, the standard command-line tools such as *ping*, *ipconfig*, *pathping*, *tracert*, *netsh*, *netstat*, and *route* have full IPv6 functionality. Use the *ping* command to check connectivity with a link-local IPv6 address on a test network. Note that if you were pinging from one host to another, you would also need to include the interface ID, for example, *ping fe80::fd64:b38b:cac6:cdd4%15*. Interface IDs are discussed later in this lesson.

> **NOTE   PING6**
>
> The *ping6* command-line tool is not supported in Windows Server 2008 R2.

Tools specific to IPv6 are provided in the *netsh* (network shell) command structure. For example, the *netsh interface ipv6 show neighbors* command shows the IPv6 interfaces of all hosts on the local subnet. You use this command in the practice session later in this lesson, after you have configured IPv6 connectivity on a subnet.

Verifying IPv6 Configuration and Connectivity

If you are troubleshooting connectivity problems or merely want to check your configuration, arguably the most useful tool—and certainly one of the most widely used—is *ipconfig*. The *ipconfig /all* tool displays both IPv4 and IPv6 configuration.

If you want to display the configuration of only the IPv6 interfaces on the local computer, you can use the *netsh interface ipv6 show address* command. Figure 1-12 shows the output of this command run on the Glasgow computer. Note the % character followed by a number after each IPv6 address. This is the interface ID, which identifies the interface that is configured with the IPv6 address.

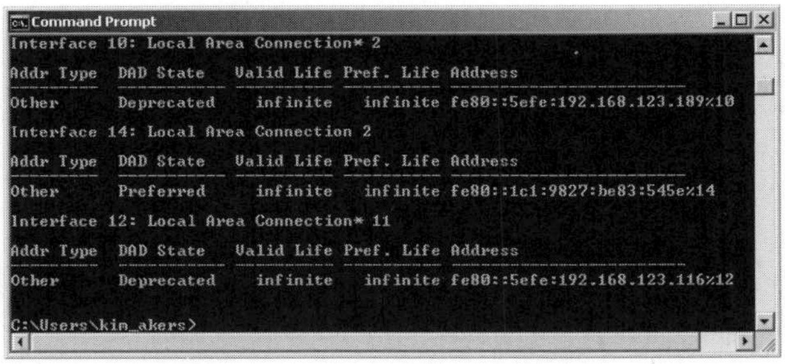

FIGURE 1-12 Displaying IPv6 addresses and interface IDs

If you are administering an enterprise network with a number of sites, you also need to know site IDs. You can obtain a site ID by using the *netsh interface ipv6 show address level=verbose* command.

Configuring IPv6 Interfaces

Typically, most IPv6 addresses are configured through autoconfiguration or DHCPv6. However, if you need to configure an IPv6 address manually, you can use the *netsh interface ipv6 set address* command, as in this example: *netsh interface ipv6 set address "local area connection 2" fec0:0:0:fffe::2*, where "local area connection 2" is the name of the network connection that you wish to configure. You need to run the command console (also known as the command prompt) as an administrator to use this command. In Windows Server 2008 R2 (as well as in Windows Vista and Windows 7), you can also manually configure IPv6 addresses from the TCP/IPv6 Properties dialog box. Figure 1-7, presented earlier in this chapter, shows this configuration.

The advantage of using the TCP/IPv6 Properties dialog box is that you can specify the IPv6 addresses of one or more DNS servers in addition to specifying the interface address. If, however, you choose to use command-line interface commands, the command to add the IPv6 addresses of DNS servers is *netsh interface ipv6 add dnsserver*, as in this example: *netsh interface ipv6 add dnsserver "local area connection 2" fec0:0:0:fffe::1*. To change the properties of IPv6 interfaces (but not their configuration), use the *netsh interface ipv6 set interface* command, as in this example: *netsh interface ipv6 set interface "local area connection 2" forwarding=enabled*. You need to run the command console (command prompt) as an administrator to use the *netsh interface ipv6 add* and *netsh interface ipv6 set* commands.

> ✔ **Quick Check**
> - Which *netsh* command lists site IDs?
>
> **Quick Check Answer**
> - *netsh interface ipv6show address level=verbose*

Verifying IPv6 Connectivity

To verify connectivity on a local network, your first step should be to flush the neighbor cache, which stores recently resolved link-layer addresses and might give a false result if you are checking changes that involve address resolution. You can check the contents of the neighbor cache by using the *netsh interface ipv6 show neighbors* command. The *netsh interface ipv6 delete neighbors* command flushes the cache. You need to run the command console as an administrator to use the *netsh* tool.

You can test connectivity to a local host on your subnet and to your default gateway by using the *ping* command. You can add the interface ID to the IPv6 interface address to ensure that the address is configured on the correct interface. Figure 1-13 shows a *ping* command using an IPv6 address and an interface ID.

To check connectivity to a host on a remote network, your first task should be to check and clear the destination cache, which stores next-hop IPv6 addresses for destinations. You can display the current contents of the destination cache by using the *netsh interface ipv6 show destinationcache* command. To flush the destination cache, use the *netsh interface ipv6 delete destinationcache* command. You need to run the command console as an administrator to use this command.

FIGURE 1-13 Pinging an IPv6 address with an interface ID

Your next step is to check connectivity to the default router interface on your local subnet. This is your default gateway. You can identify the IPv6 address of your default router interface by using the *ipconfig, netsh interface ipv6 show route*, or *route print* commands. You can also specify the zone ID, which is the interface ID for the default gateway on the interface on which you want the ICMPv6 Echo Request messages to be sent. When you have ensured that you can reach the default gateway on your local subnet, ping the remote host by its IPv6 address. Note that you cannot ping a remote host (or a router interface) by its link-local IPv6 address because link-local addresses are not routable.

If you can connect to the default gateway but cannot reach the remote destination address, trace the route to the remote destination by using the *tracert –d* command followed by the destination IPv6 address. The *–d* command-line switch prevents the *tracert* tool from performing a DNS reverse query on router interfaces in the routing path. This speeds up the display of the routing path. If you want more information about the routers in the path, and particularly if you want to verify router reliability, use the *pathping –d* command, again followed by the destination IPv6 address.

> ✔ **Quick Check**
> - Which *netsh* command could you use to identify the IPv6 address of your default router interface?
>
> **Quick Check Answer**
> - *netsh interface ipv6 show route*

Troubleshooting Connectivity

As an experienced administrator, you know that if you cannot connect to a remote host, you (or more probably a more junior member of your team) first want to check the various hardware connections (wired and wireless) in your organization and ensure that all network devices are running. If these basic checks do not find the problem, the IPsec configuration might not be properly configured, or firewall problems (such as incorrectly configured packet filters) might exist.

You can use the IP Security Policies Management MMC snap-in to check and configure IPsec policies, and the Windows Firewall with Advanced Security snap-in to check and configure IPv6-based packet filters. Figures 1-14 and 1-15 show these tools.

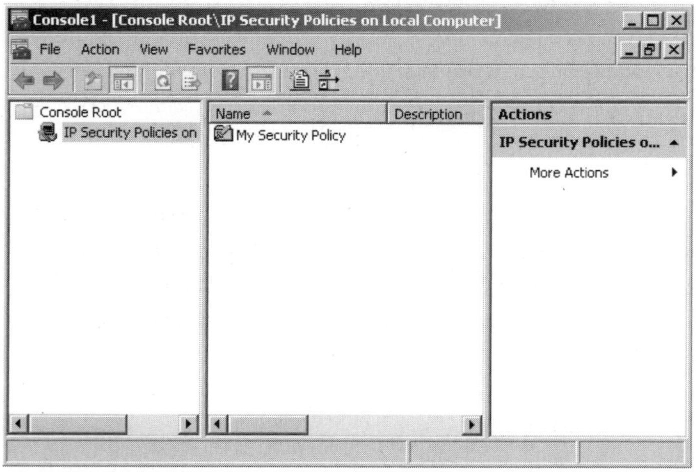

FIGURE 1-14 The IP Security Policies Management snap-in

NOTE **IPSEC6**

The IPSec6 tool is not implemented in Windows Server 2008 or in Windows Server 2008 R2.

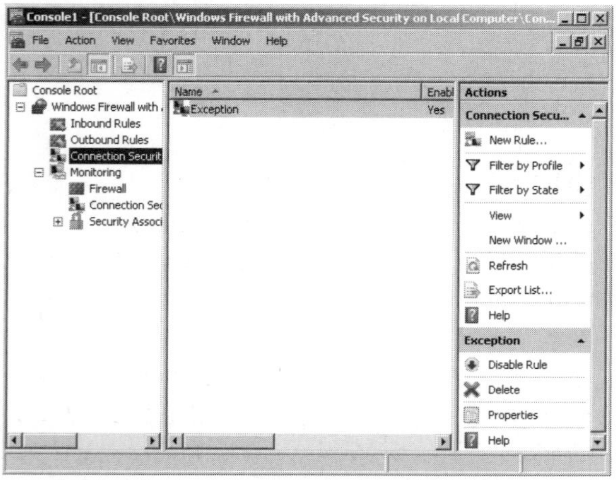

FIGURE 1-15 The Windows Firewall with Advanced Security snap-in

You might be unable to reach a local or remote destination because of incorrect or missing routes in the local IPv6 routing table. You can use the *route print*, *netstat –r*, or *netsh interface ipv6 show route* commands to view the local IPv6 routing table and verify that you have a route corresponding to your local subnet and to your default gateway. Note that the *netstat –r* command displays both IPv4 and IPv6 routing tables.

If you have multiple default routes with the same metric, you might need to modify your IPv6 router configurations so that the default route with the lowest metric uses the interface that connects to the network with the largest number of subnets. You can use the *netsh interface ipv6 set route* command to modify an existing route. To add a route to the IPv6 routing table, use the *netsh interface ipv6 add route* command. The *netsh interface ipv6 delete route* command removes an existing route. You need to run the command console as an administrator to use these commands.

If you can access a local or remote host by IPv4 address but not by hostname, you might have a DNS problem. Tools to configure, check, and debug DNS include *dnscmd, ipconfig, netsh interface ipv6 show dnsservers, netsh interface ipv6 add dnsserver, nslookup,* and the TCP/IPv6 Properties dialog box. This chapter has discussed these tools in earlier sections of both lessons.

Verifying IPv6-Based TCP Connections

If the Telnet client tool is installed, you can verify that a TCP connection can be established to a TCP port by entering the *telnet* command followed by the destination IPv6 address and the TCP port number, as in this example: *telnet fec0:0:0:fffe::1 80*. If Telnet successfully creates a TCP connection, the telnet> prompt appears, and you can type Telnet commands. If the tool cannot create a connection, it will return an error message.

> **MORE INFO** **INSTALLING THE TELNET CLIENT**
>
> For more information about Telnet, including how to install the Telnet client, search Windows Server 2008 R2 Help for "Telnet: frequently asked questions."

Configuring Clients Through DHCPv6

You can choose stateless or stateful configuration when configuring hosts by using DHCPv6. Stateless configuration does not generate a host address—which is instead autoconfigured—but it can, for example, specify the address of a DNS server. Stateful configuration specifies host addresses.

Whether you choose stateful or stateless configuration, you can assign the IPv6 addresses of DNS servers through the DNS Recursive Name Server DHCPv6 option (option 0023). If you choose stateful configuration, the IPv6 addresses of DNS servers can be configured as a scope option, so different scopes could have different DNS servers. Scope options override server options for that scope. This is the preferred method of configuring DNS server IPv6 addresses, which are not configured through router discovery.

With DHCPv6, an IPv6 host can receive subnet prefixes and other configuration parameters. A common use of DHCPv6 for Windows-based IPv6 hosts is to configure the IPv6 addresses of DNS servers automatically.

Currently, when you configure an IPv6 scope, you specify the 64-bit prefix. By default, DHCPv6 can allocate host addresses from the entire 64-bit range for that prefix. This allows for IPv6 host addresses that are configured through adapter hardware. You can specify exclusion ranges, so if you wanted to allocate only host addresses in the range fec0::0:0:0:1 through fec0::0:0:0:fffe, you would exclude addresses fec0::0:0:1:1 through fec0::ffff:ffff:ffff:fffe.

Several DHCPv6 options exist. Arguably the most useful option specifies the DNS server. Other options are concerned with compatibility with other systems that support IPv6, such as the UNIX Network Information Service (NIS).

DHCPv6 is similar to DHCP in many respects. For example, scope options override server options, and DHCPv6 requests and acknowledgments can pass through BootP-enabled routers and layer-3 switches (almost all modern routers and switches act as DHCP relay agents) so that a DHCPv6 server can configure clients on a remote subnet.

> **_NOTE_ CONFIGURING A DHCP RELAY AGENT**
>
> If you want to configure a Windows Server 2008 R2 server as a DHCP relay agent, you need to install the Routing and Remote Access Services (RRAS) role service, available under the Network Policy and Access Services role.

As with DHCP, you can implement the 80:20 rule so that a DHCPv6 server is configured with a scope for its own subnet that contains 80 percent of the available addresses for that subnet and a second scope for a remote subnet that contains 20 percent of the available addresses for that subnet. A similarly configured DHCPv6 server on the remote subnet provides failover. If either server fails, the hosts on both subnets still receive their configurations.

For example, the Tailspin Toys Melbourne office network has two private virtual local area networks (VLANs) that have been allocated the following site-local networks:

- VLAN1: fec0:0:0:aaaa::1 through fec0:0:0:aaaa::fffe
- VLAN2: fec0:0:0:aaab::1 through fec0:0:0:aaab::fffe

Exceptions are defined so that IPv6 addresses on the VLANs can be statically allocated to servers. In this case, you could implement the 80:20 rule by configuring the following DHCPv6 scopes on the DHCP server on VLAN1:

- fec0:0:0:aaaa::1 through fec0:0:0:aaaa::cccb
- fec0:0:0:aaab::cccc through fec0:0:0:aaab::fffe

You would then configure the following DHCPv6 scopes in the DHCP server on VLAN2:

- fec0:0:0:aaab::1 through fec0:0:0:aaab::cccb
- fec0:0:0:aaaa::cccc through fec0:0:0:aaaa::fffe

DHCP servers, and especially DHCP servers that host 20-percent scopes, are excellent candidates for virtualization because they experience only limited I/O activity. Additionally, you can deploy this role on a Server Core installation of Windows Server 2008. This technique is particularly applicable to more complex networks.

For example, Trey Research is a single-site organization but has five buildings within its site, which are connected by fiber optic links to a layer-3 switch configured to allocate a VLAN to each building. VLAN1, allocated to the main office, supports the majority of the company's computers. VLAN3 supports most of the remainder. VLAN2, VLAN4, and VLAN5 each support only a few computers.

In this case, you can configure the DHCP server on VLAN1 to host 80 percent of the VLAN1 address range. You can configure a virtual DHCP server on the same VLAN to host 20 percent of the VLAN2 through VLAN5 address ranges. On VLAN3, you can configure a DHCP server to host the 80 percent ranges for VLAN2 through VLAN5 and a virtual server to host the 20 percent range for VLAN1. If either server fails, hosts on all the VLANs can continue to receive their configurations through DHCP.

Installing the DHCP Server role and configuring a DHCPv6 scope are practical procedures and are, therefore, covered in detail in the practice session later in this lesson.

Planning an IPv6 Network

Configuring IPv6 and implementing IPv6 are relatively straightforward. Planning an IPv6 network is more complex. Every scenario has unique features, but, in general, you might want to deploy IPv6 in conjunction with an existing IPv4 network. You might have applications that require IPv6, although your network is principally IPv4. You might want to design a new network or restructure a current one so it is primarily IPv6. You could be designing a network for a large multinational company with multiple sites and thousands of users or for a small organization with a head office and a single branch office.

Whatever the scenario, you will need to maintain interoperability with former functions and with IPv4. Even in a new IPv6 network, it is (currently) unlikely that you can ignore IPv4 completely.

Analyzing Hardware Requirements

An early step in the design process is to identify and analyze the required network infrastructure components. Hardware components could include the following:

- Routers
- Layer-3 switches
- Printers
- Faxes
- Firewalls
- Intrusion-detection equipment
- Hardware load balancers
- Load-balancing server clusters
- Virtual private network (VPN) entry and exit points
- Servers and services
- Network interconnect hardware
- Intelligent NICs

This list is not exhaustive, and you might need to consider other hardware devices, depending on the scenario. Which of these hardware devices store, display, or allow the input of IP addresses? Can all the necessary hardware be upgraded to work with IPv6? If not, what are the workarounds? If you need to replace hardware, is there a budget and a time frame for hardware refresh?

Analyzing Software and Application Requirements

From the software and applications viewpoint, network management is the area most likely to be affected by the version of IP used, although some line-of-business (LOB) applications could also be affected. You might need to consider the IPv6 operation and compatibility of the following components:

- Network infrastructure management, such as WINS
- Network management systems, such as systems based on Simple Network Management Protocol (SNMP)
- Performance management systems
- High-level network management applications (typically third-party applications)
- Configuration management, such as DHCP and DHCPv6
- Security policy management and enforcement
- LOB applications
- Transition tools

Consideration of transition tools implies the requirement—except in a new IPv6 network—of determining the transition strategy you want to deploy. Transition strategies were discussed earlier in this lesson and depend largely on the planned scenario and whether both IPv4 and IPv6 stacks are available. If some previous components do not support IPv6, you need to consider how to support them while transitioning is in progress and whether you will continue to support them in a dual-stack network when transitioning is complete. You need to ensure interoperability between IPv4 and IPv6 components.

Possibly your first step in configuration management is to decide whether to use stateful or stateless configuration. With IPv6, it is possible to have every component on your network configured with its own global unicast address. Security is implemented by firewalls, virus filters, spam filters, IP filtering, and all the standard security methods. IPsec provides end-to-end encryption. You can configure peripheral zones in IPv6 networks like you can in IPv4 networks. DHCPv6 in stateless mode can configure options—for example, DNS servers—that are not configured through router discovery. In either case, you need to ensure that your ISP is IPv6-compliant and obtain a range of IPv6 addresses.

Integrating DHCP with Network Access Protection

You can further increase security on your network by integrating DHCP and DHCPv6 with Network Access Protection (NAP). NAP provides policy enforcement components that help ensure that computers connecting to or communicating on a network comply with administrator-defined requirements for system health and limit the access of computers that do not meet these requirements to a restricted network. The restricted network contains the resources needed to remediate computers so that they meet the health requirements. When you integrate DHCP with NAP, a computer must be compliant to obtain an unlimited access IP address configuration from a DHCP server. Network access for noncompliant computers is limited through an IP address configuration that allows access only to a restricted network. DHCP enforcement ensures that clients conform to health policy requirements every time a DHCP client attempts to lease or renew an IP address configuration. DHCP enforcement also actively monitors the health status of the NAP client and renews the IP address configuration for access to only the restricted network if the client becomes noncompliant.

When planning DHCP integration with NAP, you must decide whether DHCP NAP enforcement will be enabled on all DHCP scopes, selected DHCP scopes, or no DHCP scopes at all. In addition, you must configure which NAP profile to use for DHCP NAP enforcement. Last, you must determine how a DHCP server will behave when the Network Policy Server (NPS) is unreachable. A DHCP server can be configured to allow full access, allow restricted access, or drop client packets when the NPS server is unreachable.

To learn more about NAP, see *http://technet.microsoft.com/en-us/network/bb545879.aspx*.

You might decide that exposing the global unicast addresses of all your network components to the Internet represents a security risk. This is a matter of debate in the networking community and is outside the scope of this book. If you do make that decision, you can choose to implement site-local IPv6 addresses on your internal subnets, assuming your NAT servers support IPv6. You can choose stateful configuration by DHCPv6. Assuming that your routers or layer-3 switches can pass DHCP traffic, you can follow the 80:20 rule across your subnets or VLANs to ensure that configuration still occurs if a DHCP server is down.

When you have made the basic decisions about network infrastructure and transitioning strategy, and have discovered whether your current network (or proposed new network) is capable of supporting IPv6, you then need to address other requirements and considerations. For example, unless you are implementing a new IPv6 network, you need to ensure that IPv4 infrastructure is not disrupted during the transition. With this requirement in mind, it might not be feasible to deploy IPv6 on all parts of your network immediately.

Alternatively, if your only requirement is to deploy a set of specified IPv6 applications (such as peer-to-peer communication), your IPv6 deployment might be limited to the minimum required to operate this set of applications.

Documenting Requirements

Your next step is to determine and document exactly what is required. For example, you might need to address the following questions:

- Is external connectivity (to the Internet, for example) required?
- Does the organization have one site or several sites? If the latter, what are the geographical locations of the sites, and how is information currently passed securely between them?
- What is the current IPv4 structure of the internetwork?
- What IPv6 address assignment plan is available from the provider?
- What IPv6 services does the provider offer?
- How should prefix allocation be delegated in the enterprise?
- Are site-external and site-internal IPv6 routing protocols required? If so, which ones?
- Does the enterprise currently use an external data center? (For example, are servers located at the provider?)
- Is IPv6 available using the same access links as IPv4?
- Which applications need to support IPv6 and can they be upgraded to do so? Will these applications need to support both IPv4 and IPv6?
- Do the enterprise platforms support both IPv4 and IPv6? Is IPv6 installed by default on server and client platforms?
- Is NAT v4–v6 available, and do the applications have any issues with using it?
- Do the applications need globally routable IP addresses?
- Will multicast and anycast addresses be used?

You also need to analyze and document the working patterns and support structure within the organization. You need to obtain the following information:

- Who takes ownership of the network? For example, is network support in-house or outsourced?

- Does a detailed asset management database exist?

- Does the organization support remote workers? If so, how?

- Is IPv6 network mobility used or required for IPv6?

- What is the enterprise's policy for geographical numbering?

- Do separate sites in the enterprise have different providers?

- What is the current IPv4 QoS policy (assuming you are not designing a new IPv6-only network)? Will this change when IPv6 is implemented?

- What proposals are in place for training technical staff in the use of IPv6?

Documenting and analyzing this information will take some time. However, without this documentation, you will not know the precise requirements for IPv6 implementation, and the project will take much longer and result in a less satisfactory outcome. When you have gathered the information, you can plan the tasks you and your team need to perform and the requirements for each. You will have a better idea of the time and cost of the project and whether it should be implemented in stages.

Your next step is to draw up and implement a project plan. Project planning is beyond the scope of this book. However, you would be wise to heed this warning: Do not ignore what might seem to be peripheral or not time-critical activities. Training your technical staff is a good example. Every part of the final plan is important, and unless every aspect is implemented, the result will be less than optimal. In the worst case, the project can fail completely because of an unconsidered component.

> **MORE INFO** **IPV6 NETWORK SCENARIOS**
>
> For more information about IPv6 planning and specific scenario examples, see RFC 4057, "IPv6 Enterprise Network Scenarios," at *http://www.ietf.org/rfc/rfc4057*.

PRACTICE Configuring IPv6 Connectivity

In this practice, you configure a site-local IPv6 address on your client computer interface that connects to your private subnet (the IPv4 10.0.0.0/24 subnet). You test IPv6 connectivity between your client and domain controller. You then install the DHCP Server role on your domain controller and configure a DHCPv6 scope.

NOTE **LOGGING ON TO THE DOMAIN CONTROLLER**

You perform the server configurations in this practice session by interactively logging on to the domain controller with an administrative-level account. However, in a production network, this would be bad practice. If you want to make the exercises more realistic, you can log on to your client computer and connect to your server through Remote Desktop or run Administrative Tools on a client and specify the server within the tool.

EXERCISE 1 Configure IPv6

In this exercise, you configure IPv6 site-local addresses on your client computer and test connectivity. You need to have configured the IPv6 settings on your domain controller in Lesson 1 before you start this exercise.

1. Log on to your client computer, Melbourne, on the *contoso.internal* domain by using the Kim_Akers account.
2. From Control Panel, access Network And Sharing Center. If you are not using Classic View, first click Network And Internet, and then click Network And Sharing Center. Click Change Adapter Settings.
3. Right-click the interface that connects to your private network and choose Properties.
4. If a UAC dialog box appears, click Continue.
5. Select Internet Protocol Version 6 (TCP/IPv6) and click Properties.
6. Configure a static site-local IPv6 address, fec0:0:0:fffe::a.
7. Configure a DNS server address, fec0:0:0:fffe::1. The Properties dialog box should look similar to Figure 1-16.

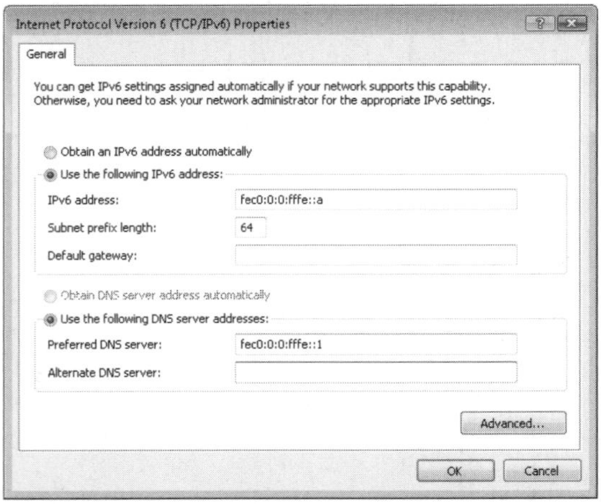

FIGURE 1-16 IPv6 configuration on the client

8. Click OK. Close the Local Area Connections Properties dialog box.

9. Close the Network Connections dialog box.

10. Close Network And Sharing Center.

> **NOTE VIRTUAL MACHINES**
>
> If you are using a virtual machine to implement your server and client on the same computer, it is a good idea to close your virtual machine and restart your computer after configuring interfaces.

11. Open the command console on the client computer. Enter **ping fec0:0:0:fffe::1**. You should get the response from the domain controller shown in Figure 1-17.

FIGURE 1-17 Pinging the domain controller from the client

> **NOTE FIREWALL CONFIGURATION**
>
> If the firewall on either your Glasgow domain controller or your Melbourne client blocks ICMP traffic, you need to reconfigure this setting (or settings) before this command will work.

12. Enter **ping glasgow**. Note that the domain controller hostname resolves to the IPv6 address.

13. Log off from the client computer.

14. Log on to your domain controller, using the Kim_Akers account.

15. Open the command console on your domain controller.

16. Enter **ping fec0:0:0:fffe::a**. You should get the response shown in Figure 1-18.

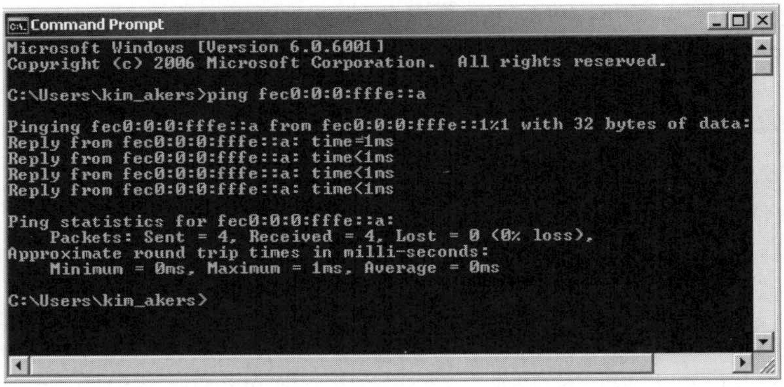

FIGURE 1-18 Pinging the client from the domain controller

17. Enter **netsh interface ipv6 show neighbors**. Figure 1-19 shows the fec0:0:0:fffe::a interface as a neighbor on the same subnet as the domain controller.

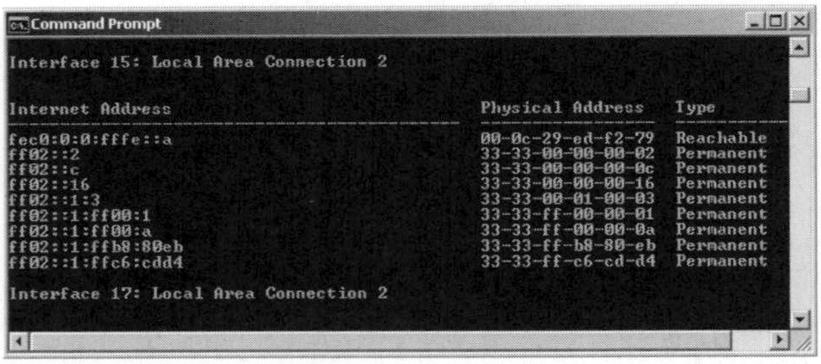

FIGURE 1-19 Showing the domain controller neighbors

EXERCISE 2   Install the DHCP Server Role

In this exercise, you install the DHCP Server role and specify that DHCPv6 can provide stateful IPv6 configuration.

1. If necessary, log on to the domain controller by using the Kim_Akers account.

2. If the Initial Configuration Tasks window opens when you log on, click Add Roles. Otherwise, from Administrative Tools, open Server Manager, right-click Roles in the console tree, and choose Add Roles.

3. The Add Roles Wizard starts. If the Before You Begin page appears, click Next.

4. Select the DHCP Server check box, as shown in Figure 1-20, and click Next. On the Introduction To DHCP Server page, click Next.

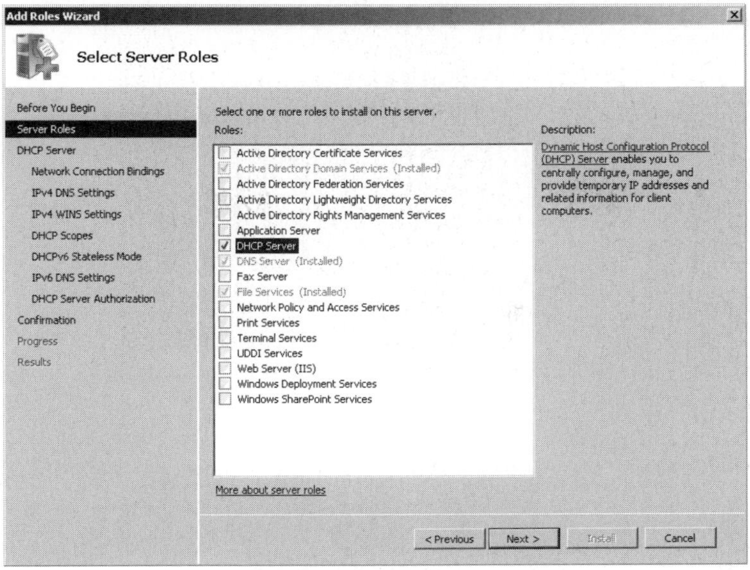

FIGURE 1-20 Selecting to install the DHCP Server role

5. On the Select Network Connection Bindings page, ensure that only the 10.0.0.11 IPv4 interface check box is selected for DHCP. Click Next.

6. On the Specify IPv4 DNS Server Settings page, verify that the domain is *contoso .internal* and the Preferred DNS Server IPv4 Address is 10.0.0.11. Click Next.

7. On the Specify IPv4 WINS Settings page, verify that WINS Is Not Required For Applications On This Network is selected. Click Next.

8. On the Add Or Edit DHCP Scopes page, you can define only IPv4 scopes, so the scope list should be empty. Click Next.

9. On the Configure DHCPv6 Stateless Mode page, select Disable DHCPv6 Stateless Mode For This Server. This enables you to use the DHCP Management Console to configure DHCPv6 after the DHCP Server role has been installed. Figure 1-21 shows this setting. Click Next.

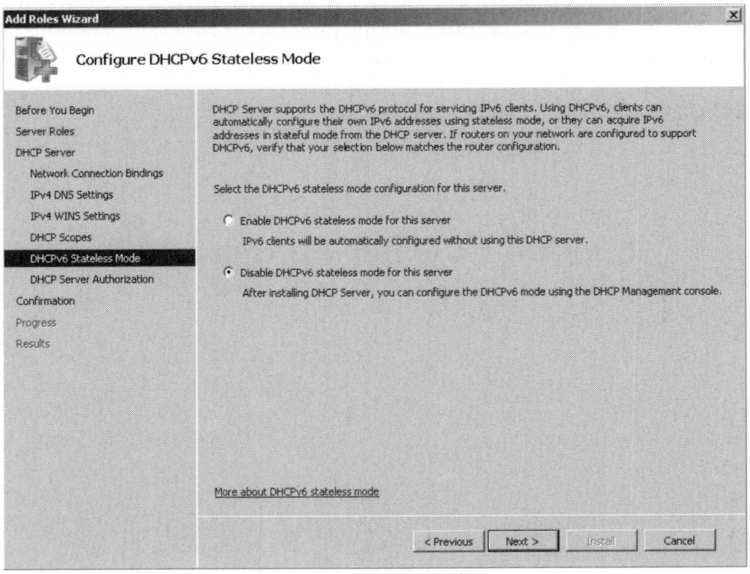

FIGURE 1-21 Disabling DHCPv6 stateless mode

10. On the Authorize DHCP Server page, ensure that Use Current Credentials is selected. Click Next.

11. On the Confirm Installation Selections page, check your settings.

12. Click Install. Click Close when installation completes.

13. Restart the domain controller.

    Note that a reboot is always a good idea after you have installed a server role, even if you are not prompted to do so, especially if you are using virtual machines.

EXERCISE 3   Set Up a DHCPv6 Scope

In this exercise, you configure a DHCPv6 scope. You need to have configured the IPv6 settings on your client and domain controller computers and installed the DHCP Server role on your domain controller before you carry out this exercise.

1. If necessary, log on to the domain controller by using the Kim_Akers account.

2. In Administrative Tools, choose DHCP.

3. If a UAC dialog box appears, click Continue to close it.

4. Expand *glasgow.contoso.internal*. Expand IPv6. Ensure that a green check mark appears beside the IPv6 icon. This confirms that the DHCPv6 Server is authorized.

5. Right-click IPv6 and choose New Scope. The New Scope Wizard opens. Click Next.

6. Give the scope a name (such as **Private Network Scope**) and type a brief description. Click Next.

7. Set Prefix to **fec0::fffe**. You are configuring only one IPv6 scope on this subnet and do not need to set Preference. Your screen should look similar to Figure 1-22. Click Next.

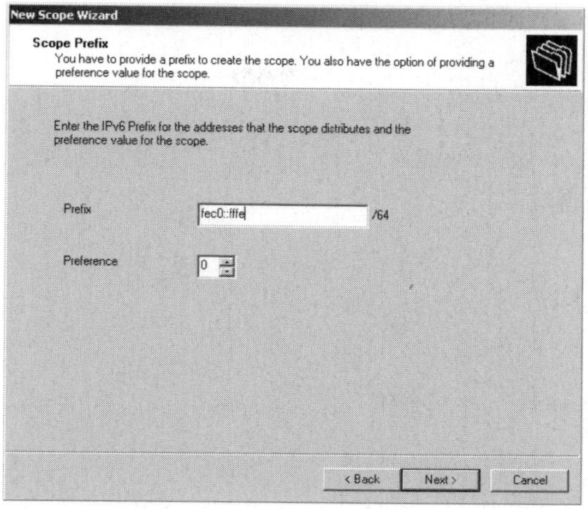

FIGURE 1-22 Setting a DHCPv6 prefix

8. You want to exclude IPv6 addresses fec0:0:0:fffe::1 through fec0:0:0:fffe::ff from the scope. Specify a Start Address of **0:0:0:1** and an End Address of **0:0:0:ff** on the Add Exclusions page and click Add, as shown in Figure 1-23.

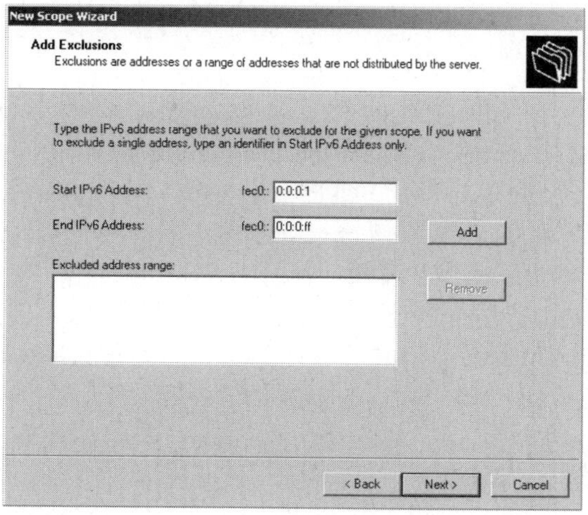

FIGURE 1-23 Configuring DHCPv6 scope exclusions

9. Click Next. You can set the scope lease on the Scope Lease page. For the purposes of this practice, the lease periods are acceptable. Click Next. Check the scope summary, ensure that Yes is selected under Activate Scope Now, and then click Finish.

10. In the DHCP console, expand the scope, right-click Scope Options, choose Configure Options, and examine the available options. Select Option 0023 DNS Recursive Server

IPv6 Address List. Specify fec0:0:0:fffe::1 as the DNS Server IPv6 address, as shown in Figure 1-24.

11. Click Add, and then click OK. Close the DHCP console.

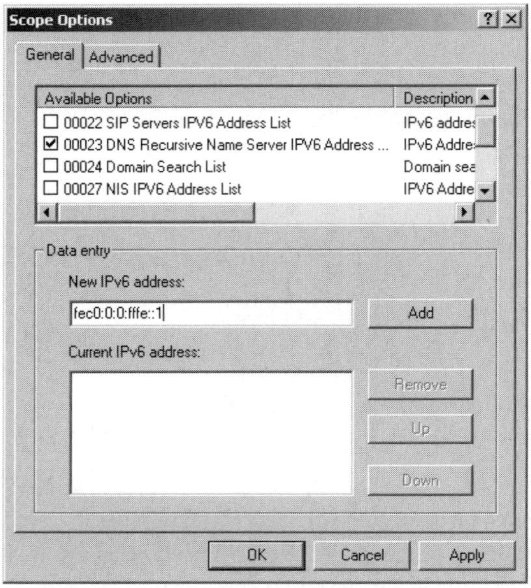

FIGURE 1-24 Specifying a DNS server for DHCPv6 configuration

Lesson Summary

- IPv6 supports unicast, multicast, and anycast addresses. Unicast addresses can be global, site-local, link-local, or special. IPX and NSAP mapped addresses are also supported.

- IPv6 is fully supported in Windows Server 2008 R2 and addresses problems, such as lack of address space, that are associated with IPv4.

- IPv6 is designed to be backward-compatible, and IPv4-compatible addresses can be specified. Transitioning strategies include dual stack, configured tunneling, automatic tunneling, 6to4, Teredo, and ISATAP.

- IPv6 addresses can be configured through stateful (DHCPv6) and stateless (autoconfiguration) methods. DHCPv6 can also be used statelessly to configure (for example) DNS servers when hosts are autoconfigured.

- Tools to configure and troubleshoot IPv6 include *ping*, *ipconfig*, *tracert*, *pathping*, and *netsh*. You can also configure IPv6 by using the TCP/IPv6 Properties GUI.

Lesson Review

Use the following questions to test your knowledge of the information in Lesson 2, "Planning Internet Protocol Addressing." The questions are also available on the companion CD if you prefer to review them in electronic form.

> **NOTE** **ANSWERS**
>
> Answers to these questions and explanations of why each answer choice is correct or incorrect are located in the "Answers" section at the end of the book.

1. Which type of IPv6 address is the equivalent of a public unicast IPv4 address?
   - **A.** Unique-local
   - **B.** Global
   - **C.** Link-local
   - **D.** Special

2. A node has a link-local IPv6 address of fe80::6b:28c:16a7:d43a. What is its corresponding solicited-node address?
   - **A.** ff02::1:ffa7:d43a
   - **B.** ff02::1:ff00:0:16a7:d43a
   - **C.** fec0::1:ff a7:d43a
   - **D.** fec0::1:ff00:0:16a7:d43a

3. Which protocol uses ICMPv6 messages to manage the interaction of neighboring nodes?
   - **A.** ARP
   - **B.** EUI-64
   - **C.** DHCPv6
   - **D.** ND

4. Which IPv6-to-IPv4 transition strategy uses preconfigured tunnels and encapsulates an IPv6 packet within an IPv4 packet?
   - **A.** Configured tunneling
   - **B.** Dual stack
   - **C.** ISATAP
   - **D.** Teredo

5. Which command enables you to configure an IPv6 address manually on a specified interface?
   - **A.** *netsh interface ipv6 show address*
   - **B.** *netsh interface ipv6 add address*

C. *netsh interface ipv6 set interface*

D. *netsh interface ipv6 set address*

6. Trey Research is an innovative research organization that prides itself on being at the forefront of technology. The company currently has 82 client computers all running Windows Vista Ultimate. All its servers—including its domain controllers—have recently been upgraded to Windows Server 2008 R2 Enterprise. Trey's site consists of two buildings linked by a fiber optic cable. Each building has its own VLAN, and Trey's peripheral zone is on a separate VLAN. All Trey's clients receive their IPv4 configurations through DHCP, and the 80:20 rule is used to implement failover if a DHCP server fails. All servers and router interfaces are configured manually, as are the company's network printers and network projectors. Trey has a Class C public IPv4 allocation and sees no need to implement NAT. It uses a network management system based on SNMP. It uses a number of high-level graphics applications in addition to business software and the Microsoft Office 2010 suite. The company wants to introduce IPv6 configuration and access the Internet. It has verified that its provider and all its network hardware fully support IPv6. Which of the following are likely to form part of Trey's IPv6 implementation plan? (Choose all that apply.)

   A. Trey is likely to adopt a dual-stack transition strategy.

   B. Trey is likely to adopt a configured tunneling transition strategy.

   C. Trey is likely to configure its internal network hosts with unique-local unicast addresses.

   D. Trey is likely to configure its internal network hosts with global unicast addresses.

   E. Trey needs to ensure that its servers and clients support IPv6.

   F. Trey needs to ensure that its network projectors and network printers support IPv6.

   G. Trey needs to ensure that its network management system is compatible with IPv6.

   H. Trey needs to ensure that its graphic applications are compatible with IPv6.

Chapter Review

To further practice and reinforce the skills you learned in this chapter, you can perform the following tasks:

- Review the chapter summary.
- Review the list of key terms introduced in this chapter.
- Complete the case scenarios. These scenarios set up real-world situations involving the topics in this chapter and ask you to create a solution.
- Complete the suggested practices.
- Take a practice test.

Chapter Summary

- IPv6 is fully supported in Windows Server 2008 R2 and is installed by default. It supports unicast, multicast, and anycast addresses. It is backward-compatible with IPv4 and offers a selection of transitioning strategies.
- IPv6 addresses can be configured through stateful and stateless configuration. Both GUI and command-line interface tools are available to configure IPv6 and check network connectivity.
- Windows Server 2008 R2 DNS fully supports IPv6 in addition to offering several new and enhanced features. It conforms to all current standards. GUI and command-line interface tools are available to configure DNS and check DNS functionality.

Key Terms

Do you know what these key terms mean? You can check your answers by looking up the terms in the glossary at the end of the book.

- 6to4
- AAAA forward lookup record
- Active Directory integrated zone
- Anycast
- BIND server
- Conditional forwarding
- DNS Cache Locking
- DNS Devolution
- DNS Socket Pool
- dnscmd
- DNSSEC

- Dual stack
- Forwarder
- Global unicast address
- GlobalNames zone
- ISATAP
- Link-local address
- Loopback address
- Multicast/broadcast
- Network Address Translation
- NS record
- nslookup
- Primary zone
- Read-only zone
- Reverse look-up zone
- Root hints
- Secondary zone
- SRV record
- Start of Authority (SOA)
- Stub zone
- Teredo
- Unicast
- Unique-local address
- Unspecified address
- WINS replication partners
- Zone transfer

Case Scenarios

In the following case scenarios, you apply what you have learned about planning name resolution and IP addressing. You can find answers to these questions in the "Answers" section at the end of this book.

Case Scenario 1: Configuring DNS

You administer the Windows Server 2008 R2 AD DS network at Blue Yonder Airlines. When the company upgraded to Windows Server 2008 R2, it also introduced Active Directory–integrated DNS, although two BIND servers are still used as secondary DNS servers. Answer the following questions.

1. Blue Yonder has set up wireless hotspots for the convenience of its customers. However, management is concerned that attackers might attempt to register their computers in the company's DNS. How can you ensure against this?

2. Your boss is aware of the need to replicate DNS zones to the two stand-alone BIND servers. She is concerned that an attacker might attempt to replicate DNS zone information to an unauthorized server, thus exposing the names and IP addresses of company computers. How do you reassure her?

3. For additional security, Blue Yonder uses RODCs at its branch locations. Management is concerned about keeping DNS zone information on these computers up to date. What information can you provide?

4. Blue Yonder wants to use an application that needs to resolve IPv6 addresses to hostnames. How do you implement this functionality?

Case Scenario 2: Implementing IPv6 Connectivity

You are a senior network administrator at Wingtip Toys. Your corporate network consists of two subnets with contiguous private IPv4 networks configured as VLANs connected to a layer-3 switch. Wingtip Toys accesses its ISP and the Internet through a dual-homed server running Internet Security and Acceleration (ISA) Server that provides NAT and firewall services and connects through a peripheral zone to a hardware firewall and, hence, to its ISP. The company wants to implement IPv6 connectivity. All of the network hardware supports IPv6, as does the ISP. Answer the following questions.

1. What options are available for the type of unicast address used on the subnets?

2. Given that the Wingtip Toys network can support both IPv4 and IPv6, what is the most straightforward transition strategy?

3. You decide to use stateful configuration to allocate IPv6 configuration on the two subnets. How should you configure your DHCPv6 servers to provide failover protection?

Suggested Practices

To help you successfully master the exam objective presented in this chapter, complete the following tasks.

Configure DNS

Do both practices in this section.

- **Practice 1** Use the command-line interface tools. It would take an entire book to do justice to the *nslookup*, *dnscmd*, *ipconfig*, and *netsh* tools. The only way to become familiar with these tools is to use them.

- **Practice 2** Configure IPv6 reverse lookup zones. This procedure was described earlier in the lesson. Specifying IPv6 reverse lookup zones in DNS can be an error-prone procedure because of the way the prefixes are specified. You will become comfortable with this notation only through practice.

Configure IPv6 Connectivity

Complete Practice 1 and Practice 2. Practice 3 is optional.

- **Practice 1** Investigate *netsh* commands. The *netsh* command structure provides you with many powerful commands. In particular, use the help function in the command console to investigate the *netsh interface ipv6 set*, *netsh interface ipv6 add*, and *netsh interface ipv6 show* commands. Also investigate the *netshdhcp* commands.

- **Practice 2** Find out more about DHCPv6 scope and server options. Use the DHCP administrative tool to list the DHCP scope and server options. Access Windows Server 2008 R2 Help and the Internet to find out more about these options. In the process, you should learn something about NIS networks. Although the 70-647 exam objectives do not cover NIS, you should, as a network professional, know what it is.

- **Practice 3** Test DHCPv6 address allocation. If you have access to additional computers with suitable client operating systems, connect them to your network and configure them to obtain IPv6 configuration automatically. Ensure that the DHCPv6 scope you have configured provides configuration for these computers. Ensure that the host IPv6 addresses configured fall outside the fec0:0:0:fffe::1 through fec0:0:0:fffe::ff range, which includes the IPv6 addresses for the Glasgow and Melbourne computers.

Take a Practice Test

The practice tests on this book's companion CD offer many options. For example, you can test yourself on just one exam objective, or you can test yourself on all the 70-647 certification exam content. You can set up the test so that it closely simulates the experience of taking a certification exam, or you can set it up in study mode so that you can look at the correct answers and explanations after you answer each question.

> ***MORE INFO*** **PRACTICE TESTS**
>
> **For details about all the practice test options available, see the "How to Use the Practice Tests" section in this book's introduction.**

CHAPTER 2

Designing Active Directory Domain Services

Active Directory Domain Services (AD DS) is arguably one of the most important server roles in Windows Server 2008 R2. AD DS provides the basis for authentication and authorization for virtually all other server roles in Windows Server 2008 R2 and is the foundation for the Microsoft Identity and Access solutions. Additionally, a number of enterprise products, such as Microsoft Exchange Server and Microsoft Windows SharePoint Services, require AD DS.

As an enterprise administrator, you are likely accountable for the architecture of AD DS in your organization. Even though virtually all large organizations have already deployed AD DS, you will inevitably need to design it because of constantly changing business and technical requirements. Designing AD DS for large organizations is a complex task. As an enterprise administrator, you must be able to gather the relevant business and technical requirements, and you must design AD DS to meet these requirements.

This chapter empowers you to design AD DS forests and domains as well as the AD DS physical topology.

Exam objectives in this chapter:

- Design Active Directory forests and domains.
- Design Active Directory physical topology.
- Design for data management and data access.

Lessons in this chapter:

Before You Begin

No special setup is required for this chapter.

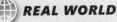 **REAL WORLD**

John Policelli

When Active Directory directory service was first released as part of the Microsoft Windows 2000 Server operating system, many organizations quickly made a decision to migrate from Microsoft Windows NT 4.0 to Active Directory. The buzz on the street was that Active Directory was a more robust directory service than the security accounts manager (SAM) database used in Windows NT 4.0, it provided significant scalability, and it promised to reduce administrative overhead. Unfortunately, many organizations failed to realize the full benefits of Active Directory because they did not spend enough time gathering requirements; therefore, their design was inadequate.

When moving from Windows NT 4.0 to Active Directory, most organizations failed to reassess business and technical requirements and, as a result, were left with an Active Directory structure that was almost identical to the Windows NT 4.0 structure from which they were trying to move away. Many of these same organizations have since realized that insufficient planning and lack of business-requirements gathering has left them with a bloated Active Directory structure. A number of these organizations have multiple-year plans to consolidate the number of forests and domains so that they can fully realize the benefits of Active Directory Domain Services (AD DS).

Designing AD DS requires a thorough understanding of business and technical requirements. Investing the time to gather these requirements properly at the outset and then designing AD DS based on these requirements can save you a significant amount of time and expense in the future.

Lesson 1: Designing AD DS Forests and Domains

When designing AD DS in Windows Server 2008 R2, you need to start with forests and domains. Forests and domains act as the security, administration, and replication boundary for AD DS and are required before you can design the physical topology.

The first part of your design will be the forest structure. To design the forest structure, you need to start by gathering a number of requirements. When you have gathered the relevant forest requirements, you can determine the number of forests you require and, finally, design the forest model. After you have completed the forest design, you need to design the domain structure. Designing the domain structure also starts with gathering a set of business and technical requirements that will enable you to determine the domain model and the number of domains you require. Because most organizations already have AD DS, you will also need to decide whether to upgrade existing domains or deploy new ones. Last, you will need to design the forest root domain and domain trees. When you have designed the forest and domain structure, you need to design forest and domain functional levels, design the schema, and design trusts to optimize intraforest authentication.

This lesson provides you with the knowledge needed to gather relevant business and technical requirements and then to create a forest and domain design in Windows Server 2008 R2 based on these requirements.

> **After this lesson, you will be able to:**
> - Gather forest and domain design requirements.
> - Determine the number of forests and domains required.
> - Design the forest model.
> - Design the domain model.
> - Decide whether to upgrade existing domains or deploy new ones.
> - Design the forest root domain.
> - Design forest and domain functional levels.
> - Design the AD DS schema.
> - Design trusts to optimize intraforest authentication.
>
> **Estimated lesson time: 45 minutes**

Designing the Forest Structure

Every AD DS design starts with designing the forest structure. Without a design for the forest structure, you will not be able to design the subsequent logical and physical components within AD DS. Designing the forest structure consists of identifying the role of AD DS in your organization; gathering business, technical, security, and network requirements; gathering autonomy and isolation requirements; determining the number of forests required; and designing the forest model.

> **MORE INFO** **WHAT'S NEW IN AD DS IN WINDOWS SERVER 2008 R2?**
>
> For more information about the changes in AD DS functionality in Windows Server 2008 R2, go to *http://technet.microsoft.com/en-us/library/dd378796(WS.10).aspx.*

Identifying the Role of AD DS

Before you can design the forest structure, you need to understand the role AD DS will have in your organization. It can be used in a variety of ways. For example, it can be used as a network operating system (NOS), as an enterprise directory, or as an Internet directory. Also, an organization can have requirements to use AD DS for more than one purpose; for instance, as an NOS directory and as an enterprise directory. How AD DS will be used in your organization will have an effect on the forest structure.

When AD DS will be used strictly as an NOS directory, a single forest is usually sufficient. However, as you will see, there are exceptions to this general rule when diverse organizational structure, operational, or legal requirements exist within an organization.

When AD DS will be used as an enterprise directory, you must consider a number of factors before you will be able to design the forest structure, and you must understand the requirements to store information within the enterprise directory. First, identify whether the enterprise directory will store confidential employee information such as payroll information. If so, determine whether access to this information needs to be restricted, because authenticated users have ready access to virtually all attributes in AD DS. If the enterprise directory will store confidential employee information, and access to this information should be restricted, it is more effective to deploy a separate forest for the enterprise directory or deploy an Active Directory Lightweight Directory Services (AD LDS) instance, both of which will affect the design of the forest structure. Although it is technically possible to modify permissions on attributes, doing so can be very complex when attributes are shared by both an NOS directory and an enterprise directory.

After you have an understanding of the requirements to store confidential information, determine whether the enterprise directory will require custom attributes and classes. Enterprise directories usually store more information, such as organizational information and payroll information, than NOS directories. Because this information varies for each organization, most enterprise directories introduce a requirement to modify the default AD DS schema, and you must identify any requirements for custom attributes and classes and assess the impact of these modifications on the schema when designing the forest structure. As previously mentioned, new attributes are visible to authenticated users. If the enterprise directory requires custom attributes, and access to these attributes must be restricted, a separate AD DS forest or an AD LDS instance is better suited to be the enterprise directory. By using either a separate AD DS forest or a separate AD LDS instance, the enterprise directory will have a dedicated schema that will not conflict with the schema for the NOS directory.

Last, when AD DS will be used as an Internet directory, there are a number of additional factors to consider as part of the design of the forest structure. Internet directories are typically used to store customer or partner identity information, which is accessed through publicly accessible servers and applications. Most organizations are legally required to restrict access to customer information. Additionally, most organizations want to separate customer and partner identities from employee identities for organizational structure and operational and security requirements. If AD DS will be used as an Internet directory, a separate AD DS forest or an AD LDS instance is required to meet organizational structure and operational, legal, and security requirements.

Gathering Business, Technical, Security, and Network Requirements

After you have a thorough understanding of the role that AD DS will have in your organization, you must gather the business, technical, and security requirements. These requirements for the forest structure typically fall into one or more of the following categories:

- Organizational structural requirements
- Operational requirements
- Legal requirements
- Limited connectivity requirements

A proper understanding of the organizational structure is essential in designing the forest structure. For example, there might be a requirement for a particular business unit to operate independently from the rest of the organization so that the business unit can be divested in the future with minimal effort. Also, a particular business unit might have a requirement to install a number of directory-enabled applications that require changes to the AD DS schema. In both cases, the business unit's unique requirements might have a negative impact on the rest of the organization if the business unit belongs to the same forest as the rest of the organization. To gather organizational structure requirements, start by identifying the various groups within the organization that will take advantage of AD DS. Next, determine whether any of these groups require the ability to operate separately from the rest of the organization. If you do find organizational structure requirements that are unique to a specific group, you must determine whether these requirements will adversely affect the rest of the organization. In most cases, this impact can be mitigated only by deploying a separate forest for each business unit that has diverse requirements from the rest of the organization.

After you have identified the organizational structure requirements, gather the operational requirements that will influence the forest structure design. Organizations such as the military and hosting companies that use AD DS are commonly bound by unique operational requirements. To identify operational requirements, start by inventorying the operational teams in the organization along with the operational requirements for each team. By completing this inventory of requirements, you will be able to select the appropriate forest design model.

You must also have an understanding of the legal requirements to which an organization must adhere in order to design the forest structure. Some organizations, such as financial institutions and government organizations, have legal requirements to function in a specific way, such as restricting access to certain information as specified in a business contract. Failure to meet these requirements can result in loss of the contract and possible legal action. When gathering legal requirements as part of your forest structure design, start by identifying the legal obligations with which the organization must comply. Next, determine whether these legal obligations can be met by using a single AD DS forest. If not, a separate forest will be required as part of the forest structure design.

Finally, identifying any limited connectivity requirements is essential in the design of the forest structure. Some organizations have limited connectivity requirements, such as groups that are located on restricted or isolated networks. Start by identifying all groups within the organization that have such limitations. For each group with limited connectivity requirements, gather the details of which networks these groups are permitted to connect to or are restricted from accessing.

Gathering Autonomy and Isolation Requirements

In addition to the forest design requirements, you must identify the autonomy and isolation requirements to design the forest structure effectively.

Autonomy involves independent control of a resource. With autonomy, the control is not exclusive. When you achieve autonomy, administrators have the authority to manage resources independently; however, there are administrators with greater authority who also have control over those resources and can take away control if necessary. The forest structure can be designed to achieve the following types of autonomy:

- **Service autonomy**   *Service autonomy* involves control over all or part of service management. Service autonomy might be required for a group within an organization that wants to be able to control the service level of AD DS by adding and removing domain controllers as needed.

- **Data autonomy**   *Data autonomy* involves control over all or part of the data stored in the directory or on member computers (member computers implies they are joined to the directory). Data autonomy does not prevent service administrators in the forest from accessing the data.

Isolation consists of independent, exclusive control of a resource. When you achieve isolation, administrators have the authority to manage a resource independently, and no other administrators can take away control of the resource. The forest structure can be designed to achieve the following types of isolation:

- **Service isolation**   *Service isolation* prevents administrators other than those specifically designated to control service management from controlling or interfering with service management. Operational or legal requirements typically create a need for service isolation.

- **Data isolation** *Data isolation* prevents administrators other than those specifically designated to control or view data from controlling or viewing a subset of data in the directory or on member computers. Because data stored in AD DS and on computers joined to AD DS cannot be isolated from service administrators, the only way for a group within an organization to achieve complete data isolation is to create a separate forest for that data.

> **MORE INFO   AUTONOMY VS. ISOLATION**
>
> For more information about autonomy versus isolation, go to *http://technet.microsoft.com /en-us/library/cc770331(WS.10).aspx*.

Determining the Number of Forests Required

After you have collected the forest design requirements, the next step is to determine the number of forests required. Start by reviewing the role of AD DS in your organization. If you are designing a forest for an NOS directory, a single forest can be used. If you are designing a forest as an enterprise directory, determine whether the existing NOS directory can be extended to act as an enterprise directory also. As previously mentioned, if the schema and data confidentiality of the enterprise directory will differ from those of the NOS directory, a separate forest is required for the enterprise directory. Alternatively, if the schema and data confidentiality requirements of the NOS directory and of the enterprise directory are consistent, a single forest will suffice. Finally, if you are designing the forest as an Internet directory, you will need to deploy a dedicated forest to ensure the separation of employee and client data.

After you have reviewed the role of AD DS in your organization, review the autonomy and isolation requirements to determine the number of forests required. Remember that with autonomy, control is not exclusive. As such, if you have identified data autonomy and service autonomy requirements, use a single forest. Conversely, if you have identified data isolation and service isolation requirements, deploy a separate forest because isolation consists of independent control.

When determining the number of forests required, it is also imperative to incorporate the cost and administrative differences between a single-forest model and a multiple-forest model into your design decision. A single forest requires the least amount of hardware and administrative effort, which makes this model the most cost effective. Multiple forests require additional hardware and administrative effort. When determining the number of forests required, you must weigh the costs of additional forests against the requirements to deploy these additional forests.

> **MORE INFO   DETERMINING THE NUMBER OF FORESTS REQUIRED**
>
> For more information about determining the number of forests required, go to *http://technet.microsoft.com/en-us/library/cc731528(WS.10).aspx*.

Designing the Forest Model

When you have collected the forest design requirements, select the appropriate forest model to meet them by first understanding the different forest models that exist. You can select from three forest models when designing the forest structure:

- **Organizational forest model**   In the *organizational forest model*, user accounts and resources exist in the same forest and are managed separately. The organizational forest model is used to provide service autonomy, service isolation, or data isolation. Figure 2-1 illustrates the organizational forest model.

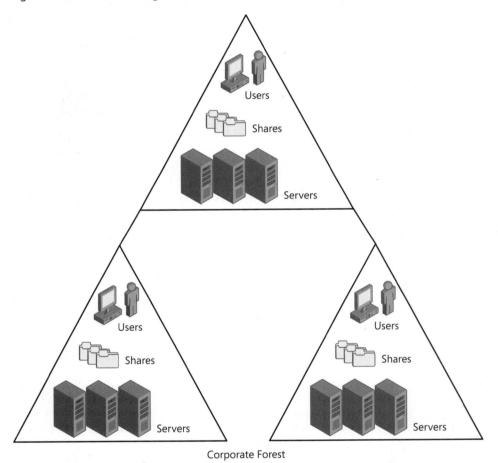

Corporate Forest

FIGURE 2-1 Organizational forest model

Use the organizational forest model when you need to provide exclusive or inclusive control of the AD DS infrastructure or when you need to prevent administrators from controlling or viewing a subset of data in the directory or on member computers joined to the directory.

- **Resource forest model**   In the *resource forest model*, a separate forest is used to manage resources. Resource forests do not contain user accounts other than those required for services. Forest trusts are established so that users from other forests can access the resources contained in the resource forest. Resource forests, illustrated in Figure 2-2, provide service isolation.

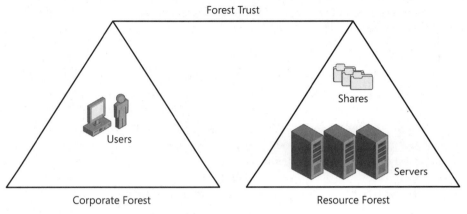

FIGURE 2-2 Resource forest model

Use the resource forest model when you need to provide exclusive control of the AD DS infrastructure.

- **Restricted access forest model**   In the *restricted access forest model*, illustrated in Figure 2-3, a separate forest is created to contain user accounts and data that must be isolated from the rest of the organization. Restricted access forests provide data isolation.

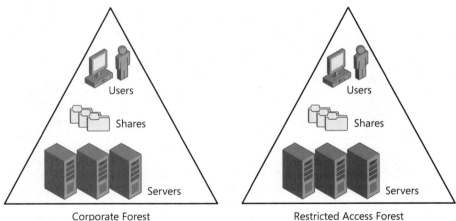

FIGURE 2-3 Restricted access forest model

Use the restricted access forest model when you need to prevent administrators from controlling or viewing a subset of data in the directory or on member computers joined to the directory.

> **MORE INFO** **FOREST DESIGN MODELS**
>
> For more information about forest design models, go to *http://technet.microsoft.com /en-us/library/cc770439(WS.10).aspx.*

Now that you have an understanding of the three existing forest models, you are ready to map the forest design requirements to the appropriate design model. Some organizations might have a single forest requirement that maps directly to a forest design model, which makes the selection of a forest design model straightforward. However, there will be cases in which an organization has multiple design requirements, which will make mapping these requirements to a forest design model more complex. You can use the information in Table 2-1 to map forest design requirements to the appropriate forest design model.

TABLE 2-1 Mapping Forest Design Requirements to Forest Design Models

LIMITED CONNECTIVITY	DATA ISOLATION	DATA AUTONOMY	SERVICE ISOLATION	SERVICE AUTONOMY	SCENARIO
No	No	Yes	No	No	Join an existing forest for data autonomy.
No	No	N/A	No	Yes	Use an organizational forest or domain for service autonomy.
No	No	N/A	Yes	N/A	Use an organizational or resource forest for service isolation.
N/A	Yes	N/A	N/A	N/A	Use an organizational or restricted access forest for data isolation.
Yes	No	N/A	No	No	Use an organizational forest or reconfigure the firewall for limited connectivity.
Yes	No	N/A	No	Yes	Use an organizational forest or domain and reconfigure the firewall for service autonomy with limited connectivity.
Yes	No	N/A	Yes	N/A	Use a resource forest and reconfigure the firewall for service isolation with limited connectivity.

MORE INFO   **MAPPING DESIGN REQUIREMENTS TO FOREST DESIGN MODELS**

For more information about mapping design requirements to forest design models, go to *http://technet.microsoft.com/en-us/library/cc732563(WS.10).aspx.*

Designing the Domain Structure

After you have designed the forest structure, you are ready to design the domain structure for each forest. Every AD DS forest must contain at least one domain. Designing the domain structure consists of gathering domain design requirements, designing the domain model, determining the number of domains required, determining whether to upgrade existing domains or deploy new domains, designing the forest root domain, and designing domain trees.

Gathering Domain Design Requirements

Because AD DS domains are used primarily to partition a large forest into smaller components for administration and replication purposes, you must gather the security, administration, and replication requirements before you can design the domain structure. It is these requirements that will aid you in determining how best to partition the AD DS data through domains.

Gathering security requirements is essential when designing the domain structure. Certain security policies, such as the domain-wide password policy, can be applied only at the domain level. When gathering security requirements, you must assess the domain-wide security requirements for the various groups in the organization. Because these security settings are domain-wide, you need to determine whether the different groups in the organization can use the same security settings. In reality, it is difficult in large organizations to have several groups agree on a common security policy. If there are groups in your organization that represent a subset of the users and have unique security requirements, you can use fine-grained password policies. Alternatively, if the group represents a large portion of your organization, it might be more efficient to deploy a dedicated domain to satisfy the group's unique security requirements. The administrative effort required to maintain the security groups used for fine-grained password policies increases substantially when the number of users to which the fine-grained password policy applies is large. Generally, any group that has unique security requirements that can be applied only at the domain level requires a dedicated domain.

After you have gathered the relevant security requirements, gather the administration requirements for the domain structure. Gathering these administrative requirements will enable you to better understand how the domains will be managed and will effectively aid you in designing the domain structure. Start by identifying the team or teams that will be responsible for AD DS service management in your organization. If you determine that a single team will require administrative access to AD DS, you can deploy a single domain to meet the administrative requirements. However, if multiple teams require administrative access to AD DS, you then need to determine whether a single domain will meet those requirements. To do this, establish the level of administrative access that is required by each team and whether the required access must be exclusive. If the access does not need to be exclusive, deploy a single AD DS domain to meet the administrative requirements, because all teams will have the same level of access. Alternatively, if the level of access needs to be exclusive to one or more teams, deploy a dedicated domain for each team.

Because the domain partition is a writable copy of all attributes on every object in the domain, you need to ensure that you account for the replication requirements when designing the domain structure so that you can partition the AD DS forest into smaller portions that will replicate more efficiently on your network. Start by identifying each location that will contain AD DS users. Then determine the number of users in each location and the business unit to which each user belongs. Next, gather the relevant network configuration information for each location. When designing a domain structure, it is important to understand how each location is connected to the remainder of the network. Collect the available bandwidth, network usage, and connection information for each location in your organization. If all the locations are interconnected through high-speed network links that have ample bandwidth, the additional network bandwidth consumed by AD DS replication will not be a concern, and a single domain will suffice. However, if there are one or more locations that have limited network bandwidth or saturated network connections, then partitioning that location through a dedicated domain will ensure that AD DS replication operates more efficiently.

Designing the Domain Model

Now that you have gathered the relevant domain structure design requirements, you can design the domain model for AD DS. To select the appropriate domain design model, you must first understand the different models that exist. You can select from two when designing the domain structure:

- **Single-domain model**   The *single-domain model*, illustrated in Figure 2-4, consists of a forest with a single domain. Any domain controller can authenticate any user in the forest, and all domain controllers can be global catalog servers. In this model, all directory data is replicated to all locations that host domain controllers. The single-domain model is the simplest because it is easier to administer and less expensive to maintain. However, it creates the most replication traffic, especially when domain controllers are decentralized. It is sufficient when security requirements, administrative requirements, and replication requirements are consistent across the organization.

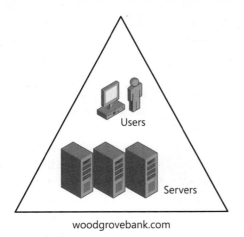

woodgrovebank.com

FIGURE 2-4 Single-domain model

Use the single-domain model when fast network connections exist between domain controllers, bandwidth consumption is not a concern, the administration of AD DS is centralized, and security requirements are consistent across the organization.

■ **Regional domain model** The *regional domain model* consists of a forest root domain and one or more regional domains, which represent the geographic locations within an organization. The regions used to define the domains in this model typically represent fixed elements, such as countries. Wide area network (WAN) connectivity is a key factor when planning to use a regional domain model, which is more complex to design and requires a thorough analysis of the WAN connectivity and the number of users in each region. However, because all object data within a domain is replicated to all domain controllers in that domain, regional domains can reduce network traffic over the WAN link. This model is better suited when diverse security requirements, administrative requirements, or replication requirements exist across the organization. Figure 2-5 illustrates the regional domain model.

Use the regional domain model when not all domain controllers are connected to the rest of the network through fast connections, network traffic needs to be minimized, the administration of AD DS is decentralized, and security requirements are diverse across the organization.

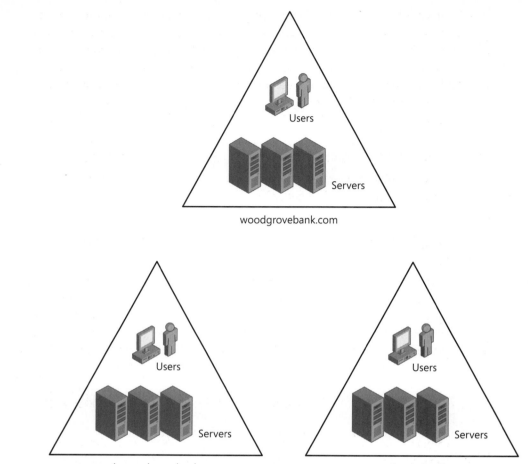

woodgrovebank.com

canada.woodgrovebank.com

us.woodgrovebank.com

FIGURE 2-5 Regional domain model

MORE INFO   **REVIEWING THE DOMAIN MODELS**

For more information about domain models, go to *http://technet.microsoft.com/en-us /library/cc731718(WS.10).aspx*.

Determining the Number of Domains Required

After you have selected a domain model, determine the number of domains required, which will vary depending on the domain model you choose. Additionally, the maximum number of users that a domain can contain will vary depending on the slowest link that must accommodate replication between domain controllers and the amount of network bandwidth you can allocate to AD DS replication. For example, if all the domain controllers are connected by network links that have a speed of 1,500 kilobits per second (Kbps), and you are able to allocate 5 percent of bandwidth to AD DS replication, the domain can contain approximately 100,000 users while maintaining efficient replication. However, if you have a domain controller connected with a 64-Kbps link, and you are able to allocate 5 percent of bandwidth to AD DS replication, the domain can contain only approximately 50,000 users while maintaining efficient replication. If you are unable to accommodate all users in a single domain, use the regional domain model so you can divide your organization into regions in a way that makes sense for your organization and your existing network.

> **MORE INFO** **DETERMINING THE NUMBER OF DOMAINS REQUIRED**
>
> For more information about determining the number of domains required, go to *http://technet.microsoft.com/en-us/library/cc732201(WS.10).aspx.*

Determining Whether to Upgrade Existing Domains or Deploy New Ones

As part of your domain structure design, determine whether to upgrade existing domains or deploy new domains. AD DS in Windows Server 2008 R2 can be installed as a new domain or by upgrading an existing domain, which is known as an in-place upgrade. If you choose to install a new domain as opposed to using the in-place upgrade path, you must migrate users from the existing domain to the new domain. User account migrations between domains can be a costly and time-consuming task and could potentially affect end users.

> **MORE INFO** **DETERMINING WHETHER TO UPGRADE EXISTING DOMAINS OR DEPLOY NEW ONES**
>
> For more information about determining whether to upgrade existing domains or deploy new domains, go to *http://technet.microsoft.com/en-us/library/cc730800(WS.10).aspx.*

You must consider a number of factors when determining whether to upgrade existing domains or deploy new ones. First, you need to determine whether the existing domain model still meets the requirements of your organization. In large organizations, requirements tend to change over time, which is why you need to determine your satisfaction level with the existing domain model. If no major changes to the domain model are desired as part of the upgrade to Windows Server 2008 R2, and the existing domain structure meets the business and technical requirements, the in-place upgrade will provide the easiest migration path. Conversely, if the existing domain structure does not meet the business and migration goals of the organization, the deployment of a new domain is required. By deploying a new domain, you can design and deploy the domain according to the current domain structure requirements and then migrate objects from the old domain into the new domain structure.

Next, determine how much downtime can be incurred when moving to Windows Server 2008 R2 and how much downtime is acceptable in your organization. Review any service-level agreements (SLAs) that exist for AD DS in your organization in order to identify the acceptable downtime and maintenance windows. The in-place upgrade performs an upgrade of the operating system on each domain controller. Although this can be phased, the in-place upgrade does result in downtime. Alternatively, the deployment of a new domain does not require you to take the existing domain or any domain controllers offline, so downtime is minimal. If downtime is a concern, deploy a new domain instead of upgrading an existing domain.

The next key criterion to consider is time constraints. You need to know how much time you have been allocated to upgrade to Windows Server 2008 R2. If the upgrade to Windows Server 2008 R2 needs to occur sooner rather than later, the in-place upgrade is the right path to take. The in-place upgrade takes roughly 60 to 90 minutes per domain controller. The deployment of new domains and migrating objects to them is time intensive and should be avoided if time constraints exist.

Last, consider budget. Determine the budget you have been allocated to upgrade to Windows Server 2008 R2. If budget is limited, use the in-place upgrade because the costs are typically lower than those of a new domain deployment. Because the existing domain controllers are upgraded, in-place upgrades do not require additional hardware or software. Also, in-place upgrades require less resource time to perform. If budget is not a concern, and you have other factors that will make the deployment of a new domain more beneficial, use the new-domain deployment strategy.

Designing the Forest Root Domain

If you decide to deploy new AD DS domains, you must first design the *forest root domain*, which is the first domain you deploy in an AD DS forest. After you deploy the forest root domain, it remains the forest root domain for the life of the AD DS deployment. It is not possible to change the forest root domain, so designing it involves determining whether you need to deploy a dedicated one.

A *dedicated forest root domain* is an AD DS domain created exclusively to function as the forest root domain. A dedicated forest root domain does not contain any end-user accounts and allows the separation of forest-level service administrators from domain-level service administrators. Additionally, a dedicated forest root domain is not usually affected by organizational changes that can result in the restructuring or renaming of domains. However, the use of a dedicated forest root domain introduces additional management overhead.

> **MORE INFO** **SELECTING THE FOREST ROOT DOMAIN**
>
> For more information about selecting the forest root domain, go to *http://technet .microsoft.com/en-us/library/cc726016(WS.10).aspx.*

If you will not use a dedicated forest root domain, you must select a regional domain to function as the forest root domain. That regional domain will be the first domain in the forest to be deployed. Using a regional domain as a forest root domain does not generate the additional management overhead that a dedicated forest root domain does, as Figure 2-6 illustrates.

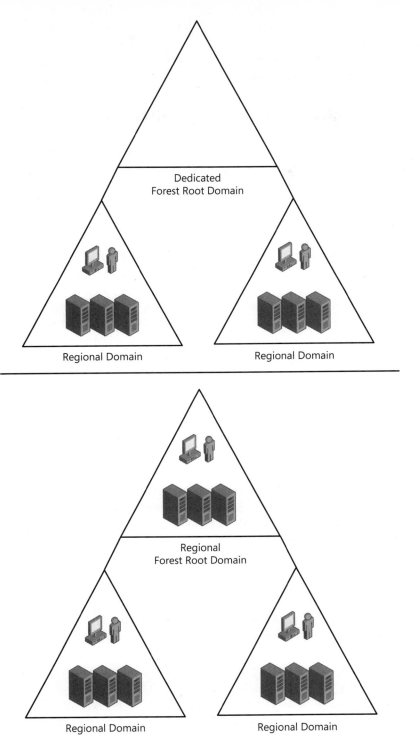

FIGURE 2-6 Dedicated forest root domain vs. regional forest root domain

MORE INFO   DEPLOYING A WINDOWS SERVER 2008 R2 FOREST ROOT DOMAIN

For more information about deploying a Windows Server 2008 R2 forest root domain, go to *http://technet.microsoft.com/en-us/library/cc731174(WS.10).aspx*.

Use a dedicated forest root domain to separate the responsibilities of forest management and domain management.

Designing Domain Trees

When the forest root domain is in place, additional domains can be added to the forest in the same domain tree as the forest root domain or in additional domain trees. All domains in the same domain tree will share a contiguous namespace, whereas domains that are added through a new domain tree will have a different namespace.

Using the same domain tree or a new domain tree does not provide any difference in functionality. In both cases, each domain within an AD DS forest will share a transitive trust with all other domains, and each domain will share the schema directory partition, configuration directory partition, and global catalog directory partition. The principles for deciding whether to use existing domain trees or additional domain trees are the same as those for planning a Domain Name System (DNS) namespace for AD DS. A domain tree is warranted when one group in the organization has a requirement for a DNS namespace that is not contiguous with the existing DNS namespace that AD DS uses. Consider the example of an AD DS forest that has an existing domain with the DNS name of *tailspintoys.com*. If the business unit called Wingtip Toys needs to have its own DNS domain name for AD DS, you would deploy a second domain tree that has a DNS domain name of *wingtiptoys.com*.

Designing Functional Levels

When you have designed the forest structure and the domain structure, you are ready to design the functional levels, which provide a way to enable domain-wide features or forest-wide AD DS features. Different levels of domain functionality and forest functionality are available, depending on your network environment. Designing functional levels includes designing domain functional levels and then designing forest functional levels.

MORE INFO   UNDERSTANDING AD DS FUNCTIONAL LEVELS

For more information about AD DS functional levels, go to *http://technet.microsoft.com /en-us/library/understanding-active-directory-functional-levels(WS.10).aspx*.

EXAM TIP

Before you take the 70-647 exam, make sure you are familiar with the different AD DS features available at each functional level.

Designing Domain Functional Levels

Designing functional levels starts with designing domain functional levels. Domain functional levels enable features that affect the entire domain and are dependent on the version of Windows that is installed on the domain controllers in the domain. Therefore, start by identifying the version of Windows that is installed on each domain controller in each domain in the forest. If you have domain controllers in a domain that have Windows 2000 Server installed on them, the highest domain functional level you can set for that domain is Windows 2000 Native. If the domain controllers in a domain have Windows Server 2003 installed on them, the highest domain functional level you can set for that domain is Windows Server 2003. If all domain controllers in the domain have Windows Server 2008 installed on them, you can set the domain functional level to Windows Server 2008. If all domain controllers in the domain have Windows Server 2008 R2 installed on them, then you can set the domain functional level to Windows Server 2008 R2.

> **NOTE DETERMINING THE OPERATING SYSTEM INSTALLED ON EXISTING DOMAIN CONTROLLERS**
>
> In large environments, it is not practical to log on to each domain controller to determine the version of the operating system it is running. The *Systeminfo* command in Windows Server 2008 R2 enables you to retrieve operating system information remotely from multiple computers. For more information about the *Systeminfo* command in Windows Server 2008 R2, go to *http://technet.microsoft.com/en-us/library/cc771190(WS.10).aspx*.

Table 2-2 lists the domain functional levels and their corresponding supported domain controllers.

TABLE 2-2 Domain Functional Levels and Supported Domain Controllers

DOMAIN FUNCTIONAL LEVEL	DOMAIN CONTROLLERS SUPPORTED
Windows 2000 Native	Windows 2000 Server
	Windows Server 2003
	Windows Server 2008
	Windows Server 2008 R2
Windows Server 2003	Windows Server 2003
	Windows Server 2008
	Windows Server 2008 R2
Windows Server 2008	Windows Server 2008
	Windows Server 2008 R2
Windows Server 2008 R2	Windows Server 2008 R2

When designing domain functional levels, determine which advanced AD DS features you need to enable in each domain. If you find that the domain functional level you require cannot be achieved because of domain controllers with earlier versions of Windows, you will have to upgrade those domain controllers or decommission them from the domain. Table 2-3 lists the domain-wide features that are enabled for the domain functional levels.

TABLE 2-3 Domain-Wide Features for Domain Functional Levels

DOMAIN FUNCTIONAL LEVEL	ENABLED FEATURES
Windows 2000 Native	All default Active Directory features and the following features: ■ Universal groups for both distribution groups and security groups ■ Group nesting ■ Group conversion, which makes conversion between security groups and distribution groups possible ■ Security identifier (SID) history
Windows Server 2003	All default Active Directory features, all features from the Windows 2000 Native domain functional level, plus the following features: ■ The availability of the domain management tool, *Netdom.exe*, to prepare for a domain controller rename ■ Update of the logon time stamp ■ The ability to set the *userPassword* attribute as the effective password on the *inetOrgPerson* object and user objects ■ The ability to redirect Users and Computers containers ■ Authorization Manager, to store its authorization policies in AD DS ■ Constrained delegation ■ Support for selective authentication
Windows Server 2008	All default Active Directory features, all features from the Windows Server 2003 domain functional level, plus the following features: ■ Distributed File System (DFS) Replication support for SYSVOL ■ Advanced Encryption Services (AES 128 and 256) support for the Kerberos authentication protocol ■ Last Interactive Logon Information ■ Fine-grained password policies

Windows Server 2008 R2	All default Active Directory features, all features from the Windows Server 2008 domain functional level, plus the following features:
	■ Authentication mechanism assurance
	■ Automatic service principal name (SPN) management for services running on a particular computer under the context of a Managed Service Account when the name or DNS host name of the machine account changes

---

IMPORTANT **RAISING THE DOMAIN FUNCTIONAL LEVEL**

When the domain functional level is raised, domain controllers running earlier operating systems cannot be introduced into the domain.

✔ **Quick Check**

1. Which domain functional levels are supported if your forest functional level is set to Windows 2008 R2?

2. Which operating systems are supported on domain controllers when the domain functional level is set to Windows Server 2008?

Quick Check Answer

1. Windows Server 2008 R2

2. Windows Server 2008 and Windows Server 2008 R2

Designing Forest Functional Levels

After you have designed the domain functional levels, you are ready to design the forest functional levels. Forest functional levels enable features that affect the entire forest and are dependent on the domain functional levels of the domains in the forest. To design forest functional levels, start by identifying the domain functional level for each domain in the forest. If domains in the forest have a domain functional level of Windows 2000 Native, the highest forest functional level that can be set is Windows 2000. If domains in the forest have a domain functional level of Windows Server 2003, the highest forest functional level that can be set is Windows Server 2003. If all domains in the forest have a domain functional level of Windows Server 2008, the forest functional level can be set to Windows Server 2008. If all domains in the forest have a domain functional level of Windows Server 2008 R2, the forest functional level can be set to Windows Server 2008 R2. Table 2-4 lists the forest functional levels and their corresponding supported domain functional levels.

TABLE 2-4 Forest-Wide Features for Forest Functional Levels

FOREST FUNCTIONAL LEVEL	DOMAIN FUNCTIONAL LEVELS SUPPORTED
Windows 2000	Windows 2000 Native
	Windows Server 2003
	Windows Server 2008
Windows Server 2003	Windows Server 2003
	Windows Server 2008
Windows Server 2008	Windows Server 2008
Windows Server 2008 R2	Windows Server 2008 R2

When designing forest functional levels, determine which advanced AD DS features you need to enable across the forest. If you find that the forest functional level you require cannot be achieved because of domains with earlier, lower-level domain functional levels, you will have to upgrade the domain functional level for these domains. Table 2-5 lists the forest-wide features that are enabled for the forest functional levels.

TABLE 2-5 Forest Functional Levels Features

FOREST FUNCTIONAL LEVEL	DOMAIN FUNCTIONAL LEVELS SUPPORTED
Windows 2000	All default Active Directory features
Windows Server 2003	All default Active Directory features, plus the following features:

- Support for forest trusts
- Support for renaming domains
- Support for linked-value replication, which enables domain controllers to replicate individual property values for objects instead of the complete objects to reduce network bandwidth usage
- The ability to deploy a *read-only domain controller* (RODC) that runs Windows Server 2008 or Windows Server 2008 R2
- Improved Knowledge Consistency Checker (KCC) algorithms and scalability
- The ability to create instances of the dynamic auxiliary class called *dynamicObject* in a domain directory partition
- The ability to convert an *inetOrgPerson* object instance into a *User* object instance and the reverse
- The ability to create instances of the new group types, called application basic groups and Lightweight Directory Access Protocol (LDAP) query groups, to support role-based authorization
- Deactivation and redefinition of attributes and classes in the schema

Windows Server 2008	All the features available at the Windows Server 2003 forest functional level but no additional features
Windows Server 2008 R2	All the features that are available at the Windows Server 2003 forest functional level, plus the following features: ■ Active Directory Recycle Bin

> **IMPORTANT RAISING THE FOREST FUNCTIONAL LEVEL**
>
> When the forest functional level is raised, domain controllers running earlier operating systems cannot be introduced into the forest.

Designing the Schema

After you have designed the forest structure, domain structure, and functional levels, you are ready to design the AD DS schema. Because there is a single schema for the entire forest and schema changes are global, designing the schema requires careful planning and testing and consists of designing a schema modification process, upgrading the schema to support Windows Server 2008 R2, and designing schema attributes and classes.

Designing a Schema Modification Process

Because schema modifications are global changes that cannot be reversed, designing a schema modification process is imperative when designing the schema. A properly designed schema modification process will aid in mitigating the impact of a problematic schema modification.

To start, determine the requirement for a schema modification. If it is required for an enterprise-wide application such as Exchange Server, then it is usually warranted. However, if it is required for an application that will be used by only a small population of the organization, determine whether you want to deploy a global change to satisfy the needs of those users. As previously mentioned, schema modifications are global, so schema modifications that are required for a non-enterprise-wide product will still require a global change that is not reversible. Additionally, schema modifications that are required for a subset of users in the organization are typically required on a short-term basis, so you must analyze the duration of the requirement. Although schema attributes can be deactivated at a later time, attributes still consume space in the schema partition, which is replicated to all domain controllers in the forest. Whenever possible, aim to limit schema changes to requirements that are enterprise-wide and long-term.

When you have decided to proceed with a proposed schema modification, you are ready to test it, an absolutely critical process that should never be ignored in view of the permanent nature of the change. When testing a schema modification, ensure that the test environment has a schema that is consistent with production. After you have deployed the schema change in your test environment, perform a level of regression testing against AD DS to determine that the schema change was not problematic. When performing regression testing, verify that AD DS is still able to replicate the schema partition to all domain controllers in the test environment. Next, modify the object type or object class that was changed as part of the schema modification. For example, if you created a new attribute and added it to the User class, you must modify it on a user object as part of your regression testing. Next, verify that you are still able to modify attributes that existed prior to the schema modification.

When you have thoroughly tested the schema modification in a test environment, you are ready to modify the schema in the production AD DS forest. By this time, you should have thoroughly reviewed and tested the schema modification in your preproduction environments, so you should be in a position to simply follow your standard change management process.

Upgrading the Schema to Support Windows Server 2008 R2

AD DS in Windows Server 2008 R2 introduces a number of changes to the schema. If you are installing a new Windows Server 2008 R2–based AD DS forest, you do not need to prepare the forest for Windows Server 2008 R2. However, if you are installing Windows Server 2008 R2 domain controllers into an existing Windows 2000 Server, Windows Server 2003, or Windows Server 2008 forest, you need to perform a number of tasks to prepare it for Windows Server 2008 R2.

Before you can add the first Windows Server 2008 R2 domain controller to an existing Windows 2000 Server, Windows Server 2003, or Windows Server 2008 forest, you must prepare the existing forest, introducing a number of schema changes and forest-wide changes by running the *adprep /forestprep* command on the server that holds the schema master operations master role.

After you have prepared the forest for Windows Server 2008 R2, prepare each domain in which you will install Windows Server 20008 R2 domain controllers. Doing so introduces a number of domain-wide changes and consists of running the *adprep /domainprep /gpprep* command on the server in each domain that holds the infrastructure operations master role.

Finally, if you are installing RODCs into an existing Windows Server 2003 forest, you must also prepare the forest for them by modifying the permissions in each domain. You do this by running the *adprep /rodcprep* command on any computer in the forest.

> **MORE INFO**   **PREPARE YOUR INFRASTRUCTURE FOR UPGRADE**
>
> For more information about schema changes in Windows Server 2008 R2, go to
> *http://technet.microsoft.com/en-us/library/cc771461(WS.10).aspx.*

Designing Trusts to Optimize Intraforest Authentication

The final component in forest and domain design consists of designing trusts to optimize intraforest authentication. In a complex forest with multiple-domain trees, intraforest authentication can take a substantial amount of time because the authentication request must traverse the trust path. Figure 2-7 shows the default trust path in a complex forest.

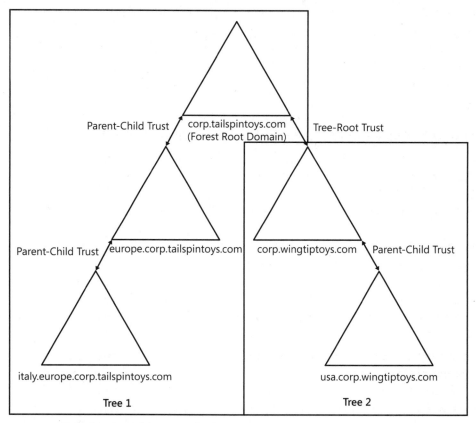

FIGURE 2-7 Default trust path in a complex forest

In this example, when a user in the *usa.corp.wingtiptoys.com* domain needs to access a resource in the *italy.europe.corp.tailspintoys.com* domain, the authentication request must traverse the following path:

1. *corp.wingtiptoys.com* domain
2. *corp.tailspintoys.com* domain
3. *europe.corp.tailspintoys.com* domain
4. *italy.europe.corp.tailspintoys.com* domain

This amount of time can be reduced significantly by using a shortcut trust. Figure 2-8 shows a shortcut trust in the same forest.

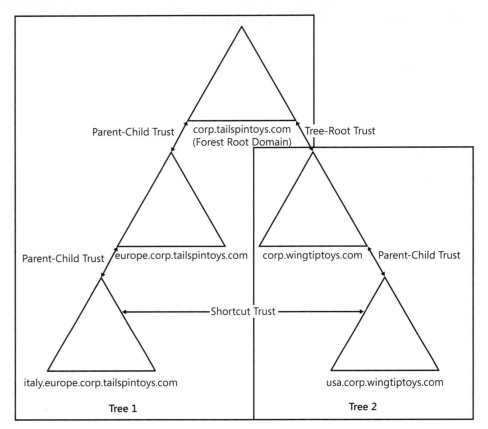

FIGURE 2-8 Shortcut trust

A shortcut trust between the *usa.corp.wingtiptoys.com* domain and the *italy.europe.corp .tailspintoys.com* domain optimizes intraforest authentication because the authentication request does not have to traverse the default trust path, but rather is sent directly between these two domains.

When designing trusts to optimize intraforest authentication, start by identifying each domain in the forest that has frequent cross-domain resource access requirements. For these domains, deploy a shortcut trust. When deploying the shortcut trust, you can use a one-way trust or a two-way trust. To determine the direction of the trust, you need to understand the resource access requirements in your organization. If bidirectional resource access is required, use a two-way shortcut trust. If unidirectional resource access is required, use a one-way shortcut trust.

> **MORE INFO** **UNDERSTANDING WHEN TO CREATE A SHORTCUT TRUST**
>
> For more information about when to create a shortcut trust, go to *http://technet.microsoft .com/en-us/library/cc754538.aspx*.

Designing AD DS Forests and Domains

You are the enterprise administrator at Contoso, Ltd. Contoso is a large corporation with offices located throughout the United Kingdom. As an enterprise administrator, it is your role to design AD DS for Contoso and its subsidiaries.

Contoso's head office is located in Glasgow, Scotland, and contains 15,000 employees. It has remote offices in England, Wales, and Northern Ireland, each containing approximately 5,000 employees. Each of the remote offices is connected to the head office through the corporate WAN.

All the Windows-based workstations and servers for Contoso and its subsidiaries will use AD DS for authentication and authorization. Contoso has a number of publicly accessible applications that require customer accounts to reside in AD DS for authentication and authorization.

For legal and security reasons, Contoso must separate employee information from customer information. The company has an IT department, located in its head office, which will be responsible for AD DS forest service management. Local IT departments situated in each location are responsible for the AD DS service management and data management in their respective location.

To comply with Contoso's IT security policies, forest-level service management and domain-level service management must be performed by different teams. Each of Contoso's locations has its own password policy requirements. The amount of bandwidth AD DS replication uses must be minimized. The domain controllers for the NOS directory will be decentralized, but the domain controllers for the Internet directory will be centralized. Contoso plans to implement fine-grained password policies in the future. It also wants to use AES 128 and 256 for the Kerberos authentication protocol for its publicly accessible applications. All AD DS domain controllers will have Windows Server 2008 R2 installed.

Contoso recently acquired a subsidiary named Fabrikam, Inc., with an office in Seattle, Washington, containing 5,000 employees. Fabrikam has diverse requirements for the internal DNS name used for resources in AD DS. Active Directory service management and data management for Fabrikam will be performed by Contoso's IT departments. Fabrikam's employees will frequently access resources located on servers in the Wales remote office. Contoso wants to ensure that the authentication process for Fabrikam users accessing resources in the Wales Contoso remote office is fast.

EXERCISE 1   **Design the Forest Structure**

In this exercise, you review the business and technical requirements to design the forest structure for Contoso and its subsidiaries.

1. What are the relevant forest design requirements for Contoso and its subsidiaries?

    The relevant forest design requirements for Contoso and its subsidiaries are as follows:

    - AD DS will act as the NOS directory and as an Internet directory for Contoso and its subsidiaries.

- Service management requirements suggest the need for service autonomy. Multiple teams will be managing the AD DS infrastructure, but control for any one team does not need to be exclusive.

- Data management requirements suggest the need for data autonomy. Multiple teams will be managing the AD DS data, but control for any one team does not need to be exclusive.

- Data management requirements also suggest the need for data isolation in the case of customer information. Employee information must be separated from customer information.

2. Based on your analysis of the requirements, how many forests are required for Contoso and its subsidiaries?

Two AD DS forests are required to meet the business and technical requirements. The first forest will be used as the NOS directory for Contoso and its Fabrikam subsidiary. Both companies can reside in the same forest because they have consistent data autonomy and services autonomy requirements; the AD DS data and service will be managed by the same IT departments.

A second forest is required to serve as Contoso's Internet directory. The Internet directory requires a dedicated forest because of the data isolation requirement; Contoso must separate employee information from customer information.

3. Which forest model(s) will be used in the design?

The first forest, which will be used as the NOS directory, will use the organizational forest model because user accounts will be stored in this forest and managed separately. There are no limited connectivity or service isolation requirements to suggest the need for a resource forest model.

The second forest, which will be used as the Internet directory, will use the restricted access forest model because there are data isolation requirements.

EXERCISE 2 Design the Domain Structure

In this exercise, you review the business and technical requirements to design the domain structure for Contoso and its subsidiaries.

1. What are the relevant domain design requirements for Contoso and its subsidiaries?

The relevant domain design requirements for Contoso and its subsidiaries are as follows:

- The security requirements state that each Contoso location has its own password policy requirements.

- The security requirements state that forest-level service management and domain-level service management must be performed by different teams.

- The business requirements state that the DNS name used for the Fabrikam subsidiary must be different from the DNS name used for the rest of the organization.

- The technical requirements state that the amount of bandwidth used by AD DS replication must be minimized.
- The technical requirements state that the domain controllers for the NOS directory forest will be decentralized, but the domain controllers for the Internet directory forest will be centralized.

2. Which domain model will be used for each forest?

   The forest used as the NOS directory will use the regional domain model because users are distributed throughout various remote locations. Additionally, by using the regional domain model for this forest, the amount of bandwidth AD DS replication uses will be minimized in accordance with the technical requirement to minimize it.

   The forest used as the Internet directory will use the single-domain model because all domain controllers will be centralized.

3. What will the forest root domain design be for the NOS directory forest?

   The forest root design for the NOS directory forest will consist of a dedicated forest root domain, which is necessary to meet the security requirement to have forest-level and domain-level service management performed by different teams.

4. Based on your analysis of the requirements, how many domains are required for each forest?

   The forest used as the NOS directory will require six domains. The first domain in this forest will be the dedicated forest root domain. Four additional domains are required for the remote Contoso locations in Scotland, England, Wales, and Northern Ireland because of the security requirement to create separate password policies for each location. Additionally, the Fabrikam subsidiary requires its own domain in this forest because of the business requirement to use a different DNS name for Fabrikam's resources.

   The forest used as the Internet directory will have a single domain to store customer information, and there are no technical or business requirements that suggest the need for multiple domains.

5. How many domain trees will be required for each forest?

   The forest used as the NOS directory will require two domain trees because there are diverse DNS namespace requirements between Contoso and its Fabrikam subsidiary. A separate domain tree is required for the Fabrikam subsidiary to meet its unique DNS namespace requirements.

EXERCISE 3   Design the Functional Levels

In this exercise, you review the business and technical requirements to design the functional levels for Contoso and its subsidiaries.

1. What are the relevant functional level design requirements for Contoso and its subsidiaries?

The relevant functional level design requirements for Contoso and its subsidiaries are as follows:

- Contoso plans to implement automatic SPN management in the future.
- Contoso wants to use authentication mechanism assurance for its publicly accessible applications.
- Contoso plans to use the Active Directory Recycle Bin in each forest.
- All AD DS domain controllers will have Windows Server 2008 R2 installed.

2. What will the domain functional level design be for each forest?

The domain functional level design for the NOS directory forest will consist of a domain functional level of Windows Server 2008 R2 for each domain so that Contoso can use automatic SPN management in the future. This functional level is also recommended for this forest because all the domain controllers will have Windows Server 2008 R2 installed.

The domain functional level design for the Internet directory forest will consist of a domain functional level of Windows Server 2008 R2 so that Contoso can use authentication mechanism assurance for its publicly accessible applications. This functional level is also recommended for this forest because all the domain controllers will have Windows Server 2008 R2 installed.

3. What will the forest functional level design be for each forest?

Both forests will have a forest functional level of Windows Server 2008 R2. This is recommended because all the domains will have a domain functional level of Windows Server 2008 R2, and this is required to use the Active Directory Recycle Bin.

EXERCISE 4   Design Shortcut Trusts

In this exercise, you review the business and technical requirements for the shortcut trusts for Contoso and its subsidiaries.

1. What are the relevant shortcut trust design requirements for Contoso and its subsidiaries?

The relevant shortcut trust design requirements for Contoso and its subsidiaries are as follows:

- Fabrikam employees will frequently access resources located on servers in the Wales remote office.
- Authentication should be optimized for Fabrikam employees accessing resources in the Wales remote office.

2. What will the shortcut trust design be?

The shortcut trust design will consist of a shortcut trust between the Wales Contoso domain and the Fabrikam domain. This is required in order to optimize authentication between Fabrikam users and resources in the Wales Contoso domain.

Lesson Summary

- Gathering forest design requirements consists of identifying the role of AD DS in your organization and gathering business, technical, security, network, autonomy, and isolation requirements.
- You can choose the organizational forest model, resource forest model, or the restricted access forest model when designing forests.
- You can choose either the single-domain model or the regional domain model when designing the domains within a forest.
- A dedicated forest root domain enables the separation of forest-level service administrators from domain-level service administrators.
- Domain functional levels enable features that affect the entire domain, and forest functional levels enable features that affect the entire forest.
- Before you can add the first Windows Server 2008 R2 domain controller to an existing Windows 2000, Windows Server 2003, or Windows Server 2008 forest, you must prepare the existing forest by using the *adprep* command. If you are installing RODCs into an existing Windows 2000 Server or Windows Server 2003 forest, you must also prepare the forest for RODCs.
- You can use shortcut trusts to optimize intraforest authentication.

Lesson Review

The following questions are intended to reinforce key information presented in this lesson. The questions are also available on the companion CD if you prefer to review them in electronic form.

> **NOTE ANSWERS**
>
> Answers to these questions and explanations of why each answer choice is correct or incorrect are located in the "Answers" section at the end of the book.

1. How can you achieve data autonomy when designing the forest structure?
   - **A.** Create a new forest by using the resource forest model.
   - **B.** Join an existing forest.
   - **C.** Create a new forest by using the organizational forest model.
   - **D.** Create a new forest by using the restricted access forest model.

2. How can you achieve service autonomy when designing the forest structure?
   - **A.** Create a new forest by using the restricted access forest model.
   - **B.** Create a new forest by using the resource forest model.
   - **C.** Create a new forest by using the organizational forest model.
   - **D.** Join an existing forest.

3. You are examining an existing AD DS environment to determine whether to upgrade the existing domains or deploy new domains. What factors must you consider? (Choose all that apply.)

   A. Existing domain model

   B. The amount of downtime that can be incurred

   C. Time constraints

   D. Budget

Lesson 2: Designing the AD DS Physical Topology

Now that you have designed the forest and domain structure in Lesson 1, you are ready to complete the AD DS design by designing the physical topology, which is required so that AD DS can replicate the directory data to domain controllers in the various locations on your network. Also, the physical topology defines how clients are directed to the appropriate domain controller for authentication and enables clients to search for printers based on location information.

The design of the physical topology starts with designing the site structure, which represents the physical structure of your network. AD DS uses that structure to build the most efficient replication topology. Designing the site structure consists of selecting a site model based on the relevant site design requirements. After you have designed the site structure, you must design replication to control how the directory data is replicated between the various domain controllers on your network. Designing replication involves designing the replication topology as well as site links, site link properties, and site link bridging. Next, you must design the placement of domain controllers—specifically, forest root domain controllers, regional domain controllers, read-only domain controllers, global catalog servers, and operations master role holders. Last, you must design printer location policies so that users can search for printers based on location information stored in AD DS.

This lesson provides you with the knowledge needed to gather relevant business and technical requirements and then to design the AD DS physical topology in Windows Server 2008 R2.

After this lesson, you will be able to:

- Gather site design requirements.
- Design the site model.
- Select a replication topology.
- Design site links and site link properties.
- Design site link bridging.
- Design the placement of forest root domain controllers, regional domain controllers, RODCs, global catalog servers, and operations master role holders.
- Design a location schema for printer location policies.

Estimated lesson time: 35 minutes

REAL WORLD

John Policelli

I recently spearheaded a site and replication redesign initiative, which emphasized the importance of reevaluating networking information and location data on an ongoing basis as part of an AD DS physical topology design.

When our client, a large financial institution with a global presence, first deployed Active Directory seven years ago, a requirement forced it to disable the Intersite Topology Generator (ISTG) on all sites. Effectively, all intersite replication connections had to be created manually. As you would expect, the network topology and location data had changed drastically from the time when the original replication design was created. However, because the client did not experience any issues with replication, it never reevaluated these requirements or its AD DS physical topology design.

We were faced with a major initiative to replace 25 percent of our client's former domain controllers with new domain controllers that would be located in a new datacenter. To make this even more complex, this was being driven by a time-sensitive data center consolidation project, which would result in a significant change to the physical topology design.

I made a conscious decision to reevaluate our client's network topology, location data, and requirements as part of the site and replication redesign initiative I was leading. As a result, I was able to validate that ISTG could be reenabled. Given the benefits of ISTG in a large environment, we decided to reenable the ISTG on all sites as part of our AD DS site and replication redesign. We saved a significant amount of time introducing the new domain controllers and decommissioning the earlier domain controllers during the data center consolidation project. Furthermore, the decision to reenable the ISTG on all sites improved the client's disaster recovery readiness. All this was exactly what I expected, knowing the benefits of ISTG. However, what surprised me the most was the fact that the forest convergence time—the time it takes for a change to the AD DS database to reach all domain controllers in the forest—was reduced by almost 40 percent as a result of reenabling the ISTG on all sites. Effectively, changes to the database were being replicated faster and more efficiently.

As you will see in this lesson, one of the most important tasks when designing the AD DS physical topology is collecting network information and location data. However, as was true in the site-and-replication redesign initiative that I led, this is not only required during the initial design phase but rather is something you need to do on an ongoing basis to ensure that your physical topology meets the constantly changing needs of your organization.

Designing the Site Structure

Designing the AD DS physical topology begins with designing the site structure, which is the foundation for the physical topology AD DS uses. Designing the site structure consists of gathering site design requirements, designing the site model, and designing site settings.

> **MORE INFO**   **DESIGNING THE SITE TOPOLOGY FOR WINDOWS SERVER 2008 AD DS**
>
> For more information about designing the site topology for Windows Server 2008 R2 AD DS, go to *http://go.microsoft.com/fwlink/?LinkId=89026*.

Gathering Site Design Requirements

To begin the site structure design, you need to gather the existing network information. Because sites in AD DS represent the physical structure of your network, AD DS uses network topology information to build the most efficient replication topology. Domain controllers are placed into sites according to where the domain data is needed, and sites are used for replication, authentication, and service location.

Start by creating a location map that represents the physical network infrastructure of your organization. Most large organizations have a network group with which you will need to consult in order to obtain the necessary information. On the location map, identify the geographic locations that contain groups of computers and users. For each location, gather the relevant network information, including the type of communication link, the link speed, and the available bandwidth between locations. Figure 2-9 shows a sample location map.

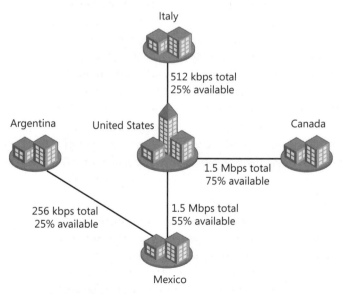

FIGURE 2-9 Sample location map

When you have collected the relevant network information, collect location data as part of your site design. Location data is required in order to determine the placement of domain controllers. Begin by gathering the IP subnets in each location; the AD DS authentication process uses IP subnets to direct clients to the closest domain controller. If you do not know the subnet mask and network address within each location, consult your networking group. Next, for each location, detail the number of users for each domain, the number of workstations, and the number of servers. Table 2-6 is a sample table you can use to document the relevant network information and location data for each region.

TABLE 2-6 Sample Network Information and Location Data Gathering Table

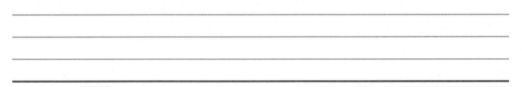

NAME OF REGION	TOTAL BANDWIDTH	AVAILABLE BANDWIDTH	NETWORK SEGMENTS	NUMBER OF USERS	DOMAINS

The location map you create and the location data you collect are required in order to identify the site model that best matches the physical topology of your network and to design the site structure. By collecting this information, you will be able to determine which physical locations need a dedicated site object and which physical locations can be combined into a single site object. Additionally, you'll use this information to design the placement of domain controllers and global catalog servers.

> **MORE INFO** **COLLECTING NETWORK INFORMATION**
>
> For more information about collecting network information, go to *http://technet.microsoft.com/en-us/library/cc771466(WS.10).aspx*.

Designing the Site Model

When you have obtained or created a location map and collected the location data, you are ready to design the site model AD DS replication will use. The two available site models are as follows:

- **Single site model** The *single site model* consists of a single site object. In this model, all domains in the forest belong to the same site object, and all IP subnets are associated with this site object. In the single site model, all authentication requests are directed to domain controllers in the same site. Additionally, all replication occurs through intrasite replication.

  The goal of the single site model is to reduce AD DS replication latency by ensuring that all domain controllers in the site are updated as quickly as possible. Through intrasite replication, replication occurs more or less immediately after a change has been made; replication traffic is not compressed; the replication process is initiated by a notification from the sending domain controller; replication traffic is sent to several replication partners during each replication cycle; and replication traffic within a single site requires virtually no customization. Use the single site model when all domain controllers are interconnected through fast network connections and there is ample available bandwidth.

- **Multiple sites model** The *multiple sites model* consists of domain controllers distributed across two or more site objects. IP subnets are associated with sites based on network information and location data. As a result, authentication requests are directed to domain controllers in the site closest to the authenticating client. Replication between domain controllers in the same site occurs through intrasite replication, but replication between domain controllers in different sites occurs through intersite replication.

The goal of the multiple sites model is to reduce the amount of bandwidth used for AD DS replication. Through intersite replication, replication is initiated according to a schedule; replication traffic is compressed; the replication schedule determines when domain controllers will replicate; replication can use either IP or Simple Mail Transfer Protocol (SMTP) transport; and replication traffic is sent through bridgehead servers rather than to multiple replication partners. However, the multiple sites model requires more configuration than the single site model. Use the multiple sites model when the physical network topology on your network includes locations that are not connected through fast connections and bandwidth consumption is a concern.

> **NOTE** **HOW DOES AUTOMATIC SITE COVERAGE WORK?**
>
> There can be cases in which sites do not contain domain controllers for each domain in the forest. The clients in these sites still need to locate a domain controller for their domain for authentication. Through automatic site coverage, Windows Server 2008 R2 registers DNS service location (SRV) resource records to ensure that clients can locate a domain controller in the nearest available site. These resource records map to the sites that contain no domain controller for the domain of which they are members. Automatic site coverage uses an algorithm that factors in the cost associated with the site links of a site that does not contain a domain controller. As a result, the appropriate domain controller registers its SRV resource records for that site.

Now that you have an understanding of the available site models, you must determine which model best meets the requirements of your AD DS physical topology. To map the appropriate site model to the site design requirements you gathered earlier, you need to examine each location independently. Start by reviewing the number of users in the location. Assess whether this number warrants the costs and administrative effort of a domain controller.

Next, review the business continuity requirements for each location. If the location needs to continue to operate if the WAN link is down, then deploying a dedicated site object for that location is a necessity. Users in a location that is not represented by a dedicated site object and does not have a local domain controller must cross the WAN when authenticating to AD DS.

You must also identify and incorporate site-aware applications when designing the site model. Site-aware applications, such as Microsoft Exchange Server and DFS, publish service information in the Sites container in AD DS so that clients can locate the services provided by these applications more efficiently. Then, determine where the servers hosting these site-aware applications will be physically located. You will need to create a dedicated site object for each location that will include servers hosting site-aware applications.

A site object should be created for each location that has 100 or more users so that users in such locations can continue to authenticate even if the WAN link is unavailable. A site object is also required for each location that will contain one or more domain controllers and for each location that will have site-aware applications installed locally. Last, if a site is not required for a location, ensure that you add the subnet of the location to a site for which the location has the maximum WAN speed and available bandwidth.

Designing Replication

After you have designed the site structure, design replication so that data is synchronized between the domain controllers in the forest and domains. Designing replication includes designing the replication topology, designing site links, designing site link properties, and designing site link bridging.

Designing the Replication Topology

The first step in designing replication is designing the replication topology, which defines the logical connections that AD DS replication uses to replicate among domain controllers. To minimize the network bandwidth required for replication, identify where bandwidth is highest and lowest on the network and model the replication topology after the physical topology of the network. There are three AD DS replication topologies:

- **Hub and spoke**   In the *hub and spoke replication topology*, one site is designated as the hub, and other sites, called spokes, connect to the hub. In this topology, AD DS replicates from the hub servers to the spoke servers and vice versa, but replication does not occur directly between two spoke servers. When you choose this topology, you must decide which site will act as the hub. If you want to set up multiple hubs, use a hybrid topology. Figure 2-10 shows an example of the hub and spoke replication topology.

  Use the hub and spoke replication topology for WANs that consist of faster network connections between major computing hubs and slower links connecting branch offices.

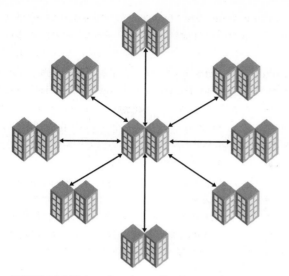

FIGURE 2-10 Hub and spoke replication topology

- **Full mesh**   In a *full mesh replication topology*, every site connects to every other site. An AD DS change on a domain controller in one site replicates directly to all other domain controllers in all other sites. Figure 2-11 shows an example of the full mesh replication topology.

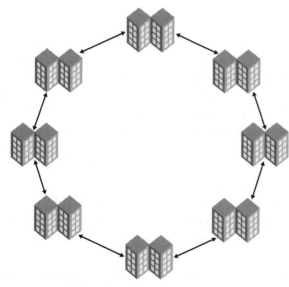

FIGURE 2-11 Full mesh replication topology

Because each site connects to every other site, the propagation of change orders for replicating AD DS can impose a heavy burden on the network. To reduce unnecessary traffic, use a different topology or delete connections you do not actually need.

- **Hybrid** The *hybrid replication topology* is a combination of a hub and spoke topology and a full mesh topology. One example of a hybrid topology is a redundant hub and spoke topology. In this configuration, a hub site might contain two domain controllers that are connected by a high-speed link. Each of these two hub servers might connect with four branch domain controllers in a hub and spoke arrangement. Figure 2-12 shows an example of a hybrid replication topology.

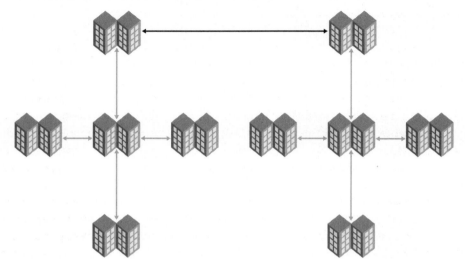

FIGURE 2-12 Hybrid replication topology

Use the hybrid replication topology to provide redundancy for a hub and spoke topology. Using the hybrid replication topology instead of only the hub and spoke replication topology eliminates a single point of failure (the hub).

EXAM TIP

Expect to see questions related to replication topologies on the 70-647 exam.

Designing Site Links

After you have designed the site model and the replication topology, design site links. *Site links* connect the sites to form the desired replication topology. Without site links, intersite replication cannot occur, which means domain controllers in different sites will not be able to replicate with one another.

To design site links, identify the sites you need to connect and create a site link for each connection. For example, if you identify the need to connect a site named Seattle and a site named Redmond, create a site link called Seattle-Redmond and associate the Seattle and Redmond sites with this site link. Next, ensure that the sites are not members of any other site links. When sites are created, they are usually added to the Default-First Site Link by default. When you associate the site with another site link, remember to change the original site link membership of the site. Ensuring site link membership accuracy is important because the KCC will make routing decisions based on the membership of both site links, which might result in incorrect routing.

MORE INFO   **CREATING A SITE LINK DESIGN**

For more information about creating a site link design, go to *http://technet.microsoft.com /en-us/library/cc732837(WS.10).aspx*.

When designing site links, you need to design the transport the site links use. The Inter-Site Transports container provides the means for mapping site links to that transport. When you create a site link object, you create it in either the IP container, which associates the site link with the remote procedure call (RPC) over IP transport, or the SMTP container, which associates the site link with the SMTP transport. When you create a site link object in the respective Inter-Site Transports container, AD DS uses RPC over IP to transfer both intersite and intrasite replication between domain controllers. To keep data secure while in transit, RPC over IP replication uses both the Kerberos authentication protocol and data encryption. When a direct IP connection is not available, you can configure replication between sites to use SMTP. However, SMTP replication functionality is limited and requires an enterprise certification authority (CA). SMTP can replicate only the configuration, schema, and application directory partitions and does not support the replication of domain directory partitions. Use RPC over IP for site links if possible. Use SMTP when a direct IP connection is not available. Avoid using SMTP if possible; use it only as an interim solution because SMTP replication will not be supported in future versions of AD DS, and SMTP replication has many limitations, as previously mentioned.

Designing Site Link Properties

After you have designed site links, design site link properties by determining the cost, the schedule, and the replication interval.

Designing site link properties starts with determining the cost for each site link. Determining the cost associated with that replication path is required because the KCC uses cost to determine the least expensive route for replication between two sites that replicate the same directory partition. To start, refer to the network map and location data you collected earlier. For each network connection in each location, determine the available bandwidth. Assign the lowest cost to the highest available bandwidth. For example, assign a cost of 283 when the available bandwidth is 4,096 Kbps and assign a cost of 1,042 when the available bandwidth is 9.6 Kbps.

MORE INFO   **DETERMINING THE COST**

For more information about determining the cost, go to *http://technet.microsoft.com /en-us/library/cc753764(WS.10).aspx*.

When you have determined the cost of each site link, determine the schedule so you can control site link availability. To design the site link schedule, create two overlapping schedules between site links that contain domain controllers that directly replicate with each other. Use the default (100 percent available) schedule on those links unless you want to block replication traffic during peak hours. By blocking replication, you give priority to other traffic, but you also increase replication latency.

> **MORE INFO   DETERMINING THE SCHEDULE**
>
> For more information about determining the schedule, go to *http://technet.microsoft.com /en-us/library/cc731931(WS.10).aspx.*

After you have determined the schedule, determine the interval to indicate how frequently you want replication to occur during the times when the schedule allows replication. Consider the example of a schedule that allows replication between the hours of midnight and 7:00 A.M. with the replication interval set to 60 minutes. In this example, replication can occur up to seven times. When determining the schedule, remember that a small interval decreases latency but increases the amount of WAN traffic. Conversely, a large interval increases latency but decreases WAN traffic. If you need to keep domain partitions up to date, you can minimize latency by setting a shorter interval, such as 15 minutes. If you need to decrease WAN traffic, increase latency by setting a larger interval, such as 360 minutes.

> **MORE INFO   DETERMINING THE INTERVAL**
>
> For more information about determining the interval, go to *http://technet.microsoft.com /en-us/library/cc730961(WS.10).aspx.*

Designing Site Link Bridging

The final component in designing replication is designing site link bridging. A *site link bridge* connects two or more site links and enables transitivity between site links. Each site link in a bridge must have a site in common with another site link in the bridge. Site link transitivity enables the Knowledge Consistency Checker (KCC) to reroute replication when necessary. When site links are bridged, the cost of replication from a domain controller at one end of the bridge to a domain controller at the other end is the sum of the costs on each of the intervening site links. Site link transitivity is enabled by default and should remain enabled unless the IP network contains segments that are not fully routed or unless you need to control the replication flow of the changes made in AD DS.

If your IP network is composed of IP segments that are not fully routed, you can disable the Bridge All Site Links option for the IP transport. In this case, all IP site links are considered nontransitive, and you can create and configure site link bridge objects to model the actual routing behavior of your network. A site link bridge has the effect of providing routing for a disjointed network. When you add site links to a site link bridge, all site links within the bridge can route transitively. Each site link in a manual site link bridge must have at least one site in common with another site link in the bridge. Otherwise, the bridge cannot compute the cost from sites in one link to the sites in other links of the bridge. If bridgehead servers that are capable of the transport used by the site link bridge are not available in two linked sites, a route is not available.

> **MORE INFO** **CREATING A SITE LINK BRIDGE DESIGN**
>
> For more information about creating a site link bridge design, go to *http://technet .microsoft.com/en-us/library/cc753638(WS.10).aspx.*

Designing the Placement of Domain Controllers

After you have designed the site structure and replication, design the placement of domain controllers, including forest root domain controllers, regional domain controllers, RODCs, global catalog servers, and operations master role holders.

 REAL WORLD

John Policelli

I have spent a great deal of my career both identifying and mitigating AD DS security risks. Through my many AD DS security assessments, I saw a common theme that was independent of the size of the AD DS deployment, the type of organization, or the administrative model used. For business and technical reasons, a significant number of organizations have had to deploy domain controllers in locations where physical security cannot be guaranteed. In these cases, the entire AD DS forest was at risk. Prior to Windows Server 2008, organizations have had very few options to mitigate this risk adequately.

RODCs in Windows Server 2008 now provide organizations with an adequate means to mitigate the security risk associated with placing domain controllers in locations where physical security cannot be guaranteed. The introduction of the RODC is one of the most important new features related to the AD DS physical topology in Windows Server 2008. Prior to Windows Server 2008, if users in a branch office could not authenticate over the WAN, a writable domain controller was required in the branch office. This has always presented a significant risk because physical security in branch offices is usually nonexistent. As with most software, if an attacker gains physical access to a domain controller, he or she can compromise it. Additionally, if an attacker gains access to a writable domain controller, the security of the entire forest is in jeopardy.

As an enterprise administrator, it is inevitable that you will design the placement of new domain controllers. However, you should also use the guidelines in this section to reevaluate the existing physical topology design in your organization.

Designing the Placement of Forest Root Domain Controllers

When designing the placement of domain controllers, you must start with the forest root domain controllers. They are the first domain controllers you deploy because the forest root domain is the first domain you add to the forest. The primary role of forest root domain controllers is to create trust paths for clients that need to access resources in domains other than their own. Regardless of whether you choose to deploy a dedicated forest root domain or to use a regional domain as the forest root domain, the placement of forest root domain controllers is imperative for end-user authentication.

Start by placing forest root domain controllers in hub locations and at datacenter locations. Next, examine the intraorganizational authentication requirements for your organization. If users in a remote location need to access resources from other domains, they need to contact the forest root domain controllers. Because you began by placing the forest root domain controllers in the hub and datacenter locations, these users will have to cross the WAN for this intraorganizational authentication. At this point, you need to determine whether the reliability of the WAN link between the remote location and the hub and datacenter locations is sufficient. If reliability is sufficient, and the WAN links are fast, you do not need to deploy additional forest root domain controllers. However, if reliability issues exist, you can either deploy a forest root domain controller in the remote location or use a shortcut trust. By deploying a forest root domain controller in the remote location, users will not have to cross the WAN for intraorganizational authentication, and the authentication time will be optimized. However, deploying forest root domain controllers in remote locations will introduce additional hardware, software, and administrative costs. Additionally, deploying forest root domain controllers in remote locations can introduce unwanted security risks. As an alternative, you can use a shortcut trust to optimize the intraorganizational authentication.

Designing shortcut trusts was discussed in the section, "Designing Trusts to Optimize Intra-forest Authentication," earlier in this chapter.

Designing the Placement of Regional Domain Controllers

Now that you have designed the placement of forest root domain controllers, you need to design the placement of regional domain controllers, which is applicable only if you are using the regional domain model. The single-domain model does not require regional domain controllers. To minimize hardware and software costs, plan to deploy as few regional domain controllers as possible. Because every AD DS site needs to have a domain controller, the placement of regional domain controllers is heavily dependent on site design and replication topology.

Start by placing regional domain controllers in every location that has an associated site object. If there are locations that contain users from multiple domains, place a regional domain controller for each domain in that location. During the authentication process, users will try to authenticate against a domain controller in the domain to which they belong in their local site. Finally, examine the organization's business continuity requirements. If they state that users should not cross the WAN in the event of a domain controller failure, place multiple-domain controllers for each domain to which users in the location belong.

Designing the Placement of RODCs

The placement of RODCs is also imperative when designing the placement of domain controllers. An RODC makes it possible for organizations to deploy a domain controller easily in scenarios in which physical security cannot be guaranteed. An RODC helps with the lack of physical security that is a common concern for domain controllers in the branch offices. An RODC must replicate domain data from a domain controller running Windows Server 2008 or Windows Server 2008 R2. Consequently, replication is among the most important considerations for determining where to place RODCs. Start by identifying the locations where physical security cannot be guaranteed, such as branch offices. Review network information and location data you previously collected for these locations. The locations that are not connected to the rest of the network through fast links, or those that have bandwidth limitations, will benefit from a local domain controller. Because the physical security cannot be guaranteed in these locations, deploy an RODC as opposed to a writable domain controller. Next, for each location that will have an RODC, you need to ensure that a writable domain controller running Windows Server 2008 or Windows Server 2008 R2 is in an adjacent site. Each RODC requires a writable domain controller running Windows Server 2008 or Windows Server 2008 R2 for the same domain from which the RODC can directly replicate. Typically, this requires that a writable domain controller running Windows Server 2008 or Windows Server 2008 R2 be placed in the nearest site in the topology, which is defined as the site that has the lowest-cost site link for the site that includes the RODC.

Designing the Placement of Global Catalog Servers

Next, design the placement of global catalog servers. The design of global catalog server placement is applicable only if the domain model you have selected is a single-domain model. Because every domain controller stores the only domain directory partition in the forest, configuring each domain controller as a global catalog server does not require any additional disk space usage, CPU usage, or replication traffic. In a multiple-domain model, the design of global catalog server placement must incorporate the application requirements, number of users, available bandwidth, and universal group membership caching for each site.

Start by reviewing network information and location data you previously collected to identify locations that are connected to the rest of the network through fast networks and that have ample bandwidth available. These locations do not require a local global catalog server, because users can access a global catalog server over the WAN link. Next, determine whether any applications need a local global catalog server. Certain applications, such as Exchange Server, Message Queuing, and applications using Distributed Component Object Model (DCOM) need a global catalog infrastructure to provide low query latency. Deploy a global catalog server in each location containing applications that need a local global catalog server. Next, review the location data to determine the number of users in each location. When the number of users exceeds 100, communication to global catalog servers is substantial, so deploy a global catalog server in each of these locations. Last, consider universal group membership caching to eliminate the need for a local global catalog server. For locations that include fewer than 100 users and that do not include a large number of roaming users nor applications that require a global catalog server, you can deploy domain controllers that are running Windows Server 2008 R2 and enable universal group membership caching.

> **MORE INFO** **HOW THE GLOBAL CATALOG WORKS**
>
> For more information about how universal group caching works, go to *http://go.microsoft .com/fwlink/?LinkId=107063*.

Designing the Placement of Operations Master Role Holders

To complete the placement of domain controller design, you need to design the placement of operations master role holders. The most important operations master for day-to-day operations is the primary domain controller (PDC) emulator. The PDC emulator receives priority updates for user password changes. Therefore, the PDC emulator should be placed in a central location where the maximum number of clients can connect to the server. The placement of the other operations masters is not as crucial as the PDC emulator; however, you must still properly design the placement of these role holders.

The schema master, domain naming master, and relative identifier (RID) master should be located in a site where another domain controller is a direct replication partner. This will provide adequate disaster recovery. If one of these servers fails, you might have to seize the operations master role on another domain controller. Ideally, you would like to seize the role on another domain controller that is fully replicated with the original operations master. This is more likely to be the case if the two domain controllers are in the same site and are configured as directory replication partners. The RID master must be accessible to all domain controllers through an RPC connection. When a domain controller requires more RIDs, it will use an RPC connection to request them from the RID master.

The placement of the infrastructure master role is dependent on the number of domains in the forest, the forest model, and whether all domain controllers are global catalog servers. As a general rule, the infrastructure master should not be located on a global catalog server that has a direct connection object to some global catalog in the forest, preferably in the same site. The role of the infrastructure master is to update user display name references between domains. Because the global catalog server holds a partial replica of every object in the forest, the infrastructure master, if placed on a global catalog server, will never update anything because it does not contain any references to objects that it does not hold. There are two exceptions to this general rule:

- **Single-domain forest**   In a forest that contains a single AD DS domain, there are no phantoms, so the infrastructure master has no work to do. The infrastructure master can be placed on any domain controller in the domain, regardless of whether that domain controller hosts the global catalog.

- **Multiple-domain forest where every domain controller in a domain holds the global catalog** If every domain controller in a domain that is part of a multiple-domain forest also hosts the global catalog, there are no phantoms or work for the infrastructure master to do. The infrastructure master can be put on any domain controller in that domain.

The Infrastructure Master Role and Global Catalog Servers

Recommendations regarding the placement of the infrastructure master role have been confusing and contradictory since the introduction of Active Directory in Windows 2000 Server. Most of the confusion stems from ambiguous wording. In some documentation, you will read that the infrastructure master can never be placed on a server that hosts the global catalog. In other documentation, you will read that the infrastructure master role can be placed on a global catalog server provided that all domain controllers in the domain are global catalog servers. To an extent, neither statement is entirely accurate.

The infrastructure master role is a domain-level operations master role. Its role is to compare objects of the local domain with objects in other domains in the same forest. The global catalog server holds a partial copy of every object in the forest. If the server holding the infrastructure master role is also a global catalog server, it will never see any differences. As a result, the infrastructure master will not make any changes in its local domain. Alternatively, if every domain controller in the domain is also a global catalog server, there is nothing for the infrastructure master to do, given that the global catalog already knows about the objects in the other domains.

In a single-domain AD DS forest model, there is no need for the infrastructure master to pull updates from other domains. In that case, the infrastructure master can reside on a global catalog server.

In a multiple-domain forest that has all domain controllers configured as global catalog servers, there is no need for the infrastructure master to pull updates from other domains because, as a global catalog server, it knows about all objects already. Therefore, the infrastructure master role can reside on a global catalog server.

Designing Printer Location Policies

After you have designed the placement of domain controllers, the final step for the physical topology involves designing printer location policies. Printers can be published in AD DS so that clients can locate printers based on their name, location, and other criteria. Designing printer location policies consists of creating a location schema, associating locations with subnets in AD DS, and enabling physical location tracking.

Designing printer location policies starts with creating a location schema, which enables users across the organization to search for locations. Location information for large organizations can change frequently, so you must ensure that the design for the location schema is flexible enough to describe all locations in which printers can be placed and to facilitate future changes in your organization. Because end users use location names, it is important to select simple and recognizable names as part of the location schema. Use the following guidelines when selecting names for the location schema:

- Use the name/name/name/name/... form for location names. (The slash (/) must be the dividing character.)
- Use any characters except for the slash (/).
- Avoid using special characters in the name.
- Keep names to a maximum of 32 characters to ensure visibility of the entire name in the user interface.
- Remember that the number of levels to a name is limited to 256.
- Remember that the maximum length of an entire location name is 260 characters.

Now that you have an understanding of the role of the location schema and the guidelines to follow when creating it, you are ready to create a location schema. To start, examine the network map and location data you collected earlier for your organization in order to determine the top-level geographic locations. Use static locations for the top-level geographic locations in your location schema, such as continents or countries. Next, use static locations for the second-level geographic locations, such as countries, states, or provinces. Next, for the third-level geographic locations, use fairly static locations, such as cities or buildings. Last, identify as many additional levels as are required according to the geographical boundaries of your organization. For levels four and beyond, use locations, divisions, and departments, all of which can change more frequently than the previous levels.

To understand fully how to create the location schema, consider the following example, shown in Table 2-7, of an organization that has a worldwide presence. The organization operates in a number of countries throughout North America, South America, and Europe. The organization has multiple offices in some countries and multiple offices in some states throughout the United States. In some offices, the organization occupies multiple floors of a building.

TABLE 2-7 Sample Network Information and Location Data-Gathering Table

TOP LEVEL	SECOND LEVEL	THIRD LEVEL	FOURTH LEVEL	FIFTH LEVEL	SIXTH LEVEL
North America	United States	Washington	Redmond	Building 40	Floor 1
North America	United States	Washington	Redmond	Building 40	Floor 2
North America	United States	New York	New York	Finance	

North America	United States	New York	New York	Marketing
North America	Canada	Ontario	Ottawa	
North America	Canada	Ontario	Toronto	Bloor Street
North America	Canada	Ontario	Toronto	Bay Street
South America	Argentina	Mendoza	Mendoza	
South America	Chile	Santiago	Santiago	
Europe	Italy	Lazio	Rome	Development
Europe	Italy	Lazio	Rome	HR
Europe	Spain	Madrid	Madrid	

- Continent names are used for the top-level locations.
- Country names are used for the second-level locations.
- State and province names are used for the third-level locations.
- City names are used for the fourth-level locations.
- Department names are used for the fifth-level locations when more than one department exists in a location.
- Building names are also used for the fifth-level locations when more than one building exists in a given city.
- Floor names are used for the sixth-level locations when more than one floor exists in a building.

This location schema provides the organization with the flexibility to add locations to the schema in the future. Additionally, users can perform searches based on broad location details such as continent, country, state or province, or city, and they can perform searches based on granular location details, such as department or floor. Also, the tree varies in depth depending on the location. For example, the full name of Floor 1 in Redmond is North America/United States/Washington/Redmond/Building 40/Floor 1, whereas the full name of the HR building in Rome is Europe/Italy/Lazio/Rome/HR.

Now that you have created the location schema, you must associate locations with subnets in AD DS. By setting location information about subnets, AD DS automatically associates a printer to a location based on the subnet on which the printer is located. Figure 2-13 shows the location information for a subnet in AD DS.

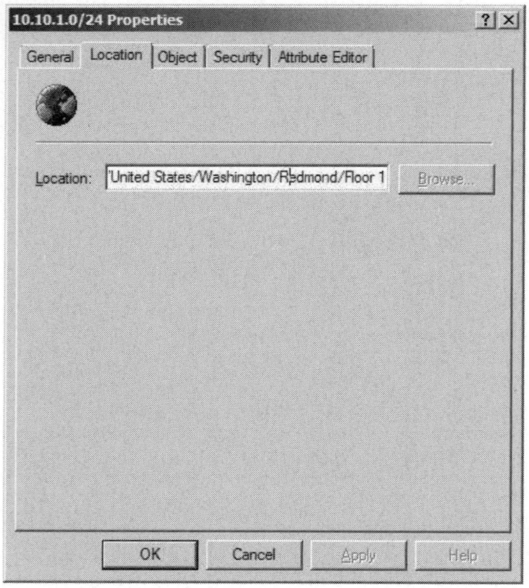

FIGURE 2-13 Subnet location information

Ensure that you define a location on all subnets in AD DS so that users can search printers based on the location information.

The last step in designing printer location policies consists of enabling physical location tracking, a feature that was introduced in Windows 2000 Server that enables users to browse for printers based on the location schema. Because physical location tracking is not enabled by default, you must enable it through Group Policy. Then, a *Browse* button appears beside the Location field in the Find Printers dialog box. When designing printer location policies, you must decide the Group Policy level in which physical location tracking will be enabled. Because printers are usually installed at the computer level as opposed to the user level, physical location tracking is a Group Policy setting that is definable under the Computer Configuration settings, as shown in Figure 2-14.

Designing an enterprise Group Policy strategy is discussed in Chapter 4, "Designing Active Directory Administration and Group Policy Strategy."

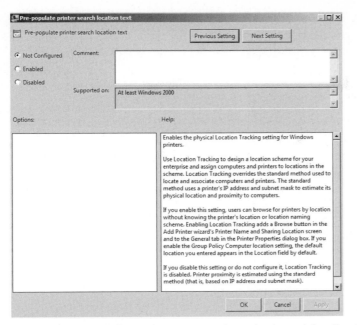

FIGURE 2-14 Group Policy setting to prepopulate printer search location text

Designing the Active Directory Domain Services Physical Topology

You are an enterprise administrator at Blue Yonder Airlines, a large multinational corporation with office locations in five countries. It is currently running Windows Server 2003 but is beginning to implement Windows Server 2008 R2. As an enterprise administrator, it is your role to design the AD DS infrastructure for Blue Yonder Airlines.

Since it implemented Windows Server 2003, the company has expanded significantly to different countries located in different regions of the world and has acquired several subsidiaries. As a result, the organization has decided to evaluate the current AD DS design to determine whether that infrastructure should be modified as part of the migration project.

Blue Yonder Airlines has a single AD DS forest that has a dedicated forest root domain named *blueyonderairlines.com*. The forest functional level in the *blueyonderairlines.com* forest is set to Windows Server 2003 and contains users from the five countries in which Blue Yonder Airlines operates. This includes 25,000 users from the United States, 10,000 users from Canada, 5,000 users from Mexico, 3,000 users from Italy, and 100 users from Argentina. Users in the United States belong to the *us.blueyonderairlines.com* regional domain. Likewise, users in Canada belong to the *canada.blueyonderairlines.com* regional domain, but those in both Mexico and Argentina belong to the *mexico.blueyonderairlines.com* regional domain.

The Canada location has a direct connection to the United States location through a 1.5-Mbps network link. The average available bandwidth on this network link is 75 percent. The Mexico location also has a direct connection to the United States location through a 1.5-Mbps network link. The average available bandwidth on this network link is 55 percent. The Italy location has a direct connection to the United States location through a 512-Kbps network link. The average available bandwidth on this network link is 25 percent during business hours and 5 percent between 2:00 A.M. and 6:00 A.M. AD DS replication should not occur after business hours. Blue Yonder Airlines has a retail outlet in Argentina where physical security is a concern. The Argentina location is connected to the Mexico location through a 256-Kbps network connection, which has an average available bandwidth of 25 percent. Blue Yonder Airlines does not want users in Argentina to authenticate over the WAN; however, it does want to ensure that users in each region are able to log on even if a network outage occurs.

EXERCISE 1   Design the Site Structure

In this exercise, you review the business and technical requirements to design the site structure for Blue Yonder Airlines.

1. Based on your analysis of the network location, draw a location map for Blue Yonder Airlines.

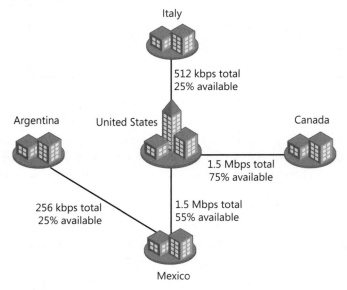

FIGURE 2-15 Location map for Blue Yonder Airlines

2. Use the following table to record the relevant location information for Blue Yonder Airlines.

NAME OF REGION	TOTAL BANDWIDTH	AVAILABLE BANDWIDTH	NETWORK SEGMENT	# OF USERS	DOMAINS

NAME OF REGION	TOTAL BAND-WIDTH	AVAILABLE BANDWIDTH	NETWORK SEGMENT	# OF USERS	DOMAINS
U.S.	1.5 Mbps	75%	10.10.1.0/24	0	blueyonderairlines.com
				25,000	us.blueyonderairlines.com
Canada	1.5 Mbps	75%	10.10.2.0/24	10,000	canada.blueyonderairlines.com
Mexico	1.5 Mbps	55%	10.10.3.0/24	5,000	mexico.blueyonderairlines.com
Italy	512 Kbps	25% (day) 5% (night)	10.10.4.0/24	3,000	italy.blueyonderairlines.com
Argentina	256 Kbps	25%	10.10.5.0/24	100	mexico.blueyonderairlines.com

3. Which site model will be used for Blue Yonder Airlines?

The multiple sites model will be used because Blue Yonder Airlines wants to ensure that users in each region are able to log on even if a network outage occurs. Additionally, each region has its own domain, so the multiple sites model will ensure that domain data is replicated only to domain controllers for a given domain instead of across the WAN.

EXERCISE 2   Design Replication

In this exercise, you review the business and technical requirements to design replication for Blue Yonder Airlines.

1. What are the relevant replication design requirements for Blue Yonder Airlines?

The relevant replication design requirements for Blue Yonder Airlines are as follows:

- Domain data for the *blueyonderairlines.com* domain is required in the U.S. location.
- Domain data for the *us.blueyonderairlines.com* domain is required in the U.S. location.

- Domain data for the *canada.blueyonderairlines.com* domain is required in the Canada location.
- Domain data for the *italy.blueyonderairlines.com* domain is required in the Italy location.
- Domain data for the *mexico.blueyonderairlines.com* domain is required in the Mexico and Argentina locations.
- The Canada location has a direct connection to the U.S. location through a 1.5-Mbps network link that has an average available bandwidth of 75 percent.
- The Mexico location has a direct connection to the U.S. location through a 1.5-Mbps network link that has an average available bandwidth of 55 percent.
- The Italy location has a direct connection to the U.S. location through a 512-Kbps network link that has an average available bandwidth of 25 percent during business hours and 5 percent between 2:00 A.M. and 6:00 A.M.
- AD DS replication should not occur between the Italy location and the U.S. location after business hours.
- The Argentina location is connected to the Mexico location through a 256-Kbps network connection that has an average available bandwidth of 25 percent.
- Blue Yonder Airlines wants to ensure that users in each region are able to log on even if a network outage occurs.

2. Which replication topology will be used for the replication design?

   The hub and spoke replication topology will be used for the replication design. It's best suited for this design because the locations that will have a writable domain controller all have a direct connection to the U.S. location, which is the hub.

3. Which site links are required to facilitate the replication design?

   The following site links are required for the replication design:

   U.S.–Canada

   U.S.–Mexico

   U.S.–Italy

   Argentina–Mexico

4. What will the cost of each site link be?

   There are no requirements to have diverse costs on the site links. Therefore, the cost of each site link can remain at the default of 100.

5. What will the replication schedule design be for each site link?

   The replication schedule design for each site link will be as follows:

   The U.S.–Canada site link will have a default replication schedule.

   The U.S.–Mexico site link will have a default replication schedule.

The U.S.–Italy site will have a custom replication schedule, preventing AD DS replication between the hours of 2:00 A.M. and 6:00 A.M.

The Argentina–Mexico site link will have a default replication schedule.

6. What will the replication interval design be for each site link?

The replication interval design for each site link will be as follows:

- The U.S.–Canada site link will have the default replication interval of 180.

- The U.S.–Mexico site link will have the default replication interval of 180.

- The U.S.–Italy site link will have the default replication interval of 180.

- The Argentina–Mexico site link will have a replication interval of 360.

EXERCISE 3   Design the Placement of Domain Controllers

In this exercise, you review the business and technical requirements to design placement of domain controllers for Blue Yonder Airlines.

1. Where will the forest root domain controllers be placed as part of the design?

The forest root domain controllers will be placed in the U.S. location. This is the only location that has users for the forest root domain. Additionally, because all domains belong to the same tree, forest root domain controllers do not need to be placed in any of the remote locations to speed up authentication.

2. Where will the regional domain controllers be placed as part of the design?

The placement of regional domain controllers for the remote offices will be as follows:

- The domain controllers for the *us.blueyonderairlines.com* domain will be placed in the U.S. location.

- The domain controllers for the *canada.blueyonderairlines.com* domain will be placed in the Canada location.

- The domain controllers for the *mexico.blueyonderairlines.com* domain will be placed in the Mexico location.

- No writable domain controllers will be placed in the Argentina location because of the lack of physical security in this location.

3. Where will global catalog servers be placed as part of the design?

Global catalog servers are required in each location except the Argentina location because of the lack of physical security there. The remaining locations (U.S., Canada, Italy, and Mexico) all require local global catalog servers because of the requirement to ensure that users do not cross the WAN for authentication.

4. Where will RODCs be placed as part of the design?

An RODC will be placed in the Argentina location because of the lack of physical security in this location.

5. Where will the operations master role holders be placed as part of the design?

The placement of operations master role holders will be as follows:

- Because the schema master and the domain naming master role are forest-level roles, and the forest root domain is in the U.S. site, these roles will reside on a server in the U.S. site.

- Because the infrastructure master role, RID master role, and PDC emulator role are domain-level roles, and the *blueyonderairlines.com* domain is in the U.S. site, these roles will reside on a server in the U.S. site.

- Because the infrastructure master role, RID master role, and PDC emulator role are domain-level roles, and the *us.blueyonderairlines.com* domain is in the U.S. site, these roles will reside on a server in the U.S. site.

- Because the infrastructure master role, RID master role, and PDC emulator role are domain-level roles, and the *canada.blueyonderairlines.com* domain is in the Canada site, these roles will reside on a server in the Canada site.

- Because the infrastructure master role, RID master role, and PDC emulator role are domain-level roles, and the *italy.blueyonderairlines.com* domain is in the Italy site, these roles will reside on a server in the Italy site.

Lesson Summary

- Gathering site design requirements consists of creating a location map and gathering location data.

- You can implement sites using the single site model to reduce AD DS replication latency or the multiple sites model to reduce the amount of bandwidth used for AD DS replication.

- Configure intersite replication topology using the hub and spoke, full mesh, or hybrid replication topology.

- Place forest root domain controllers in hub locations and at datacenter locations. Place regional domain controllers in every location that has an associated site object. Place RODCs in locations that require a local domain controller but lack physical security.

- At least one global catalog server should be placed in each location that has an associated site object unless universal group caching is enabled on the site object.

- Place the PDC emulator in a central location where the maximum number of clients can connect to the server.

- The schema master, domain naming master, and RID master should be located in a site where another domain controller is a direct replication partner.

- In a forest that contains a single AD DS domain, the infrastructure master can be placed on any domain controller in the domain. If every domain controller in a domain that is part of a multiple-domain forest also hosts the global catalog, you can place the infrastructure master on any domain controller in that domain.

Lesson Review

The following questions are intended to reinforce key information presented in this lesson. The questions are also available on the companion CD if you prefer to review them in electronic form.

> **NOTE** **ANSWERS**
>
> Answers to these questions and explanations of why each answer choice is correct or incorrect are located in the "Answers" section at the end of the book.

1. Which of the following uses intrasite replication only?
   - **A.** Single site model
   - **B.** Multiple sites model
   - **C.** Hub and spoke replication topology
   - **D.** Full mesh replication topology

2. Which replication topology would you use if your network consists of faster network connections between major computing hubs and slower links connecting branch offices?
   - **A.** Single site model
   - **B.** Ring replication topology
   - **C.** Hub and spoke replication topology
   - **D.** Full mesh replication topology

3. You have a single AD DS forest with a single domain that is using the hub and spoke replication topology. Where should you place the server that holds the PDC emulator operations master role?
   - **A.** In the location represented by the hub site
   - **B.** In one of the locations represented by a spoke site
   - **C.** In every location represented by a spoke site
   - **D.** On the server that holds the global catalog server role in a location represented by a spoke site

Chapter Review

To further practice and reinforce the skills you learned in this chapter, you can perform the following tasks:

- Review the chapter summary.
- Review the list of key terms introduced in this chapter.
- Complete the case scenarios. These scenarios set up real-world situations involving the topics of this chapter and ask you to create a solution.
- Complete the suggested practices.
- Take a practice test.

Chapter Summary

- Gathering forest design requirements consists of identifying the role of AD DS in your organization and gathering business, technical, security, network, autonomy, and isolation requirements.
- The three forest models are the organizational forest model, the resource forest model, and the restricted access forest model.
- Domain design requires you to consider an organization's security, administrative, and replication requirements. You can implement two domain models: the single-domain model and the regional domain model.
- Gathering site design requirements consists of creating a location map and gathering location data. You can implement two site models: the single site model and the multiple sites model.
- The three replication topologies are the hub and spoke replication topology, the full mesh replication topology, and the hybrid replication topology.
- Place the PDC emulator in a central location where the maximum number of clients can connect to the server.
- The schema master, the domain naming master, and the RID master should be located in a site where another domain controller is a direct replication partner.

Key Terms

Do you know what these key terms mean? You can check your answers by looking up the terms in the glossary at the end of the book.

- Data autonomy
- Data isolation
- Dedicated forest root domain
- Forest root domain

- Full mesh replication topology
- Hub and spoke replication topology
- Hybrid replication topology
- Multiple sites model
- Organizational forest model
- Read-only domain controller (RODC)
- Regional domain model
- Resource forest model
- Restricted access forest model
- Service autonomy
- Service isolation
- Single-domain model
- Single site model
- Site links
- Site link bridge

Case Scenarios

In the following case scenarios, you apply what you've learned about designing AD DS forests and domains and their topologies. You can find the answers to these questions in the "Answers" section at the end of this book.

Case Scenario 1: Designing the AD DS Forest

You work as an enterprise administrator at Tailspin Toys, which has an existing AD DS forest supported by the Tailspin Toys IT department. Tailspin Toys recently purchased Wingtip Toys.

Wingtip Toys does not use AD DS. It has been mandated, however, to move to a centralized model for authentication and authorization and thus will begin using AD DS. Wingtip Toys has its own IT department that will support AD DS.

You have been asked to design a forest for Wingtip Toys. The administrators from Tailspin Toys should be permitted to manage the AD DS forest only for Tailspin Toys. The administrators from Wingtip Toys should be permitted to manage the AD DS forest only for Wingtip Toys.

1. Will joining the Wingtip Toys computers to the existing Tailspin Toys forest meet the requirements?

2. Will creating a new organizational forest for Wingtip Toys meet the requirements?

Case Scenario 2: Designing AD DS Sites

You are an enterprise administrator at Woodgrove Bank, which has a single AD DS forest with a dedicated forest root domain named *woodgrovebank.com*.

The *woodgrovebank.com* forest contains users from the five countries in which Woodgrove Bank operates. The Canada location has a direct connection to the United States location through a 1.5-Mbps network link with an average available bandwidth of 75 percent. The Mexico location has a direct connection to the United States location through a 1.5-Mbps network link with an average available bandwidth of 55 percent. The Italy location has a direct connection to the United States location through a 512-Kbps network link with an average available bandwidth of 25 percent. The Argentina location is connected to the Mexico location through a 256-Kbps network connection with an average available bandwidth of 25 percent. Woodgrove Bank does not want users in Argentina to authenticate over the WAN.

You need to determine which AD DS site replication topology to use for Woodgrove Bank.

1. Will using a hub and spoke AD DS replication topology meet the requirements?
2. Will using a hybrid AD DS replication topology meet the requirements?

Case Scenario 3: Designing the Placement of Domain Controllers

You are an enterprise administrator at Woodgrove Bank, which has a single AD DS forest with a dedicated forest root domain named *woodgrovebank.com*.

The *woodgrovebank.com* forest contains users from the five countries in which Woodgrove Bank operates. This includes 25,000 users from the United States, 10,000 users from Canada, 5,000 users from Mexico, 3,000 users from Italy, and 100 users from Argentina. Users in the U.S. location belong to the *us.woodgrovebank.com* regional domain. Users in the Canada location belong to the *canada.woodgrovebank.com* regional domain. Users in both the Mexico and Argentina locations belong to the *mexico.woodgrovebank.com* regional domain.

Woodgrove Bank has a retail outlet in Argentina where physical security is a concern. The Argentina location is connected to the Mexico location through a network connection. Woodgrove Bank does not want users in Argentina to authenticate over the WAN.

You need to determine how users in the Argentina location will authenticate without compromising physical security.

1. Will placing a global catalog server in the Argentina location meet the requirements?
2. Will placing an RODC in the Argentina location meet the requirements?

Suggested Practices

To help you successfully master the exam objectives presented in this chapter, complete the following tasks:

Implement Forests, Domains, and the Physical Topology

- **Practice 1**   Implement an AD DS forest with a child domain by performing the following procedure. Using either virtual or physical machines, install the Active Directory Domain Services Server role on two installations of Windows Server 2008 R2. On the first server, install a new AD DS forest and domain. On the second server, install a new AD DS domain, following the same namespace as the first domain.

- **Practice 2**   Implement an AD DS site and replication design by performing the following procedure. Using either virtual or physical machines, create a multiple-domain AD DS forest. Create one site object for each domain controller in the forest. Create site links between all site objects by using the full mesh topology. Configure the cost, schedule, and frequency on each site link.

- **Practice 3**   Implement a domain controller placement design by performing the following procedure. Using either virtual or physical machines, create a multiple-domain AD DS forest. Transfer the schema master role. Transfer the domain naming master role. Transfer the RID master role in each domain in the forest. Transfer the infrastructure master role in each domain in the forest. Transfer the PDC emulator role in each domain in the forest.

Watch a Webcast

- **Practice 1**   Watch the "Active Directory Domain Services in Windows Server 2008 R2 Technical Overview" webcast. You can find this by searching *http://msevents .microsoft.com* for event ID # 1032416407 or by visiting *https://msevents.microsoft.com /CUI/WebCastEventDetails.aspx?EventID=1032416407&EventCategory=5&culture =en-US&CountryCode=US*.

Read a White Paper

- **Practice 1**   Read the "AD DS Installation and Removal Step-by-Step Guide" white paper from Microsoft at *http://technet.microsoft.com/en-us/library/cc755258(WS.10).aspx*.

- **Practice 2**   Read the "Active Directory Recycle Bin Step-by-Step Guide" white paper from Microsoft at *http://technet.microsoft.com/en-us/library/dd392261(WS.10).aspx*.

- **Practice 3**   Read the "Authentication Mechanism Assurance for AD DS in Windows Server 2008 R2 Step-by-Step Guide" white paper from Microsoft at *http://technet .microsoft.com/en-us/library/dd378897(WS.10).aspx*.

Take a Practice Test

The practice tests on this book's companion CD offer many options. For example, you can test yourself on just one exam objective, or you can test yourself on all the 70-647 certification exam content. You can set up the test so that it closely simulates the experience of taking a certification exam, or you can set it up in study mode so that you can look at the correct answers and explanations after you answer each question.

> **MORE INFO** **PRACTICE TESTS**
>
> For details about all the practice test options available, see the "How to Use the Practice Tests" section in this book's introduction.

CHAPTER 3

Planning Migrations, Trusts, and Interoperability

This chapter focuses on how to get Microsoft Windows Server 2008 R2 working with other technologies and other operating systems. In the first lesson, you learn which factors you need to consider when planning an organization's move from an existing Active Directory directory service environment to one based on Windows Server 2008 R2 Active Directory Domain Services (AD DS). You will also learn what steps to consider when planning a trust relationship between one AD DS environment and another. The second lesson in this chapter focuses on the topic of interoperability, which includes ensuring that users of Windows-based and UNIX-based computers are able to work seamlessly together. This lesson also includes information about technologies by which you can migrate services and applications that traditionally run on UNIX-based computers only, so that they can be hosted on computers on which the Windows Server 2008 R2 operating system is installed.

Exam objectives in this chapter:

- Plan for domain or forest migration, upgrade, and restructuring.
- Plan for interoperability.

Lessons in this chapter:

Before You Begin

To complete the lessons in this chapter, you must have installed a Windows Server 2008 R2 Enterprise domain controller named Glasgow as described in Chapter 1, "Planning Name Resolution and Internet Protocol Addressing." No additional configuration is required for this chapter.

REAL WORLD

John Policelli

In the 10 years that I have been working with Active Directory, I have been involved in countless migrations and upgrades. Over these years, I have had the opportunity to see the evolution of Active Directory migrations. As one would expect, the migration processes have improved with the progression of the technology and the maturity of the product. I have also seen the complexity of migrations increase substantially over the years. Organizations have had to migrate and upgrade for fairly basic technical reasons, such as staying within support and leveraging new features, as new versions of the Windows Server operating system have been released. However, organizations in this day and age have important business drivers, such as mergers and acquisitions and increased pressure to consolidate, which often result in very complex migrations. I've come to realize that the most complex and difficult migrations are much more achievable through proper planning.

Lesson 1: Planning for Migration, Upgrade, and Restructuring

Although it is possible to add a member server running Windows Server 2008 R2 to an existing Microsoft Windows Server 2003 domain, at some point in your organization's migration to Windows Server 2008 R2, you are going to want to upgrade your organization's domain controllers.In this lesson, you learn which steps you need to take to move from a network environment that is dependent on a previous version of Microsoft Windows to a Windows Server 2008 R2 Active Directory–based network infrastructure.

> **After this lesson, you will be able to:**
> - Prepare the environment for Windows Server 2008 R2.
> - Migrate objects.
> - Plan domain consolidation.
>
> **Estimated lesson time: 40 minutes**

Migration Paths

You can take one of three general paths to move from an existing AD DS environment to a Windows Server 2008 R2 AD DS environment. These paths are known as the *domain upgrade*, the *domain restructure*, and the *upgrade-then-restructure*. When planning which method to use, consider factors such as the amount of time the migration should take and the availability of new server hardware. An operating system upgrade is an ideal time to reassess your business requirements and compare these to your existing AD DS design, and potentially identify opportunities for increased efficiencies and cost savings.

Domain Upgrade Migration Path

The *domain upgrade migration path* involves upgrading the operating system of a domain controller running Windows Server 2003 or Windows Server 2008 to Windows Server 2008 R2 or installing Windows Server 2008 R2 domain controllers into a Windows 2000 Server or Windows Server 2003 domain. If you are planning to add Windows Server 2008 R2 domain controllers to a domain, you need to ensure that domains in your organization are at the Windows 2000 Native functional level or higher. Domains at the Windows 2000 mixed or Windows Server 2003 interim functional level do not support Windows Server 2008 R2 domain controllers. There is no direct upgrade path between Windows 2000 Server and Windows Server 2008 R2. Plan to use the domain upgrade migration path when you will not have access to a significant amount of new server hardware on which to install new deployments of Windows Server 2008 R2.

Domain Restructure Migration Path

The *domain restructure migration path* involves copying AD DS objects from the original domain or forest to the new Windows Server 2008 R2 domain or forest, using tools, such as the Active Directory Migration Tool, covered later in this lesson. After all objects are migrated, the domain controllers in the original domain or forest are decommissioned. The domain restructure migration path includes the following advantages:

- The original environment remains the same until the migration is completed. Users are not forced to the new environment until it is tested and ready.

- It enables the selective migration of objects. When you perform a domain upgrade, all objects are upgraded, including those that are redundant, inactive, and no longer necessary. Domain restructure migrations enable organizations to clean up their environments as they transition to the new technology.

The domain restructure migration requires you to have enough new server hardware to support both the original and destination environments concurrently. If the budget does not allow for new server hardware, the domain upgrade migration path is a more feasible alternative. Although it is possible to perform a domain restructure migration using virtualization, you should avoid this approach unless you are planning an AD DS deployment that primarily involves virtualized domain controllers.

Upgrade-Then-Restructure Migration Path

The upgrade-then-restructure migration path, also known as a two-phase migration, involves upgrading the original domain or forest and then migrating AD DS objects to a new Windows Server 2008 R2 domain or forest. This process essentially combines the domain upgrade and domain restructure approaches, enabling an organization to benefit immediately from a Windows Server 2008 R2 upgrade and then to transition to new Windows Server 2008 R2 domain controller hardware at some point in the future, with the added benefit of removing unnecessary AD DS objects through the selective migration process.

Active Directory Migration Tool

You can use the Active Directory Migration Tool v3.2 (ADMT v3.2) to migrate AD DS objects within a forest, referred to as an *intraforest migration*, or to migrate objects to another forest, referred to as an *interforest migration*. You can use the ADMT to migrate users, groups, managed service accounts, computers, and trusts. The ADMT has a simulation mode that enables administrators to evaluate the results of planned migrations prior to performing the actual migrations.

> **MORE INFO** **OBTAIN THE ACTIVE DIRECTORY MIGRATION TOOL**
>
> You can obtain the Active Directory Migration Tool from the Microsoft Web site at *http://www.microsoft.com/downloads/en/details.aspx?FamilyID=20c0db45-db16-4d10 -99f2-539b7277ccdb.*

Upgrading an Existing Domain to Windows Server 2008 R2

There are two basic strategies for transitioning from an existing domain to a Windows Server 2008 R2 AD DS domain. The first strategy is to introduce new Windows Server 2008 R2 domain controllers into the forest and then either to retire or upgrade existing Windows Server 2003 or Windows Server 2008 domain controllers. The second strategy is simply to perform an in-place upgrade of all existing Windows Server 2003 or Windows Server 2008 domain controllers. Both of these strategies are useful when pursuing the domain upgrade migration path.

Preparing the Environment

You need to perform several steps prior to adding a Windows Server 2008 R2 domain controller to an existing AD DS environment, even if you do not intend to change the current domain or forest functional level. These steps include ensuring that existing domain controllers in the environment have appropriate patches and service packs installed and that the AD DS schema has been appropriately prepared for the introduction of Windows Server 2008 R2 domain controllers.

If you are planning to add a Windows Server 2008 R2 domain controller to a domain that has active Windows 2000 Server domain controllers, which is possible when using the Windows 2000 Native domain and forest functional level, you must ensure that all Windows 2000 Server domain controllers have Service Pack 4 installed.

To prepare a forest for the installation of Windows Server 2008 R2 domain controllers, run the *adprep /forestprep* command on the schema master. To execute this command successfully, the user account must be a member of the Enterprise Admins, Schema Admins, and Domain Admins groups.

To prepare a forest for the installation of a read-only domain controller (RODC), run the *adprep /rodcprep* command on the schema master. This command needs to be run only once on the schema master and does not need to be run in each domain in the forest in which you intend to install Windows Server 2008 R2 RODCs. As is the case with *adprep /forestprep*, to execute this command successfully, the user account must be a member of the Enterprise Admins, Schema Admins, and Domain Admins groups.

After you have completed the forest-level preparation tasks, you must prepare each domain in the forest where you plan to install Windows Server 2008 R2 domain controllers. A user who is a member of that domain's Domain Admins group must run the *adprep /domainprep /gpprep* domain preparation command on the domain controller that holds the infrastructure master role. After this command has been run, Windows Server 2008 R2 domain controllers can be introduced to that domain.

In-Place Domain Controller Upgrade

Upgrading each domain controller in the domain from Windows Server 2003 or Windows Server 2008 to Windows Server 2008 R2 works well within the limitations of the types of upgrades you can perform. The ability to perform in-place upgrades becomes slightly more complicated with Windows Server 2008 R2 because of the fact that Windows Server 2008 R2 only includes x64 support; there are no x86 editions of Windows Server 2008 R2. It is quite likely that you have existing domain controllers that have an x86 edition of Windows Server installed. Cross-architecture in-place upgrades, for example x86 to x64, are not supported. Additionally, in-place upgrades from computers that have operating systems prior to Windows Server 2003 SP2 are not supported.

EXAM TIP

For the 70-647 exam, ensure that you understand the upgrade paths from previous versions of Windows Server to Windows Server 2008 R2 because these affect the Active Directory Domain Services upgrade paths.

✔ **Quick Check**

1. On which domain controller should you perform the first forest preparation task?
2. Which of the Windows Server 2003 domain functional levels do not support the introduction of Windows Server 2008 R2 domain controllers?

Quick Check Answers

1. You must run *adprep /forestprep* on the domain controller hosting the schema master role.
2. The Windows Server 2003 interim domain functional level does not support Windows Server 2008 R2 domain controllers.

Cross-Forest Authentication

The forest is the ultimate security boundary for AD DS. Organizations often have multiple AD DS forests or have partners with AD DS forests, for which the security boundary must be extended. Cross-forest authentication consists of enabling users in one forest to access resources in another forest. Cross-forest authentication is usually achieved by using forest trust relationships. Forest trust relationships are transitive; they allow users in any domain in one forest to access resources in any domain in another forest. In addition to forest trust relationships, external trusts can be used to provide cross-forest authentication. External trusts are created between domains in two separate forests and enable users in one domain to access resources in the other domain. Active Directory Federation Services (AD FS) also provides a method of granting access to forest resources; you will learn about this technology in Lesson 2, "Planning for Interoperability."

When planning a trust, you must consider the following factors:

- Whether a forest trust or external trust is required
- The direction of the trust
- The level of authentication that will be allowed through the trust
- Whether Security Identifier (SID) filtering should be implemented

Because trust relationships extend the AD DS security boundary, it is important to ensure that you grant only the minimum required access needed to meet business and technical requirements.

You can determine whether a forest trust or external trust is required by assessing the location of the users requiring access and the resources to which they require access. As previously mentioned, forest trusts are transitive. Therefore, if users from any domain in one forest require access to resources in any domain in another forest, then a forest trust is required. On the other hand, if users from a single domain in one forest require access to resources in a single domain in another forest, an external trust is better suited.

Once you've determined whether a forest trust or external trust is required, you must decide on the direction of trust. Forest trusts and external trusts can be one-way or two-way. A two-way trust is only required when users in each forest or domain need to access resources located in the other domain or forest. One-way trusts will suffice when bidirectional access is not required.

Trust relationships provide a pathway for all authentication requests between the forests or domains. By default, any user can authenticate over a trust relationship. However, selective authentication enables you to restrict which users can authenticate over a trust. Effectively, selective authentication can be used to limit the groups of users who are able to access resources across the trust and enables you to limit which computers in the trusting forest can be accessed across the trust. You can configure selective authentication when you first create the trust or alter the properties of an existing trust, as shown in Figure 3-1. If you choose not to implement selective authentication, plan to remove the Authenticated Users group from all sensitive resources in the trusting domain.

SID History is a feature that supports the migration of user and group accounts between domains and allows the user accounts to retain access to resources in their original domain. SID filtering prevents users from using SIDs stored in the *SIDHistory* attribute when accessing resources in a trusting forest. A new SID will be assigned to the account when it is moved to the new domain, and that new SID will not be assigned access to the resources that are yet to be migrated from the original domain. SID filtering can block the *SIDHistory* attribute across the forest trust, which ensures that accounts that have been migrated to a trusted forest no longer have access to resources in the original forest unless explicitly specified. When enabled, any SIDs from domains other than the trusted domain are ignored. For example, SID filtering is enabled by default on any trust created using a computer running Windows Server 2008 R2. Disable SID filtering only during the migration of user and group accounts from one forest to another. This allows access to resources during the migration process. After the migration is complete, plan to reenable SID filtering.

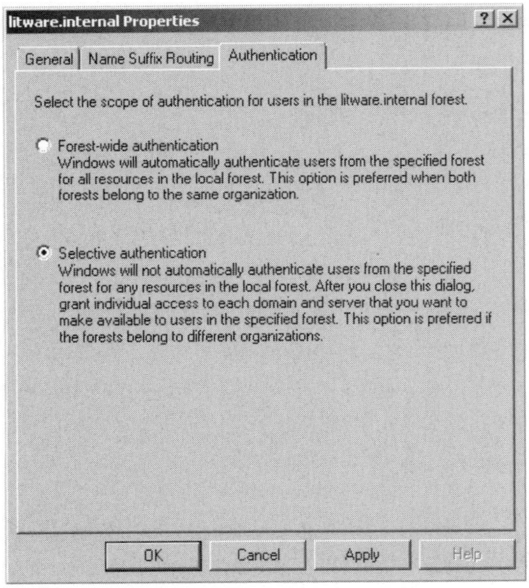

FIGURE 3-1 Configuring selective authentication

PRACTICE Planning Forest Migration to Windows Server 2008 R2

Tailspin Toys has a 15-domain AD DS forest that contains a mix of domains running at the Windows 2000 Mixed, Windows Server 2003 Interim, and Windows Server 2003 functional levels. You are planning the transition of the Tailspin Toys environment so that the forest operates at the Windows Server 2008 R2 functional level.

The *trafalgar.tailspintoys.internal*, *warragul.tailspintoys.internal*, and *bairnsdale.tailspintoys .internal* domains are running at the Windows Server 2003 Interim level.

The *yarragon.tailspintoys.internal*, *traralgon.tailspintoys.internal*, and *morwell.tailspintoys.internal* domains contain only Windows 2000 Server domain controllers. The existing domain controller hardware in each of these domains will support Windows Server 2008 R2 domain controllers if they are running the Server Core installation. You want to deploy RODCs at several sites within these domains, and budget is available for one new Windows Server 2008 R2 domain controller, including hardware, for each of these domains.

EXERCISE   Plan the Migration of the Tailspin Toys Forest to Windows Server 2008

In this exercise, you review the aforementioned business and technical requirements as part of planning a migration to Windows Server 2008 R2 AD DS at Tailspin Toys.

1. Which steps should you include in your plans with respect to the *tailspintoys.internal* root domain?

   - Join a Windows Server 2008 R2 member server to the domain.
   - Run *adprep /forestprep* on the schema master.
   - Run *adprep /rodcprep* on the schema master.

   This is because you must deploy RODCs in several domains in the forest.

2. Which steps should you include in your plans to transition the *yarragon.tailspintoys.internal* domain to the Windows Server 2008 R2 functional level?

   - Ensure that all Windows 2000 Server domain controllers have Service Pack 4 installed.
   - Ensure that *adprep /rodcprep* has been run on the schema master.
   - Join the Windows Server 2008 R2 member server to the domain.
   - Run *adprep /domainprep /gpprep* on the infrastructure master in the domain.
   - Promote the Windows Server 2008 R2 member server to domain controller. Seize all domain operations master roles for this domain controller.
   - Demote existing Windows 2000 Server domain controllers.
   - Upgrade the domain functional level to Windows Server 2008 R2.
   - Perform clean installations of Windows Server 2008 R2 Server Core on the hardware originally used by the Windows 2000 domain controllers.
   - Promote these computers running Windows Server 2008 R2 Server Core to domain controllers or RODCs as necessary.

Lesson Summary

- Run *adprep /forestprep* on the domain controller hosting the schema master role.
- To upgrade a domain in a forest that has been prepared using *adprep /forestprep*, run the *adprep /domainprep /gpprep* command on the domain controller that holds the infrastructure master role.

- Selective authentication stops users from trusted domains from being treated automatically as members of the Authenticated Users group in the trusting domain.
- SID filtering ensures that only SIDs from the trusted domain can be used when users attempt to access resources in the trusting domain. SID filtering is enabled by default on trusts created between Windows Server 2008 R2 domains. SID filtering is often disabled during cross-forest migration, allowing migrated user accounts access to resources in the source environment until the migration is complete.
- You can use the Active Directory Migration Tool to migrate objects between domains and forests.

Lesson Review

You can use the following questions to test your knowledge of the information in Lesson 1, "Planning for Migration, Upgrade, and Restructuring." The questions are also available on the companion CD if you prefer to review them in electronic form.

> **NOTE ANSWERS**
>
> Answers to these questions and explanations of why each answer choice is correct or incorrect are located in the "Answers" section at the end of the book.

1. Assuming that the operations master roles are distributed across Windows Server 2003 domain controllers in the forest root domain so that no one domain controller hosts more than a single role, on which of the following computers should you run the *adprep /forestprep* command?

   A. Domain controller hosting the PDC emulator role

   B. Domain controller hosting the schema master role

   C. Domain controller hosting the RID master role

   D. Domain controller hosting the infrastructure master role

   E. Domain controller hosting the domain naming master role

2. You have upgraded the forest root domain so that it now has Windows Server 2008 R2 domain controllers. You now plan to upgrade a child domain in the same forest. Assuming that no domain controller in the forest hosts more than one flexible single master operations (FSMO) role, on which domain controller in the child domain should you run the *adprep /domainprep /gpprep* command?

   A. Domain controller hosting the PDC emulator role

   B. Domain controller hosting the schema master role

   C. Domain controller hosting the RID master role

   D. Domain controller hosting the infrastructure master role

   E. Domain controller hosting the domain naming master role

3. You are planning the migration of several thousand user accounts from the *maffra .contoso.internal* domain to the *traralgon.fabrikam.internal* domain. Each domain is in a separate AD DS forest. Each AD DS forest is configured to run at the Windows Server 2008 R2 functional level, and the forests share a two-way forest trust. During the migration, you want to ensure that migrated user accounts are able to access resources in both domains. Which of the following should you plan to do during the migration?

   A. Disable SID filtering.

   B. Enable SID filtering.

   C. Configure Selective Authentication.

   D. Configure name suffix routing.

4. You are planning a two-way forest trust between the Contoso and Fabrikam organizations. You want to ensure that only authorized users from each trusted forest have access to resources in the trusting forest. Many resources are available to authenticated users in each forest. These resources should not be available to users in the trusted forest unless explicitly allowed. Which of the following plans should you make?

   A. Implement selective authentication.

   B. Implement SID filtering.

   C. Implement user principal name (UPN) suffix routing.

   D. Implement forest-wide authentication.

Lesson 2: Planning for Interoperability

Organizations of all sizes are increasingly collaborating with partners and customers. Traditionally, this collaboration results in the need to manage multiple user accounts and groups, as well as the exchange of private information. The interoperability capabilities built into Microsoft's Identity and Access solutions now enable organizations to securely collaborate with partners and vendors without users having to exchange private information. Moreover, it enables users to move seamlessly between applications across the enterprise and other organizations through consistent, persistent identity and credentials. This capability allows organizations to more securely establish and extend trust with partners and other external groups while reducing the complexity of managing multiple identities. Part of an enterprise administrator's job is to make the user experience seamless. In this lesson, you will learn how you can use Windows Server 2008 R2 to enable disparate technologies to interoperate.

> **After this lesson, you will be able to:**
> - Determine the types of scenarios in which it is necessary to deploy AD FS 2.0.
> - Determine which interoperability technology to deploy for UNIX-based computers, based on organizational needs.
>
> **Estimated lesson time: 40 minutes**

Planning Active Directory Federation Services

AD FS allows organizations to more securely establish and extend trust with partners and other external groups while reducing the complexity of managing multiple identities. AD FS accomplishes this by securely sharing digital identity and entitlement rights across a set of preconfigured security boundaries. For example, AD FS enables you to configure a web application on your network to use a directory service on a trusted partner organization's network for authentication. AD FS enables user accounts from one organization to access the applications of another organization while still enabling full administrative control to each organization's IT departments. Rather than having to create a new account for a person when you need to grant access to a web application that you manage, you trust the partner organization's directory service. Users from the partner organization can then authenticate to your organization's web application using their own organization's credentials.

Windows Server 2008 and Windows Server 2008 R2 include AD FS 1.1, which can be installed through Server Manager. Microsoft released AD FS 2.0 after Windows Server 2008 R2 was released. AD FS 2.0 is not integrated into the Windows Server 2008 R2 operating system or Service Pack 1 for Windows Server 2008 R2. AD FS 2.0 must be downloaded and installed separately. For information on downloading and installing the software, visit the following link: *http://technet.microsoft.com/en-us/library/dd807096(WS.10).aspx*.

AD FS 2.0 has the following features:

- An enterprise claims provider for claims-based applications
- A Federation Service for identity federation across domains
- Improved support for federation trusts
- An enhanced snap-in management console

An AD FS deployment can include the following components:

- **Federation Server**   A computer running Windows Server 2008 or Windows Server 2008 R2 that has been configured using the AD FS 2.0 Federation Server Configuration Wizard to act in the federation server role. A federation server issues tokens and serves as part of a Federation Service.

- **Federation Server Proxy**   A computer running Windows Server 2008 or Windows Server 2008 R2 that has been configured using the AD FS 2.0 Proxy Configuration Wizard to act in the federation server proxy role. A federation server proxy provides an additional layer of security to the Federation Service.

- **Claim**   A statement that one subject makes about itself or another subject. For example, the statement can be about a name, identity, key, group, privilege, or capability. Claims have a provider that issues them, and they are given one or more values. They are also defined by a claim value type and, possibly, associated metadata.

- **Claim Rule**   A rule that is created with a claim rule template or that is written using the claim rule language in AD FS 2.0 that defines how to generate, transform, pass through, or filter claims.

- **Attribute Store**   A database or directory service that contains attributes about clients. These attributes can be used to issue claims about the clients. For example, AD FS 2.0 supports the use of either AD DS or Microsoft SQL Server as the attribute store for a claims provider.

- **Claims Provider**   A Federation Service that issues claims for a particular transaction.

- **Relying Party**   A Federation Service or application that consumes claims a particular transaction.

- **Certificate**   The Federation Service in AD FS 2.0 uses certificates for issuing and receiving tokens, publishing federation metadata, or communicating through Secure Sockets Layer (SSL).

- **Endpoints**   Endpoints provide access to the federation server functionality of AD FS 2.0, such as token issuance, and the publishing of federation metadata.

- **Information Card**   Information cards, which a claims provider can issue, that represent a user's digital identity.

One of the most important aspects of designing AD FS 2.0 is selecting the appropriate AD FS 2.0 design. To do so, you must first identify your deployment goals. Typically, AD FS 2.0 deployment goals fall into one of the following three categories:

- Provide your Active Directory users access to your claims-aware applications and services
- Provide your Active Directory users access to the applications and services of other organizations
- Provide users in another organization access to your claims-aware applications and services

After you have identified your deployment goals, you can go ahead and map your deployment goals to an AD FS 2.0 design. AD FS 2.0 includes the following designs:

- Web Single Sign-On (SSO) design
- Federated Web SSO design

In the Web SSO design, users must authenticate only once to access multiple AD FS–secured applications or services. In this design, all users are external and no federation trust exists because there are no partner organizations. Typically, you deploy this design when you want to provide individual consumer or customer access to one or more AD FS 2.0–secured services or applications over the Internet. With the Web SSO design, an organization that typically hosts an AD FS–secured application or service in a perimeter network can maintain a separate store of customer accounts in the perimeter network, which makes it easier to isolate customer accounts from employee accounts.

The Federated Web SSO design involves secure communication that spans multiple firewalls, perimeter networks, and name-resolution servers, in addition to the entire Internet routing infrastructure. Typically, this design is used when two organizations agree to create a federation trust relationship to allow users in one organization (the account partner organization) to access web-based applications or services, which are secured by AD FS 2.0, in the other organization (the resource partner organization).

> **MORE INFO** **MORE ON AD FS 2.0 DESIGN**
>
> To learn more about designing AD FS 2.0, consult the following link: *http://technet .microsoft.com/en-us/library/adfs2-design-guide(WS.10).aspx.*

> ✔ **Quick Check**
> 1. What does the deployment of AD FS 2.0 enable you to accomplish?
> 2. Which role services are included with AD FS 2.0?

Planning for UNIX Interoperability

As an enterprise administrator, you are aware that many companies do not settle on a single company's operating system solutions for the clients and servers. In some cases, your organization might choose an alternative solution because it meets a particular set of needs at a particular point in time; in other cases, you might inherit a diverse operating system environment when your company acquires a subsidiary. In either situation, it is your job as enterprise administrator to ensure that these diverse systems interoperate in a seamless manner. Windows Server 2008 R2 includes several features and role services that can assist in integrating UNIX-based operating systems in a Windows Server 2008 R2 infrastructure.

Identity Management

Identity Management for UNIX is a role service, available under the Active Directory Domain Services role, that enables you to integrate your Windows users in existing environments that host UNIX-based computers. You are most likely to deploy this feature in predominantly UNIX-based environments and where Windows users and computers running Windows must integrate in an existing UNIX-based infrastructure. Identity Management for UNIX is compatible with Internet Engineering Task Force (IETF) Request for Comments (RFC) 2307, "An Approach for Using LDAP as a Network Information Service." A Lightweight Directory Access Protocol (LDAP) server resolves network password and Network Information Service (NIS) attribute requests. LDAP is a directory services protocol commonly used in UNIX environments in a way very similar to how AD DS is used on Windows networks.

> **MORE INFO**   **MORE ON IDENTITY MANAGEMENT FOR UNIX**
>
> To learn more about Identity Management for UNIX, consult the following TechNet link:
> *http://technet2.microsoft.com/windowsserver2008/en/library/ffad69a4-4a3f-4161-8a0c-dd6c1b9f288f1033.mspx?mfr=true.*

Password Synchronization

The Password Synchronization component of Identity Management for UNIX simplifies the process of maintaining secure passwords in environments in which computers running UNIX and Windows are present and used by staff. When Password Synchronization is deployed, the user's password on all UNIX computers in the environment will also be changed when a user changes his or her password in AD DS. Similarly, you can configure the Password

Synchronization component to change a password automatically in AD DS when a user's UNIX password is changed. You configure the direction of password synchronization by setting the password synchronization properties as shown in Figure 3-2. Access the Password Synchronization Properties dialog box using the Microsoft Identity Management for UNIX console.

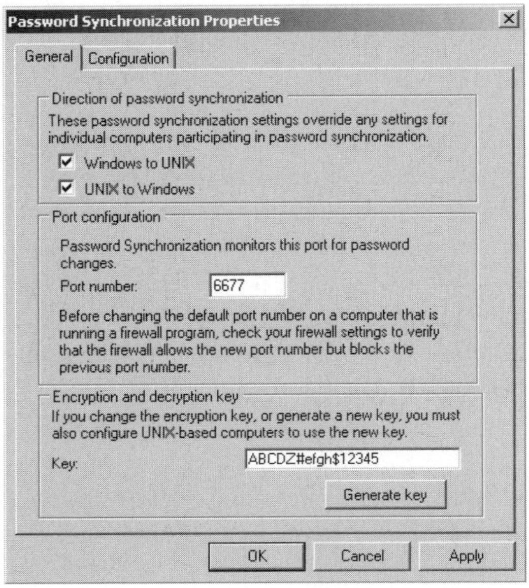

FIGURE 3-2 Configuring Password Synchronization Properties

Password Synchronization is supported between Windows Server 2008 R2 and the following UNIX-based operating systems:

- Hewlett Packard HP UX 11i v1
- IBM AIX version 5L 5.2 and 5L 5.3
- Novell SUSE Linux Enterprise Server 10
- Red Hat Enterprise Linux 4 Server
- Sun Microsystems Solaris 10 (SPARC architecture only)

You should deploy Password Synchronization on all domain controllers in a domain in which it is needed. Any newly deployed domain controllers in the domain should also have this feature installed. Microsoft also recommends that you demote a domain controller before removing Password Synchronization. Ensure that the password policies on the UNIX computers and within the Windows domain are similarly restrictive. Inconsistent password policies will result in a synchronization failure if a user is able to change a password on a less-restrictive system because the password will not be changed on the more-restrictive system due to the password policy. When configuring Password Synchronization, best practice is to ensure that the passwords of sensitive accounts, such as those of administrators from both UNIX and Windows environments, are not replicated. By default, members of the local Windows Administrators and Domain Administrators groups are not replicated.

> **MORE INFO**   **MORE ON PASSWORD SYNCHRONIZATION**
>
> To learn more about Password Synchronization, consult the following TechNet document: *http://technet2.microsoft.com/windowsserver2008/en/library/e755c195-e7e0-4a38-9531 -47a31e6e2aea1033.mspx?mfr=true.*

Subsystem for UNIX-Based Applications

Subsystem for UNIX-Based Applications (SUA) is a Windows Server 2008 R2 feature that enables enterprises to run UNIX-based applications on computers running Windows Server 2008 R2. SUA provides a UNIX-like environment, including shells, a set of scripting utilities, and a software development kit (SDK). SUA also provides support for case-sensitive file names, compilation tools, job control, and more than 300 popular UNIX utilities, commands, and shell scripts. You can install SUA as a Windows feature by using the Add Features Wizard.

A computer running Windows Server 2008 R2 that has the SUA feature installed enables two separate command-line environments: a UNIX environment and a Windows environment. Applications execute within a specific environment. A UNIX command executes within the UNIX environment, and a Windows command executes within the Windows environment. Although the environments are different, commands executing in these environments can manipulate files stored on Windows volumes normally. For example, you can use the UNIX-based *grep* command under SUA to search a text file stored on an NTFS volume.

UNIX applications that run on existing computers can be ported to run on Windows Server 2008 R2 under the SUA subsystem. This enables organizations to migrate existing applications that run on UNIX computers to Windows Server 2008 R2. SUA supports connectivity to Oracle and SQL Server databases by using the Oracle Call Interface (OCI) and Open Database Connectivity (ODBC) standards. SUA also includes support that enables developers to debug Portable Operating System Interface (POSIX) processes by using Microsoft Visual Studio. POSIX is a collection of standards that define the application programming interface (API) for software that is compatible with UNIX-based operating systems.

> **MORE INFO**   **MORE ON SUBSYSTEM FOR UNIX-BASED APPLICATIONS**
>
> To learn more about the Windows Server 2008 R2 Subsystem for UNIX-Based Applications, consult the following TechNet link: *http://technet2.microsoft.com/windowsserver2008/en /library/f808072e-5b17-4146-8188-f0b3b7e5c6291033.mspx?mfr=true.*

Server for NIS

Server for NIS enables a Windows Server 2008 R2 domain controller to act as a master NIS server for one or more NIS domains. Server for NIS provides a single namespace for NIS and Windows domains that an enterprise administrator can manage by using a single set of tools. Server for NIS stores the following NIS map data in AD DS:

- Aliases
- Bootparams
- Ethers
- Hosts
- Group
- Netgroup
- Netid
- Netmasks
- Networks
- Passwd
- Protocols
- Rpc
- Services
- Pservers
- Shadow

It is possible to deploy Server for NIS on other domain controllers located in the same domain as the master NIS server. This enables these domain controllers to function as NIS subordinate servers, and NIS data is replicated through AD DS to the servers hosting the Server for NIS role. UNIX-based computers can also function as NIS subordinate servers because Server for NIS uses the same replication protocol to propagate NIS data to UNIX-based subordinates as a UNIX-based NIS master server does. When considering the deployment of Server for NIS in an integrated environment, remember that a computer running Windows Server 2008 R2 must hold the master NIS server role. A computer running Windows Server 2008 R2 cannot function as an NIS subordinate server to a UNIX-based NIS master.

When planning the migration from UNIX-based NIS servers to Windows-based NIS servers, your first task is to move the NIS maps to the new Windows Server 2008 R2 NIS server. After you do this, the computer running Windows Server 2008 R2 can function as an NIS master. It is possible to move multiple NIS domains to a single Windows Server 2008 R2 domain controller. Although you can configure Server for NIS to support multiple NIS domains concurrently, you can also merge the domains after they have been migrated to the Windows Server 2008 R2 domain controller running Server for NIS.

You are likely to plan the deployment of Server for NIS when you want to retire an existing NIS server infrastructure even though NIS clients are still present on your organizational network. Server for NIS enables you to consolidate your server infrastructure around the Windows Server 2008 R2 operating system while enabling UNIX-based NIS client computers to continue functioning normally on your organizational network.

When planning the deployment of Server for NIS, remember that this component is installed as a role service under the AD DS server role. Server for NIS can be installed only on a Windows Server 2008 R2 domain controller. You cannot deploy Server for NIS on a standalone computer running Windows Server 2008 R2 or on a member server running Windows Server 2008.

> **MORE INFO**   **MORE ON SERVER FOR NIS**
>
> To learn more about Server for NIS, consult the following TechNet link:
> *http://technet2.microsoft.com/windowsserver2008/en/library/f8ce4afa-e9b4-4e1c
> -95bd-d8de161c414b1033.mspx?mfr=true.*

Services for Network File System

Services for Network File System (NFS) enables file sharing between Windows-based and UNIX-based computers. Plan to deploy Services for NFS if your environment contains a large number of UNIX-based client computers that need to access the same shared files as the Windows-based client computers on your organization's network. Figure 3-3 shows the NFS Advanced Sharing dialog box on a computer running Windows Server 2008 R2 configured with Services for NFS.

During the deployment of Services for NFS, you must configure AD DS lookup resolution for UNIX group ID and UNIX user ID (GID and UID). You do this by installing the Identity Management for UNIX Active Directory schema extension that is included in Windows Server 2008 R2. Lesson 1 of this chapter covered extending the schema in preparation for the deployment of the first Windows Server 2008 R2 domain controller in a domain. You can then configure identity mapping by configuring the properties of Services for NFS and specifying the domain in the forest in which Identity Management for UNIX has been installed. Figure 3-4 shows identity mapping configuration for Services for NFS.

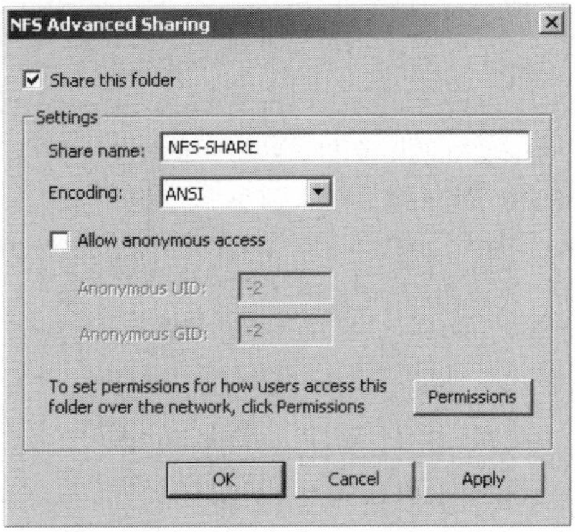

FIGURE 3-3 Configuring an NFS share

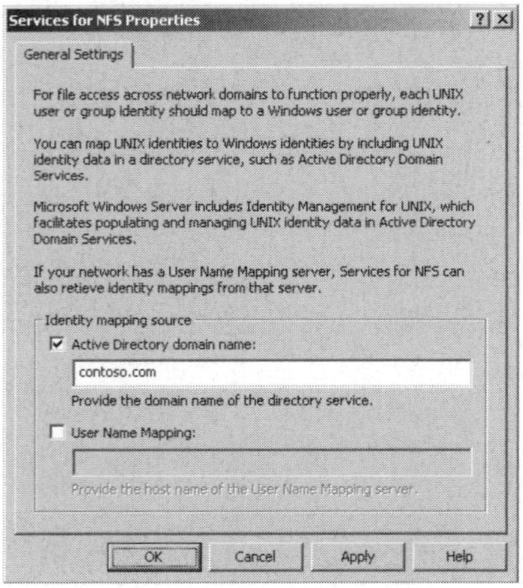

FIGURE 3-4 Configuring NFS identity mapping

> **MORE INFO**   **MORE ON SERVICES FOR NFS**
>
> To learn more about Services for NFS, consult the following TechNet document:
> *http://technet2.microsoft.com/windowsserver2008/en/library/1f02f8b2-e653-4583*
> *-8391-84d3411badd11033.mspx?mfr=true.*

PRACTICE   Planning for Interoperability

Wingtip Toys is a moderate-sized enterprise that has 15 branch offices located across the
southeastern states of Australia. Wingtip Toys wants to move away from its existing network
infrastructure that includes both Windows-based and UNIX-based computers to a more

homogeneous operating system environment. The company has a mixture of UNIX-based client and server computers at each branch office. UNIX-based client computers authenticate against the NIS service running on a UNIX server at each branch location. All existing UNIX-based client computers currently access shared files from UNIX servers. These shared files should be moved to a Windows-based platform. Previous attempts to achieve this have failed due to problems synchronizing user accounts and passwords between the disparate platforms. Because of budgetary constraints, management has asked that the UNIX servers at Wingtip Toys be decommissioned first, with a gradual transition from UNIX-based client computers to computers running Windows Vista over the next 24 months.

EXERCISE Plan the Interoperability Strategy for Phasing Out UNIX-Based Computers at Wingtip Toys

In this exercise, you review the preceding business and technical requirements as part of a planned a migration from UNIX-based computers at Wingtip Toys.

1. What steps must you perform to ensure that the NIS master server is a computer running Windows Server 2008 R2 rather than a UNIX-based computer?
    - Install Server for NIS on a Windows Server 2008 R2 domain controller at each site. Configure one Windows Server 2008 R2 domain controller as the master NIS server.
    - Migrate NIS maps to the new master NIS server.
    - Decommission existing NIS servers.

2. What steps must you perform to ensure that users who switch between Windows-based and UNIX-based client computers use the same passwords for their user accounts?
    - Install Password Synchronization.
    - Ensure that password policies are compatible.

3. What steps must you perform prior to decommissioning the UNIX-based file servers that UNIX-based client computers use?
    - Install Services for NFS on the file servers running Windows Server 2008 R2 that will replace the UNIX file servers.
    - Migrate files and permissions from the NFS shares on the UNIX-based computers to the NFS shares on the computers running Windows Server 2008 R2.
    - Decommission the UNIX file servers.

Lesson Summary

- Active Directory Federation Services (AD FS) 2.0 provides consistent, persistent identity and credentials that can flow between organizations, which helps reduce the need to manage multiple user accounts or group memberships.
- Services for Network File System (NFS) enables UNIX-based computers to access shared files hosted on a computer running Windows Server 2008 R2.

- Subsystem for UNIX-Based Applications (SUA) enables POSIX-compliant applications to execute on a computer running Windows Server 2008 R2.

- Server for Network Information Service (NIS) enables a computer running Windows Server 2008 R2 to act as a master NIS server. A computer running Windows Server 2008 R2 cannot function as a subordinate NIS server to a UNIX-based NIS master server.

- Identity Management for UNIX enables Windows-based computers to perform lookups on UNIX-based directories for authentication. The Identity Management for UNIX role service encompasses Server for Network Information Service, Password Synchronization, and Administration Tools components.

- Password Synchronization enables user account passwords on UNIX-based computers and Windows-based computers to be synchronized. Password policies on both UNIX-based and Windows-based computers must be similar; otherwise, synchronization errors can occur.

Lesson Review

You can use the following questions to test your knowledge of the information in Lesson 2, "Planning for Interoperability." The questions are also available on the companion CD if you prefer to review them in electronic form.

> *NOTE* **ANSWERS**
>
> **Answers to these questions and explanations of why each answer choice is correct or incorrect are located in the "Answers" section at the end of the book.**

1. In which of the following situations would you plan to deploy Active Directory Federation Services 2.0?

   A. You need to share files on a computer running Windows Server 2008 R2 to clients running UNIX-based operating systems.

   B. You need to synchronize user account passwords between computers running AD DS and UNIX-based computers.

   C. You need to run POSIX-compliant applications on a computer running Windows Server 2008 R2.

   D. You need to provide single sign on for a group of related web applications to users in a partner organization.

2. The organization that you work for wants your assistance in planning the deployment of a solution that will ensure that new employee data entered in the human resource Oracle 9i database is synchronized with your organization's Windows Server 2008 AD DS and Exchange Server 2007 deployments. Which of the following solutions would you consider deploying to meet this need?

A. AD FS

   B. Microsoft Identity Lifecycle Manager 2007 Feature Pack 1

   C. Server for NIS

   D. Services for NFS

3. Your predominantly Windows-based organization has recently acquired a company that uses UNIX-based computers for all client and server computers. The recently acquired company has a significant amount of spare office space. A nearby branch office has older facilities, so there is a plan to redeploy staff from this older facility to the recently acquired company's site. As part of this redeployment, it will be necessary to introduce computers running Windows Server 2008 R2 functioning as file servers. Which of the following Windows Server 2008 R2 role services or functions should you plan to deploy so that UNIX-based client computers will be able to access files hosted on a Windows Server 2008 R2 file server?

   A. Subsystem for UNIX-Based Applications

   B. Server for NIS

   C. Services for NFS

   D. Network Policy Server

4. You are putting the finishing touches on a plan to migrate several branch offices to Windows Server 2008 R2. Each branch office currently has an old UNIX-based computer that hosts several POSIX-compliant applications. You want to minimize the amount of hardware present at each branch office. Which of the following items should you include in your Windows Server 2008 R2 branch office migration plan? (Choose two. Each answer forms part of the solution.)

   A. Deploy the Remote Desktop Services role.

   B. Deploy the Hyper-V role.

   C. Deploy the Subsystem for UNIX-Based Applications feature.

   D. Deploy the Active Directory Federation Services role.

   E. Migrate the applications from the UNIX-based computer to Windows Server 2008 R2.

Chapter Review

To further practice and reinforce the skills you learned in this chapter, you can perform the following tasks:

- Review the chapter summary.
- Review the list of key terms introduced in this chapter.
- Complete the case scenario. This scenario sets up a real-world situation involving the topics of this chapter and asks you to create a solution.
- Complete the suggested practices.
- Take a practice test.

Chapter Summary

- Run *adprep /forestprep* on the schema master and *adprep /domainprep /gpprep* on each domain's infrastructure master.
- Limit the scope of trusts so that they meet the necessary requirements only. Do not create a two-way trust when a one-way trust is all that is required.
- Selective authentication enables administrators in a trusting forest or domain to allow limited access to specific users from a trusted forest or domain.
- AD FS 2.0 enables partner organizations to have single sign on for local web applications without configuring forest-based or domain-based trusts.
- Server for NIS enables a computer running Windows Server 2008 R2 to function as an NIS server for UNIX-based computers.
- Services for NFS enables a computer running Windows Server 2008 R2 to function as a file server for a UNIX-based computer.
- The Password Synchronization component enables account passwords for AD DS–based and UNIX-based computers to be the same.
- SUA enables POSIX-compliant applications to run on computers running Windows Server 2008 R2.

Key Terms

Do you know what these key terms mean? You can check your answers by looking up the terms in the glossary at the end of the book.

- Active Directory Federation Services (AD FS)
- Active Directory Migration Tool
- Attribute store
- Certificate
- Claim rule

- Claim
- Claims provider
- Domain restructure migration path
- Domain upgrade migration path
- Endpoints
- Federation Server proxy
- Federation Server
- Identity Management for UNIX
- Information card
- Interforest migration
- Intraforest migration
- Relying party
- Server for NIS
- Services for Network File System (NFS)
- SID History
- Subsystem for UNIX-Based Applications (SUA)
- Upgrade-then-restructure migration path

Case Scenario

In the following case scenario, you apply what you have learned about restructuring and interoperability. You can find answers to these questions in the "Answers" section at the end of this book.

Case Scenario: Phasing Out a UNIX-Based Computer at Tailspin Toys

You are assisting Tailspin Toys to integrate the recently purchased Wingtip Toys company in its network infrastructure. The integration will proceed over time, with some tasks of higher priority to the management of Tailspin Toys than others. One high-priority task involves an aging UNIX-based computer at Wingtip Toys that hosts a POSIX-compliant payroll application. This is the only UNIX-based computer in either organization, and management would prefer not to replace the computer with another UNIX-based computer unless absolutely necessary. Wingtip Toys is using Lotus Notes 7.0, and Tailspin Toys uses Exchange Server 2007. The HR department at Tailspin Toys uses an SQL Server 2008–based database to manage employee data. The HR department at Tailspin Toys will now be responsible for managing all new and existing employee data for both organizations. Although the HR database will be managed centrally, each organization's accounting teams will be kept separate, although they will use the existing Tailspin Toys financial web applications. One problem with this is that the Wingtip Toys accountants find the authentication process quite complicated, and management hopes that you might offer some recommendations to make it simpler. With this information in mind, answer the following questions.

1. What plans could you make to simplify authentication to the Tailspin Toys accounting applications for Wingtip Toys staff?

2. What plans could you make to migrate the Wingtip Toys payroll application to Tailspin Toys?

Suggested Practices

To help you successfully master the exam objectives presented in this chapter, complete the following tasks.

Plan for Domain or Forest Migration, Upgrade, and Restructuring

Complete the following practice exercise.

■ **Practice** Upgrade a Windows Server 2008 single-domain forest to Windows Server 2008 R2.

- Using evaluation software, create a Windows Server 2008 single-domain forest.
- Join a Windows Server 2008 R2 member server to this single-domain forest.
- Use the *adprep* command to prepare the Windows Server 2008 single-domain forest.
- Promote the Windows Server 2008 R2 member server to domain controller.
- Transfer FSMO roles from the Windows Server 2008 domain controller to the Windows Server 2008 R2 domain controller.
- Demote the Windows Server 2008 domain controller to member server.

Plan for Interoperability

Complete the following practice exercise.

■ **Practice** Work with Services for NFS.

- Install the Services for Network File System (NFS) role service on a computer running Windows Server 2008 R2.
- Configure an NFS share that will be accessible to UNIX-based operating systems.

Take a Practice Test

The practice tests on this book's companion CD offer many options. For example, you can test yourself on just one exam objective, or you can test yourself on all the 70-647 certification exam content. You can set up the test so that it closely simulates the experience of taking a certification exam, or you can set it up in study mode so that you can look at the correct answers and explanations after you answer each question.

> **MORE INFO** **PRACTICE TESTS**
>
> For details about all the practice test options available, see the "How to Use the Practice Tests" section in this book's introduction.

CHAPTER 4

Designing Active Directory Administration and Group Policy Strategy

In most cases, a default installation of Active Directory Domain Services (AD DS) does not meet the administration and security enforcement requirements for each enterprise. Designing and planning AD DS administration and Group Policy is central to the operation of an enterprise network.

Group Policy enables enterprises to manage configurations for users and computers. Through Group Policy, enterprises can configure options for registry settings, security settings, software deployment, scripts, folder redirection, Windows Deployment Services, and Microsoft Internet Explorer maintenance. A properly designed enterprise-level Group Policy can enable you to significantly reduce your organization's total cost of ownership. However, if designed incorrectly, Group Policy can cause detrimental effects for your network.

This chapter enables you to properly design the AD DS administration model, an enterprise-level Group Policy strategy, and data management and data access.

Exam objectives in this chapter:

- Design the Active Directory Domain Services administrative model.
- Design an enterprise-level Group Policy strategy.
- Design for data management and data access.

Lessons in this chapter:

Before You Begin

To complete the lessons in this chapter, you must have done the following:

- Installed a Windows Server 2008 R2 Enterprise domain controller named Glasgow as described in Chapter 1, "Designing Name Resolution and Internet Protocol Addressing."
- Installed a Windows Server 2008 R2 Enterprise domain controller in the *litware.internal* domain. The computer name is Brisbane. Configure a static IPv4 address of 10.0.0.31 with a subnet mask of 255.255.255.0. The IPv4 address of the Domain Name System (DNS) server is 10.0.0.31. Other than IPv4 configuration and the computer name, accept all the default installation settings. It is recommended that you use a virtual machine to host this server. To download an evaluation version of Virtual Server 2005 R2 or Hyper-V Server 2008 R2, visit *http://www.microsoft.com/windowsserversystem /virtualserver/downloads.aspx*. You can obtain an evaluation version of Windows Server 2008 R2 Enterprise from the Microsoft Download Center at the following address: *http://www.microsoft.com/downloads/search.aspx*.
- Created the Kim_Akers administrator-level account in the *contoso.internal* domain as described in Chapter 1.
- Created a Tom_Perry administrator-level account with the password P@ssw0rd in the *litware.internal* domain. This account should be a member of Domain Admins, Enterprise Admins, and Schema Admins.

REAL WORLD

John Policelli

Whenever I think of AD DS delegation, I can't help but recall a project I worked on a few years ago. I executed an Active Directory security assessment for a client, which identified several vulnerabilities. The most alarming finding was that there were more than 150 user accounts that had membership in the highly privileged built-in AD DS groups, such as Domain Admins and Enterprise Admins. Effectively, any one of these user accounts could be used to take down the client's AD DS environment. As you can imagine, mitigating this was given very high priority. The combination of default user rights assignments, built-in groups, several levels of group nesting, and no delegation model had resulted in this excessive number of user accounts with high privileges in AD DS.

After modifying the user rights assignments assigned to domain controllers, and implementing a group strategy, we were able to reduce this number by about 50 percent. However, this was still too high, given that there were only five individuals who required this level of access. Our next task was to design and implement an AD DS service management delegation model, which allowed us to significantly reduce the number of privileged user accounts. However, the delegation model also enabled us to implement the *principle of least privilege* for AD DS administration at this client. It was a great feeling to see the Domain Admins and Enterprise Admins groups virtually empty by the end of this project.

Lesson 1: Designing the Active Directory Domain Services Administrative Model

As an enterprise administrator, you will plan and design the administrative model for AD DS within your enterprise. You are unlikely to perform the day-to-day administration tasks yourself, but you will design a delegation model so that data administrators and service administrators can carry out the tasks required to perform their jobs using the principle of least privilege.

Designing and planning an AD DS administrative model in the enterprise is a complex task. This lesson discusses the aspects of this task.

> **After this lesson, you will be able to:**
> - Determine a delegation policy that facilitates efficient AD DS administration but does not allocate unnecessary rights and permissions.
> - Plan an AD DS group strategy.
> - Plan a compliance auditing strategy to include Group Policy and AD DS auditing.
> - Plan the administration of AD DS groups.
> - Plan an organizational structure that includes the design of organizational unit (OU) and group structure.
>
> **Estimated lesson time: 55 minutes**

Delegating Active Directory Domain Services Administration

The successful management of AD DS environments requires the distribution of administrative responsibilities among multiple administrators according to organizational, operational, legal, and administrative requirements. Most organizations today leverage a centralized IT infrastructure that spans multiple organizational and geographic boundaries. In such cases, these organizations might have the following requirements:

- **Organizational structure requirements**   Part of an organization might participate in a shared infrastructure to save costs but require the ability to operate independently from the rest of the organization.

- **Operational requirements**   An organization might place unique constraints on directory service configuration, availability, or security.

- **Legal requirements**   An organization might have legal requirements to operate in a specific manner, such as restricting access to confidential information.

- **Administrative requirements**   Different organizations might have different administrative needs, depending on existing and planned IT administration and support models.

The first three requirements express themselves as needs for autonomy and isolation. *Autonomy* is the ability of the administrators of an organization to independently manage all or part of service management (service autonomy) and all or part of the data stored in or protected by AD DS (data autonomy). *Isolation* is the ability of an administrator or an organization to prevent other administrators from controlling or interfering with service management (service isolation) and controlling or viewing a subset of data in AD DS or on member computers that are joined to AD DS (data isolation).

Having the necessary background information, requirements, practices, and recommendations will enable you to delegate administration to more securely and efficiently manage AD DS services and data.

Delegation Benefits and Principles

By efficiently delegating administrative responsibilities among various administrative groups, you can address the specific requirements of administrative autonomy and successfully manage an AD DS environment. When you are planning the *delegation* of administration, adhere to the following principles:

- **Distribute administrative responsibilities on the basis of least privilege** This ensures that the individual or group of individuals to whom the tasks have been delegated can perform only the tasks that have been delegated and cannot perform tasks that have not been explicitly delegated or authorized.

- **Increase administrative efficiency** Many of the responsibilities for managing AD DS content can be assigned to the directory service itself. This automates management and increases efficiency.

- **Reduce administrative costs** You can do this by facilitating shared administrative responsibility. For example, you could allocate administrative responsibility for providing account support to all accounts in the organization to a specific group. You need to ensure, however, that the organization's autonomy requirements are met.

Managing Active Directory Domain Services through Delegation

The primary reason for delegating administrative authority is to allow organizations to efficiently manage their AD DS environments and the data stored in AD DS. Delegation of administration makes AD DS management easier and enables organizations to address specific administrative needs.

The administrative responsibilities of managing an AD DS environment fall into two categories:

- **Service management** Administrative tasks involved in providing secure and reliable delivery of the directory service

- **Data management** Administrative operations involved in managing the content stored in or protected by the directory service

SERVICE MANAGEMENT

Service management includes managing all aspects of the directory service that are essential to ensuring the uninterrupted delivery of the directory service across the enterprise. Service management includes the following administrative tasks:

- Adding and removing domain controllers
- Managing and monitoring replication
- Ensuring the proper assignment and configuration of operations master roles
- Performing regular backups of the directory database
- Managing domain and domain controller security policies
- Configuring directory service parameters, such as setting the functional level of a forest or putting the directory in the special List-Object security mode

DATA MANAGEMENT

Data management includes managing the content stored in AD DS as well as content protected by AD DS. Data management tasks include the following:

- Managing user accounts
- Managing computer accounts
- Managing security groups
- Managing application-specific attributes for AD DS–enabled and AD DS–integrated applications
- Managing workstations
- Managing servers
- Managing resources

You delegate AD DS administrative functions such as service and data management in response to the geographical, business, and technical infrastructure of an enterprise. A well-implemented delegation model provides coverage for all aspects of AD DS management, meets autonomy and isolation requirements, efficiently distributes administrative responsibilities (with a limited subset of tasks delegated to nonadministrators), and delegates administrative responsibilities in a security-conscious manner.

Defining the Administrative Model

To manage an enterprise environment effectively, you need to define how tasks will be assigned and managed. Your plan for delegating responsibility for the network defines the enterprise's administrative model. Microsoft identifies the following three types of administrative models that you can use to allocate the management of the enterprise network logically between individual administrators or departments within the enterprise's IT function:

- Centralized
- Distributed
- Mixed

To identify the correct administrative model, determine which services are needed in each location in the enterprise and where the administrators with the skills to manage these services are located.

CENTRALIZED ADMINISTRATION MODEL

In the centralized administration model, IT-related administration is controlled by one group. In this model, all critical servers are housed in one location, which facilitates central backup and an appropriate IT staff member being available when a problem occurs.

The centralized administration model is typically used in organizations that have one large central office with a few branch offices. Delegation is by function rather than by geographical location, and most tasks are allocated to IT staff.

THE DISTRIBUTED ADMINISTRATION MODEL

In the distributed administration model, tasks are delegated to IT in various locations. The rights to perform administrative tasks can be granted based on geography, department, or job function. Also, administrative control can be granted for a specific network service such as DNS or a Dynamic Host Configuration Protocol (DHCP) server. This enables separation of server and workstation administration without giving nonadministrators the rights to modify network settings or security. A sound, well-planned delegation structure is essential in the distributed administration model.

The distributed administration model is commonly used in enterprises that have a number of large, geographically distributed locations—for example, a multinational organization. Such organizations typically have several domains or even several forests. Although rights are delegated to administrative staff on a regional basis, a group of enterprise administrators can typically perform high-level administrative tasks across domains and across forests.

MIXED ADMINISTRATION MODEL

The mixed administration model uses both centralized and distributed administration. For example, you could define all security policies and standard server configurations from a central site but delegate the implementation and management of key servers by physical location. Administrators can configure servers in their own location but cannot configure servers in other locations. You can distribute the rights to manage only local user accounts to local administrators and restricted rights over specific OUs to nonadministrative staff. As with the distributed administrative model, an enterprise administrators group would have rights in all locations. This model is used in medium-sized organizations with a few fairly large sites that are geographically separated but in which the main office wants to keep control of certain aspects of the operation.

Using Group Strategy to Delegate Management Tasks

A user to whom you delegate a specific management task or set of tasks is known as a *management stakeholder*. Such users can be enterprise-level administrators who can perform tasks across multiple domains or multiple forests if the appropriate forest trusts are configured. However, most day-to-day administration in a well-organized enterprise network is carried out by users who do not have administrative rights to an entire domain, forest, or multiple forests. Instead, these users have sufficient rights to carry out specifically defined tasks, typically within a single OU and any child OUs. This follows the principles of autonomy (stakeholders can perform predefined tasks) and isolation (stakeholders can perform only the tasks that are predefined) that were discussed earlier in this lesson.

Stakeholders might be delegated rights to determine who in the organization has permission to read, write, and delete data in a shared folder on a file server. They might be delegated rights to reset passwords in a departmental OU so that they can deal with the situation when a user forgets a password without needing to call in an administrator. An administrator can be delegated the rights to create and change the membership of a global distribution group and, hence, to determine the membership of a mailing list, but have no rights to reconfigure security policies.

A responsible staff member who is nevertheless not an administrator might be delegated permission to configure a member server as a *read-only domain controller* (RODC) on a specified site. An administrator at a remote location might be able to configure servers at that location and restore a server from backup but have no rights at other locations. A domain administrator might have rights to a specific domain but not to any of the domains in a separate forest in the enterprise.

Typically, the rights and permissions of stakeholders are conferred through membership in security groups. It is possible to give an individual user rights, but this is bad practice. Familiarize yourself with the built-in domain-wide local security groups that confer limited rights, such as Account Operators and Backup Operators. Figure 4-1 shows the built-in local security groups in the Builtin AD DS container. You cannot change the group type or scope of built-in local security groups.

Allocate user rights to domain local security groups. You can allocate rights to global security groups, universal groups, and even to individual users, but this is bad practice. By the same token, you should not add users directly to local groups. You learned this rule in your very first days of training to be an administrator. Now that you are an experienced administrator looking at high-level planning tasks, the rule is every bit as important.

Add users to global groups. Nest global groups in other global groups. If you use universal groups, add global groups (not users) to universal groups. Add global and universal groups to domain local groups. Assign rights to domain local groups.

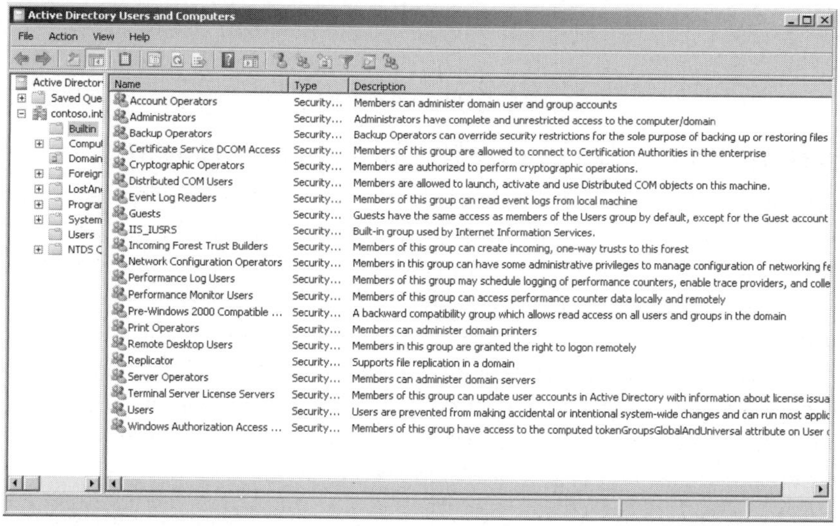

FIGURE 4-1 Built-in local security groups

Universal groups can contain users or (preferably) global security groups from multiple domains and can be allocated rights and permissions across domains. If forest trusts are set up correctly, they can operate across forests.

To an enterprise administrator, universal groups might seem at first to provide an easy answer to cross-domain and cross-forest design, but beware. Universal groups need to be replicated across domains and forests, typically over slow wide area network (WAN) links. They can increase network traffic and thus reduce performance.

Microsoft recommends using as few universal groups as possible. With careful planning, you can do most of what you want to do with global and domain local groups. If you must use a universal group, do not add users. Every time the group membership changes, this triggers more replication traffic. Use only global groups, for example, the Domain Admins group from each of your domains, as members of a universal group. Even if the membership of a Domain Admins group changes, the membership of the universal group—which contains groups and not individual users—remains the same.

Management Roles

Roles are collections of rights and permissions, and you should use them in your planning rather than relying on individual rights. For example, Server Manager is a role that consists of a number of rights such as logging on to servers interactively and configuring servers. In general, a role is implemented by a built-in or domain local security group.

Microsoft recommends a number of roles for *service management*. These role recommendations take into account defined sets of logically related administrative tasks and the security sensitivity and impact of these tasks. The following is the set of recommended roles for delegating service management:

- Forest Configuration Operators
- Domain Configuration Operators
- Security Policy Administrators
- Service Administration Managers
- Domain Controller Administrators
- Backup Operators
- Schema Administrators
- Replication Management Administrators
- Replication Monitoring Operators
- DNS Administrators

> **MORE INFO   SERVICE MANAGEMENT**
>
> For more information about service management and the recommended service manage-
> ment roles, see *http://technet.microsoft.com/en-us/library/dd349801(WS.10).aspx*.

In addition, Microsoft has engineered a set of recommended roles for delegating data management. These role recommendations take into account the sets of logically related administrative tasks and the security sensitivity and impact of these tasks. The following is the set of recommended roles for delegating data management:

- Business Unit Administrators
- Account Administrators
- Workstation Administrators
- Server Operators
- Resource Administrators

- Security Group Administrators
- Help Desk Operators
- Application-Specific Administrators

> **MORE INFO**   **DATA MANAGEMENT**
>
> For more information about data management and the recommended data management roles, see *http://technet.microsoft.com/en-us/library/dd349801(WS.10).aspx*.

Planning Forest-Level Trusts

A forest trust (or forest-level trust) allows every domain in one forest to trust every domain in a second forest. Forest trusts can be one-way incoming, one-way outgoing, or two-way. For example, you can configure all the domains in Forest A to trust all the domains in Forest B by creating a one-way trust in either Forest B or Forest A. If, in addition, you want all the domains in Forest B to trust all the domains in Forest A, you need to create a two-way trust.

You can use forest trusts with partner or closely associated organizations. For example, Contoso, Ltd., and Litware, Inc., have merged but do not choose to amalgamate their AD DS structures in a single forest. Instead, you are asked to plan a forest trust to give employees of one organization rights and permissions in the other.

Forest trusts can form part of an acquisition or takeover strategy. Northwind Traders has acquired Coho Winery. The eventual plan is to reorganize the domain structures of both companies into a single forest, but, until this process is complete, you might plan a forest trust between the organizations.

You can also use forest trusts for AD DS isolation. You might, for example, want to run Exchange Server 2010 as part of a migration strategy to try out the new features and familiarize your technical staff. However, you do not want to install Exchange Server 2010 into your production forest because this could affect your current Exchange Server 2007 deployment. You can create a separate forest in which you can run Exchange Server 2010 but access resources in your production forest while doing so by setting up a forest trust.

Planning Trust Type and Direction

The most common type of trust that operates across forests is the forest trust, and this is the type of trust discussed in this lesson. You should, however, be aware of the other types of trusts that can be set up with entities outside your forest. These include the following:

- **Shortcut trust**   A forest trust will enable any domain in one forest to trust any domain in another forest. However, if forests are complex, with several layers of child domains, it might take some time for a client in a child domain to locate resources in a child domain in another forest, especially when the operation happens over a WAN link. If users in one child domain frequently need to access resources in another child domain in another forest, you might decide to create a shortcut trust between the two domains.

- **External trust**   You set up an external trust when a domain within your forest requires a trust relationship with a domain that does not belong to a forest. Typically, external trusts are used when migrating resources from Microsoft Windows NT domains, many of which still exist. Windows NT does not use the concept of forests, and a Windows NT domain is a self-contained, autonomous unit. If you plan to migrate resources from a Windows NT domain into an existing AD DS forest, you can establish an external trust between one of the AD DS domains and the Windows NT domain.

- **Realm trust**   If a UNIX realm uses Kerberos authentication, you can create a realm trust between a Windows domain and a UNIX realm. This is similar to an external trust, except that it is between a Windows domain and a UNIX realm.

When you have selected the type of trust you require, you then need to decide whether the trust is one-way or two-way and, if it is the former, what the trust direction is. One-way trusts can be incoming or outgoing.

If users in Forest A must access resources in Forest B, and users in Forest B must access resources in Forest A, you need to create a two-way trust. Because this is bidirectional, you do not need to specify a direction.

If, however, users in Forest A require access to resources in Forest B, but users in Forest B do not require access to resources in Forest A, Forest A is the trusted forest and Forest B is the trusting or resource forest. Forest B trusts the users in Forest A and allows them to access its resources. If you are creating a one-way forest trust in a resource forest, it is an incoming trust. If you are creating a one-way forest trust in a trusted forest, it is an outgoing trust.

Creating Forest Trusts

Before you create a forest trust, ensure that the forest functional level of both forests is Windows Server 2003 or higher. Forest functional levels were discussed in Chapter 2, "Designing Active Directory Domain Services, Identity Management, and Authentication." Your next step is to ensure that each forest's root domain can access the root domain of the other forest. You need to create the required DNS records and use the *nslookup* tool to ensure that you can resolve domain names in the other forest. You also need to know the username and password for an enterprise administrator account (an administrator account in the root domain) in each forest unless you are setting up only one side of the trust, and an administrator in the other forest is setting up the other side. You create a forest trust in this lesson's practice.

Planning Data Management

In many enterprise organizations, the AD DS administration structure is not the main concern of the majority of users. They are not concerned about who can configure what. They are concerned about how their data is administered and whether they have the appropriate permissions to read, update, and delete files. A list of data management roles was given earlier in this lesson. It remains only to discuss group management in this context.

Suppose, for example, you have a shared folder on a server called Data Files. In practice, this will probably be a data structure, and you could plan whether to block permission inheritance on subfolders. Your administrators can configure share and NTFS permissions on the folder or folder tree through the Sharing and Security tabs. On the Security tab shown in Figure 4-2, Sample Group has the Modify permission on the folder. Standard users can read the files.

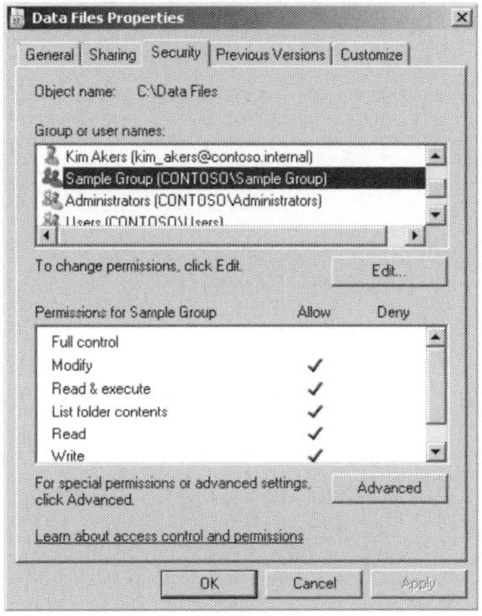

FIGURE 4-2 Sample Group permissions

You can delegate the management of Sample Group to one of its members. For example, Figure 4-3 shows the management of Sample Group delegated to Don Hall. Don can change the group membership.

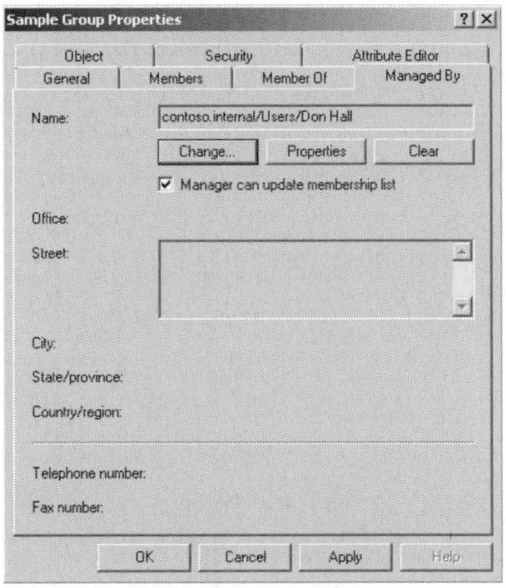

FIGURE 4-3 Sample Group management

The consequences of this configuration are significant. Don Hall is a standard user with no administrative rights other than the delegated right to manage the Sample Group membership. He cannot set permissions. He cannot manage any other groups. The permissions on the Data Files folder have been set by an administrator. Members of Sample Group have *Modify* permission. Don cannot change this.

However, he can change the membership of Sample Group. So, safely, and without allocating any administrative rights to anything else, you have delegated to the user Don Hall the facility to determine who can modify files in the Data Files folder. This is a valuable technique. Use it in your planning.

> **MORE INFO** **DELEGATING DATA MANAGEMENT**
>
> Space considerations prevent a full discussion of data management and how to delegate it—a topic that could easily fill an entire book. For more information, go to *http://technet .microsoft.com/en-us/library/dd349801(WS.10).aspx* and follow the links on the left side of the console pane.

Using Starter GPOs

Windows Server 2008 Group Policy introduced starter *Group Policy objects* (GPOs); incorporate these in your group strategy planning. Starter GPOs enable you to save baseline templates that you can use when you create new GPOs. You can also export starter GPOs to domains other than those in which they were created.

When you open Group Policy Management Console in Windows Server 2008 R2, you can locate the Starter GPOs container in the left pane below a domain. Until you populate it, this container is empty. You create a starter GPO by right-clicking the Starter GPOs container and selecting New. You can configure GPOs in this container like you would configure any GPO, except that only the Administrative Templates settings are available in both Computer Settings and User Settings.

When you create a new starter GPO, you are prompted to name it, and you can add a comment. You can edit your starter GPO and set the Administrative templates you require. When you create a starter GPO, you automatically create a new folder on the domain controller to which Group Policy Management Console is connected by default in the C:\Windows \SYSVOL\domain \StarterGPOs path. This is replicated to other domain controllers as part of SYSVOL replication.

You can create a new (normal) GPO by using a starter GPO as a template by right-clicking the starter GPO and selecting New GPO From Starter GPO. Alternatively you can right-click the Group Policy Objects container, select New, and then specify a starter GPO from the Source Starter GPO drop-down list. You can access the same dialog box and specify a starter GPO if you right-click an OU (or the domain) and select Create A GPO In This Domain, And Link It Here. From a starter GPO, you can easily create multiple GPOs with the same baseline configuration. You need only to configure settings in these GPOs that are not contained in Administrative Templates.

Starter GPOs are not backed up when you choose Back Up All on the Group Policy Management Console Action menu or right-click the Group Policy Objects container and select Back Up All. You must back up starter GPOs separately by right-clicking the Starter GPOs container and selecting Back Up All or by right-clicking individual starter GPOs and selecting Back Up.

Using Group Policy Modeling and Results

You or one of your administrators can use the *Group Policy Modeling* node of the Group Policy Management Console to verify that planned *Group Policy settings* have been correctly configured prior to deployment. You can delegate the rights to perform this operation to a member of your team by assigning that user account the *Perform Group Policy Modeling Analysis* permission.

You can use the *Group Policy Modeling* node to simulate policy settings that will be applied to a computer that is not currently logged on. You can use the *Group Policy Results* node (or Group Policy Results tool) to display policy settings that are applied to computers or users that have actually logged on. If you want to delegate the ability to use planning mode, a user account must be assigned the Perform Group Policy Modeling Analysis right. The *Read Group Policy Results* permission is required to use the Resultant Set of Policy (RSoP) snap-in tool in logging mode.

Using Migration Tables

You use migration tables when you import or copy a GPO from one domain or forest to another. These tables deal with domain- and forest-specific information that specifies where the GPO was created. Such information does not apply to the domain or forest in which the GPO is being copied or into which it is being imported. GPOs copied within the same domain, being backed up, or being restored to their original location do not require migration tables.

Your plan would include migration tables if you need to import GPOs that were created in another forest or to copy a GPO to another domain within the same forest. If you want to export a GPO from one forest to another and you need to account for all domain-specific settings that exist for the GPO that you want to export, you would use the Migration Table Editor tool to populate a migration table automatically with domain-specific Group Policy values so that these can be accounted for when the GPO is imported into the target environment.

EXAM TIP

For the 70-647 exam, remember that you can manage both local and domain Group Policy by using the Group Policy Management Console (GPMC) on computers running Windows 7 and Windows Server 2008 R2. GPMC can be installed with the Remote Server Administration Tools (RSAT) on Windows 7 and added as a feature through Server Manager on Windows Server 2008 R2.

Planning to Audit AD DS and Group Policy Compliance

In Windows Server 2008 R2, the global audit policy Audit Directory Service Access is enabled by default. This policy controls whether auditing for directory service events is enabled or disabled. You can configure this policy setting by modifying Default Domain Controllers Policy and then specifying whether to audit successes, audit failures, or not audit at all. You can control which operations to audit by modifying the system access control list (SACL) on an object. You can set an SACL on an AD DS object on the Security tab of that object's Properties dialog box.

Plan how your administrators should configure audit policy. Enabling success or failure auditing is a straightforward procedure. Deciding which objects to audit; whether to audit success, failure, or both; and whether to record new and old values if changes are made is much more difficult. Auditing everything is never an option—too much information is as bad as too little. Your plan needs to be selective.

In Windows 2000 Server and Windows Server 2003, an administrator can specify only whether Active Directory directory service access is audited. Windows Server 2008 and Windows Server 2008 R2 give more granular control. Your auditing policy can include the following:

- AD DS access
- AD DS changes (old and new values)
- AD DS replication

Auditing AD DS replication is further subdivided so that you can choose two levels of auditing—normal or detailed.

✔ **Quick Check**

- One of your administrators is setting up AD DS replication auditing. What are the two auditing levels from which she can choose?

Quick Check Answer

- Normal or detailed

If a new object is created, AD DS logs the values of the attributes that are configured or added at the time of creation. Attributes that take default values are not logged. If an object is moved within a domain, your auditing policy can ensure that the previous and new locations are logged. When an object is moved to a different domain, a *Create* event is generated and logged on the domain controller in the target domain. If an object is undeleted, your auditing policy can identify the location to which the object is moved. If attributes are added, modified, or deleted during an *Undelete* operation, your administrators can determine the values of those attributes from the Security event log.

If auditing of Directory Service Changes is enabled, AD DS logs events in the Security event log when changes are made to objects that one of your administrators has set up for auditing. Table 4-1 lists these events.

TABLE 4-1 Security Events Related to AD DS Objects

EVENT ID	TYPE OF EVENT	EVENT DESCRIPTION
5136	*Modify*	A successful modification has been made to an attribute in the directory.
5137	*Create*	A new object has been created in the directory.
5138	*Undelete*	An object has been undeleted in the directory.
5139	*Move*	An object has been moved within the domain.

Plan whether to react to such events and how to do so. By default, the events are logged in the Security event log, and members of the Domain Admins, Builtin\Administrators, and Enterprise Admins groups can view them by opening Event Viewer. However, you can design your auditing policy so that an event written to the Security event log initiates a task such as generating an alert or starting an executable program. An administrator can select the event in Event Viewer and choose Attach Task To This Event on the Action menu. Figure 4-4 shows this function.

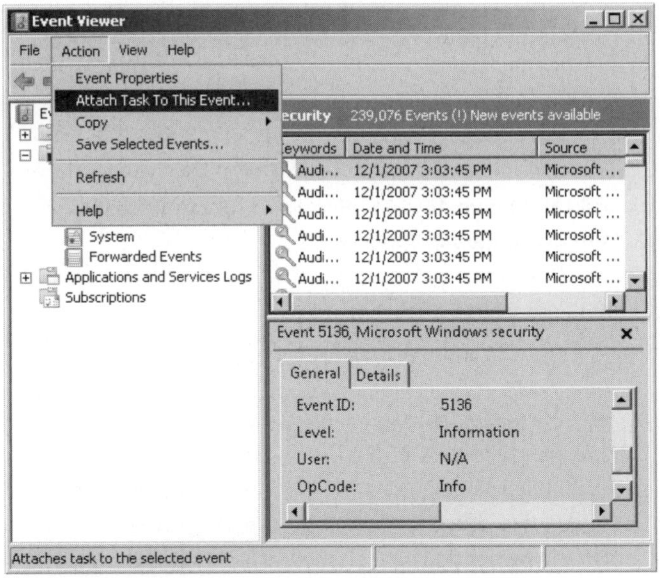

FIGURE 4-4 Attaching a task to an AD DS *Modify* event

MORE INFO **ACTIVE DIRECTORY LIGHTWEIGHT DIRECTORY SERVICE**

You can also plan to use the new Directory Service Changes audit policy subcategory when planning to audit Active Directory Lightweight Directory Services (AD LDS). For more information about AD LDS, see *http://technet2.microsoft.com/windowsserver2008/en /servermanager/activedirectorylightweightdirectoryservices.mspx* and follow the links.

Planning Organizational Structure

When planning your organizational structure, one of your primary aims is to organize the logical design of your OU hierarchy so that it facilitates the management of Group Policy. This OU hierarchy need not mirror your enterprise's departmental hierarchy. Instead, plan every OU so it has a defined purpose such as delegation of authority or the application of Group Policy. Business needs must drive the OU hierarchy. Plan to delegate administrative authority and designate groups of users to have control over the users and computers or other objects in an OU.

You can add users or groups to user rights policies in a GPO that links to an OU or OU hierarchy, as was discussed earlier in this lesson. You can also plan to delegate control of OUs. You do not need to delegate control of an OU, which is the smallest AD DS container, to an administrative user. Many of the tasks that can be carried out within an OU are straightforward (for example, resetting passwords when users have forgotten them) and can be easily carried out by nonadministrative users. It is also relatively safe to delegate authority to an OU. Other than to child OUs, delegated authority over an OU does not give a user rights to any other part of AD DS.

Figure 4-5 shows the Delegation of Control Wizard, which is currently delegating control of the Sample OU to Sample Group. You can plan a very simple delegation, such as the right to reset passwords and to require users to change a password at next logon, to more advanced features, such as the ability to link this OU to other GPOs.

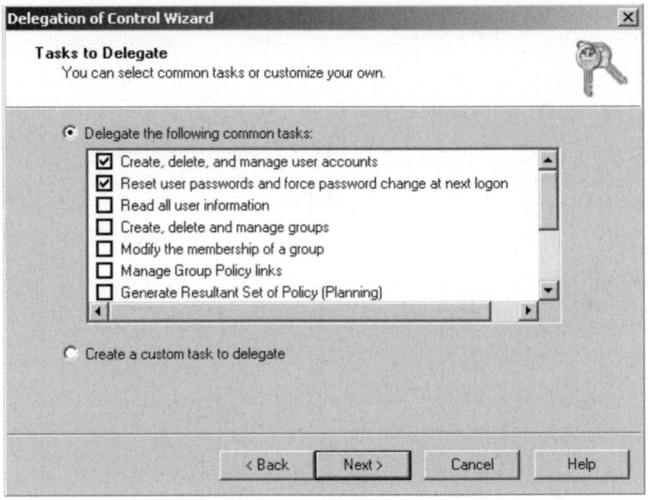

FIGURE 4-5 Delegating control of an OU

Your planned organizational structure should link GPOs to sites, domains, and OUs to implement Group Policy settings as broadly or as narrowly in the organization as necessary. Keep in mind how Group Policy is applied when you plan the scope of application of GPOs. You are probably aware of the following facts, but a spot of review never goes amiss:

- The policy settings in GPOs are inherited and cumulative and apply to all users and computers in an AD DS container.

- GPOs are processed in the following order: local GPO, site, domain, and OU.

- By default, Group Policy inheritance is evaluated starting with the AD DS container farthest from the computer or user object. The AD DS container closest to the computer or user overrides Group Policy set in a higher-level AD DS container unless you enable the Enforced option for that GPO.

- If you link more than one GPO to an AD DS container, the GPO processing order (priority) is as follows: the GPO highest in the Group Policy Object Links list, displayed in the Group Policy section of the AD DS container's Properties page, has precedence by default. If you enable the Enforced option in one or more of the GPOs, the highest GPO that is set to Enforced takes precedence.

PRACTICE Creating a Forest Trust

In this practice, you create a forest trust between the *contoso.internal* and *litware.internal* forests. You then experiment with adding groups from one forest to groups in another.

EXERCISE Create a Forest Trust

You need two forests on your network before you can carry out this exercise. Ensure that the forest functional levels of your two forests are at least Windows Server 2003. You might need to raise the domain functional levels of your domains before you can raise forest functional levels. You should also create a conditional forwarder for *litware.internal* on Glasgow and a conditional forwarder for *contoso.internal* on Brisbane, using the servers' respective DNS consoles. If you are unsure how to perform these tasks, refer to the Windows Server 2008 R2 Help files.

1. Log on to the Glasgow domain controller with the Kim_Akers account.

2. Open Active Directory Domains And Trusts from Administrative Tools. Click Continue to clear the User Account Control (UAC) dialog box and ensure that the tool is connected to the Glasgow domain controller in the *contoso.internal* domain.

3. Right-click the *contoso.internal* domain in the tool's left pane, and choose Properties. On the Trusts tab, click New Trust, as shown in Figure 4-6, to launch the New Trust Wizard. Click Next.

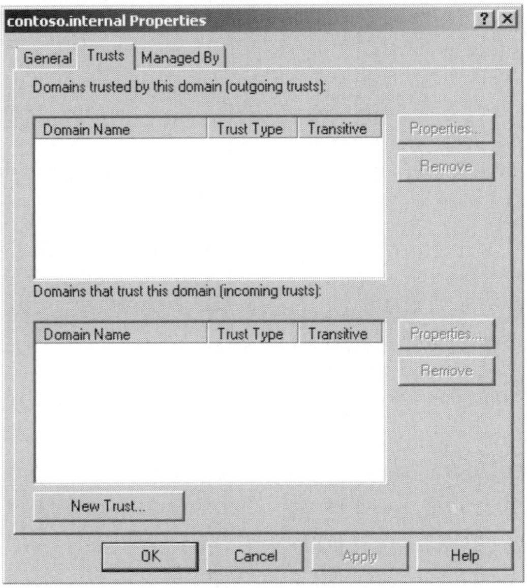

FIGURE 4-6 Launching the New Trust Wizard

The wizard prompts you to enter the domain, forest, or realm name of the trust.

4. Enter the domain name **litware.internal** for the root domain in the forest with which you want to establish the trust, as shown in Figure 4-7.

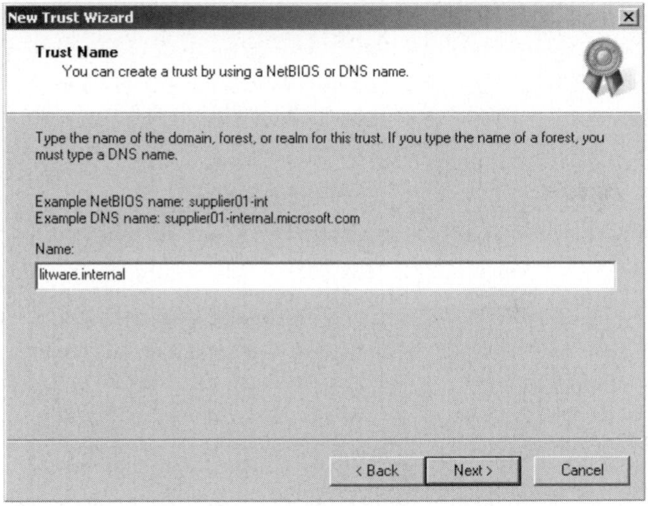

FIGURE 4-7 Specifying the trust endpoint

5. Click Next. The wizard asks whether you are creating a realm trust or a trust with a Windows domain.

6. Select the Trust With A Windows Domain option, as shown in Figure 4-8, and click Next.

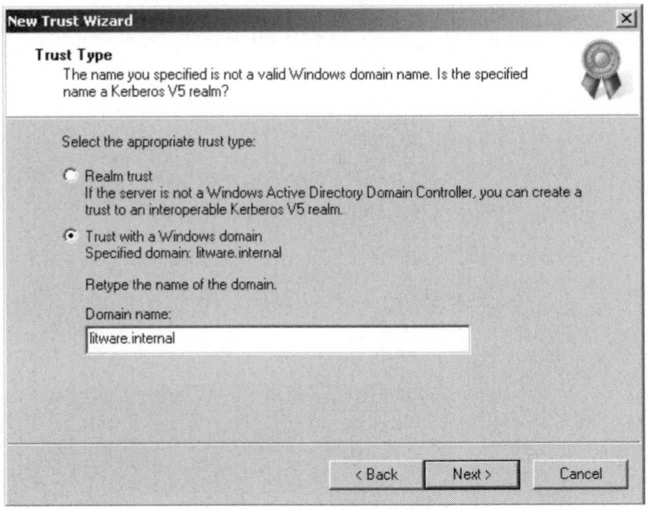

FIGURE 4-8 Specifying a Windows domain trust

You are given the choice of creating a forest trust or an external trust.

7. Choose the Forest Trust option, and click Next. At this point, the wizard asks you whether you want to establish a one-way incoming, one-way outgoing, or two-way trust.

8. Select Two-Way, and click Next to create a two-way trust.

   The wizard now asks whether you want to configure only your own side of the trust or both sides of the trust. An administrative password for both forest root domains is required to establish the trust.

9. Choose to configure both sides of the trust, and then click Next.

10. When prompted, enter the username **Tom_Perry** and the password **P@ssw0rd**, and then click Next.

11. You now need to choose between Forest-Wide Authentication and Selective Authentication. Selective Authentication enables you to specify the authentication process in more detail, but it involves much more work. On the Outgoing Trust Authentication Level—Local Forest page, choose Forest-Wide Authentication. Click Next.

12. On the Outgoing Trust Authentication Level—Specified Forest page, choose Forest-Wide Authentication, and then click Next.

> **MORE INFO**   SELECTIVE AUTHENTICATION
>
> For more information about selective authentication, see *http://technet.microsoft.com /en-us/library/dd349801(WS.10).aspx*. Although this document and linked documents are part of the Windows Server 2003 library, the information they provide is relevant to Windows Server 2008 R2.

   The wizard displays a summary of the options you have chosen.

13. Click Next to establish the trust. Click Next again.

14. On the Confirm Outgoing Trust page, you can confirm the outgoing link by selecting Yes, Confirm The Outgoing Trust and clicking Next.

15. On the Confirm Incoming Trust page, confirm the incoming trust link by selecting Yes, Confirm The Incoming Trust and clicking Next.

16. On the Completing The New Trust Wizard page, click Finish to close the wizard. Click OK to close the Properties dialog box for the *contoso.internal* domain.

17. Create a universal security group in the *contoso.internal* domain. Add this universal security group to the Administrators built-in security group in the *litware.internal* domain. Experiment to discover the rights and permissions Tom Perry and Kim Akers have in both domains.

Lesson Summary

- Delegation is the transfer of administrative responsibility for a specific task from a higher to a lower authority. It increases administrative efficiency and reduces administrative costs. Delegation needs to provide both isolation and autonomy.

- When delegating AD DS administration, you use built-in local, domain local, global, and (sometimes) universal security groups. You can assign rights to security groups and delegate control of OUs to groups.

- Windows Server 2008 R2 includes the ability to audit changes to Group Policy and AD DS structure.

- You can delegate the management of groups to a group member without assigning any additional rights over any other part of the enterprise.

- The design of your OU and GPO structure depends on how the organization is structured (geographically or by department) and which administrative model is used.

Lesson Review

Use the following questions to test your knowledge of the information in Lesson 1, "Designing the Active Directory Domain Services Administrative Model." The questions are also available on the companion CD if you prefer to review them in electronic form.

> **NOTE ANSWERS**
>
> Answers to these questions and explanations of why each answer choice is correct or incorrect are located in the "Answers" section at the end of the book.

1. Northwind Traders is a large multinational company with offices located in a number of countries spread over several continents. Each national office has a high degree of autonomy and its own administrative staff. Some Group Policy settings are specified by the head office in Detroit, but the vast majority are configured on a national basis. AD DS structure is based on geographical structure. Which administrative model does Northwind Traders use?

   A. The centralized model

   B. The hybrid model

   C. The distributed model

   D. The mixed model

2. Which of the following management roles does Microsoft recommend for delegating data management? (Choose all that apply.)

   A. Business Unit Administrators

   B. Security Policy Administrators

   C. Service Administration Managers

   D. Resource Administrators

   E. Security Group Administrators

   F. Application-Specific Administrators

   G. Replication Management Administrators

3. Which Windows Server 2008 R2 global audit policy controls whether auditing for directory service events is enabled or disabled, and what is the default setting?

   A. Audit Directory Service Access. This is disabled by default.

   B. Audit Directory Service Access. This is enabled by default.

   C. Directory Service Changes. This is enabled by default.

   D. Directory Service Changes. This is disabled by default.

4. You administer a Windows Server 2008 R2 single-domain AD DS forest. Your organization recently acquired another company that uses a Windows NT 4.0 domain. You need to set up a trust relationship with the Windows NT 4.0 domain. What sort of trust do you use?

   A. Forest trust

   B. Realm trust

   C. Shortcut trust

   D. External trust

5. You are designing a Group Policy strategy and plan to give members of the software developers' security group permission to link certain GPOs that have already been created to specific OUs within your organization. You do not want to allow members of the software developers' security group to be able to edit these GPOs. Which of the following permissions should you delegate?

   A. Permission to link GPOs

   B. Permissions on a GPO

   C. Permission to generate Group Policy modeling data

   D. Permission to generate Group Policy results

Lesson 2: Designing Enterprise-Level Group Policy Strategy

Group Policy enables you to systematically apply and enforce security and configuration settings on sets of users and computers. By using Group Policy, enterprises can reduce the total cost of ownership associated with day-to-day management and configuration.

This lesson focuses on planning Group Policy and defining a Group Policy hierarchy. It looks at how you control device installation, authentication and authorization, and fine-grained password policies.

After this lesson, you will be able to:

- Plan a Group Policy hierarchy and implement scope filtering.
- Control device installation through Group Policy.
- Distinguish between multifactor authentication and multifactor authorization.
- Plan a password policy, including the use of fine-grained passwords.
- Plan an authentication policy that uses security certificates and smart cards.

Estimated lesson time: 40 minutes

REAL WORLD

John Policelli

I worked on a project several years ago that proved the importance of proper planning when it comes to Group Policy. The project involved migrating mission-critical applications from Windows NT 4.0 to Windows Server 2003. The roughly 100 mission-critical applications were distributed across dozens of NT 4.0 domains, and each had a different level of security. The goal of the project was to move these applications to new hardware, which would run Windows Server 2003 and reside in a centralized Active Directory domain.

Before I joined the project, the project team had tried to gather all of the existing security settings for the legacy environment and design a Group Policy strategy that would meet these requirements. However, this proved to be unsuccessful quite early. Moreover, they had created an OU structure in the target environment, which also proved to be inadequate.

When I joined the project, I took a much different approach, which you will find throughout this chapter. I gathered the operational, legal, and administrative requirements for the target environment. I then started to design a Group Policy strategy that could meet these requirements. Thereafter, I created a Group Policy hierarchy that allowed the GPOs to be applied according to the strategy. What resulted was a role-based Group Policy strategy, which applied and enforced the new security policies. More interesting to me, though, this same Group Policy strategy and hierarchy is still in place today and is being used to apply and enforce security settings to more than 500 servers.

Planning a Group Policy Hierarchy

Group Policy is applied by linking GPOs to specific types of AD DS objects, including sites, domains, and OUs. Group Policy hierarchy and structure is closely linked with AD DS logical structure.

Group Policy is made up of multiple elements that are applied to user objects and to computer objects. You must manage your GPOs to keep them well organized and make it as simple as possible to determine which policy elements apply in a given situation.

GPOs that apply at the domain and site level can be combined with GPOs that apply to OUs, OU hierarchies, and local computer settings. Several GPOs can link to a single OU, and you need to determine the order in which they are applied. If Group Policy settings in multiple GPOs conflict, the GPO that is applied last defines the settings. This applies unless a GPO earlier in the order has been configured to be enforced. When a GPO is configured to be enforced, its settings override those applied later. You can apply site policy, domain policy, and OU policy. Figure 4-9 shows multiple GPOs linked to a single OU.

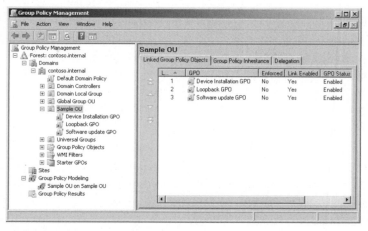

FIGURE 4-9 Linking multiple GPOs to an OU

The link precedence is shown in Figure 4-10. You can change the order of precedence by selecting a GPO link and moving it up or down, as shown on the Linked Group Policy Objects tab in Figure 4-9.

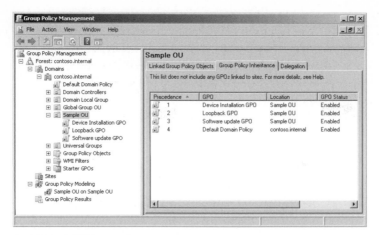

FIGURE 4-10 GPO precedence

Filtering GPOs

When planning your Group Policy structure, bear in mind that you can further refine the application of the policy settings in a GPO by specifying that they should be applied only to specified security groups. These security groups need to be in the container or containers (for example, OU or domain) to which the GPO is linked. They can contain user or computer accounts. If a security group contains user accounts, remove Authenticated Users from the policy scope before you add the security group to the scope.

Figure 4-11 shows the scope of the Device Installation GPO limited to computers in the USA Computers security group. Take note of this facility because it could play a part in your Group Policy design, but, like the Enforced option, it is an exception and should be used sparingly.

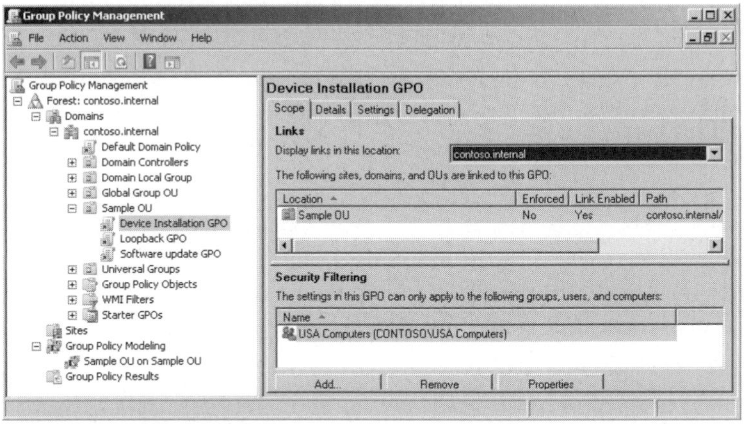

FIGURE 4-11 GPO filtering

Controlling Device Installation

When you are formulating a plan to control the installation of devices in your enterprise, you can use Group Policy to specify whether devices can be installed and, if so, which criteria should be applied. Depending on company policy, your plan could have one of the following outcomes:

- Prevent users (except for administrators) from installing any device.

- Allow users to install only devices that are on an approved list. If a device is not on the list, the user cannot install it.

- Prevent users from installing devices that are on a prohibited list. If a device is not on the list, the user can install it.

- Deny read or write access to users for devices that are removable or that use removable media, such as CD and DVD burners, external hard drives, and portable devices such as media players, smartphones, or Pocket PC devices.

You need to be familiar with the device installation process and the identification strings that match a device with the device driver packages available on a computer. Obtaining device identities (IDs) and global unique identifiers (GUIDs) is discussed later in this section.

By restricting the devices that users can install, you can reduce the risk of data theft. Users will find it more difficult to make unauthorized copies of company data if they cannot install unapproved devices that support removable media on their computers. You can plan to use Group Policy to deny write access to users for devices that are removable or that use removable media. Restricting device installation can also reduce support costs. You can ensure that users install only those devices that your help desk is trained and equipped to support. This reduces both support costs and user confusion.

In an enterprise environment in which you manage a large number of client computers, you can apply Group Policy settings to manage device installation on computers that are members of a domain or of an OU in a domain. You can choose one of the following strategies:

- **Prevent installation of all devices**   You plan to prevent standard users from installing any device but to allow administrators to install or update devices. In this scenario, you configure two computer Group Policy settings. The first prevents all users from installing devices, and the second exempts administrators from the restrictions.

- **Allow users to install authorized devices only**   You plan to allow users to install only the devices included on a list of authorized devices. In this scenario, you initially prevent standard users from installing any device. You then create a list of authorized devices and configure Group Policy so that standard users can install only specified devices.

- **Prevent installation of prohibited devices only**   You plan to allow standard users to install most devices but prevent them from installing devices included on a list of prohibited devices. In this scenario, you do not use Group Policy to prohibit installation of all devices; instead, you create a list of prohibited devices and configure Group Policy so that standard users can install any device except those on the list.

- **Control the use of removable media storage devices**   You plan to prevent standard users from writing data to removable storage devices or to devices with removable media, such as USB memory drives or CD or DVD burners. In this scenario, you configure a computer Group Policy to allow read access but deny write access to USB memory devices and to any CD or DVD burner device on users' computers. You can then configure a setting that prevents this policy from affecting users who are members of the Administrators group.

Group Policy Settings That Control Device Installation

Windows Vista and Windows Server 2008 introduced new policy settings that enable you to control device installation. You can configure these policy settings individually on a single computer, but, in the enterprise environment, you are more likely to apply them to a large number of computers through Group Policy in an AD DS domain. These are computer policies and affect any user logged on to a computer, except for the Allow Administrators To Override Device Installation Policies setting, which exempts members of the built-in local Administrators group from any of the device installation restrictions. The following policy settings allow you or members of your administrative team to implement your device installation plan:

- **Prevent Installation Of Devices Not Described By Other Policy Settings**   If this policy setting is enabled, users cannot install or update the drivers for devices unless they are described by either the Allow Installation Of Devices That Match Any Of These Device IDs policy setting or the Allow Installation Of Devices Using Drivers That Match These Device Setup Classes policy setting. If your plan involves disabling or not configuring this policy setting, users can install and update the driver for any device that is not described by the Prevent Installation Of Devices That Match Any Of These Device IDs policy setting, the Prevent Installation Of Devices Using Drivers That Match These Device Setup Classes policy setting, or the Prevent Installation Of Removable Devices policy setting.

- **Allow Administrators To Override Device Installation Restriction Policies**   If this policy setting is enabled, it allows members of the local Administrators group to install and update the drivers for any device, regardless of other policy settings. Administrators can use the Add Hardware Wizard or the Update Driver Wizard to install and update the drivers for any device. If your plan disables or does not configure this policy setting, administrators are subject to all policy settings that restrict device installation.

- **Prevent Installation Of Devices That Match Any Of These Device IDs** This policy setting enables you to specify a list of Plug and Play hardware IDs and compatible IDs for devices that users cannot install. Enabling this policy setting prevents users from installing or updating the driver for a device if any of its hardware IDs or compatible IDs are included in the list. If your plan disables or does not configure this policy setting, users can install devices and update their drivers as permitted by other policy settings for device installation. This policy setting takes precedence over any other policy settings that allow users to install a device, and prevents users from installing a device even if its ID matches another policy setting that would allow installation.

- **Prevent Installation Of Devices Using Drivers That Match These Device Setup Classes** This policy setting enables you to specify a list of Plug and Play device setup class GUIDs that define devices users cannot install. If you enable this policy setting, users cannot install or update drivers for a device that belongs to any of the listed device setup classes. If your plan disables or does not configure this policy setting, users can install and update drivers for devices as permitted by other policy settings for device installation. This policy setting takes precedence over any other policy settings that allow users to install a device and prevents users from installing a device with a GUID on the list even if its ID matches another policy setting that would allow installation.

- **Allow Installation Of Devices That Match Any Of These Device IDs** If you enable this policy setting, you can specify a list of Plug and Play hardware IDs and compatible IDs that describe devices users can install. Plan to use this setting only when the Prevent Installation Of Devices Not Described By Other Policy Settings policy setting is enabled and does not take precedence over any policy setting that would prevent users from installing a device. If you enable this policy setting, users can install and update any device with a hardware ID or compatible ID that matches an ID in this list if that installation has not been specifically prevented by the Prevent Installation Of Devices That Match These Device IDs policy setting, the Prevent Installation Of Devices Using Drivers That Match These Device Setup Classes policy setting, or the Prevent Installation Of Removable Devices policy setting. If another policy setting prevents users from installing a device, users cannot install it even if the device is also described by a value in this policy setting. If your plan involves disabling or not configuring this policy setting, and no other policy describes the device, the Prevent Installation Of Devices Not Described By Other Policy Settings policy setting determines whether users can install the device.

- **Allow Installation Of Devices Using Drivers That Match These Device Setup Classes** If you enable this policy setting, you can specify a list of device setup class GUIDs that describe devices users can install. Plan to use this setting only when the Prevent Installation Of Devices Not Described By Other Policy Settings policy setting is enabled and does not take precedence over any policy setting that would prevent users from installing a device. If you enable this setting, users can install and update any device with a device setup class that matches one of the device setup class GUIDs in this list unless that installation has not been specifically prevented by the Prevent Installation Of Devices That Match Any Of These Device IDs policy setting, the Prevent Installation Of Devices Using Drivers For These Device Setup Classes policy setting, or the Prevent Installation Of Removable Devices policy setting. If another policy setting prevents users from installing a device, users cannot install it even if the device is also described by a value in this policy setting. If your plan involves disabling or not configuring this policy setting, and no other policy setting describes the device, the Prevent Installation Of Devices Not Described By Other Policy Settings policy setting determines whether users can install the device.

> **NOTE   PLANNING DEVICE INSTALLATION**
>
> The way the device installation computer policies interact with each other is fairly intuitive and not as complex as it seems when described on paper. If you are formulating plans in this area, practice using these policies until you are familiar with what they do and how they interact. This is a suggested practice later in this chapter and is one of the few instances when an enterprise administrator should carry out configuration rather than delegate it.

Figure 4-12 shows the Device Installation Restriction policies in Group Policy Management Editor. Figure 4-13 shows one of the simplest and most widely used sets of policy settings that prevents standard users from installing devices but permits administrators to do so.

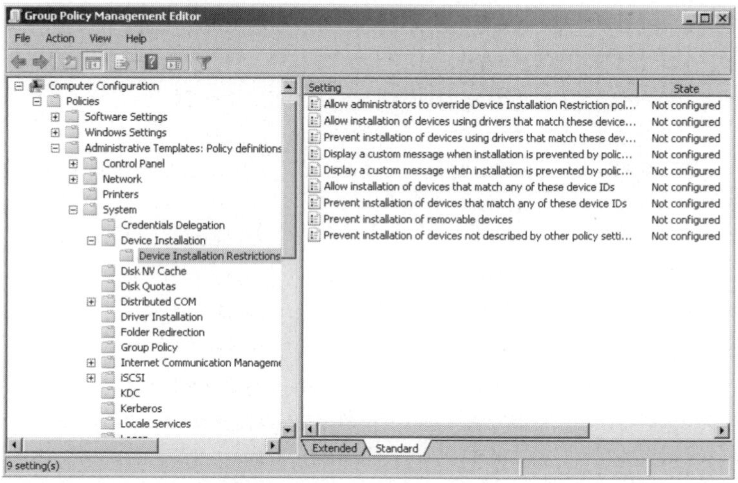

FIGURE 4-12 Device Installation Restriction policies

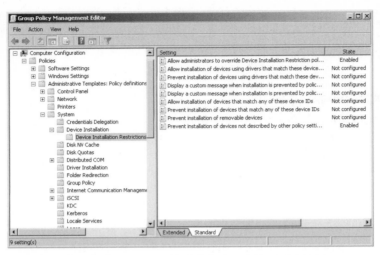

FIGURE 4-13 Standard users cannot install devices, but administrators can

Obtaining Hardware IDs, Compatible IDs, and GUIDs

You can allow or prevent the installation of specific devices by enabling the appropriate Group Policy setting and adding a list of hardware IDs, compatible IDs, or both. You can also specify device setup class GUIDs that describe devices users can install.

HARDWARE IDS

Hardware IDs provide the most exact match between a device and a driver package. The first string in the list of hardware IDs is referred to as the device ID because it matches the exact make, model, and version of the device. The other hardware IDs in the list match the details of the device less exactly. For example, a hardware ID might identify the make and model of the device, but not the specific version. This scheme allows Windows to use a driver for a different version of the device if the driver for the correct revision is not available. Figure 4-14 shows the list of hardware IDs for a USB flash memory device. You can access this from the device's Properties dialog box in Device Manager.

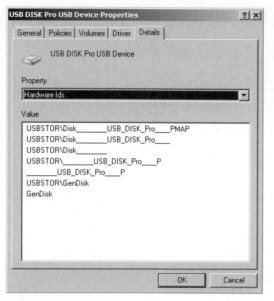

FIGURE 4-14 Hardware IDs

COMPATIBLE IDS

Windows Server 2008 R2 uses compatible IDs to select a device driver if the operating system cannot find a match for the device ID or any of the other hardware IDs. Compatible IDs are listed in the order of decreasing suitability. These strings are optional and, when provided, they are generic, such as *Disk*. When a match is made using a compatible ID, you can typically use only the most basic functions of the device. Figure 4-15 shows the list of hardware IDs for a USB flash memory device.

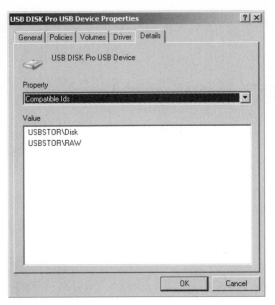

FIGURE 4-15 Compatible IDs

GUIDS

A GUID defines a device setup class, which the device manufacturer assigns to a device in the device driver package. The device setup class groups devices that are installed and configured in the same way. For example, all CD drives belong to the CDROM device setup class and use the same co-installer. When Windows Server 2008 R2 starts, it builds a tree structure in memory with the GUIDs for all the detected devices.

In addition to the GUID for the device setup class of the device itself, Windows Server 2008 R2 might need to insert the GUID for the device setup class of the bus to which the device is attached (for example, USB). When you use device setup classes to control users' installation of device drivers, you must specify the GUIDs for all the device's device setup classes, or you might not achieve the results you want. In addition, GUIDs are held in the HKLM\SYSTEM\CurrentControlSet\Control\Class\{*ClassGUID}* registry key and are not as easily obtained as hardware IDs.

For these reasons, hardware IDs, rather than GUIDs, are typically used to specify the devices that can or cannot be installed. Figure 4-16 shows a hardware ID list specified for the Allow Installation Of Devices That Match Any Of These Device IDs setting.

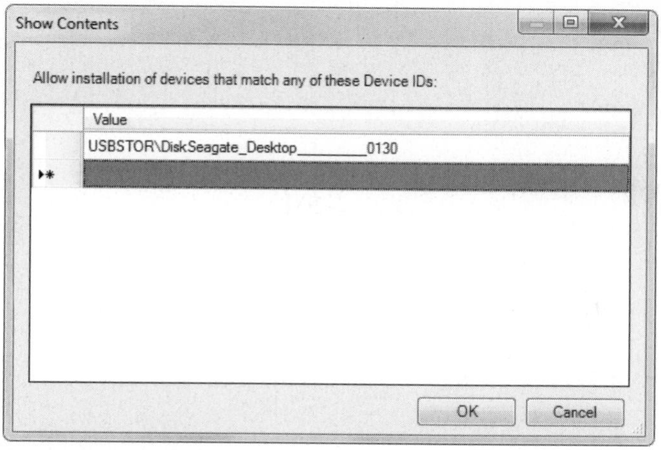

FIGURE 4-16 Specifying hardware IDs

Planning Authentication and Authorization

Authentication involves checking that users are who they say they are. It uses username and password or a security certificate installed on a smart card. *Authorization* determines whether a user has access to resources through permissions or administrative rights through group membership and delegation. Authorization can happen within a domain, across a domain tree, or between forests. It involves the Security Accounts Manager (SAM), access control lists (ACLs), and protocols such as Kerberos v5.

> **MORE INFO   KERBEROS AUTHENTICATION**
>
> For more information about Kerberos authentication, see *http://technet.microsoft.com /en-us/library/dd349801(WS.10).aspx.*

Multifactor Authentication and Authorization

Multifactor authentication occurs when you must use two or more distinct methods to authenticate an identity. For example, you are logged on to a domain with an administrative-level account. You need to access a stand-alone Berkley Internet Daemon (BIND) server through Remote Desktop. You are asked for credentials. They are the same credentials that you used to log on to the domain, but you need to enter them again. This is multifactor authentication.

Multifactor authorization occurs when you need to authenticate two people to accomplish a stated aim. For example, you need to create a two-way forest trust between the *contoso.internal* and *litware.internal* forests. You create one end of the trust logged on to the *contoso.internal* forest as Kim_Akers. To create the other end, you need to provide the credentials for Tom_Perry in the *litware.internal* forest. This is multifactor authorization.

Using Password Authentication

You can authenticate a user through a username and password. Before you plan a password policy, you need to know what the default settings are. Figure 4-17 shows the default settings for the *contoso.internal* domain.

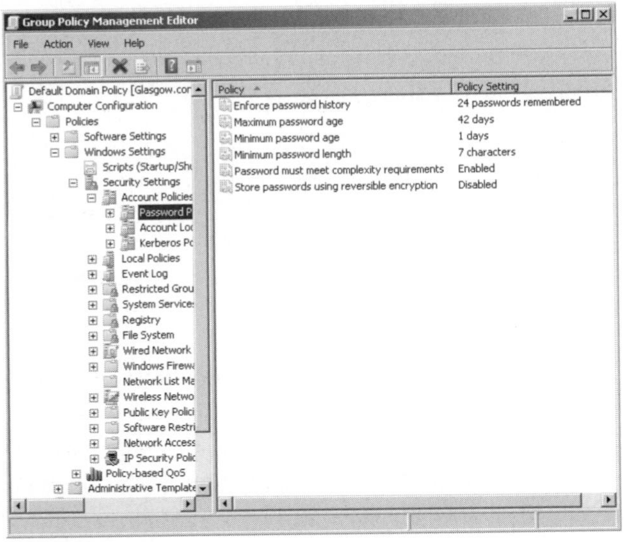

FIGURE 4-17 Default password settings

Configuring Fine-Grained Password Policies

As a first step in planning *fine-grained password* and account lockout policies, decide how many password policies you need. At a minimum, you would probably want to configure the following:

- An administrative-level password policy with strict settings: for example, a minimum password length of 12, a maximum password age of 28 days, and password complexity requirements enabled.

- A user-level password policy with, for example, a minimum password length of 6, a maximum password age of 90 days, and password complexity requirements based on business or security policies.

- A service account password policy with a minimum password length of 32 characters and complexity requirements enabled. (Service account passwords are seldom typed in.) Because of their complexity, service account passwords can typically be set to not expire or to have very long password ages.

You also need to look at your existing group structure. If you have existing Administrators and Users groups, there is no point creating new ones. Ultimately, you need to define a group and AD DS structure that maps to your fine-grained password and account lockout policies.

You cannot apply *Password Setting objects* (PSOs) to OUs directly. If your users are organized into OUs, consider creating *shadow groups* for these OUs and then applying the newly defined fine-grained password and account lockout policies to them. A shadow group is a global security group that is logically mapped to an OU to enforce a fine-grained password and account lockout policy. Add OU users as members to the newly created shadow group and then apply the fine-grained password and account lockout policy to this shadow group. If you move a user from one OU to another, you must update user memberships in the corresponding shadow groups.

> **NOTE   SHADOW GROUPS**
>
> You will not find an *Add Shadow Group* command in Active Directory Users and Computers. A shadow group is simply an ordinary global security group that contains all the user accounts in one or more OUs. When you apply a PSO to a shadow group, you are effectively applying it to users in the corresponding OU.

Microsoft applies PSOs to groups rather than to OUs because groups offer better flexibility for managing various sets of users. Windows Server 2008 R2 AD DS creates various groups for administrative accounts, including Domain Admins, Enterprise Admins, Schema Admins, Server Operators, and Backup Operators. You can apply PSOs to these groups or nest them in a single global security group and apply a PSO to that group. Because you use groups rather than OUs, you do not need to modify the OU hierarchy to apply fine-grained passwords. Modifying an OU hierarchy requires detailed planning and increases the risk of errors.

If you intend to use fine-grained passwords, you probably need to raise the functional level of your domain. To work properly, fine-grained password settings require a domain functional level of Windows Server 2008 or higher. Planning domain and forest functional levels is discussed in Chapter 2. Changing functional levels involves irreversible changes. You need to be sure, for example, that you will never want to add a Windows Server 2003 domain controller to your domain.

By default, only members of the Domain Admins group can create PSOs and apply a PSO to a group or user. You do not, however, need to have permissions on the user object or group object to be able to apply a PSO to it. You can delegate Read Property permissions on the default security descriptor of a PSO to any other group (such as help desk personnel). This enables users who are not domain administrators to discover the password and account lockout settings applied through a PSO to a security group.

You can apply fine-grained password policies only to user objects and global security groups (or *InetOrgPerson* objects if they are used instead of user objects). If your plan identifies a group of computers that requires different password settings, consider techniques such as password filters. Fine-grained password policies cannot be applied to computer objects.

If you use custom password filters in a domain, fine-grained password policies do not interfere with these filters. If you plan to upgrade Windows 2000 Server or Windows Server 2003 domains that currently deploy custom password filters on domain controllers, you can continue to use those password filters to enforce additional password restrictions.

If you have assigned a PSO to a global security group, but one user in that group requires special settings, you can assign an exceptional PSO directly to that particular user. For example, the CEO of Northwind Traders is a member of the senior managers group, and company policy requires that senior managers use complex passwords. However, the CEO is not willing to do so. In this case, you can create an exceptional PSO and apply it directly to the CEO's user account. The exceptional PSO will override the security group PSO when the password settings (*msDS-ResultantPSO*) for the CEO's user account are determined.

✔ **Quick Check**

- By default, members of which group can create PSOs?

Quick Check Answer

- Domain Admins

Finally, you can plan to delegate management of fine-grained passwords. When you have created the necessary PSOs and the global security groups associated with these PSOs, you can delegate management of the security groups to responsible users or user groups. For example, a human resources (HR) group could add user accounts to or remove them from the managers group when staff changes occur. If a PSO specifying fine-grained password policy is associated with the managers group, in effect the HR group is determining to whom these policies are applied.

> **MORE INFO** **FINE-GRAINED PASSWORD AND ACCOUNT LOCKOUT POLICY CONFIGURATION**
>
> For more information about fine-grained password and account lockout policies, see *http://technet2.microsoft.com/WindowsServer2008/en/library/2199dcf7-68fd-4315-87cc -ade35f8978ea1033.mspx#BKMK_7.*

Using Smart Card Authentication

If you are using smart cards in your organization to provide additional security and control over user credentials, your users can use those smart cards with authentication credentials to obtain rights account certificates (RACs) and use licenses from an Active Directory Rights Management Services (AD RMS) server (or, more commonly in the enterprise environment, an AD RMS cluster), provided a Secure Sockets Layer (SSL) certificate has already been installed.

> **MORE INFO** **AD RMS CLUSTER**
>
> For more information about installing an AD RMS cluster, see *http://technet2 .microsoft.com/windowsserver2008/en/library/a65941cb-02ef-4194-95ce -7fd213b1e48c1033.mspx?mfr=true.*

To use smart card authentication, you must also add the Client Certificate Mapping Authentication role service in Server Manager. This is part of the Web Server (IIS) server role. Your next step is to configure the authentication method in IIS. Perform these steps to do so.

1. Click Start, point to Administrative Tools, and then click Server Manager.

2. Under Roles Summary, click Add Roles.

3. Use the Add Roles Wizard to add the Web Server (IIS) role.

4. In Internet Information Services (IIS) Manager, expand the server name in the console tree and, in the server Home page, under IIS, double-click Authentication to open the Authentication page.

5. In the Authentication page, right-click Active Directory Client Certificate Authentication, and then choose Enable.

6. Enable client authentication for the website that is hosting AD RMS. In IIS Manager, expand the server name in the console tree, expand Sites, and then expand the website that is hosting AD RMS. By default, the website name is Default Web Site.

7. In the console tree, expand _wmcs, right-click either the certification virtual directory (to support RACs) or the licensing virtual directory (to support user licenses), and then choose Switch To Content View.

8. Right-click certification.asmx or license.asmx, as appropriate, and then choose Switch To Features View.

9. In the Home page, double-click SSL Settings, and choose the appropriate client certificates setting (Accept or Require).

   Accept client certificates if you want clients to have the option to supply authentication credentials by using either a smart card certificate or a username and password. Require client certificates if you want only clients with client-side certificates such as smart cards to be able to connect to the service.

10. Click Apply. If you want to use client authentication for both certification and licensing, repeat this procedure but select the alternate virtual directory the second time.

11. Close IIS Manager. If you are using an AD RMS cluster, repeat the procedure for every other server in the cluster.

Your next task is to force the authentication method to use Client Certificate Mapping Authentication for the AD RMS cluster. Before you do that, back up the Applicationhost.config file in the %windir%\System32\Inetsrv\Config folder.

1. Open an elevated command prompt, and change the directory to %windir%\System32\Inetsrv\Config.

2. Enter **notepad applicationhost.config** and locate the section similar to Default Web Site/_wmcs/Certification/Certification.asmx.

3. If you want to allow smart card authentication in addition to Windows authentication, change

   ```
   access sslFlags="Ssl, SslNegotiateCert, SslRequireCert, Ssl128"
   ```

to

```
access sslFlags="Ssl, SslNegotiateCert, Ssl128"
```

4. Add a new line under windowsAuthentication enabled="true". In this line, type:

```
clientCertificateMappingAuthentication enabled="true"
```

5. If you want to allow only smart card authentication, ensure that SSL client authentication with IIS is required. Add a new line under windowsAuthentication enabled="true." In this line, type:

```
clientCertificateMappingAuthentication enabled="true"
```

6. Change

```
windowsAuthentication enabled="true"
```

to

```
windowsAuthentication enabled="false"
```

7. Click File, choose Save, and then close Notepad.

8. At the command prompt, enter **iisreset**.

Note that running *iisreset* from a command prompt will restart the services associated with IIS.

Again, if you are using an AD RMS cluster, you repeat the procedure for every other server in the cluster.

After you have configured these settings, a user who attempts to open rights-protected content published by the AD RMS server or cluster is prompted to provide authentication credentials before the server or cluster provides the user with an RAC or user license.

PRACTICE **Implementing Fine-Grained Password Policies**

To complete this practice, the domain functional level of the *contoso.internal* domain must be set to Windows Server 2008 or higher. If you are unsure how to do this, consult the Windows Server 2008 R2 Help files.

EXERCISE Create a PSO

In this exercise, you create a PSO with password policies that are not the same as the default password policies for the *contoso.internal* domain. You associate this with a global security group called special_password that contains the user Don_Hall. Do not attempt this practice until you have raised the domain functional level of the *contoso.internal* domain to Windows Server 2008 or higher.

1. Log on to the Glasgow domain controller with the Kim_Akers account.

2. If necessary, create a user account for **Don_Hall** with a password of **P@ssw0rd**. Create a global security group called **special_password**. Make Don_Hall a member

of special_password. If you are unsure how to do this, consult the Windows Server 2008 R2 Help files.

3. In the Run box, type **adsiedit.msc**.

4. If this is the first time you have used the ADSI Edit console on your test network, right-click ADSI Edit, and then choose Connect To. Type **contoso.internal** in the Name box, and then click OK.

5. Double-click *contoso.internal*.

6. Double-click DC=contoso,DC=internal.

7. Double-click CN=System.

8. Right-click CN=Password Settings Container. Choose New. Choose Object, as shown in Figure 4-18.

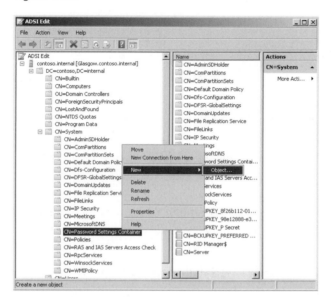

FIGURE 4-18 Creating a password settings object

9. In the Create Object dialog box, ensure that msDS-PasswordSettings is selected. Click Next.

10. In the Value box for the *CN* attribute, type **PasswdSettings01**. Click Next.

11. In the Value box for the *msDS-PasswordSettingsPrecedence* attribute, type **10**. Click Next.

12. In the Value box for the *msDS-PasswordReversibleEncryptionEnabled* attribute, type **FALSE**. Click Next.

13. In the Value box for the *msDS-PasswordHistoryLength* attribute, type **6**. Click Next.

14. In the Value box for the *msDS-PasswordComplexityEnabled* attribute, type **TRUE**. Click Next.

15. In the Value box for the *msDS-MinimumPasswordLength* attribute, type **6**. Click Next.

16. In the Value box for the *msDS-MinimumPasswordAge* attribute, type **1:00:00:00**. Click Next.

17. In the Value box for the *msDS-MaximumPasswordAge* attribute, type **20:00:00:00**. Click Next.

18. In the Value box for the *msDS-LockoutThreshold* attribute, type **2**. Click Next.

19. In the Value box for the *msDS-LockoutObservationWindow* attribute, type **0:00:15:00**. Click Next.

20. In the Value box for the *msDS-LockoutDuration* attribute, type **0:00:15:00**. Click Next.

21. Click Finish.

22. Open Active Directory Users and Computers, choose View, and then choose Advanced Features.

23. Expand *contoso.internal*, expand System, and then select Password Settings Container.

24. In the details pane, right-click *PasswdSettings01*. Choose Properties.

25. On the Attribute Editor tab, select *msDS-PSOAppliesTo*, as shown in Figure 4-19.

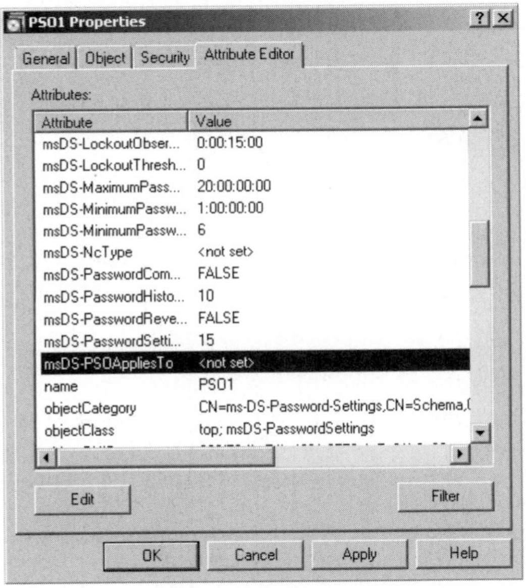

FIGURE 4-19 Selecting an attribute to edit

26. Click Edit.

27. Click Add Windows Account.

28. In the Enter The Object Names To Select box, type **special_password**. Click Check Names.

29. Click OK. The Multi-valued Distinguished Name With Security Principal Editor dialog box should look similar to Figure 4-20.

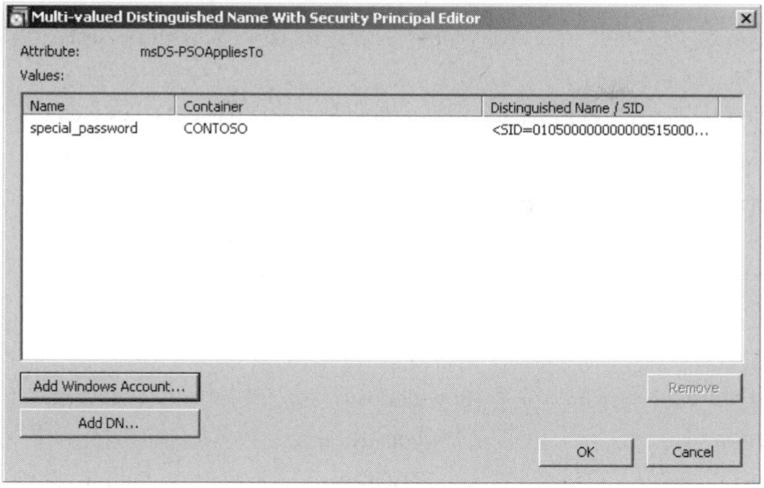

FIGURE 4-20 Adding the special_password global security group to PSO1

30. Click OK, and then click OK again to close the PasswdSettings01Properties dialog box.

31. Test your settings by changing the password for the Don_Hall account to a noncomplex, six-letter password such as **simple**.

Lesson Summary

- When planning a Group Policy structure, keep it as simple as possible and minimize the use of exceptions. Do not link GPOs to OUs across site links.
- Scope filtering enables you to apply the policy settings in a GPO to selected groups or users in the OU.
- You can use Group Policy to control who can install devices on client workstations and what devices they can install.
- You can authenticate users by username and password or by security certificates held on smart cards. Windows Server 2008 R2 enables you to use fine-grained password policies.

Lesson Review

Use the following questions to test your knowledge of the information in Lesson 2, "Designing Enterprise-Level Group Policy Strategy." The questions are also available on the companion CD if you prefer to review them in electronic form.

1. You are planning your Group Policy structure. Which of the following statements represents good advice?

    A. Keep the number of GPOs to an absolute minimum by having many configuration settings in a single GPO.

    B. If you have two OUs at geographically remote sites that have the same Group Policy settings, link a single GPO to both OUs.

    C. Give your OUs and GPOs meaningful names.

    D. Use features such as the Block Inheritance, Enforced, Security Filtering, and Loopback Policy settings on GPOs extensively.

2. Which of the following interfaces are components of the AD DS data store? (Choose all that apply.)

    A. Directory Server Agent (DSA)

    B. Messaging Application Programming Interface (MAPI)

    C. Security Accounts Manager (SAM)

    D. Replication (REPL)

    E. Lightweight Directory Access Protocol (LDAP)

    F. Extensible Storage Engine (ESE)

3. You want to use Group Policy to control device installation in accordance with company policy. You want administrators to be able to install any device. You do not want standard users to be able to install any devices except for one device that has been approved by the company. You know the Hardware ID for that device. Which of the following configuration steps would you implement? (Choose all that apply.)

    A. Enable Prevent Installation Of Devices Not Described By Other Policy Settings.

    B. Disable or do not configure Prevent Installation Of Devices Not Described By Other Policy Settings.

    C. Enable Allow Administrators To Override Device Installation Restriction Policies.

    D. Disable or do not configure Allow Administrators To Override Device Installation Restriction Policies.

    E. Enable Prevent Installation Of Devices That Match Any Of These Device IDs, and add the Hardware ID of the approved device to the policy setting.

    F. Enable Allow Installation Of Devices That Match Any Of These Device IDs, and add the Hardware ID of the approved device to the policy setting.

Chapter Review

To further practice and reinforce the skills you learned in this chapter, you can perform the following tasks:

- Review the chapter summary.
- Review the list of key terms introduced in this chapter.
- Complete the case scenarios. These scenarios set up real-world situations involving the topics in this chapter and ask you to create a solution.
- Complete the suggested practices.
- Take a practice test.

Chapter Summary

- Delegation increases administrative efficiency and reduces administrative costs. It provides both isolation and autonomy. You can assign rights to security groups and delegate control of OUs to groups.
- You can delegate the management of groups to a group member and delegate rights to an OU to users or groups without granting rights to any other part of the enterprise.
- Avoid exceptions when planning Group Policy. You can use scope filtering to apply the policy settings in a GPO to selected groups or users in the OU. You can use Group Policy to control device installation.
- New features in Windows Server 2008 enable you to audit changes to Group Policy and AD DS structure and to use fine-grained password policies.
- The design of your OU and GPO structure depends on how the organization is structured (geographically or by department) and which administrative model is used.

Key Terms

Do you know what these key terms mean? You can check your answers by looking up the terms in the glossary at the end of the book.

- Authentication
- Authorization
- Autonomy
- Data management
- Delegation
- Fine-grained password policies
- Group Policy object (GPO)
- Group Policy setting
- Group Policy

- Isolation
- Organizational unit (OU)
- Password Settings object (PSO)
- Principle of least privilege
- Read-only domain controller (RODC)
- Service management
- Shadow group
- Starter Group Policy objects (GPOs)

Case Scenarios

In the following case scenarios, you will apply what you have learned about designing AD DS administration and Group Policy strategy. You can find answers to these questions in the "Answers" section at the end of this book.

Case Scenario 1: Designing a Delegation Strategy

You are an enterprise administrator at Northwind Traders. You have just upgraded your domain to Windows Server 2008 R2. You are planning to delegate administrative tasks to members of your team and nonadministrative tasks to security groups that contain standard user accounts. Answer the following questions:

1. Historically, the administrator team has mostly been involved in emergency resolution, and changes were made to AD DS that were not well documented. The technical director requires you to maintain an audit trail of AD DS changes, including what the original configurations are before changes are made. How do you reassure him?

2. You have identified an OU that contains several security groups. You ask one of your administrators to create a GPO and to link it to the OU. However, the policy settings in the GPO should apply to only two of the groups and not to the remaining groups. Your team member is unsure how to do this. What do you advise?

3. A member of your team uses Group Policy to deploy isolation policies to a group of servers in your organization. After deploying the servers, you have determined that the isolation policies are not being applied to several of the servers. Which Group Policy Management Console tool should your team member use to diagnose this problem?

Case Scenario 2: Planning Authentication and Authorization

You are the enterprise manager at Litware, Inc. Litware has recently upgraded all its domain controllers to Windows Server 2008 R2, and you are planning authentication and authorization policies that take advantage of the new features Windows Server 2008 R2 provides. Answer the following questions:

1. Some members of staff (for example, the CEO) want to use simple passwords, although the default policy for the *litware.com* domain enforces complex passwords. This is possible in Windows Server 2003, but it is difficult to configure, and, therefore, was never implemented by Litware. You are asked whether Windows Server 2008 R2 makes this configuration easier. What is your reply?

2. A member of your administrative team informs you that she cannot get the fine-grained password policy to work, even though all domain controllers now run Windows Server 2008 R2. What do you advise her to do?

3. Currently, all staff at Litware can install USB flash memory devices on their client workstations and upload and download files. The technical director sees this as a security risk and wants only administrators to be able to install such devices. However, he does not want to lose the ability to boost Windows Vista or Windows 7 client performance through the Windows ReadyBoost feature. What do you tell him?

Suggested Practices

To help you successfully master the exam objectives presented in this chapter, complete the following tasks.

Designing the Active Directory Domain Services Administrative Model

Complete both practices in this section.

- **Practice 1**   Investigate management roles. Microsoft-engineered roles for data and system management are listed in this chapter, and a link is given for more information. Follow this link and investigate on the Internet. Find out more about these roles.

- **Practice 2**   Investigate compliance auditing. This chapter discusses AD DS and Group Policy auditing, but space prohibits a detailed discussion of every possible setting and option. Search the Internet for more information on this topic.

Designing Enterprise-Level Group Policy Strategy

Do both practices in this section.

- **Practice 1**   Work with device installation policy settings. The only good way to become familiar with them and how they interact is to configure them and observe the results. Experiment with these settings.

- **Practice 2**   Configure PSOs. A PSO can contain a large number of settings, of which you configured only a small subset in the practice in Lesson 2. Experiment with PSO settings and determine the effects each has on the security policies that affect the users associated with the GPO.

Take a Practice Test

The practice tests on this book's companion CD offer many options. For example, you can test yourself on just one exam objective, or you can test yourself on all the 70-647 certification exam content.
You can set up the test so that it closely simulates the experience of taking a certification exam, or
you can set it up in study mode so that you can look at the correct answers and explanations after
you answer each question.

> **MORE INFO** **PRACTICE TESTS**
>
> For details about all the practice test options available, see the "How to Use the Practice Tests"
> section in this book's introduction.

CHAPTER 5

Designing a Network Access Strategy

In the past, designing an access strategy for your network involved only three considerations: who should be able to access the network, how they should access the network, and which resources should be made available to these users. Unfortunately, this limited set of criteria falls far short of what should be included when designing an access strategy. With the advent of more insidious types of attacks through viruses and Trojan horse programs in recent years, it is quite evident that additional requirements are needed prior to allowing a computer access to your secure network.

Methods for protecting the internal network from the ever-increasing number of attacks have evolved over the years. From the beginning of the very first stateful firewalls in the mid-1990s to the complex security services offered today, network security experts have steadfastly attempted to keep up with the various threats produced daily. Firewalls; perimeter networks; antivirus, anti-spam, and antispyware programs; and software updates all contribute to the security of networks. All of these are much easier to administer and control when computers attached to the network remain stationary. Newer attacks over the past several years have targeted computers that are not part of the network and have placed dormant pieces of malware on them. When these computers attach to secure networks, some of these newer pieces of malicious software, using various techniques, become active and begin infecting computers and devices on the internal network. Able to penetrate the various layers of defense at the perimeter network by using this newer attack vector with impunity, malware writers can now concentrate on attacking computers that have fewer defense mechanisms.

An initial concern in remote connectivity is the setup of the network perimeter. Perimeter network design has undergone relatively few changes, considering the topology of the perimeter itself. What have changed are the devices and services that are constantly being added to and used in the perimeter network. The discussion in this chapter focuses on the devices to deploy in the perimeter to aid in designing a Network Access Protection (NAP) solution. The initial lesson discusses deployment options for a Remote Authentication Dial-In User Service (RADIUS) solution that adequately meets the demands of the environment.

This chapter discusses the components necessary to provide secure remote access connectivity, while ensuring the health of the computers and their compliance with stated network policy, to help you design a network perimeter when deploying a NAP solution.

Exam objectives in this chapter:

- Design for network access.

Lessons in this chapter:

Before You Begin

To complete the lessons in this chapter, you should have:

- Experience creating Layer 2 Tunneling Protocol (L2TP) and Point-to-Point Tunneling Protocol (PPTP) virtual private network (VPN) connections.

- An understanding of authentication protocols used for remote access.

- Working knowledge of implementing encryption technologies for VPNs.

- An understanding of firewalls, rules, and security policies for perimeter networks.

- An understanding of RADIUS and a simple RADIUS configuration.

 **REAL WORLD**

Paul Mancuso

Prior to undertaking any project involving the design of network security services, I constantly research any new or recently available documentation regarding
the features and services of any component involved in the project. Remote access
connectivity is quite a fluid subject when it comes to new and innovative devices
and services constantly being delivered by the various vendors within the industry.
Research becomes even more important due to NAP features and services just arriv-
ing to market. There are so many components involved in the process that reading
the white papers and studying the example scenarios is imperative because there
are so few actual working examples on which to draw at this time. This will rapidly
change because Microsoft Windows Server 2008 brings with it an entire solution
that enables third-party vendor solutions to be integrated in the mix.

In addition to the research, you should set up a working lab with a bare minimum of half a dozen virtual machines that you can readily assemble into a working design. This enables you to assemble a working solution to which you can always return when issues arise in a RADIUS or NAP implementation. The interaction of the various components of a NAP solution requires time spent studying the interaction and knowledge of the flow of communication through each of the components involved with the solution. A deep understanding of RADIUS and the attributes involved in each of the NAP enforcement types will aid in designing your NAP solution.

One final note: Ensure that you have checked with any third-party vendor for its compliance with NAP when using its features within your NAP infrastructure. You do not want to be deep into a NAP deployment only to realize that certain attributes you assumed would interact appropriately do not function the way you thought they would. Microsoft also publishes a list of all its partners that support NAP at *http://www.microsoft.com/windowsserver2008/en/us/nap-partners.aspx*.

Lesson 1: Perimeter Networks and Remote Access Strategies

Providing secure remote connectivity involves designing access through a perimeter network. Therefore, design a secure perimeter network and decide which services will reside within it first. Services to consider deploying within the perimeter network will most likely include various RADIUS components, VPN servers, publicly accessible application servers, wireless devices, and supporting network infrastructure devices.

Due to the current security-minded environment, your network undoubtedly contains a firewall along with one or more supporting infrastructure devices, such as switches and routers, and application servers such as web and File Transfer Protocol (FTP) servers that are publicly accessible. In addition, the network might also have a RADIUS server to authenticate VPN connections, partner access to existing extranets, or possibly to provide secure authentication for a preexisting wireless infrastructure. These network devices and application servers will make up the perimeter network that you inherit or are currently administering.

As the enterprise administrator, you are responsible for upgrading the current environment to provide support for the following:

- An updated RADIUS solution to provide support for an eventual NAP solution
- A remediation network for the NAP solution

This lesson provides the background necessary to build a remote access solution and to help lay the groundwork for designing a NAP solution.

> **After this lesson, you will be able to:**
> - Understand the technical requirements when designing perimeter networks.
> - Understand which services to provide in a perimeter network.
> - Determine appropriate firewall services to provide for various types of perimeter networks.
> - Design VPN solutions.
> - Design a RADIUS solution for a small enterprise.
> - Design a RADIUS solution to support branch offices within the same forest.
> - Design a RADIUS solution to support a multiforest environment.
>
> **Estimated lesson time: 45 minutes**

Designing the Perimeter Network

Most perimeter network designs involve one or two firewall devices to protect the edge network. Traffic from the outside passes through one or more inspection points before it is allowed into the perimeter network to access services deployed there or into the secure environment. Typical designs involve a single perimeter device with two or more network interfaces or two inspection points with two security devices, one inspecting traffic into the perimeter network from an untrusted external environment and another inspecting traffic as it enters the secure environment from the perimeter network.

As the enterprise administrator, you must assess the type of traffic you allow into your perimeter network and what traffic is permitted into the secure network. You need to determine how and at what layer you inspect this traffic to fulfill your security requirements successfully. You must assess the services to be deployed in the perimeter network for public accessibility and for a secure remote access solution.

Types of Perimeter Network Architectures

There are many types of perimeter network layouts. The design guides here provide descriptions of the basic security feature sets included in most designs. Network architectures will generally include three distinct regions or zones:

- Border network
- Perimeter network
- Internal network

The border network provides the direct connection to the external environment, which is usually a connection to an Internet service provider (ISP), often through a router. The border router can offer some protective features, such as access lists, to manage specific unwanted traffic from certain Internet Control Message Protocol (ICMP) types, such as echo requests associated with pinging. A perimeter firewall along with associated security devices and services provides the bulk of protection for the border network. Other than a switch used to provide connectivity to the perimeter security services, there are usually no other network application services of significance within this zone.

The perimeter network is a semiprotected area secured by a perimeter firewall and, possibly, an internal firewall. Services located in this area include web servers for public access that connect to internal SQL servers, along with many other application servers. Most of the discussion in this lesson focuses on other services located within this area.

The internal network is the location of the secure environment. It houses the corporate user and server environment. Some security designs include another firewall service separating the internal user network from the server farms.

Figure 5-1 displays the typical architecture of the three-zone network environment, using two firewall services.

If the perimeter firewall is composed of three or more network interfaces, an internal firewall is a more logical association, with the same physical device providing the services for the perimeter firewall, than a physical association with its network interfaces. Figure 5-2 displays an alternative architecture of the network environment employing three or more zones, using a single physical firewall service dividing separate logical security domains.

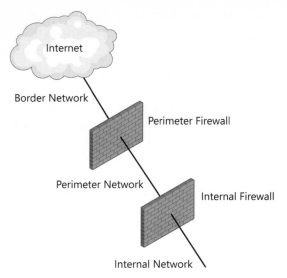

FIGURE 5-1 Perimeter network design employing two firewall devices

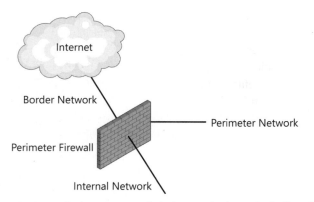

FIGURE 5-2 Perimeter network design employing a single firewall device

These logical designs display a basis for targeting services and security features when designing the perimeter network. As the enterprise administrator, you are responsible for the security of the services that are deployed in the perimeter network. Consider questions such as these:

- Which services should be deployed in the perimeter network to provide secure VPN connections?
- Which supporting services are necessary to provide secure VPN connections?
- Do internal users require a secured wireless connection?
- Should the access points for wireless users be deployed as part of the perimeter network design?

- If RADIUS is to be used to centralize management of authentication for remote access and wireless users, which RADIUS components, if any, should be deployed in the perimeter network?

Securing the Perimeter Network

What is not shown in either design is the type of security services offered by the firewall devices at the perimeter, nor the internal location in the two firewall device designs. Knowing the types of security devices used to secure access into the perimeter network as well as into the internal environment offers you, the enterprise administrator, a better idea of how services deployed in the perimeter network can be protected. Different types of security devices provide varying levels of security. This lesson focuses only on enterprise-class devices. These devices typically provide one or more of the following:

- Network Address Translation (NAT)
- Stateful inspection
- Circuit-level inspection
- Proxy services
- Application-layer firewalls

NAT uses private IP addresses that have significant meaning when used within your organization. When traffic is sent out to the Internet, these addresses require translation to an acceptable public IP address. NAT was originally devised to overcome the anticipated shortage of public IP addresses. One of the benefits of using NAT in your firewall design is that your internal addressing structure is hidden from outside attackers—not a major source of security, but a significant fact. A possible detriment when using NAT is that certain services, when run through it, have problems and require services such as NAT editors for PPTP tunnels or NAT Traversal (NAT-T) for IPsec tunnels and L2TP tunnels.

Stateful inspection firewalls provide an accounting of all traffic that originated on an interface in a state table. When the connection traffic is returned, the state table determines whether the traffic originated on that interface.

Circuit-level firewalls provide a more in-depth inspection of traffic than stateful firewalls do. Circuit-level firewalls provide session maintenance and enable the use of protocols that require secondary connections such as FTP. Circuit-level firewalls are usually the way stateful inspection services are carried out in today's retail firewalls.

Proxy servers are intermediaries that provide security by requesting a service on behalf of a client; the client is not directly connected to the service. The proxy service can inspect all headers involved in the transaction, providing an extra layer of protection. Frequently requested content can be cached and reused to reduce bandwidth. Proxy servers can also provide authenticated requests, NAT, and authentication request forwarding.

The ultimate in protection is an application-layer firewall. Not only are all the incoming and outgoing packet headers inspected and state tables maintained, but the data streams can also be inspected to provide security against attacks hidden in the data payloads of ordinary web service packets such as HTTP, other web-related request and data packets, and many other application-specific request and response packets.

MORE INFO   **TYPES OF FIREWALL SERVICES**

The information presented here on types of firewall services is just an overview to provide a basis for discussion on perimeter network design and services deployed within the perimeter network. There is much additional information about firewall types that you can view at *http://technet.microsoft.com/en-us/library/cc700828.aspx*.

PLANNING FOR MICROSOFT FOREFRONT THREAT MANAGEMENT GATEWAY SERVER

Protecting the internal network has been a primary focus of Microsoft Forefront Threat Management Gateway (TMG) Server. Forefront TMG 2010 Server is the current version and provides an integrated edge security gateway for remote access, branch office connectivity, and Internet access protection. Forefront TMG 2010 Server figures prominently in any Microsoft solution because it integrates well with Microsoft remote access services and provides secure tunneling for site-to-site VPNs.

NOTE   **FOREFRONT SECURITY**

Forefront TMG and the earlier Microsoft ISA Server 2006 are now part of the new Microsoft Forefront product line. The Microsoft Forefront line of products provides a comprehensive set of security products from the edge of the network, starting with Forefront TMG 2010 Server, all the way to the desktop (Forefront Endpoint Protection), providing firewall services, protection from malware and spyware, network edge security services, and much more. Microsoft Forefront Unified Access Gateway (UAG) provides the recommended solution for remote access and reverse proxy to publish applications such as Microsoft SharePoint and Microsoft Exchange.

Microsoft positions Forefront TMG in one of two ways depending on your network topology:

- **Edge firewall**   Forefront TMG in this topology is the perimeter security device that sits between the Internet and the internal network. Forefront TMG provides all possible network security services, such as the Internet proxy for internal clients, remote access server for VPNs, and, finally, the reverse proxy for internally hosted applications available for external access.

- **3-leg firewall**   The Forefront TMG server provides access to a minimum of three networks: the external network, one or more perimeter networks, and the internal network. The perimeter network hosts the usual Internet services and edge Simple Mail Transfer Protocol (SMTP) services. The Forefront TMG server can provide remote access services for VPNs if needed.

- **Back firewall** The Forefront TMG server is the back-end security appliance in a back-to-back firewall configuration. A front-end security device secures the perimeter network from the external network. Forefront TMG's primary responsibility is to provide secure Internet-related connectivity for internal clients.

Figures 5-3 and 5-4 display some of the roles that Forefront TMG can play when deployed in the perimeter network.

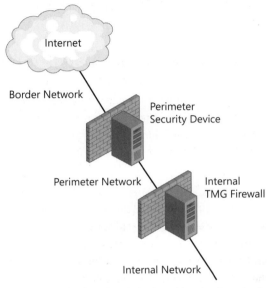

FIGURE 5-3 Forefront TMG deployed in a back-to-back firewall design

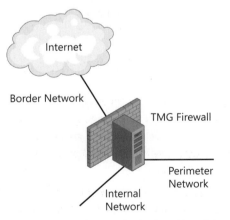

FIGURE 5-4 Forefront TMG deployed in a 3-leg firewall design

If Microsoft Forefront TMG is providing VPN for remote access, then it can also provide quarantine control for VPN clients by using either its Remote Access Quarantine Service or NAP provided by Windows Server 2008 R2.

ISA Server 2006 supports Network Access Quarantine Control as a complementary service to Microsoft Windows Server 2003. ISA Server 2006, when installed on Windows Server 2003 SP1 or later, can use Quarantine Control, which is provided by the Routing and Remote Access Service of Windows Server 2003 and is limited to providing access control to VPN and remote access clients only. The service requires custom connection profiles on the clients, along with server-side scripts to check for compliance by remote access clients. The Quarantine Control Service for ISA Server does not allow for integration with the newer NAP service and Network Policy Server (NPS) services in Windows Server 2008 other than NPS providing RADIUS services to VPN clients using ISA Server as the VPN server.

> **MORE INFO** **ISA SERVER AND FOREFRONT TMG HELP**
>
> A site with helpful ideas that involve ISA Server is *http://www.isaserver.org*. This site is well maintained and well organized and offers a wealth of ideas about design, add-ons, and configuration in ISA Server.

> **NOTE** **ISA SERVER 2006, FOREFRONT TMG, AND WINDOWS SERVER 2008**
>
> ISA Server 2006, at the time of this writing, is not available for installation on Windows Server 2008 and is available as a 32-bit application server only. Forefront Security products are tailored for Windows Server 2008 and are available for 64-bit platforms.

Forefront TMG provides several enhanced capabilities compared to previous ISA Server products. Forefront TMG can provide the following additional features:

- Installation on Windows Server 2008 64 bit
- Web antimalware filtering for enhanced deep packet inspection in the application layer
- HTTPS inspection
- Email security
- Network Inspection System, which provides traffic inspection for exploits of Microsoft vulnerabilities
- Advanced Quarantine enhancements as well as VPN Quarantine capabilities

THIRD-PARTY FIREWALL PRODUCTS

With the security field growing at an increasing pace, third-party firewall products are plentiful. Many of these products fit a paradigm similar to Forefront TMG. Many of the major firewall product vendors have also included multiple feature sets in their firewall product offerings. This makes it even more attractive to pair a firewall product from one of these top-selling vendors with Forefront TMG. A common scenario is to use a firewall appliance for the perimeter firewall and a Forefront TMG cluster for the internal firewall. Many of these third-party products provide an integrated assortment of security services such as the following:

- Stateful firewall services
- Intrusion prevention services

- Antimalware services
- Application-layer firewall services

At a minimum, the firewall appliance should provide circuit-level services along with an inline intrusion prevention service module to ensure inspection at the application layer for inbound requests from the border network. Forefront products installed as the internal firewall can provide proxy, packet filtering, circuit-level firewall services, and application-layer inspection of packets originating from either the border network or the perimeter network for access to internal hosts or responses returned to internal clients.

Deploying Strategic Services in the Perimeter Network

The perimeter network was originally designed to contain web services for public use. Over time, the decision to deploy specific applications and services there has changed significantly. The perimeter network might contain not only web services but also many of the following suggested services:

- Application servers for extranets
- VPN servers for remote access
- Wireless access points to provide public wireless access in your enterprise and wireless local area networks (WLANs) for internal corporate use
- Remote Desktop (RD) Gateway role service
- Components of RADIUS to provide authentication for wireless access, VPNs, and application servers
- Online Certificate Status Protocol (OCSP) servers to provide timely information regarding the revocation status of a certificate in use

This list is not exhaustive but does describe the more commonly deployed services in the perimeter network. This lesson focuses on the Microsoft best practices for perimeter network design and server placement of these services.

Planning Web Services Deployment in the Perimeter Network

Web server services commonly deployed in the perimeter network consist of the following:

- Web servers for Internet and extranet access
- FTP servers
- Publicly accessible Domain Name System (DNS) servers

Web servers offer access over HTTP and HTTPS. Even custom applications built for delivery through a web server use the same ports, minimizing the number of ports to be opened through the perimeter firewall. This is the strength of using application servers running Microsoft Internet Information Services (IIS) 7.0 as the application platform for delivery.

Extranet application servers using Secure Sockets Layer (SSL) connections might require the services of an OCSP responder, a server responding to requests for certificate revocation similar to what is provided by a lookup on a certificate revocation list (CRL), although an OCSP request and response is less resource intensive and more timely concerning the currency of the information. An OCSP responder can be deployed in the perimeter network because there is usually little concern over security. The OCSP responder signs its response, and the one waiting for the response can check its validity by using the public key of the OCSP responder.

DNS servers deployed in the perimeter network provide name resolution for publicly accessible web services and should be restricted to providing responses only to DNS requests for those services. A host-based firewall that includes antimalware services along with the removal of all unnecessary services is part of the preliminary setup of a secured host in the perimeter zone.

These web server services should be deployed at the corporate site and can include an alternate site for site redundancy when providing a solution for a disaster recovery plan. Services at the alternate site should be provided the same considerations regarding security.

PLANNING IPV6 ACCESS FOR WEB SERVICES

Windows Server 2008 provides complete support for all related web services over IPv6 although no special consideration is required because all Internet-related services require an IPv4 address for appropriate access for the immediate future. Options for migration to IPv6 are already available in Windows Server 2008 for networks employing IPv6 alongside IPv4 for all web services.

Designing a Remote Access Strategy

In designing remote access, an enterprise administrator must consider all required avenues of access. The traditional methods of access have given way to various types of VPN connections and Remote Desktop connections. These two general categories involve many considerations. This portion of the lesson concentrates on deploying VPN servers and providing access for Remote Desktop clients.

Planning for VPN Remote Access Connections

As the enterprise administrator, you must make decisions concerning the following:

- Which VPN protocols for remote access are available?
- Which authentication methods should be supported when considering an eventual NAP deployment?
- How should VPN servers deployed for Internet and extranet access be secured?
- What public key infrastructure (PKI) support is needed for VPN access methods?
- How should NAP be integrated with VPN enforcement?

Each of these items has its own unique set of requirements and dependencies. A decision about one can affect the decisions about others. For instance, choosing to use authentication involving certificates can require a supporting PKI. You must then decide how this choice affects your deployment of a NAP solution. In addition, you might require multiple encryption or authentication protocols and services if you are supporting guest access, extranets with partner firms, and your own remote access clients. Each of these groups of users can have different requirements.

You might want to enforce a stringent security policy, but other factors always come into play. These factors, not necessarily in this order, include the following:

- Cost
- Compatibility with existing operating systems
- Compatibility with existing application services
- The inevitable politics involved with enforcing security features on guests and extranets

Designing a VPN Protocol Solution

Deciding which VPN protocols to use for your remote access policies depends on several issues such as these:

- Which operating systems do your VPN clients use?
- Which security requirements exist regarding encrypted communications?
- Which security policies exist to secure communication through your corporate firewall?
- Which authentication mechanisms are acceptable?
- Is there a need to deploy a PKI to support the VPN infrastructure?

VPN TUNNELING PROTOCOLS

Windows Server 2008 provides support for three tunneling protocols when configuring remote access connections:

- Point-to-Point Tunneling Protocol (PPTP)
- Layer 2 Tunneling Protocol (L2TP)
- Secure Sockets Tunneling Protocol (SSTP)

Windows Server 2008 R2 Routing and Remote Access (RRAS) supports the previously listed Windows Server 2008 RRAS tunneling protocols along with a new tunneling protocol named IPsec Tunnel Mode with Internet Key Exchange version 2 (IKEv2), also referred to as *VPN Reconnect*.

POINT-TO-POINT TUNNELING PROTOCOL

PPTP still provides a high level of security as a VPN tunneling protocol. Many of the past arguments concerning vulnerabilities were addressed long ago. Its simplicity of deployment as a solution is one of its greatest assets. It is well supported by the following operating systems: Microsoft Windows 2000 Professional, Windows 2000 Server, Windows XP, Windows Server 2003, Windows Vista, Windows 7, and Windows Server 2008. PPTP has garnered broad support from the IT industry as well as from many vendors who support its use within their products. PPTP is still considered by most security experts to be less than ideal for high-security deployments because authentication in most cases occurs outside of a secure encrypted tunnel. With the use of Extensible Authentication Protocol/Transport Layer Security (EAP-TLS) certificate-based authentication, these concerns are diminished somewhat but the level of complexity in your VPN design greatly increases.

PPTP, when used in a perimeter network, engenders some concerns when a NAT service is between a PPTP client and a server connection. The NAT service must include a NAT editor such as the one found in the Routing and Remote Access Service of Windows Server 2003 and Windows Server 2008. Because ISA Server 2004 and ISA Server 2006 both run on Windows Server 2003 and use the services of the Routing and Remote Access Service of Windows Server 2003, a NAT editor is also available for use through ISA Server. Forefront TMG also supports the use of PPTP clients behind the firewall by using its NAT editor.

> **NOTE USE OF NAT EDITORS**
>
> Most Microsoft administrators experienced in the use and configuration of VPNs using Microsoft's remote access solutions will usually tell you that PPTP is one of the easiest VPN protocols to configure because it almost feels like a Plug and Play protocol for VPNs. Use of NAT in the past many years has taught these same administrators that PPTP is not easy to configure through many firewall products. Microsoft includes NAT editors in its Windows Server 2003, Windows Server 2008, and Forefront TMG products that require some effort in their configuration to ensure inside PPTP clients can make successful outbound connections through firewall services offered in Microsoft products.

To secure the connections to the VPN server, establish inbound and outbound filters for all communication to ensure that only VPN traffic is allowed. Table 5-1 displays filters you should configure to ensure the security of the VPN server.

TABLE 5-1 PPTP Filters on Firewall for VPN Server Deployed in the Perimeter Network

FILTER DIRECTION	SOURCE PORT AND IP ADDRESS	DESTINATION PORT AND IP ADDRESS	FILTER ACTION
Inbound	Greater than TCP 1023 and source IP address (any) of client	TCP 1723 and IP address of perimeter interface of VPN server	Allows PPTP tunnel maintenance traffic from the PPTP client to the PPTP server
Inbound	IP 47 and Source IP address (any) of client	IP 47 and IP address of perimeter interface of VPN server	Defines the PPTP data tunnel from the PPTP client to the PPTP server

| Outbound | TCP Port 1723 and IP address of perimeter interface | TCP port of client request (any) and IP address of client (any) | Allows PPTP tunnel maintenance traffic from the PPTP server to the PPTP client |
| Outbound | IP 47 and IP address of perimeter interface | IP 47 and IP address of client (any) | Defines the PPTP data tunnel from the PPTP server to the PPTP client |

LAYER 2 TUNNELING PROTOCOL

L2TP provides a more secure connection than PPTP due to several aspects. L2TP provides the same user authentication that PPTP provides and computer authentication using IPsec authentication. L2TP with IPsec uses 168-bit triple DES (3DES) encryption for the data and provides per-packet data origin authentication, proving the identity of the user and providing data integrity and replay protection while providing a high level of confidentiality.

L2TP has some constraints, however. Every computer must have a computer certificate. The certificate used by the VPN server and the VPN client computer must come from the same trusted root certification authority (CA). If both the VPN server and the VPN client computer are members of a domain, both computers can use autoenrollment to acquire the necessary computer certificate. If one or both computers are not domain members, an administrator must request certificates on their behalf by using the CA Web enrollment tool. The administrator then needs to install the certificate on the computers by using a flash drive or some other external, but secure, access method. At the time of this writing, computer certificates cannot be issued to smart cards for use with L2TP certificate authentication of the tunnel.

> *NOTE* **PRESHARED KEY VERSUS A COMPUTER CERTIFICATE**
>
> Although you can use a preshared key instead of a computer certificate for L2TP/IPsec computer authentication, it is considered to be a test lab feature only. This is because using a preshared key is significantly less secure.

L2TP also has an issue with firewall services using NAT. L2TP requires NAT Traversal (NAT-T) to pass through a NAT. This means that an extra User Datagram Protocol (UDP) port, UDP 4500, must be open on the firewall. The clients connecting to a VPN server behind a firewall using L2TP must also support NAT-T. L2TP requires the filters in Table 5-2 for the perimeter firewall's Internet interface.

TABLE 5-2 L2TP Filters on Firewall for VPN Server Deployed in the Perimeter Network

FILTER DIRECTION	SOURCE PORT AND IP ADDRESS	DESTINATION PORT AND IP ADDRESS	FILTER ACTION
Inbound	Source IP address (any IP address) of client	UDP port 500 and IP address of perimeter interface of VPN server	Allows IKE traffic to the VPN server
Inbound	Source IP address (any IP address) of client	IP 47 and IP address of perimeter interface of VPN server	Allows IPsec NAT-T traffic to the VPN server
Inbound	Source IP address (any IP address) of client	IP 50 and IP address of perimeter interface of VPN server	Allows IPsec Encapsulating Security Protocol (ESP) traffic to the VPN server
Outbound	UDP port 500 and IP address of perimeter interface of VPN server	IP address (any IP address) of client	Allows IKE traffic from the VPN server
Outbound	UDP port 4500 and IP address of perimeter interface of VPN server	IP address (any IP address) of client	Allows IPsec NAT-T traffic from the VPN server
Outbound	IP 50 and IP address of perimeter interface of VPN server	IP address (any IP address) of client	Allows IPsec ESP traffic from the VPN server

SECURE SOCKETS TUNNELING PROTOCOL

SSTP is a new VPN tunnel supported by Windows Vista SP1, Windows 7, and Windows Server 2008. It uses SSL-encrypted HTTP connections for the VPN connection. More specifically, Point-to-Point Protocol (PPP) sessions are encrypted by SSL and transferred over an HTTP connection. This makes using SSTP a great benefit because most companies and organizations such as hotels, Internet cafes, and other Internet hotspots allow TCP port 443 for outbound access. Thus, changes to the firewall are not a great concern when implementing SSTP and deploying the VPN server in the perimeter network.

Another advantage is that SSTP is quite secure. An SSL tunnel is initially formed prior to the transfer of user credentials. SSTP also supports the EAP types, EAP-TLS, and Protected Extensible Authentication Protocol-Transport Layer Security (PEAP-TLS) for user authentication and the Microsoft Challenge Handshake Authentication Protocol (MS-CHAP) v2 authentication methods.

There are some drawbacks to using SSTP. It is supported on Windows Vista SP1 and Windows 7 as a VPN client only and on Windows Server 2008 as a VPN client or server. SSTP support will not be added to Windows XP, which still has a considerable installed user base. In addition, users must trust the root CA that issued the certificate to the VPN server. VPN clients must have the root CA certificate installed as one of their trusted root CAs to validate this certificate.

Allowing access to a VPN server offering SSTP is fairly simple. More than likely, your firewall is already set to allow access through TCP port 443 for HTTPS. An additional rule is needed only to ensure the passage of TCP port 443 from the border network into the perimeter network to the VPN server perimeter interface.

IPSEC TUNNEL MODE WITH IKEV2 AND VPN RECONNECT

Windows Server 2008 R2 introduces VPN Reconnect provided by support for IPsec Tunnel Mode with IKEv2. This protocol now provides for the VPN session to remain active in the event that an IP address change occurs during the connection. Loss of a VPN connection is a common issue with mobile wireless users when switching hotspots or changing from wireless to wired connections. The user, after the change in IP address, would be required to reestablish the VPN connection and then reopen applications that were closed with possible data loss due to the disruption caused by the loss of the original VPN connection.

This VPN connection requires a Windows 7 client and a Windows Server 2008 R2 VPN server. IKEv2 supports only client VPN connections and not site-to-site VPN connections. Other considerations when deploying the IKEv2 VPN tunneling protocol include the following:

- VPN server should be configured with a network connection to the Internet and a separate network connection to the intranet.
- VPN server has been joined to the domain.
- Configure routing on the VPN server to provide connectivity for the incoming remote access clients.
- Active Directory Certificate Services and Web Server (IIS) server roles for computer enrollment.
- Certificates need to be issued to the VPN server by using a certificate template configured with the Enhanced Key Usage option for Server Authentication
- Ensure the trusted root certificate is present on the VPN server and remote access clients.
- If EAP-based authentication will be used, the NPS server role is also required to be installed and an NPS policy configured to grant EAP-MSCHAPv2 authentication for IKEv2-based VPN connections.

VPN reconnect is enabled on the Windows 7 client by first configuring a VPN connection using the Set Up a New Connection or Network Wizard in the Network and Sharing Center. Reconfigure the VPN connection by selecting the IKEv2 option on the Security tab from the Type Of VPN drop-down menu. The VPN reconnect feature works for either IPv4 or IPv6 mobile connections as long as the Mobility check box is selected on the Advanced Settings for the VPN connection.

DIRECTACCESS: THE NO VPN SOLUTION

Administering remote access is one of the more complex duties of an enterprise administrator. Microsoft has enabled use of most of the standard-based VPN services available today through the RRAS role service in Windows Server 2008. DirectAccess adds one more solution in Windows Server 2008 R2.

DirectAccess enables remote users to connect to their intranet applications, websites, and enterprise shares without the use of a traditional VPN connection. A DirectAccess-enabled computer creates a seamless connection that is established the moment the user connects to the Internet. The user then has bidirectional connectivity to some or all of the enterprise resources normally available to a locally connected LAN user. The user is not required to set up the intermediate VPN connection, wait for it to be established, and possibly troubleshoot it. In addition, due to the bidirectional capabilities of the DirectAccess feature, enterprise administrators are able to manage systems remotely as if they were located within the local LAN. The enterprise administrator does not require the remote access client to maintain a VPN connection and the Internet connection for maintenance.

DirectAccess does have several selective requirements:

- Requires Windows 7 Enterprise or Windows 7 Ultimate for the client and Windows Server 2008 R2 for the server.
- One Windows Server 2008 R2 server configured as a DirectAccess server.
- DirectAccess clients must be members of the AD DS domain.
- A PKI to issue computer certificates for authentication and possibly health certificates for NAP interoperability.
- IPv6 must be enabled and configured on both the client and the server.
- IPsec is required to provide secure, flexible network connections.
- If Forefront UAG is not included in the solution, then a NAT64 device is used to provide connectivity to IPv4-only resources.

DirectAccess uses two IPsec-encrypted tunnels for its functionality. An initial tunnel is set up to manage the connection and access to resources for authentication, such as DNS servers, NAP if employed, a domain controller to authenticate the DirectAccess client computer, and the DirectAccess server to establish the connection. Certificates are used during this process to authenticate the computer and provide a health certificate from a *Health Registration Authority* (HRA), which is used to prove system health requirements mandated by the Network Policy Server and presented to the DirectAccess server. The second IPsec tunnel is initiated by the user logon process. The DirectAccess server, after successful authentication of the user, forwards the traffic between the DirectAccess client and intranet resources authorized for access by the DirectAccess user. Figure 5-5 displays a simplified overview of a DirectAccess connection showing the two IPsec tunnels, the client's access of Internet servers, and access to the enterprise intranet servers.

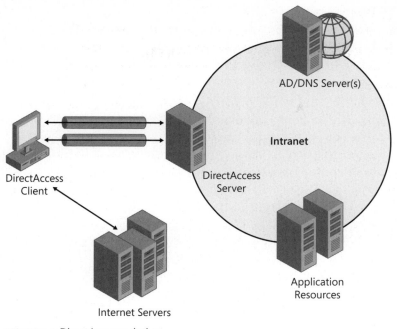

FIGURE 5-5 DirectAccess solution

Other complications can arise if the DirectAccess user is behind a firewall or proxy server preventing the initial DirectAccess tunnel from forming. Another protocol, Internet Protocol over Secure Hypertext Transfer Protocol (IP-HTTPS) is then automatically called on by the DirectAccess client to perform the attempted connection. If IP-HTTPS is used, the initial IPv6 traffic is encapsulated within an SSL connection for delivery to the DirectAccess server.

Normal VPN tunnels often require additional consideration for splitting the remote access user's requests for internal resource access and the user's Internet access. Split tunnel is often used to ensure communication is directed to the appropriate destination. DirectAccess employs DNS, Name Resolution Policy Table (NRPT), and network location detection to determine the separation of traffic between the Internet and the corporate network connected by IPsec tunnels.

To access intranet resources using IPv4 addressing, the DirectAccess solution requires the use of either IPv6 transition technologies, such as Teredo, 6to4 tunnels, or IntraSite Automatic Tunnel Addressing Protocol (ISATAP), or a NAT64 device acting as an IPv6-to-IPv4 translator. IPsec tunnels to the intranet resources could end the IPsec portion of the connection at the edge on the DirectAccess server or, more securely, end at each accessible resource on the intranet.

OTHER DEPLOYMENT CONSIDERATIONS FOR DIRECTACCESS

The requirements of allowing only Windows 7 clients and Windows Server 2008 R2 servers to participate in the use of DirectAccess will initially limit its use. Non-Windows clients and earlier Windows operating systems will still require the use of standardized VPNs. Also, DirectAccess only provides for user remote access connections. Site-to-site remote access connections will require the use of a VPN to provide the secure tunnels in those situations.

Deploying DirectAccess using Forefront UAG allows for easier enterprise deployments of DirectAccess. Forefront UAG incorporates into its management console a series of wizards designed to support DirectAccess tunnel options, Group Policy management, NAP interaction, and the DirectAccess Connectivity Assistant (DCA), which allows easy distribution of DCA policy to DirectAccess clients.

AUTHENTICATION PROTOCOLS

Windows Server 2008 provides support for quite a few authentication protocols. The list now includes the following:

- Password Authentication Protocol (PAP)
- MS-CHAP
- MS-CHAPv2
- PEAP-MSCHAPv2/EAP-MSCHAPv2
- EAP-TLS
- PEAP-TLS

The list has dwindled a little because support for Shiva Password Authentication Protocol (SPAP) and the Extensible Authentication Protocol-Message Digest have been removed as client choices from Windows Server 2008, Windows 7, and Windows Vista VPNs. It was thought that these two types of authentication provided little value in securing authentication.

> *NOTE* **MS-CHAP AND SPAP SUPPORT IN WINDOWS SERVER 2008 R2**
>
> In Windows Server 2008 R2, MS-CHAP (also known as MS-CHAPv1) and SPAP were still included in the Routing and Remote Access Microsoft Management Consoles (MMCs) Connection Policies, although EAP-MD5 is not available. Documentation at *http://technet .microsoft.com/en-us/library/bb726965.aspx#ECAA* states that support was removed for all three. Please note the last section that states the removal of certain technologies. From a VPN client perspective for Windows Vista, Windows 7, and Windows Server 2008 R2, EAP-MD5, MS-CHAP, and SPAP are no longer available as choices.

From a security perspective, do not choose PAP and MS-CHAP unless necessary to support an incompatible client. MS-CHAPv2 should be used only when strong passwords are enforced.

Among the supported EAP types, EAP-TLS and PEAP-TLS use certificate-based authentication. PEAP supports two EAP types, PEAP-TLS and PEAP-MSCHAPv2. When PEAP is used with the EAP-MSCHAPv2 type, passwords are used to authenticate the user for the connection. Once again, strong passwords should be enforced to ensure a higher level of security for the connection.

To provide support for certificates when employing certificate-based authentication with either EAP-TLS or PEAP-TLS, users require a user certificate on either a smart card or on their computers. Issuing a certificate through a smart card is not too difficult. Issuing certificates to users who are mostly remote to store on their computers requires one of three solutions:

- Have each user manually request a certificate through either the certificate authority Web enrollment service or the Certificates MMC snap-in.

- Have an administrator request a certificate on the user's behalf and manually install the certificate in the personal store on the user's computer.

- Use Group Policy to distribute a certificate to users.

Having each user perform the request individually solves the dilemma of distributing certificates in most cases. The issue becomes a support problem if too many users need assistance or other technical difficulties arise. The final answer, to use Group Policy, is probably the most efficient, but can also be problematic. Some laptop users might not be connected to the network, or the computer itself might not be part of the corporate domain for one reason or another. In most cases, Group Policy works for the majority of users. Traveling users using laptops that are part of the domain need to connect and log on to the domain as part of the process of acquiring a certificate through Group Policy.

Another concern when setting up the environment for remote access connectivity is whether NAP will be instituted in the near future. For VPN connections, NAP includes a VPN enforcement point, which requires a connecting client to use one of the PEAP types for authentication. In choosing which PEAP type to use, PEAP-MSCHAPv2 or PEAP-TLS, PEAP-TLS holds the advantage as a superior authentication protocol for two reasons:

- It uses a certificate, rather than a password, for authentication, as previously noted..

- PEAP-TLS is superior to EAP-TLS because the exchange of certificates for authentication takes place after the client and the server have created an encrypted tunnel.

The disadvantage of using PEAP-TLS instead of PEAP-MSCHAPv2 is that all users now require a certificate, whereas PEAP-MSCHAPv2 requires only a server certificate. An issue in using PEAP-MSCHAPv2 concerns the certificate issued to the VPN server performing the authentication. If the certificate issued to it is from one of the established trusted public root CAs, no work is required other than purchasing the certificate itself. If the certificate is issued from a stand-alone root CA by the internal enterprise PKI, then a copy of its certificate needs to be installed on all computers connecting to the VPN using PEAP-MSCHAPv2 for authentication. If the certificate is issued from an enterprise CA, the certificate for the root CA must be distributed through the Web enrollment, the Certificates console, or another manual method.

Designing Secure VPN Server Deployment

When considering the placement of VPN servers, it has become customary for the VPN servers to be deployed in the perimeter network. Although there are established guidelines for deploying the VPN server outside of the perimeter firewall, it is considered a best practice to deploy the VPN server inside the perimeter zone, behind the perimeter firewall. The previous IP filter tables, Tables 5-1 and 5-2, outline the best practices for opening up access to the VPN servers deployed inside the perimeter network.

If the branch offices need VPN connectivity, two choices are available:

- Direct VPN connectivity to VPN servers located at the branch offices
- Centralized management of VPN access to one main office and ensured VPN client access to resources located in their respective branch offices

VPN SERVER DEPLOYMENT AT BRANCH OFFICES

If VPN servers are to be deployed at the branch offices, you must give the same consideration to setting up access through the firewall there. The VPN server should be deployed in a perimeter network often termed a screened subnet, as Figure 5-6 displays. Availability of affordable firewalls, such as ISA Server, can provide a perimeter network and secure access to resources, such as a VPN server, making it easier to secure a collocated VPN server. Companies can standardize how branch office access is achieved to relieve the complications involved in planning each deployment.

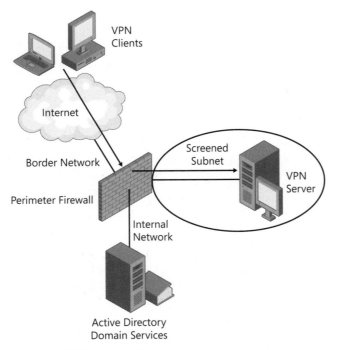

FIGURE 5-6 VPN server deployed in the screened subnet

CENTRALIZED MANAGEMENT OF VPN ACCESS

Clients accessing resources through VPN servers that are centrally located can still access resources anywhere within the enterprise. Because a VPN connection to a VPN client is essentially offering a local area network (LAN) connection remotely, a VPN client will also have access anywhere on that LAN where a normal wired LAN client has access. This is both an advantage and a plausible security issue.

The obvious advantage is the ease in offering resources to the remote client. The VPN client can be anywhere Internet access is available to gain access to data and application servers on your enterprise network in a secure manner. To mediate any possible security issues, the VPN server can enforce strict network routing rules to allow the client access to specific segments of the network. In addition, filter rules can be applied to the VPN connection to disallow a curious VPN client from wandering into areas of the network that are deemed out of bounds. Because a user with sufficient rights locally can administer his or her own routing tables, the VPN administrator needs to be aware that such users can circumvent simple security applied through routing rules. Inbound IP filters and policies applied to the VPN connection can disable a user's ability to browse networks that are not authorized by the connection.

✓ Quick Check

1. Which VPN solution can be used with computers running Windows XP?
2. Which VPN solution provides a solution allowing commonly used web-based protocols?

Designing a RADIUS Solution for Remote Access

In designing a VPN solution, authentication of VPN clients becomes a paramount concern. In deciding which protocols to use for the tunnel and which authentication protocols are configured for access, the next step is how to manage the authentication of those users.

Managing authentication services for multiple services and for multiple points of access for each of these services rapidly becomes a drain on an administrator's time. As the enterprise administrator, you can see the wisdom in centrally managing authentication and authorization of access to resources.

Microsoft has had an evolving RADIUS strategy ever since the introduction of Routing and Remote Access Service (RRAS) in Windows 2000 Server. Internet Authentication Service (IAS) was the next iteration and brought huge improvements. One of the advances was support for a RADIUS proxy. With Windows Server 2008, the VPN and RADIUS solutions are now part of its newly renamed NPS.

NPS encompasses many facets of remote access services. It provides the following services:

- RADIUS client
- RADIUS proxy
- RADIUS server
- RADIUS accounting
- VPN administration for access and polices
- Primary console for administering NAP services

Therefore, when designing your RADIUS solution for VPNs and remote access policies, think about eventually using NAP because NPS plays a central role in this feature.

Designing a RADIUS Solution for the Main Office

In designing a RADIUS solution, consider all the components of a RADIUS infrastructure that provide authentication, authorization, and accounting. Starting with the access clients and moving all the way through the RADIUS infrastructure to the back-end user database, an enterprise administrator must carefully plot the location of each of these services. Figure 5-7 displays a real RADIUS design from a high-level overview.

From this overall design, you can see that RADIUS can support authentication for a variety of services and a variety of access client and access servers. Users of web-based applications from either extranets with partners or publicly accessible application servers can be authenticated using the *RADIUS client* support built into ISA Server. VPN and dial-up clients can be authenticated through an NPS server configured as a RADIUS client. Finally, wireless clients, either guests or WLAN for the corporate environment, can also use the built-in RADIUS client support in wireless access points to relay RADIUS requests.

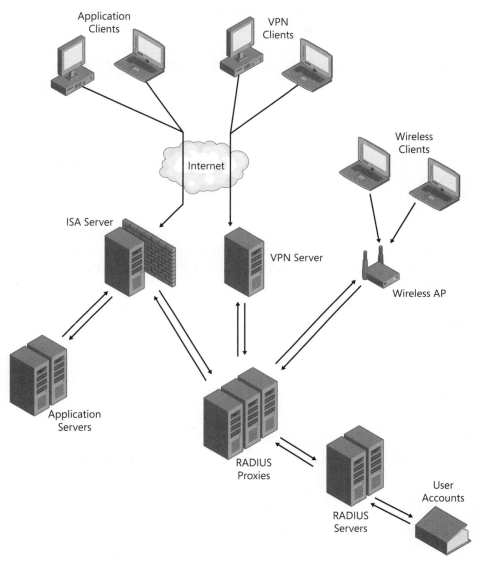

FIGURE 5-7 RADIUS infrastructure, support elements, and example application support

DEPLOYMENT LOCATION FOR RADIUS SERVICES

Securing your RADIUS solution involves deploying only the essential services in the perimeter network and placing the rest of the services in the secured, internal network. Using Figure 5-7 as a basis for this discussion, you would want to place only the following services in the perimeter network and deploy the rest of the services behind the internal firewall:

- ISA Server/Forefront TMG
- Application servers (probably in a screened subnet connected through Forefront TMG or Forefront UAG, leaving any SQL servers containing the data inside the trusted environment)
- VPN server
- Wireless access point
- RADIUS proxies

PLANNING RADIUS COMMUNICATION

ISA Server and Forefront TMG have built-in capabilities to forward authentication requests to a *RADIUS server* in order to centralize authentication for users of published web servers, web application servers, and Windows SharePoint Services websites. The application servers can exist in a screened subnet or in the perimeter network but have access only through an authenticated request from Forefront TMG. The data that the application servers draw on can be secured in SQL servers behind the internal firewall.

VPN servers with the NPS role installed can be set up as RADIUS clients and forward all requests to back-end *RADIUS proxies*. The VPN servers can use a RADIUS server group configuration to ensure high availability and load balancing of requests.

The wireless access points using 802.1x, WPA Enterprise, or WPA2 Enterprise authentication services act as RADIUS clients to forward all RADIUS requests through the RADIUS proxies. The RADIUS proxies then forward those requests to an internal RADIUS server.

LOAD BALANCING AND HIGH AVAILABILITY OF A RADIUS INFRASTRUCTURE

Using RADIUS proxies in your RADIUS design is a strong asset in a RADIUS solution for several reasons. There is a fine line between a RADIUS client and a RADIUS proxy. To the RADIUS client, the RADIUS proxy appears to be the RADIUS server where authentication would normally occur. Thus, the communication between the RADIUS clients and the RADIUS proxies is through the RADIUS protocol.

Typically, RADIUS clients do not have a reliable mechanism built into their client architecture for load balancing their requests across multiple RADIUS servers. Load balancing the RADIUS client requests is achieved by configuring some of the RADIUS clients to use specific RADIUS proxy servers as their primary RADIUS servers and configuring other RADIUS clients to use the remaining RADIUS proxy servers as their primary servers. Each of these two RADIUS client groups can then use the other's primary RADIUS server as its secondary RADIUS server.

This type of load balancing is sufficient for the front end of your RADIUS infrastructure. To load balance the back end, the RADIUS proxy servers load balance their requests by round robin with servers of a RADIUS server group.

NPS role service also provides the VPN server role. You can load balance the VPN service, if necessary, by creating a Network Load Balancing (NLB) cluster and ensuring that you set the port rule to single or network affinity. The port range for the port rule should encompass the proper TCP port (1723) for PPTP, the UDP ports (500/4500) for L2TP, and TCP port (443) for SSTP.

> **MORE INFO** **IP ADDRESS AND SUBJECT NAME CONFIGURATION FOR SSTP NLB CLUSTER**
>
> To ensure proper setup for NLB when using SSTP, the certificate must be the same computer certificate on all VPN servers in the NLB cluster. You can find additional information regarding IP address and subject name configuration for the SSTP NLB cluster at *http://support.microsoft.com/kb/947029/en-us*.

Designing a RADIUS Solution for Branch Office Remote Access

If your deployment design calls for distributed VPN remote access, the VPN servers can route their RADIUS requests to the central office's RADIUS server. You can use RADIUS proxies if necessary. To secure the RADIUS communication from the VPN servers through a public network, such as the Internet, you can use VPNs linking the branch offices to the main office to carry the RADIUS communication. Because the RADIUS protocol encrypts only select portions of the RADIUS protocol communication, be sure to encrypt the entire RADIUS communication pathway whenever you need RADIUS communication over great distances. This is another advantage that ISA Server delivers when you use it to secure access to the branch offices. ISA Server can also establish the secure VPN that can carry the RADIUS communication between the branch office VPN servers and the main office RADIUS servers.

Scaling RADIUS Authentication for Multiple Domains and Forests

If your enterprise requires you to authenticate VPN clients from different forests, you have another issue. RADIUS by default provides authentication for users from the same realm of which the RADIUS server is a member. To provide RADIUS authentication for multiple realms, trust relationships must be constructed, or a RADIUS proxy can enable authentication.

For multiple domains of the same forest, no extra trusts are required. For multiple domains with no trusts or one-way trusts, either create the needed trusts or employ a RADIUS proxy.

A RADIUS proxy can resolve the issue if trust relationships are not possible. A RADIUS server in a domain foreign to that of the user receives a RADIUS request for authentication. The RADIUS server without trusts with the foreign domain in place cannot forward the request to an appropriate realm to authenticate the user. By implementing a RADIUS proxy in the communication pathway, the RADIUS requests from the RADIUS clients in specific realms can be proxied to the correct RADIUS servers to provide a successful authentication for the user. Figure 5-8 displays the design details.

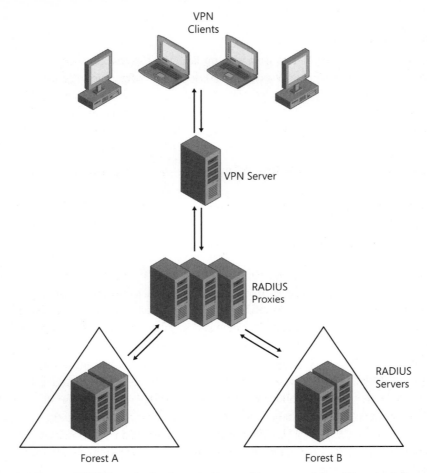

FIGURE 5-8 RADIUS proxies implemented to provide a successful multiforest solution

RADIUS Enhancements in Windows Server 2008 R2

Windows Server 2008 R2 includes several enhancements to RADIUS features provided by NPS role service. These features improve management and monitoring as well as upgrade and migrations options.

The NPS templates feature allows an administrator to provide consistent configuration elements of an NPS solution to be exported and reused on another server running NPS. The templates are managed within the NPS console on a node for Template Management. You are capable of exporting and importing configuration elements such as the following:

- RADIUS clients
- Shared secrets

- Remote RADIUS servers
- IP filters
- Health Policies
- Remediation server groups

Also included within the improved NPS console is an update to the *Accounting* node that contains an Accounting Configuration Wizard. The Accounting Configuration Wizard will guide an NPS administrator in configuring RADIUS logging to a text file, a SQL Server database, or both. The wizard is also capable of configuring the SQL Server database used for logging so that very little SQL Server expertise is necessary to complete the setup.

PRACTICE   **Designing a RADIUS Solution for a Midsize Enterprise**

You are the enterprise administrator at Contoso, Ltd. Contoso is a midsize corporation with offices located in the southeastern United States and the Caribbean. As an enterprise administrator, you are charged with the task of constructing a VPN solution for all branch offices and the main office in Fort Lauderdale, Florida, for Contoso.

With branch offices in Atlanta, Georgia; New Orleans, Louisiana; Orlando, Florida; St. Thomas in the Virgin Islands; and Grand Cayman in the Cayman Islands, Contoso employs more than 2,000 employees. Offices in the United States are connected by the corporate wide area network (WAN). Offices in the Caribbean are connected by a site-to-site VPN connection to the Fort Lauderdale office.

A single Active Directory Domain Services (AD DS) forest with two domains currently exists for Contoso. The two domains are *contoso.com* and *caribbean.contoso.com*. The Grand Cayman branch office is a recent acquisition from a competing firm, Fabrikam, Inc. Fabrikam has one Active Directory forest with one domain, *fabrikam.com*. You have already moved all Fabrikam domain controllers to the Fort Lauderdale office in anticipation of centralized management. The branch office at Grand Cayman is being sent a read-only domain controller (RODC) for secure local authentication.

An overall goal is to provide a secure and efficient remote access solution for users in all offices. Certificate authentication of both users and computers is required for the remote access solution instead of the current user password-only authentication provided by MS-CHAP. No dial-up services are offered because all users should connect to their offices through the Internet. Remote access is administered by each office. Administration of remote access policies must be simplified and duplicated on every VPN server. The remote access setup must allow users to authenticate to VPN servers at any of the branch offices or the main office.

Contoso wishes to enforce a level of health for all computers connecting through the VPN. Initially, only a monitored solution is needed to determine the extent of the security problems with VPN clients.

All domains are run internally by a mixture of Windows Server 2003 and Windows Server 2008 domain controllers. All VPN servers are running on Windows Server 2003.

EXERCISE 1 Design the VPN Solution

In this exercise, you review the current enterprise and, based on the requirements for the new remote access solution, plan a new solution.

1. What are important factors in the current environment to consider when forming a remote access solution?

   - Multiple forests with no established trusts between them

   - Management's desire to simplify the distributed management of the current authentication scheme used for remote access

   - Use of the Internet for all remote access connections

   - Employment of the highest security by all connections, implying a VPN connection

   - Security requirements to use a certificate-based authentication service

2. Which authentication protocols can you choose? Why?

   - EAP-TLS and PEAP-TLS are the only authentication protocols that provide certificate-based solutions.

3. Which VPN protocol should you use?

   - L2TP, because it will provide the security required for both the computer and the user. SSTP provides a secure and encrypted tunnel using only a server certificate.

EXERCISE 2 Design the RADIUS Solution

1. What are the primary considerations in moving the VPN connection toward a RADIUS solution in line with Contoso's overall goals?

   - Windows Server 2003 VPN servers need to be upgraded to Windows Server 2008.

   - In the RADIUS solution, you must consider that a NAP solution will ultimately be deployed.

   - Remote access is currently administered in a distributed fashion. Central administration of remote access policies is a primary goal.

2. Which components are required of a RADIUS solution for each branch office and for the main office?

   - For all U.S.-based branch offices, only a VPN server is necessary because it will act as the RADIUS client, forwarding the authentication requests to the Fort Lauderdale–based RADIUS proxy servers.

   - For all Caribbean branch offices, only a VPN server is necessary because it, too, will act as a RADIUS client by forwarding the authentication requests to the Fort Lauderdale–based RADIUS proxy servers.

   - At the Fort Lauderdale main office, you need a hierarchy of VPN servers acting as RADIUS clients forwarding requests to RADIUS servers, along with RADIUS proxy servers receiving requests from the Cayman Islands, to forward those requests to the appropriate RADIUS servers in the appropriate domain.

Lesson Summary

- Perimeter networks serve as the external barrier between the unsecured Internet and the secure internal network.

- Servers deployed in the perimeter network service direct requests from public computers. Servers in the perimeter network are semiprotected by a perimeter firewall.

- Servers containing sensitive data, such as SQL database servers, should be located on the internal network.

- Network Policy Server (NPS) has replaced Internet Authentication Server (IAS) to provide authentication, authorization, and accounting for RADIUS, management of connection request policies, and network connection policies.

- Computer certificates can be distributed through Group Policy for managed computers.

- Newer remote access technologies, such as VPN Reconnect and DirectAccess, exist for companies adopting Windows 7 desktops.

- VPN servers providing the initial point of access for VPN clients should be deployed in the perimeter network. A VPN server can provide the authentication or forward the authentication request to a central location by using RADIUS.

- RADIUS can provide centralized authentication, authorization, and accounting for remote access, 802.1x, and application services.

- A RADIUS configuration involves an access client (which is actually an access server) that forwards the authentication request to a RADIUS server or a RADIUS proxy. If a RADIUS proxy is involved, it also acts much like a RADIUS client and forwards the request to a RADIUS server.

- The RADIUS clients and the RADIUS proxy are usually deployed in the perimeter networks.

Lesson Review

You can use the following questions to test your knowledge of the information in Lesson 1, "Perimeter Networks and Remote Access Strategies." The questions are also available on the companion CD if you prefer to review them in electronic form.

> **NOTE ANSWERS**
>
> Answers to these questions and explanations of why each answer choice is correct or incorrect are located in the "Answers" section at the end of the book.

1. Which of the following performs RADIUS authentication?

   A. Access client

   B. Access server

   C. RADIUS proxy

   D. RADIUS server

2. Which of the following does not describe an appropriate function of a RADIUS proxy?

   A. Processing requests from access servers and forwarding them to a RADIUS server

   B. Processing incoming connection attempts from access clients

   C. Load balancing RADIUS requests among servers of the RADIUS server group

   D. Providing support for multiforest authentication

3. Which of the following are true statements regarding authentication protocols used for remote access? (Choose all that apply.)

   A. EAP-TLS uses only the server certificate to create secure communication between an authenticating client and the authentication server prior to the computer authenticating.

   B. With PEAP-TLS, the computer and server certificates are exchanged over a secure encrypted tunnel created by only the server certificate.

   C. MS-CHAPv2 uses only a user password to authenticate the user attempting a remote access connection.

   D. MS-CHAPv2 provides for mutual authentication of client and server.

Lesson 2: Designing Network Access Policy and Server and Domain Isolation

The IT industry long ago anticipated the issue of network vulnerability due to problematic computers connecting to the network and has been furiously investigating solutions to physically enforce company security policies. Network Access Control (NAC) was created to combat this very issue. NAC provides a framework for vendors to produce services and features that can interrogate a computer prior to a connection to the secure, internal network and ensure a computer's compliance with stated health requirements and security settings.

Microsoft has introduced its version of controlling network access with NAP, which provides an enforcement service for health requirement policies prior to network access. NAP offers services, components, and an application programming interface (API) that provide an inherent solution for ensuring the health of servers and networks running Windows Server 2008 and computers running Windows 7, Windows Vista, and Windows XP SP3 as clients.

> **After this lesson, you will be able to:**
> - Describe NAP and the various scenarios for its implementation.
> - Describe the architecture and components of NAP.
> - Identify purposes for specific NAP enforcement methods.
> - Describe the process for implementing NAP policies.
>
> **Estimated lesson time: 45 minutes**

Network Access Protection Overview

NAP provides a platform for validating the health of computer systems prior to allowing access to protected networks. In doing so, a level of assurance can be attained that a computer has at least been "inspected" prior to accessing the private network every time a new connection is made. The validation a computer undergoes can now be logically enforced.

Prior to NAP, a typical connection from an external computer would involve a client connecting across a public network, such as the Internet, by using a VPN connection. The client connection would initially pass through a firewall or be forwarded by a proxy using the appropriate communication ports required by the chosen security protocol. An authentication service would then examine the credentials of the remote access client. If the credentials were successfully authenticated, the client would be connected to whatever portion of the protected network the connection was previously set up to accomplish.

This scenario has a major flaw. If the remote access client is exactly who it purports to be, provides all the necessary credentials appropriately, and performs only the tasks on the private network that the connection was set up to do, would there still be a problem? Maybe. Suppose the remote access client performs unintended service requests, discovery, research, or—worse—invasive software installations without the knowledge of the user of the computer making the remote access connection. This has become one of the primary reasons for implementing a NAP solution.

REAL WORLD

Paul Mancuso

After spending a considerable amount of time, effort, and money, you have deployed the following security services across an entire network:

- A top-of-the-line perimeter firewall device
- An antivirus module inside the firewall device whose services you have configured to check for updates once every hour
- An automated update service for workstations and servers to call on periodically for updates to the operating system and installed applications
- An enterprise antimalware service that installed antimalware agents on all client workstations and servers within the environment, with centralized management for setting and configuring changes and updating installed software and agents on deployed computers

Feeling that the enterprise has a reasonable level of security, you go home and think that tomorrow should be a relatively peaceful day.

In the evening, a salesman visiting a branch office connects his laptop to the protected network. The salesman's laptop is considered safe merely because it is corporate property. A worm that was released into the wild that day had infected the corporate offices of another corporation, where the salesman had plugged the laptop in while delivering a presentation. The worm can now perform functions inside the network from a device considered to be a secure system. Tomorrow comes, and virus reports are coming out of the woodwork.

Several factors could have caused the salesman's laptop to become infected. First, it is presumed that the salesman does not alter the basic security settings of either the security software or the operating system. Also, the laptop is part of the domain; internal group policies were set to ensure the timely scheduling of updates to either the operating system or the security software on all computers, including those the salesman uses. This last presumption leads to missed updates when the salesman is traveling and is not connected to the network.

These periodic lapses in acquiring updates provide opportunities for infections when the salesman connects the laptop to unknown environments. The salesman's laptop can acquire all kinds of Trojan horse programs, viruses, and worms. The salesman travels back to the office, plugs the infected laptop into the protected network, and unknowingly unleashes the malicious programming on the laptop into the protected network. The salesman has bypassed all the security precautions the enterprise administrator has painstakingly set up in the network.

With a NAP solution, the possibilities of a traveling employee or guest unleashing an infection into your secured network are reduced. The standard communication flow from a computer being introduced to a network for its initial connection to the network would be altered to pass through a perimeter network as the components of the NAP platform engage. The NAP platform would now involve an entire NAP ecosystem with the connection request of an external client now referred to as a NAP client. The perimeter network would still include the same security services and devices as before, but now the NAP client's request for access takes a detour while the various components of the NAP platform engage to determine the health status of the connecting client. Figure 5-9 shows the difference between a traditional remote access connection and one involving a NAP platform.

Figure 5-9 shows that not only are NAP components now involved in the communication flow, but also that the NAP client might be restricted to an external network referred to as the remediation network, where additional servers using health resources update the client and bring it into compliance.

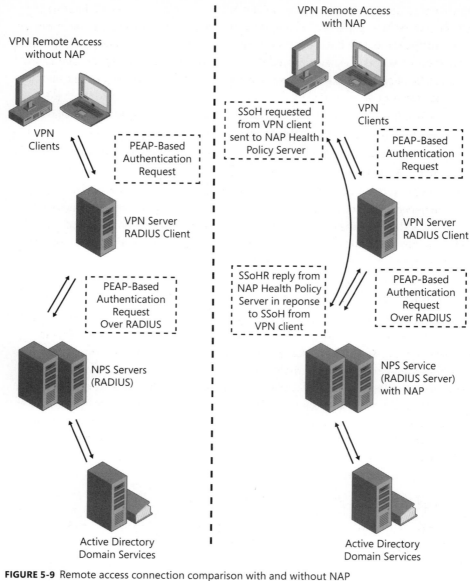

FIGURE 5-9 Remote access connection comparison with and without NAP

A complete NAP solution involves three distinct features:

- Health state validation
- Health policy compliance
- Limited access

Health state validation is the process of validating a computer's health and determining its compliance. If the NAP platform is configured for a remediation network, a noncompliant computer is restricted to only the remediation network's subnet until it meets compliance. If the NAP platform has been initially implemented with logging only to quantify compliance issues, the health compliance of a computer is logged, and it is allowed to proceed with the normal connection routine.

To monitor and possibly enforce health policy requirements, administrators create health policies. The health policy component is the heart of a NAP solution. Health policies mandate the level of software updates, operating system build, antivirus revision, and firewall features implemented, and many other possible health compliance factors.

When computer systems do not meet the level of health compliance necessary to connect to the private network, an administrator can mandate one of two outcomes, either to allow the connection and log the noncompliant issues or to shunt the connection to a remediation network to configure and update any noncompliant aspect of the computer. This is the limited-access feature of NAP.

> **NOTE** **NETWORK ACCESS QUARANTINE**
>
> Limited access has some similarities to Network Access Quarantine Control, but only in one principal feature: limiting access for noncompliant computers when making dial-up and VPN connections. Limited access, when implemented with a NAP platform, provides more capability and a standardized structure. This structure facilitates the addition of third-party enhancements and services. NAP also extends beyond VPN and dial-up communication to include protection when computer systems connect on the LAN. For more information about the older Network Access Quarantine Control, please visit the Cable Guy article on Network Access Quarantine Control at *http://technet.microsoft.com/en-us/library /bb877976.aspx.*

Overview of NAP Infrastructure

The NAP infrastructure for all types of enforcement provides a similar architectural overview, as displayed in Figure 5-10. Only the devices and regions of interest to a NAP solution are pictured.

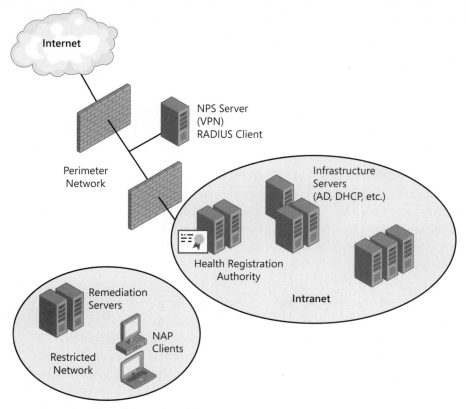

FIGURE 5-10 Overview of the NAP architecture

- The Internet lies outside the perimeter network and is separated by the perimeter firewall.

  VPN clients access the internal network from this region.

- The perimeter network is segregated by a perimeter and an internal firewall.

  VPN servers reside here and provide the initial point of enforcement for a *NAP VPN enforcement point*. For security purposes, no other NAP service is needed in this location.

- The restricted network is logically separated from the intranet for computers that, although having passed authentication for the NAP enforcement points that require authentication, have not yet acquired the necessary authorization to access the secure intranet. Servers deployed here can include quite a range of NAP support services:

  - The usual DNS, Windows Internet Name Service (WINS), Active Directory domain controllers, and Dynamic Host Configuration Protocol (DHCP) servers, along with other supporting network infrastructure devices, can be deployed.

  - Servers supporting software updates, such as Windows Server Update Services (WSUS) SP3 or WSUS server role on Windows Server 2008, can be deployed.

- For wired switches employing 802.1x enforcement, any switch ports can be associated logically with the restricted network.
- For wireless access points employing 802.1x enforcement, the entire access point might be logically associated with the restricted network because, at any time, it can be servicing compliant and noncompliant computers.

- The intranet is considered the secured network for most NAP enforcement methods and contains the corporate environment. NAP IPsec enforcement includes an additional logical boundary between two of its zones that is necessary for IPsec enforcement operation.
  - The boundary network is where HRA servers and, possibly, NAP CAs, NPS servers, and IPsec remediation servers reside.
  - The secure network is where the remaining portion of all NAP enforcement components resides. These components are the NAP health policy servers, the health requirement servers, the RADIUS proxy servers, and the NPS servers' endpoints. The *System Health Validators* (SHVs), which are used by the Health policies to define an acceptable health status, are configured on the NAP policy servers.

Windows Server 2008 R2 includes an enhancement to configuring SHVs. Multiconfiguration SHVs allow an SHV to be configured with multiple settings depending on the type of NAP enforcement. This allows Health policies to select the same SHVs but specify different sets of health requirements depending on the type of connection. For instance, an IPsec enforcement policy might contain an SHV that requires antispyware to be enabled, but that same SHV can be configured in a VPN enforcement policy to not only be enabled but to also require a specific signature status.

Where NAP Works

NAP can be implemented in any scenario in which a computer or network device has left a network and requires a new connection when brought back to the network. The following are specific scenarios of this type of event:

- Desktop computers that have been dormant for periods of time
- Laptops for roaming users
- Personal desktops and laptops of corporate users when connecting to the network to retrieve email and other data
- Laptops of guests
- Laptops and desktops from users of partner firms connected by an extranet

This list includes the general categories in which a NAP solution would provide a level of assurance about the health of a connected computer. Due to the diversity of these categories, the same level of enforcement of noncompliant computers might not be possible in all situations. Computers that are unmanaged, such as partner computers, home computers, laptops, and those of guests, would be sent to the restricted network and might not be required to undergo remediation, but would not be allowed into the private network. Managed computers provided by the corporation could institute automatic remediation for any of its computers moved into the restricted network. Options to remediate would vary, depending on the situation.

Considerations for NAP Enforcement

When deliberating between the types of NAP enforcement methods to institute within your network, you need to know the strengths and weaknesses of each method. How does each method deal with computers that are not NAP-capable? What is required in each method to administer unmanaged computers (computers not part of the internal AD DS)? In planning a NAP solution, consider that all the NAP enforcement methods have one or more of the following aspects:

- NAP does not stop attackers.
- NAP, to some degree, implies a trust with the NAP client.
- NAP does not remove harmful software from connecting computers.
- NAP should be treated as an assurance feature.

NAP cannot stop an attacker. A malicious user, whether an employee, guest, or outside user, might provide all the necessary compliance for access to your network but still launch an attack when inside your network.

NAP indirectly assumes that the client has not provided false settings, configurations, or modifications to installed software to attain a false positive of compliance. Remember, you are essentially asking the computer owner whether everything on the computer is fine and confirming that he or she has not falsified, concealed, or knowingly allowed anyone to configure or install software on this computer. Does this sound similar to the security warnings you might hear a dozen times an hour at any airport?

NAP provides a health statement based on the appearance of sound security configurations, settings, and installed software. It does not scan the computer for malicious software but, rather, assumes that the verified health state of a computer means that another subsystem or configuration on an installed security software application performs that feature.

Finally, NAP is an assurance feature. You are determining that the computers connecting to your network and communicating with the secure internal environment have applied the necessary security precautions to prevent an outbreak. Remember, if someone with malicious intent were to circumvent your NAP solution, the assurance that all other computers have complied with your NAP policies will help deter an attacker from damaging your environment or possibly acquiring sensitive information. As an enterprise administrator, realize that your NAP solution was not meant to stop an employee or would-be attacker intent on stealing information; that is not the role a NAP infrastructure is meant to play.

EXAM TIP

NAP is an ideal solution to determine that the following health requirements are fulfilled:

- Windows Firewall is enabled
- Antivirus and Antispyware software is installed, enabled, and up to date
- Microsoft Update Services is enabled
- The most recent Microsoft Updates are installed

Planning NAP IPsec Enforcement

When looking for the strongest enforcement method to apply within your network, NAP IPsec enforcement provides the most robust and tamper-resistant solution compared to all other NAP enforcement methods. IPsec enforcement has these advantages:

- Tightly controlled enforcement that not even the local administrator is capable of bypassing
- Upgrades to network infrastructure devices such as hubs, switches, and routers to support NAP are unnecessary
- Granular control to network access
- Easier avenue to end-to-end encryption of sensitive communications

Even by manipulating the settings and the configuration of the local computer, administrators cannot bypass health certificates issued by the HRA. Because all other computers are also protected by the same means, there is no way to subvert this requirement. Introducing new switches or other network devices provides no means around the required legitimate health certificate to communicate with hosts expecting the certificate during the IPsec negotiation.

IPsec works at layer 3 and uses a logical connection that is above the physical layers in the network; bypassing it would require modification or extensive reconfiguration of physical hardware.

IPsec allows an administrator to control communication pathways end to end. An administrator can create hardened IPsec policies that dictate source and destination IP addresses along with source and destination ports that are allowed for communication and must be encrypted. IPsec enforcement can also stringently control access to the network but use a general approach to managing communication. If you use IPsec enforcement to tightly control access to the secure network, you have already taken a large leap toward encrypting sensitive traffic within your environment.

The disadvantages of an IPsec enforcement solution deserve serious consideration as well:

- It requires creation and maintenance of network zones for the logical separation of network communication.
- It requires the establishment of an internal PKI. If one already exists, it might need a minor overhaul if its creator did not anticipate the additional load that an IPsec enforcement solution will incur.

- It requires another series of servers, which must be managed for configuration, load balancing, and high availability. Loss of the ability to issue health certificates would mean a catastrophic loss of communication within the environment.

When weighing the advantages and disadvantages of a NAP solution using IPsec enforcement, an organization has to consider the increased security that would be provided. IPsec enforcement provides not only the direct benefits offered by a NAP solution, but also the increased benefits of data confidentiality when communicating throughout the network environment.

Designing NAP IPsec Enforcement

When planning NAP IPsec enforcement for any organization, you need to establish the security zones first and determine which services to offer in the boundary network. The three security zones for an IPsec solution are the following:

- Restricted network
- Boundary network
- Secure network

RESTRICTED NETWORK

The restricted network, also referred to as the remediation network, is not the same as the perimeter network. The restricted network is a select network where noncompliant computers have limited access to services to perform remediation. Computers placed into the restricted network consist of either noncompliant NAP clients or non-NAP-capable clients. For IPsec enforcement, the restricted network includes only these devices.

Computers in the restricted network can initiate communication with computers in the restricted and boundary networks. Neither type of communication is protected by IPsec. Computers in all three networks, however, can initiate communication with computers in the restricted network. This communication is not protected by IPsec either.

Computers that are not NAP-compliant have already attempted communication with an HRA and have received a System Statement of Health Response (SSoHR) that contains the Statement of Health Responses (SoHRs) stating which *system health agents* (SHAs) are non-compliant. The non-NAP-compliant computer in the restricted network will initiate contact with servers in the boundary network to perform remediation. After remediation has been performed, the non-NAP-compliant computer will try again to attain a health certificate. The computer will go through the process of accumulating, across all SHAs, a *Statement of Health* (SoH) and submit a System Statement of Health (SSoH) to an HRA. The HRA, by using SHVs, will process all SoHs on the SSoH to formulate its SSoHR.

When it receives the SSoHR that shows the NAP client as compliant, the HRA also issues a health certificate so that the NAP client is now part of the secure network and initiates IPsec-authenticated communication with computers in either the boundary network or the secure network.

Non-NAP-capable computers are those of guests and other unsupported operating systems, such as any version of Windows earlier than Windows XP SP3, Apple Macintosh computers, and UNIX computers. A guest computer can be NAP capable but, because it is unmanaged (not part of AD DS), it will more than likely be treated like a non-NAP-capable computer unless network policies dictate otherwise.

BOUNDARY NETWORK

The boundary network contains computers responsible for remediation and for the HRAs; support services such as DNS, AD DS, and DHCP servers; WSUS; and possibly the NAP CAs. Because the boundary network requires communication from computers residing in the restricted and secure networks, IPsec policies should allow for IPsec-authenticated traffic and for unauthenticated traffic. Computers in the boundary network should be managed computers. This enables them to receive their IPsec policies and changes to those policies through Group Policy.

Boundary servers, when communicating with computers in the restricted network, allow unauthenticated communication because computers in the restricted network do not contain the necessary health certificates. When boundary servers communicate with servers in the restricted network, IPsec-authenticated traffic is required.

There is a twist to this last statement. The boundary computers themselves are the ones that offer the update services, have the necessary configuration for compliance, and are part of the NAP components. To ensure that they are capable of initiating IPsec-authenticated communication, they also require a health certificate. To provide these computers with a health certificate, create an IPsec NAP exemption group with membership that includes all the computers of the boundary network. Configure a Group Policy setting that sets the NAP IPsec exemption group for certificate autoenrollment to acquire the necessary health certificate. Because the computers of the exemption group need to hold onto this certificate for the period of time they are performing their services, ensure that the template used to issue the certificate has been set for an extended period of time.

Computers from the restricted network as well as the computers in the boundary network need authentication services. Domain controllers located in the boundary network should be RODCs.

SECURE NETWORK

The secure network includes all computers that have passed health validation and have acquired a health certificate. The remaining portion of the NAP components related to IPsec enforcement also resides here. These components consist of the following:

- NAP Health Policy servers
- Health Requirement servers
- Root CAs
- RADIUS proxy servers

Computers within this network should be managed computers (part of AD DS). This enables them to acquire their IPsec policies and any configuration changes to your NAP environment through Group Policy.

Scaling NAP IPsec Enforcement for Small Environments

When deploying components for NAP IPsec enforcement, you have the opportunity to decide which components can be installed together. In smaller environments, it might be appropriate to consolidate several services on one computer. The issue becomes deciding which services to install together.

The HRA must be able to support unprotected communication from NAP clients, and you should, therefore, install the HRA in the boundary network. Because the load on the HRA in a small environment might not be that heavy, you might decide to install it on a computer that has one or more of the following services other computers in the boundary network also need:

- RODCs
- NPS configured with NAP Health Policies
- NAP CA

If your environment is expected to grow, it would be wise to move some of these components to another server. You can then assume that the server installed with the HRA would be deployed in the boundary network, and another computer with the remaining services would be deployed in the secure network.

> **IMPORTANT** **SPLITTING THE HRA AND THE NAP HEALTH POLICY SERVER ROLE**
>
> If you split the HRA and the NAP Health Policy Server role to two computers, you still need to install the NPS role on the HRA computer. Then configure a RADIUS server group and a connection request policy for the local NPS service to forward requests to the remote RADIUS server group in the secure network.

Administrators of extremely small sites of 15 or fewer computers might consider employing Forefront TMG. Forefront TMG can create a site-to-site VPN link to the main office boundary network. The connection from the VPN server in the boundary network can be treated like any other local connection requiring IPsec enforcement to obtain a certificate initially. After a computer at the remote office has obtained a health certificate, IPsec rules can be managed granularly to ensure that the branch office computer is able to communicate only with the necessary services at the remote office, through the site-to-site VPN, and in the boundary network for remediation and renewal of certificates. Forefront TMG would require a certificate as well and should probably be included in the IPsec exemption group. Ensure that a computer certificate is issued to the computer running Forefront TMG for an extended period of time.

Scaling NAP IPsec Enforcement for Larger Environments

For larger environments, several components require a thorough design review to ensure high availability and load balancing of specific components. You can begin by deciding which of the following services will be installed individually on at least two computers in the boundary network at the corporate office:

- HRA
- RODC
- Remediation server services
- Subordinate NAP CA
- Configuring the use of Databaseless CA for the NAP CA

By providing fault tolerance for the HRA, the RODCs, and the NAP CA, you are ensuring a healthy environment. Remember that by employing IPsec enforcement, you are required to have these services running constantly. If one or more of these services become unavailable, health certificates will expire, and communication within the network will fail. Ensuring the ability of NAP clients to acquire health certificates is essential because all communication depends on each computer presenting a valid health certificate when attempting to communicate with another computer.

In the secure network, deploy at least two NAP health policy servers. Configure the HRA computers as RADIUS clients of the NAP health policy servers. To ensure proper load balancing when configuring the remote RADIUS server group of the NPS service on the HRA computers, use the same priority and weight settings for all members of the RADIUS server group on each of the HRA computers.

For deployments at the branch offices, consider using the deployment models discussed previously for a small company. The services offered at the branch offices would model the same considerations given to a smaller company with a single site.

PKI Support for IPsec Enforcement

IPsec enforcement use of health certificates requires you, as the enterprise administrator, to reexamine the role PKI currently has within your environment. If a PKI does not exist, you need to deploy one. If one already exists, consider the additional load balancing and management that will be needed.

Smaller environments that already have a PKI probably require only the creation of a subordinate CA for NAP. This CA can be deployed in the boundary networks on the HRA to conserve server resources.

Larger environments require more planning because you need to consider additional aspects of the PKI when employed for use with NAP IPsec enforcement. The load on the CA issuing health certificates will be directly proportional to the following:

- The number of NAP clients in the environment
- The lifetime of the health certificate

The number of NAP clients is not something that you can truly control because deploying a NAP solution would entail using it pervasively throughout the environment.

The lifetime of the health certificate is something you can administer, and it has a direct influence over the load on your NAP CAs. Microsoft best practice recommends keeping the lifetime at a minimum, preferably four hours. Reducing this time increases the load on the NAP CAs for renewals. Increasing the time, although it reduces the load on the NAP CAs, also increases the likelihood that a computer can be out of compliance for a longer period due to changes in the health requirement policy.

STRUCTURE OF THE PKI

For most environments, adding an additional subordinate CA to issue health certificates for NAP is sufficient. Microsoft recommends that, in large environments, administrators create an entirely new PKI for NAP. You need to install a new root CA on a server within the secure environment and secure its private key with a hardware security module (HSM). Create subordinate CAs for NAP to issue the health certificates. These can be deployed in the boundary network and given the same security consideration as the RODCs deployed there. This would mean the removal of all unnecessary services and provide a limited attack surface. Securing its private key is not as critical as securing the root CA, because certificates issued by it will have a limited lifetime.

You do not need to worry about issuing timely CRLs for this portion of your PKI because the certificates will expire long before the CRLs are published. In addition, an OCSP responder service is also unnecessary due to the limited lifetime of your health certificates.

Microsoft noticed a performance issue when employing IPsec enforcement in its environment with the NAP CA. The NAP CA might have to issue and maintain a database of IPsec certificates for IPsec enforcement that last only a short time, such as 72 hours. Therefore, maintaining the database of issued certificates is of little critical value. Microsoft created out of its own need a new feature for the NAP CA, a Databaseless CA. This removes a terrible burden on the CA to maintain previously issued certificates that will expire within a short time, which causes additional overhead when cleaning up the database or just maintaining the certificates. Additional discussion on the uses of a Databaseless CA is found in Chapter 10, "Planning and Designing a Public Key Infrastructure."

CONFIGURING ADDITIONAL NAP COMPONENTS ON CLIENTS

System health agents from third-party members need to be installed on all NAP clients. A variety of software distribution methods are available to an administrator. You can use any one of the following not only for IPsec enforcement but also for VPN enforcement, 802.1x enforcement, and DHCP enforcement, which are discussed later in this chapter:

- Software deployment or logon scripts through Group Policy.
- Desktop management software, such as Microsoft System Center Configuration Manager 2007.
- Manual installation for unmanaged computers.

- Shares on remediation servers. Configure the troubleshooting URLs to instruct the user to install the missing SHAs.

CONFIGURING NAP HEALTH POLICY SERVERS

The NPS server running the NAP health policy server can be configured with additional third-party SHVs. Installation instructions for the third-party SHVs are provided by the third-party vendor. The SHVs must be installed on all NAP health policy servers participating in the NAP solution for IPsec and for VPN enforcement, 802.1x enforcement, and DHCP enforcement, which are discussed later in this chapter. Windows Server 2008 provides the default Windows Security Health Validator SHV that provides security settings for the Windows Security Center on Windows NAP clients.

Planning NAP VPN Enforcement

VPN enforcement in NAP is supported for VPN remote access connections by using PPP, specifically by working in conjunction with the PPP authentication phase. Windows XP SP3, Windows Vista, Windows 7, Windows Server 2008, and Windows Server 2008 R2 support the remote access quarantine enforcement client for NAP clients.

VPN enforcement design requires you, the enterprise administrator, to consider the following:

- VPN authentication methods
- VPN servers in use
- VPN clients compliant with VPN enforcement
- Configuration of the restricted network for remediation
- Other VPN enforcement considerations such as these:
  - Non-NAP-capable VPN clients
  - Configuring exemptions
  - Migration from Network Access Quarantine Control to VPN enforcement
  - Installing support for additional SHAs on NAP clients
  - Installing support for additional SHVs on NAP Health Policy servers

When VPN enforcement is employed, VPN clients are evaluated for compliance with health policy immediately after successful PPP authentication. Therefore, VPN clients are left in one of four stages after an attempt to connect through remote access:

- Clients fail authentication and the PPP session ends.
- Clients succeed in authenticating but do not possess a VPN enforcement client.
- Clients succeed in authenticating but do not pass the health inspection and therefore become noncompliant.
- Clients succeed in authenticating, pass the health inspection, and become compliant.

Planning VPN Authentication Protocol Use for VPN Enforcement

Microsoft supports the use of the two PEAP-based authentication protocols, PEAP-TLS and PEAP-MSCHAPv2, for VPN enforcement. This is due to PEAP-TLS messages used to transmit system health state information between the VPN client and the NAP health policy server.

Your current VPN remote access solution can use PEAP-TLS and PEAP-MSCHAPv2 as you ramp up the environment to support NAP. PEAP-TLS requires support for a computer certificate on each computer within the environment and on the NPS server performing RADIUS authentication. PEAP-MSCHAPv2 requires a computer certificate for authentication on the RADIUS server only. The VPN enforcement clients are required to trust the certificate issued to the RADIUS server and need to have the certificate of the root CA in their Trusted Root CA store. You can use Group Policy to issue a required certificate to each computer and to update the local computers' trusted root CAs.

If a PKI already exists, configuring PEAP-based support for managed computers is a bit easier administratively. Within AD DS, you can use a variety of ways to deliver Group Policy to select accounts. The following are the two easiest methods to accomplish this goal without extensive Group Policy filtering:

- Create a computer group and add all the computer accounts that participate as VPN enforcement clients to the group membership.
- Create an organizational unit (OU) and move the computer accounts that participate as VPN enforcement clients into the OU.

Next, apply Group Policy and ensure that the container to which the Group Policy is applied is the one that contains only the necessary computer accounts or contains the computer group containing the respective computer account members. If using a computer group to assemble the necessary computer accounts, you can filter Group Policy by ensuring that the specific computer group has the required Read and Apply Group Policy permissions assigned to it.

Other VPN Enforcement Considerations

Setting up support for VPN enforcement requires you to consider several remaining elements:

- Non-NAP-capable VPN clients
- Migration from Network Access Quarantine Control

- Installing or updating SHAs on clients
- Installing additional SHVs on NAP Health Policy servers

NON-NAP-CAPABLE VPN CLIENTS

VPN clients not capable of performing NAP and VPN enforcement need to be treated in one of two ways:

- Allow unlimited access by creating an exemption group.
- Allow only limited access to the restricted network.

To allow unlimited access, create an exemption group that includes the non-NAP-capable computer accounts. Create a network policy by using the Windows Groups condition and selecting the newly created exemption group. On the settings for NAP enforcement on this network policy, ensure that the computer group is allowed full network access for an unlimited time or for a specified time period. Using a specified time period allows a period during which a non-NAP-capable client is upgraded to support VPN enforcement.

Using that same policy, you could switch the settings to ensure that the client is allowed only limited access. This would ensure a safer environment but a restriction in access for non-NAP-capable computers. This might severely restrict guests and partner access to a company. Ensure that this is the desired effect prior to implementing this decision.

MIGRATING FROM NETWORK ACCESS QUARANTINE CONTROL

Moving to VPN enforcement is a natural progression from Network Access Quarantine Control, which is supported on Windows Server 2003 with the IAS RADIUS server.

When upgrading to Windows Server 2008 from Windows Server 2003 running IAS and configured with Network Access Quarantine Control, all the Network Access Quarantine Control settings are brought over. To move toward NAP using VPN enforcement, you must upgrade all the computers running Windows Server 2003 that are running IAS. Although Windows Server 2008 supports Network Access Quarantine Control, Windows Server 2003 with IAS does not support NAP. During the migration from Network Access Quarantine Control to VPN enforcement, you can run them simultaneously. Upgrade your existing clients to support NAP and the clients configured for VPN enforcement.

CONFIGURING ADDITIONAL NAP COMPONENTS ON CLIENTS AND NAP HEALTH POLICY SERVERS

The same considerations enumerated in the sections "Configuring Additional NAP Components on Clients" and "Configuring NAP Health Policy Servers" earlier in this chapter apply to VPN enforcement as well.

Planning NAP 802.1x Enforcement

Using 802.1x enforcement means employing NAP at layer 2 over your network and entails both wired and wireless NAP clients configured with an EAPHost NAP enforcement client. Other key components involve an 802.1x-compliant access point and a NAP Health Policy server. An 802.1x-compliant access point can be either a wireless access point or a wired switch; both are capable of performing 802.1x authentication.

Five Microsoft operating systems provide 802.1x enforcement clients:

- Windows Server 2008 R2 Extensible Authentication Protocol (EAP) Quarantine enforcement client
- Windows Server 2008 Extensible Authentication Protocol (EAP) Quarantine enforcement client
- Windows 7 Extensible Authentication Protocol (EAP) Quarantine enforcement client
- Windows Vista Extensible Authentication Protocol (EAP) Quarantine enforcement client
- Windows XP SP2 with two 802.1x enforcement clients
  - A wired client named EAP Quarantine enforcement client
  - A wireless client named Wireless EAPoL Quarantine enforcement client

Design Considerations for 802.1x Enforcement

The first step toward designing your 802.1x enforcement for NAP is to assess your current access points within your environment. Questions to answer include the following:

- Are all the switches used at the access layer and back-end server farms 802.1x compatible?
- Which RADIUS attributes do they support for your 802.1x enforcement?
- Which 802.1x authentication methods will you use?
- Which type of 802.1x enforcement—access control list (ACL) or virtual local area network (VLAN)—will you use?
- Must you support Pre-Boot Execution Environment (PXE) boot?

Using the inventory list from the documentation of your switches, you can begin assessing the switches involved in the 802.1x enforcement. Contact the vendor's website to find out about any known issues with employing NAP and about any necessary updates.

Access Point Considerations

As 802.1x authentication proliferates, more and more vendors are adding NAP support. There are even blogs devoted to listing security vendors supporting NAP. Finding hardware is not the problem; discerning whether the hardware currently in use is or can be made compliant is the issue. Purchasing new hardware is always an easy way to achieve compliance, but it is also the most expensive.

> **MORE INFO**   **802.1X ENFORCEMENT**
>
> The Microsoft NAP team has provided a specific blog that lists switches tested for 802.1x enforcement. This list is not meant to be exhaustive; in fact, it appears rather to be a list about a single device from the major network infrastructure vendors that was tested for 802.1x enforcement abilities. The assumption is that there is support from each of these

When examining compliance, look for specific RADIUS support. The Microsoft NAP supports the following vendor-specific attributes (VSAs) and RADIUS attributes for defining the restricted network with 802.1x enforcement:

- Filter-ID for identifying the ACL
- Tunnel-Medium-Type
- Tunnel-Pvt-Group-ID
- Tunnel-Type
- Tunnel-Tag

For setting the periodic reauthentication interval, the standard *Session-Timeout* RADIUS attribute has broad support from most of the hardware vendors.

ACLs vs. VLANs

802.1x enforcement can implement ACLs or VLANs for restricted access. Which enforcement method you use depends on your access point or switches' support and which type provides the restriction desired within your environment.

Using ACLs, an administrator can define a specific set of packet filters that enable a noncompliant NAP client to communicate only with a specific subset of servers. Because the 802.1x enforcement process occurs over layer 2, the noncompliant NAP client still attempts automatic configuration for its IPv4 configuration or autoconfiguration for IPv6. It attains an address for its usual subnet, but now is confined to limited access to specific servers for remediation. The big advantage here is that the ACL also prevents a rogue noncompliant NAP client from attempting to infect other noncompliant NAP clients. Because all the remediation servers should be up to date with their security software and configuration settings, the remediation servers should be fairly impervious to attack as well. This creates an isolated network on a per-port basis because the noncompliant client sees only the remediation network servers until fully compliant.

Using VLANs, an administrator can define a VLAN for remediation. Noncompliant NAT clients and 802.1x NAP clients failing a health check are forced into this VLAN by the wireless access point or a wired switch port on the switch. The VLAN is composed of remediation servers along with other noncompliant NAP clients. This restriction prevents communication outside the VLAN until the NAP client passes its health check. Ensure that this restricted VLAN is used solely for noncompliant NAP clients. Do not configure non-NAP-capable or unauthenticated NAP clients to use this VLAN. Normally, if an EAPHost NAP enforcement client fails authentication, the computer will not be allowed to communicate through the access point, so these unauthenticated computers will not be placed in the VLAN designated as the restricted network either.

Planning Authentication Protocols for 802.1x Enforcement

The only two supported authentication protocols for 802.1x enforcement included in Windows XP SP3, Windows Vista, Windows 7, and Windows Server 2008 are the PEAP types, PEAP-TLS and PEAP-MSCHAPv2. If implementing third-party vendor add-ons for 802.1x enforcement, you need to test their solutions because Microsoft NAP supports only PEAP-based solutions.

When implementing an 802.1x enforcement solution, you must consider the PKI when choosing between PEAP-TLS and PEAP-MSCHAPv2. If you're using PEAP-TLS, it will probably be more cost effective to implement an internal Microsoft-based PKI. You need computer certificates for the NPS servers performing RADIUS authentication and for the NAP clients using 802.1x enforcement. You can acquire certificates for computer accounts through autoenrollment using Group Policy, by importing a certificate file by using either a group certificate (considered less secure) or an individual certificate per computer, or, finally, by using Web enrollment.

The RADIUS servers require a certificate for PEAP-MSCHAPv2. You must install the root CA certificate on all computers employing 802.1x enforcement. For managed computers, it is fairly easy to have clients trust the root CA by using Group Policy. For unmanaged computers, you need to import the root CA certificate into the local computer's Trusted Root CA store.

Using 802.1x enforcement also requires you to consider the reauthentication interval. If health policy changes, there is no standard way to enforce client remediation after an 802.1x enforcement client is considered compliant. Setting a time interval that requires clients to reauthenticate provides a reliable means of forcing clients to seek compliance when the health policy is modified. As mentioned earlier, shorter intervals place a greater stress on the NAP infrastructure components, such as RADIUS. Microsoft best practice recommends a four-hour interval. You can enforce a reauthentication interval by the following techniques:

- Direct manipulation of the access point's 802.1x configuration
- A VSA configured on the RADIUS server and supported by the 802.1x access point
- The *Session-Timeout* RADIUS attribute

REAL WORLD

Paul Mancuso

When using PEAP-MSCHAPv2, two PKI considerations come to mind. First, using an internal PKI gives you far greater control over which computer will trust the root CA. Managed computers can easily be configured to trust the root CA through Group Policy. This also establishes a nice baseline so that only managed computers have this trust.

However, this creates a lot of work for an IT department when all that is really necessary to make 802.1x function in relation to a PKI is to purchase a certificate from a PKI vendor whose root CA is already trusted. This eliminates much work on the back end of an 802.1x authentication configuration. The dollar cost is pennies when compared to the time, effort, and additional troubleshooting necessary to set up your own internal PKI and configure Group Policy for managed computers (the easy part) or to use one of the manual methods (Web enrollment or importing a certificate file) for unmanaged computers.

Other 802.1x Enforcement Considerations

802.1x enforcement is not without some issues. One of them is the problem of not allowing the use of PXE boot on switch ports where 802.1x enforcement is configured. Also, there might be certain noncapable 802.1x clients within your environment, such as printer servers, fax servers, or computers installed with an operating system that is noncompliant for 802.1x enforcement. You must exempt them from 802.1x enforcement. Configuring exemptions can be as easy as configuring the specific ports used by these network clients to be exempt from 802.1x authentication and 802.1x enforcement or from just 802.1x enforcement if they support 802.1x authentication but not 802.1x enforcement.

Using 802.1x is not the security panacea that will solve all your concerns about keeping out attackers. As stated earlier, NAP is not designed to stop attackers; it is mainly designed to prevent malware outbreaks. In fact, 802.1x authentication has one known flaw regarding man-in-the-middle attacks, but this requires some physical access to your access ports. In addition, 802.1x does not provide the end-to-end security that IPsec enforcement can provide.

802.1x provides the assurance that compliant computers on the network, if attacked by invading malware, are better equipped to ward off the attack. It helps maintain a stable and secure environment.

CONFIGURING ADDITIONAL NAP COMPONENTS ON CLIENTS AND NAP HEALTH POLICY SERVERS

The same considerations enumerated in the sections "Configuring Additional NAP Components on Clients" and "Configuring NAP Health Policy Servers" earlier in this chapter apply to 802.1x enforcement.

Planning NAP DHCP Enforcement

DHCP enforcement provides for NAP enforcement before an IPv4 client receives its automatic configuration information from a DHCP server. DHCP enforcement uses a limited IPv4 configuration to restrict a DHCP client to a restricted network to perform remediation.

DHCP enforcement combines the use of Windows Server 2008 running the DHCP Server service, the NPS service for RADIUS client capabilities, and the supported Windows clients:

- Windows XP SP3
- Windows Vista
- Windows 7
- Windows Server 2008

DHCP enforcement uses the following configurations of IPv4 to restrict a noncompliant client:

- Sets the router option to 0.0.0.0 for noncompliant clients
- Sets the subnet mask for the IPv4 address to 255.255.255.255
- Uses the Classless Static Routes DHCP option to set host routes to specified computers on the restricted network

DHCP enforcement is simple to set up but has some considerable disadvantages when compared to other forms of NAP enforcement:

- It is the weakest form of NAP enforcement.
- A local administrator can override the settings by setting an appropriate manual IPv4 configuration to access the network.
- It does not provide support for IPv6 environments. Currently, DHCP enforcement is an IPv4-only solution.

Design Considerations for DHCP Enforcement

Several items need to be in place for a successful DHCP enforcement solution:

- All DHCP servers need to be upgraded to Windows Server 2008.
- All DHCP servers need to add the NPS role and configure a Remote Servers group containing the NAP Health Policy servers.
- Installation of RADIUS infrastructure is necessary if one is not already deployed.
- Consideration is necessary for how to implement exemptions for non-NAP-capable computers.

The network infrastructure, switches, routers, and Active Directory domain controllers require no updates or upgrades. Only the DHCP servers need to be upgraded to Windows Server 2008; install the NPS service and configure the service to function as a RADIUS proxy for the back-end NAP Health Policy servers.

- The DHCP scopes need to be appropriately configured:
  - NAP needs to be enabled for the specified scopes where DHCP enforcement is to function.
  - DHCP scopes need to be configured with the options for noncompliant NAP clients.

- Using either specific Vendor classes or the Default Network Access Protection Class User class, configure the Classless Static Routes option (Option 249) for clients that are noncompliant.

CONFIGURING ADDITIONAL NAP COMPONENTS ON CLIENTS AND NAP HEALTH POLICY SERVERS

The same considerations enumerated in the sections "Configuring Additional NAP Components on Clients" and "Configuring NAP Health Policy Servers" earlier in this chapter apply to DHCP enforcement as well.

Final Say on DHCP Enforcement

Despite all the disadvantages of DHCP enforcement, it can provide a fine solution for a small company intent on enhancing its malware protection services. For larger environments, DHCP enforcement can provide an inexpensive reporting solution, assuming the necessary Windows Server 2008 components can be installed. For a small environment, as well as for branch offices in larger enterprises, one server can be used to deploy all the necessary components: DHCP, NPS, and NAP Health Policy server. This is an inexpensive solution to provide at least a fine reporting tool by which to monitor your noncompliant clients' health in your environment and provide a step toward a more secure environment.

Domain and Server Isolation

Domain isolation and server isolation, introduced initially with Windows Server 2003, are effective means of improving secure communications within an enterprise. By ensuring which computers can communicate with other computers, you provide secure end-to-end authenticated communication. Securing end-to-end communication is not addressed through VPN enforcement, DHCP enforcement, or 802.1x enforcement. NAP IPsec enforcement does provide the same end-to-end authenticated communication service as isolation and, thus, can implement a similar style of security while adding support for health policies.

With domain and server isolation, IPsec-authenticated communication defends a computer against network attacks, protection that application-layer user authentication security services do not offer. User authentication does prevent users from attacking specific files and applications, but it is not true security at the lower layers. IPsec authentication helps prevent attacks against services running at the network layer.

You might be asking yourself why you wouldn't just implement tightened host-based firewalls instead. Firewalls are a fine security feature when you are attempting to protect physical or even geographically isolated environments. Firewalls were not created as a solution for the logically distributed network environments of today. Host-based firewalls should still be used and managed centrally, but they do not provide the highest method of ensuring which users from specific computers should have access to specific applications and services on other computers. What is needed for this type of isolation is a logical solution. Domain and server isolation provide this capability.

Domain vs. Server Isolation

Domain isolation is a way of ensuring that computers that need to communicate are members of the domain and have received the necessary IPsec policies through Group Policy. This isolates trusted computers from untrusted computers. All incoming requests and subsequently transferred data must be authenticated and protected by IPsec. Using Windows Firewall with Advanced Security policy settings, you can define IPsec and connections security rules that either require or request all inbound traffic to be authenticated with IPsec.

Server isolation is a more selective isolation method than domain isolation. Server isolation enables the enterprise administrator to designate specific hosts within the environment that should require that all client connection requests to them be authenticated by IPsec, much like domain isolation. In addition, you can designate select servers to allow communication with specific clients and servers through the following:

- Selective certificates used for IPsec authentication
- Specific IP addresses, using Windows Firewall with Advanced Security policy settings
- Windows Server 2008, creating firewall rules that permit traffic from computers or users who are members of a select Active Directory security group
- Windows Server 2003, using the local Group Policy Access This Computer From The Network user right to specify users and computer accounts

When using either domain or server isolation, exemptions can be made for computers that are not capable of performing IPsec authentication or are not members of AD DS.

Comparing Server and Domain Isolation to IPsec Enforcement

From a high-level perspective, these technologies are more similar than different. Both technologies use IPsec to provide logical network segmentation. Both server isolation and domain isolation attempt to make the network safer by ensuring that only trusted computers can communicate. IPsec enforcement ensures that computers trusted by health validation are allowed to communicate. Both use IPsec authentication to mutually assure communicating computers of their ability to trust and be trusted. Both technologies can use the default Kerberos authentication or deploy certificates for computer authentication prior to establishing IPsec security associations.

Server isolation enables an administrator to segment high-value servers further for granular control within the trusted environment. IPsec NAP can define specific zones of security to tighten access even further to high-value servers. Figure 5-11 displays the logical network segmentation that both forms of IPsec isolation can provide.

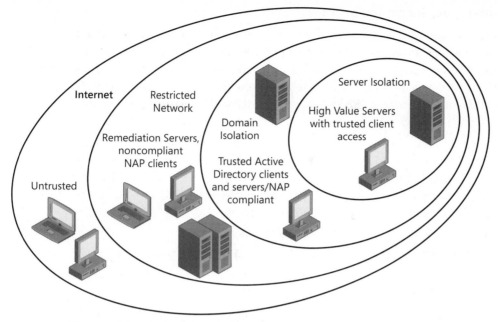

FIGURE 5-11 IPsec providing the logical network segmentation

Adding NAP technology to your IPsec isolation solution now provides the following additional security aspects:

- Formalizes policy validation for healthy computers
- Further restricts computer trust to computers that are managed and healthy
- Uses remediation to enable updating for unhealthy managed computers
- Creates a system of ongoing enforced compliance that offers flexible management for defining trust

Moving from Server and Domain Isolation to IPsec NAP

If your environment is using Windows 2000 Server or later, you can use IPsec NAP to provide a trusted environment to enforce logical network segmentation for the creation of trusted zones. For networks that have already upgraded to Windows XP SP3, Windows Vista, or Windows 7 on the desktop and have begun the upgrade to Windows Server 2008 or Windows Server 2008 R2, a steady migration toward NAP can begin.

You can begin introducing health validation in network locations that have already upgraded their operating systems to NAP-capable clients by implementing a pilot program. This pilot program should initially use reporting and should quickly move toward the implementation of restriction. After a predominant portion of each network location—branch offices or the main office—has upgraded to NAP-capable clients, you can introduce a NAP solution using reporting. Finally, each office in the network can eventually turn on restriction after a careful review of logs gathered during the implementation of reporting only.

It is essential to plan the implementation to consider other factors:

- Which computers require IPsec enforcement?
- Which computers should be exempt from NAP IPsec enforcement?
- Consider creating NAP IPsec client groups for computers that require NAP IPsec enforcement and for those that should be exempt.
- Issue the appropriate certificates for each of the previous two groups to ensure proper identity for determining which systems require NAP IPsec enforcement.
- Run an extensive limited trial prior to broader implementation to ensure that possible issues that you might encounter have been appropriately addressed.

Proper planning is essential to a NAP implementation. It is conceivable that if IPsec NAP is your choice of NAP enforcement, then first instituting server and domain isolation in phases throughout your environment would be a good starting place.

> **MORE INFO** **IPSEC ENFORCEMENT**
>
> An excellent source for a limited lab and possible pilot implementation that is completely documented step-by-step can be found at *http://www.windowsecurity.com/articles/Deploying-IPsec-Server-Domain-Isolation-Windows-Server-2008-Group-Policy-Part1.html*. At the end of this article are the additional links for all four parts to the configuration.

Lesson Summary

- Gathering the design requirements for a NAP solution involves collecting a list of items necessary to perform each of the desired NAP enforcement types.
- For all NAP enforcement types, ensure that your RADIUS servers are all upgraded to Windows Server 2008. Upgrade only the necessary components of your RADIUS solution, the RADIUS clients and proxies, when required in your design.
- You can implement NAP enforcement through a VPN, 802.1x, DHCP, or IPsec.
- For all NAP enforcement types, determine non-NAP-capable clients. Segment all the types of non-NAP-capable clients into respective groups so you can create policies for each type. Determine a NAP solution for the security policies prescribed for each group.
- Maintain adequate supervision for the servers providing remediation in your restricted network.

Lesson Review

You can use the following questions to test your knowledge of the information in Lesson 2, "Designing Network Access Policy and Server and Domain Isolation." The questions are also available on the companion CD if you prefer to review them in electronic form.

1. Choose the appropriate decision points when deciding to implement NAP. (Choose all that apply.)

    A. Provides a safer environment for trusted computers

    B. Enforces a policy on the health level of the computers in the trusted environment

    C. Provides a firewall block against would-be attackers

    D. Ensures that internal computers are more likely to be protected from an attack

2. Choose the correct statement when determining which NAP enforcement method meets a stated policy goal of that NAP enforcement type.

    A. 802.1x enforcement provides end-to-end secure communications of NAP-compliant clients.

    B. DHCP enforcement enables an administrator to mandate the use of a VLAN ID in the restricted network on failure of a NAP client for compliance.

    C. VPN enforcement provides for confidentiality of each packet's data along its entire path.

    D. IPsec prevents the replay of any portion of a session between two trusted clients.

Chapter Review

To further practice and reinforce the skills you learned in this chapter, you can perform the following tasks:

- Review the chapter summary.
- Review the list of key terms introduced in this chapter.
- Complete the case scenario. This scenario sets up a real-world situation involving the topics of this chapter and asks you to create a solution.
- Complete the suggested practices.
- Take a practice test.

Chapter Summary

- Design a perimeter network with servers that receive access requests from clients in the border network. Servers on the perimeter network include VPN servers, servers providing web services, web application servers, proxy servers servicing web applications serving as RADIUS clients, and the firewall and network infrastructure devices.
- If you need a PKI to support a remote access solution, determine whether you can scale an existing PKI to support those needs.
- Review the load on your RADIUS servers to determine high availability and load-balancing needs, especially if you intend to expand the VPN to support additional remote users.
- Determine the security requirements for your choice of VPN protocols. If the highest level of security is required for the VPN due to security policy, and mutual authentication is required for the user and the computer, consider using an EAP-based type of authentication with L2TP to provide the highest level of security for the tunnel, the data, and the VPN client.
- NAP is not designed to lock attackers out of your environment. NAP is designed to ensure that, if attacked, your computers have a well-managed security policy that enhances their ability to fend off an attack.
- You can implement NAP enforcement through IPsec, DHCP, VPN, or 802.1x. IPsec NAP enforcement is the strongest form of NAP enforcement. DHCP enforcement is the weakest form of NAP enforcement.
- Be sure to test a well-documented pilot deployment extensively prior to implementing an enterprise deployment of any NAP solution.

Key Terms

Do you know what these key terms mean? You can check your answers by looking up the terms in the glossary at the end of the book.

- DirectAccess
- Health Registration Authority (HRA)
- NAP enforcement point
- RADIUS client
- RADIUS proxy
- RADIUS server
- Statement of Health (SoH)
- System Health Agent (SHA)
- System Health Validator (SHV)
- VPN Reconnect

Case Scenario

In the following case scenario, you apply what you've learned about designing a network access strategy. You can find answers to these questions in the "Answers" section at the end of this book.

Case Scenario: Designing a NAP Solution for a Large Enterprise

Contoso, Ltd., is a corporation with ten branch offices and a main office in Fort Lauderdale, Florida. The company employs 3,500 people across all its locations. Seven of the branch offices are substantial in size with more than 50 employees and computers for all employees at these locations. There is one Active Directory domain in a forest named *contoso.com*.

The company maintains a large data center at the Fort Lauderdale office. A set of servers at the seven larger branch offices supports authentication, local profiles, data shares, and printing. All servers are for local use only. Remote salespeople and traveling representatives of the company use the three smaller branch offices for meetings. No domain controllers are stationed at any of the branch offices.

The seven larger branch offices are connected to the main office with multiple T1 links to form a link speed between 5 and 10 Mbps. The smaller offices use a business broadband connection through either DSL or cable with asymmetric speeds exceeding 1 Mbps for uploading and 6 Mbps for downloading. At these smaller offices, ISA Server 2006 running on Windows Server 2003 provides local DHCP and firewall services and a site-to-site VPN connection to the main office. Clients at the smaller branch offices consist of a small staff of users for support of the salespeople who travel into the area and for a few local salespeople who reside in the area. All the salespeople, including corporate officers, use these smaller offices for meetings.

Remote access is provided through an L2TP VPN that is centrally managed at the Fort Lauderdale office. A RADIUS solution is already in use because all offices forward their authentication requests to the main office. Each of the branch offices has a single VPN server running Windows Server 2003. The main office has four RADIUS servers running Windows Server 2008.

The company plans to implement NAP using IPsec enforcement at the main office and is currently in the test phase of an IPsec enforcement deployment. Server isolation has been proposed for high-value servers at the main office. All corporate officers and a smaller, exclusive group of users spread across the enterprise will have access to these servers. IT must complete the NAP IPsec deployment at the main office and evaluate NAP enforcement at the branch offices.

1. Clients at the larger branch offices access servers at the main office. Several users at two of the branch offices access one of the database clusters that has been deemed a high-value server. How would you apply an IPsec NAP solution at these offices?

2. Support staff at the branch office require access to the servers running Exchange Server and access to file servers that all reside at the main office. None of these resource servers have been deemed high-value servers. Will an IPsec NAP enforcement solution be necessary at these branch offices?

Suggested Practices

To help you successfully master the exam objectives presented in this chapter, complete the following tasks.

Implement VPNs, RADIUS Solution, and NAP Enforcement

In Practice 1, implement an L2TP VPN by using a VPN access server and a RADIUS server with directory database. In Practice 2, implement NAP by using DHCP, VPN, IPsec, and 802.1x enforcement.

- **Practice 1** Using either virtual or physical computers, install the Active Directory Domain Services Server role on one installation of Windows Server 2008. Install an enterprise CA on this same instance with Web enrollment. Install on this same server the Network Policy Server role. Acquire a computer certificate for authentication.

  On a second installation of Windows Server 2008, keep it as a workgroup computer and install NPS. Create a connection request policy by using the remote access server as the type of network access server, specifying L2TP as the tunnel type, and enabling the server for 24/7 in day and time restrictions. Ensure that you place the policy at the top of the Connection Request Policies list. Also on this second instance, create a Remote RADIUS Server group, specifying the first Windows Server 2008 as a RADIUS server. (Use only a single subnet and adapter for all computers in this test lab; alternately, you can configure Routing and Remote Access Services and a second adapter on the second instance of Windows Server 2008.)

  On the first instance, create a RADIUS client, specifying the second instance of Windows Server 2008 as the RADIUS client. Create a connection request policy stating

L2TP as the tunnel type. Create a network policy, using the NAS type of remote access server, VPN as the NAS port type, Authentication Methods set to only Microsoft Protected EAP (PEAP), and edit to ensure that only a certificate is used. Select the option for the client to be assigned a static IPv4 address and type in an appropriate address for connection to this server through the VPN.

Create a Windows 7 installation and maintain the computer as a workgroup member. Configure an L2TP VPN connection, using PEAP-TLS as the only authentication protocol. Ensure that an appropriate IPv4 address is configured for its connection to the RADIUS client VPN server. Acquire an appropriate user certificate (user authentication for the PEAP-TLS) and computer certificate (computer authentication for L2TP) by using Web enrollment. Ensure that you also acquire the root CA certificate and make sure that it is stored in the Trusted Root CA store. Test your connection.

- **Practice 2** Using the Microsoft Step-by-Step guides and either virtual machines or physical computers, practice implementing each of the NAP enforcement types and the newer VPN connection types.

  Practice NAP DHCP:

  http://go.microsoft.com/fwlink/?Linkid=85897

  Practice NAP VPN enforcement:

  http://go.microsoft.com/fwlink/?Linkid=85896

  Practice NAP IPsec enforcement:

  http://go.microsoft.com/fwlink/?Linkid=85894

  Practice NAP 802.1x enforcement:

  http://go.microsoft.com/fwlink/?Linkid=86036

  Practice Remote Access with VPN Reconnect:

  http://technet.microsoft.com/en-us/library/dd637783(WS.10).aspx.

Watch a Webcast

For these practices, watch two webcasts about Active Directory Domain Services in Windows Server 2008.

- **Practice 1** Watch the Support webcast, "Support Webcase: Introduction to Network Access Protection," at *http://support.microsoft.com/kb/921070.*
- **Practice 2** Watch the TechNet webcast, "How Microsoft Does IT: Managing Network Access Protection (Level 300)," at *https://msevents.microsoft.com/CUI /WebCastEventDetails.aspx?culture=en-US&EventID=1032391121&CountryCode=US.*

Read a White Paper

In Practice 1, read a white paper about NAP in Windows Server 2008. In Practice 2, read a security guide detailing the steps to creating a security risk management program.

- **Practice 1** Read the "Network Access Protection Policies in Windows Server 2008" white paper from Microsoft at *http://www.microsoft.com/downloads/details .aspx?FamilyID=8e47649e-962c-42f8-9e6f-21c5ccdcf490&displaylang=en.*

- **Practice 2** Read the "Managing Network Access Protection at Microsoft" at *http://www.microsoft.com/downloads/en/details.aspx?FamilyID=7f137f24 -8921-4862-a315-db5ee889d4ef.*

Take a Practice Test

The practice tests on this book's companion CD offer many options. For example, you can test yourself on just one exam objective, or you can test yourself on all the 70-647 certification exam content. You can set up the test so that it closely simulates the experience of taking a certification exam, or you can set it up in study mode so that you can look at the correct answers and explanations after you answer each question.

> **MORE INFO** **PRACTICE TESTS**
>
> For details about all the practice test options available, see the "How to Use the Practice Tests" section in this book's introduction.

CHAPTER 6

Design a Branch Office Deployment

I t seems that every enterprise eventually confronts this issue: Whether through the need to have representation in many locations, whether by acquiring another company, or whether by outgrowing the existing office space, at some point you will need to design, deploy, and manage a branch office. The *branch office* presents a unique collection of challenges. It requires the enterprise administrator to develop a specialized vision and understanding of the many facets of the information system design and the administration demanded by this isolated, and often unsupported and unsecure, facility.

This chapter describes the various real-world pressures and issues that you might face regarding the branch office. It also explains the tools and techniques provided by Microsoft Windows Server 2008 R2 to help you properly analyze, design, deploy, and maintain a branch office environment. You should develop balanced solutions that address the need for connectivity, performance, and resource access, along with the need for control and security and for legal and regulatory compliance to mitigate the pressures and risks associated with the branch office. Windows Server 2008 R2 has introduced several new features to further enhance security and performance in the branch office.

Exam objectives in this chapter:

- Design the branch office deployment.

Lessons in this chapter:

Before You Begin

To complete the lessons in this chapter, you should have:

- An understanding of Windows Server 2008 Active Directory Domain Services (AD DS) and its required infrastructure.
- An understanding of network communications.
- An understanding of the concepts of a security policy.

To complete the lessons in this chapter, you might want to have:

- A lab environment with a Windows Server 2008 R2 Active Directory domain.
- Internet access.
- Access to Microsoft TechNet.

REAL WORLD

David R. Miller

In my experience as an enterprise administrator, branch offices are a natural point of vulnerability for an enterprise. They often connect to the organization's most critical information assets, but they are usually not supported, monitored, or secured as thoroughly as the headquarters (HQ) facility. There is an increased likelihood that, because of these vulnerabilities, the branch office will be the point of attacks. These attacks can be through electronic means, through improper disposal of information assets, or through the outright theft of computer or network hardware. A successful attack on the branch office can lead to the compromise not only of valuable information assets located at the branch office, but also of valuable information assets located at HQ and the entire connected information systems infrastructure.

Many branch office locations are too small to warrant dedicated, full-time, highly skilled, local technical support. Branch offices are typically supported by the more skilled and remote administrative crew at HQ. It is not uncommon for a local junior administrator to provide support services for the branch office. These junior administrators often have lesser skills and might not even be trusted. Very often, the branch office junior administrators provide support only as a part of their daily responsibilities. This can (and often does) lead to a conflict of interest in their decision-making processes as the local administrator. They will need guidelines and rigid boundaries to manage, control, and monitor their authority and actions in this isolated environment.

These controls might be in the form of written policies, or they might be technical controls implemented at HQ. These technical controls should begin with the delegation of authority to branch office administrators, following the principle of least privilege: providing only the barest level of authority and access for junior administrators to perform their limited tasks and meet their limited set of responsibilities. Other controls might include Group Policy object (GPO) restrictions on desktop, applications, software installation, hardware installation, and the like. Still other controls might be implemented on infrastructure systems, like *Network Access Protection* (NAP) policies and firewall rules on browsing and downloads.

NOTE **PRIVILEGE**

Privilege is defined as the collection of rights (the ability to perform system-related functions) and permissions (the ability to access resources and objects) granted to a user or a group of users. A user's level of privilege defines that user's access to an information system.

Users in the branch office need a local network infrastructure, like workstations and switches, and at least a firewall and router. They probably also need virtual private network (VPN) capabilities to provide secure connectivity to HQ. They need proper and controlled system configuration. They need application deployment and they might need access to local and remote resources. They need access to the network infrastructure services, like Dynamic Host Configuration Protocol (DHCP) and the AD DS infrastructure, either locally, remotely, or both. They also need a way to locate these resources and the network infrastructure.

There is a need to implement controls on these users to maintain the stability and functionality of the information system, to protect the confidentiality and integrity of the valuable information assets, and to conform to legal and regulatory compliance requirements. HQ administrators must balance the need for resource access and performance (availability) with the often conflicting need for control and security (confidentiality and integrity) of the information system.

Together, these branch office issues represent a potential downstream liability for the organization.

Lesson 1: Branch Office Deployment

In this lesson, you are presented with scenario-like branch office issues and the tools and techniques that Windows Server 2008 R2 provides to help resolve those issues.

After this lesson, you will be able to:

- Describe the server roles and their uses in the branch office implementation.
- Identify the network infrastructure services and know how to deploy them in a branch office environment.
- Describe the components required to provide reliable and secure authentication to branch offices.
- Describe the concept of Administrator Role Separation.
- Describe the advantages and disadvantages of using full, read-only, and Server Core domain controllers in a branch office.
- Describe the benefits and ramifications of performing forest restructuring when implementing branch offices.
- Describe the mechanisms used to improve the availability of information system services and resources in the branch office.

Estimated lesson time: 50 minutes

Branch Office Services

Designing the Active Directory Structure for Branch Office Administration

The first issue to consider in the branch office is the establishment of the proper level of access and authority for the branch office administrator. The branch office administrator is generally less skilled and less trusted than the administrators in the corporate HQ. Branch office administrators are responsible for lower-level administrative functions related to application installation, performing operating system and application updates, and restarting servers and domain controllers. However, the branch office administrator is generally not authorized to perform Active Directory–related administrative functions. Because branch office administrators are not as skilled or as trusted as the HQ administrators and because they typically are responsible only for their local branch office systems, it is generally not desirable to add the branch office administrators to the Domain Admins group or to other domain-related built-in groups. This is usually too much privilege.

As in Windows Server 2003, you can use the *Delegation of Control* Wizard in Windows Server 2008 to delegate preconfigured levels of privilege at the Active Directory site, the domain, and the organizational unit (OU). Several additional preconfigured levels of privilege have been added at the domain level to the wizard in Windows Server 2008.

Because the branch office almost always represents an Active Directory site, it might seem that the Delegation of Control Wizard should be used at the site level to delegate privilege to the branch office administrator. However, the preconfigured privileges available at the site level number exactly one—Manage Group Policy Links, just like in Windows Server 2003. The Delegation of Control Wizard enables you to create custom tasks to delegate, but when privilege is delegated at the site level, the branch office administrator's level of authority would approximate that of an Enterprise Admin. Enterprise Admin is far too much authority for the branch office administrator and is usually not a good choice for delegation in this case.

If the branch office is configured in Active Directory as its own domain, the branch office administrator can be granted Domain Admin status in his or her home domain. This might or might not be too much authority because members of the Domain Admins group can write GPOs, delegate authority, and define a great deal of policy and control over the domain. Delegation at the domain level would require a skilled and trusted branch office administrator. If the branch office administrator is up to this level of challenge, responsibility, and authority in the enterprise in which the branch office is its own domain, making the branch office administrator a domain administrator in his or her home domain could be a viable option.

It is generally better to delegate administrative authority at the lowest possible container within the Active Directory structure—the OU. For more granular administrative control, create an OU for each branch office and delegate authority to the branch office administrator at the OU level. Then place all local branch office users and computers into the proper branch office OU. At the OU level, the Delegation of Control Wizard has about a dozen preconfigured levels of privilege. Members of the Enterprise Admins group can still create and link GPOs at the Site level, with the optional Enforced setting enabled, for high-level, enterprise administrative control. Members of the Domain Admins group can also create and link GPOs at the domain level, also with the optional Enforced setting enabled, for high-level administrative control.

> **NOTE DOMAIN RESTRUCTURING**
>
> Windows Server 2008 provides for domain restructuring in an entirely new way. Branch offices are often isolated from the main office not only geographically but also financially (like a different cost center) or administratively (politically), with different network administration, and they might even have different requirements regarding security and compliance concerns.
>
> No matter how the branch office is configured within Active Directory, the branch office might be restructured to better fit the business needs of the enterprise with the control and administration models supported by the different Active Directory containers.
>
> The topic of restructuring domains is covered in Chapter 3, "Planning Migrations, Trusts, and Interoperability."

Although you can use delegation of authority at the site, domain, or OU levels to provide administrative control over member computers and users, what about the domain controller that is physically located in the branch office? Domain controllers should never be moved from the Domain Controllers OU. How can the local branch office administrator manage that operating system and applications? You don't want the local administrator working with Active Directory, but you need his or her help in maintaining the server operating system underlying Active Directory. Windows Server 2008 introduced Administrator Role Separation specifically to address this issue.

Administrator Role Separation

A new feature of Windows Server 2008 is the ability to delegate local administrative privilege on a domain controller. This grants the delegated user or group local administrator privilege on the server, with the ability to log on to the server, update drivers, and restart the server, but disallows the delegated user or group from being able to manage Active Directory or Directory Services. This is called *Administrator Role Separation*.

You must perform Administrator Role Separation delegation on a server-by-server basis. The delegated user or group will not have any administrative privileges on other domain controllers in the domain. You will implement Administrator Role Separation in the practice section of this lesson.

EXAM TIP

For the 70-647 exam, make sure you understand how to use Administrator Role Separation to allow a branch office administrator the ability to manage the operating system of a local domain controller, but not allow them to manage Active Directory.

Components and Services in the Branch Office

The branch office typically has relatively few users, relatively few computers, a smaller budget for information services, fewer network infrastructure devices (like servers and firewalls), and, most unfortunately, lesser security and less skilled administration. The users in the branch office will still need access to enterprise resources, along with a reasonable level of performance, coupled with an appropriate level of security for the information systems. Furthermore, there might be the need to provide additional infrastructure in the branch office to remain in compliance with industry regulations and laws. There has to be a balance between the needs of the users in the branch office and the cost of providing infrastructure, support, performance, and reliability for the network. It is not prudent business practice to spend money on the issue, hoping that the complaints and other problems will go away.

Consequently, a branch office will need an infrastructure to provide information services. This section explores some of the options and discusses the benefits, along with the price you'll pay to implement the service in the remote and potentially unsupported and nonsecure branch office. As a branch office grows, the need for local services and support also grows.

The following is a list of information-system components and services that might be desirable in the branch office:

- Client computers
- Servers
  - Member or stand-alone, to support services like File Services, Print Services, and other infrastructure services
  - Full server or Server Core installation
- Domain controller
  - Full Installation: domain controller or *read-only domain controller* (RODC)
  - Server Core Installation: domain controller or RODC
- Global catalog
- Operations master roles
- Domain Name System (DNS)
- DHCP
- Multisite cluster nodes
- Distributed File System (DFS) or Distributed File System with Replication
- Routing and Remote Access Services (RRAS)
  - For dial-in and VPN, DHCP relay agent, and Network Address Translation (NAT) support
- Windows Server Update Services to provide Microsoft operating system and application updates
- Windows Server Virtualization (WSV) services

In addition, the branch office will typically need at least one firewall/router and a wide-area-network (WAN) link to provide connectivity to the HQ networks, as well as to the Internet. A more detailed discussion of the elements on this list follows.

The branch office network typically connects to the HQ over dedicated WAN links, like a T1 or a T3, or it connects through VPNs over the Internet's public network. In either case, for performance and reliability reasons, it is often desirable to place network infrastructure systems in the branch office.

Windows Deployment Services

What is the value of a branch office without computers? How do you get those standardized operating system and application installations to the branch office? Microsoft has redesigned the earlier Remote Installation Services (RIS) in Windows Server 2008 to enhance the remote deployment and reimaging of computers using preconfigured images complete with applications and settings. Windows Deployment Services (WDS) is a server role that can be added to any Windows Server 2008 server.

Windows Deployment Services is optimized to deploy Windows 7, Windows Vista, and Windows Server 2008, but it can deploy earlier versions of Windows operating systems as well. It relies on preboot execution environment (PXE) technology and requires Transmission Control Protocol/Internet Protocol (TCP/IP) connectivity between the Windows Deployment Services server and the target client. Windows Deployment Services can deploy remote clients using multicast transmission to deploy an image to a large number of client computers simultaneously.

Windows Server 2008 R2 provides new support for driver provisioning during deployment or to boot images, and has improved the multicasting functionality over slow links and through the use of a stripped down, stand-alone, PXE-based transport server. Further, support has been added for deploying Windows Server 2008 R2 from virtual hard disk images (.vhd files) as part of unattended installations.

WINDOWS SERVER 2008 R2 SERVER—MEMBER OR STAND-ALONE

In the enterprise, the most common deployment of client and server class computers is to make them members of the domain by joining them to the domain. This must be done on the local computer by script or by answer file during an unattended installation. Joining these systems to the domain implements the administrative control desired (required) by the administration and by the enterprise security policy. The majority of administrative control is accomplished through the GPO within Active Directory. The benefit to the user of the system is single sign-on to access resources enterprise-wide. The impact of joining the domain for a computer is giving up administrative control of the computer. The administrators in the enterprise now own the control of the system.

For the administrator in the enterprise, almost the only circumstances in which it might be desirable to have a company computer remain a stand-alone system and not join the domain is when there is little or no need to access enterprise resources and when there is significant risk of the computer being compromised. The compromise could be physical theft or access, or it could be an attack through the network.

WINDOWS SERVER 2008 R2 SERVER CORE

Server Core is the most secure installation of Windows Server 2008 R2. Server Core installs a minimal operating system, providing minimal services and applications, with no Windows shell and a limited graphical user interface (GUI). This reduces the maintenance, management, and hardware requirements of the server. (Server Core requires only about 1 GB of hard disk space for installation and about 2 GB for ongoing server operations.)

Perhaps more significantly, Server Core reduces the attack surface of the server, making it the securest installation of Windows Server 2008. It is designed as a bastion host or hardened server, already minimizing the attack vectors of the operating system. In almost all cases, the way a hacker is able to compromise a computer is through vulnerabilities in services and applications (program code) running (in memory) on the computer. These vulnerabilities are inherent in all program code. By reducing the number of services and applications on a computer, you are reducing the number of attack vectors available to the hacker is exactly what Server Core does. It operates with a bare minimum of services and programs running in memory.

Furthermore, if a hacker can break into a running process, the hacker's level of privilege is that of the user account that initially launched the compromised process. After a hacker accesses a computer through one of the vulnerabilities in running program code, the hacker's next objective is to elevate his or her level of privilege to acquire greater control over the computer. This is commonly accomplished by triggering the execution of a service (or other process) that runs at a higher level of privilege. Because vulnerabilities are inherent in all program code, the hacker now breaks into the process that runs at the higher level of privilege, acquiring a higher level of privilege on the computer. Again, because Server Core has a reduced set of services and applications installed and available on the computer, the hacker has fewer targets with elevated privilege to exploit. This reduces the likelihood that a hacker can elevate his or her level of privilege on the Server Core server, keeping the hacker at a lower level of privilege. These are the principal mechanisms that make Server Core the securest implementation of Windows Server 2008.

> **NOTE THE MANY FACETS OF SECURITY**
>
> The reduction of programs in memory and on the hard disk alone does not ensure security of the computer. These features, combined with a comprehensive, multilayered, and monitored security structure, are the best defense against hacker compromise of the computer system.
>
> It takes only one vulnerability in a system to enable a hacker to exploit the system. You must attempt to secure them all. Many of these other security measures are addressed later in this chapter.

Because Server Core has no Explorer shell and a limited GUI, local administration and administration through a Remote Desktop (Terminal Services) connection must be performed using commands at a command prompt. Figure 6-1 shows the Server Core console.

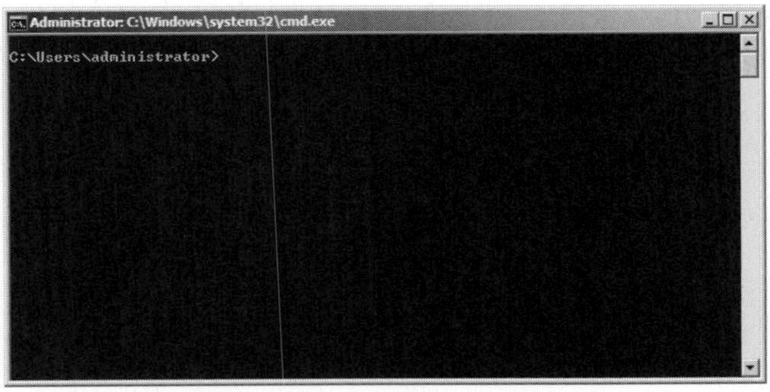

FIGURE 6-1 The Windows Server 2008 Server Core console

Many Control Panel items are available in Server Core. Type the name of the .cpl item at the command prompt, like **intl.cpl** and **timedate.cpl**. These Control Panel items provide about the only limited GUI for local server administration. Other useful administrative tools are RegEdit.exe, RegEdt32.exe, and Bcdedit.exe. You can also use scripts, based on Extensible Markup Language (XML), to configure the Server Core server.

You can also manage the Server Core server remotely, using the Microsoft Management Console (MMC), remote command-line tools, or Remote Server Administration Tools (RSAT). The MMC and RSAT used through a remote connection to the Server Core server are the only ways to administer the Server Core server through a GUI.

Server Core supports the following server roles:

- Active Directory Domain Services (AD DS)
- Active Directory Lightweight Directory Services (AD LDS)
- DHCP Server
- DNS Server
- File Server
- Print Server
- Streaming Media Services
- Web Server (IIS)

You must select Server Core Installation during the installation of the operating system. Figure 6-2 shows the selection menu from which you need to select the Server Core Installation during the Windows Server 2008 installation.

Windows Server 2008 Server Core in the branch office, whether configured as a stand-alone, member, domain controller, or RODC server, provides the securest Windows Server 2008 operating system platform because of its server hardening by design. You should use this implementation when the server has a significant risk of being either physically or electronically exposed to compromise or when the server will be supporting the most sensitive data or processes, even in a well-protected local area network (LAN) or branch office environment. The potential minor cost savings in hardware should typically not be a consideration in making this decision.

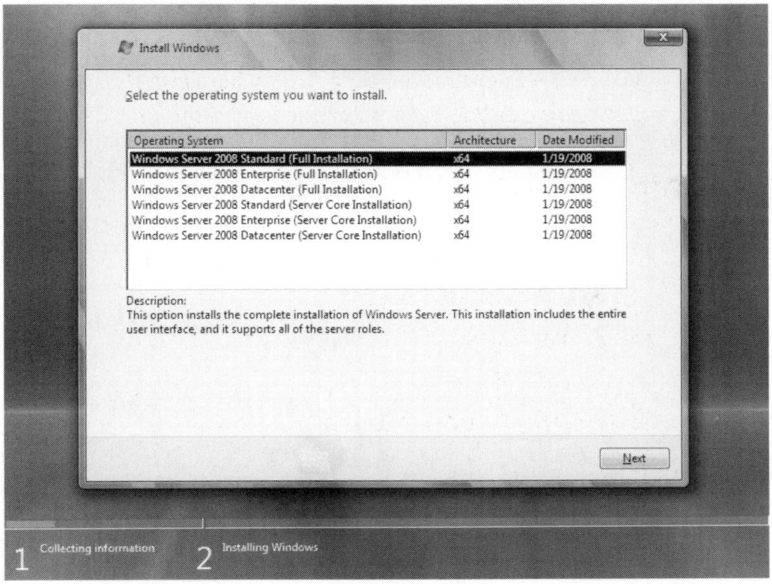

FIGURE 6-2 Selecting Windows Server 2008 Full Installation or Server Core Installation

WINDOWS SERVER 2008—FULL INSTALLATION

The full installation of Windows Server 2008 is what most administrators are used to. It provides all of the desired features through a familiar GUI. Unfortunately, all the gadgets, GUIs, tools, utilities, and applications that make life easy for the administrator create a substantially greater number of opportunities for unauthorized users to break into and take over a server, as previously described.

A Windows Server 2008 full installation is generally safe to use on a well-protected LAN or in a branch office environment where the threat of compromise is reduced and where the server is supporting less highly sensitive data and processes.

Adding a Domain Controller

Access to the domain controller server is required for successful authentication of users and computers in the enterprise. Adding a domain controller to a branch office introduces increased risk, cost, and administrative overhead in human terms. In terms of directory services, it involves the following:

- There is additional hardware (cost) at the branch office.
- Enterprise Admins must create, configure, and maintain a site in Active Directory for the branch office.
- There will be Active Directory replication traffic over the WAN link between HQ and the branch office.

- There will be the need for additional infrastructure devices, services, or both.
- The remote domain controller must be maintained (at the server level), requiring that Administrator Role Separation be configured.
- There are security concerns about having a copy of the entire Active Directory database, complete with user names and passwords, along with the additional infrastructure systems and services in this potentially unsecure facility.

On the other hand, having a domain controller in the branch office provides a notable improvement in performance and reliability for the branch office for the following reasons:

- Branch office users can authenticate more quickly and can authenticate even if the WAN link is down.
- All other local requests of AD DS are handled more quickly and are successful even if the WAN link is down.
- Not having a domain controller in the branch office means the branch office relies more heavily on the performance and reliability of the WAN link.
- The domain controller provides an additional level of fault tolerance to the Active Directory database.

Microsoft recommends the addition of a domain controller in any site (like a branch office) in the following situations:

- More than 100 users are in the site.
- The site is using an application that relies on a custom Active Directory partition for replication.
- Domain logons must be successful (typically expressed as the requirement to access domain resources) even if the WAN link is down.

> **NOTE ACTIVE DIRECTORY DOMAIN SERVICES BINARIES**
>
> A new process that runs prior to initializing the Active Directory Installation Wizard is the installation of the DCPromo binaries (executables) onto the server. You can initiate this by adding the AD DS server role. Then you can execute DCPromo from a command prompt. Alternatively, if you don't first install the AD DS server role, you'll see it automatically initiate.

In situations where the domain controller is required in the branch office, the next decision is what type of domain controller should be deployed. This question has new potential answers in Windows Server 2008. Windows Server 2008 can now provide the following types of domain controllers, engineered to help satisfy reliability, performance, and security concerns in the branch office.

FULL DOMAIN CONTROLLER

Based on a Full Installation of Windows Server 2008 (as opposed to a Server Core Installation), the full domain contains all of the standard components of Active Directory, just like in Windows Server 2003. These domain controllers perform bidirectional replication with other domain controllers in the domain and forest, just like in earlier versions of the operating system.

The full domain controller is the least secure implementation of the domain controller. It has the full operating system, with many opportunities for hackers to exploit. It has the full Active Directory database, complete with user names and passwords. The Active Directory database is writable, providing the opportunity for inappropriate modification, which is a violation of the integrity of the data in the Active Directory database. These potential violations of integrity can be the result of either an authorized user's accidental misconfiguration or willful misuse or an unauthorized user's manipulation of Active Directory.

READ-ONLY DOMAIN CONTROLLER

The RODC is a more secure version of a domain controller. Based on a full installation of Windows Server 2008 (as opposed to a Server Core Installation), the RODC contains all of the standard components of Active Directory, except for account passwords. Clients are not able to write any changes to the RODC, however. Lightweight Directory Access Protocol (LDAP) applications that perform write operations are referred to writable domain controllers that are located in the nearest site over an available WAN link. RODCs receive only inbound, one-way domain data replication from Windows Server 2008 domain controllers in the domain. A common approach to implementing an RODC in the branch office is to include the global catalog (GC) and a DNS server service. This collection of services provides fast and reliable authentication and access to remote Active Directory components, while keeping the domain controller specialized enough to improve its security. Adding many more features or services to the RODC increases its vulnerability to attack.

In addition to the read-only Active Directory database and the one-way replication, RODC features include the following:

- **Credential caching** Limited contents are stored in the password database in case of compromise. Administrators must configure a Password Replication Policy to allow password replication of only specified accounts to occur to the RODC.
- **Administrator Role Separation** This was described earlier in this lesson.
- **RODC filtered attribute set** This is used to allow administrators to selectively filter attributes on Active Directory objects, typically for security purposes.
- **Read-only DNS** All Active Directory–integrated zones get replicated to the read-only DNS server; however, the zones are nondynamic. When clients attempt to update their DNS information, the read-only DNS server returns a referral to the client with the address of a DNS server with a writable copy of the zone.

NOTE INCREASED RODC SECURITY COMES AT A PRICE

Although the RODC provides additional security against unauthorized changes to Active Directory and minimizes the number of passwords that might be compromised if the domain controller gets stolen from the branch office, the RODC cannot be used to make any changes to Active Directory data. If the WAN link is down, no changes can be made to Active Directory through the RODC.

The RODC was largely designed for branch office implementation. It can be installed on the Full Installation or the Server Core Installation of Windows Server 2008—Server Core, of course, being the more secure of the two. The option to install the domain controller as an RODC is a new setting in the DCPromo utility, as shown in Figure 6-3.

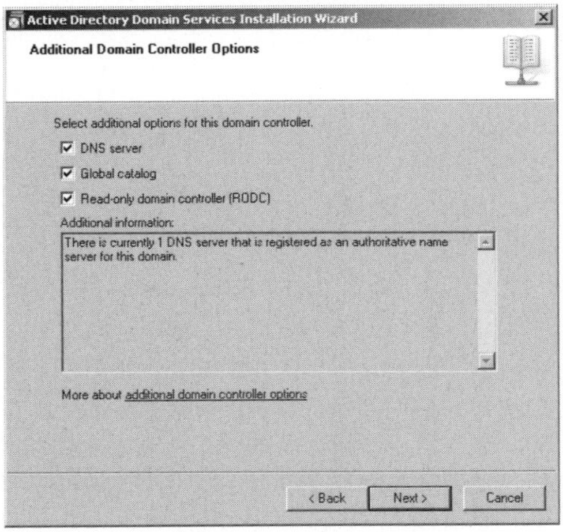

FIGURE 6-3 Selecting the RODC during DCPromo

NOTE THE RODC COMPATIBILITY PACK

To improve compatibility with RODCs and domain member systems, you can install the RODC compatibility pack on Windows Server 2003 and Windows XP member systems. To learn more about the RODC compatibility pack, go to *http://technet.microsoft.com/en-us/library/cc725669(WS.10).aspx*. You can obtain the RODC compatibility pack at *http://go.microsoft.com/fwlink/?LinkId=120375*.

The RODC is covered in more detail in Lesson 2, "Branch Office Server Security."

SERVER CORE DOMAIN CONTROLLER

As stated previously, Server Core is the most secure installation of Windows Server 2008. Server Core installs a minimal operating system, providing minimal services and applications, with no Windows shell and a limited GUI.

Server Core is not a domain controller by default, but AD DS can be added to the Server Core Installation. When the more secure RODC role is added to the Server Core Installation, you have the most secure domain controller installation possible, optimized for the risky branch office implementation. You add the AD DS role to the Server Core server using the **DCPromo /unattend <unattend.txt>** command, along with a preconfigured answer file (Unattend.txt) for the DCPromo utility.

Windows Server 2008 Server Core in the branch office, whether configured as a stand-alone, member, domain controller, or RODC server, provides the most secure Windows Server 2008 operating system platform due to its server hardening by design.

✔ **Quick Check**

1. Which installation of a domain controller provides increased security and a full graphical user interface?

2. Which installation of a domain controller provides the most security?

Quick Check Answers

1. Read-only Domain Controller installed on a Windows Server 2008 R2 Full Installation server.

2. Read-only Domain Controller installed on a Windows Server 2008 R2 Server Core server.

GLOBAL CATALOG

The global catalog server is required for successful authentication of users and computers in the enterprise. The global catalog must reside on a domain controller. Microsoft recommends that you place a global catalog in a branch office in the following situations:

- There is a domain controller in the branch office, and:
  - The WAN link is unreliable.
  - There are more than 100 users in the branch office.
  - Universal group membership caching is not enabled.
  - The branch office supports Active Directory–aware or Distributed Component Object Model (DCOM) applications.

Placing a global catalog in the branch office will improve the performance of Lightweight Directory Access Protocol (LDAP) queries, user logons, and Active Directory–aware and DCOM applications for users in the branch office.

Placing a global catalog in the branch office requires a domain controller in the branch office, raising the risk of the domain controller being compromised. Furthermore, it increases the risk of compromise of sensitive global catalog data and it increases the amount of AD DS replication traffic to and from the branch office over the WAN links.

OPERATIONS MASTERS

Few situations would warrant placing one or more operations masters in a branch office. Operations masters are significant components within Active Directory that reside on domain controllers within the AD DS environment, and placing them in an isolated and potentially disconnected branch office could cause problems for the entire forest. About the only cases in which it might be appropriate are the following:

- There is a domain controller in the branch office, and:
  - The branch office is its own domain. A domain controller in the branch office would hold the relative ID (RID) master, the infrastructure master, and the primary domain controller (PDC) emulator operations master roles.
  - The branch office is its own forest. A domain controller in the branch office would hold the domain naming master, the schema master, the RID master, the infrastructure master, and the PDC emulator operations master roles.
  - The branch office has the bulk of down-level clients in the enterprise. A domain controller in the branch office would hold the PDC emulator operations master roles.

In almost every other case, the operations master roles should typically remain on the well-secured, stable, and well-connected HQ network.

DOMAIN NAME SYSTEM

The DNS server is required for successful authentication of users and computers in the enterprise and for Internet access. Clients in the branch office will need to locate AD DS servers and other infrastructure services. It is useful, and can be a requirement, that a DNS server be placed in the branch office. This provides rapid registration and query responses, even if the WAN link to HQ is down or busy.

Providing a DNS server in the branch office is a requirement if the branch office is configured as its own domain in AD DS. Local clients will need local DNS to locate domain-related services. From the perspective of the user or computer, the act of locating AD DS is accomplished through service location (SRV) records within the DNS zone for the domain. In addition, other AD DS DNS zones throughout the forest must meet the following requirements:

- Be configured as Active Directory–integrated DNS zones with proper replication partitions configured
- Have secondary DNS zones and zone transfers configured
- Have forwarders or stub zones configured
- If the branch office domain is a child domain, have a delegation record in the parent DNS zone configured

DHCP SERVICES

Another network infrastructure service that is often required is DHCP for the dynamic assignment of IP addresses and other configuration settings to clients. Again, for performance and reliability reasons, placing a DHCP server in the branch office is often desirable. This aids IP connectivity for branch office clients even if the WAN link is down for extended periods.

MULTISITE (BRANCH OFFICE) CLUSTERING WITH MICROSOFT CLUSTER SERVICES

Failover clusters provide server fault tolerance for highly available applications and services, such as Microsoft SQL Server, Microsoft Exchange Server, Windows Server Virtualization (also known as Hyper-V or WSV) servers, DHCP servers, and file and print services. You can place cluster nodes in each branch office site to provide local access with increased availability to applications, services, and data.

DFS REPLICATION FOR DATA FAULT TOLERANCE

Another fault-tolerant mechanism that can be used in the branch office is Distributed File System (DFS) replication. DFS replication is typically used to replicate data files to multiple and geographically dispersed DFS replica sets, which is ideal for the branch office deployment. DFS replication has been overhauled in Windows Server 2008, with improvements in performance, data reliability, and replication on demand (called Replicate Now), and it can be used on the new Windows Server 2008 RODC server. DFS replication is so much better than the earlier (Windows 2000 Server and Windows Server 2003) File Replication Service (FRS) that it replaces FRS for SYSVOL replication for domains configured to use the Windows Server 2008 domain functional level.

Windows Server 2008 R2 also provides read-only DFS replica content to provide integrity protection of the original data.

ROUTING AND REMOTE ACCESS SERVICES

The Routing and Remote Access Services (RRAS) server hosts several useful but potentially risky services. It is now a component of the Network Policy and Access Services server role, but it can be installed independently of NAP. New in Windows Server 2008 is support for IPv6.

RRAS can be particularly useful in the branch office because it includes the following services:

- VPN server
- Demand-dial routing for use with establishing on-demand VPNs
- NAT with:
  - IP routing (small scale; perfect for satisfying the limited routing needs in the branch office)
  - DHCP relay agent

...n be configured to perform as a Network Policy Server (NPS) used to support ...elated, supplemental services include the following:

- ...registration authority
- ...Credential Authorization Protocol

...ion, RRAS provides support for these typically lesser used but sometimes helpful

- ...Dial-in connections
- ...Internet Group Management Protocol (IGMP)—Multicast routing
- Routing Information Protocol (RIP) version 1 and version 2

If you decide to place an RRAS server in the branch office, if it doesn't exist in the branch office already, you'll want to consider the potential placement of a domain controller in the branch office. If the RRAS server will be authenticating users and VPN connections, you might prefer to provide local authentication services.

The VPN server component of the RRAS server provides tremendous benefits in securing information in transit between the branch office and HQ, between two branch offices, and between the branch office and remote authorized users. It can provide core network infra- structure services with NAT, IP routing, and the DHCP relay agent.

However, remember that a dial-in server, like RRAS, allows remote users, both authorized and unauthorized, to gain access to the internal network and its resources. This device is a gap in the security fortress and must be implemented with careful consideration and plan- ning. It requires ongoing monitoring and analysis to maintain and maximize security on this portal into your network infrastructure.

WINDOWS SERVER UPDATE SERVICES

Microsoft Windows Server Update Services (WSUS), currently v3.0 SP2, enables administrators to deploy the latest Microsoft product updates to computers running the Windows operating system. This server downloads, stores, and distributes approved Microsoft operating system and application updates to computers in the enterprise. Placing a WSUS server in a branch office reduces update traffic, either from the HQ or from the Internet. The WSUS server in the branch office can be managed from HQ, so no administrative privilege is required other than local administrator privilege (see Administrator Role Separation, which was covered earlier in this chapter) for underlying server support. HQ administration can, of course, grant update approval authority to the branch office administrator, if appropriate.

The downside, again, is the hardware cost, the slightly increased local administration over- head, and the increased attack surface of the server and the branch office network.

VIRTUALIZATION IN THE BRANCH OFFICE

Another new technology that can be a major benefit in the branch office is Microsoft Hyper-V. Hyper-V provides support for running multiple virtual machines (VMs) on a single physical computer host. This is referred to as server consolidation. Because most computers operate using only 10 to 25 percent of a computer system's available resources, such as RAM and CPU clock cycles, the hardware is severely underutilized. By running multiple VMs on a single physical server host, these server resources are much better utilized, requiring fewer physical servers and providing better return on investment. Having fewer physical devices in the branch office reduces the difficulty of physically securing those devices.

Microsoft's virtualization technology provides for rapid and easy deployment of VMs and simplifies the migration of VMs from one physical host to another. These features can be essential components of the enterprise's business continuity and disaster recovery plans. Hyper-V can be implemented on Windows Server 2008 Server Core servers for increased security and can be clustered to provide server failover fault tolerance.

Hyper-V is included with Windows Server 2008 Standard, Windows Server 2008 Enterprise, and Windows Server 2008 Datacenter. Windows Server 2008 Standard includes one virtual instance per license. Windows Server 2008 Enterprise includes four virtual instances per license. With Windows Server 2008 Datacenter, customers receive unlimited virtual instances per license. You can buy these versions without Hyper-V, but the savings are negligible.

Additional improvements to virtualization have been introduced in Windows Server 2008 R2, with technologies that include the upgraded Virtual Desktop Infrastructure (VDI; formerly Terminal Services), which provides client desktops to remote systems, application delivery, and a new collection of VDI management and deployment tools. These technologies, when used in branch offices, provide for centralized administration and excellent control over the operating systems and applications available in the branch office.

> **NOTE** VDI
>
> **VDI is covered in detail in Chapter 8, "Designing Virtualization."**

Branch Office Communications Considerations

Branch office networks need to connect to resources in the HQ network. This connection can be on dedicated lines, like T1 or T3 lines, or it can be over the public wires of the Internet. In either case, these channels of communication should be protected from sniffers and eavesdroppers. Furthermore, it is not uncommon for the WAN link between the branch office and HQ to go down, forcing the network administrator to view WAN links as unreliable. These unsecure and unreliable WAN links might be required to carry sensitive corporate, medical, financial, and otherwise private data requiring protection by laws and regulations, as well as data to support AD DS. The types of data an enterprise must consider in its branch office deployment design are the following:

- AD DS replication data—if the branch office holds a domain controller
- Global catalog replication data—if the branch office holds a global catalog
- DNS data—either within AD DS replication Active Directory–integrated zones or in zone transfers

- Virtualization and remote access communications, including VDI communications, RemoteApp and Desktop (RAD) connections, RemoteFX, Remote Workspace, Presentation Virtualization, and Remote Desktop Gateway

- User data—accessed over the WAN links and for centralized backups at HQ

- DFS replicated data and BranchCache data

- Multisite clustering heartbeat data

Site Link Considerations for the Branch Office

Each defined site must connect to AD DS by means of a site link. A site link is the logical connection object between sites for AD DS replication. This logical connection, of course, requires physical connectivity to be in place and to be functioning properly for replication to succeed. Due to the security constraints on different types of data that must be replicated and to provide redundancy for failed replication servers, there are often replication paths for Active Directory replication data that would fail without the addition of site link bridges.

The good news is that, as early as Windows 2000 Server, site link bridging is enabled by default on all site links. If tighter control over replication paths is required, the Bridge All Site Links option can be disabled. The administrator must then manually construct any specific site link bridges required to provide the proper connectivity and redundancy on these logical connections.

Another aspect of AD DS replication, new to Windows Server 2008, is the need to ensure replication to the new RODC. Unfortunately, down-level domain controllers (Windows 2000 Server and Windows Server 2003) do not recognize an RODC because of its one-way replication processes and will not replicate data to it. This requires that any site with only RODCs (one or more) must have a site link directly to a site with at least one Windows Server 2008 domain controller. The Windows Server 2008 domain controller does recognize the RODC and will replicate AD DS data to it appropriately.

Confidentiality for Data in Transit

No matter what type of connection you use, you should employ VPNs to secure data in transit between the branch office and HQ and between remote clients and the branch office. Windows Server 2008 provides VPN support for the following VPN protocols:

- **Point-to-Point Tunneling Protocol (PPTP)** The early and original Microsoft VPN protocol. This VPN is easy to set up and provides reasonable security based on the RC4 cipher for encryption. It uses TCP port 1723.

- **Layer 2 Tunneling Protocol (L2TP)** Operates at layer 2 of the Open Systems Interconnection (OSI) model, so no IP network is required. L2TP provides strong authentication, nonrepudiation, and strong integrity validation by using X.509 digital certificates on the endpoint servers. It does not provide confidentiality (encryption). It uses TCP port 1701.

- **IP Security (IPsec)** Operates at layer 3 of the OSI model, so an IP network is required. It has become the de facto VPN protocol of choice. With Windows Server 2008, it uses triple Data Encryption Standard (3DES) or Advanced Encryption Standard (AES) for encryption and can provide weak authentication and integrity validation based on Kerberos. It can be strengthened to provide strong authentication, nonrepudiation, and integrity validation based on X.509 digital certificates. It uses User Datagram Protocol (UDP) port 500.

- **Secure Sockets Transport Protocol (SSTP)** This is a new feature in Windows Server 2008. This VPN protocol is based on the very popular Hypertext Transfer Protocol (HTTP) over Secure Sockets Layer (SSL) and Transport Layer Security (TLS), but it has been refined for use on the LAN (versus its original use for web-based services and applications). It can provide only client-to-server functionality and provides strong authenticity, nonrepudiation, and integrity validation of the server (only), along with weak authentication and integrity validation of the client. SSTP has native support for IPv6. It is based on an X.509 digital certificate on the server, uses the popular RC4 and AES ciphers, and runs over TCP port 443.

- **DirectAccess** Introduced in Windows Server 2008 R2, DirectAccess securely and automatically connects remote Windows 7 Ultimate and Enterprise domain clients to the corporate intranet, eliminating the complexity and confusion of client-initiated VPNs. Based on IPsec and IPv6, DirectAccess incorporates IPv6-in-IPv4 tunneling and 6-to-4 translation where necessary to accommodate whatever version of IP is running in the intranet and between the client and intranet.

- **VPN Reconnect** (previously called Agile VPN) Also introduced in Windows Server 2008 R2, VPN Reconnect reestablishes broken VPN connections for Windows 7 users without user intervention when the connection path resumes. It takes advantage of features within IPsec Tunnel mode and Internet Key Exchange version 2 (IKEv2) technology to automatically reauthenticate a previously authenticated VPN connection. This transparent VPN break and reconnect is most useful in high-mobility environments where mobile clients might change their connection to wireless access points or cellular connections, forcing a change in their IP address and causing traditional VPNs to fail and require manual reconnection.

Improve Branch Office Performance Using BranchCache

A new feature to improve performance in branch offices is BranchCache. Available in Windows 7 and Windows Server 2008 R2, *BranchCache* works with centralized applications and stores a copy of data retrieved from intranet file and web servers on systems within the branch office. If a branch office server is available, BranchCache can operate in hosted mode, storing cached data on the server. If no server is available, BranchCache can operate in distributed mode, storing cached data on one or more client computers in the branch office. These cached copies of files are now automatically provided to local clients when they might normally pull another copy over the WAN to the corporate network, improving performance and reducing WAN link load.

BranchCache is easily configured on systems using GPO settings or by using the *netsh branchcache* command-line utility. BranchCache must first be enabled and set to distributed or hosted mode. The amount of disk space to use for cached data defaults to 5 percent of the disk, but can be configured. If you are using hosted mode, you can specify the location of the hosted cache on the host server(s).

BranchCache data can be encrypted while in transit using VPNs, which might already be in place between the branch office and the corporate intranet. Either BitLocker or Encrypting File System (EFS) can be configured if encryption for the cached content is required while at rest.

EXAM TIP

For the 70-647 exam, make sure you understand how to use BranchCache to improve file access performance in the branch office and to reduce bandwidth consumption over WAN links.

PRACTICE **The Branch Office Administrator**

In this practice, you assign server administration privilege on a branch office domain controller without granting domain administration privilege to the user.

EXERCISE 1 Implementing Administrator Role Separation

To implement Administrator Role Separation on a single domain controller, at a command prompt on the domain controller, type:

DSMGMT.exe

and press Enter. At the DSMGMT prompt, type:

```
local roles
```

and press Enter. You can type a question mark (**?**) to get help at any level in the DSMGMT application. Next, type:

```
list roles
```

to view the possible delegations on the server. Now, for the delegation, type:

add <domain>\<user name or group name> administrators

You should receive the following response:

Successfully Updated Local Role

Next, to confirm the delegation, type:

show role administrators

You should see the user or group that has been delegated the Administrator Role Separation role. Keep in mind that this grants the delegated user or group administrative privilege on only this one domain controller. To grant administrative privilege to the branch office administrator over users and computers in the branch office, you will also need to delegate privilege at the site, domain, or OU level for the branch office, as appropriate.

Lesson Summary

- The branch office is typically isolated, with minimal support, infrastructure, and security relative to the enterprise HQ. Therefore, the branch office system is more likely to be compromised than systems at the more developed HQ.

- Delegate privilege to the branch office administrator following the principle of least privilege, using Administrator Role Separation and the Delegation of Control Wizard at the lowest level in the Active Directory hierarchy.

- Consider restructuring the AD DS to optimize administrative control and limit exposure in the branch office.

- Analyze the need for information systems services in the branch office. Balance the needs and benefits of placing these infrastructure services in the remote and less secure branch office with the associated costs and risks.

- Understand the dependencies that services installed in the branch office might require, along with their associated costs and risks.

- Carefully plan and understand the connectivity (WAN links) between the branch office and HQ so that proper security and fault-tolerant measures can be implemented.

Lesson Review

You can use the following questions to test your knowledge of the information in Lesson 1, "Branch Office Deployment." The questions are also available on the companion CD if you prefer to review them in electronic form.

> **NOTE ANSWERS**
>
> Answers to these questions and explanations of why each answer choice is correct or incorrect are located in the "Answers" section at the end of the book.

1. What new feature of Windows Server 2008 gives a branch office administrator the privilege of logging onto a domain controller for server administration but does not give the administrator the privilege of administering Active Directory?

   A. Read-only domain controller (RODC)

   B. Server Core domain controller

   C. Administrator Role Separation

   D. BitLocker

2. Which of the following provides user data fault tolerance in a branch office?

   A. Read-only domain controller (RODC)

   B. Clustering

   C. Server Core

   D. DFS replication

3. Your HQ has a DHCP server. You are designing a new branch office. You need to provide dynamic IP addressing to branch office clients, even if the WAN link fails between HQ and the new branch office. What should you do?

   A. Install a DHCP relay agent in the branch office.

   B. Configure a superscope on the DHCP server in HQ.

   C. Install DHCP on a multisite cluster node in the branch office.

   D. Install demand-dial routing in the HQ.

Lesson 2: Branch Office Server Security

The branch office should initially be considered inherently unsecure, both physically and electronically. It is a mistake to make assumptions about any level of security until the site has been physically inspected and a comprehensive security policy and program has been defined and implemented specifically for each branch office. Unfortunately, what you'll probably discover, in some cases, is that the information technology component of the branch office is understaffed, underbudgeted, unplanned, and unmonitored.

The pressing need for the security policy and resulting program should be driven by senior management's security posture for the enterprise. The security policy should include disaster recovery planning and business continuity planning and should address every law and regulation with which the company must comply.

Implementation and maintenance of security for the branch office should be the responsibility of an entity other than the IT administration. The security professional and the IT administrator have common concerns, up to a point. The point where they diverge is the one at which you realize that IT's philosophy is "Availability at all cost!" and the security professional's philosophy is "If it isn't secure, pull the plug."

Although the security professional is responsible for the overall security of the branch office, the security professional will usually be located in a distant office, typically HQ. It is the responsibility of local administration and management to become the enforcers of the security policy and program that is handed down from the security professional's team. They are the ones with the intimate knowledge and vision of the people, procedures, and structure of the branch office. Although the protection of the confidentiality, integrity, and availability of valuable information assets will be the major content of this lesson, the primary consideration for the security program is human safety. People come first; the issue of protecting the assets of the enterprise immediately follows.

> **After this lesson, you will be able to:**
> - Describe the major components of physical security for the branch office.
> - Identify the basic components that establish electronic security on a network.
> - Describe the features in Windows Server 2008 that you can use to satisfy specific security targets.
> - Describe how to use an RODC to provide increased security in the branch office.
> - Describe how to design a Password Replication Policy to maximize security on the RODC.
> - Describe how to use the Windows Server 2008 Server Core and the Windows Server 2008 Server Core domain controller server installation to provide increased security in the branch office.
> - Describe how to secure data in storage on servers in the branch office.
>
> **Estimated lesson time: 50 minutes**

Overview of Security for the Branch Office

The first component of the security policy and program used to implement security at the branch office is a definition of adequate physical security. Physical security is intended to keep intruders out and to keep the valuable information system assets in. Physical security is implemented by obvious things like solid walls, fences, doors and locks, guards and guard dogs, and internal security zones, like a secure server room with card swipes in and out, designed to provide differing levels of security as users enter the different security zones. Physical security is also implemented by more technical components, like the use of strong passwords, smart cards, and biometrics.

Next, acceptable use policies should be created to include any device or system in the facility and any device owned by the enterprise that gets issued to the worker. One of the most effective security measures that can be implemented, after the security policy, the security program, and the acceptable use policies, is security awareness training for all users. This should cover facility safety training and an overview of the security policy. Employees should understand that they have specific responsibilities related to the security program and that they must know what the rules of the policy are. They must further understand that violation of any security policy could be grounds for termination. Employees should be constantly reminded about and aware of the security concerns of the organization. For example, this can be accomplished through posters or a highlighted story on the corporate intranet citing recent violations and threats, as well as through feedback from IT and management when users are identified to be in violation of acceptable use of the computers and information systems.

Security awareness training should be performed at least annually for all employees and should be provided at a higher level and more often as the role of the user rises in the organizational structure in the enterprise. Management personnel must understand their responsibility to know the relevant security policies, as well as their roles as the enforcers of the security policy in their departments. Middle management must provide enforcement at the lower levels of management, and so on.

When employees know what the acceptable use rules are and understand their responsibilities, the security structure should include auditing and monitoring of the facility and as much of the environment as is legal. It should be explained that this monitoring is for the safety and security of the employees as well as for the assets of the enterprise.

> **NOTE** **A WARNING ABOUT EMPLOYEE MONITORING**
>
> Laws in the United States on employee monitoring vary greatly from state to state and even county to county. Typically, the employee must be aware of, and agree to, the monitoring. Furthermore, the monitoring cannot target specific individuals, which would amount to discrimination. The monitoring should be performed routinely and randomly.
>
> Always consult the local legal department for documented guidelines on how, what, and who can be monitored, and do not exceed these guidelines.

You will, of course, enable a comprehensive audit policy on the information systems. You might want to monitor by using closed-circuit cameras and recording devices, and you might want to record network and Internet usage for any and all employees. You might want to have access to monitor the display on the computer monitor (these can indeed be shadowed by the administration) and be able to search any hard disk drive on the corporate network. You should monitor employees' company email and voice mail. You should monitor the employees any time they are on the company premises, any time they are using company-owned resources (such as cell phones and portable computers), and any time they are acting as representatives of the organization—again, only within the limits of the law. Don't forget that, in most cases, the organization is legally responsible, and therefore liable, for anything inappropriate that an employee does while on company business or while using any of the organization's devices.

Recording all of this information is beneficial, but it is useless unless someone is specifically responsible for the review of the audit logs, the intrusion detection system (IDS) and intrusion prevention system (IPS) logs, the videotapes, the call logs, the firewall logs, and so on. This is the difficult part. Because the reviewers are looking at the actual map of attacks, exploits, violations, and events that occurred on the system, they must decipher what these many logs and events actually say. The responsible person must identify violations, attempted violations, and unexpected vulnerabilities in the environment and develop proposals for the implementation of new and appropriate countermeasures to mitigate the risks and defend against these attacks in the future.

Furthermore, in many cases, these logs must be tightly secured, with their integrity protected and provable, and retained in archives for several years to satisfy legal and regulatory compliance requirements.

Securing Windows Server 2008 in the Branch Office

Now that the foundation of security is in place, including the security policies, employee safety, physical security, awareness training, and monitoring, the next security objective is the electronic security of the information systems. The threats to information systems that are covered in this section include threats from willful and malicious hacker attack, malware, willful or accidental modification of data or system configuration, and privilege misuse.

Security Overview for the Information System in the Branch Office

Each branch office implementation must be individually and carefully designed, implemented, and maintained. There are, however, several core security components that virtually every branch office network installation should include.

INFRASTRUCTURE FIREWALLS

The branch office network should be isolated from external networks, including the network at HQ, through one or more firewalls. They can be placed in series (one behind the other) to construct a perimeter network (also known as DMZ, demilitarized zone, and screened subnet) for public resources or resources shared with HQ. They can be placed in parallel and through different Internet service providers (ISPs) to provide redundancy for the WAN link connections to the Internet or to HQ.

HOST-BASED FIREWALLS

In addition to the network-based firewalls, Windows Server 2003, Windows Vista, Windows 7, and Windows Server 2008 all have a built-in, host-based firewall (often called a personal firewall). In general, these host-based firewalls should all be enabled and properly configured to allow only the minimum required traffic into and out of the Windows-based computers. Windows Vista, Windows 7, and Windows Server 2008 provide for advanced configuration in the host-based Windows Firewall with Advanced Security.

THE INTRUSION DETECTION SYSTEM/INTRUSION PROTECTION SYSTEM

Another infrastructure device that you should consider on the branch office network is the IDS/IPS. These are third-party devices (or systems). The IDS monitors network traffic, logs data about the traffic, analyzes the traffic based on signatures and anomalies, recognizes potential attacks, and alerts the administrative staff to the perceived attack. In addition, the IPS has the capability to react to the perceived attack. This reaction can be an adjustment to the rule base on one or more firewalls to reject the attacker's frames, the transmission of TCP NACK to the victim, or the transmission of deauthentication frames to an 802.1x port-based authentication switch to disconnect the victim from the attacker.

SERVER HARDENING

The next routine security target on all computer systems is *server hardening*, or creating the bastion host. This reduces the attack surface of the computer by reducing the number of targets available on the system to a hacker. In general, server hardening includes the following:

- Stopping and disabling all unnecessary services and applications
- Renaming the Administrator account
- Creating a new, useless, and disabled user account named Administrator and securing it with an impossible password
- Removing or disabling all unnecessary user accounts
- Delegating remaining user accounts based on the principle of least privilege
- Requiring strong authentication of users
- Performing regular firmware, operating system, and application updates
- Installing, running, and regularly updating antivirus and anti-spyware applications
- Regularly documenting and then reconfirming the system configuration
- Implementing routine auditing on logons, network connections, object access, and system configuration changes

This is the basic hardened server configuration that should be implemented on every computer in the enterprise. However, for critical or exposed servers, you should implement additional lockdowns. These include the following:

- Deleting or uninstalling all nonessential executables (binaries) from the computer
- Deleting or uninstalling all administration tools
- Configuring a GPO to disable and further restrict unused services
- Creating scripts to lock down services and schedule them to run each hour
- Implementing a routine or process to detect changes to the system files or system configuration (You can use the Microsoft System File Checker [SFC.exe] for this purpose. A popular third-party tool named Tripwire is available to validate the integrity of system files, as well.)
- Monitoring system activity and network traffic to and from the hardened server
- Implementing more detailed auditing on logons, network connections, object access, and system configuration changes

The list could go on, but you undoubtedly get the idea. Windows Server 2008 Server Core is a specially designed, hardened server on installation, as was described in Lesson 1, "Branch Office Deployment."

Securing Windows Server 2008 in the Branch Office

Windows Server 2008 has introduced several significant enhancements to improve security in installations like the branch office. The most important new additions are the following:

- The Server Core Installation
- The RODC
- The Password Settings Object (PSO)
- NAP
- Administrator Role Separation

Server Core and Administrator Role Separation were covered in detail in Lesson 1, and NAP is covered in Chapter 5, "Designing Network Access." The RODC and the setting of fine-grained password policies with the PSO remain to be discussed in this lesson.

THE RODC

A new security-related feature in Windows Server 2008 is the RODC. It is designed for implementation in environments where:

- There is a need for local access to Active Directory by users, computers, applications, or other entities.
- The physical security of the server cannot be guaranteed.
- The server might be exposed to a hazardous network environment, such as an extranet.

- There are relatively few users.
- WAN link connectivity to the main network might be unreliable.
- Local technical support skills might be limited.

As you review this list, you will undoubtedly realize that it sounds like a branch office environment. The RODC differs from the full domain controller in the following ways; the RODC:

- Holds a read-only copy of the Active Directory database.
- Participates in only one-way replication of all replication partitions, including domain data from a Windows Server 2008 domain controller.
- Participates in only one-way replication of schema, configuration, and application directory partitions, and the global catalog from a Windows Server 2003 domain controller but not the domain partition.
- Does not receive user or computer credentials (passwords) from Active Directory by default.
- Can cache only selected user and computer credentials for accounts specified in a Password Replication Policy.
- Supports the removal of specified sensitive attributes from replication through the RODC filtered attribute set.
- Supports Administrator Role Separation.
- Supports read-only SYSVOL folders
- Supports a read-only instance of the DNS zones.

RODC DISADVANTAGES

Because of the read-only nature of the RODC, it cannot be used as an operations master or a replication bridgehead server. In addition, if Active Directory–aware applications need to write data to Active Directory, the RODC cannot accept those write commands and the application's process will fail. Microsoft Exchange Server is an example of this type of application. An Active Directory write process fails if the request is sent to an RODC. Active Directory–aware applications should be tested with the RODC prior to deployment into production.

The RODC might fail to authenticate smart card logons by default. For any domain controller to be able to authenticate smart card logons, the domain controller must receive a domain controller X.509 digital certificate from a trusted certification authority. These digital certificates are typically distributed to the domain controllers through certificate autoenrollment. The permissions on the certificate template must be modified to allow the RODC to receive this certificate.

The RODC does not advertise properly as a time source, causing the clocks on the branch office client computers to become desynchronized. The simple solution is to configure a Windows Server 2008 Full Installation domain controller as the PDC emulator operations master for the domain, making it the time master for the domain. Another solution is to manually configure a time master for the domain.

INSTALLING AN RODC

You need to take a few steps before you can install the first RODC in a domain:

1. Ensure that the forest functional level is Windows Server 2003 or higher. Remember that this means you must purge the forest of any Windows NT Server 4.0 and Windows 2000 Server domain controllers.

2. Run *ADPrep/RODCPrep*. This can only be done on the Schema Operations master for the forest and only by a member of the Enterprise Admins group. This step is not required if this is a new Windows Server 2008 forest. Copy the contents of the \Sources\Adprep folder from the installation media to the schema master domain controller and execute the command from there.

3. Install a Windows Server 2008 domain controller into the domain. This domain controller is the replication source for the RODC. The Windows Server 2008 domain controller must hold the PDC emulator operations master role and be located in the site nearest the site of the RODC, based on site-link cost.

After taking these steps, you can install the RODC on a Windows Server 2008 server. You can install the RODC on a Windows Server 2008 Full Installation or on a Windows Server 2008 Server Core Installation. Installing the RODC on the Server Core Installation provides the greatest level of security because of the hardened server nature of the Server Core Installation.

DELEGATED INSTALLATION OF THE RODC

The RODC computer object can be created in, or moved to, the domain controller OU during the installation of the RODC, but this will require membership in the Domain Admins group in the domain for the installer. However, this level of privilege is often not desirable for users in the remote office.

Because the RODC is often located in a remote office with a nondomain administrator user as the installer, it is possible to precreate the RODC account in the Domain Controllers OU in Active Directory Users and Computers and delegate authority to the remote, nondomain administrator installer who completes the DCPromo portion of the installation. Furthermore, you can specify details about the DCPromo installation that get stored on this unoccupied domain controller account object. These details get pushed down to the remote RODC during the DCPromo installation.

In Active Directory Users and Computers, on the Domain Controllers OU, right-click and select the Pre-Create Read-Only Domain Controller Account option, as shown in Figure 6-4. You now see the Active Directory Domain Services Installation Wizard.

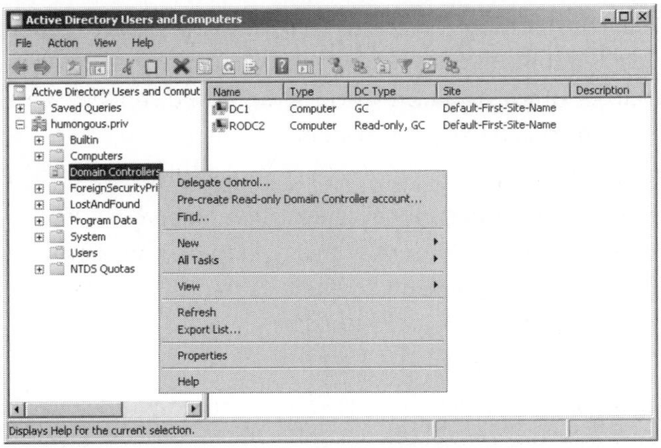

FIGURE 6-4 The delegated RODC installation

To see all configurable options for the RODC, on the Welcome page, select the Use Advanced Mode Installation check box. After a few standard DCPromo pages, such as the Network Credentials page, you are prompted to define information, such as the necessary credentials to precreate the domain controller account, computer name, site location, and whether you want to configure the RODC to host services such as DNS or the global catalog. Next, you can specify the Password Replication Policy for the RODC server, as shown in Figure 6-5.

This policy defines the list of passwords that can be replicated to, and cached on, the RODC. This *Password Replication Policy* will be explained in more detail later in this lesson.

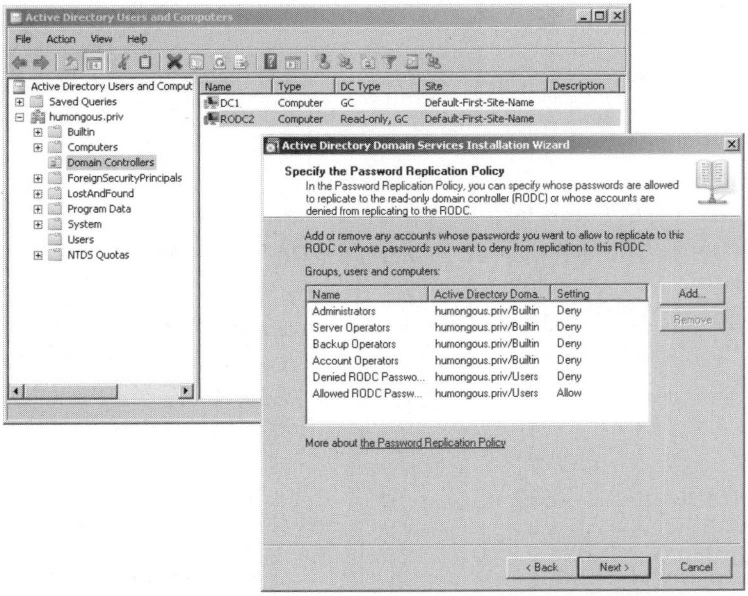

FIGURE 6-5 Specifying the Password Replication Policy for the RODC installation

The Active Directory Domain Services Installation Wizard next prompts you to specify which user or group of users are delegated the authority to run the DCPromo process on the Windows Server 2008 server in the remote office, as shown in Figure 6-6. The delegated users do not require any additional privileges to complete the installation.

The recommendation for granting privilege, including the privilege to install an RODC, is, as always, to follow A-G-DL-P: Place user accounts into global groups, place global groups into domain local groups, and then grant the necessary privileges to the domain local group. The Summary dialog box has an *Export* button to generate an answer file for use in other similar unattended installations.

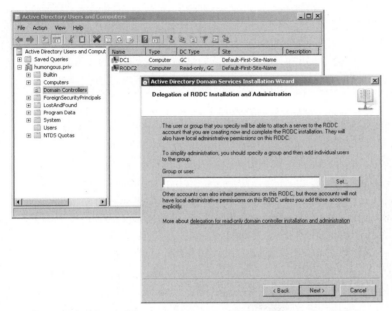

FIGURE 6-6 Specifying the nonadministrator installer of the remote RODC

INSTALLING THE RODC FROM CUSTOMIZED MEDIA

As you probably recall from Windows Server 2003, the DCPromo utility could be executed using the */ADV switch.* This allowed the remote domain controller to acquire the Active Directory database (NTDS.dit) from a system state data backup copy of a domain controller in the same domain. This feature has been replaced in Windows Server 2008 with what is called *Install From Media* (IFM). By using the Ntdsutil.exe utility with the IFM subcommand, you can create a copy of the NTDS.dit database and remove "cached secrets"—that is, passwords that you do not want to cache on the RODC server.

The RODC installation methods that can use the custom IFM media with passwords re-moved from the Active Directory database include the following:

- The Active Directory Domain Services Installation Wizard (DCPromo.exe) where the media can be specified

- From the command line by using *DCPromo /ReplicationSourcePath*
- Within an Answer file

THE RODC AUTHENTICATION PROCESS

In Windows Server 2008, the authentication processes have been changed in environments like a branch office where the only domain controller is an RODC. When a member computer boots up or when a user attempts to log on to a domain account, the request is sent to the local domain controller—in this case, it is an RODC. The RODC does not cache user or computer credentials by default. The RODC, acting as a relay agent, will then refer the authentication request across the WAN link to a Windows Server 2008 Full Installation (writable) domain controller in the nearest site. This can be slow and will fail the authentication process if the WAN link is down.

To improve performance and reliability, an administrator can create a Password Replication Policy that will replicate the passwords of the users and computers in the remote branch office to the branch office RODC. Now when a member computer boots up or when a user attempts to log on to a domain account, the local RODC can complete the authentication process within the local branch office. A different Password Replication Policy can be created for each RODC.

If a member server boots up or a user attempts to log on to a domain account and the local RODC does not have its credentials cached, after the authentication process completes through the referral process, the RODC will request that the writable domain controller replicate the credentials to the RODC for caching. If the account (user or computer) is on the Allowed list of the Password Replication Policy for that RODC, the credentials are replicated from the writable domain controller to the database of the RODC in the branch office.

If the account is not on the Allowed list of the Password Replication Policy for that RODC, the credentials are not replicated from the writable domain controller to the RODC, and the authentication process will need to be completed over the WAN link through the referral process every time.

The Password Replication Policy maintains four lists, as follows:

- **Allowed list** These passwords (secrets or credentials) can be replicated to the RODC.
- **Denied list** These passwords (secrets or credentials) cannot be replicated to the RODC.
- **Revealed list** A list of accounts, the passwords for which are cached on RODCs. This list can be used to reset passwords of accounts on RODC servers that become compromised.
- **Authenticated list** A list of accounts that have been successfully authenticated against the RODC.

You can view these lists in Active Directory Users and Computers by displaying the properties of the RODC server's computer object. On the Password Replication Policy tab, you can see the allowed and denied entities by examining the Setting column, as shown in Figure 6-7.

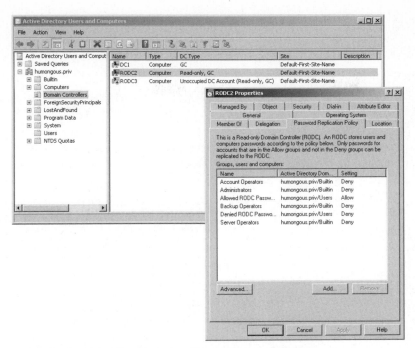

FIGURE 6-7 Accessing the Allowed and Denied lists on the RODC

Click Advanced to access the Revealed and Authenticated lists, as shown in Figure 6-8.

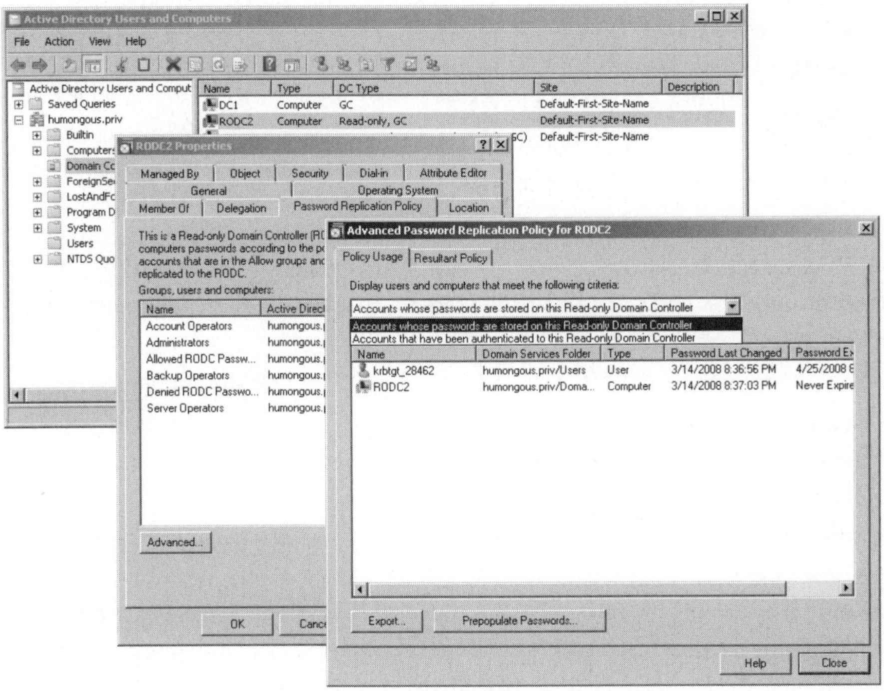

FIGURE 6-8 Accessing the Revealed and Authenticated lists on the RODC

REPLICATION CONCERNS WITH THE RODC

As stated previously, the RODC can receive domain replication data only from a Windows Server 2008 Full Installation (writable) domain controller. The site with the RODC must be connected to a site with a Windows Server 2008 Full Installation (writable) domain controller in the same domain by a site link with the lowest cost. If the nearest site (again, based on site link cost) does not contain a Windows Server 2008 Full Installation (writable) domain controller in the same domain, domain data replication to the RODC will fail.

The RODC can receive all other partitions of replication from a Windows Server 2008 domain controller or a Windows Server 2003 domain controller.

AUTOMATIC SITE COVERAGE

Sites are defined in Active Directory by mapping IP subnets to specific sites. Active Directory clients authenticate against and otherwise access domain controllers in their local site based on their IP addresses. To ensure that all Active Directory clients are able to identify the appropriate local domain controller, DNS SRV records are created for domain controllers and mapped to each site within the DNS zone for the domain.

Because it is possible to create a site without placing a domain controller in the site, Windows 2000 Server, Windows Server 2003, and Windows Server 2008 perform a service called *automatic site coverage*. If a site is recognized to be without a domain controller, a domain controller in the nearest site, based on site link cost, registers an SRV record for the remote site. This allows the Active Directory clients in the remote site without a local domain controller to connect to the domain controller nearest to their site.

However, Windows 2000 Server and Windows Server 2003 do not recognize a Windows Server 2008 RODC and might register an SRV record for a remote site with only an RODC in it. This is a problem. In DNS for the branch office site, there is an SRV record for the RODC that is actually in the branch office site and an SRV record for a Windows 2000 Server domain controller or a Windows Server 2003 domain controller in a site remote from the branch office. With DNS round robin (enabled by default), 50 percent of the time Active Directory clients in the branch office site will commute the WAN link to access Active Directory when they have their own RODC locally. This causes increased and unnecessary traffic on the WAN link, degrades performance, and can cause Active Directory–related failures for clients in the branch office site if the WAN link is down.

At the time of this writing, Microsoft recommends using one of five adjustments to resolve this problem:

- Wait for a hotfix from Microsoft.
- Use only Windows Server 2008 domain controllers in the site nearest to the RODC site.
- Disable automatic site coverage on the Windows 2000 Server domain controllers and the Windows Server 2003 domain controllers.
- Adjust the weight of the Windows Server 2003 domain controller SRV records (this is only a partial solution).

- Use a GPO to adjust the weight of the Windows Server 2003 domain controller SRV records (this is only a partial solution).

MORE INFO   RODC ISSUES AND WORKAROUNDS

To see a list of known RODC issues and the workarounds, review the RODC compatibility pack at *http://support.microsoft.com/kb/944043*.

RODC COMPROMISE

The main reason to use the RODC is the increased threat of compromise of the domain controller in an unsecure environment, either by physical theft or access of the system or electronic attack. If the RODC is stolen or becomes otherwise compromised and the hacker gets into the Active Directory database, the hacker has access to only a few account passwords, so the number of accounts potentially compromised is reduced. By using the Revealed list for the RODC in Active Directory Users and Computers, you can quickly reset the potentially compromised passwords.

Because the RODC cannot replicate to other domain controllers, there is no risk of a hacker modifying anything in Active Directory, such as permissions and group membership, and then poisoning the legitimate Active Directory through replication.

If your RODC is stolen, you can easily delete the RODC computer object in Active Directory Users and Computers without a successful DCPromo to remove the domain controller from Active Directory and without using the Ntdsutil *MetadataCleanup* command. (Using the Ntdsutil *MetadataCleanup* command to remove Active Directory objects leaves broken links from processes that refer to the now-removed object. These broken links will generate numerous errors about the missing object in event logs of domain controllers for the life of the domain.) To delete the RODC computer object, in Active Directory Users and Computers, right-click the RODC computer object in the Domain Controllers OU, and select Delete. Click Yes to continue. You are presented with the Deleting Domain Controller dialog box, and can then export a list of all accounts that were cached on the RODC and force the resetting of user and computer passwords for all accounts that were cached on the RODC, as shown in Figure 6-9.

To summarize, a Windows Server 2008 domain controller in the branch office will maximize performance by having a local copy of all passwords, accepting Active Directory changes, and performing two-way replication. However, it also maximizes the amount of sensitive data loss and the risk of poisoning the legitimate Active Directory in the case of compromise.

A Windows Server 2008 RODC in the branch office will support most Active Directory requirements in the branch office while minimizing the amount of sensitive data loss and the risk of poisoning the legitimate Active Directory in the case of compromise. The more accounts you cache, the better the performance but the greater the risk of exposure. The fewer accounts you cache, the poorer the performance but the less the risk of exposure.

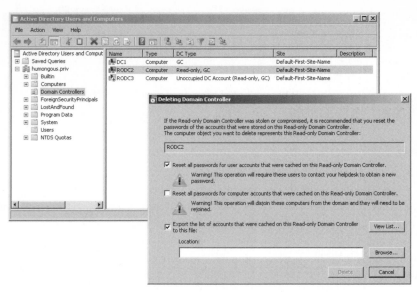

FIGURE 6-9 Deleting a stolen RODC from Active Directory Users and Computers

Installing the RODC on a Windows Server 2008 Server Core Installation in the branch office provides the greatest level of security in the branch office by reducing the attack surface of the server and minimizing the amount of sensitive data loss and the risk of poisoning the legitimate Active Directory in the case of compromise.

The RODC supports delegated installation as well as Administrator Role Separation for increased security.

THE PASSWORD SETTINGS OBJECT

New to Microsoft Windows Server 2008 is the ability to define different password and account lockout policies to users in the domain. This support for different policies for different users is called fine-grained password policies. In earlier versions of Windows, only one password and account lockout policy could be effective for all users in the domain. It is a common concern that different users in the domain, like the users in a branch office, require different strengths of passwords and more or less strict account lockout policies. These differing password policies are defined in PSOs and are applied to users and (preferably) groups of users. PSOs cannot be applied to computer objects or to OUs.

To utilize fine-grained password policies in the branch office, the domain functional level must be set to Windows Server 2008. This requires that all domain controllers in the domain run Windows Server 2008. Next, create one or more global security groups, one for each different PSO required in the branch office, and populate the group(s) with the appropriate users. Chapter 4, "Designing Administration and Group Policy," explains in detail how to configure fine-grained password policies.

Using fine-grained password policies, you can configure values, including the following:

- Maximum Password Age
- Minimum Password Age
- Minimum Password Length
- Password History
- Password Complexity
- Reversible Encryption Enabled
- Account Lockout Threshold
- Account Lockout Window
- Account Lockout Duration
- Users or global security groups to which the PSO applies

If you don't like ADSI Edit, you can use LDIFDE. LDIFDE uses a script to configure the new PSO. Save the following script to an ASCII text file and apply an .ldf file extension. Adjust the parameters as desired. For example, you will need to replace the domain name specified in the "dn:" line with your domain name.

```
dn: CN=BoPSO, CN=Password Settings
Container,CN=System,DC=dc1,DC=litware,DC=internal
changetype: add
objectClass: msDS-PasswordSettings
msDS-MaximumPasswordAge:-1728000000000
msDS-MinimumPasswordAge:-864000000000
msDS-MinimumPasswordLength:8
msDS-PasswordHistoryLength:24
msDS-PasswordComplexityEnabled:TRUE
msDS-PasswordReversibleEncryptionEnabled:FALSE
msDS-LockoutObservationWindow:-18000000000
msDS-LockoutDuration:-18000000000
msDS-LockoutThreshold:0
msDS-PasswordSettingsPrecedence:10
msDS-PSOAppliesTo:CN=BOusers,CN=Users,DC=dc1,DC=litware,DC=internal
```

The time values are calculated using the I8 format. The I8 format breaks the time units into negative 100 nanoseconds (billionths of a second), so all forward-looking time values must be negative. To convert time into I8 values:

- Multiply minutes by -6,000,000,000.
- Multiply hours by -36,000,000,000.
- Multiply days by -864,000,000,000.

MORE INFO **SETTING I8 VALUES**

Learn more about setting I8 values at *http://support.microsoft.com/kb/954414*.

After you create the PSO, you can adjust the users and groups to which it is applied by using Active Directory Users and Computers. Complete the following steps:

1. From the View menu, select Advanced Features.

2. Expand the Active Directory Users And Computers tree to <Domain Name>, System, and then select the Password Settings Container.

3. In the right pane, right-click the PSO and choose Properties.

4. On the Attribute Editor tab, select the *msDS-PsoAppliesTo* attribute and click Edit.

5. Add the distinguished name of the user or global security group to which you want to apply the PSO or remove the desired entry.

Fine-grained password policies allow administrators to define unique password and account lockout policies for users and global security groups in a domain. They are well suited for application to users in the branch office environment, which commonly requires a different level of security.

> **MORE INFO** **CREATING THE PASSWORD SETTINGS OBJECT**
>
> For more detail on the creation of the PSO, see the Technet article at
> *http://technet.microsoft.com/en-us/library/cc770842(WS.10).aspx.*

Security for Data in Storage

Another area of security for the nonsecure branch office that you should address is security for data in storage. If a computer is stolen from a branch office, the thief could crack user accounts on the system and access data stored locally on the hard disk drives. If the thief removes the hard disk drives from the original computer and mounts them in another computer where he or she is the administrator, the thief can access all the content. Windows Server 2008 provides three ways to secure this stored data:

- Read-only DFS replicas
- The EFS
- BitLocker

READ-ONLY DFS REPLICAS

DFS replica sets are often used in the branch office to provide fast and reliable access to current data. However, with security concerns in branch offices, you might need to provide integrity protection of the data by making the data read only. Another new feature in Windows Server 2008 R2 is the ability to configure the DFS replica set as read-only. This eliminates the need to manually adjust access control lists (ACLs) in the branch offices on shared folders, reducing administrative overhead.

THE ENCRYPTING FILE SYSTEM

EFS was introduced in Windows 2000. It provides encryption for data files and folders only. It requires that the underlying volume (partition) be formatted with NTFS. It uses self-generated X.509 digital certificates associated with the user account to secure encryption keys for the encrypted content. Ultimately, one accesses the decryption key by knowing the user's password. If the hacker can crack the password, the hacker can decrypt all of the user's EFS-protected content.

By default, the local administrator (stand-alone) or the domain administrator (domain member) is the EFS recovery agent and can decrypt any EFS-secured content. EFS cannot be applied to system or AD DS–related files. All other users who attempt to access another user's EFS content receive an Access Denied error, even if proper permissions are granted.

BITLOCKER

BitLocker was introduced in Windows Vista and is available in Windows Server 2008. A specific partition structure must be configured prior to the installation of the operating system for BitLocker to be available for implementation on a system. *BitLocker* encrypts the entire volume and can be applied to system, boot, and data volumes. BitLocker encryption remains intact even if the hard disk drive is installed in another computer and is mounted by another operating system.

BitLocker is based on the Trusted Platform Module (TPM), currently version 1.2. TPM is a microchip that holds the encryption/decryption key and a piece of code in the BIOS used to perform the encryption/decryption process on the specified disk volumes. You can also implement BitLocker on systems without TPM support by storing the encryption/decryption key on a USB thumb drive.

In either case, a recovery key, recovery password, or both should be exported to external media in case the original encryption/decryption key(s) are lost. By default, no recovery information is backed up. The recovery password is a 48-character numeric value that can be typed into the BitLocker Recovery Console. The recovery key is stored on a USB thumb drive and can be accessed by the BitLocker Recovery Console. In addition, you can generate and store the recovery passwords in AD DS by means of a GPO. The recovery key and recovery password should be securely stored separate from the computer.

> **MORE INFO** **BITLOCKER VOLUME RECOVERY**
>
> For detailed instructions on backing up BitLocker recovery keys in AD DS and on the BitLocker recovery process, see the following Technet article: *http://technet.microsoft.com /en-us/library/cc766015(WS.10).aspx.*

> **Quick Check**
>
> 1. Encryption for data in storage can be provided by which Microsoft technologies in Windows Server 2008 R2?
>
> 2. What tool does Windows Server 2008 R2 provide to reset passwords of accounts on RODC servers that become compromised?
>
> **Quick Check Answers**
>
> 1. The Encrypting File System (EFS) and BitLocker
>
> 2. The Revealed List

Securing the Branch Office with Network Access Protection

In Windows Server 2008, administrators can use NAP to ensure that remote, local, and branch office clients meet minimum security and configuration compliance requirements for secure connections to branch office and HQ networks. NAP checks the client's health status regarding the state of its firewall, updates, antivirus protection, and anti-spyware protection for the Windows XP SP3, Windows Vista, Windows 7, and Windows Server 2008 operating systems.

> **NOTE** **NETWORK ACCESS PROTOCOL**
>
> NAP is covered in detail in Chapter 5.

Lesson Summary

- Introduce all the requisite physical security measures in the branch office to establish a reasonably secure physical environment.
- Reduce the number of passwords that might be exposed in the branch office by using an RODC along with a minimal list of objects in the Password Replication Policy for that RODC.
- Implement the delegated installation of the RODC by precreating the RODC account in Active Directory Users and Computers.

- Create custom NTDS.dit content on installation media using the IFM subcommand in Ntdsutil.exe. IFM stands for installation from media. This replaces the *DCPromo /ADV* switch used by Windows Server 2003.

- Implement Administrator Role Separation to limit the administrative privileges to the operating system only and not to the AD DS.

- Implement an RODC on a Windows Server 2008 Server Core Installation to reduce the attack surface of the RODC.

- Understand the need for a Windows Server 2008 Full Installation domain controller in the site nearest to the RODC.

- Consider the impact of automatic site coverage on the registration of SRV records for the site by Windows Server 2003 domain controllers in nearby sites.

- Implement fine-grained password policies by creating a PSO and assigning it to users and global security groups.

- Use EFS to encrypt data content while in storage.

- Use BitLocker to encrypt the operating system, the Active Directory database file NTDS.dit, and data content. This protects the operating system's Active Directory database and data even if the drive is mounted in another computer.

- Archive the BitLocker recovery keys in Active Directory to recover data if the TPM module on a system fails.

Lesson Review

You can use the following questions to test your knowledge of the information in Lesson 2, "Branch Office Server Security." The questions are also available on the companion CD if you prefer to review them in electronic form.

> **NOTE ANSWERS**
>
> Answers to these questions and explanations of why each answer choice is correct or incorrect are located in the "Answers" section at the end of the book.

1. What type of domain controller should be implemented in the branch office for maximum security?

   A. RODC on a Windows Server Full Installation

   B. RODC on a Server Core Installation domain controller

   C. Full (writable) domain controller on a Windows Server Full Installation

   D. Full (writable) domain controller on a Server Core Installation domain controller

2. How can you ensure that replication will successfully occur to a site with only one Windows Server 2008 RODC?

   A. Place a Windows Server 2008 full (writable) domain controller in the site nearest to the RODC.

   B. Place a Windows Server 2008 R2 RODC in the site nearest to the RODC.

   C. Make the site-link cost to the adjacent site higher than all other costs on site links.

   D. Construct a site-link bridge.

3. What is the first action to take if you receive a report that one of the branch offices has had an RODC stolen?

   A. Implement Administrator Role Separation on the replacement RODC.

   B. Use ADSI Edit to construct a new PSO.

   C. Construct a new IFM disk.

   D. In Active Directory Users and Computers, delete the RODC.

Chapter Review

To further practice and reinforce the skills you learned in this chapter, you can perform the following tasks:

- Review the chapter summary.

- Review the list of key terms introduced in this chapter.

- Complete the case scenarios. These scenarios set up real-world situations involving the topics of this chapter and ask you to create a solution.

- Complete the suggested practices.

- Take a practice test.

Chapter Summary

- The branch office has an increased number of physical and network vulnerabilities.

- The resource access needs of the branch office users can vary greatly and must be carefully considered and planned for accordingly.

- The branch office will have specific network infrastructure system and service requirements that must be carefully considered and planned.

- The branch office deployment must be designed for the securest implementation and provide only the required services.

- You can restructure the branch office within Active Directory as necessary to maximize security.

- You can provide redundancy of services by installing multisite cluster nodes in the branch office.

- You can provide integrity protection and redundancy of data by configuring DFS replication and read-only DFS replicas in the branch office.

- RemoteApp and Desktop (RAD) is a new virtualization technology that provides easy deployment and centralized management of branch office Windows 7 client computers and applications.

- BranchCache improves the performance of branch office Windows 7 and Windows Server 2008 R2 clients' access to data and reduces load on WAN links.

- BranchCache can operate in Distributed or Hosted mode and can transport data using HTTP, HTTPS, or SMB, including signed SMB.

- Placement of a Windows Server Update Services (WSUS) server in the branch office minimizes update-related network traffic to HQ and to the Internet.

- Installing Windows Server 2008 R2 Server Core Installations in the branch office reduces the attack surface of the servers.

- You can install RODC domain controllers in the branch office to reduce the risk of exposing passwords.

- Delegate installation of the RODC by precreating the RODC account in Active Directory Users and Computers.

- Use Administrator Role Separation to give the branch office administrator the privilege of maintaining Windows Server 2008 but not access to modify Active Directory.

- Use VPNs to secure data in transit between the branch office and HQ.

- The different types of VPNs supported by Windows Server 2008 R2 are PPTP, L2TP, IPsec/IKEv2, and SSTP.

- DirectAccess transparently connects remote Windows 7 users to intranet resources like web content, file shares, and applications.

- VPN Reconnect, primarily used for mobile Windows 7 clients, transparently reconnects broken VPNs.

- You can use EFS to secure data in storage in the branch office.

- You can use BitLocker to secure data in storage for the operating system, the Active Directory database, and data in the branch office.

- You should archive BitLocker keys in Active Directory to support BitLocker recovery in case the TPM module fails on a computer.

Key Terms

Do you know what these key terms mean? You can check your answers by looking up the terms in the glossary at the end of the book.

- Administrator Role Separation
- Automatic site coverage
- BitLocker
- Branch office
- BranchCache
- Credential caching
- Delegation of control
- Domain restructuring
- Encrypting File System (EFS)
- Install From Media (IFM)
- Network Access Protection
- Ntdsutil
- Password Replication Policy

- Primary read-only DNS zones
- Privilege
- Read-only DFS replicas
- Read-only domain controller (RODC)
- Revealed list
- RODC filtered attribute set (FAS)
- Server core
- Server hardening

Case Scenarios

In the following case scenarios, you apply what you've learned about designing a branch office infrastructure. You can find answers to these questions in the "Answers" section at the end of this book.

Case Scenario 1: Contoso Trucking, Part 1

Contoso is a trucking company with its HQ in Oshkosh, Wisconsin. Contoso will be adding branch offices in Syracuse and Schenectady, New York. There will be 150 users in Syracuse and 90 users in Schenectady. The tracking program used to schedule trucks and drivers will be required in each office and uses the Active Directory database. All servers in HQ run Windows Server 2008 R2. The IDS on your HQ network shows repeated attacks from your competitor. You have hired a junior administrator for each location.

1. What type of servers should be used in the branch offices?
2. What type of domain controllers should be used in the branch offices?
3. What privileges should the administrators in the branch offices be granted?

Case Scenario 2: Contoso Trucking, Part 2

After the two new branch offices are up and running, you grow concerned that the servers in Syracuse could easily be stolen. Furthermore, you decide that the users in Schenectady should have a stronger password policy because of the concentration of financial information they use and process daily.

1. How can you improve security on the operating system and data files that reside on the domain controllers in Syracuse?
2. How should you satisfy the need for a stronger password policy for users in Schenectady?

Case Scenario 3: Contoso Trucking, Part 3

You plan to add another office in Saskatchewan. The junior administrator in Saskatchewan will be buying the server that is to be the local RODC there.

1. What steps should you take to securely deploy the new RODC in Saskatchewan?

2. How should you configure delegated authority for the administrator in Saskatchewan?

Suggested Practices

To help you successfully master the exam objectives presented in this chapter, complete the following tasks.

Branch Office Deployment

The branch office introduces many challenges regarding functionality, performance, reliability, and security. The following practices help you understand the many new features of Windows Server 2008 that improve branch office deployment.

- **Practice 1**

    - On a Windows Server 2008 Full Installation, implement server hardening techniques, including stopping and disabling services, uninstalling or disabling unnecessary applications (especially those that launch at startup), installing all required operating system and application updates, configuring automatic updates, installing antivirus software, installing anti-spyware software, enabling and verifying settings on the host-based firewall, configuring auditing of successful and failed logon attempts and successful and failed object access on a test folder, documenting the system configuration and storing it apart from the server, and minimizing the number of user accounts by deleting and disabling as many as possible.

    - Install a Windows Server 2008 RODC and explore the relevant interfaces.

    - Configure a Password Replication Policy with two or three user accounts allowed for replication and two or three user accounts denied for replication.

    - Install a Windows Server 2008 Server Core and explore the relevant interfaces.

    - Install an RODC on a Windows Server 2008 Server Core Installation.

    - Configure Administrator Role Separation on an RODC server.

    - Create a PSO and assign it to a sample global security group.

    - Perform a fresh installation of Windows Server 2008 Full Installation and configure it for BitLocker. Remember that a specific partition structure must be created prior to the operating system installation.

Read a White Paper

- **Practice 2** Read overviews and step-by-step guides for installing and configuring the following components.

  - Windows Server 2008 RODC
    http://technet.microsoft.com/en-us/library/cc754629(WS.10).aspx

  - Configuring Windows Server 2008 Server Core
    http://technet.microsoft.com/en-us/library/cc753802(WS.10).aspx

  - Configuring fine-grained password policies
    http://technet.microsoft.com/en-us/library/cc770842(WS.10).aspx

  - Configuring Administrator Role Separation
    http://technet.microsoft.com/en-us/library/cc732301(WS.10).aspx

  - Configuring BitLocker
    http://technet.microsoft.com/en-us/library/dd835565(WS.10).aspx

Take a Practice Test

The practice tests on this book's companion CD offer many options. For example, you can test yourself on just one exam objective, or you can test yourself on all the 70-647 certification exam content. You can set up the test so that it closely simulates the experience of taking a certification exam, or you can set it up in study mode so that you can look at the correct answers and explanations after you answer each question.

> **MORE INFO** **PRACTICE TESTS**
>
> For details about all the practice test options available, see the "How to Use the Practice Tests" section in this book's introduction.

CHAPTER 7

Designing Remote Desktop Services and Application Deployment

Application deployment would be a simple affair if all you needed to do was deploy the same set of applications to all users in your environment. The realities of software licensing mean that large organizations can realize significant cost savings by ensuring that only those workers who need an application have it deployed to their computers. In this chapter, you learn how to plan the distribution of applications to the workers in your environment by using several tools, each of which is appropriate for a certain set of circumstances. Methods of deploying applications to users discussed in this chapter include Remote Desktop Session Host (RD Session Host), Microsoft System Center Essentials 2007 SP1, Microsoft System Center Configuration Manager 2007, and traditional deployment through Active Directory Domain Services (AD DS) software publishing functionality.

Exam objectives in this chapter:

- Plan for Remote Desktop.
- Plan for application delivery.

Lessons in this chapter:

Before You Begin

Ensure that you have installed a Microsoft Windows Server 2008 R2 Enterprise domain controller named Glasgow as described in Chapter 1, "Designing Name Resolution and Internet Protocol Addressing." No additional configuration is required for this chapter.

REAL WORLD
Paul A. Mancuso

Working in the field for more than 20 years has shown me that most companies struggle with ways to provide remote connectivity to network resources. Companies are constantly looking for easy and inventive ways to allow access without having to retrain entire staffs on the use of remote access software. Starting from the beginning, remote access clients evolved many times, mostly morphing from one type or variation of virtual private network (VPN) clients. Users would require constant training and support to ensure the smooth access of the VPN client and the administration of the VPN services and devices. Providing seamless but secure access from a user's desktop with lowered costs has been the ultimate goal. Starting with Remote Desktop Services in Windows Server 2008 and continuing with the enhancements provided in Windows Server 2008 R2, Remote Desktop Services has evolved to meet that ultimate goal. With Remote Desktop Services, a user from any remotely connected location merely needs to click an associated document of an application running on a server located within the user's internal corporate network and a secure connection over Secure Sockets Layer (SSL) through a firewall can be initiated and authenticated seamlessly to the user. This removes the two biggest barriers to deploying applications for remote use: a user's knowledge of how to access the applications as well as the overhead of training the user, and the ability to secure the access with reasonable costs for both the solution and the continued administration of the services and devices associated with the solution. My clients have shown a surprising increase in remote use of their applications due to the increased convenience and lowered costs.

Lesson 1: Designing Remote Desktop Services

Planning the deployment of Remote Desktop Services in your enterprise environment means taking into consideration licensing, server resilience, how clients connect, and how applications are deployed to the Remote Desktop Session Host. In this lesson, you learn how each of these factors influences the plans you develop to deploy Remote Desktop Services in your own organization's enterprise environment.

> **After this lesson, you will be able to:**
> - Plan Remote Desktop Session Host deployment.
> - Plan Remote Desktop Session Host server farms.
> - Plan Remote Desktop Services session availability.
> - Plan RemoteApp deployment.
> - Plan secure remote client connections to Remote Desktop Services.
>
> **Estimated lesson time: 45 minutes**

Planning a Remote Desktop Session Deployment

As an experienced enterprise administrator, you are aware of the role *Remote Desktop Services* plays on your organizational network. You understand how client computers connect using Remote Desktop Connections, how to install applications on a Remote Desktop Session Host, and the basics of managing and configuring an individual Remote Desktop Session server. In this lesson, you go beyond the maintenance and configuration of this technology and learn how to plan the deployment of Remote Desktop Services so that it best meets the needs of your organization.

The first step in planning a deployment is understanding how the following Remote Desktop Services components fit together:

- **Remote Desktop Session Host**   The Remote Desktop Session Host (RD Session Host) role service, formerly the Terminal Server role service, is the core component of a Remote Desktop Services deployment. This is the server to which clients connect so they can access their applications.

- **Remote Desktop Session Host server farm**   The RD Session Host server farm, formerly called the Terminal Server farm, is a collection of RD Session Host servers used to provide high availability and load balancing to clients on the organizational network. Client connections to RD Session Host server farms are mediated by Remote Desktop Connection Brokers. RD Session Host server farms are more likely to be deployed at large sites than are individual RD Session Host servers.

- **Remote Desktop Licensing**   The Remote Desktop Licensing (RD Licensing) role service, formerly called the Terminal Server Licensing role service, provides Remote Desktop Session client access licenses (CALs) to RD Session Host servers on the network. Unless an RD Licensing role service is deployed, clients are able to connect using Remote Desktop Services for only a limited amount of time (120 days).

- **Remote Desktop Gateway**   The Remote Desktop Gateway (RD Gateway) role service was formerly called the Terminal Server Gateway role service. This role service provides access to authorized remote users from untrusted networks. In enterprise networks, the RD Gateway server provides a bridge between the protected internal network and the internal corporate network where the RD Session Host server farm resides. The RD Gateway role service enforces secure, encrypted connections between remote users and internal resources.

- **RemoteApp and Desktop Connection**   The service formerly called RemoteApp programs in Windows Server 2008 Terminal Services provided the ability to run applications that appear to be running locally. With RemoteApp and Desktop Connection, you now have the ability to group and manage the applications so that they are personalized for the individual remote users and accessible to the remote users from their Start menus.

- **Remote Desktop Virtualization Host**   The Remote Desktop Virtualization Host (RD Virtualization Host) is a new role service included in Windows Server 2008 R2 that integrates with Hyper-V to provide access to a unique virtual machine for every individual user through RemoteApp and Desktop Connection. The RD Virtualization Host role service will not install if you are running or testing Remote Desktop Services on a virtual machine—you must be running on supported physical hardware.

- **Microsoft RemoteFX**   RemoteFX is a new client enrichment feature provided in Windows Server 2008 R2 with Service Pack 1. RemoteFX provides the ability to add a fuller complement of codecs, device support, USB redirection, and additional 3D experience to an enterprise desktop accessing applications through a remote desktop connection.

When planning the deployment of individual RD Session Host servers and RD Session Host server farms, ensure that the software applications installed on the RD Session Host servers that will be used by the remote clients are installed after the RD Session Host role is deployed. Many applications perform a check during installation to determine whether the target of the installation is an RD Session Host. In some cases, different executable files will be installed when the installation target is an RD Session Host using the Remote Desktop Web Access role service for application deployment. Alternatively, some applications will generate a pop-up dialog box informing you that installing the application on a Remote Desktop server is not recommended and that the vendor does not support this deployment configuration.

Applications that are deployed on a RD Session Host server might conflict with one another in unexpected ways. Your Remote Desktop Services deployment plan should include a testing period so that you can verify that each Remote Desktop server's application configuration does not lead to unforeseen conflicts. If conflicts are detected, you will need to plan to either deploy conflicting applications on separate terminal servers or to deploy applications by using Microsoft Application Virtualization (App-V), which is covered in more detail in Chapter 8, "Designing Virtualization."

Remote Desktop Licensing

Perhaps the most critical aspect of planning the deployment of Remote Desktop Services in enterprise environments is ensuring that licensing is configured appropriately. The loss of one RD Session Host server in an environment in which there are 100 RD Session Host servers is a potential problem. The loss of a license server in an environment in which there are 100 RD Session Host servers is a potential disaster.

All clients that connect to an RD Session Host server require a Remote Desktop Services CAL. This license is not included with Windows Vista or Windows 7 and is not a part of the standard CALs that you use when licensing a Windows-based server. Remote Desktop Services CALs for the RD Licensing role service are managed by the RD Licensing Manager. When planning a Remote Desktop services deployment, answer the following questions when considering the deployment of a Remote Desktop license server:

- What will be the anticipated deployment size for remote users and devices?
- Will there be a need to provide Remote Desktop Session licensing for Windows Server 2008 Terminal Services? If so, what is the scope of the license server? Will it service clients in the domain or workgroup, or manage the licenses for all clients in the forest?
- How will the license server be activated with Microsoft? How will additional licenses be purchased and installed?
- How many license servers are required to service the needs of your organization?
- What type of licenses will be deployed?

License Server Deployment

An RD Session Host server must be able to contact a Remote Desktop License server to fulfill requests by remote users or devices connecting to the RD Session Host server. Automatic discovery of Remote Desktop License servers is no longer supported for Windows Server 2008 R2 running RD Session Host server. An RD Session Host server is permitted to request RDS CALs from a license server running either Windows Server 2008 R2 or Windows Server 2008.

To determine the need for multiple RD Licensing servers, you should determine the necessity for fault-tolerant connectivity in your environment. It is usually a best practice to install any critical service with servers configured for redundancy. To configure redundancy for the RD Licensing server, you only need to install more than one RD Licensing server and configure each of the RD Session Host servers to use more than one RD Licensing server.

environments, you can deploy the RD Licensing server on the RD Session Host
...ger environments, where there will be substantial overhead with providing Remote
...rvices CALs for remote users and devices, should consider separating the role
...to separate Windows Server 2008 R2 servers. Figure 7-1 displays the dialog box
...rom the RD Session Host Configuration console.

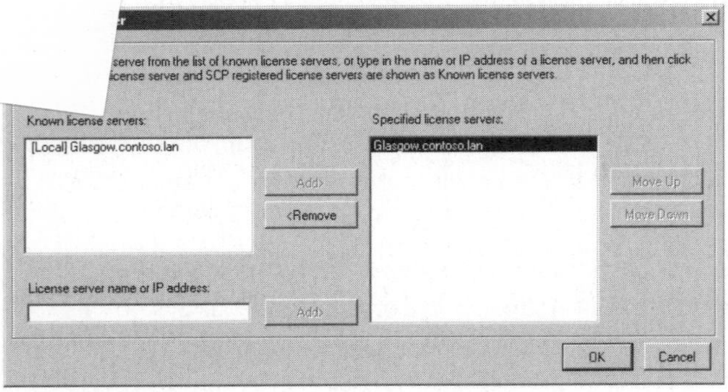

FIGURE 7-1 Manually specifying a license server

If Windows Server 2008 Terminal Servers, Windows Server 2003, or Windows 2000 is still in
use, it will be necessary to specify a license server's discovery scope. This is used by previous
versions of terminal servers and remote desktop clients to automatically detect the license
server. You configure the license server scope during the installation of the Remote Desktop
Licensing role service, as shown in Figure 7-2. You can change the scope after it is set. The
three possible discovery scopes are This Workgroup, This Domain, and The Forest.

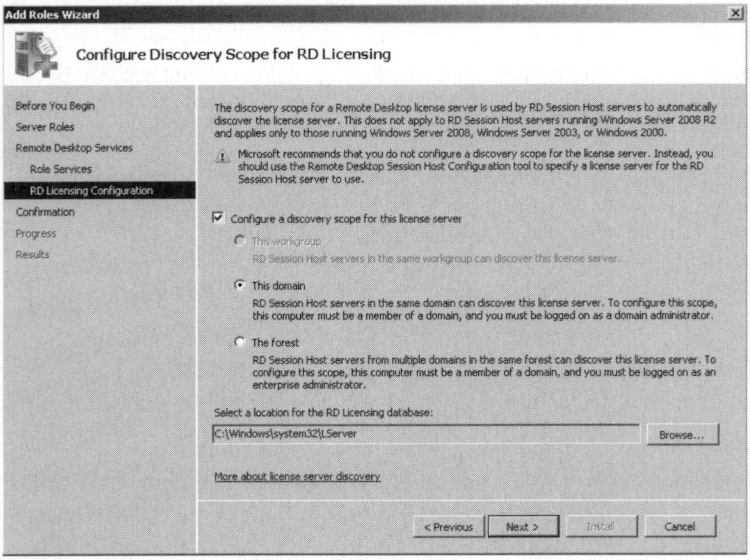

FIGURE 7-2 License server discovery scope

- **This Workgroup** This scope is not available if the license server is joined to an Active Directory service domain. This discovery scope is most often installed on a computer that hosts the RD Session Host service. RD Session Hosts and clients in the same workgroup can automatically discover this license server.

- **This Domain** The domain discovery scope enables RD Session Hosts and clients that are members of the same domain to acquire Remote Desktop Services CALs automatically. Plan to use this scope if Remote Desktop Services CALs in your organization are going to be purchased and managed on a per-domain basis.

- **The Forest** The forest discovery scope enables RD Session Hosts and clients located anywhere in the same Active Directory forest to acquire Remote Desktop Services CALs automatically. You should plan to use this scope when licensing issues are handled at the organizational level rather than at the domain level.

For example, if your organization has a single forest with a separate domain for each state division, but all software purchasing and licensing is handled centrally, you would plan to deploy a license server set to the forest discovery scope. This enables the people responsible for licensing to check a central location to determine your organization's compliance with its Remote Desktop client licensing responsibilities. It saves them from having to check each state division's Remote Desktop license server. If, however, your nationwide organization has software and purchasing managed on a regional basis, it makes sense to deploy RD Licensing servers on the same basis. In that case, you would plan to deploy RD Licensing servers by using the domain discovery scope.

License Server Activation

Another important component of a Remote Desktop server deployment plan is choosing a license server activation method. Before a Remote Desktop license server can issue Remote Desktop Services CALs, it must be activated with Microsoft in a procedure similar to Windows product activation. During the activation process, a Microsoft-issued digital certificate validating both server ownership and identity is installed on the Remote Desktop license server. This certificate will be used in transactions with Microsoft for the acquisition and installation of further licenses. As shown in Figure 7-3, a license server can be activated through three methods.

The first method occurs transparently through a wizard, like Windows product activation. This method requires the server to be able to connect to the Internet directly, using an SSL connection, which means that it will not work with certain firewall configurations.

The second method involves navigating to a webpage. This method can be used on a computer other than the license server and is appropriate in environments in which the network infrastructure does not support a direct SSL connection from the internal network to an Internet host.

The third method involves placing a telephone call to a Microsoft clearinghouse operator. This is a toll-free call from most locations. The method you use for activation will also validate Remote Desktop Services CALs that are purchased at a later date, although you can change this method by editing the Remote Desktop license server's properties. If a license server is not activated, it can issue temporary CALs only, which are valid for 120 days.

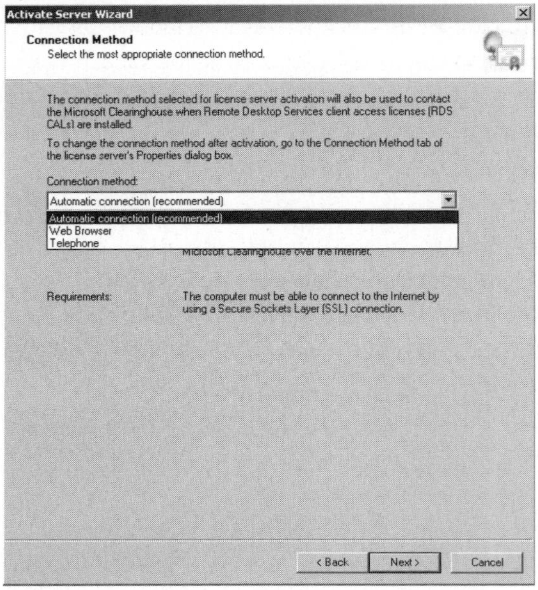

FIGURE 7-3 Three methods of activating a Remote Desktop license server

When planning disaster recovery contingencies for your Remote Desktop Services deployment, consider that if the certificate acquired during the activation process expires or becomes corrupted, you might need to deactivate the license server. A deactivated license server cannot issue permanent Remote Desktop Services per-device CALs, although it can still issue Remote Desktop Services per-user CALs and temporary Remote Desktop per-device CALs. You can deactivate Remote Desktop license servers by using the automatic method or over the telephone, but you cannot deactivate them by using a web browser on another computer.

Remote Desktop Services Client Access Licenses

When planning the deployment of Remote Desktop Services, you must determine which sort of Remote Desktop Services CAL is most appropriate for your organization. A Windows Server 2008 Remote Desktop license server can issue two types of CALs: the per-device CAL and the per-user CAL. The differences between these licenses are as follows:

- **Remote Desktop Services per device CAL** The Remote Desktop Services per-device CAL gives a specific computer or device the ability to connect to a terminal server. Remote Desktop Services per-device CALs are automatically reclaimed by the RD Licensing server after a random period ranging from 52 to 89 days. This will not affect clients that regularly use these CALs because any available CAL will simply be reissued the next time the device reconnects. In the event that you run out of available

CALs, you can revoke 20 percent of issued Remote Desktop Services per-device CALs for a specific operating system by using the Remote Desktop Licensing Manager console on the license server. For example, 20 percent of issued Windows Vista Remote Desktop Services per-device CALs or 20 percent of issued Microsoft Windows Server 2003 per-device CALs can be revoked at any one time. Revocation is not a substitute for ensuring that your organization has purchased the requisite number of Remote Device Services per-device CALs for your environment.

- **Remote Desktop Services per user CAL**   A Remote Desktop Services per-user CAL gives a specific user account the ability to access any terminal server in an organization from any computer or device. Remote Desktop Services per-user CALs are not enforced by Remote Desktop Services licensing, and it is possible to have more client connections occurring in an organization than actual Remote Desktop Services per-user CALs installed on the license server. Failure to have the appropriate number of per-user CALs is a violation of license terms. You can determine the number of per-user CALs in use by using the Remote Desktop Licensing Manager console on the license server. You can either examine the Reports node or use the console to create a Per-User CAL Usage report.

When planning the deployment of Remote Desktop license servers, remember that Remote Desktop Services CALs can be purchased directly from the server if the Remote Desktop server is capable of making a direct SSL connection to the Internet. Alternatively, it is possible to use a separate computer that is connected to the Internet to purchase Remote Desktop Services CALs by navigating to a website or to call the Microsoft clearinghouse directly.

> **MORE INFO**   **MORE ON REMOTE DESKTOP SERVICES CALS**
>
> To learn more about TS CALs, see the following TechNet website: *http://technet.microsoft .com/en-us/library/ff710460(WS.10).aspx*

Backing Up and Restoring a License Server

To back up a Remote Desktop license server, you need to back up the system state data and the folder in which the Remote Desktop licensing database is installed. You can use Review Configuration, shown in Figure 7-4, to determine the location of the Remote Desktop licensing database. To restore the license server, rebuild the server, and reinstall the Remote Desktop Licensing Server role, restore the system state data and then restore the Remote Desktop licensing database. When restored to a different computer, unissued licenses will not be restored, and you will need to contact the Microsoft clearinghouse to get the licenses reissued.

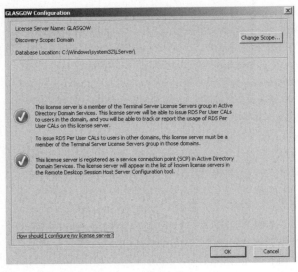

FIGURE 7-4 Reviewing the configuration

License Server Deployment

When planning the deployment of Windows Server 2008 R2 Remote Desktop Services in an environment with Terminal Services running on earlier versions of a Microsoft-based server operating system, consider that Windows Server 2003 Terminal Services license servers and Microsoft Windows 2000 Server Terminal Services license servers cannot issue licenses to Windows Server 2008 terminal servers or Windows Server 2008 R2 RD Session Host servers. Windows Server 2008 R2 Remote Desktop license servers, however, support the licensing requirements of earlier versions of Terminal Services. If your organization's Windows Server 2003 terminal servers or Windows Server 2008 terminal servers will coexist with Windows Server 2008 R2 RD Session Host servers for a time, upgrade your organization's license servers to Windows Server 2008 R2 so that they can support both the new RD Session Host servers and previously installed terminal servers.

License Server High Availability

When planning a high-availability strategy for license servers supporting versions of Terminal Services prior to Windows Server 2008 R2, plan the deployment of two separate Remote Desktop license servers configured with the appropriate scope (domain versus enterprise) and install 50 percent of the Terminal Services CALs on each license server. Because the location of previous versions of license servers is published within AD DS, it is not necessary to use a technology such as Domain Name System (DNS) round robin, Network Load Balancing (NLB), or failover clustering for the deployment of license servers. Current versions of Windows Server 2008 R2 RD Session Host servers will be manually configured for each of the deployed Remote Desktop license servers.

Your deployment plan for license servers should include regular backups so that if a license server does fail, the purchased licenses can be quickly recovered and redeployed. Remember that licenses that have been installed but not issued will be lost when a server is recovered. It is possible to recover these licenses from the Microsoft clearinghouse, but your license deployment plan should ensure that only the required number of licenses is purchased. You should not purchase a significant number of extra licenses for possible future use. It is easier to purchase those licenses when they will actually be used than to worry about recovering unused licenses if the license server fails.

✔ **Quick Check**

1. Which type of Remote Desktop Services CAL can be revoked?

2. At what point should you install the applications that will be used by Remote Desktop Services clients on the RD Session Host server?

Quick Check Answers

1. Per-device CALs can be revoked.

2. After the RD Session Host server role has been installed on the server.

Deploying Applications Using Remote Desktop Web Access

Windows Server 2008 Terminal Services included Terminal Services Web Access (TS Web Access). TS Web Access enables clients to connect to a terminal server through a webpage link rather than by entering the terminal server address in the Remote Desktop Connection client software. This enables you to deploy applications through the publication of URLs, which can be distributed through Group Policy.

Unlike the similar functionality that was available in Windows Server 2003, TS Web Access in Windows Server 2008 does not rely on an ActiveX control to provide the Remote Desktop client connection, but instead uses the Remote Desktop Client (RDC) software that is installed on client computers. This means that to use TS Web Access, client computers need to be running Windows XP SP2, Windows Vista, Windows Server 2003 SP1, or Windows Server 2008.

A drawback to deploying TS Web Access in an enterprise environment is that it must be installed on the terminal server to which it is providing access. It is not possible to connect to a second terminal server by using TS Web Access installed on the first. When considered from the perspective of planning the deployment of applications in an enterprise environment, it means you must distribute a different set of URLs to groups of clients as a method of limiting the number of simultaneous connections to TS Web Access.

In general, you should not plan to use DNS round robin or NLB with TS Web Access. Although these technologies will balance incoming connections, they will cause problems with reconnections, with clients occasionally reconnected to servers that are not hosting a currently active session. An exception to this rule is TS Web Access servers located at branch office locations. If your organization has single TS Web Access servers deployed at each branch office location, using DNS round robin and netmask ordering will ensure that branch office clients will be connected to their local TS Web Access server.

In Windows Server 2008 R2, Remote Desktop Web Access now has the ability to be installed on a separate server from the RD Session Host server role. You are able to configure high availability for the Remote Desktop Web Access service by using either an NLB cluster or DNS round robin.

A user or an administrator is able to configure specific RD Session Host servers hosting applications using RemoteApp. In addition, a user is able to target any computer allowing Remote Desktop access. Thus, a user with only a browser is able to connect to any remote desktop or RemoteApp configured for that user.

With the added advantage of connecting to any available Remote Desktop Services–enabled application or desktop from a browser, an administrator is assured of providing a secure connection to an application from managed and unmanaged desktops. As an enterprise administrator, you are now more focused on securing the connections and less concerned with the securing the user's desktop.

Planning the Deployment of Applications Using RemoteApp

RemoteApp differs from a normal terminal server session in that instead of connecting to a window that displays a remote computer's desktop, an application being executed on the terminal server appears as if it's being executed on the local computer. For example, Figure 7-5 shows WordPad running both locally and as a RemoteApp on the same computer running Windows Vista. The visible difference between these two is that one does not have the Windows Vista borders, and it retains the Windows Server 2008 appearance.

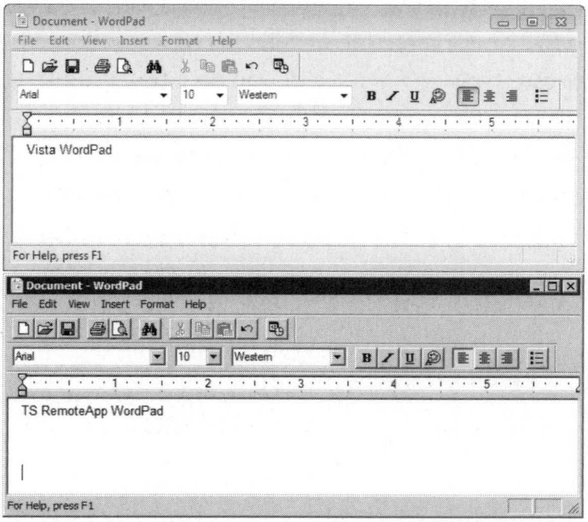

FIGURE 7-5 Two different instances of WordPad

When planning the deployment of applications using RemoteApp, you can use one of three methods:

- Create a Remote Desktop Protocol (RDP) shortcut file and distribute this file to client computers. You can do this by placing the RDP shortcut in a shared folder. This distribution method is inefficient in enterprise environments, although it can work well in smaller, branch office situations.

- Create and distribute a Windows Installer package using Group Policy or a file share.

- Have clients connect to an RD Web Access server and launch the RemoteApp application from a link on the page. The drawbacks of previous versions of TS Web Access as an application deployment platform have been largely reduced with the enhancements added to Remote Desktop Web Access in Windows Server 2008 R2.

Deploying RemoteApp allows application administrators the freedom to deploy applications without worry of conflicting dynamic link libraries associated with applications already installed on users' computers. In addition, RemoteApp offers users the ability to resize the window of the application as if it is running locally. Notifications, custom print settings, and redirection of various devices, along with the ability to customize access to the RemoteApp programs, provide a rich user experience.

Another RemoteApp enhancement for Windows Server 2008 R2 is the ability to provide per-user authentication and authorization for each application. With per-user authorization for each RemoteApp, an enterprise administrator is now able to granularly control application access from the RemoteApp management console.

A complete solution for offering remote users access to authorized applications within the corporate environment is now more complete:

- Configure an RD Session Host server to host applications through RemoteApp.

- Configure additional RD Session Host servers as a session farm for redundancy and load balancing (discussed later in this chapter).

- Configure on a separate computer for the Remote Desktop Web Access server to publish through links on the page applications available for access on the internal network. This provides browser-based clients to access internally published applications.

- Configure RemoteApp with RemoteApp Manager from an RD Session Host server to publish the applications (multiple publishing options are available, as noted earlier).

- Configure a Remote Desktop Gateway server to allow secure access for the external clients using either RD Web Access or the RD Gateway server directly with a remote desktop connection.

> **MORE INFO   REMOTEAPP AND REMOTEAPP MANAGER**
>
> For more information, go to *http://technet.microsoft.com/en-us/library/cc755261.aspx*.

Planning RD Session Host Server Farms

The RD Connection Broker role service simplified the process of adding capacity to an existing RD Session Host deployment in Windows Server 2008 R2. RD Connection Broker enables load balancing of RD Session Host servers in a group referred to as a load balanced RD Session Host server farm.

The RD Connection Broker maintains a database of RD sessions. RD Connection Broker can work with DNS round robin or with NLB to distribute clients to RD Session Host servers. When configured with load balancing, the RD Connection Broker service monitors all RD Session Hosts in the group and allocates new clients to the RD Session Host servers that have the largest amount of free resources. When used with DNS round robin, clients are still distributed; the main benefit is that RD Connection Broker remembers where a client is connected. Thus, a disconnected session is reconnected appropriately rather than a new session being created on a different RD Session Host. The limitation of the load balancing service of RD Connection Broker is that it can be used only with Windows Server 2008 RD Session Hosts. Windows Server 2003 terminal servers cannot participate in an RD Connection Broker server farm.

When planning the deployment of RD Connection Broker load balancing in your organization, you must ensure that clients support RDC 5.2 or later. It is also necessary to ensure that each RD Session Host in a particular farm has the same application configuration. Configure separate RD Session Host server farms when it is necessary to deploy different groups of applications. For example, application A and application B conflict when deployed together on a single RD Session Host server and must be deployed on separate ones. It would be necessary to plan the deployment of two RD Session Host server farms, one for each application, if you need to extend client capacity by adding additional RD Session Host server farms to support each application.

Planning the Migration to Remote Desktop Connection Broker

Remote Desktop Connection Broker in Windows Server 2008 R2 provides the previously discussed load balancing and session reconnection service as TS Session Broker, but now provides a unified management service for the user's access to RemoteApp and Desktop Connection and virtual desktops (discussed in Chapter 8). Proper planning and configuration of Remote Desktop Connection Broker using Remote Desktop Connection Manager will still provide the same enhanced user experience for the desktop and single sign-on authentication provided by RemoteApp and Desktop Connection.

To ensure proper configuration for the digital signing files used for virtual desktop connections and to provide single sign-on for RemoteApp and Desktop Connections, make certain these few relatively simple configurations are implemented:

- Configure digital signing of .rdp files using the RemoteApp Manager on RD Session Host. If public access to RemoteApp and Desktop Connections will be needed, it will be necessary to use Trusted Root Certification Authorities (CAs) for the certificate. An Enterprise CA was used to issue the signing certificate (in this case, the server authentication certificate) displayed in Figure 7-6.

- Also configure digital signing of .rdp files using the Remote Desktop Connection Manager. To maintain single sign-on for access to RemoteApp and Desktop Connections, use the same digital signing certificate for .rdp files that was configured on the RD Session Host for RemoteApp in the Digital Signature settings. Configure the Digital Certificate setting as shown in Figure 7-7.

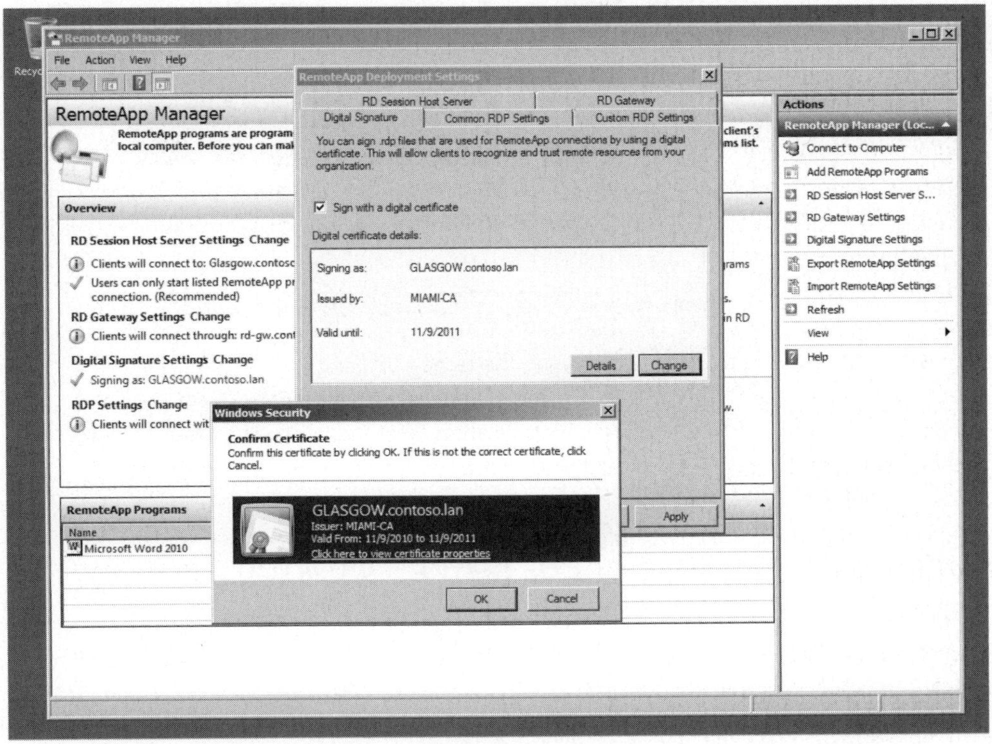

FIGURE 7-6 Configuring the digital signing file for RemoteApp

In planning the use of RD Connection Broker to manage access to RD Session Host farms, ensure all remote clients connecting will be using at least RDC 7.0 or a web browser with RD Web Access configured. The RD Session Host servers must be configured to use a farm in Remote Desktop Connection Broker. All servers configured for the farm must be running Windows Server 2008 or Windows Server 2008 R2. You should configure the use of load balancing using the relative weight value that the RD Connection Broker will use. Each server in the farm will receive connections based on a proportional value by comparing the relative weights of the RD Session Host servers in the farm. Otherwise, DNS round robin, NLB clustering, or a third-party load balancer will be needed to administer proper load distribution within the farm.

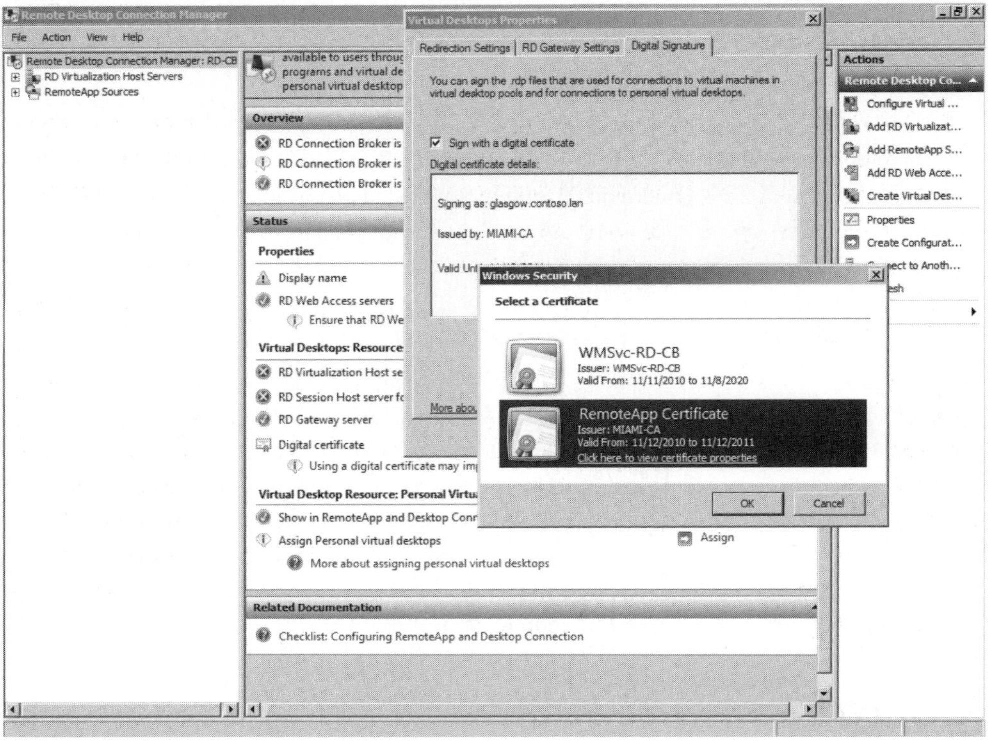

FIGURE 7-7 Configuring the digital signing file for the RD Connection Broker

Planning the Deployment of Remote Desktop Gateway Servers

Plan the deployment of Remote Desktop Gateway (RD Gateway) servers when you need to enable Remote Desktop Protocol over HTTPS connections to RD Session Host servers located on protected internal networks from remote clients on the Internet or untrusted networks.

RD Desktop Gateway Services for Windows Server R2

Remote Desktop Gateway Services in Windows Server 2008 R2 provides enterprise administrators the following enhancements for remote desktop deployment over the previous Terminal Server Gateway server of Windows Server 2008:

- You are now able to configure idle timeouts to reclaim resources from user sessions that are no longer in use.

- Using the configurable session timeouts, you can provide the enforcement of security policy changes in your environment in a timelier manner.

- Background session authentication and authorization allows a user to reestablish the use of a disconnected session without the need for interaction with a new authentication process.

- Device redirection enforcement provided in RD Session Host servers is now available through RD Gateway Services for clients running Remote Desktop Connection 7.0 or better. The RD Gateway Server will direct connections to RD Session Host servers that enforce device redirection.

- Network Access Protection (NAP) remediation can be enforced through an RD Gateway Server (using an RD connection authorization policy) to manage clients not in compliance with the corporate health policy.

EXAM TIP

For the 70-647 exam, in questions stating security requirements mandating that desktops must have version-specific antimalware software installed, specific Windows updates installed, and other specific requirements, VPN services with NAP would not be a good fit due to the number of items that may require remediation in order to allow a secure connection. The use of an SSL connection provided by a Remote Desktop Gateway server to a managed desktop will provide a secure connection.

Planning Connection Authorization Policies

RD Gateway servers enforce Remote Desktop connection authorization policies (RD CAPs) that specify which users are allowed to connect through the RD Gateway server to resources located on a protected network. One requirement of an RD CAP is to specify which users of a domain from groups within AD DS are authorized to connect through the RD Gateway. In addition, an optional configuration item is to configure the client computers users are allowed to use for connection through the RD Gateway. RD CAPs also specify whether remote clients use a password or a smart card for authentication to access internal network resources through the RD Gateway. RD CAPs can also be used to ensure remote clients that are trusted are redirected to RD Session Host servers that enforce RD Gateway device redirection. To be granted access to internal resources, a remote user must meet the conditions of at least one RD CAP prior to being denied access from a list of policies in the Network Policy Server.

You can use RD CAPs in conjunction with NAP to ensure that clients pass a system health check before being allowed to connect to terminal servers on a protected network. Automatic remediation is configurable for remote clients not passing a health check. In addition, a remediation server group can be configured to automatically redirect the remote client computer for remediation.

Planning Resource Authorization Policies

RD Gateway also provides configurable Remote Desktop resource authorization policies (RD RAPs) to determine the specific resources on the protected network that an incoming RD Gateway client is able to use. You create an RD RAP and specify a group of computers that you want to allow access to a specified group of users. For example, you could create a group of computers called AccountsComputers that will be accessible to members of the Accountants user group. To be granted access to internal resources, a remote user must meet the conditions of at least one RD RAP configured on the RD Gateway Manager.

For example, for a sample configuration to satisfy the connection requirements for access through an RD Gateway, you might create an RD CAP that specifies that the Accountants group, members of which have authenticated using smart cards and whose computers have passed a health check, are also users of a configured group of an RD RAP that is requesting access to approved RD Session Hosts groups also configured in the RD RAP.

> **MORE INFO**   **MORE ON CONFIGURING RD GATEWAY ROLE SERVICE**
>
> To learn more about configuring RD Gateway, see *http://technet.microsoft.com/en-us /library/cc754191.aspx*.

Planning for Secure Communications

Configuring the use of Transport Layer Security (TLS) on the RDP-Tcp property settings of an RD Session Host has been shown to be an easy solution for securing communications within the corporate environment. Also, securing communications for external clients has been briefly discussed with the use of RD Gateway services.

The RD Gateway, formerly TS Gateway Services, was introduced by Microsoft to replace the complex solution often implemented when using RDC in the past. Most RDC solutions involving access through an untrusted network and requiring a secure solution required the initial use of a VPN connection into the internal environment. Then the remote user initiates a remote desktop connection through the VPN. This convoluted solution is too time consuming for performing minimal tasks and would drive users away from accessing corporate resources when only minimal access was needed if time was an issue. Another obstacle for this solution might be that the use of the VPN client configured for access was prohibited by the policy of the location from which the remote user was attempting access.

The RD Gateway service allows a remote user to connect to the RD Gateway host using an SSL connection over TCP port 443, a very common port to configure for access through a firewall. The RD Gateway server then provides the connection to the secure RD Session Host servers in the internal network. The solution appears easy, but the complexity of the back end of the connection, the connection between the RD Gateway server and the internal RD Session Host servers, causes a bit of anxiety for security administrators because the RD Gateway server still needs access to the following services using the following destination ports:

- To provide for authentication of users: TCP port 88 for Kerberos.

- The RPC Endpoint Mapper: TCP port 135. This communication provides the TCP port for communicating with the NTDS RPC service for AD DS.

- Communicating with the NTDS RPC service for AD DS. This TCP port must be configured statically in the registry of the RD Gateway server.

- Information to authorize the user using the Lightweight Directory Access Protocol (LDAP) service: TCP port 389.

- DNS Traffic for name resolution: User Datagram Protocol (UDP) port 53.

- RDP Traffic for communicating with the back-end RD Session Hosts: TCP port 3389.

- RADIUS traffic if a central Network Policy Server server is used for authentication and authorization of the remote connection: UDP ports 1812 and 1813 for RADIUS and RADIUS accounting, respectively.

- Finally—yes, this list is pretty exhausting—if checking for the certificate revocation list is necessary: LDAP or HTTP (80) or FTP (21) might be necessary.

An easier and more secure solution would be to employ a security server or security device to provide a secure reverse proxy of all the above communication from the perimeter network to an RD Gateway service on the internal network. This would alleviate using firewall rules to provide communication for the RD Gateway server in the perimeter network to all of the previously listed servers and services. Microsoft Forefront Threat Management Gateway 2010, formerly ISA Server, provides an elegant solution to this problem by receiving the remote client's request and providing a secure web gateway through the firewall separating the perimeter network and the internal network. All of these rules can be provided within a predefined rule set preconfigured for use with the RD Gateway server.

Designing for RD Virtualization Host Servers

To provide further integration of all remote user access to applications, desktops and now virtual desktops, Microsoft introduced *Remote Desktop Virtualization Host* (RD Virtualization Host). RD Virtualization Host utilizes Hyper-V as its platform and RD Connection Broker as the management piece to provide redirection for a user to the user's virtual desktop. RD Virtualization Host can also provide via RD Connection Broker access to dynamic pools and session reconnection if a user has an existing session with a virtual desktop within a pool. RD Virtualization Host also provides the ability to access applications enabled with RemoteFX in the virtual machines.

In planning the deployment of the RD Virtualization Host role service, the administrator must also plan for the associated deployment of Hyper-V because the Hyper-V role is also installed on the same server. First, the server has to meet the following hardware specifications for the Hyper-V role:

- x64-based processor and Windows Server 2008 R2 SP1 x64-based versions

- Hardware-assisted virtualization from Intel, Intel VT, or AMD, AMD-V

- Hardware-enforced Data Execution Prevention, otherwise known as NX/XD, No eXecute (AMD), eXecute Disable (Intel)
- Hyperthreading is enabled in the BIOS of the RD Virtualization Host

In addition, the hardware specifications must also comply with the requirements for running RemoteFX. The requirements for installing the RemoteFX role service are discussed later in this chapter.

In addition to ensuring these software and hardware specifications required for the individual roles and role services, the enterprise administrator must plan for the scalability of the design when deploying a Virtual Desktop Infrastructure (VDI). Because all application execution and data processing occurs on the server on a virtual machine, the hardware of the server hosting the RD Virtualization Host must be able to satisfy all of the requirements for the proposed number of virtual desktops planned for use on this server. This is discussed more thoroughly in Chapter 8.

Designing for RemoteFX Content

The ability to improve remote user experience to the point that it feels as if the user is experiencing the same multimedia, 3D graphics, Windows Aero, full-fidelity video and all rich media content provided through service features such as Silverlight and DirectX has finally arrived with RemoteFX. RemoteFX is really a set of RDP technologies that provides the platform for technologies enabling the rich content normally experienced by a local user. Microsoft RemoteFX is available for RD Session Host servers running on Windows Server 2008 R2 Service Pack 1.

RemoteFX technology can be embedded into a thin client device to provide an extremely rich environment when used for access to a remote desktop using Remote Desktop virtualization. A user with this type of thin client device will be capable of running truly powerful applications such as AutoCAD 2011 or even games requiring extensive 3D graphics. This has not been previously possible for any environment using a remote desktop or a virtual desktop.

The requirements for deploying RemoteFX include deploying RemoteFX on a Windows Server 2008 R2 Service Pack 1 installation including the Hyper-V and RD Virtualization Host role services. The RemoteFX is also a role service of the Remote Desktop Services role. The computer requirements for providing the RemoteFX role service are as follows:

- A Second-Level Address Translation (SLAT)–enabled processor that provides virtualized environment hardware-assisted memory enhancements to reduce the overhead in memory mapping and memory I/O for the memory space of each individual virtual machine running on the computer.
- A high-performance graphics processing unit (GPU) capable of quickly rendering 3D graphics because all graphic rendering is performed on the server back end for a RemoteFX–enabled application. The graphics adapter requires an amount of dedicated video memory that is directly dependent on the number of monitors used for the virtual machines hosted on the computer. If multiple GPUs per computer will be used to increase scalability, then the GPUs must be identical.

- An optional RemoteFX hardware encoder can be installed to increase scalability. This requires installation in a PCI Express x4 slot, or greater, on the server.
- A Windows Display Driver Model (WDDM) compliant driver is needed.

> **NOTE** **WDDM VS. XDDM**
>
> A current limitation exists when using a WDDM driver and a server with a baseboard management controller (BMC). The BMC usually requires the use of an XP Display Driver Model (XDDM) driver. A GPU running on a server is not capable of using both drivers simultaneously. Therefore, a current workaround is to install a RemoteFX cap driver that disables use of the XDDM driver for the integrated display adapter used by the BMC during normal function of the computer. If the computer suffers a severe error, the BMC is accessible remotely because the WDDM driver will not be in use.

Deployment considerations for the client to run RemoteFX–enabled applications require one of two solutions:

- Client software that includes a software client for RemoteFX. The Remote Desktop Client update for Windows 7 included in Windows Server 2008 R2 with Service Pack 1 contains a RemoteFX–enabled client.
- A hardware decoder for RemoteFX that can be included in thin client devices as an embedded application-specific integrated circuit (ASIC) to provide a hardware-based RemoteFX decoder.

PRACTICE   Planning Use of the Remote Desktop Gateway

Tailspin Toys is an Australian company headquartered in Sydney. The company uses a single Active Directory forest. Regional branches are located in each Australian state and territory as well as on both of New Zealand's islands. Each regional branch has its own domain in the Tailspin Toys forest. Responsibility for software purchasing and licensing is handled on a branch-by-branch basis by a designated licensing officer. The licensing officer is responsible for ensuring that his or her regional branch complies with its licensing responsibilities.

Tailspin Toys has an existing Remote Desktop Services infrastructure, which you plan to expand as the need for applications installed on Remote Desktop Session Hosts continues to grow. Although Tailspin Toys has more than 10,000 employees spread across offices in Australia and New Zealand, only a small percentage of employees ever need to access applications hosted on RD Session Hosts and terminal servers running on Windows Server 2008; however, they often do so from multiple computers. These employees primarily use two applications. Extensive testing has revealed that installing application Alpha and application Beta on the same RD Session Host leads to application instability. At present, RD Session Hosts are deployed with either application Alpha or application Beta in each regional office. There are no plans to use Microsoft App-V at Tailspin Toys.

Another application that runs from an RD Session Host, called application Gamma, is used with the company's financial database. This application is used at the Sydney office only. As a method of protecting the company's financial database, you are planning to move all servers that support the database, including the RD Session Host that hosts application Gamma, to an organizational unit (OU) named Secure Servers. The Secure Servers OU has a Group Policy object (GPO) applied that enforces TLS 1.0 to secure communications with all RD Session Hosts.

EXERCISE   Plan Tailspin Toys Remote Desktop Services Deployment

In this exercise, you review the business and technical requirements to plan a Remote Desktop Services deployment for Tailspin Toys.

1. Twenty members of the accounting team need access to the front-end financial application installed on the RD Session Host. Which steps can you take to allow only these users access from anywhere, using the required TLS security layer for communications, and not configure certificates for each individual remote client?

    - Configure an RD Gateway Server to use a certificate to enforce the use of SSL for all traffic between the remote client and RD Gateway Server.

    - Configure the use of TLS communications for the security layer on the RDP-Tcp properties of the RD Session Host.

    - Configure an RD RAP and RD CAP that allow only the 20 authorized users from the accounting team to use the RD Gateway server to connect to the RD Session Host that publishes the database front-end application through RemoteApp.

2. What plans should you make for the deployment of Remote Desktop license servers on the Tailspin Toys network to mirror the company's current software purchasing arrangements and to ensure that a license server is still accessible in the event of a hardware failure?

    - Place two RD Licensing servers in each domain in the forest. Set the scope on each license server to Domain because there is a mix of Windows Server 2008 Terminal Servers and Windows Server 2008 R2 RD Session Hosts. License purchasing is done on a regional basis, and each domain represents a region.

    - Instruct the licensing officers to purchase per-user Remote Desktop Services CALs. These are appropriate because only a small number of users actually access Remote Desktop Services but often do so from multiple computers.

    - Instruct the license administrator in each domain to install 50 percent of the licenses on each RD Licensing server.

3. Clients connecting to RD-Alpha and RD-Beta at the Sydney head office site are reporting that performance has degraded significantly. It is likely that the number of users at the head office that need to use application Alpha and application Beta will increase

threefold in the next financial year. What changes can you implement to improve capacity on RD-Alpha and RD-Beta to meet this projected growth in demand?

- Install two RD Session Host farms, one for RD-Alpha and one for RD-Beta. Add RD Session Hosts to each farm as required.
- Install an RD Connection Broker to establish load balancing and session reconnection.
- It is necessary to use separate farms because application Alpha and application Beta conflict when installed on the same RD Session Host. Each server in an RD Session Host farm must have an identical application configuration.

Lesson Summary

- Remote Desktop Licensing servers must be activated before you can install Remote Desktop Services CALs. The discovery scope of a license server is still required for Terminal Servers running on Windows 2000 Server, Windows Server 2003, and Windows Server 2008. The discovery scope determines which clients and Terminal Services servers can automatically detect the server. RD Session Host servers running on Windows Server 2008 R2 do not use a discovery scope because RD Session Host servers must be individually configured for a license server.
- RD Connection Broker enables you to manage load balancing in an RD Session Host farm. RD Connection Broker can be paired with DNS round robin or NLB for load balancing and ensures that disconnected clients are always reconnected to the correct session on the appropriate server.
- RD Web Access allows clients to connect to an RD Session Host by using a browser for remote clients not using RDC.
- RD Gateway servers can enable clients from unprotected networks to connect to RD Session Hosts on protected networks.

Lesson Review

You can use the following questions to test your knowledge of the information in Lesson 1, "Designing Remote Desktop Services." The questions are also available on the companion CD if you prefer to review them in electronic form.

> **NOTE ANSWERS**
>
> Answers to these questions and explanations of why each answer choice is correct or incorrect are located in the "Answers" section at the end of the book.

1. You are planning the deployment of Remote Desktop licensing for your organization's Australian subsidiary. Your organization has two offices, one located in Brisbane and one located in Adelaide. A data center in Hobart hosts infrastructure servers. Both the Brisbane and Adelaide offices have their own RD Session Host farms. The offices are connected by a high-speed wide area network (WAN) link. Each office has its own AD DS domain, and both are a part of the same forest. The forest root domain is located in the Hobart data center and does not contain standard user or computer accounts. For operational reasons, you want to ensure that Remote Desktop Services CALs purchased and installed at each location are allocated to devices at that location only. All RD Session Hosts are running on Windows Server 2008 R2. Which of the following license server deployment plans should you implement?

   A. Deploy a license server to each location and set the discovery scope of each license server to Domain.

   B. Deploy a license server to each location and set the discovery scope of each license server to Forest.

   C. Deploy a license server to the Hobart data center and set the discovery scope of the license server to Forest.

   D. Deploy a license server at each site and configure each RD Session Host server at each site to use the local RD Licensing server.

2. You are planning the deployment of RD Licensing servers. Which of the following steps do you need to take prior to installing Remote Desktop Services CALs on an RD Licensing server?

   A. Set the forest functional level to Windows Server 2008.

   B. Set the domain functional level of each domain in the forest to Windows Server 2008.

   C. Activate the license server.

   D. Install Internet Information Services (IIS).

3. The organization for which you work is going through a period of growth. Users access business applications from client terminals. You are concerned that the growth in users will outstrip the processing capacity of the RD Session Host. Which of the following solutions enables you to increase the client capacity without requiring client reconfiguration?

   A. Use Windows System Resource Manager (WSRM) to ensure that all users are able to access resources equally.

   B. Install Hyper-V on a computer running Windows Server 2008 Enterprise and add virtualized servers as required.

   C. Add RD Session Hosts as required and reconfigure clients to use specific ones.

   D. Create an RD Session Host farm and RD Session Hosts as required.

4. You need to ensure that clients connecting to your RD Session Hosts have passed a health check. Which of the following deployments should you implement?

   A. Install Microsoft Forefront Client Security on the RD Session Hosts.

   B. Implement an RD Connection Broker.

   C. Mediate access using an RD Gateway server.

   D. Mediate access using Forefront Threat Management Gateway.

Lesson 2: Designing Application Deployment

A constant challenge for enterprise administrators in large organizations is ensuring that staff members within the organization have access to the specific applications they need to perform their job functions but not to applications they do not need. Just as a missing application costs the organization money in terms of lost productivity, an installed application that is never used costs the organization money in terms of licensing fees. In this lesson, you learn about three application deployment technologies that can simplify the rollout of important productivity software to users in your enterprise environment. You learn the benefits and drawbacks of each method and which of these solutions is appropriate for a given situation or network environment.

After this lesson, you will be able to:

- Design application deployment using Group Policy.
- Design application deployment using System Center Essentials.
- Plan the deployment of applications using System Center Configuration Manager.

Estimated lesson time: 40 minutes

Designing Application Deployment using Group Policy

As an enterprise administrator, you are aware that Group Policy enables you to publish software to users, assign software to users, or assign software to computers. You can use a combination of these methods to ensure that applications are available to users on the network, that the software automatically repairs if it becomes corrupted, and that updates and new revisions are installed as appropriate.

Publishing a software installation package to users in a site, domain, or OU enables users to use Programs and Features in Control Panel to install the software. The Auto-Install publishing option deploys the application when the user attempts to open an associated document. This process is known as document invocation.

You can assign software to users on demand, assign software to users on logon, or assign software to computers. If you assign software to deploy on demand, it is advertised on the desktop. The user installs the software by double-clicking the desktop shortcut, by accessing the software through the Start menu, or by document invocation. If Control Panel is available, the user can also install the software through Programs and Features. You can also assign software to users so that it installs the next time a user logs off (or reboots the computer) and logs on again. Even if the user removes the software, it becomes available again at logon. Updates and new versions are automatically installed at logon.

If you assign software to users in an OU and users in different OUs use the same computer, then the software might be available to one user and not to another. If you want the software to be available to all users of a computer or group of computers, you can assign software to computers. The software is installed when the computer powers on, and any updates or revisions are installed on reboot. If you assign software to a computer, the computer user cannot remove it. Only a local or domain administrator can remove the software, although a user can repair it.

When planning the deployment of applications, you might have to consider the automatic removal of the application if the computer or user is reassigned. For example, the computer a manager uses in one department is reassigned to an administrative assistant in another department when the manager receives a newer computer. The set of applications the manager uses might be significantly different from the set of applications the administrative assistant uses. If you have configured Group Policy software deployment just to install applications, the set of applications assigned for the administrative assistant are added to those already assigned to the manager. For example, if the manager is assigned applications A, B, C, and D and the administrative assistant is assigned applications C, D, E, and F, the computer now has applications A, B, C, D, E, and F installed after reassignment. By configuring software to be removed when the policy falls out of scope, as shown in Figure 7-8, applications A, B, C, and D are removed and applications C, D, E, and F are installed when the computer is reassigned to a new user.

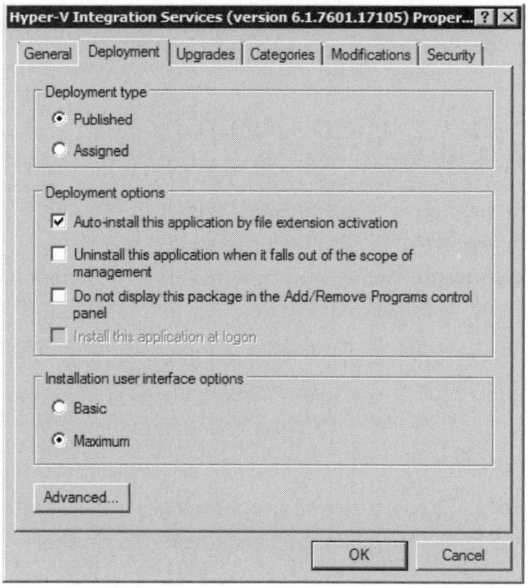

FIGURE 7-8 Ensuring that applications are removed when they fall out of scope

When planning software deployment using Group Policy, it is important to remember the impact WAN bandwidth limitations will have on deployment. If not configured properly, application files might be pushed to clients across WAN connections, clogging them with traffic and causing the deployment to fail. When planning software deployments, remember that technologies such as distributed file system (DFS) enable you to replicate application packages to branch office locations prior to using Group Policy to publish them. Similarly, use Group Policy filtering to target application deployment precisely when using Group Policy. An excellent tool that assists you with planning application deployment using Group Policy is the Group Policy Modeling node of the Group Policy Management Console. With this tool, you can simulate an application deployment using Group Policy without having to perform the actual deployment to verify its efficacy.

Group Policy is another way to deploy applications configured as a RemoteApp. Applications added as a RemoteApp within the RemoteApp Manager can then be made into an .msi file for distribution using one of the previously discussed methods of application deployment for Group Policy. The user's desktop or Start menu can be populated with these applications published as RemoteApps. The user does not need to wait for long installation routines because the only options necessary for the deployment as a RemoteApp are where the application will be deployed and whether the application will be configured for document invocation. This allows the RemoteApp to be associated with various extensions of documents that, when selected by the user on the remote client, will open up the associated RemoteApp. The user will feel as if the application was installed locally.

> **MORE INFO** **MORE ON PLANNING APPLICATION DEPLOYMENT USING GROUP POLICY**
>
> For more information about using Group Policy to deploy software, access the following address: *http://technet.microsoft.com/en-us/library/cc725828(WS.10).aspx.*

Planning Application Deployment with System Center Essentials

System Center Essentials 2010 is an application deployment solution suitable for organizations that have fewer than 500 clients. Although this number is significantly below what most people would consider an enterprise environment, your particular enterprise might include multiple domains or forests that have fewer than 500 clients, in which case it makes sense to consider System Center Essentials 2010 in your application deployment plans. A migration path to Microsoft System Center Configuration Manager 2007 is also available for organizations growing beyond the needs of managing more than 50 servers and 500 client management limits.

System Center Essentials 2010 provides a single server solution for managing an organization's servers, clients, hardware, and software. The tool provides an upgrade from Windows Server Update Services (WSUS) 2.0 or 3.0 as well as requiring access to a Microsoft SQL Server database to store configuration and reporting data. If your organization does not have a SQL Server 2008 instance, the System Center Essentials 2010 installation routine installs SQL Server 2008 Express Edition as well as its own instance (not shared) of SQL Server Reporting Services.

An administrator can use the System Center Essentials 2010 console to assess, configure, and deploy software to targeted groups and computers. System Center Essentials 2010 also simplifies the task of deploying operating system upgrades or installing application suites (for example, Office 2010) by providing a wizard that walks you through the process of deploying software by creating a package and targeting installation on clients and servers in your network. You can deploy Microsoft software installation (MSI) and non-MSI applications, drivers, and Microsoft and non-Microsoft hotfix releases. You can target software installations by grouping computers and defining command-line configurations.

Application deployment using System Center Essentials 2010 is configured through a wizard that enables you to deploy .msi or .exe packages to clients and servers within your organization. The wizard asks you to specify the destination of the application to be deployed and the application installation deadline. It then enables you to track installation progress and troubleshoot any problems that arise with the deployment.

Application deployment requires that the computers have an installed agent for management and be configured for Automatic Updates. To deploy the software packages, a computer group consisting of managed computers is required. The installation schedule for the package deployment is dependent on the configuration of Automatic Updates on the managed computers. Application packages can be installed automatically, on approval to download the application package via a notification from Automatic Updates, or any time a notification is given that the download of the package is complete and that the local user is configured to provide a manual installation of any software approved and downloaded through Automatic Updates. All of these options are consistent with the different configuration options for Automatic Updates. Automatic Updates configuration can also be controlled through System Center Essentials 2010.

System Center Essentials 2010 automates software and hardware inventory so you can review assets and optimize configuration and ensure that software deployed within your organization meets compliance requirements. You can perform searches, define filters, and generate reports that include up-to-date lists of all installed software applications and installed hardware. This is useful if you want to generate hardware readiness reports for the deployment of major applications or new operating systems.

From the perspective of planning application deployment for large network environments, System Center Essentials 2010 sits between using the Active Directory software deployment functionality and the greater functionality of System Center Configuration Manager 2007. System Center Essentials 2010 works best for single-domain environments with between 300 and 500 client computers. It is possible to deploy only one System Center Essentials 2010 server per domain, so when planning application deployment for domains with more than 500 clients, you will need to implement System Center Configuration Manager 2007.

System Center Essentials 2010 can be an appropriate application deployment solution for organizations with multiple domains, but only when the domains each have fewer than 500 client computers and software application deployment will be managed at the domain rather than at the organizational level. This is because System Center Essentials 2010 cannot be used in a hierarchy and each System Center Essentials 2010 server is essentially a stand-alone solution.

Planning the Deployment of Applications Using System Center Configuration Manager 2007

The Microsoft top-tier application deployment solution is *System Center Configuration Manager 2007.* If planned correctly, you can use a System Center Configuration Manager 2007 installation to manage the application deployment needs of thousands of clients across an enterprise network. This is possible because System Center Configuration Manager 2007 can be deployed in a hierarchy, with multiple software distribution points across different sites. System Center Configuration Manager 2007 also enables you to delegate the deployment of applications to administrators in regional offices.

System Center Configuration Manager 2007 is not limited to application deployment; you can also use it to deploy server and client operating systems and software updates. The software update functionality of System Center Configuration Manager 2007 is covered in more detail in Chapter 11, "Designing a Software Update Infrastructure and Managing Compliance." The extensive reporting functionality of System Center Configuration Manager 2007 enables administrators to meter and evaluate software usage, which is very important when you are attempting to assess which computers in an organization have a specific application already deployed.

System Center Configuration Manager 2007 can be configured to work with the Windows Server 2008 R2 Network Policy Server to restrict network access to computers that do not meet specified requirements, for example, when installing required security updates. System Center Configuration Manager 2007 can also be configured to perform automatic client remediation, removing unapproved software from clients and installing applications to meet the organization's software configuration policies.

System Center Configuration Manager 2007 is an agent-based solution, and you must install the agent software on client computers before they can be managed. You can do this automatically for client computers that are members of the same Active Directory forest as the System Center Configuration Manager 2007 server.

System Center Configuration Manager 2007 is deployed on a per-site basis. System Center Configuration Manager 2007 sites can be the same as Active Directory sites or can be independent of the Active Directory structure, so it is important to understand that the same term can be used differently, depending on whether it relates to System Center Configuration Manager 2007 or to AD DS. System Center Configuration Manager 2007 sites have the following properties:

- **Primary site**   A primary site always stores the System Center Configuration Manager 2007 data for itself and for all sites below it in a System Center Configuration Manager hierarchy using a SQL Server database. This database is typically located on the same local area network as the initial System Center Configuration Manager 2007 server and is called the Configuration Manager 2007 site database. The first site in which System Center Configuration Manager 2007 is deployed is always a primary site.

- **Secondary site** A secondary System Center Configuration Manager site has no local SQL Server database because all configuration data is stored in the database at the primary site. The secondary site is attached to the primary site and administered from the primary site. Secondary sites require no additional System Center Configuration Manager 2007 license and cannot have other sites below them in the hierarchy.

- **Parent sites** Parent sites have other sites attached to them in a hierarchy.

- **Child sites** Child sites are attached to sites above them in the hierarchy. A child site can be either a primary site or a secondary site.

- **Central site** Central sites have no parent sites. These sites are sometimes called stand-alone sites.

MORE INFO **MORE ON SITES**

To understand more about System Center Configuration Manager 2007 sites, consult the TechNet article at *http://technet.microsoft.com/en-us/library/bb632547.aspx*.

System Center Configuration Manager 2007 Client Deployment

Before you can use System Center Configuration Manager 2007 to deploy an application to a computer on your network, the client computer must have the System Center Configuration Manager 2007 agent software installed. You can use a number of methods to deploy this software on computer systems in your network. Table 7-1 lists and briefly describes these methods.

TABLE 7-1 Methods of Deploying System Center Configuration Manager 2007 Client

INSTALLATION METHOD	DESCRIPTION
Client push installation	Targets the agent to assigned resources
Software update point installation	Installs the agent by using the System Center Configuration Manager 2007 software updates feature
Group Policy installation	Installs the agent by using Group Policy
Logon script installation	Installs the agent by means of a logon script
Manual installation	Installs the agent manually
Upgrade installation	Installs upgrades to the agent software by using the software distribution feature in System Center Configuration Manager 2007
Client imaging	Prestages the agent installation as part of an operating system image

Deploying Applications with System Center Configuration Manager 2007

You can use the System Center Configuration Manager 2007 software distribution functionality to push applications and updates to client computers. It uses packages (for example, MSI packages) to deploy software applications. Within those packages, commands known as programs tell the client what executable file to run. A single package can contain multiple programs. Packages can also contain command lines to run files already present on the client. Advertisements specify which clients receive the program and the package. The distribution of applications using System Center Configuration Manager 2007 involves creating the software distribution package, creating programs to be included in the package, selecting package distribution points, and then creating an advertisement for a program.

A significant difference between using System Center Configuration Manager 2007 and deploying applications through Group Policy is software metering, by which administrators collect software usage data from System Center Configuration Manager 2007 clients. Software metering will inform you of which applications are actively being used as well as which applications are being installed. This enables organizations to rationalize their software licensing, removing applications that have been deployed but are not used from client computers throughout the organization.

Another advantage of System Center Configuration Manager 2007 over traditional software deployment methods is the ability to use a feature known as Wake On LAN. Wake On LAN can send a wake-up transmission prior to the configured deadline for a software deployment. This enables deployment of applications to computers when their users are not present rather than waiting for installation to proceed when the user first logs on.

> **MORE INFO**   **WAKE ON LAN**
>
> For System Center Configuration Manager 2007 to use Wake On LAN, the System Configuration Manager 2007 client software must be installed on the computer, the client network card must support magic packet format, and the client BIOS must be configured for wake-up packets on the network card. For more information and example scenarios, access *http://technet.microsoft.com/en-gb/library/bb932183.aspx*.

PRACTICE   Planning Application Deployment

The Wingtip Toys Active Directory infrastructure consists of three forests, each of which shares a forest trust. As enterprise administrator, you are responsible for planning the software deployment infrastructure for all three forests, although the actual software deployment tasks will be carried out by systems administrators who report directly to you and who have administrative rights only at the forest level.

The *wingtiptoys.internal* forest consists of 20 Active Directory domains, each of which has between 400 and 1,000 computer accounts. These 20 domains are spread across seven

Active Directory sites. No domain spans more than a single site. Because of the large number of clients in this forest, the chief information officer has asked that application usage be strictly monitored to ensure that only applications that are used are deployed to computers within the organization. All application deployment and configuration data should be stored centrally. Application deployment will also be handled by administrators in the *wingtiptoys.internal* forest root domain and will not be handled by staff at individual sites.

The *wingtiptoys.development* forest consists of five Active Directory domains, one for the development department in each regional head office. Each domain has between 400 and 450 computer accounts and a maximum of 20 servers. Each domain is deployed at a single Active Directory site.

The *wingtiptoys.design* forest consists of a single-site Active Directory domain with 150 computer accounts. It is necessary to deploy several custom applications that are not in MSI format to all computers in the *wingtiptoys.design* domain.

Where possible, the technology with the lowest cost should be used. Assume that it costs the least to use software deployment through Group Policy and the most to use System Center Configuration Manager 2007. Although it will be necessary in some instances to deploy third-party applications, your application deployment plans should avoid tools and deployment mechanisms that use third-party products.

EXERCISE   Plan the Appropriate Application Deployment Technology

In this exercise, you review the business and technical requirements as a precursor to planning an application deployment strategy for the various divisions of Wingtip Toys.

1. Which application deployment method would be most appropriate for use in the *wingtiptoys.design* forest, and why?

   - System Center Essentials 2010 is the most appropriate for use in the *wingtiptoys.design* forest. The forest has a single domain, fewer than 500 client computers, and the necessity to install software packages that are not in MSI format. Software packages that are not in MSI format cannot be deployed using standard Group Policy software deployment tools. Some technologies allow conversion of third-party applications to MSI format, but the business and technical requirements specify that these must be avoided. You can learn more about creating MSI packages for third-party products by accessing the following link: *http://support .microsoft.com/default.aspx/kb/257718.*

2. Which application deployment infrastructure plans would you make for the *wingtiptoys.internal* forest? Include information about the infrastructure that will be deployed at each Active Directory site.

   - Deploy a System Center Configuration Manager 2007 primary site at the *wingtiptoys.internal* forest root site. Application deployment will be managed from here. This site will also host the System Center Configuration Manager 2007 configuration database.

- Deploy a System Center Configuration Manager 2007 secondary site at the other six Active Directory sites so that application deployment can be managed centrally from the primary site.

- Configure System Center Configuration Manager 2007 software metering to monitor application usage.

3. Under what circumstances would it be necessary to use System Center Configuration Manager 2007 rather than System Center Essentials 2010 as an application deployment solution for the *wingtiptoys.development* forest?

- You would use System Center Configuration Manager 2007 rather than System Center Essentials 2010 when administration needs to be performed in a top-down manner. System Center Essentials 2010 is limited to 500 clients, which means it would be necessary to deploy a System Center Essentials 2010 server in each domain for application deployment, each of which would be managed on an individual basis.

- It would be necessary to use System Center Configuration Manager 2007 if the number of clients in each domain grows to more than 500. Each System Center Essentials 2010 instance can be used to deploy applications to a maximum of only 500 client computers.

- It would be necessary to use System Center Configuration Manager 2007 if centralized reporting for the entire forest is necessary. System Center Essentials 2010 can perform reports only for the clients it manages. System Center Configuration Manager 2007 could be generated for every client in the forest.

Lesson Summary

- Group Policy software deployment enables applications prepared as MSI packages to be distributed to clients by linking GPOs.

- Group Policy software deployment provides no reporting functionality.

- You can target deployments by using GPO filtering.

- System Center Essentials 2010 can be used to perform application deployment and reporting, but it is limited to 500 clients.

- System Center Essentials 2010 deployment can be targeted to specific computers or users irrespective of OU membership.

- Only one System Center Essentials 2010 server can be installed in an Active Directory domain.

- System Center Configuration Manager 2007 can perform sophisticated application deployment and reporting and has no client limitation.

- Like System Center Essentials 2010, System Center Configuration Manager 2007 can target specific computers or users for application deployment irrespective of OU membership.

- Software metering enables administrators to rationalize application software licensing.

Lesson Review

You can use the following questions to test your knowledge of the information in Lesson 2, "Designing Application Deployment." The questions are also available on the companion CD if you prefer to review them in electronic form.

> **NOTE ANSWERS**
>
> Answers to these questions and explanations of why each answer choice is correct or incorrect are located in the "Answers" section at the end of the book.

1. You are planning an application deployment strategy for a single domain forest that has 600 client computers spread across five Active Directory sites. Which of the following technologies can you use to deploy applications to all client computers in this environment? (Choose two. Each correct answer forms a complete solution.)

   A. Group Policy software deployment

   B. System Center Essentials 2010

   C. System Center Operations Manager 2007

   D. System Center Configuration Manager 2007

   E. System Center Virtual Machine Manager 2007

2. You are planning to use Group Policy software deployment to deploy several important applications to client computers on your organization's network. Before performing the actual deployment, you want to verify that the Group Policy configuration will behave in the planned manner. Which of the following tools can you use to verify that the application deployment strategy has been correctly configured prior to application rollout?

   A. Group Policy Results

   B. Group Policy Modeling

   C. Active Directory Users and Computers

   D. Active Directory Sites and Services

3. You are planning the deployment of an important computer-aided design (CAD) application to a select group of users within your organization. You need to ensure that the application will be removed from the users' computers if they are transferred to another department and their user accounts are moved to a new OU within the Active Directory structure. Which of the following plans should you make?

   A. Plan to use the Published, rather than Assigned, deployment type.

   B. Plan to use the Ignore Language When Deploying This Package advanced deployment option when configuring the software deployment.

C. Plan to use the Install This Application At Logon option when configuring software deployment.

D. Plan to use the Uninstall The Application When It Falls Out Of The Scope Of Management option when configuring software deployment.

4. As part of your application deployment plans, you want to review application deployment every six months to ensure that your organization is using software licenses efficiently. You want to locate those computers in your organization that have unused applications. Which of the following tools enables you to accomplish this?

A. System Center Configuration Manager 2007

B. Windows Server Update Services 3.0 SP1

C. Group Policy Management Console

D. Active Directory Users and Computers

Chapter Review

To further practice and reinforce the skills you learned in this chapter, you can perform the following tasks:

- Review the chapter summary.
- Review the list of key terms introduced in this chapter.
- Complete the case scenario. This scenario sets up a real-world situation involving the topics of this chapter and asks you to create a solution.
- Complete the suggested practices.
- Take a practice test.

Chapter Summary

- RD Licensing servers must be activated before they can have Remote Desktop Services per-device and Remote Desktop Services per-user CALs installed.
- RD RemoteApp displays just the application, rather than the entire remote desktop, on the Remote Desktop client and now provides single sign-on.
- RD Gateway servers enable clients on the Internet to connect to protected terminal servers without requiring the setup of a VPN.
- RD Connection Broker provides the management of RD Session Host farms and ensures that clients are reconnected to the correct session if they become disconnected.
- Group Policy software deployment enables applications prepared as MSI packages to be distributed to clients by linking GPOs to appropriate Active Directory containers.
- You can use System Center Essentials 2010 to perform application deployment and reporting, but it is limited to 500 clients. Only one System Center Essentials 2010 server can be installed in an Active Directory domain.
- System Center Configuration Manager 2007 can perform sophisticated application deployment and reporting and has no client limitation. You can use System Center Configuration Manager 2007 reporting to examine how deployed applications are used in an environment so that licensing can be rationalized.

Key Terms

Do you know what these key terms mean? You can check your answers by looking up the terms in the glossary at the end of the book.

- Remote Desktop Services
- RemoteFX
- RD Virtualization Host

- System Center Essentials 2010
- Systems Center Configuration Manager 2007

Case Scenario

In the following case scenario, you apply what you have learned about Remote Desktop Services and application and server virtualization. You can find answers to these questions in the "Answers" section at the end of this book.

Case Scenario: Planning a Remote Desktop Services Strategy for Wingtip Toys

You are planning the deployment of Remote Desktop Services for Wingtip Toys. The company has an office in each state of Australia. Because of the decentralized nature of the Wingtip Toys organization, each state office has its own domain in the *wingtiptoys.internal* forest. All clients in the organization are using Windows Vista without any service packs applied. Taking this into consideration, how will you resolve the following design challenges?

1. The purchase and management of Remote Desktop Services CALs should be handled separately. What plans should be made for an RD Licensing server deployment?

2. The RD Session Host in the Queensland office is reaching capacity and cannot be upgraded further. How can you continue to service clients in the Queensland office and ensure that interrupted sessions are reconnected?

3. What steps must you take to ensure that Windows Vista clients can access RemoteApp applications through RD Web Access?

Suggested Practices

To help you successfully master the exam objectives presented in this chapter, complete the following tasks.

Provision Applications

Complete all the practices in this section.

- **Practice 1** Create a Windows Installer package for Notepad and access the deployed application with a remote client by performing these steps:
  - Install the RD Session Host role on another member server within the Active Directory domain with the Glasgow computer already acting as the domain controller for the domain. Call the new system RDSH-1.
  - Using the RD RemoteApp manager, create the Windows Installer package for the Notepad application.

- From a third computer installed as a domain member running Windows 7, access the deployed application using the Remote Desktop client and try accessing the application using a browser.
- **Practice 2** Install and activate an RD Licensing server by performing these steps:
  - Install the RD License role service on the Glasgow computer.
  - Activate the RD Licensing server by using the webpage method, using another computer that is connected to the Internet
- **Practice 3** Install and configure an RD Connection Broker (on another computer system called Paris that is joined to the domain) by performing these steps:
  - Install the RD Connection Broker role service on the Paris computer
  - Configure the use of the RD Connection Broker and ensure the appropriate group membership has been configured for the TS Web Access group on Glasgow and the appropriate group settings for the TS Web Access group on Paris.
  - Configure the RD Web Access servers setting in Remote Desktop Connection Manager on Paris.

Take a Practice Test

The practice tests on this book's companion CD offer many options. For example, you can test yourself on just one exam objective, or you can test yourself on all the 70-647 certification exam content. You can set up the test so that it closely simulates the experience of taking a certification exam, or you can set it up in study mode so that you can look at the correct answers and explanations after you answer each question.

> **MORE INFO** **PRACTICE TESTS**
>
> For details about all the practice test options available, see "How to Use the Practice Tests" in this book's introduction.

CHAPTER 8

Designing Virtualization

Of all the new technologies introduced in Windows Server 2008, few will affect the way you design your network deployment as much as server and application virtualization. Although virtualization products have existed on the Windows Server platform for some time, Hyper-V ties virtualization directly into the operating system. In this chapter, you learn about Hyper-V functionality and how this technology will influence the decisions you make about deploying Windows Server 2008. The second part of this chapter covers application virtualization. In most deployments, applications are installed and interact directly with the operating system. In application virtualization, a virtualization layer exists between the application and the operating system. This allows the operating system to run applications that might not be compatible if installed in a traditional manner. It also allows applications to be run in a partitioned environment, which means that applications that would normally conflict with each other when run concurrently can be executed side by side without any problems.

Exam objectives in this chapter:
- Design an operating system virtualization strategy.

Lessons in this chapter:

Before You Begin

To complete the lessons in this chapter, you should have installed a Windows Server 2008 R2 Enterprise domain controller named Glasgow, as described in Chapter 1, "Planning Name Resolution and Internet Protocol Addressing." No additional configuration is required for this chapter.

Lesson 1: Designing Operating System Virtualization

In this lesson, you learn how to design an operating system virtualization strategy. This includes learning how to assess which existing server deployments make good candidates for virtualization, learning how to plan the migration of servers from traditional hardware-based installations to virtual hosts, and learning the most effective locations in an existing network infrastructure to deploy servers that host virtual machines (VMs). This lesson not only explains Hyper-V but also examines Remote Desktop Virtualization Host and System Center Virtual Machine Manager 2007. To effectively design an operating system virtualization strategy, you need to understand how these separate components can be integrated to meet your organization's needs.

> **After this lesson, you will be able to:**
> - Understand the differences among operating system virtualization technologies.
> - Understand the benefits of deploying System Center Virtual Machine Manager 2007.
> - Design a server consolidation strategy.
> - Design a virtual host and VM deployment strategy.
>
> **Estimated lesson time: 40 minutes**

Every year the hardware that vendors make available becomes more powerful and scalable. These hardware improvements change the way that enterprise administrators plan the deployment of server resources. In the past, server utilization patterns and performance meant that only a single server role or application could be deployed on computer hardware. Today's server hardware can cope with a much larger workload. This means that fewer servers are required to do the same amount of work. Virtualization allows you to fully utilize the increased computing power made available by modern hardware without worrying about the conflicts that might occur if you cohosted important applications and server roles on a single instance of Microsoft Windows Server 2008 R2. Virtualization provides the following benefits over traditional installations:

- **More efficient use of hardware resources**   Services such as Dynamic Host Configuration Protocol (DHCP) and Domain Name System (DNS), although vital to network infrastructure, are unlikely to push the limits of your server's processor and RAM. Although it is possible to colocate the DNS and DHCP roles on one Windows Server 2008 R2 computer, the strategy of separating network roles onto separate partitions allows you to relocate those partitions to other host computers if the circumstances and usage of those roles changes.

- **Improved availability**   Consolidating these services onto a single hardware platform can reduce costs and maintenance expenses. Although moving from many platforms to one might look as though it would lead to a single point of failure, implementing redundancy technologies (clustering and hot-swappable hardware such as processors, RAM, power supplies, and hard disk drives) provides a greater level of reliability at a lower cost. Consider the following situation: Four Windows Server 2008 R2 computers are each running a separate application provided to users on your network. If a hardware component fails on one of those servers, the application that the server provides to users of the network is unavailable until the component is replaced. Building one server with redundant components is less expensive than building four servers with redundant components. If a component fails, the built-in redundancy allows all server roles to remain available.

- **Servers need to be only intermittently available**   Some servers need to be available only intermittently. For example, the best practice with a root certificate authority (CA) is to use subordinate CAs to issue certificates and to keep the root CA offline. With virtualization, you could keep the entire virtualized root CA server on a removable USB hard disk drive in a safe, only turning it on when necessary and thereby ensuring the security of your certificate infrastructure. Virtualization frees up existing hardware that is rarely used—or makes it unnecessary to buy it.

- **Role sandboxing**   Sandboxing is a term used to describe the partitioning of server resources so that an application or service does not influence other components on the server. Without sandboxing, a failing server application or role has the capacity to bring down an entire server. Just as web application pools in Microsoft Internet Information Services (IIS) sandbox web applications so that the failure of one application will not bring all of them down, running server applications and roles in their own separate virtualized environment ensures that one errant process does not bring down everything else.

- **Greater capacity**   Adding significant hardware capacity to a single server is less expensive than adding incremental hardware upgrades to many servers. You can increase capacity by adding processors and RAM to the host server and then allocating those resources to a virtual server as needed.

- **Greater portability**   After a server has been virtualized, migrating it to another host if the original host's resources become overcommitted is relatively simple. For example, suppose that the disks on a Windows Server 2008 R2 Enterprise computer hosting 10 virtualized servers are reaching their input/output (I/O) capacity. Migrating some of the virtualized servers to another host is simpler than upgrading a server. Tools such as System Center Virtual Machine Manager, covered later in the chapter, make the process even simpler.

- **Easier backup and restore** Tools such as volume shadow copy allow you to back up an entire server's image while the server is still operational. If a host computer fails, the images can be rapidly restored on another host computer. Rather than backing up individual files and folders, you can back up the entire virtualized computer in one operation. System Center Virtual Machine Manager (SCVMM) 2007 allows you to move VMs back and forth to the storage area network (SAN) and even migrate VMs between host computers. SCVMM 2007 is covered in more detail later in this lesson.

Planning for Hyper-V

Hyper-V is a Windows Server 2008 feature that allows you to run virtualized computers under x64 versions of Windows Server 2008. Hyper-V is a hypervisor-based technology. A *hypervisor* is a software layer between the hardware and the operating system that allows multiple operating systems to run on a *host* computer simultaneously. Hyper-V has many similarities to Microsoft Virtual Server 2005 R2 in terms of functionality. Unlike Virtual Server 2005 R2, Hyper-V is built directly into the operating system as a role and does not sit above the operating system as an application. In addition to being a feature included with the operating system, Hyper-V has the following advantages as a virtualization platform:

- Hyper-V allows you to run 64-bit VM guests. Hyper-V can concurrently host 32-bit and 64-bit VM guests.
- Hyper-V supports symmetric multiprocessor (SMP) in the VM environment.
- Hyper-V can be installed on Windows Server 2008 R2 Datacenter and Windows Server 2008 R2 Enterprise editions with up to 2 TB of memory.
- Hyper-V can host as many concurrent VMs as the underlying hardware resources support.
- Hyper-V can be configured as a part of a failover cluster, so that a VM fails over across the network to a server running Hyper-V in a recovery site.
- Hyper-V can be used on a Windows Server 2008 R2 computer installed using the Server Core option. You can manage Hyper-V on a Server Core computer using the Windows Management Instrumentation (WMI) interface or a remote session using the Hyper-V manager console.
- Hyper-V guests can have a maximum of four virtual Small Computer System Interface (SCSI) controllers per VM.
- Hyper-V guests can have a maximum of 12 virtual network adapters per VM.
- The Enterprise and Datacenter editions of Windows Server 2008 R2 include licenses to run virtualized instances of the Windows Server operating systems using Hyper-V.

Windows Server 2008 R2 added the following features to Hyper-V:

- Live Migration of running VMs between two virtualization host servers without interrupted access to the client guest.
- Dynamic VM storage.

- Enhanced processor support for up to 64 logical processors.
- Enhanced networking support enables VMs to take advantage of the newer networking features available in Window Server 2008 R2.

Windows Server 2008 R2 SP1 delivers the exciting new RemoteFX technology. RemoteFX brings rich end user desktop virtualization experience with enhanced video content to server-hosted virtual desktops. Another new feature of Windows Server 2008 R2 SP1 is dynamic memory. This provides for direct management for a VM's memory allocation while it is running.

Hyper-V Considerations

Decision issues arise when planning the appropriate hardware for your Hyper-V deployment. Hyper-V requires a 64-bit platform with support for hardware-assisted virtualization. The Intel platform provides this support with its Intel Virtualization Technology (Intel VT). AMD refers to its version as AMD Virtualization (AMD-V) technology. Both Intel VT and AMD-V technologies must be enabled in the BIOS of the hardware platform prior to the installation of Hyper-V. Both of these technologies improve the performance of 64-bit client guests running on Hyper-V. There is no support for installation of Windows Server 2008 R2 or Hyper-V on 32-bit (x86) hardware platforms.

An additional requirement for the hardware platform is support for hardware-enforced Data Execution Prevention (DEP). Again, each of the major CPU vendors has different names for this hardware-assist feature. Intel refers to its version as Intel XD (eXecute Disable), and AMD names its version AMD NX (No eXecute). DEP provides support for preventing code execution from a region memory marked as nonexecutable. This is also designed to stop buffer overflow attacks.

Ensure that you are familiar with your particular vendor's implementation of these hardware-assist features, because each vendor references various aspects of Intel VT and AMD-V in many different ways and also provides various additional settings. Hardware-assist virtualization (Intel VT and AMD-V) and DEP must be enabled prior to the installation of the Hyper-V server role.

Planning for Guest Operating Systems

Guest operating systems support in Windows Server 2008 R2 has been expanded to include support for Windows Server 2008 R2 and Windows 7. Support has also been added for several Linux operating systems: Red Hat 5.x 32-bit and 64-bit guests, and SUSE 10.x SP3 and 11.x 32-bit and 64-bit guest VMs.

> **MORE INFO** **MORE ON CLIENT GUEST OPERATING SYSTEM SUPPORT**
>
> To view a complete list of client guest operating systems supported by Windows Server 2008 R2, see *http://technet.microsoft.com/en-us/library/cc794868(WS.10).aspx.*

Guest operating system support is further enhanced by the software package Integration Services. Integration Services enhances several aspects of the VM environment. Depending on the operating system, enhanced support for the following devices and services is available:

- Up to four Integrated Development Environment (IDE) devices and four virtual SCSI controllers

- Up to 12 virtual network adapters, eight of which are the *network adapter* type and four of which can be the legacy *network adapter* type

- Use of a mouse within the guest VM

- Improved video resolution capabilities and performance

- Managing operating system shutdown

- Time Synchronization

- Increased data exchange and I/O

- Heartbeat monitoring of the client guest operating system

- Online backup, which requires support for Volume Shadow Copy Service from the guest operating system

Planning Your Virtual Machine Deployment

Deciding how you will deploy your guest operating systems within your virtual environment begins with a discussion on how to create VMs. There are several ways to create a VM, and the following are a few of the methods integrated into Windows Server 2008 R2 server roles and the Hyper-V management console:

- The New Virtual Machine Wizard from the Hyper-V management console is the simplest method to create a base VM's components from scratch. The wizard is very limited and will usually require you to modify the VM components after creation of the VM.

- Import a previously created VM by using the Import Virtual Machine Wizard from the Hyper-V management console.

- Use the Windows Deployment Services (WDS) server role to deploy VMs.

Using the New Virtual Machine Wizard to create a VM provides the basic ability to create a VM on a Hyper-V host and is relatively simple. It involves running the New Virtual Machine Wizard from the Virtualization Management console. To deploy your VMs, several decisions must be made prior to the deployment:

- Storage location of the VMs

- Memory configuration of the VMs

- Network configuration for VM use

- The disk controller and hard disk configuration of the VMs

- The operating system selection and installation

PLANNING YOUR VIRTUAL MACHINE STORAGE

You will need storage locations on which to place your deployed VMs that are accessible by your Hyper-V hosts. Storage devices used for your VMs should be configured for high availability and redundancy using an appropriate RAID option that meets your desired performance and availability requirements. You should avoid placing VMs on the same volumes as the host operating system, because loss of the system volume of the host could cause loss of the VMs.

Hyper-V does support the use of local storage devices either within the local server cabinet or within an accessible external storage cabinet. The obvious benefit here is low cost and easy deployment of VMs per each host. The drawback to using local drives is their inability to be shared in a cluster and to provide high-availability features.

The best practice for storage is using a SAN. Fibre channel or iSCSI SAN storage appliances provide the capability required for use as shared storage for a cluster of Hyper-V hosts along with the corresponding performance necessary to ensure appropriate disk I/O. A Hyper-V failover cluster will require that any VM requiring failover to another Hyper-V node in the cluster be initially deployed on shared storage. There are also a number of SAS technologies that are approved storage appliances for Hyper-V.

The storage media used for the VMs cannot have the Encrypting File System (EFS) enabled. A storage device configured with BitLocker Drive encryption can be used by the Hyper-V host. Also, compression cannot be enabled on the storage media.

Hyper-V in Windows Server 2008 R2 and Windows Server 2008 R2 SP1 does not provide support for network attached storage (NAS) appliances or network file system (NFS) access. This is usually not a significant drawback because most NAS appliances and storage devices appropriate for storage use in your Hyper-V environment will be capable of iSCSI access.

> **MORE INFO** **PLANNING FOR DISK AND STORAGE**
>
> To view the different storage options for Hyper-V, please see *http://technet.microsoft.com /en-us/library/dd183729(WS.10).aspx*.

PLANNING PROCESSOR AND MEMORY SETTINGS FOR YOUR VIRTUAL MACHINES

When creating your VMs, you will initially specify the memory allocation for the VM, which determines the maximum amount of RAM available to the guest operating system. This allows the administrator of your virtual environment to provision only the necessary RAM needed for each VM. Remember that each active VM must be allocated RAM and that the total amount of allocated RAM for all active VMs on a single Hyper-V host cannot exceed the physical amount of memory installed on the host computer, less the RAM allocated to the host operating system. A VM will only consume RAM when it is running or paused.

When configuring the processors, determine in advance the actual workload and multi-threaded capability of the operating system and applications that will run within the VM. Up to four virtual processors can be configured for a VM depending on the support by the guest operating system. In addition, up to eight virtual processors per every one logical processor of the Hyper-V host can be provisioned to your VMs running on the host. Windows 7 VMs support up to 12 virtual processors per every logical processor. When calculating the number of logical processors available on a Hyper-V host, a logical processor is equal to the number of physical cores on a Hyper-V host without hyperthreading enabled. A host with hyper-threading enabled counts each physical core as two logical cores (two logical processors per every physical core with hyperthreading enabled).

Processor compatibility must also be considered when using the new feature Live Migration. A VM is capable of being migrated while running between two different Hyper-V hosts if the physical processors are compatible between the two hosts. If migration of VMs between Intel hosts and AMD hosts is required, but these cluster nodes vary in their proces-sor families of their respective vendors, it might be necessary to set the Migrate To A Physical Computer With A Different Processor Version option to ensure successful Live Migrations. This setting becomes highly useful when maintenance and other administrative tasks need to be completed in heterogeneous Hyper-V environments.

One final consideration is whether nonuniform memory architecture (NUMA) is enabled on your Hyper-V hosts. NUMA provides for specially designed high-speed memory regions specifically mapped to physical cores on the system board of the Hyper-V host. Do not create VMs that would require use and assignment of processors or memory outside the size of a single NUMA region. Review your host's configuration guide to determine the exact NUMA setup on your system board.

PLANNING THE VIRTUAL NETWORK CONFIGURATION

To begin configuring the network services for your virtual environment, you must first config-ure the virtual networks that will be used as communication channels by the VMs running on your Hyper-V hosts. The next step is to configure the use of a network adapter(s) on your VMs for use of one or more of the communication channels you have previously configured on the host.

Determining the network configuration for your VMs requires a number of questions to be answered:

- What are the security requirements for the VMs?
- What are the VMs' external connectivity requirements, both for bandwidth and for individual virtual local area networks (VLANs)?
- What high-availability needs are there in regard to accessibility?
- What network connection option best suits the needs of the previous considerations?

There are three types of communication channels you can configure for VM use by using the Virtual Network Manager feature of Hyper-V:

- A private network that allows for communication only among VMs on the Hyper-V host

- An internal network that allows for communication among the VMs and between the host and the VMs

- An external network that provides the VMs bidirectional connectivity to your physical network

Use of each of the three types of communication channels depends on the communication requirements for the VMs. The virtual networks function at Layer 2 of the Open Systems Interconnect (OSI) model of the International Organization for Standardization (ISO). If a VM will only communicate with other VMs, then configure a private network and configure the virtual adapters of those VMs for its use. The virtual switch created for the private network use will not have a virtual adapter of the management operating system bound to it. The VMs bound to the private network will be able to communicate if they are configured with Internet Protocol (IP) addresses of the same IP subnet. If different IP subnets are configured for use on two or more different private virtual networks, then a VM running a routing service will be required to provide communication between the two virtual networks.

If VMs on the host require communication with the management operating system of the Hyper-V host, an internal network will be required. An internal network switch provides the same Layer 2 communication of the internal network but also allows communication between the Hyper-V host and the VMs configured for its use. The same constraints of the internal switch apply and the host firewall settings might require exceptions to be configured for communication with the running VMs.

An external network type provides for communication between the VMs and the external environment. For each external network configured, a physical network adapter is required. This requires the administrator to account for each external network needed for communication to production LAN segments, IP storage (iSCSI SAN), and the additional physical network interface cards (NICs) needed by the management operating system of the Hyper-V host.

After configuring the necessary virtual networks on the host, the VMs will require use of these virtual networks through a virtual adapter device. A small overview of Hyper-V's network adapters for use by the VMs when configuring the VMs' devices shows two options:

- Legacy network adapter
- Network adapter

The legacy network adapter is provided for operating systems that have one or more of the following needs:

- A network adapter is needed without the installation of the integration services because the legacy network adapter emulates DEC 21140 10/100TX NIC.

- A network-based installation such as the ability to boot to the Pre-Execution Environment (PXE) is needed to install an operating system within the guest VM.

- There is a compatibility issue with using the integration software.

- More than the maximum of eight network adapter interfaces are required for use within the VM. The legacy network adapter allows for a VM to have four additional network interfaces for a combined total of 12 network adapters.

Also note that the use of the legacy network adapter consumes additional CPU resources when providing emulation of the physical network adapter. The legacy network adapter should be used only when needed. All other network adapters utilized by VMs should be of the high-speed network adapter type.

The network adapter is provided by the integration services from Hyper-V and offers superior performance. Some of the more recent versions of Windows, Windows Server 2008 R2 and Windows 7, also provide the driver. The network adapter also consumes fewer CPU resources because this driver provides full functionality without requiring assistance from the management operating system.

PLANNING THE VIRTUAL HARD DISKS CONFIGURATION

Determining the configuration of your VMs requires you to decide where the *virtual hard disks* (VHDs) should be stored. Shared storage provided by SANs allows the greatest portability of the VM as well as use of failover in a failover cluster and the new Live Migration feature.

VMs can be configured to use flat files to store hard disk data. Hyper-V mounts the file systems used to store VHDs. VHDs appear to the VM as normal hard disk drives to be formatted and partitioned. If you decide not to use a fixed (often referred to as thick provisioning) solution, another option for VHDs is a storage disk drive that dynamically grows (often referred to as thin provisioning). When configuring the size of a VHD for a VM, you should specify enough space for the operating system to grow when using the dynamic disk option.

A third type of VHD is a *differencing disk*. A previously created VM can be used as the basis for deployment of multiple VMs by using differencing disks. The VHD of a fully configured VM is needed to create one or more differencing disks. The differencing disks can then be used as the VHD when creating a new VM. This allows for rapid deployment of new VMs. The original base VHD needs to be marked as read-only in its file attributes. Differencing disks are also used by the Hyper-V snapshot feature.

One additional option allows for the selection of an actual physical disk. The physical disk must be configured on the Hyper-V host and set to be offline prior to adding the disk drive to the VM. The drive can be a local drive or a logical unit number (LUN) on a SAN.

All of the preceding VHD and physical drive options can now be configured dynamically while the VM is running. The only stipulation is that the VM must have a source drive to run its operating system, and all other drives can be added or removed while the VM is running without any downtime.

INSTALLING THE GUEST OPERATING SYSTEMS

In the final stage of setting up a VM, you specify how you will install the operating system if you are creating a new VM. You will have several choices starting with the use of an image file, such as an .iso file or one from a CD/DVD-ROM; or from a network-based installation server, such as WDS.

Operating system installation from an ISO image is the most common method, but it is less than desirable for an extensive deployment. Microsoft System Center Virtual Machine

Manager (SCVMM) 2008 presents the opportunity to rapidly deploy VMs with guest operating systems through a variety of methods as well as the ability to deploy VMs on a Hyper-V host by cloning the physical computers in your original environment.

Managing Virtualized Servers

You use the Hyper-V Manager console to deploy and manage Hyper-V and VMs, as shown in Figure 8-1. You can also use this console to create and manage virtual networks, edit and inspect disks, take snapshots, revert to snapshots, and delete snapshots, as well as to edit the settings for individual VMs. You can also have the option to mount VHDs as volumes on the host server. Several of these functions were already discussed in the earlier section "Planning Your Virtual Machine Deployment."

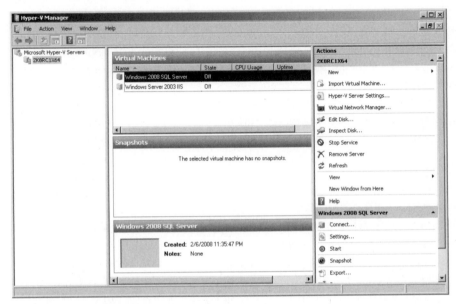

FIGURE 8-1 Virtualization Management console

Snapshots

Snapshots are similar to a point-in-time backup of a virtualized machine. The great benefit of snapshots is that they allow you to roll back to an earlier instance of an operating system far more quickly than any other technology. For example, assume that your organization hosts its intranet web server as a VM hosted by Hyper-V. A snapshot of the intranet web server is taken every day. Because of an unforeseen problem with the custom content management system, the most recent set of updates to the intranet site has wiped the server completely. In the past, as an administrator, you would have to go to your backup tapes and restore the files. With Hyper-V, you can just roll back to the previous snapshot and everything will be in the state it was in when the snapshot was taken.

Snapshots use differencing disks to store all changes to the original VHD. The VHD is frozen in time. Loss of the original VHD on which snapshots were based causes loss of all access to the VHD and any dependent differencing disks. It is important not to use snapshots as a means of backup. Snapshots should be used only as a point in time for reference. All data and production VMs should be backed up properly. Snapshots can also cause a performance penalty due to the inherent fragmentation that might result from their long-term use.

Licensing

All operating systems that run in a virtualized environment need to be licensed. Windows Server 2008 Standard allows for one physical system license and one additional VM instance (also referred to as a software instance). Windows Server 2008 Enterprise additionally allows for a single physical instance of the operating system installation and four additional software instances of the operating system installation. Windows Server 2008 Datacenter is licensed per processor and allows for an unlimited number of software instances to run on the physical host. The applications that run on the virtualized servers also need licenses. As with all licensing queries, in more complicated situations you should check with your software vendor if you are unsure whether you are in compliance.

> **MORE INFO**   **LICENSING FOR VIRTUAL MACHINES**
>
> To learn more about what you need to consider when licensing a VM, see *http://www .microsoft.com/licensing/about-licensing/virtualization.aspx*.

Modifying Hardware Settings

You can edit VM settings. This allows you to add additional resources like VHDs and RAM and to configure other settings, such as the Snapshot File Location. Figure 8-2 shows the Integration Services for a specific VM. Integration Services allow information and data to be directly exchanged between host and VM. To function, these services must be installed on the guest operating system. This task is performed after the guest operating system is installed. You can edit certain settings, such as the DVD drive settings, while the VM is running. Other settings, such as assigning and removing processors from a VM, require you to power off the VM.

You can limit the amount of processor usage by a particular VM. You do this with the Processor settings shown in Figure 8-3. By doing this, you can prevent a VM that has relatively high processing needs from monopolizing the host server's hardware. You can also use the Processor settings to assign a relative weight to a hosted VM. Rather than specifying a percentage of system resources to which the VM is entitled, you can use ratios to weight VM access to system resources. The benefit of using relative weight is that you do not have to recalculate percentages each time you add or remove VMs from a host. You simply add a new VM, assign a relative weight, and let Hyper-V work out the specific percentage of system resources to which the VM is entitled.

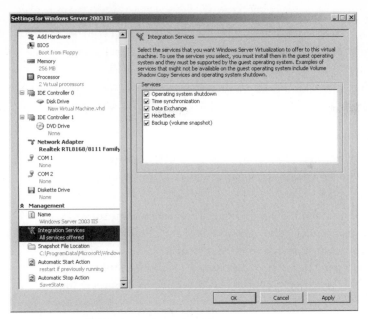

FIGURE 8-2 Modifying the settings of a VM

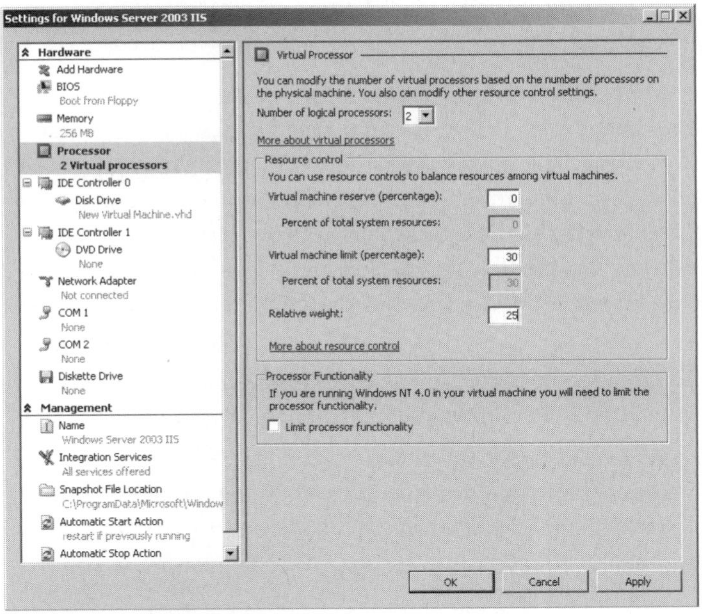

FIGURE 8-3 VM processor allocation

Candidates for Virtualization

When you are considering server deployment options, it will be more beneficial in some situations to deploy a virtualized server rather than the real thing. One factor is cost: A Windows Server 2008 Enterprise license includes the licenses for four hosted virtual instances. Although you need to consider many other costs when making a comparison, from a licensing perspective, one Windows Server 2008 Enterprise license will cost less than five standard licenses. Also remember that enterprise-class server hardware will always cost significantly more than a Windows Server 2008 Enterprise license, especially if your organization has a licensing agreement with Microsoft.

Although each situation will be different, in certain archetypical situations, including the following, you would plan a virtualized server rather than a traditional physical installation:

- You want to use WDS at a branch office location for a rollout that will last several days, but you do not have the resources to deploy extra hardware to that location. In this case, you could virtualize a WDS server and power on the VM only when it is needed. If more operating systems need to be rolled out later, the VM could be powered on.

- You have two applications hosted on the same server that conflict with each other. Because custom applications do not always work together well, sometimes you need to place each application in its own VM. Applications hosted on separate computers are unlikely to conflict with each other! Another solution is to virtualize the application itself. Virtualizing applications is covered later in this chapter.

- You are working with developers who need to test an application. If you have worked as a systems administrator in an environment with developers, you know that some projects are not stable until they are nearly complete, and, until that time, they are prone to misbehavior. Giving developers their own VM with which to work allows them the flexibility they need to recover from corruption, while protecting other users and services.

Some server deployments make poor candidates for virtualization. Servers that have high I/O requirements or high CPU requirements make poor candidates. A server that monopolizes CPU, memory, and disk resources on a single computer will require the same level of resources when virtualized, and a traditional server installation will provide better performance than virtualization. In general, you are reasonably safe in deciding to deploy virtual servers if the server does not have a large performance footprint. When a server is expected to have a significant performance footprint, you will need to develop further metrics to decide whether virtualization offers an advantage.

Planning for Server Consolidation

When you plan the deployment of Windows Server 2008 R2 at a particular site that has an existing Windows server infrastructure, you will be making an assessment about which of the existing physical servers can be virtualized, which need to be migrated, and which need to be upgraded. If you have deployed System Center Operations Manager in your environment, you can use its features to generate a Virtualization Candidates report, which will give you a list of servers in your environment that make good candidates for virtualization, given their current usage levels.

When you have determined the need to virtualize a server, the next step is to move that server from its existing hardware to a virtualized partition running under Windows Server 2008 R2. You can use two tools to virtualize a server installed on traditional hardware: the Virtual Server Migration Toolkit (VSMT) and SCVMM. Both tools are compatible with Hyper-V. Virtualizing a physical server is commonly referred to as physical-to-virtual (P2V).

Virtual Server Migration Toolkit

VSMT is the best tool to use when you have a small number of servers that need to be virtualized. The tool is command line-based and uses Extensible Markup Language (XML) files to store configuration data that is used during the migration process. You cannot use the VSMT tool to manage virtualized servers—it is purely a tool for migrating physical servers to a virtualized environment.

Unlike the SCVMM 2008 migration tools, it is not possible to use the VSMT to perform migrations without downtime. The VSMT was primarily designed for migrating servers to the Virtual Server 2005 platform. It is because Virtual Server 2005 virtualized operating systems are compatible with Hyper-V that you can use this tool to perform migrations to Windows Server 2008 virtual hosts.

MORE INFO   VIRTUAL SERVER MIGRATION TOOLKIT FREQUENTLY ASKED QUESTIONS

To find out more about how you can use VSMT to virtualize servers, see the following TechNet article: *http://www.microsoft.com/technet/virtualserver/evaluation/vsmtfaq.mspx*.

System Center Virtual Machine Manager 2008 R2

You should plan to use SCVMM 2008 R2 when you have a large number of VMs to manage in a single location. SCVMM requires a significant infrastructure investment and is primarily designed to manage enterprise-sized virtual server deployments rather than to migrate a few branch office servers into a virtual environment. If you are planning to virtualize a large number of servers, you will find the extra functionality of SCVMM 2008 valuable. Unlike VSMT, SCVMM is fully integrated with Windows PowerShell, giving you more flexibility in migrating servers from physical to virtualized environments.

You should note that deployment of SCVMM requires a connection to a SQL Server database. The Express edition of SQL Server 2005 SP3 is included with the SCVMM 2008 R2 installation files. Alternately, you can use an existing SQL Server 2005 SP2 or SQL Server 2008 instance. SCVMM 2008 uses this database to store VM configuration information.

In addition to virtualizing traditional server installations, you can use SCVMM to do the following:

- Monitor all of the virtualized servers in your environment. A single SCVMM server can be used to manage up to 8,000 VMs.
- Monitor all Hyper-V hosts in your environment. A single SCVMM server can be used to manage up to 400 Hyper-V or Virtual Server 2005 R2 host computers.
- When connected to a Fibre Channel SAN environment, move virtualized servers from one Hyper-V host to another.
- Move virtualized servers to and from libraries.
- Delegate permissions so that users with nonadministrative privileges are able to create and manage their own VMs.
- Migrate servers from physical to virtual without any downtime.
- Provide support for the use of Live Migration.
- Automatically enable the Hyper-V role on a Windows Server 2008 R2 host added to the SCVMM console.
- Support Clustered Shared Volumes (CSVs).
- Perform Fibre Channel and iSCSI SAN transfers to migrate VMs into and out of a cluster.
- Provide support for Hyper-V's dynamic disk addition and removal.
- Manage VMware ESX 3.0, 3.5, and 4.0 hosts. Currently, there is no support for VMware ESX 4.1.

- Support storage migration of a VM's virtual disks on either a Hyper-V host or a VMware ESX host.

- Support maintenance mode that allows the ability to migrate VMs on a host to perform maintenance tasks on the host.

- Support Windows PowerShell 2.0.

SCVMM 2008 R2 includes capacity planning technology that allows you to assign VMs to the virtual hosts in your environment that have the appropriate available resources based on VM performance data. For example, if you have ten Windows Server 2008 R2 hosts that each host multiple VMs, the capacity planning technology in SCVMM 2008 R2 can make recommendations about where each VM should be hosted based on observed performance data metrics.

SCVMM 2008 R2 increases your operating system virtualization planning options because it includes tools that allow you to make the most efficient use of your virtual infrastructure. As Figure 8-4 shows, the capacity planning tools available in SCVMM 2008 R2 can be customized, allowing administrators to prioritize the importance of specific resources. For example, you can configure the capacity planning tools to prioritize servers that have available memory over those that have lower CPU utilization.

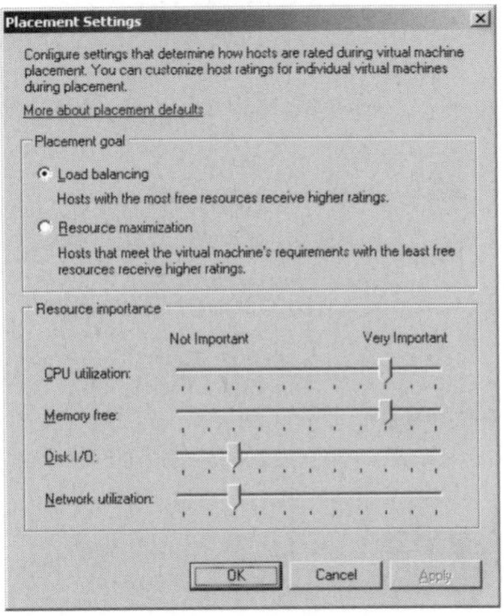

FIGURE 8-4 Configuring capacity planning

Components of a System Center Virtual Machine Manager 2008 R2 Deployment

An SCVMM 2008 R2 deployment consists of several components that can all be installed on a single server or on several servers throughout the enterprise. SCVMM 2008 R2 components include the following:

- **SCVMM server** This is the server on which the SCVMM software is installed. You should install this component first. Except under unusual circumstances, there is usually only one SCVMM server in an environment, so you should plan redundancy using failover clustering rather than the deployment of multiple servers. Although it is possible to deploy multiple SCVMM servers in a forest, each SCVMM server requires a separate database; however, these databases can be hosted on the same SQL Server instance. An SCVMM server cannot be installed in a forest that has a disjointed DNS namespace (multiple separate domain trees within the same forest).

- **SCVMM agent** This component is installed on a host running Virtual Server 2005 R2 or Hyper-V and SCVMM library servers. To be automatically managed, all VMs must be members of the same forest as the SCVMM server. It is possible to install the SCVMM agent on a computer that is not a member of the same forest and configure a connection manually to the SCVMM server. This is usually done when a virtual host is deployed on a perimeter network. A single SCVMM server can manage a maximum of 400 servers running Hyper-V, Virtual Server 2005 R2 SP1, or both. A Hyper-V or Virtual Server 2005 R2 SP1 host can be managed only by a single SCVMM server.

MORE INFO **INSTALLING AN SCVMM AGENT LOCALLY**

For more information about installing the SCVMM agent locally, consult the following TechNet document: *http://technet.microsoft.com/en-us/library/cc764218.aspx*.

EXAM TIP

For the 70-647 exam, remember that the SCVMM agent is an agent installed on Hyper-V servers for administration and monitoring of the Hyper-V host. Agents to administrate and monitor the VMs are installed by Microsoft System Center Operations Manager R2.

- **SCVMM database** The SCVMM database can be hosted either on SQL Server 2005 or SQL Server 2008. If no SQL Server instance is specified, the setup routine installs SQL Server Express 2005 SP3 on the SCVMM server. One drawback of using SQL Server Express is that the advanced reporting functionality will be unavailable. In addition to using SQL Server 2005 SP2 or higher, or SQL Server 2008, if you plan to use the advanced reporting functionality of the product, you must also deploy System Center Operations Manager 2007 in the same forest. If the SCVMM database is remote from the SCVMM server, you should secure the connection between the two servers using Secure Sockets Layer (SSL).

MORE INFO **CONFIGURING A REMOTE INSTANCE OF SQL SERVER**

For more information on the specific steps involved in configuring a remote instance of SQL Server to support SCVMM 2007, consult the following TechNet document: *http://technet.microsoft.com/en-us/library/bb740749.aspx*.

- **SCVMM Administrator console** The SCVMM Administrator console can be installed on an administrator workstation to manage SCVMM remotely or can be used directly on whichever SCVMM components are installed.

- **SCVMM self-service portal** This portal allows users who are not SCVMM administrators to manage VMs for which they have been delegated permissions. The portal is web based and should be installed on a server that has IIS 7.0 or later and is a member of the same forest as the SCVMM server.

- **SCVMM library server** The library is a catalog of resources that are used to create VMs using SCVMM. These resources include ISO images, scripts, hardware profiles, VM templates, VHDs, and stored VMs. A VM template includes a guest operating system profile, a hardware profile, and VHDs. These resources are hosted on a set of shares that are managed through the SCVMM console. The library can be stored across multiple physical servers in an enterprise deployment. If the SCVMM library is not deployed on the VM host server, then the network connection between a VM host server and the library is recommended to ensure speed and reliability. A default library share called VMMLibrary is created on the SCVMM server during the installation process unless an administrator determines otherwise. An SCVMM library server can be managed by only one SCVMM server. You cannot directly share resources among different SCVMM environments.

SCVMM 2008 R2 in the Branch Office

SCVMM 2008 R2 is usually deployed in a datacenter environment, with all components, including VM hosts, located at the same site. If SCVMM 2008 R2 is going to be used to create, run, and manage VMs at a branch or satellite office, you should deploy a VMM library server and a VM host at the branch office site. This will allow you to deploy new VMs directly from the library to the VM hosts without having to transfer large amounts of data across a wide area network (WAN) link.

In branch office deployments, the SCVMM library is usually deployed on the same server as the VM host. This allows for rapid deployments by eliminating the need for files used to build VMs to be copied over the network. The drawback of this type of deployment is that it requires a significant amount of disk storage for both the library data and the deployed VMs.

> **MORE INFO   PLANNING YOUR VMM DEPLOYMENT**
>
> For more information on planning an SCVMM 2008 R2 deployment, consult the following TechNet web page: *http://technet.microsoft.com/en-us/library/cc793146.aspx*.

PRACTICE Designing Virtual Server Deployment

Fabrikam, Ltd., is a large Australian company that has three sites spread across the state of Victoria. The headquarters site is in the city of Warrandyte, with branch offices in Yarragon and Traralgon. As a part of a shareholder initiative to reduce Fabrikam's carbon footprint, the company has been looking for ways to reduce its consumption of electricity. An audit of the company's computer hardware resources has found that it has large numbers of servers deployed throughout all locations, the resources of which are severely underutilized. Reducing the number of physical servers will reduce the company's use of electricity and achieve the shareholder initiative.

Both the Traralgon and Yarragon sites have a large number of Windows Server 2003 computers. All of these computers were originally upgraded from Windows 2000 Server and hardware that was purchased in early 2001, and are therefore underpowered in comparison to today's available hardware. Management believes that the amount of hardware located at the Traralgon and Yarragon sites can be significantly rationalized.

Although operating system virtualization is not being used at the branch office sites, an administrator who has since left the organization realized significant efficiencies by virtualizing 200 existing servers in the Warrandyte datacenter and retiring aging hardware. There are 200 Windows Server 2003 VMs currently hosted on 10 Windows Server 2003 Enterprise edition computers. The hosting platform is Virtual Server 2005 R2 SP1. Part of the virtualization plan will involve moving these VMs so that they are hosted on Hyper-V rather than Virtual Server 2005 R2 SP1. The previous administrator determined that all 200 Windows Server 2003 VMs could be hosted on two computers running Windows Server 2008 R2 Datacenter if the computers were configured with the appropriate hardware. The administrator left the company before this project moved beyond the early planning stage, so you will need to further develop the plan.

EXERCISE Planning an Operating System Virtualization Strategy for Fabrikam

In this exercise, you review the business and technical requirements to plan a virtualized application deployment for Fabrikam, Ltd.

1. What strategy should you use to determine which servers at Fabrikam will make good virtualization candidates and what steps should be taken to virtualize these servers?

- Plan the deployment of System Center Operations Manager 2008 R2 in the Fabrikam forest. Generate a Virtualization Candidates report.

- Deploy SCVMM 2008 R2 and use its features to virtualize existing physical servers. To do this, each candidate must be a member of the same forest or have the SCVMM 2008 agent installed.

2. What plans should you make to ensure that it is possible to rapidly deploy virtualized servers at the Traralgon and Yarragon branch offices?

- It will be necessary to deploy an SCVMM 2008 library at both the Traralgon and Yarragon branch office sites.

- It will be necessary to configure distributed file system (DFS) to replicate updated library data to the library site over the WAN links during off-peak period.

3. What plans should you make to migrate the VMs hosted at the Warrandyte datacenter from Virtual Server 2005 R2 to Hyper-V?

- Deploy a high-speed SAN at the Warrandyte datacenter.

- Deploy a Windows Server 2008 R2 Datacenter host at the Warrandyte datacenter.

- Use SCVMM 2008 R2 to migrate the VMs hosted on Virtual Server 2005 R2 to Hyper-V, transferring them across the SAN.

Lesson Summary

- Hyper-V is an available server role for 64-bit versions of Windows Server 2008 that you can use to host and manage virtualized operating systems.

- Snapshots allow the state of a server to be taken at a specific point in time, such as prior to the deployment of an update, so that the server can be rolled back to that state in the future.

- The best candidates for virtualization are servers that do not intensively use processor, RAM, and disk resources.

- The Virtual Server Migration Toolkit (VSMT) provides tools you can use to virtualize existing servers. The toolkit uses XML-based files to assist in the transition from a physical to a virtualized installation. Use this option if you have a small number of existing servers to virtualize.

- System Center Virtual Machine Manager (SCVMM) allows you to manage many VMs and Hyper-V hosts at once. It includes tools that allow you to move VMs between hosts, allow nonprivileged users to create and manage their own VMs, and perform bulk virtualizations of servers installed on physical hardware. Use SCVMM only with medium-to-large VM deployments.

Lesson Review

You can use the following questions to test your knowledge of the information in Lesson 1, "Designing Operating System Virtualization." The questions are also available on the companion CD if you prefer to review them in electronic form.

> **NOTE ANSWERS**
>
> Answers to these questions and explanations of why each answer choice is correct or incorrect are located in the "Answers" section at the end of the book.

1. Which of the following scenarios provides the most compelling case for the planned deployment of SCVMM 2008 R2?

   A. You need to virtualize four Windows 2000 Server computers.

   B. You want to be able to move virtualized servers between hosts on your Fibre Channel SAN.

   C. You are responsible for managing 10 virtualized Windows Server 2008 servers at your head office location.

   D. You need to automate the deployment of five Windows Server 2008 Enterprise computers with the Hyper-V server role installed.

2. On which of the following platforms can you install the Hyper-V server role?

   A. A Server Core installation of the x64 version of Windows Server 2008 R2 Enterprise

   B. A Server Core installation of the x86 version of Windows Server 2008 R2 Datacenter

   C. A standard installation of the x86 version of Windows Server 2008 R2 Enterprise

   D. A standard installation of the x86 version of Windows Server 2008 R2 Datacenter

3. Which of the following are the management limits of a single-server SCVMM 2008 R2 deployment? (Choose two. Each correct answer forms a complete solution.)

   A. 400 virtual machine hosts

   B. 800 virtual machine hosts

   C. 1,200 virtual machine hosts

   D. 16,000 virtual machines

   E. 8,000 virtual machines

4. Which of the following SCVMM 2008 R2 components should you plan to install at branch office locations where you will need to be able to rapidly deploy new VMs to virtual hosts at those sites?

   A. SCVMM database

   B. SCVMM self-service portal

   C. SCVMM server

   D. SCVMM library server

5. You are planning the deployment of SCVMM 2008 R2 to manage several hundred VMs hosted by Windows Server 2008 R2 computers with Hyper-V. Approximately 30 VMs are hosted on two Windows Server 2008 R2 computers in your organization's screened subnet. Which of the following plans should you make to ensure that all VMs hosted in your environment can be managed using SCVMM 2008 R2 without installing unnecessary instances of the product?

   A. Install the SCVMM agent manually on the two Windows Server 2008 R2 host computers and configure the internal firewall with the required ports.

   B. Install the SCVMM agent manually on the 30 VMs and configure the internal firewall with the required ports.

   C. Install Active Directory Lightweight Directory Services (AD LDS) and configure the internal firewall with the required ports.

   D. Install SCVMM 2008 R2 on each Windows Server 2008 R2 host computer and configure the internal firewall with the required ports.

Lesson 2: Designing Application Virtualization

This lesson discusses Microsoft Application Virtualization (App-V). Formerly called Microsoft Softgrid Application Virtualization, App-V is a technology that allows applications that would otherwise conflict or have issues with running directly from a Remote Desktop Session host that will be virtualized and delivered to clients over the network. This technology differs from the RemoteApp presentation virtualization technology covered in Chapter 7, "Designing Remote Desktop Services and Application Deployment," because the application executes on the client rather than executing on the server, with only the visual output being displayed on the client.

> **After this lesson, you will be able to:**
> - Understand the benefits of application virtualization.
> - Plan the deployment of application virtualization.
> - Understand the components required for the deployment of Microsoft App-V.
>
> **Estimated lesson time: 40 minutes**

Microsoft Application Virtualization

Instead of creating a separate partitioned space for the entire operating system, *Microsoft Application Virtualization* (App-V) creates a separate partitioned space for a specific application when it is run on an App-V client. This allows applications that would otherwise be incompatible with each other to execute concurrently. For example, if it was necessary in your organization to run two versions of the same application on the same Windows 7 computer, you could use App-V to ensure that there were no conflicts between them.

Similarly, if it was necessary in your environment to deploy two versions of the same application using RemoteApp, which was covered in Chapter 7, you would need to use two separate Remote Desktop Session Host sessions, wasting resources and providing the application, as well as additional administrative overhead, to publish the other version of the application to specific users. This is because, generally speaking, if you install two versions of the same application on the same Remote Desktop Session Host, you will run into configuration problems and conflicts. Applications deployed through App-V can share data with locally installed applications, although they cannot perform complex interactions beyond file associations, cut-and-paste, and Object Linking and Embedding (OLE) integration. If your organization uses applications that require more complex integration, it will be necessary to use App-V to deploy applications within a sequenced group called a suite. In a suite configuration, a group of applications runs within the same silo. Silos are discussed later in this lesson.

Applications deployed through App-V can be executed on client computers that have the Microsoft Application Virtualization Desktop client installed. The client functions like VM software, although instead of hosting a virtualized operating system locally, it hosts a virtualized application that is streamed from a computer that has Microsoft Application Virtualization Management Server installed. It is also possible to install Microsoft Application Virtualization for Remote Desktop Services (RDS), which allows you to deploy multiple versions of the same application, or applications, that conflict from a Remote Desktop Session Host deployment. These applications are streamed to the individual Remote Desktop Session Host from the computer with Microsoft Application Virtualization Management Server installed, as shown in Figure 8-5. An important advantage of App-V is that it allows applications that cannot normally be deployed through Remote Desktop to be deployed in this manner.

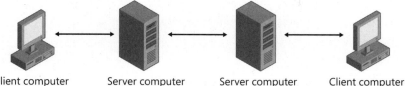

Client computer
with Microsoft
Application
Virtualization
Desktop Client

Server computer
with Microsoft
Application
Virtualization
Management Server

Server computer
with Microsoft
Application
Virtualization
for RDS

Client computer
with Microsoft
Application
Virtualization
Desktop Client

FIGURE 8-5 Streaming applications using App-V

> **MORE INFO   MICROSOFT APP-V APPLICATION VIRTUALIZATION FOR TERMINAL SERVICES**
>
> At the time of the writing of this book, Microsoft has yet to update the technical documentation to the newest iteration for Microsoft Application Virtualization for RDS. The most current information can be found on the site for Microsoft Application Virtualization for Terminal Services at *http://www.microsoft.com/systemcenter/appv/terminalsvcs.mspx*.

You should deploy Microsoft App-V in your environment when you need to do the following:

- Run multiple versions of the same application on the same local client as the silos, ensuring that the differing versions of the applications will not conflict. This is especially useful in application development environments where different versions of the same application need to be tested simultaneously.

- Deploy applications that would normally conflict to the same client.

- Deploy multiple versions of the same application from the same terminal server or Remote Desktop Session Host.

- Deploy applications that are not compatible with RDS from Remote Desktop Session Hosts. When Microsoft App-V Application Virtualization for RDS is installed on a Remote Desktop Session Host, you can deploy applications that are incompatible with Remote Desktop Session Hosts.

greater control over which users can execute specific applications. Each time a
attempts to execute an application, App-V will query Active Directory Domain
vices (AD DS) to verify that the user has been authorized to use that application.
udit-based license tracking and strict license enforcement are built into App-V and
an be configured to ensure that your organization remains compliant with its application licensing responsibilities.

MORE INFO   MICROSOFT APP-V APPLICATION VIRTUALIZATION TECHCENTER

You can learn more about Microsoft App-V and how you can plan for the deployment of
this technology in your environment at *http://technet.microsoft.com/en-us
/appvirtualization/default.aspx*.

Planning the Deployment of Application Virtualization

Planning the deployment of App-V for an organization requires understanding the available
components and how they interact with one another. A Microsoft Application Virtualization
deployment has the following components:

- **Microsoft Application Virtualization Sequencer**   The sequencer is used to package
  an existing application so it can be deployed through App-V. This component should
  be installed on a clean computer installation with only the necessary components
  required for the operating system. Generally, it is necessary to have only a single
  sequencer because this component is used only when preparing applications for their
  deployment to the Microsoft System Center Virtual Application server. The computer
  used for the sequencer should be imaged to allow for fast restore of the base installation for continuous application sequencing of other applications. The Application
  Virtualization Sequencer now supports both 32-bit and 64-bit computing platforms.
  The computer operating system should be configured and updated identically to those
  of the desktops to which the virtualized application will be streamed.

- **Microsoft Application Virtualization Management Server**   This server maintains
  application packages and streams parts of the application to the client using Real-Time
  Streaming Protocol (RTSP) or Real-Time Streaming Protocol Secure (RTSPS) when security is needed. After certain portions of the application are transmitted to the client,
  the components are cached and do not need to be retransmitted when the application
  is used again. This server also handles authentication and licensing. High availability
  should be achieved by load balancing identical Microsoft Application Virtualization
  Management servers. This server must be a member of an AD DS forest.

MORE INFO   OVERVIEW OF APPLICATION VIRTUALIZATION

To learn about application virtualization, consult the application virtualization white
paper at *http://technet.microsoft.com/en-us/library/ee958112.aspx*.

- **Microsoft Application Virtualization Data Store** The App-V component maintains application information in a SQL Server database. It is possible to use SQL Server 2005 SP3 Express to support the App-V data store, although enterprise organizations will want to use SQL Server 2005 SP2 or SQL Server 2008 to store their data. This App-V component can be installed on the same server as the Virtualization Application Management Server component or on another computer if more sufficient I/O is required.

- **Microsoft Application Virtualization Management Console** This Microsoft Management Console (MMC) 3.0 snap-in is used for Microsoft Application Virtualization Management.

- **Microsoft Application Virtualization Management Web Service** The web component communicates read/write requests to the App-V Data Store. This component is usually installed with the Application Virtualization Management Server.

- **Microsoft Application Virtualization Streaming Server** The server component provides streaming functionality in the absence of an Application Virtualization Management Server. This server can work in conjunction with a previous installation of Application Virtualization Management Server and Application Virtualization Web Management Server.

- **Microsoft Application Virtualization Client for Desktops** Microsoft Application Virtualization Client for Desktops can be installed on Microsoft Windows 2000 Professional, Windows XP Professional, Windows Vista, and Windows 7. This software is necessary if the client computer is going to execute an App-V application directly. This client software can be deployed to client operating systems by using traditional application deployment methods. Microsoft Application Virtualization for RDS is installed on Windows Server 2008 R2 with the Remote Desktop Session Host server role installed. App-V RDS client is installed by using the normal install mode required for the installation of nonvirtualized application on a Remote Desktop Session Host server.

> **MORE INFO** **MICROSOFT APPLICATION VIRTUALIZATION 4.6 GUIDE**
>
> To determine the number of Virtual Application servers required for an enterprise environment that uses App-V, consult the following guide: *http://technet.microsoft.com /en-us/library/ee354207.aspx*.

App-V Branch Office Deployments

When planning the deployment of App-V for enterprises that have a centralized management mode but require virtualized applications to be streamed into branch offices, App-V 4.6 already provides a solution out of the box. Because WAN links, even today, are too slow to support the streaming of application data to client computers, App-V provides a distribution model that streams applications locally in the branch office. All components of the full App-V infrastructure are installed in the main office. This includes the SQL server and all management components. In the branch office, install the Microsoft Application Virtualization Streaming Server and the associated desktop clients. The application for streaming at the branch office will be staged on the local Application Virtualization Streaming Server.

In some cases, there will be enough bandwidth from a central location to a branch office to support a Remote Desktop Session Host session, and using the App-V RDS component on a local Remote Desktop Session Host might be the best application deployment solution. Alternatively, if there are only a few clients, you might configure them to access Remote Desktop Session Hosts across the Internet through a Remote Desktop Gateway server located on a screened subnet at your organization's datacenter site.

Alternatively, if the branch offices will provide a full App-V infrastructure, planning for the rollout of newly sequenced applications to the branch office Virtual Application servers should leverage existing Windows Server 2008 R2 replication tools like DFS. Once they are replicated out to the branch offices, the App-V administrator can configure the local Virtual Application servers with the new App-V packages. App-V is not currently able to distribute packages intelligently across WAN links.

> **MORE INFO**   **APPLICATION VIRTUALIZATION WHITE PAPERS**
>
> To learn more about the deployment of App-V and branch office deployments, consult the TechNet web page at *http://technet.microsoft.com/en-us/appvirtualization/cc843994*.

> **MORE INFO**   **WINDOWS 7 VIRTUAL LABS**
>
> To learn more about Microsoft App-V Application Virtualization, you should review the following TechNet Virtual Labs that are available on Microsoft's website: *http://technet .microsoft.com/en-us/virtuallabs/ee862412.aspx*.

PRACTICE   Planning Application Virtualization

You are being retained as a consultant for the development of an application virtualization strategy for Contoso, Ltd. Contoso is a large corporation with offices located throughout Australia. As an enterprise administrator, it is your role to design an operating system virtualization strategy. Contoso's head office in Melbourne has 15,000 employees. Contoso has remote offices in Sydney, Adelaide, and Brisbane, each with approximately 5,000 employees. Each remote office is connected to the head office through a leased line WAN.

Approximately 75 percent of the client computers at Contoso have Windows XP Professional SP3 installed. The rest of the client computers at Contoso have Windows 7 Enterprise with SP1 installed. All servers at Contoso have been upgraded to Windows Server 2008 R2.

Contoso is dependent on four line-of-business applications. After these applications recently received security updates to deal with several important security issues, it was found that when two or more of these applications run concurrently on a Windows XP or Windows 7 computer, a conflict occurs that causes the computer to experience a STOP error. After further testing of these applications, you have determined that two of these applications cannot be installed on a Windows Server 2008 R2 computer with the Remote Desktop Session Host role service. The other two applications can be installed on Remote Desktop Session Host, but the server will encounter a STOP error if any single user executes these applications concurrently.

Almost all users in the Contoso environment will need access to two or more of these applications to perform their daily tasks, and the company's compliance auditors consider rolling back to the versions of the applications that have not received the security updates unacceptable. At present, users have been instructed to execute only one application at a time, but there is a growing need to be able to run them concurrently and to cut and paste data between these programs.

Additionally, several groups of users in the organization telecommute. Management wants these users to be able to access these applications while telecommuting, but it will be necessary to ensure that these users' computer operating system updates and antivirus and spyware definitions are up-to-date before they are granted access to the corporate network. Management would prefer any proposed solution to work without deploying a virtual private network (VPN) or dial-up-based remote access solution.

Finally, any solution that you plan to deploy should be fault-tolerant and should be able to survive the loss of a single server.

EXERCISE Planning a Virtualized Application Deployment

In this exercise, you review the business and technical requirements to plan a virtualized application deployment for Contoso, Ltd.

1. What aspects of Contoso's operation strongly indicate the necessity of using an application deployment strategy that leverages Microsoft App-V Application Virtualization over other application deployment alternatives?

   - Several line-of-business applications conflict and cause STOP errors when they are run concurrently on a Remote Desktop Session Host or on a client computer.

   - Several applications cannot be installed on a Remote Desktop Session Host by using the standard application deployment method.

   - Using Microsoft App-V Application Virtualization allows these applications to be installed and execute concurrently on a Windows Server 2008 R2 computer with the Remote Desktop Session Host role installed without conflicts arising, due to the virtualized nature of the execution environment.

2. What plans should you make to ensure that Contoso staff at the head and branch offices is able to access important line-of-business applications if a server and WAN links fail completely during a peak business period?

- At each branch office, plan the installation of the following:
  - A network load-balanced Microsoft Application Virtualization cluster so that App-V applications can be delivered to local Remote Desktop Session Hosts. These servers need to be local because App-V applications shouldn't be streamed over WAN links. A load-balanced cluster is necessary to meet the availability requirements. SQL Server Express should be deployed on each server.
  - Configure a two-node network load-balanced Remote Desktop Session Host server farm. Install Microsoft App-V Application Virtualization for RDS on each Remote Desktop Session Host. Load-balanced Remote Desktop Session Host servers are necessary to meet the availability requirements.
  - Client computers at each branch office need to access their applications through Remote Desktop Services.
3. What plans should you make to address the needs of the Contoso users who are telecommuting?
   - Plan the installation of a Remote Desktop Gateway server on the screened subnet at Contoso HQ. Instruct telecommuting users to connect to this server over the Internet.
   - Plan the configuration of a Remote Desktop Gateway server Network Access Protection (NAP) policy to ensure that connecting computers' System Health Validators (SHVs) report on the compliance level of software updates, and antivirus and antispyware definitions. Configure the Remote Desktop Gateway server to allow access to only the Remote Desktop Session Hosts at the HQ site.

Lesson Summary

- Microsoft Application Virtualization allows applications to be virtualized. This allows applications that might conflict with each other to be run concurrently.
- Microsoft Application Virtualization differs from Remote Desktop Services in that applications execute on the client rather than on the remote server.
- You prepare applications for deployment through App-V by using an App-V sequencer.
- A server with Microsoft Application Virtualization Management Server installed is used to stream applications to clients by using RTSP. High availability should be provided through the use of Network Load Balancing.
- The App-V data store is a SQL Server database. If no SQL Server 2005 or SQL Server 2008 database is present in the network environment during the installation of Microsoft Application Virtualization Management Server, it is possible to deploy SQL Server Express 2005 SP3 from the Microsoft Application Virtualization Management Server installation media.

- You can deploy App-V applications to Remote Desktop Session Host clients by installing Microsoft App-V Application Virtualization for RDS on a Remote Desktop Session Host computer. When configured in this way, the application is streamed to the Remote Desktop Session Host, which then presents it in a traditional way to the client.

Lesson Review

You can use the following questions to test your knowledge of the information in Lesson 2, "Designing Application Virtualization." The questions are also available on the companion CD if you prefer to review them in electronic form.

> **NOTE ANSWERS**
>
> Answers to these questions and explanations of why each answer choice is correct or incorrect are located in the "Answers" section at the end of the book.

1. Which of the following high-availability solutions should you plan to deploy to ensure that the Microsoft Application Virtualization Management Server component of your application virtualization is still available in the event of a critical hardware failure?

   A. Deploy two servers in DNS round-robin configuration.

   B. Deploy two servers in a failover cluster configuration.

   C. Deploy two servers in Network Load Balancing configuration.

   D. Deploy two servers in a Remote Desktop Session Host server farm configuration.

2. Which of the following App-V components is used to convert applications so that they can be deployed through Microsoft Application Virtualization Management Server as App-V applications for client computers?

   A. App-V data store

   B. App-V sequencer

   C. App-V Application Virtualization for RDS

   D. App-V Application Virtualization for Desktops

3. Your organization is about to open a branch office location in a suburb on the other side of the city in which the HQ site is located. You already use App-V to deploy several mission-critical applications to desktop computers at the HQ site. You plan to do the same for the new branch office location. Which of the following plans should you make to extend the existing Application Virtualization infrastructure to the new branch office? (Choose two. Each correct answer forms a part of the solution.)

   A. Plan to deploy the Microsoft App-V Application Virtualization for Clients software to all client computers at the new branch office.

   B. Plan to deploy Hyper-V at the new branch office.

   C. Plan to deploy SCVMM at the new branch office.

D. Plan to deploy a Microsoft Application Virtualization Management Server at the new branch office site.

E. Plan to deploy Microsoft Application Virtualization for RDS at the new branch office site.

4. In which of the following situations must you plan to deploy Microsoft Application Virtualization for RDS?

A. You want to deploy Microsoft Office 2007 applications by using RemoteApp from a single Remote Desktop Session Host.

B. You want to deploy both Microsoft Office 2007 and Microsoft Office XP to Windows 7 client computers.

C. You want to deploy Microsoft Office 2010 applications by using RemoteApp from a Remote Desktop Session Host server farm.

D. You want to deploy Microsoft Office 2007 and Microsoft Office XP from a Remote Desktop Session Host server farm.

5. You work as a systems administrator for a software development company. During the application development phase, it is necessary to deploy several versions of the same software from the same Remote Desktop Session Host. When you attempt to install the applications side by side, a conflict arises. Which of the following solutions should you plan to use?

A. Deploy the applications using RemoteApp.

B. Deploy a Remote Desktop Gateway Server.

C. Deploy Microsoft Application Virtualization.

D. Deploy the applications using Remote Desktop Web Access.

Chapter Review

To further practice and reinforce the skills you learned in this chapter, you can perform the following tasks:

- Review the chapter summary.
- Review the list of key terms introduced in this chapter.
- Complete the case scenarios. These scenarios set up real-world situations involving the topics of this chapter and ask you to create a solution.
- Complete the suggested practices.
- Take a practice test.

Chapter Summary

- Servers that do not have large hardware footprints can be virtualized and hosted on a Windows Server 2008 R2 64-bit computer running the Hyper-V role.
- Virtualization of servers and hosted applications can provide cost reduction in the datacenter.
- Microsoft Remote Desktop Virtualization Host can provide application hosting, virtual desktops, and failover clustering, and maintain high availability of applications in times of hardware maintenance and software updates.
- SCVMM should be deployed when an administrator must manage large numbers of VMs.
- Microsoft Application Virtualization allows applications that could not otherwise be installed or coexist on a Remote Desktop Session Host to be streamed to clients. This is achieved through application virtualization. There are a variety of deployment options to provide scalability.
- Microsoft Application Virtualization can also stream applications to Remote Desktop clients by using Microsoft Application Virtualization for RDS.

Key Terms

Do you know what these key terms mean? You can check your answers by looking up the terms in the glossary at the end of the book.

- App-V
- Differencing disk
- Guests
- Host
- Hypervisor

- Snapshot
- Virtual hard disk

Case Scenario

In the following case scenario, you apply what you have learned about Remote Desktop Services and application and server virtualization. You can find answers to these questions in the "Answers" section at the end of this book.

Case Scenario: Tailspin Toys Server Consolidation

Tailspin Toys has an aging deployment of computers running Windows 2000 Server. Management has decided to transition to a Windows Server 2008 R2 infrastructure. One goal of the transition project is to reduce the number of physical servers and to retire all existing server hardware that is now more than five years old. You have been brought in as a consultant to assist in the development of plans for server consolidation at a Tailspin Toys branch office. Each site has a unique set of needs and applications. The characteristics of each site are as follows:

1. The Wangaratta site currently hosts a Windows 2000 Server domain controller that also hosts the DHCP and DNS services. A Windows 2000 Server computer hosts a SQL Server 2000 database, and there are two additional Windows 2000 Server computers, each of which hosts custom business applications. These applications cannot be colocated with each other or with the SQL Server 2000 database. How could you minimize the number of physical servers by using virtualization, and what would the configuration of these servers be?

2. The Yarragon site currently hosts six terminal servers, each of which hosts a separate business application. One of these applications uses a SQL Server 2005 database. These applications cannot be colocated without causing problems on the host terminal servers. Because the Yarragon site has only a small number of users, the hardware resources of the terminal servers are underutilized. How can you minimize the number of terminal servers required to support the staff at the Yarragon site?

Suggested Practices

To help you successfully master the exam objectives presented in this chapter, complete the following tasks.

Windows Server Virtualization

Complete the following practice exercise.

- **Practice** Obtain a 64-bit evaluation version of Windows Server 2008 R2, and install it on a 64-bit Hyper-V–compliant computer. Join this computer to the *contoso.internal* domain. Install the Hyper-V server role. Install a 64-bit evaluation version of Windows Server 2008 R2 as a guest VM.

Download and install the System Center Virtual Machine Manager 2008 R2–Evaluation VHD file, and join it to the *contoso.internal* domain. Use it to manage the newly installed Windows Server 2008 R2 computer that has the Hyper-V server role installed. Use SCVMM 2008 R2 to virtualize server Glasgow.

> **MORE INFO**   **OBTAINING THE SCVMM VHD**
>
> You can get the System Center Virtual Machine Manager R2 – Evaluation VHD from the following website: *http://www.microsoft.com/downloads/en/details.aspx?FamilyID =ff3e3752-8906-41ed-a210-94304f9d5212&displaylang=en.*

Plan Application Virtualization

Complete the following practice exercise.

- **Practice**   Tailspin Toys has its head office in Sydney, Australia, and branch offices in Brisbane, Adelaide, Hobart, and Melbourne. All client computers at Tailspin Toys have Windows XP Professional installed, and all domain controllers have Windows Server 2008 R2 installed. Tailspin Toys uses five locally produced off-the-shelf software applications, three of which are no longer actively maintained by the respective vendors but are still mission-critical to Tailspin Toys' operations. Two of these applications have recently been updated to deal with publicly disclosed security vulnerabilities. These updates have caused problems on the client computers when these applications were run concurrently with the three applications that are no longer actively maintained. All applications need to run locally on users' Windows XP Professional computers. Plan an App-V deployment. Include in your plans the necessary server infrastructure and roles, client software deployment required at each site, and planned method of rolling out updates. Your plan should minimize the number of virtualized applications.

Watch a Webcast

- **Practice**   Watch the webcast "Technical Overview of SCVMM 2008 R2," available at *https://msevents.microsoft.com/CUI/WebCastEventDetails.aspx?EventID =1032423217&EventCategory=5&culture=en-US&CountryCode=US and MSDN.*

- **Practice**   Watch the webcast "Virtual Lab: Introduction to System Center Virtual Machine Manager 2008," available at *https://msevents.microsoft.com/CUI /WebCastEventDetails.aspx?EventID=1032448056&EventCategory=3&culture =en-US&CountryCode=US.*

Take a Practice Test

The practice tests on this book's companion CD offer many options. For example, you can test yourself on just one exam objective, or you can test yourself on all the 70-647 certification exam content. You can set up the test so that it closely simulates the experience of taking a certification exam, or you can set it up in study mode so that you can look at the correct answers and explanations after you answer each question.

> **MORE INFO**   **PRACTICE TESTS**
>
> For details about all the practice test options available, see "How to Use the Practice Tests" in this book's introduction.

CHAPTER 9

Designing Solutions for Data Sharing, Data Security, and Business Continuity

Before you deploy any new technology in a corporate network, it's important to have a clear idea of the problem that technology is intended to solve. In this way, planning for a new technology always begins with assessing your network needs. When you have defined these needs, you can conduct research to determine which feature or technology can best meet them.

This chapter reviews features in Microsoft Windows Server 2008 and Windows Server 2008 R2 that address the specific needs for data sharing, data storage security, system recoverability, and system availability.

Exam objectives in this chapter:

- Plan for business continuity.
- Design for data management and access.

Lessons in this chapter:

Before You Begin

To complete the lessons in this chapter, you must have:

- A basic understanding of Windows Server 2008 R2 and of Active Directory Domain Services (AD DS).

REAL WORLD
John Policelli

A few years back I was involved in proposing an encryption solution to a high-profile company. At the time, they decided to turn down the proposal because it was not something they felt they required. Several months later, this same company had made the news; It was reported that several hard drives had been missing and unaccounted for. That same day, we received a call from the company saying that they wanted to proceed with implementing our original encryption proposal. Data security is a requirement in virtually all organizations these days. However, the importance of data security is usually only realized after a security breach has occurred. There are several technologies built into Windows Server 2008 R2 that can protect against data loss, data theft, or both. In my experience, the effort and cost to implement these technologies is miniscule compared to the effect a public report of data loss or theft can have on an organization.

Lesson 1: Planning for Data Sharing and Collaboration

Distributed file system (DFS) and SharePoint facilitate data sharing in large organizations, but in very different ways. The main benefit of DFS is to replicate file shares to remote offices and to provide a consistent Universal Naming Convention (UNC) pathname to file shares, regardless of location in a network. SharePoint, on the other hand, provides access to data through team websites. SharePoint sites can store files and documents, but also provide version control, bulletin boards, calendaring, and many other features.

This lesson reviews the features and design strategies associated with these two data sharing technologies.

After this lesson, you will be able to:

- Determine whether DFS is a suitable solution for your network.
- Understand the DFS settings that are integral to an overall DFS design.
- Determine whether Microsoft Windows SharePoint Services 3.0 is a suitable solution for your network.
- Determine whether Microsoft Office SharePoint Server 2007 is a suitable solution for your network.

Estimated lesson time: 60 minutes

Planning a DFS Deployment

DFS is a feature in Windows Server 2008 R2 that facilitates access to shared files in a large network. As part of your overall network planning for data sharing and collaboration, you should consider your network needs for file sharing, review the features offered by DFS, and then determine whether this feature can meet those needs.

Reviewing DFS Concepts and Features

DFS enables an organization to build a single hierarchical view of file shares that remains consistent across sites in a large network. Users access DFS shares by specifying an alias pathname that remains identical, regardless of location. With DFS, shared files are replicated among multiple servers so that by specifying the same pathname, users throughout the network access a local copy of the hosted files. When permissions allow changes to a file or folder, changes made to the local copy are also replicated to other DFS servers.

IMPORTANT **DFS FUNDAMENTALS**

If you are not familiar with basic concepts related to DFS, be sure to view the introductory Flash demonstration named Dfs.swf, which you can access by visiting *http://www.microsoft .com/windowsserver2003/evaluation/demos/dfs.html*. Although this demonstration was created for Windows Server 2003, the fundamental concepts about DFS have not changed.

DFS is made up of the following network elements:

- **Namespace** The virtual view of shared folders in an organization. A namespace is made up of the remaining elements on this list.

- **Namespace server** A namespace server hosts a namespace. A namespace server can be a stand-alone server, a domain member server, or a domain controller.

- **Namespace root** The namespace root is the starting point of the namespace. A domain-based namespace can be hosted on multiple namespace servers to increase the availability of the namespace.

- **Folder** A container in a namespace that redirects clients to a folder target.

- **Folder targets** A location separate from a folder in which data and content is stored.

The elements that make up a DFS namespace are illustrated in Figure 9-1.

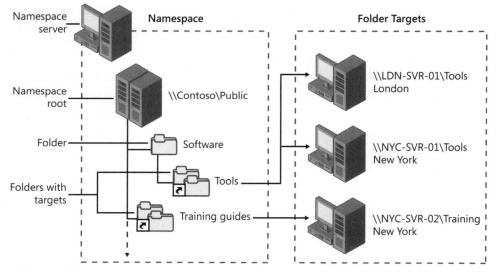

FIGURE 9-1 DFS namespace elements

When you create a new namespace, you can create it as either a domain-based namespace or a stand-alone namespace. A domain-based namespace is published to AD DS and supports the file replication and built-in fault-tolerance features. A stand-alone namespace stores its configuration information in the registry of the namespace target that hosts it. Stand-alone namespaces do not integrate with AD DS and are stored on a single namespace server. Stand-alone namespaces do not support file replication.

When you create a namespace in Windows Server 2008 mode, two enhancements are added. First, Windows Server 2008 domain-based namespaces support increased scalability (more than 5,000 folders). In addition, Windows Server 2008 namespaces support access-based enumeration. (With access-based enumeration, users can see on a file server only the files and folders for which they have proper permissions.)

To create a domain-based namespace in Windows Server 2008 mode, your servers and domain will need to meet the following requirements:

- The domain functional level must be Windows Server 2008 or higher.
- All servers hosting the namespace must run Windows Server 2008 or higher.

DFS Component Technologies

In Windows Server 2008 R2, DFS is based on two underlying technologies: DFS Namespaces and DFS Replication.

- DFS Namespaces allow administrators to group shared folders located on different servers and present them to users as a virtual tree of folders known as a namespace. A namespace provides numerous benefits, including increased availability of data, load sharing, and simplified data migration.

- *DFS Replication* is a multimaster replication engine that supports replication scheduling and bandwidth throttling. DFS Replication uses a compression protocol called Remote Differential Compression (RDC), which can be used to efficiently update files over a limited-bandwidth network. RDC detects insertions, removals, and rearrangements of data in files, thereby enabling DFS Replication to replicate only the changes when files are updated. Another important feature of DFS Replication is that in choosing replication paths, it leverages the Active Directory site links configured in Active Directory Sites and Services.

Figure 9-2 illustrates how DFS Namespaces and DFS Replication work together. In Step 1, client computers contact a namespace server and receive a referral. In Step 2, client computers access the first server provided by their referrals. The actual targets on the hosting servers are replicated with each other to allow local referrals.

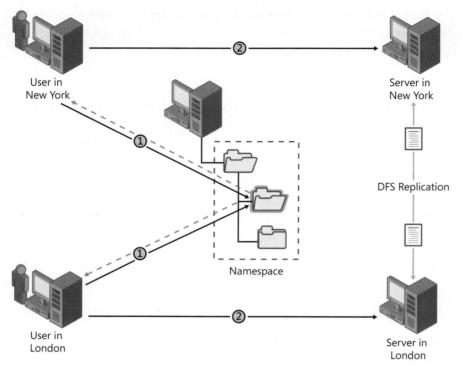

FIGURE 9-2 DFS component technologies

DFS Namespaces Advanced Settings and Features

You can customize or enable the following settings and features in DFS Namespaces as necessary to design a DFS Namespaces solution for your organization.

Referral Ordering

A *DFS referral* is an ordered list of targets, transparent to the user, which a client receives from a domain controller or namespace server when the user accesses the namespace root or a folder with targets in the namespace. The client caches the referral for a configurable period of time.

Targets in the client's Active Directory site are listed first in a referral. (Targets given the target priority "first among all targets" will be listed before targets in the client's site.) The order in which targets outside of the client's site appear in a referral is determined by one of the following referral ordering methods:

- Lowest cost
- Random order
- Exclude targets outside of the client's site

You can set referral ordering on the namespace root, and the ordering me[...] all folders with targets in the namespace. You can also override the namespace ro[...] ing method for individual folders with targets.

Failover and Failback

Client failover in DFS Namespaces is the process in which clients attempt to access another target server in a referral after one of the servers fails or is removed from the namespace. Client failback is an optional feature that enables a client to fail back to a preferred, local server after it is restored.

Failback occurs only when a client has failed over to a more expensive server (in terms of site link cost) than the server that is restored. If the restored server has the same cost as the server to which the client is currently connected, failback to the restored server does not occur. For example, if there are two servers (Server 1 and Server 2) in the client's site and Server 1 fails while the client is connected to it, the client will fail over to Server 2. However, the client will not fail back to Server 1 when it is restored because both servers are located in the same site and therefore are associated with the same site link cost.

> **NOTE** **SITE LINK COSTS**
> You can view site link costs by reviewing the site links under Inter-Site-Transports, using the Active Directory Sites and Services snap-in.

Target Priority

You can assign a priority to individual targets for a given namespace root or folder. This priority determines how the target is ordered in a referral. The options are as follows:

- First among all targets
- Last among all targets
- First among targets of equal cost
- Last among targets of equal cost

It is important to note that setting target priority on a target will result in that target always being present in a referral, even in cases where you set the Exclude Targets Outside Of The Client's Site option on the folder associated with the target.

Redundant Domain-Based Namespace Servers

Multiple namespace servers can host a domain-based namespace to increase the availability of the namespace. Putting a namespace server in remote or branch offices also allows clients to contact a namespace server and receive referrals without having to cross expensive wide area network (WAN) connections.

y Mode

...domain-based namespace across namespace servers, it is necessary ...o periodically poll AD DS to obtain the most current namespace data. ...ll use more than 16 namespace servers to host a single namespace, it ...t you enable namespace scalability mode. When this mode is enabled, ...running Windows Server 2003, Windows Server 2008, and Windows ...o not send change notification messages to other namespace servers when ...changes, nor do they poll the primary domain controller (PDC) emulator ...stead, they poll their closest domain controller every hour to discover updates ...space. (Regardless of whether namespace scalability mode is enabled, changes to ...pace are always made on the PDC emulator.)

> **NOTE ROOT SCALABILITY MODE**
>
> Namespace scalability mode is known as root scalability mode in Windows Server 2003.

Read-Only Replicated Folders

Prior to Windows Server 2008 R2, the only way to prevent users from adding or changing files was to manually set share permissions and access control lists (ACLs) on the folders, which required additional administrative effort and increased the likelihood of mistakes. In Windows Server 2008 R2, DFS now includes read-only replicated folders, which provides true read-only capabilities. In addition, read-only replicated folders are also used by read-only domain controllers (RODCs) to keep the SYSVOL shared folder updated while preventing local changes.

Support for Access-Based Enumeration

Windows Server 2008 R2 also introduces support for enabling access-based enumeration within DFS. Effectively, only the files and folders that a user has permissions to access will be displayed within DFS. Access-based enumeration can be enabled on a shared folder by using Share and Storage Management and on a DFS namespace.

> **EXAM TIP**
>
> On the 70-647 exam, expect to see questions in which you must understand the features and options of DFS Namespaces described in this section.

DFS Replication Advanced Settings and Features

You can customize or enable the following settings and features in DFS Replication as necessary to design a DFS Replication solution for your organization.

RDC

Remote Differential Compression (RDC), which is the basis for DFS replication, is a protocol that can be used to efficiently update files 64 KB or larger over a limited-bandwidth network. RDC detects insertions, removals, and rearrangements of data in files, regardless of file type, enabling DFS Replication to replicate only the changes when files are updated. To compute the changes to replicate, RDC typically works on an older version of the file with the same name that exists at the appropriate location in the replicated folder tree on the receiving member.

In earlier versions of Windows Server, the protocol used to replicate files among folders in a DFS namespace was File Replication Service (FRS). Unlike RDC, FRS copied only entire files, not portions of files. As a result, DFS in earlier versions of Windows is much more bandwidth-intensive than in Windows Server 2008 R2 networks. This change in technology in Windows Server 2008 R2 provides a huge improvement in DFS replication performance, especially across WAN links. Therefore, when planning for DFS, you should plan to upgrade your DFS servers if replication will occur across WAN links.

> **NOTE RDC AND SMALL FILES**
>
> RDC is not used on files smaller than 64 KB; in this case, the file is compressed before it is replicated. You can also disable RDC on connections that are in a local area network (LAN) where network bandwidth is not contended.

Cross-File RDC

An additional function of RDC, known as cross-file RDC, can be used to further reduce bandwidth usage. Cross-file RDC is useful when a file exists on the sending member and not the receiving member, but similar files exist on the receiving member. Instead of replicating the entire file, DFS Replication can use portions of files that are similar to the replicating file to minimize the amount of data transferred over the WAN. Cross-file RDC can use multiple files as candidate files for RDC seed data.

Replication Schedule and Bandwidth Throttling

DFS Replication supports replication scheduling and bandwidth throttling in 15-minute increments during a seven-day period. When specifying a replication window, you choose the replication start and stop times as well as the bandwidth to use during that window. The settings for bandwidth usage range from 16 kilobits per second (Kbps) to 256 megabits per second (Mbps), as well as full (unlimited) bandwidth. You can configure a default schedule and bandwidth that applies to all connections between members and, optionally, create a custom schedule and bandwidth for individual connections.

Because members of a replication group are often located in different time zones, it is important to consider the time zones of the sending and receiving members when you set the schedule. The receiving member initiates replication by interpreting the schedule either coordinated Universal Time (UTC) or in the receiving member's local time, depending on which setting you choose. You can choose this setting for the replication group schedule and for custom schedules on individual connections.

Replication Filters

You can configure file and subfolder filters to prevent files and subfolders from replicating. Both types of filters are set on a per-replicated-folder basis. You exclude subfolders by specifying their name or by using the asterisk (*) wildcard character. You exclude files by specifying their name or by using the asterisk (*) wildcard character to specify file names and extensions.

Staging Folder

DFS Replication uses staging folders to act as caches for new and changed files to be replicated from sending members to receiving members. Each replicated folder uses its own staging folder, and each staging folder has a configurable quota. The quota, which governs when files are purged based on high and low watermarks, must be carefully set based on each replicated folder's replication activity and the disk space available on the server.

Conflict And Deleted Folder

DFS Replication uses a last writer wins method for determining which version of a file to keep when a file is modified on two or more members and each member has not seen the other's version. The losing file is stored in the Conflict And Deleted folder on the member that resolves the conflict. The Conflict And Deleted folder can also be used to store files that are deleted from replicated folders. Each Conflict And Deleted folder has a quota that governs when files are purged for cleanup purposes.

Disabled Memberships

A membership defines the relationship between each replicated folder/member pair. Each membership has a status, either enabled or disabled. If you do not want a replicated folder to be replicated to certain members, you can disable the memberships for those members. Doing so allows you to replicate folders to only a subset of replication group members.

> **EXAM TIP**
>
> On the 70-647 exam, expect to see questions in which you must understand the features of DFS Replication described in this section.

Overview of the DFS Design Process

If you decide to implement DFS, you can use the following general outline to plan your DFS design:

1. Identify data to replicate.

2. Make initial namespace decisions.

3. Design the replication topology.

4. Plan for high availability and business continuity.

5. Plan for delegation.

6. Design the namespace hierarchy and functionality.

7. Design replication schedules and bandwidth throttling.

8. Review performance and optimization guidelines.

9. Plan for DFS Replication deployment.

✔ **Quick Check**

- How can you keep a specific file from replicating in a DFS namespace?

Quick Check Answer

- Use replication filters.

Planning a SharePoint Infrastructure

Microsoft provides two related technologies that an organization can use to support collaborative projects among many users. The most recent versions of these technologies, Windows SharePoint Services 3.0 and Office SharePoint Server 2007, are suitable for meeting different but related organizational needs. As part of your overall network planning, you should assess the needs of your organization for collaboration and information sharing, review the features offered by these two technologies, and then decide which, if either, of these technologies is best suited to meet those needs.

Assessing Needs for Windows SharePoint Services 3.0

Windows SharePoint Services 3.0 is a free and downloadable add-on to Windows Server 2008 R2. Its purpose is to create a web-based environment in which users can share information and documents. Organizations can use Windows SharePoint Services as the basis for a company intranet or simply as an individual site to facilitate information sharing within teams and departments. Much of the power in Windows SharePoint Services is derived from its ability to integrate with Microsoft Office applications and facilitate collaboration with Office files. Beyond allowing collaboration with Office files out of the box, Windows SharePoint Services is also a platform that developers can use to write their own web-based applications or to connect to other established applications.

Windows SharePoint Services 3.0 with Service Pack 2 can be downloaded from the following location: *http://www.microsoft.com/downloads/en/details.aspx?FamilyId=EF93E453-75F1-45DF-8C6F-4565E8549C2A*.

REVIEWING WINDOWS FOR SHAREPOINT SERVICES FEATURES

Windows SharePoint Services features enable website-based document storage, collective document editing, document organization, version control, wikis, and blogs. It also includes user features like workflows, to-do lists, alerts, bulletin boards, and basic site search.

When determining whether you need to deploy Windows for SharePoint Services, consider the following points:

- **Document storage**   You should consider deploying Windows for SharePoint Services if you need a dedicated document storage site for your organization. Whether you require a special site for document storage depends on many factors, such as how many documents need to be stored, how many people are contributing documents, who needs to act on the documents, and so on.

  Document storage sites typically include the following features:

  - The ability to check documents in or out, to track changes to documents, and to keep multiple versions of documents

  - The ability to route documents for approval or through specific processes before publishing them to a larger audience

  - The ability to tag documents with metadata so that documents can be more efficiently sorted and managed

- **Communication**   You should consider deploying Windows SharePoint Services if your organization needs a communication site. Communication sites are primarily concerned with distributing information, data, and documents to groups of users. For example, a large organization might have a central site for broadcasting organization-wide information about policies or events (such as a human resources site or a company events site).

  Many communication sites are also used for gathering and sharing information. For example, a community bulletin board is primarily a communication site. People in the community come to the site to read items and to post items for others to read.

  Communication sites are often used for:

  - Describing, publicizing, or announcing an event or other information

  - Viewing calendar or event information

- Reading documents or editorial articles
- Posting or uploading information or documents
- Creating group lists
- Publishing calendar-based alerts to a group of users

- **Collaboration** Windows SharePoint Services is extremely useful in creating collaboration sites, and your needs for such a site could determine whether deploying this solution is worthwhile for your organization. Collaboration sites are primarily concerned with sharing information and documents, generating ideas, responding to other people's ideas, and tracking progress toward a goal.

  Collaboration sites can vary depending on the team type, size, complexity, or objective. For example, a small team that is working on a short-term project (such as organizing an upcoming event or planning a new product launch) has different needs than a larger team that is working on a series of long-term projects (such as a research department in a manufacturing company or the editorial staff in a publishing company). Members of an organization working together to organize an event (such as a charity event) or to encourage participation in the organization (such as a community or school organization) have their own unique needs.

  Collaboration sites often include sections for:

  - Sharing information and data
  - Sharing documents
  - Sharing calendar or event information
  - Generating ideas and discussing ideas about a project
  - Adding, assigning, and tracking tasks

In general, you can think of Windows SharePoint Services 3.0 as a free add-on technology that allows you to quickly build a team website in a way that fully integrates with Microsoft Office 2010.

MORE INFO **WINDOWS SHAREPOINT SERVICES 3.0 FEATURES**

For a fuller description of the features offered by Windows SharePoint Services 3.0, read the Microsoft Windows SharePoint Services 3.0 Evaluation Guide, available at *http://technet.microsoft.com/en-us/windowsserver/sharepoint/bb400753.aspx.*

MORE INFO **TOUR A WINDOWS SHAREPOINT SERVICES SITE**

You can view a demo Windows SharePoint Services 3.0 site at *http://www.wssdemo.com /default.aspx.*

UNDERSTANDING WINDOWS SHAREPOINT SERVICES DEPLOYMENT OPTIONS

From a systems administration standpoint, it's important to balance the ease of deployment against other features, such as scalability. To meet different needs, Windows SharePoint Services has two main types of deployment options: a stand-alone configuration and a server farm configuration.

- **Deploying Windows SharePoint Services in a stand-alone configuration**   You can quickly publish a SharePoint site by deploying Windows SharePoint Services 3.0 on a single server computer. A stand-alone configuration is useful if you want to evaluate the software's features and capabilities, such as collaboration, document management, and search. A stand-alone configuration is also useful if you are deploying a small number of websites and you want to minimize administrative overhead.

  When you deploy Windows SharePoint Services 3.0 on a single server using the default settings, the Setup program automatically installs the Windows Internal Database and uses it to create the configuration database and an initial content database for your SharePoint sites. Windows Internal Database uses SQL Server technology as a relational data store for Windows roles and features only, such as Windows SharePoint Services, Active Directory Rights Management Services (AD RMS), Universal Description, Discovery, and Integration (UDDI) Services, Windows Server Update Services (WSUS), and Windows System Resources Manager (WSRM). In addition, Setup installs the SharePoint Central Administration website and creates your first SharePoint site collection and site.

  In general, the advantage of running Windows SharePoint Services on a single computer is that doing so facilitates deployment. The primary drawback of a stand-alone configuration is that it does not support the scalability needed in larger environments.

- **Deploying Windows SharePoint Services in a server farm configuration**   You can deploy Windows SharePoint Services 3.0 in a server farm environment if you are hosting a large number of sites, if you want the best possible performance, or if you want to take advantage of the scalability of a multitier topology. A server farm consists of one or more servers dedicated to running the Windows SharePoint Services 3.0 application.

  In a multitier server farm, multiple Windows SharePoint Services front-end servers can connect to a back-end database server that hosts copies of all documents, settings, and related data. This helps organizations increase performance and provide access to data in a variety of scenarios. For example, it allows you to create an extranet that third-party users and organizations (such as business partners) can use for collaboration.

  The basic system requirements for a server farm are identical to those for deploying Windows SharePoint Services in a stand-alone configuration, with one exception. In a server farm, a SharePoint database must be stored on a computer running either Microsoft SQL Server 2000 or SQL Server 2005.

MORE INFO   DEPLOYING WINDOWS SHAREPOINT SERVICES 3.0

For a fuller description of how to deploy Windows SharePoint Services 3.0, read "Getting Started with Windows SharePoint Services 3.0," available at *http://go.microsoft.com /fwlink/?LinkId=91963*.

Assessing Needs for Microsoft Office SharePoint Server 2007

Like Windows SharePoint Services 3.0, Microsoft Office SharePoint Server 2007 allows you to create a website that facilitates collaboration, provides content management features, and provides access to information essential to organizational goals and processes. However, Microsoft Office SharePoint Server 2007 offers many more features than Windows SharePoint Services 3.0 does. Unlike Windows SharePoint Services 3.0, in fact, Microsoft Office SharePoint Server 2007 is not free; It is a separately purchased product.

To determine whether your organization needs Microsoft Office SharePoint Server 2007 and not merely Windows SharePoint Services 3.0, you should first assess your organization's need for collaboration and then determine whether the features offered by Microsoft Office SharePoint Server 2007 can best meet your organization's needs.

MORE INFO   MICROSOFT SHAREPOINT SERVER 2010

Microsoft Office SharePoint Server 2007 has been superseded by Microsoft SharePoint Server 2010. Microsoft SharePoint Server 2010 is licensed separately from Windows Server 2008 R2 and is not covered in this training kit. For more information on Microsoft SharePoint Server 2010, please go to *http://technet.microsoft.com/en-us /sharepoint/ee263917*.

DIFFERENCES BETWEEN WINDOWS SHAREPOINT SERVICES 3.0 AND MICROSOFT OFFICE SHAREPOINT SERVER 2007

Microsoft Office SharePoint Server 2007 builds on the technologies offered by Windows SharePoint Services 3.0 to enable community sites that are far more powerful, more customizable, and more tightly integrated with an organization's business processes than those enabled by Windows SharePoint Services 3.0.

First, Microsoft Office SharePoint Server 2007 facilitates the creation and deployment of powerful websites that are more feature-rich and content-rich than those that can be created with Windows SharePoint Services 3.0. Sites that are better supported by Microsoft Office SharePoint Server 2007 include organizational portal sites and Internet presence sites. Microsoft Office SharePoint Server 2007 also comes with many ready-to-use website and portal templates, Web Parts, lists, libraries, workflows, and site variations to tailor content to different cultures, markets, and geographic regions.

Microsoft Office SharePoint Server 2007 also provides greater support for the authoring, staging, and publishing of custom websites than does Windows SharePoint Services 3.0. It enables My Sites, individual mini-sites that can be quickly created to show how users are connected to one another in an organization, the tasks and skills associated with each user, user contact information, and more.

Finally, Microsoft Office SharePoint Server 2007 can be much more tightly integrated into an organization's business processes than Windows SharePoint Services 3.0 can. Solutions based on Microsoft Office SharePoint Server 2007 can provide organization-wide access to business intelligence and other information stored in the application or in line-of-business systems such as SAP. For example, the Business Data Catalog enables you to include data from back-end systems in lists, Web Parts, pages, and search results. In addition, Excel Services provides access to real-time, interactive Microsoft Office Excel 2007 spreadsheets from a web browser. Microsoft Office SharePoint Server 2007 also provides extended access to information, people, and expertise.

> **MORE INFO**   **MICROSOFT OFFICE SHAREPOINT SERVER 2007 EVALUATION GUIDE FEATURES IN DETAIL**
>
> For a full description of the features and services of Microsoft Office SharePoint Server 2007, see the Evaluation Guide for Office SharePoint Server 2007, available at *http://go.microsoft.com/fwlink/?LinkId=83060&clcid=0x409*.

EXAMPLES OF SOLUTIONS BASED ON MICROSOFT OFFICE SHAREPOINT SERVER 2007

Here are examples of typical solutions that can be built using Microsoft Office SharePoint Server 2007 (as opposed to Windows SharePoint Services 3.0):

- **Online news magazine**   A publishing organization uses Microsoft Office SharePoint Server 2007 to build its branded online magazine site. Article submissions come from inside and outside the organization to be reviewed and accepted by staff editors. This Internet site has a strong community presence because users can log on for personalized information, and it has an extensive search component.

  The Internet site includes subsites for current news and editorials; blogs; and regular columns about politics, business, health, people, personal finance, and science and technology. The site also enables users to sign in to interact with one another and to comment on articles published on the site.

- **Controlled distribution of financial data to clients and business partners**   A bank deploys a solution based on Microsoft Office SharePoint Server 2007 to take advantage of Excel Services. The solution enables bank managers to communicate efficiently with clients by providing controlled access to specified workbooks that can be rendered with view-only permissions in a web browser. The workbooks are accessible in document libraries on a portal; this enables the bank to restrict the availability of financial data to clients who have authenticated access to the portal.

- **Online permit application** A local government agency uses Microsoft Office SharePoint Server 2007 and Office InfoPath 2007 to provide permit application and approval to contractors over the Internet. Contractors use the website to apply for permits using an online service. Data entered into the permit application web form is submitted to a database in the government's Department of Building Inspections network.

  After the application data is submitted, a new permit request (a multipart Office InfoPath 2007 form) is automatically populated to a workspace. When the form is opened, the requesting contractor's company and permit application data are populated into the form's fields. If the request is approved, an electrical permit (also populated with the requestor's contact data and relevant information) is rendered in HTML and posted to the Department of Building Inspections permit site, where the contractor can view and print the permit for posting at the construction site.

- **Corporate Internet presence site** An international automobile manufacturer has headquarters in Germany; a major subsidiary in Michigan serving the North American market; and regional offices throughout Europe, Asia, and North America. The products are sold internationally, and distinct manufacturing operations serve each regional market. The company's Internet presence website is built, administered, and authored using Microsoft Office SharePoint Server 2007. It is the focal point for the corporate marketing efforts, and it includes subsites for each product line, along with areas for press releases, investment information, company information, and career opportunities.

  Each corporate brand has its own marketing department with individuals responsible for writing that brand's content and updating it on the website. The corporate communication department controls the look and feel of the site to make sure the branding and messaging are consistent. The site includes site variations that tailor its content to different languages, cultures, markets, and geographic regions.

  Using Microsoft Office SharePoint Server 2007 websites, the writers for each brand author the site's content and route it for review and approval while managing the creation of multilingual content versions. Using scheduled workflows, the approved and localized content is copied to staging sites where it is tested and ultimately deployed to the public site.

MORE INFO **DEPLOYING MICROSOFT OFFICE SHAREPOINT SERVER 2007**

Like Windows SharePoint Services 3.0, Microsoft Office SharePoint Server 2007 can be deployed as a stand-alone server or in a server farm configuration. For more information about deploying Microsoft Office SharePoint Server 2007, see "Getting Started with Office SharePoint Server," which you can download at *http://go.microsoft.com /fwlink/?LinkID=91741*.

You are an enterprise administrator for A. Datum Corporation, a multinational software company with headquarters in New York. To reduce costs, improve efficiency, and encourage creativity, management has recently introduced a plan to increase collaboration between the New York office and the branch offices in Boston, San Jose, London, and Bangalore. As an enterprise administrator, you and the other members of your team need to choose technologies and configurations that support these new interbranch projects.

The following points represent the technical requirements for each project:

- A new project with Boston will be used to develop an advertising campaign for the company. Files to be shared between the branches are expected to be very large, and local access to all files is needed.

- Collaboration with the San Jose office should be able to support as many projects as needed among the 100 members of the marketing department. The collaboration solution should enable team members to have ready access to marketing data that is updated in real time. In addition, users should be able to find and contact each other based on skill sets.

- Collaboration with the London office involves copy and tech writing. Employees at the New York and London branches should be able to work together on documents in a way that provides version control.

- Collaboration with the Bangalore office needs to support many projects related to software development. Team members should be able to have local access to large files that are frequently updated by both New York employees and Bangalore employees. All development team members should also have access to a central schedule and announcement board.

EXERCISE 1 Planning for a Data Sharing Solution

In this exercise, you make decisions about the data sharing solutions for the various projects in a manner based on the requirements given.

1. At a minimum, which solution or solutions should you implement to meet the stated requirements for the Boston project?

2. Assuming that the design goals of making files available locally are met, how can you automatically redirect users to files in the opposite branch when the local server is unavailable?

3. At a minimum, which solution or solutions should you implement to meet the stated requirements for the San Jose project?

4. At a minimum, which solution or solutions should you implement to meet the stated requirements for the London project?

5. At a minimum, which solution or solutions should you implement to meet the stated requirements for the Bangalore project?

Lesson Summary

- DFS enables an organization to build a single hierarchical view of file shares that remains consistent across sites in a large network. When you integrate DFS with AD DS, DFS folders can be replicated across sites so that users in various locations can have access to a local copy of the shared files.

- You should deploy DFS if you need to provide local access to the same files across multiple sites. You should customize the deployment by configuring features such as referral ordering, failover, and replications schedules.

- Microsoft provides two related technologies that an organization can use to support collaborative projects among many users. The most recent versions of these technologies, Windows SharePoint Services 3.0 and Microsoft Office SharePoint Server 2007, are suitable for meeting different but related organizational needs.

- You should consider deploying Windows SharePoint Services if you want a free tool that facilitates the creation of team websites that enable communication among team members and that provide version control for Office documents.

- You should consider deploying Microsoft Office SharePoint Server 2007 if you need to support more powerful community websites, such as Internet portals, or if you need to create intranet sites that provide business data that is automatically updated in real time.

Lesson Review

The following questions are intended to reinforce key information presented in this lesson. The questions are also available on the companion CD if you prefer to review them in electronic form.

> **NOTE ANSWERS**
>
> Answers to these questions and explanations of why each answer choice is correct or incorrect are located in the "Answers" section at the end of the book.

1. You have implemented a domain-based DFS namespace that spans all five sites of your company network in London, New York, Los Angeles, Toronto, and Sydney. The site link costs among all sites are configured as equal at all five sites.

    A certain folder named Marketing in the DFS namespace includes targets in all five sites. You want users to connect to the local target when available, but when users are unable to connect to the local target, you want their requests to be redirected to the associated target in the New York office.

    How should you enable this functionality?

    A. Configure the New York target priority as first among all targets.

    B. Configure the New York target priority as first among targets of equal cost.

C. At all four other sites, raise the site link cost to the New York office.

D. At all four other sites, lower the site link cost to the New York office.

2. You are planning a collaboration solution for your company. You need to ensure the solution provides access to real-time, interactive Microsoft Office Excel 2007 spreadsheets from a web browser.

How should you enable this functionality?

A. Deploy Distributed File System.

B. Deploy Windows SharePoint Services.

C. Deploy Active Directory Federation Services.

D. Deploy Microsoft Office SharePoint Server 2007.

3. Your company has a single Active Directory Domain Services forest with a single domain. The domain functional level and the forest functional level are set to Windows Server 2003. All domain controllers have Windows Server 2008 installed. You deploy new Windows Server 2008 R2–based DFS servers. You plan to create a domain-based namespace.How should you enable this functionality?

A. Raise the domain functional level to Windows Server 2008.

B. Raise the domain functional level to Windows Server 2008 R2.

C. Raise the forest functional level to Windows Server 2008.

D. Raise the domain functional level to Windows Server 2008 R2.

Lesson 2: Choosing Data Security Solutions

One of the first steps in designing security for stored data is to choose the security that you will use to protect your data in various locations on your network. A number of data security features are available to protect data, and each available technology is designed to meet specific security needs. For example, BitLocker is designed to protect data on a disk that is stolen or on a computer that has been booted with a stealth operating system. *Encrypting File System* (EFS) provides a simple method to encrypt chosen files on a disk. *Active Directory Rights Management Services* (AD RMS) is used to secure files even if they leave your network.

Data protection features vary not only in their application but also in the cost and complexity of their adoption. In general, you need to review the features of each technology and then decide whether your security needs warrant the implementation of the technology in question. In general, the higher your needs to protect specific data, the higher the cost and complexity you should consider to meet your security requirements.

This lesson reviews three data protection technologies: BitLocker, EFS, and AD RMS.

After this lesson, you will be able to:

- Understand the features and benefits of BitLocker.
- Understand the benefits of EFS and several considerations for planning an EFS implementation.
- Understand the features and benefits of AD RMS.

Estimated lesson time: 35 minutes

Protecting Volume Data with BitLocker

BitLocker is a data protection feature available in Windows Server 2008 R2 that provides data encryption for full volumes and integrity checking for early boot components. The purpose of BitLocker is to protect data on a drive that has been stolen or that has been accessed offline in a way that bypasses file permissions (for example, by booting the computer from a stealth operating system). BitLocker to Go extends BitLocker data protection to USB storage devices, enabling them to be restricted with a passphrase.

BitLocker is designed primarily for use with a Trusted Platform Module (TPM), which is a hardware module included in many new laptops (as well as some desktops) that are available today. TPM modules must be version 1.2 for use with BitLocker. The TPM module is a permanent part of the motherboard.

If a TPM 1.2 module is not available, a computer can still take advantage of BitLocker encryption technology as long as the computer's BIOS supports reading from a USB flash device before the operating system is loaded. However, you cannot use BitLocker integrity checking capabilities without a TPM 1.2 module.

BitLocker Drive Encryption

In Windows Server 2008 R2, BitLocker encrypts system volumes, data volumes, and USB storage devices. To encrypt the full volume, a cryptographic key known as the Full Volume Encryption Key (FVEK) is used. This key is stored in the volume metadata and is itself encrypted by another key known as the Volume Master Key (VMK). The VMK is then encrypted again by the TPM, if one is available, or by a startup key located on a user-provided USB flash device accessed during the startup phase.

BitLocker Performance Issues

Windows Server 2008 R2 and Windows 7 encrypt and decrypt disk sectors on the fly as data is read from and written to encrypted volumes. As a result, BitLocker does affect performance because these cryptographic operations consume some processor time. However, the actual impact depends on multiple factors, such as caching, hard disk speed, and processor grade.

Choosing a BitLocker Authentication Mode

BitLocker supports four separate authentication modes. The mode you choose depends on the computer's hardware capabilities and the level of security you desire for the computer:

- **BitLocker with a TPM only**   In this authentication mode, BitLocker uses only a TPM to unlock the VMK and enable a volume to be read. Advantages of this mode are that it requires no user intervention; It protects the data from being read if the drive is stolen, and it protects the drive against rootkits and other low-level malware. The disadvantage of this authentication mode is that it does not protect data from being read if the entire computer is stolen because the TPM is attached to the internals of the computer.

- **TPM with USB flash device**   In this mode, both a TPM and a USB flash device are required. To start the computer, a user must insert a USB flash device containing an external key. This effectively authenticates both the user and the integrity of the computer. The advantage of this method is that, in principle, it protects the data even if the entire computer is stolen (because a thief needs access to the flash device to read the data). The disadvantage is that it requires user intervention every time the computer is started.

- **TPM with PIN** This authentication mode requires both a TPM and a user to provide a personal identification number (PIN) every time the computer is started. The advantage of this method is that it protects the volume data if the entire computer is stolen and that it is often easier to provide a PIN than to provide a USB flash device during startup. The disadvantage of a PIN is that, although this mode is more secure than BitLocker with a TPM only, it is potentially less secure than providing a USB flash device on a TPM-supplied computer.

- **USB flash device only** This is the only authentication mode that can be used on computers that do not have a TPM. In this mode, the user provides a USB flash device during startup that includes an external key, enabling encrypted volumes to be read. The advantage of this method is that it can be used on all computers with a BitLocker-compatible BIOS. The disadvantage of this method is that it does not provide data integrity checking.

BitLocker Security Design Considerations

Use the following list to help you determine whether to use BitLocker, which authentication mode to implement, and which type of operating system to use.

- Only BitLocker allows you to encrypt all files on a volume, including the page file, hibernation file, registry, and temporary files. If you want to prevent these files from being read if a computer or drive is stolen, use BitLocker and not another encryption technology, such as EFS.

- If you want BitLocker to detect changes to system data, such as those that might occur from malware or rootkit infection, you must use a system supplied with a TPM. You cannot choose the USB flash device only authentication method.

- If you want to protect BitLocker with two-factor authentication, you must use a system supplied with a TPM. You can then use a USB flash device or PIN for authentication in addition to the TPM.

MORE INFO **PLANNING FOR BITLOCKER**

For in-depth information about planning the use of BitLocker in Windows, visit the Microsoft Download Center at *http://download.microsoft.com* and search for "Windows BitLocker Drive Encryption Design and Deployment Guides."

Planning for EFS

EFS is the file encryption technology built into Windows that is used optionally to encrypt files stored on NTFS volumes. When a user or program attempts to access a file that is encrypted with EFS, the operating system automatically attempts to acquire a decryption key for the content and, if successful, silently performs encryption and decryption on behalf of the user. When users do not have access to the encryption key, they are not able to open an encrypted file, even if they have been assigned Read permissions to that file.

EFS relies on both symmetric and public key cryptography. To support public key cryptography, EFS uses certificates and key pairs. In a workgroup environment, these certificates and keys are stored locally on each computer. However, in a domain environment, the certificates can be issued by an enterprise certification authority (CA) and managed by Group Policy. With an enterprise CA, a domain user can read his or her encrypted files while logged on to any computer in the domain. In addition, when EFS is deployed with an enterprise CA, a domain user designated as a data recovery agent (DRA) can recover encrypted files stored in the domain.

In general, the advantage of EFS is that it provides a simple method to protect a file from being read on a disk, even if that file is accessed offline. The biggest disadvantage of EFS is that it does not protect data sent over the wire or data copied to an alternate location. EFS can protect data only while it stays on an NTFS volume.

> **MORE INFO**   **EFS FUNDAMENTALS**
>
> For a complete overview of EFS, visit the following location: *http://technet.microsoft.com /en-us/library/cc700811.aspx.*

When you are planning EFS policy for an organization, it is useful to determine the threats to your system, how EFS handles these threats, and whether to deploy a CA.

To properly plan for and implement EFS, follow these steps:

1. Investigate EFS technology and capabilities.
2. Assess the need for EFS in your environment.
3. Investigate the configuration of EFS using Group Policy.
4. Identify the computer systems and users that require EFS.
5. Identify the level of protection that you require. For example, does your organization require using smart cards with EFS?
6. Configure EFS as appropriate for your environment using Group Policy.

In addition, be sure to follow these EFS best practices:

■   Use Group Policy to ensure that the Documents or My Documents folder is encrypted for all users. This practice secures by default the data in which most documents are stored.

- Instruct users to encrypt folders instead of individual files. Encrypting files consistently at the folder level ensures that files are not unexpectedly decrypted.

- The private keys that are associated with recovery certificates are extremely sensitive. These keys must be generated either on a computer that is physically secured, or their certificates must be exported to a .pfx file, protected with a strong password, and saved on a disk that is stored in a physically secure location.

- Recovery agent certificates must be assigned to special recovery agent accounts that are not used for any other purpose.

- Do not destroy recovery certificates or private keys when recovery agents are changed. (Agents are changed periodically.) Keep them all until all files that might have been encrypted with them are updated.

- Designate two or more recovery agent accounts per organizational unit (OU), depending on the size of the OU. Designate two or more computers for recovery, one for each designated recovery agent account. Grant permissions to appropriate administrators to use the recovery agent accounts. It is a good idea to have two recovery agent accounts to provide redundancy for file recovery. Having two computers that hold these keys provides more redundancy to allow recovery of lost data.

- Implement a recovery agent archive program to make sure that encrypted files can be recovered by using obsolete recovery keys. Recovery certificates and private keys must be exported and stored in a controlled and secure manner. Ideally, as with all secure data, archives must be stored in a controlled access vault and you must have two archives: a master and a backup. The master is kept on-site and the backup is located in a secure off-site location.

- Avoid using print spool files in your print server architecture, or make sure that print spool files are generated in an encrypted folder.

- EFS does take some CPU overhead every time a user encrypts and decrypts a file. Plan your server usage wisely. Load balance your servers when there are many clients using EFS.

✔ **Quick Check**
- As a best practice, how many EFS recovery agents should you designate per OU?

Quick Check Answer
- Two or more

Using AD RMS

Active Directory Rights Management Services (AD RMS) is a technology that allows an organization to control access to and use of confidential data. With an AD RMS–enabled application such as Office, you can create a usage policy to protect a file in the application by controlling rights to that file, even when it is moved outside of the company network.

Whenever you choose to protect data by using AD RMS, users who later want to read the data must first be authenticated against the AD RMS server. This authentication can occur anywhere in the world, as long as the AD RMS server is accessible over the network and as long as the user's computer is running the AD RMS client, which is built into Windows Vista, Windows 7, Windows Server 2008, and Windows Server 2008 R2.

> **MORE INFO** **AD RMS IN DEPTH**
>
> For in-depth information about AD RMS, see the Active Directory Rights Management Services TechCenter page at *http://go.microsoft.com/fwlink/?LinkId=80907*.

AD RMS is installed as a server role and managed through the Active Directory Rights Management Services console, shown in Figure 9-3.

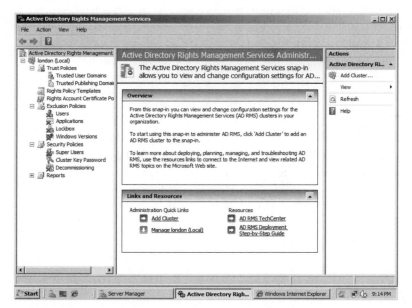

FIGURE 9-3 The Active Directory Rights Management Services console

AD RMS usage policies define three elements for protected files:

- **Trusted entities** Organizations can specify the entities, including individuals, groups of users, computers, and applications that are trusted participants in an AD RMS system. By establishing trusted entities, AD RMS can help protect information by enabling access only to properly trusted participants.

- **Usage rights and conditions** Organizations and individuals can assign usage rights and conditions that define how a specific trusted entity can use rights-protected content. Examples of usage rights are permission to read, copy, print, save, forward, and edit. Usage rights can be accompanied by conditions, such as when those rights expire. Organizations can exclude applications and entities from accessing the rights-protected content.

- **Encryption** AD RMS encrypts information, making access conditional on the successful validation of the trusted entities. When information is locked, only trusted entities that were granted usage rights under the specified conditions (if any) can unlock or decrypt the information in an AD RMS–enabled application or browser. The application will then enforce the defined usage rights and conditions.

Creating and Viewing Rights-Protected Information

To protect data with AD RMS, information workers simply follow the same workflow they already use for their information.

Figure 9-4 illustrates how AD RMS works when users publish and consume rights-protected information.

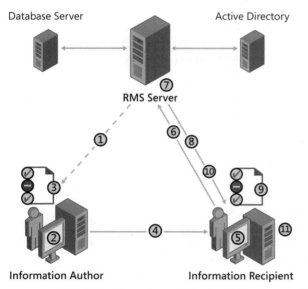

FIGURE 9-4 Workflow of creating and viewing rights-protected information

This process includes the following steps:

1. When a user chooses the option to protect data in an AD RMS–enabled application for the first time, the author receives a client licensor certificate from the AD RMS server. This is a one-time step that enables offline publishing of rights-protected information in the future.

2. Using an AD RMS–enabled application, an author creates a file and defines a set of usage rights and conditions for that file. A publishing license is then generated that contains the usage policies.

3. The application encrypts the file with a symmetric key, which is then encrypted with the public key of the author's AD RMS server. The key is inserted into the publishing license and the publishing license is bound to the file. Only the author's AD RMS server can issue use licenses to decrypt this file.

4. The author distributes the file.

5. A recipient receives a protected file through a regular distribution channel and opens it using an AD RMS–enabled application or browser.

6. If the recipient does not have an account certificate on the current computer, this is the point at which one will be issued.

7. The application sends a request for a use license to the AD RMS server that issued the publishing license for the protected information. The request includes the recipient's account certificate (which contains the recipient's public key) and the publishing license (which contains the symmetric key that encrypted the file).

8. The AD RMS licensing server validates that the recipient is authorized, checks that the recipient is a named user, and creates a use license.

9. During this process, the server decrypts the symmetric key using the private key of the server, re-encrypts the symmetric key using the public key of the recipient, and adds the encrypted session key to the use license. This step ensures that only the intended recipient can decrypt the symmetric key and thus decrypt the protected file. The server also adds any relevant conditions to the use license, such as the expiration of an application or operating system exclusion.

10. When the validation is complete, the licensing server returns the use license to the recipient's client computer.

11. After receiving the use license, the application examines both the license and the recipient's account certificate to determine whether any certificate in either chain of trust requires a revocation list. If so, the application checks for a local copy of the revocation list that has not expired. If necessary, it retrieves a current copy of the revocation list. The application then applies any revocation conditions that are relevant in the current context. If no revocation condition blocks access to the file, the application renders the data and the user can exercise the rights he or she has been granted.

This 11-step process is essentially the same whether the recipient is within the publishing organization or outside of it. The recipient is not required to be inside the author's network or domain to request a use license. All that is required is a valid account certificate for the recipient and access to the licensing server that issued the publishing license.

AD RMS Applications

AD RMS–enabled applications are those that are specifically designed to encrypt and control usage of the information through AD RMS. AD RMS–enabled applications include the following:

- Office System 2003: Word, Excel, PowerPoint, Outlook
- Office 2007: Word, Excel, PowerPoint, Outlook, InfoPath
- Office 2010: Word, Excel, PowerPoint, Outlook, InfoPath
- SharePoint Server 2007and 2010
- Exchange Server 2007 and 2010
- XPS (XML Paper Specification) v1.0
- Internet Explorer 6.0 or later (through use of the RM Add-on for IE)

For a complete list of AD RMS–aware applications visit *http://technet.microsoft.com/en-us /library/dd772697(WS.10).aspx*.

EXAM TIP

For the 70-647 exam, the most important feature to remember about AD RMS is that it enables users to provide persistent protection for data, even as the data leaves the organization. A situation in which AD RMS would be useful would be in protecting confidential email or Word documents, even if they are leaked to a third party.

PRACTICE   Designing Data Storage Security

You are an enterprise administrator for Consolidated Messenger. The company network consists of a single Active Directory domain. You, along with other members of the data security team, have been given the responsibility of choosing data security solutions for the entire corporate network.

The following points represent the design goals of the data security solutions:

A. No data on critical servers should be accessible, even if the hard disks are physically stolen.

B. To start critical servers, you must use a PIN.

C. Email marked as confidential must not be readable to unauthorized parties.

D. Users who choose to encrypt personal files must be able to read those files from any computer on the company network.

EXERCISE 1   Planning a Data Storage Security Solution

In this exercise, you make decisions about data security in a manner based on the requirements given.

1. Which security feature should you use to meet requirement A?

2. Are there any hardware prerequisites to meet requirement A? If so, what are they?

3. Which security feature should you use to meet requirement B?

4. Are there any hardware prerequisites to meet requirement B? If so, what are they?

5. Which security solution should you use to meet requirement C?

6. What technology should you deploy to meet requirement D?

Lesson Summary

- BitLocker is a full-volume data encryption feature designed to protect data on a drive that has been stolen or that has been accessed offline. BitLocker encrypts complete volumes, including page files and hibernation files. To gain the full benefits of BitLocker, you need to configure the feature on a computer that has a TPM version 1.2.

- BitLocker provides for authentication modes or methods of decrypting disk data: TPM only, TPM with a USB flash device, TPM with PIN, and USB flash device only. If you use USB flash device only mode, BitLocker does not verify the integrity of early boot components.

- EFS is the file encryption technology built into Windows that is used optionally to encrypt files stored on NTFS volumes. EFS is best deployed with an enterprise CA. Although EFS does not enable users to encrypt all files on a drive, it is easy to implement and requires no special hardware.

- AD RMS is a technology designed to protect files for AD RMS–compatible applications, such as Office. With AD RMS, protected files and emails remain protected, even when they leave the company network.

Lesson Review

The following questions are intended to reinforce key information presented in this lesson. The questions are also available on the companion CD if you prefer to review them in electronic form.

> **NOTE** **ANSWERS**
>
> Answers to these questions and explanations of why each answer choice is correct or incorrect are located in the "Answers" section at the end of the book.

1. You want to deploy Microsoft SQL Server 2008 on a database server to store confidential data that is accessed infrequently. The server itself is rack-mounted and is not likely to be stolen, but the disks are hot-swappable and could feasibly be removed by an intruder. You want to ensure that even if the server's disks are stolen, nobody will be able to read the contents of the disks. You also want the server to be able to restart without administrator assistance. What should you do to best meet the requirements of the database server?

A. Buy a server with a TPM 1.2 module and use AD RMS to protect the data.

B. Use BitLocker to protect the data. You do not need a server with a TPM 1.2.

C. Use AD RMS to protect the data. You do not need a server with a TPM 1.2.

D. Buy a server with a TPM 1.2 module and use BitLocker to protect the data.

2. You are planning to deploy BitLocker in your organization. You need to ensure data is protected if drives are stolen from computers. Additionally, this should be accomplished without user intervention. Which BitLocker authentication method should you choose?

A. BitLocker with a TPM only

B. TPM with USB flash device

C. TPM with PIN

D. USB flash device only

3. You are planning to deploy BitLocker in your organization. You need to ensure data is protected if computers are stolen. Which BitLocker authentication method should you choose?

A. BitLocker with a TPM only

B. TPM with USB flash device

C. TPM with PIN

D. USB flash device only

Lesson 3: Planning for System Recoverability and Availability

When you deploy essential servers, such as domain controllers, web servers, and database servers, you need to plan how to design the system for recoverability in the event of server failure. In the case of a domain controller, you should plan to use Windows Server Backup (or another backup application) to back up the AD DS database. With web servers and other application servers that need to support many users, you can use Network Load Balancing (NLB). For database servers, mail servers, and other application servers that use a shared database, you can use failover clustering to support recoverability and service availability.

After this lesson, you will be able to:

- Design domain controller storage for optimal recoverability.
- Understand general procedures and considerations for performing maintenance on the AD DS database.
- Know when you should seize a domain controller operations master role.
- Understand the benefits of NLB and the scenarios in which it is best used.
- Understand the benefits of failover clustering and the scenarios in which it is best used.

Estimated lesson time: 30 minutes

Planning AD DS Maintenance and Recovery Procedures

Before you deploy Windows Server 2008 R2 domain controllers, you need to plan AD DS maintenance and recovery procedures, such as backing up and restoring the AD DS database (Ntds.dit), defragmenting the AD DS database, and seizing operations master roles.

Planning for AD DS Backup

Before you install Windows Server 2008 R2 on a computer you plan to deploy as a domain controller, you should design the storage of that server in a way that best suits its recoverability. Specifically, for each domain controller you should store operating system files, the Active Directory database (Ntds.dit), and the SYSVOL directory all on separate volumes that do not contain other user, operating system, or application data.

The actual backup procedure for AD DS is different in Windows Server 2008 and Windows Server 2008 R2 than it is for earlier versions of Windows Server. In Windows Server 2008, you must back up critical volumes on a domain controller rather than backing up only the system state data.

Critical volumes are those that contain the following data:

- The volume that hosts the boot files, which consists of the Bootmgr file and the boot configuration data (BCD) store
- The volume that hosts the Windows operating system and the registry
- The volume that hosts the SYSVOL directory
- The volume that hosts the Active Directory database (Ntds.dit)
- The volume that hosts the Active Directory database log files

WINDOWS SERVER BACKUP AND *WBADMIN*

Windows Server 2008 and Windows Server 2008 R2 include a new backup application named Windows Server Backup and an associated command-line tool named *wbadmin*. These features are not installed by default. You must install them by using the Add Features option in Server Manager.

> **NOTE   YOU CANNOT BACK UP FILE ALLOCATION TABLE (FAT) VOLUMES OR PARTIAL VOLUMES**
>
> Only NTFS volumes on locally attached disks can be backed up by using Windows Server Backup. In addition, you cannot use Windows Server Backup to back up selected files or folders; you can back up only entire volumes.

You can schedule full server backups and critical-volume backups by using either Windows Server Backup or *wbadmin*. When determining the frequency for AD DS backups, consider the following:

- **The frequency of significant changes to AD DS data**   Significant changes can include changes to the schema, group membership, Active Directory replication or site topology, and policies. They can also include upgrades to operating systems, renaming domain controllers or domains, and migration or creation of new security principals.
- **The effect on business operations if data in AD DS or SYSVOL is lost**   Lost data can include updates to passwords for user accounts, computer accounts, and trusts. It can also include updates to group membership, policies, and the replication topology and its schedules.

In general, it is recommended that you perform backups nightly during times of decreased network traffic. For fault tolerance, schedule at least two trusted backups for each domain. You can start by scheduling the backups daily and then adjust the frequency of your backups depending on the previously specified criteria.

Finally, note the following considerations when choosing a storage location for your backups:

- It is recommended that you create a backup volume on a dedicated internal or attached external hard disk drive.

- The destination volume for the backup must be on a separate hard disk from the source volumes.

- In Windows Server Backup, you cannot perform a scheduled backup to a network share. Only manual backups can be performed to a network share.

- Windows Server Backup does not enable you to back up to tape.

> **NOTE CAN YOU USE WINDOWS SERVER BACKUP ON A SERVER CORE INSTALLATION?**
>
> To use the Windows Server Backup graphical user interface (GUI) for managing backup and to restore operations on a server that is running a Server Core installation of Windows Server 2008 R2, you must connect remotely from a server that is running a full installation of Windows Server 2008 R2.

Planning for AD DS Recovery

Planning for AD DS recovery entails learning the recovery procedures, learning when to perform each restore type, and deciding whether to install Windows Recovery Environment (RE) on a dedicated partition as part of domain controller deployment.

AD DS recovery includes performing nonauthoritative restores and authoritative restores. A *nonauthoritative restore* is what you should perform if the Active Directory volume becomes corrupted or is deleted. To perform a nonauthoritative restore of AD DS, you need at least a critical-volume backup. If you cannot start the server, then you must perform a full server recovery instead.

To perform a nonauthoritative restore, you must restart the domain controller in Directory Services Restore Mode (DSRM). Then you can open Windows Server Backup or use the *wbadmin* utility to perform the recovery.

> **NOTE FULL SERVER RECOVERY AND WINDOWS RE**
>
> A full server recovery requires you to start the server with the Windows Server 2008 R2 product DVD and choose the Repair Your Computer option. To avoid having to use the operating system media during recovery, use the Windows Automated Installation Kit (AIK) to install Windows RE on a separate partition. When you install Windows RE beforehand, you can simply choose it from the boot menu and access Windows Recovery options. For more information about the Windows AIK, visit *http://go.microsoft.com/fwlink/?LinkId=90643*.

> **MORE INFO PERFORMING A NONAUTHORITATIVE RESTORE**
>
> For more information about performing a nonauthoritative restore, visit *http://technet .microsoft.com/en-us/library/cc730683(WS.10).aspx*.

Unlike a nonauthoritative restore, the purpose of an *authoritative restore* is to restore an object that has accidentally been deleted. For example, you might need to perform an authoritative restore if an administrator inadvertently deletes an OU containing a large number of users. If you restore the server from backup, the normal, nonauthoritative restore process does not restore the inadvertently deleted OU because the restored domain controller is updated following the restore process to the current status of its replication partners, which have deleted the OU. Recovering the deleted OU instead requires authoritative restore. You can use authoritative restore to mark the OU as authoritative and let the replication process restore it to all the other domain controllers in the domain.

When an object is marked for authoritative restore, its version number is changed so that it is higher than the existing version number of the (deleted) object in the Active Directory replication system. This change ensures that any data that you restore authoritatively is replicated from the restored domain controller to other domain controllers in the forest.

You should not use an authoritative restore to restore an entire domain controller, nor should you use it as part of a change-control infrastructure. Proper delegation of administration and change enforcement will optimize data consistency, integrity, and security.

To perform an authoritative restore, follow this four-step procedure:

1. Start the domain controller in DSRM.

2. Restore the desired backup, which is typically the most recent backup.

3. Use *ntdsutil* to mark desired objects, containers, or partitions as authoritative.

4. Restart in normal mode to propagate the changes.

> **MORE INFO   PERFORMING AN AUTHORITATIVE RESTORE**
>
> For more information about performing an authoritative restore, visit *http://technet .microsoft.com/en-us/library/cc755296(WS.10).aspx*.

Stopping AD DS to Perform Maintenance Procedures

Windows Server 2008 introduced a new feature called restartable AD DS that facilitates some Active Directory maintenance procedures. In Windows Server 2008 and Windows Server 2008 R2, AD DS appears in the Services console as a service that can be stopped and restarted like any other service. Stopping the AD DS service enables you to perform an offline defragmentation or update of a locally stored AD DS database while you are logged on to a domain controller normally. In earlier versions of Windows, you needed to start the computer in DSRM to perform such procedures.

> **MORE INFO   OFFLINE DEFRAGMENTATION**
>
> For specific instructions on how to perform an offline defragmentation of the AD DS database by using the *ntdsutil* command-line utility, visit *http://technet.microsoft.com/en-us /library/cc794920(WS.10).aspx*.

Although AD DS is stopped on a particular domain controller, other domain controllers can still service new domain logon requests. Even on the domain controller on which AD DS is stopped, you can continue to log on to the domain if other domain controllers are available to service the logon request. If no other domain controller is available, you can still log on to the server in DSRM by using the local Administrator account and the DSRM password, like in Windows 2000 Server or Windows Server 2003.

> **NOTE CAN YOU USE *DCPROMO* TO REMOVE AD DS WHEN AD DS IS STOPPED?**
>
> You can run *dcpromo /forceremoval* to forcefully remove AD DS from a domain controller while AD DS is stopped. However, you should use this procedure only if AD DS cannot be started.

Aside from improving the convenience of performing offline maintenance procedures to the AD DS database, stopping the AD DS service provides the additional benefit of preserving the availability of other services while you are performing those maintenance tasks. For example, if a domain controller is also a Dynamic Host Configuration Protocol (DHCP) server, the domain controller can continue to service DHCP clients when you are performing offline maintenance on AD DS.

> **NOTE STOPPING AD DS AT A COMMAND LINE**
>
> To stop AD DS at a command line, type **net stop ntds**.

Seizing Operations Master Roles

Certain domain and enterprise-wide services that are not suitable for multimaster updates are performed by a single domain controller in AD DS. The domain controllers that are assigned to perform these unique operations are called operations masters or flexible single master operations (FSMO) role holders. If a domain controller that holds an operations master role is lost and cannot be brought back online, you can use the *ntdsutil* utility to seize the lost operations master role.

> **MORE INFO OPERATIONS MASTER ROLES**
>
> For an introduction to FSMO roles and for specific instructions about how to use the *ntdsutil* utility to seize FSMO roles, see *http://support.microsoft.com/kb/255504*.

A domain controller whose FSMO roles have been seized should not be permitted to communicate with existing domain controllers in the forest. In this scenario, you should either format the hard disk and reinstall the operating system on such domain controllers or forcibly demote such domain controllers on a private network and then remove their metadata on a surviving domain controller in the forest by using the *ntdsutil /metadata cleanup* command.

Using Network Load Balancing to Support High-Usage Servers

Network Load Balancing (NLB) is used to support a highly used network service or application. An installable feature of Windows Server 2008 R2, NLB transparently distributes client requests among servers in a cluster by using virtual IP addresses and a shared name. From the perspective of the clients, the NLB cluster appears to be a single server.

In a common scenario, for example, NLB is used to create a *web farm*—a group of computers working to support a website or a set of websites. In some scenarios, it might be possible that a single, powerful server could be used to support the client traffic instead of many smaller web servers in an NLB farm. However, an NLB farm enables you to gradually increase the power of your solution by adding more servers (called hosts) to the farm as the need arises. NLB also provides the advantage of high availability because in such a cluster there is no single point of failure.

Aside from web farms, you can also use NLB to create a terminal server farm, a virtual private network (VPN) server farm, or an Internet Security & Acceleration (ISA) Server firewall cluster. Figure 9-5 shows a basic configuration of an NLB web farm located behind an NLB firewall cluster.

As a load balancing mechanism, NLB automatically detects servers that have been disconnected from the cluster and then redistributes client requests to the remaining live hosts. This feature prevents clients from sending requests to the failed servers. NLB also allows you the option to specify a load percentage that each host will handle. Clients are then statistically distributed among hosts so that each server receives its percentage of incoming requests.

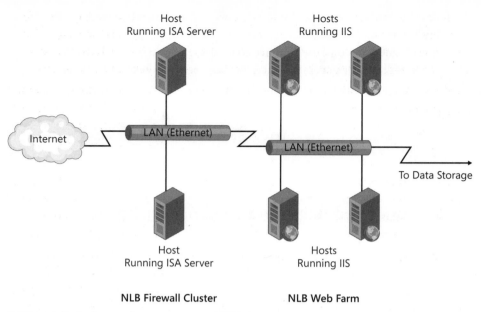

Host
Running ISA Server

Hosts
Running IIS

Internet

LAN (Ethernet)

LAN (Ethernet)

To Data Storage

Host
Running ISA Server

Hosts
Running IIS

NLB Firewall Cluster

NLB Web Farm

FIGURE 9-5 Basic diagram for two connected NLB clusters

Identifying Applications for NLB

The applications and services that run on NLB include stateful applications (those that maintain session state) and stateless applications. Maintaining session state means that the application or service collects information when first connecting to a cluster host and then retains the information for subsequent requests. During a user session, the same server must handle all the requests from the user to access that information. Applications and services that are stateless maintain no user or communication information for subsequent connections.

With a single server, maintaining session state presents no difficulty because the user always connects to the same server. However, when client requests are load balanced within an NLB cluster, without some type of persistence the client might not be directed to the same host for a series of client requests.

In NLB, you maintain session state with a *port rule affinity* between the client and a specific cluster host. Port rule affinity directs all client requests from the same IP address to the same NLB host. You can use port rules to specify the port rule affinity between clients and NLB cluster hosts.

Some of the common applications and services well-suited to run on NLB include the following:

- **Web applications** One of the most common of the solutions that use NLB is a web farm. A typical challenge in supporting web applications occurs when an application must maintain a persistent connection to a specific cluster host. For example, if a web application uses Hypertext Transfer Protocol Secure (HTTPS), the application should, for efficiency, contact the same cluster hosts within the cluster. Connecting to a different cluster host requires establishing a new Secure Sockets Layer (SSL) session, which creates excess network traffic and overhead on the client and server. NLB maintains affinity and reduces the possibility that a new SSL session needs to be established.

- **VPN remote access running on Routing and Remote Access Service (RRAS)**   Another solution that uses NLB involves using RRAS in Windows Server 2008 R2 to provide VPN remote connectivity. In the VPN solution, you combine multiple remote access servers running Windows Server 2008 R2 and RRAS to create a VPN remote access server farm.

- **Web content caching and firewall running on ISA Server**   You can also use NLB in solutions that include ISA Server to provide network security, network isolation, Network Address Translation (NAT), or web content caching. In ISA Server solutions, the design and deployment are integral parts of the ISA Server design and deployment process.

- **Application hosted on Remote Desktop Services**   When you run applications on Remote Desktop Services, the Remote Desktop Services clients can be load balanced across a number of computers running Remote Desktop Services. NLB works with the Remote Desktop Session Host role service to provide improved scalability and availability for Remote Desktop Services.

- **Custom applications**   NLB might be an appropriate method of improving scalability and availability for applications that your organization or third-party organizations have developed. Custom applications must adhere to the same criteria listed earlier in this section.

WHEN NOT TO USE NLB

In NLB, each host in the farm is connected to separate storage, and this data is not replicated among hosts. As a result, NLB is not well-suited to support services in which data is updated by users because data inconsistency among nodes could result. In particular, you should not use NLB to support database servers or file servers. However, many organizations use NLB to support a website front end to a single database server.

> **MORE INFO**   **NLB BEST PRACTICES**
>
> For a detailed list of NLB best practices, visit *http://technet.microsoft.com/en-us/library /cc740265(WS.10).aspx*. Although this information was written for earlier versions of Windows Server, the concepts are still valid.

Using Failover Clusters to Maintain High Availability

A *failover cluster* is a group of two or more computers used to minimize downtime for selected applications and services. The clustered servers (called nodes) are connected by physical cables to each other and to shared storage disks. If one of the cluster nodes fails, another node begins to take over service for the lost node in a process known as failover. As a result of failover, users connecting to the server experience minimal disruption in service.

Servers in a failover cluster can function in a variety of roles, including the roles of file server, print server, mail server, or database server, and they can provide high availability for a variety of other services and applications.

In most cases, the failover cluster includes a shared storage unit that is physically connected to all the servers in the cluster, although any given volume in the storage is accessed by only one server at a time.

Figure 9-6 illustrates the process of failover in a basic two-node failover cluster.

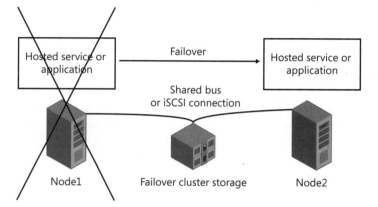

FIGURE 9-6 In a failover cluster, when one server fails, another takes over using the same storage

Server clusters can benefit your organization if:

- Your users depend on regular access to mission-critical data and applications to do their jobs.

- Your organization has established a limit on the amount of planned or unplanned service downtime that you can sustain. This is categorized by most companies as Recovery Time Objective (RTO).

- The cost of the additional hardware that server clusters require is less than the cost of having mission-critical data and applications offline during a failure.

Comparing NLB and Failover Clusters

NLB clusters and failover clusters are used for different purposes. Whereas NLB is used primarily for increased scalability of web servers, VPN servers, ISA Server firewalls, and terminal servers, failover clusters are most often used to increase the availability of database servers. Frequently, in fact, NLB clusters can work as a front end to a failover cluster, as in the case of a website that connects to a back-end database, illustrated in Figure 9-7.

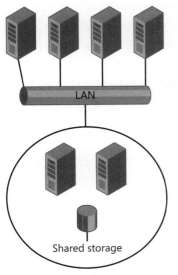

Web servers/NLB cluster

LAN

Shared storage

Database server/Failover cluster

FIGURE 9-7 An NLB cluster often acts as the front end to a back-end failover cluster

Preparing Failover Cluster Hardware

Failover clusters have fairly elaborate hardware requirements. To configure the hardware, review the following list of requirements for the servers, network adapters, cabling, controllers, and storage:

- **Servers** Use a set of matching computers that contain the same or similar components (recommended).

- **Network adapters and cabling** The network hardware, like other components in the failover cluster solution, must be compatible with Windows Server 2008 R2. If you use Internet Small Computer System Interface (iSCSI), your network adapters must be dedicated to either network communication or iSCSI, not both.

  In the network infrastructure that connects your cluster nodes, avoid having single points of failure. There are several ways to achieve this. You can connect your cluster nodes by multiple, distinct networks. Alternatively, you can connect your cluster nodes with one network that is constructed with teamed network adapters, redundant switches, redundant routers, or similar hardware that removes single points of failure.

- **Device controllers or appropriate adapters for the storage** If you are using Serial Attached SCSI or Fibre Channel, the mass-storage device controllers that are dedicated to the cluster storage should be identical in all clustered servers. They should also use the same firmware version. If you are using iSCSI, each clustered server must have one or more network adapters or host bus adapters (HBAs) that are dedicated to the cluster storage. The network you use for iSCSI cannot be used for network communication.

In all clustered servers, the network adapters you use to connect to the iSCSI storage target should be identical. It is also recommended that you use Gigabit Ethernet or higher. (Note also that for iSCSI you cannot use teamed network adapters.)

- **Storage**   You must use shared storage that is compatible with Windows Server 2008 R2. For a two-node failover cluster, the storage should contain at least two separate volumes configured at the hardware level.

  The first volume will function as the *witness disk*. A witness disk is a volume that holds a copy of the cluster configuration database. Witness disks, known as *quorum disks* in Windows Server 2003, are used in many, but not all, cluster configurations.

  The second volume will contain the files that are being shared to users. Storage requirements include the following:

  - To use the native disk support included in failover clustering, use basic disks, not dynamic disks.

  - It is recommended that you format the storage partitions with NTFS (for the witness disk, the partition must be NTFS).

  When deploying a storage area network (SAN) with a failover cluster, be sure to confirm with manufacturers and vendors that the storage, including all drivers, firmware, and software used for the storage, are compatible with failover clusters in Windows Server 2008 R2.

After you have met the hardware requirements and connected the cluster servers to storage, you can then install the Failover Cluster feature.

What Are Quorum Configurations?

Quorum configurations in a failover cluster determine the number of failures that the cluster can sustain before it stops running. In Windows Server 2008 R2, you can choose from among four quorum configurations. The first option is the node majority quorum configuration, which is recommended for clusters with an odd number of nodes. In node majority, the failover cluster runs as long as a majority of the nodes are running. The second option is the node and disk majority quorum configuration, which is recommended for clusters with an even number of nodes. In node and disk majority, the failover cluster uses a witness disk as a tiebreaker node and the failover cluster then runs as long as a majority of these nodes are online and available. The third option is the node and file share majority quorum configuration. In node and file share majority, which is recommended for clusters that have an even number of nodes and that lack access to a witness disk, a witness file share is used as a tiebreaker node and the failover cluster then runs as long as a majority of these nodes are online and available. The fourth and final option is the No Majority: Disk Only quorum configuration. In this configuration, which is generally not recommended, the failover cluster remains active as long as a single node and its storage remain online.

Lesson Summary

- You should deploy domain controllers with recovery in mind. Design storage with AD DS elements stored on dedicated volumes, and have in place a plan for recovery procedures.
- In Windows Server 2008 and Windows Server 2008 R2, you can stop AD DS as a service, which facilitates certain AD DS maintenance procedures, such as offline defragmentation.
- In NLB, many live servers simulate a single server and client requests are distributed to one host in the server farm. NLB is used to support high-usage web servers, terminal servers, ISA Server servers, and VPN servers.
- In a failover cluster, two or more servers (called nodes) share storage and only one node hosts a given service at any given time. Whenever a node fails, another node takes over the services that were hosted by the failed node. Failover clusters are typically used to support high availability for database servers, but they can also be used to support mail servers, print servers, and file servers.

Lesson Review

The following questions are intended to reinforce key information presented in this lesson. The questions are also available on the companion CD if you prefer to review them in electronic form.

NOTE ANSWERS

Answers to these questions and explanations of why each answer choice is correct or incorrect are located in the "Answers" section at the end of the book.

1. You are planning a failover cluster for a database server. You want the server to include two nodes, and you want to include a witness (quorum) disk in your design. Which quorum configuration should you choose?

    A. Node majority

    B. Node and disk majority

    C. Node and file share majority

    D. No Majority: Disk Only

2. You are designing a disaster recovery strategy for your AD DS environment. You need to ensure that your disaster recovery strategy includes steps to recovery from accidental deletions of OUs. What should you do?

   A. Plan to perform an authoritative restore.

   B. Plan to perform a nonauthoritative restore.

   C. Plan to perform a full server recovery.

   D. Plan to perform a critical volume recovery.

3. The domain controller that holds the PDC emulator role fails and you are unable to recover it. You take the domain controller offline and seize the PDC emulator role from this domain controller. You determine the cause of the failure to be a faulty motherboard. You replace the motherboard on this server. You want to bring the server back online. What should you do?

   A. Transfer the PDC emulator role back to this server.

   B. Perform an authoritative restore of the server.

   C. Perform a nonauthoritative restore of the server.

   D. Remove the server from AD DS and reinstall the operating system.

Chapter Review

To further practice and reinforce the skills you learned in this chapter, you can perform the following tasks:

- Review the chapter summary.
- Review the list of key terms introduced in this chapter.
- Complete the case scenario. This scenario sets up a real-world situation involving the topics in this chapter and asks you to create solutions.
- Complete the suggested practices.
- Take a practice test.

Chapter Summary

- When you need a solution to support data sharing, you should choose DFS if you want to provide users with local access to the same files across multiple sites.
- If you need a solution to support collaboration through team websites, you should choose Windows SharePoint Services when you want the sites to provide storage and version control for Office documents.
- If you need a solution to support collaboration through team websites, you should choose Microsoft Office SharePoint Server 2007 when you want the sites to support very advanced features, such as automated integration with business process.
- If you need a solution to encrypt full volumes in case a computer or a drive is stolen, you should choose BitLocker.
- If you need a solution that allows users to encrypt their personal files, you should choose EFS.
- If you need a solution that protects email and Office documents even if they leave your network, you should choose AD RMS.
- You should deploy domain controllers with recovery in mind. Design storage with AD DS elements stored on dedicated volumes, and have a plan in place for recovery procedures.
- NLB is used to provide high availability for web servers, terminal servers, ISA Server servers, and VPN servers.
- Failover clusters are typically used to provide high availability for database servers, but they can also be used to support mail servers, print servers, and file servers.

Key Terms

Do you know what these key terms mean? You can check your answers by looking up the terms in the glossary at the end of the book.

- Active Directory Rights Management Services (AD RMS)
- Authoritative restore
- BitLocker
- DFS folder
- DFS folder targets
- DFS namespace
- DFS namespace root
- DFS namespace server
- DFS Referral
- DFS Replication
- Distributed File System (DFS)
- Encrypting File System (EFS)
- Failover cluster
- Network Load Balancing (NLB)
- Nonauthoritative restore

Case Scenario

In the following case scenario you apply what you've learned in this chapter. You can find answers to these questions in the "Answers" section at the end of this book.

Case Scenario: Designing Solutions for Sharing, Security, and Availability

You are an IT administrator for Fourth Coffee, Inc., a specialty producer of coffee drinks based in Endicott, New York. The company has been experiencing rapid growth and has recently opened branch offices in Boulder, Austin, and Atlanta.

The *fourthcoffee.com* network consists of a single Active Directory domain. In the network, all servers are running Windows Server 2008 R2 and all clients are running Windows 7 Enterprise.

Recently, management has determined that new technical solutions are needed to meet new business needs. These needs have been specified in the following list:

- Project managers in any department of the company should be able to assemble teams made of members from any of the four sites, and every team should be able to create a team website quickly and easily. Team websites should be used to facilitate communication among team members and to provide announcements, calendars, blogs, and bulletin boards.

- Every department in the company should be associated with a single pathname to its network shares that remains consistent everywhere in the company network. All department shares should be available locally at all four sites, and queries for department shares should not cross WAN links.

- Confidential emails should be secured in a way that protects them from being read by unauthorized third parties.

- No single server failure should allow any portion of any database server deployed in the company to go offline.

You are a member of the team whose responsibility is to design solutions to meet these stated needs.

1. At a minimum, what technology should you use to meet the need to assemble team websites?

2. Which technology should you use to meet the goals for department file shares? How should you meet the requirement to avoid intersite communication for department share queries?

3. Which technology should you use to meet the requirement to protect confidential email?

4. Which feature should you use to meet the requirement for database servers?

Suggested Practices

To help you successfully master the exam objectives presented in this chapter, complete the following tasks.

Watch a Webcast

- **Practice**   Watch the webcast, "Deploying Microsoft Windows Rights Management Services," which you can access by visiting *https://msevents.microsoft.com/CUI /WebCastEventDetails.aspx?culture=en-US&EventID=1032286987&CountryCode=US*.

- **Practice**   Watch the webcast, "Planning and Deploying the Branch Office Technologies in Windows Server 2003 R2," which you can access by visiting *https://msevents .microsoft.com/CUI/WebCastEventDetails.aspx?EventID=1032283986&EventCategory =5&culture=en-US&CountryCode=US*. This webcast deals primarily with DFS, which has not changed substantially from Windows Server 2003 R2.

Read a White Paper

- **Practice**   Review the white papers, "Planning and Architecture for Office SharePoint Server 2007, Part 1," which you can download at *http://go.microsoft.com/fwlink/?LinkID =79552*, and "Planning and Architecture for Office SharePoint Server 2007, Part 2," which you can download at *http://go.microsoft.com/fwlink/?LinkId=85548*.

- **Practice** Review the white papers, "Planning and Architecture for Windows Share-Point Services 3.0 Technology, Part 1," which you can download at *http://go.microsoft.com/fwlink/?LinkId=79600*, and "Planning and Architecture for Windows SharePoint Services 3.0 Technology, Part 2,", which you can download at *http://go.microsoft.com/fwlink/?LinkId =85553*.

Take a Practice Test

The practice tests on this book's companion CD offer many options. For example, you can test yourself on just one exam objective, or you can test yourself on all the 70-647 certification exam content. You can set up the test so that it closely simulates the experience of taking a certification exam, or you can set it up in study mode so that you can look at the correct answers and explanations after you answer each question.

> *MORE INFO* **PRACTICE TESTS**
>
> For details about all the practice test options available, see the "How to Use the Practice Tests" section in this book's introduction.

CHAPTER 10

Planning and Designing a Public Key Infrastructure

Planning and designing a public key infrastructure (PKI) for a large organization is a complicated undertaking, but the process can be broken down into three general steps. First, as part of a team of stakeholders, you need to identify and assess the needs of the PKI. Second, you can design the PKI by mapping out the particular certification authorities (CAs) you need to create and the trust relationships among them. Third, you need to design the lifecycle management procedures for each CA: how certificates are issued, renewed, and revoked.

This chapter provides an overview of each of these three steps in the PKI design process.

Exam objectives in this chapter:

- Design and implement public key infrastructure.

Lessons in this chapter:

Before You Begin

To complete the lessons in this chapter, you must have the following:

- A basic understanding of Active Directory Domain Services (AD DS)
- A basic understanding of Active Directory Certificate Services (AD CS)

> ### REAL WORLD
> J.C. Mackin
>
> Windows Server 2008 and Windows Server 2008 R2 introduce a number of enhancements to AD CS: the inclusion of an Online Certificate Status Protocol (OCSP) responder, support for network device enrollment, support for Cryptography Next Generation (CNG) algorithms, and several other improvements. However, these new features are not available by default if your Active Directory directory service forest predates Windows Server 2008, which is very likely unless your network is brand new.
>
> Before you can take advantage of the new features offered by Windows Server 2008 enterprise CAs, you need to upgrade your preexisting (non-2008) Active Directory schema. (Note, however, that you *don't* need to upgrade any domain controllers or adjust any forest or domain functional levels.)

Lesson 1: Identifying PKI Requirements

In Windows Server 2008 networks, a PKI relies on one or more CAs deployed through AD CS. However, deploying a PKI is not as simple as adding the AD CS role in Server Manager. For most medium-sized and large organizations, implementing a PKI requires significant planning. Once the introduction of *PKI-enabled applications* or other needs trigger the implementation of a PKI, you need to review your organization's security policy. Then you need to assess other requirements for the PKI, such as business, external, and Active Directory requirements.

After you assess the needs of your organization in this way, you can design the PKI as a means to enforce your organization's security policies and to ensure that the new PKI remains aligned with the company's business and IT strategy.

> **After this lesson, you will be able to:**
> - Understand the function of a PKI.
> - Identify applications that require a PKI.
> - Understand many of the factors that you need to consider when performing a needs assessment for a PKI in a Windows Server 2008 network.
>
> **Estimated lesson time: 20 minutes**

Reviewing PKI Concepts

A PKI refers to the set of technologies that enable an organization to use public key cryptography. In public key cryptography, a mathematically related key pair consisting of a *public key* and a *private key* is used in the encryption, authentication, and verification processes. If the public key is used for encryption, only the private key can be used for decryption. If the private key is used for encryption, only the public key can be used for decryption. To maintain security of the PKI, the public keys can be shared with anyone, but the private key(s) must be kept private, never shared or compromised.

More specifically, a PKI is a system of *digital certificates*, CAs, and other *registration authorities* (RAs) that provides cryptographic keys for, and authenticates the validity of, each party involved in an electronic transaction. CA servers guarantee that the subject's public key belongs to the subject identity information that is contained in the certificates it issues. The certificate and its verification process add the element of trust to the functionality of the cryptographic keys, encryption algorithms, and hashes.

> **MORE INFO**   **PUBLIC KEY CRYPTOGRAPHY**
>
> For an introduction to public key cryptography, see "Understanding Public Key Cryptography," available at *http://technet.microsoft.com/en-us/library/aa998077(EXCHG.65).aspx*.

A PKI consists of the following basic components:

- **Digital certificates** Electronic credentials that include a public key and that are used to sign and encrypt data. Digital certificates are the foundation of a PKI.

- **One or more CAs** Trusted entities or services that issue digital certificates. When multiple CAs are used, they are typically arranged in a carefully prescribed order and perform specialized tasks, such as issuing certificates to subordinate CAs or issuing certificates to users.

- **Certificate policy and practice statements** These two documents outline how the CA and its certificates are to be used, the degree of trust that can be placed in these certificates, legal liabilities if the trust is broken, and so on.

- **Certificate repositories** A directory service or other location where certificates are stored and published. In a domain environment, Active Directory is the most likely publication point for certificates issued by Windows-based CAs.

- **Certificate verification systems** These include the Certificate Chain, Authority Information Access data, OCSP, certificate revocation lists (CRLs) and *CRL distribution points* (CDPs), and the *certificate verification* procedures written into PKI-enabled applications and processes.

> **MORE INFO   PUBLIC KEY INFRASTRUCTURE**
>
> For an introduction to PKI, see "Cryptography and Microsoft Public Key Infrastructure," available at *http://technet.microsoft.com/en-us/library/dd277320.aspx*.

Identifying PKI-Enabled Applications

One reason that an organization decides to deploy a PKI is that the organization introduces one or more applications that depend on a PKI. After the need for a PKI arises, you can begin to define the PKI in a way that best supports these applications. The way these *PKI-enabled applications* use a digital certificate will typically identify the certificate's intended purpose. A certificate has a predefined intended purpose that limits its possible uses. Intended purposes include Client Authentication, Server Authentication, Code Signing, Secure Email, Key Recovery Agent, and more.

The following list describes the most common applications and technologies that can lead an organization to consider deploying a PKI:

- **802.1x port-based authentication** 802.1x authentication allows only authenticated users or computers to access either an 802.11 wireless network or a wired Ethernet network. A PKI is required to support 802.1x when the Extensible Authentication Protocol-Transport Layer Security (EAP-TLS), Extensible Authentication Protocol-Tunneled Transport Layer Security (EAP-TTLS), or Protected Extensible Authentication Protocol (PEAP) authentication protocol is used.

- **Digital signatures**   A PKI is used for digital *signing. Digital signatures* secure Internet transactions by providing a method for verifying the source of the data and that content was not modified since it was signed. Depending on how a certificate is issued, digital signatures also provide nonrepudiation. In other words, data signers cannot deny that they are the data senders because they are the only users with access to the certificate's private key.

- **Encrypting File System (EFS)**   EFS provides a confidentiality service to NTFS. It employs user key pairs to encrypt and decrypt files and recovery agent key pairs for file recovery purposes. Certificates used for EFS are available from enterprise CAs. In an environment with no Microsoft enterprise CAs, all EFS certificates are created on first use of EFS by the local operating system and are self-signed.

- **Internet Protocol Security (IPsec)**   Certificates can be used to authenticate the two endpoints in an IPsec association. After authentication, IPsec can be used to encrypt and digitally sign all communications between the two endpoints. Certificates do not play a part in the actual encryption and signing of IPsec-protected data—they are used only to authenticate the two endpoints. Note also that in AD DS domains, Kerberos, not certificates, is typically used for authentication.

- **Secure email (S/MIME)**   Secure email, the industry standard for which is Secure /Multipurpose Internet Mail Extensions (S/MIME), provides confidential communication, data integrity, and nonrepudiation for email messages. S/MIME uses certificates to verify a sender's digital identity, the message's point of origin, and message authenticity. It also protects the confidentiality of messages by encrypting their content.

- **Smart card logon**   Smart cards are credit card–sized cards that contain a user certificate. You can use smart cards to provide strong authentication for interactive logons.

- **Code signing**   Code signing protects computers from the execution of unauthorized controls, drivers, or applications. Applications that support code signing, such as Microsoft Internet Explorer, can be configured to prevent execution of unsigned controls.

- **Virtual private networks (VPNs)**   VPNs allow remote users to connect to a private network by using tunneling protocols, such as Point-to-Point Tunneling Protocol (PPTP), Layer 2 Tunneling Protocol (L2TP), or Secure Socket Tunneling Protocol (SSTP). Not all VPN types use certificates. However, certificates increase the strength of user authentication and can provide authentication for IPsec if using L2TP with IPsec encryption.

- **Web authentication and encryption**   Distributing Secure Sockets Layer (SSL) certificates to a web server on either an intranet or the Internet allows a web client to validate the web server's identity and encrypt all data sent to and from the web server. All web servers offering SSL connections require a server certificate, typically issued by a third-party CA. Optionally, SSL connections can use client certificates (although this is rarely implemented).

Identifying Certificate Requirements

After you have determined which PKI-enabled applications your organization plans to deploy, you must determine who must acquire the certificates and the types of certificates that are required. Typically, certificates are deployed to the following subjects (also called end entities):

- **Users** A digital certificate uniquely identifies a user to a PKI-enabled application. A user can be assigned a single certificate that enables all applications or can receive application-specific certificates, such as an EFS encryption certificate that can be used for one purpose only. The certificates issued to the user are stored in the Current User certificate store.

- **Computers** A digital certificate uniquely identifies the computer when a user or computer connects to the computer where the certificate is installed. The certificate becomes the computer's identifier and is stored in the Local Machine certificate store. If the Client Authentication object identifier (OID) is included in the certificate in either the Enhanced Key Usage (EKU) extension or the Application Policies extension, an application can use the computer certificate to initiate connections. If the Server Authentication OID is included in the certificate in the EKU or Application Policies extension, the certificate can be used to authenticate the computer's identity when a client application connects.

- **Network devices** Several devices on a network allow the installation of certificates for client/server authentication. These devices include, but are not limited to, VPN appliances, firewalls, and routers. The actual process used to install a certificate on a network device is subject to the type of operating system and interfaces of the actual network device.

- **Signed Applications** Signing an application embeds a digital certificate into the compiled executable to verify that the executable has not been tampered with or modified since it was signed and to verify the source of the executable; it can also be used to control execution of the application. AppLocker is the new feature in Windows Server 2008 R2 and Windows 7 that manages signed applications.

EXAM TIP

Network device enrollment is a new feature offered by Windows Server 2008, and device certificate renewal is supported in Windows Server 2008 R2. Therefore, you are likely to see a general question about these topics on the 70-647 exam. Network device enrollment and renewal rely on the Network Device Enrollment Service (NDES). This service is the Microsoft implementation of the Simple Certificate Enrollment Protocol (SCEP), a communication protocol that enables software running on network devices (such as routers and switches, which cannot otherwise be authenticated on the network) to enroll for X.509 certificates from a CA.

- **Services** Some services require computer certificates for either authentication or encryption. Certificates are not actually issued to a service. Instead, the service certificate is stored either on the Local Machine store or in the user's profile of the associated service account. For example, if a certificate is installed for the World Wide Web (WWW) service of a web server, the certificate is stored in the Local Machine store. However, the EFS recovery agent certificate for the EFS service is stored in the user profile of the designated EFS recovery agent.

> **NOTE   WHERE SHOULD YOU INSTALL A CERTIFICATE FOR A SERVICE?**
>
> The easiest way to determine where to install a certificate for a service is to investigate what credentials the service uses to authenticate. If the service uses Local System, then the certificate must be stored in the Local Machine store. If the service uses a user account and password, then the certificate must be stored in that specific user's profile.

Identifying Certificate Security Requirements

Certificate requirements are driven by the PKI-enabled applications your organization plans to use. Identifying these requirements will let you determine the properties of the certificates needed. For each set of certificates, you should identify the following security requirements:

- **Length of the private key**   In a typical deployment, the lengths of private keys are nested so that each level in the PKI hierarchy has a key whose length is half that of the level above it. For example, in a PKI, issued user certificates might have 1,024-bit keys, issuing CAs might have 2,048-bit keys, and root CAs might have 4,096-bit keys. Note that because longer keys are harder to mathematically attack, they support proportionately longer lifetimes but impose lengthier calculation times during normal use.

> **MORE INFO   CA HIERARCHIES**
>
> CA hierarchies, issuing CAs, and root CAs are discussed in more detail in Lesson 2, "Designing the CA Hierarchy."

In choosing a length for each CA in the *CA hierarchy*, the biggest restriction is the set of applications that will use the CA hierarchy for certificates. Some applications are known to not support keys larger than a certain value.

- **Cryptographic algorithms that are used with certificates**   The standard settings for certificates issued by a Windows Server 2008 R2 CA can meet typical security needs. However, you might want to specify stronger security settings for certificates that are used by certain user groups. For example, you can specify longer private key lengths and shorter certificate lifetimes for certificates used to provide security for very valuable information. You can also specify the use of smart cards for private key storage to provide additional security.

- **Lifetimes of certificates and private keys and the renewal cycle**   A certificate has a predefined validity period that includes a start date and time and an end date and time. You cannot change an issued certificate's validity period after it has been issued. *Certificate lifetimes* are determined by the type of certificate, your security requirements, standard practices in your industry, and government regulations.

NOTE CERTIFICATE LIFETIMES

When determining certificate lifetimes for a PKI, a good rule of thumb is to make the validity period of the certificate for a parent CA at least twice as long as the certificate for a subordinate CA. In addition, the validity period of the certificate for an issuing CA should be at least twice as long as the maximum validity period of any certificates issued by that same CA. For example, you might give issued user certificates a lifetime of one year, the certificate for the issuing CA a lifetime of five years, and the certificate for the root CA of the PKI a lifetime of ten years.

■ **Special private key storage and management requirements** An organization's security policy can require specific security measures for a CA's private key. For example, an organization might have to implement *Federal Information Processing Standards (FIPS) 140-2* protection of the CA's private key to meet industry or organizational security requirements.

MORE INFO WHERE CAN YOU READ FIPS 140-2?

FIPS 140-2, "Security Requirements for Cryptographic Modules," can be found at *http://csrc.nist.gov/publications/fips/fips140-2/fips1402.pdf*.

Measures you can take to protect the CA's private key include using a *cryptographic service provider* (CSP), which stores the CA's private key material on the computer's local hard disk; a smart card CSP, which stores the CA's private key material on a smart card associated with a personal identification number; and a hardware security module (HSM), which provides the highest level of security for private keys in dedicated hardware devices.

✔ **Quick Check**
   ■ If the lifetime of an issued user certificate is two years, what should normally be the minimum lifetime of the certificate for the issuing CA?

Quick Check Answer
   ■ Four years

Reviewing the Company Security Policy

After the need for a PKI is established and the required certificates are identified, you should review the organization's security policy. A security policy is a document that is approved and supported by senior management and is created by members of an organization's legal, human resources, and IT departments, which defines an organization's security standards. Legal and regulatory compliance requirements must be incorporated into the company's security policies. The policies usually include the assets an organization considers valuable, the potential threats to these assets, and, in general terms, the measures that must be taken to protect these assets.

The security policy should be updated to answer high-level PKI questions, such as the following:

- What applications should be secured with certificates?
- What kind of security services should be offered by using certificates?

In general, when planning and designing a PKI, it is essential to remember that a PKI should enforce your organization's security policy. A PKI, after all, is only as secure as the policies and procedures that the organization implements.

Assessing Business Requirements

Business requirements define an organization's goals. They affect the design of the PKI by allowing the PKI to enhance business goals and processes. For example, the following business requirements can affect a CA hierarchy design.

- **Minimizing PKI-associated costs** When reviewing CA hierarchy designs, you might have to choose a CA hierarchy that deploys the fewest CAs. For example, some organizations combine the roles of policy CAs and issuing CAs into a single CA in the hierarchy, deploying a two-tier hierarchy rather than a three-tier hierarchy.

- **High availability of certificate issuance** An organization can require that a CA be consistently available to ensure that no certificate requests fail due to a CA being down for any reason. To ensure that a CA is always available, you should implement clustering on the issuing CA that issues certificates based on the defined *certificate template*. If your up-time requirements are not as stringent, you might consider publishing the certificate template at more than one CA in the CA hierarchy, protecting against the failure of a single CA.

- **Liability of PKI participants** A CA hierarchy includes policy CAs that define the liability of the CA. The liability should provide sufficient coverage for transactions that use CA-issued certificates. Your organization's legal department must review this liability definition to ensure that the definition is legally correct and binding on all participants in the PKI.

Assessing External Requirements

In some cases, an organization might have to meet external requirements, such as those defined by other organizations or by the governments of countries in which the organization conducts business.

Examples of external requirements include the following:

- **Enabling external organizations to recognize employee-used certificates**   If you need other organizations to recognize the certificates assigned to entities in your organization, you can choose not to deploy an internal PKI and instead simply obtain certificates from a *public CA*, such as VeriSign or Thawte. Alternatively, you can use *cross-certification* or *qualified subordination* to define which external certificates you trust.

- **Using your organization's certificate at partner organizations**   Your employees might use the certificates issued by your CA hierarchy for encryption or signing purposes at another organization. In this case, you might have to create custom certificates to meet the requirements of the other organization.

- **Industry or government legislation**   Several countries have legislation that affects the design of a CA hierarchy. For example, Canada enforces the Personal Information Protection and Electronic Documents Act (PIPEDA), which regulates the management of a customer's personal information when held by a private-sector company. The act requires that someone be accountable for compliance and that this person be involved in the deployment and design of the CA hierarchy to ensure that all requirements of the act are enforced in the design.

- **Certificates for nonemployees**   If you issue certificates to nonemployees, you can use a CA hierarchy to deploy a separate certificate policy that includes greater detail for external clients.

Assessing Active Directory Requirements

You should make several preparations before you install a Windows Server 2008 R2 enterprise CA in a Windows 2000 Server or Windows Server 2003 Active Directory environment. These preparations include the following:

- **Determining the number of untrusted forests in the environment**   Prior to Windows Server 2008 R2, the number of forests in your environment had a large effect on the number of enterprise CAs required in your AD CS deployment. An enterprise CA could issue certificates only to users and computers with accounts in the same forest. If multiple forests had to consume certificates from the PKI, you had to deploy at least one enterprise CA per forest. In Windows Server 2008 R2, you can support entities in multiple forests with a single CA, reducing the number of CAs. Bidirectional forest trusts are required for cross-forest Active Directory PKI, as well as the interforest replication of certificate templates.

- **Determining the number of domains in the forest**   If more than one dom[...]
  the forest, one of the major design decisions is which domain will host the[...]
  selection of which domain will host the computer accounts of the CA con[...]
  will depend largely on whether your organization uses centralized or de[...]
  management. In a centralized model, all the CAs will typically be place[...]
  domain. In a decentralized environment, you might end up deployin[...]
  domains.

- **Determining the membership of the local Administrators groups for a memb[...]
  server**   If you use CSPs to protect a CA's private key, all members of the CA's local
  Administrators group will be able to export the CA's private key. You should start
  identifying which domain or organizational unit (OU) in a domain will best limit the
  number of local administrators. For example, an organization that has deployed an
  empty forest root might choose to deploy all enterprise CAs as members of the forest
  root domain to limit the number of local administrators on the CA.

- **Determining the schema version of the domain**   To implement Windows
  Server 2008 CAs and take advantage of all the new features introduced for AD CS,
  you must implement the latest version of the Active Directory Domain Services
  schema. The Windows Servers 2008 schema can be deployed in forests that contain
  Windows 2000 Server, Windows Server 2003, and Windows Server 2008 domain
  controllers.

Assessing Certificate Template Requirements

Certificate templates provide a practical way to implement *certificate enrollment* in a managed Active Directory environment. Because of the different versions of certificate templates
released with each version of Windows Server, compatibility issues must be identified as part
of your PKI planning.

Historically, static V1 certificate templates were introduced with Windows 2000 Server.
With Windows Server 2003, customization was introduced with V2 certificate templates.
With Windows Server 2008 R2, more certificate templates and certificate template properties
(compared with the Windows Server 2003 templates) became available (including properties
related to CNG). The new template types in Windows Server 2008 are called V3 templates.

Because of dependencies to the underlying operating system, Windows Server 2008 templates can be assigned only to CAs that are running on Windows Server 2008. Only Windows
Vista client computers, Windows 7 client computers, and Windows Server 2008 computers
can enroll for V3 certificate templates.

If you have installed only V2 certificates in your AD DS forest, you should upgrade the
existing templates and add the new V3 certificate templates. If you do not have any certificate templates, all V1, V2, and V3 certificate templates are simply added to the configuration
container of your AD DS forest.

In this practice, you review your current networking environment, either at the enterprise or within your home network, and identify the various potential applications for digital certificate use to improve the security of the environment.

EXERCISE Determine Potential Use of Digital Certificates Within Your Networking Environment

In this exercise, you review your computer and network operating systems and applications and document the potential need for strong authentication, nonrepudiation, confidentiality, and integrity protection and verification by using digital certificates.

1. User authentication
   - SSL/TLS tunnels
   - IPsec tunnels
   - Smart cards
   - Digital signatures
2. Computer authentication
   - L2TP tunnels
   - SSL tunnels
   - DNS Security Extensions (DNSSEC) signatures
3. Network device authentication
   - DNSSEC signatures
4. Digital signature use: Authentication, nonrepudiation, and integrity validation
5. VPN use (securing data in transit)
   - IPsec: user authentication
   - L2TP: computer authentication and integrity validation
   - SSL: web server authentication, confidentiality, and integrity validation
6. Encryption use (securing data at rest)
   - EFS: user authentication
   - BitLocker: user authentication

Lesson Summary

- A PKI is a system of digital certificates, CAs, and other RAs that enables an organization to use public key cryptography.
- The following technologies require a PKI or digital certificates: digital signatures, EFS, SSL, S/MIME, smart cards, and code signing. In addition, the following technologies can require a PKI or digital certificates: 802.1x, IPsec, SSL, and VPNs.

- After you have determined which PKI-enabled applications your organization plans to deploy, you must determine who must acquire the certificates, the types of certificates that are required, and the security requirements for those certificates.
- As part of the process of planning a PKI for an organization, you should review the organization's existing security policy, along with its business, Active Directory, and certificate template requirements, and any other external requirements.

Lesson Review

You can use the following questions to test your knowledge of the information in Lesson 1, "Identifying PKI Requirements." The questions are also available on the companion CD if you prefer to review them in electronic form.

> **NOTE ANSWERS**
>
> Answers to these questions and explanations of why each answer choice is correct or incorrect are located in the "Answers" section at the end of the book.

1. Which of the following applications does NOT require the use of certificates?
   A. Encrypting File System (EFS)
   B. Secure/Multipurpose Internet Mail Extensions (S/MIME)
   C. Internet Protocol Security (IPsec)
   D. Secure Sockets Layer (SSL)

2. Which of the following is NOT a legitimate business reason to require the use of digital certificates or a PKI?
   A. Business partnership requirements
   B. Legal or regulatory requirements
   C. Corporate security policy requirements
   D. Corporate loan requirements

3. Which of the following is used to control the use of digitally signed executables?
   A. DirectAccess
   B. Hyper-V
   C. AppLocker
   D. OCSP

Lesson 2: Designing the CA Hierarchy

To design the CA hierarchy in a PKI means to determine the actual CAs that your PKI will use and the trust relationships between them. In most medium-sized and large networks, deploying more than one CA is recommended.

This lesson describes the considerations that go into determining how many CAs to deploy, the types of CAs to deploy, and how many tiers of CAs are suitable for your organization's PKI.

> **After this lesson, you will be able to:**
> - Understand the advantages and disadvantages of deploying an internal CA versus relying on an external CA.
> - Understand the advantages and disadvantages of enterprise CAs versus stand-alone CAs.
> - Understand the difference between a root CA and a subordinate CA.
> - Understand the advantages of using a two-tier or three-tier hierarchy in your PKI.
> - Design a PKI hierarchy for an organization.
>
> **Estimated lesson time: 30 minutes**

Planning the CA Infrastructure

Before you can implement a PKI that meets the security needs and certificate requirements for your organization, you need to make a number of decisions about how you will deploy CAs. Planning the CA infrastructure for your organization involves making decisions about the following:

- Location and protection of the root CA
- Internal versus third-party CAs
- CA types and roles
- Number of CAs required

> **NOTE   CAS IN BRANCH OFFICES**
> A new capability in Windows Server 2008 R2 is that you can install the Certification Authority service on a Windows Server 2008 R2 Server core server.

Designing Root CAs

A CA infrastructure consists of a hierarchy of CAs that are trusted by a common root CA, making the root CA the pinnacle of trust for the PKI. The root CA certifies other CAs to publish and manage certificates within the organization. Because of the devastating results if they are compromised, root CAs are typically stand-alone (not integrated with Active Directory) and typically are never connected to a network (the offline root CA).

Selecting Internal CAs vs. Third-Party CAs

Depending on the functionality that you require, the capabilities of your IT infrastructure and IT administrators, and the costs that your organization can support, you might choose to base your CA infrastructure on internal CAs, third-party CAs, or a combination of internal and third-party CAs.

INTERNAL CERTIFICATION AUTHORITIES

If your organization conducts most of its business with partner organizations and wants to maintain control of how certificates are issued, internal CAs are the best choice. Internal CAs:

- Allow an organization to maintain direct control over its security policies.
- Allow an organization to align its certificate policy with its overall security policy.
- Can be integrated with the AD DS infrastructure of the organization.
- Can be expanded to include additional functionality and users at relatively little extra cost.

The disadvantages of using internal CAs include the following:

- The organization must manage its own certificates.
- The deployment schedule for internal CAs might be longer than that for CAs available from third-party service providers.
- The organization must accept liability for problems with the PKI.

EXTERNAL CERTIFICATION AUTHORITIES

If your organization conducts most of its business with external customers and clients and wants to outsource certificate issuing and management processes, you might choose to use third-party CAs. Third-party CAs:

- Allow customers a greater degree of confidence when conducting secure transactions with the organization.
- Allow the organization to take advantage of the expertise of a professional service provider.
- Allow the organization to use certificate-based security technology while developing an internally managed PKI.
- Allow the organization to take advantage of the provider's understanding of the technical, legal, and business issues associated with certificate use.

The disadvantages associated with the use of third-party CAs include the following:

- They typically involve a high cost per certificate.
- They might require the development of two management standards—one for internally issued certificates and one for commercially issued certificates.

- They allow less flexibility in configuring and managing certificates.

- The organization must have access to the third-party CAs in order to access the CRLs.

- Autoenrollment is not possible.

- They allow only limited integration with the internal directories, applications, and infra-structure of the organization.

Defining CA Types and Roles

To plan your CA infrastructure, you need to understand the different types of CAs available with Windows Server 2008 and the roles that they can play. Windows Server 2008 R2 Certificate Services supports the following two types of CAs:

- Enterprise
- Stand-alone

Enterprise and stand-alone CAs can be configured as either root CAs or subordinate CAs. Subordinate CAs can further be configured as either intermediate CAs (also referred to as policy CAs) or issuing CAs.

Before you create your CA infrastructure, you need to determine the type or types of CAs that you plan to use and define the specialized roles that you plan to have each CA assume.

ENTERPRISE VS. STAND-ALONE CERTIFICATION AUTHORITIES

Enterprise CAs are integrated with Active Directory and are typically used if the subjects of the certificates to be issued are in your Active Directory environment. Enterprise CAs can publish certificates and CRLs to Active Directory. Enterprise CAs use information stored in Active Directory, including user accounts and security groups, to approve or deny certificate requests. When a certificate is issued, the enterprise CA uses information in the certificate template to generate a certificate with the appropriate attributes for that certificate type.

If you want to enable automated certificate approval and automatic user certificate enroll-ment, you must use enterprise CAs to issue certificates. Additionally, only enterprise CAs can issue certificates that enable smart card logon, because this process requires that smart card certificates be mapped automatically to the user accounts in Active Directory.

Stand-alone CAs are typically used if the subjects of the certificates to be issued are not in your Active Directory environment. Stand-alone CAs do not require Active Directory and do not use or provide certificate templates if the server is not a member of a domain. If you use stand-alone CAs in this manner, all information about the requested certificate type must be included in the certificate request. Root CAs are often stand-alone CAs to avoid the network-ing requirement of Active Directory. By default, all certificate requests submitted to stand-alone CAs are held in a pending queue until a CA administrator approves them.

You can configure stand-alone CAs to issue certificates automatically on request, but this is less secure and is usually not recommended because the requests are not authenticated. From a performance perspective, using stand-alone CAs with automatic issuance enables you to issue certificates more quickly than you can by using enterprise CAs. However, using

stand-alone CAs to issue a high volume of certificates usually comes at a h
cost, because an administrator must manually review and then approve or
cate request. For this reason, stand-alone CAs are best used with public key
tions on extranets and the Internet, when users do not have Windows accou
volume of certificates to be issued and managed is relatively low.

In addition, you must use stand-alone CAs to issue certificates when you ar
party directory service or when Active Directory is not available.

> **NOTE MIXING STAND-ALONE AND ENTERPRISE CAS**
>
> You can use both enterprise and stand-alone CAs in your organization.

Table 10-1 lists the options that each type of CA supports.

TABLE 10-1 Options for Enterprise vs. Stand-Alone CAs

OPTION	ENTERPRISE CA	STAND-ALONE CA
Publish certificates in Active Directory and use Active Directory to validate certificate requests	X	
Take the CA offline		X
Configure the CA to issue certificates automatically	X	
Administrators approve certificate requests (default)		X
Use certificate templates	X	X (nondomain member)
Authenticate requests to Active Directory	X	

In general, you should deploy a stand-alone CA if:

- The CA is an offline root or offline intermediate CA.
- Support of templates that you can customize is not required.
- A strong security and approval model is required.
- Fewer certificates are enrolled and the manual work that you must do to issue certificates is acceptable.
- Subjects are heterogeneous and not members of Active Directory.
- The CA is combined with a third-party RA solution in a multiforest or heterogeneous environment.
- The CA issues certificates to routers through NDES SCEP.

You should deploy an enterprise CA if:

- A large number of certificates should be enrolled and approved automatically.
- Availability and redundancy are mandatory.

jects are Active Directory members.

- Features such as autoenrollment or modifiable templates are required.
- Key archival and recovery are required to escrow encryption keys.

THE ROOT CA

A *root CA* is required in each PKI hierarchy and is at the top of a certification hierarchy. Clients in your organization trust the root CA unconditionally by definition.

Because there is no higher certifying authority in the certification hierarchy, the root CA certificate is self-signed. The root CA is typically used only to certify subordinate CAs, but in smaller environments, it can also issue certificates to end entities, like computers and users.

A root CA serves as the foundation on which you base your CA trust model. Different CAs might also verify this relationship by using different security standards based on its policy; therefore, it is important to understand the policies and procedures of the root CA before choosing to trust that authority to verify public keys.

The root CA is the most important CA in your hierarchy. If your root CA is compromised, every other CA and certificate in your hierarchy might be compromised. You can maximize the security of the root CA by keeping it disconnected from the network (always offline) and using subordinate CAs to issue certificates to other subordinate CAs or to end users. Certify your subordinate CAs by using the good old sneaker net and a USB thumb drive.

THE SUBORDINATE CA

CAs that are not root CAs are considered *subordinate CAs*. The first subordinate CA in a hierarchy obtains its CA certificate from the root CA. In a two-tier PKI hierarchy, the subordinate CA is an *issuing CA* that provides certificates to end entities (subjects). In a three-tier PKI hierarchy, the second-tier subordinate CAs (referred to as intermediate CAs) are subordinate to a root CA (top tier), but also serve as a higher certifying authority to one or more subordinate CAs (third tier). In this scenario, this intermediate CA issues CA server certificates only to third-tier subordinate CAs.

Intermediate CAs are typically used to create branches in the PKI hierarchy, providing different levels of security and trust within the PKI hierarchy. Intermediate CAs are often referred to as *policy CAs* because they define their security structure and intended trust level by policy. The need for multiple intermediate CAs is defined by the need for differing levels of security and trust to be provided by an individual intermediate CA and its subordinate issuing CAs, for instance, a policy CA for governmental PKI use versus a policy CA for commercial PKI use. A policy CA can be online or offline.

> **NOTE POLICY CAS**
>
> Many commercial organizations use one offline root CA and two policy CAs—one to support internal subjects (enterprise) and another to support external subjects (stand-alone). If the organization must also provide certificates for governmental use, a third policy CA might be required.

The next level in the three-tier CA hierarchy contains issuing CAs. The issuing CA issues certificates to end entities, such as users and computers, and is almost always online. You might need multiple issuing CAs to provide services in multiple geographic locations or to provide greater capacity and availability.

Another component of the PKI hierarchy is the RA. The RA is used to verify the identity of a user who is applying for a certificate and to submit the request for a certificate to the issuing CA. Unlike a CA, however, an RA does not issue certificates or CRLs; it merely processes transactions on behalf of the CA.

The hierarchy consisting of a root CA, policy CAs, and issuing CAs is illustrated in Figure 10-1.

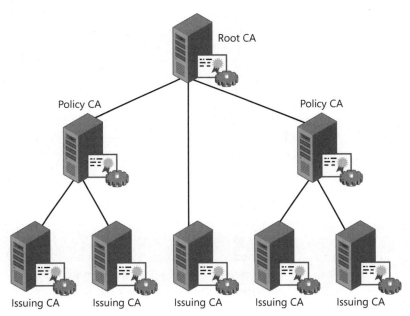

FIGURE 10-1 CA hierarchy roles

Using Offline CAs

Securing your CA hierarchy is critical. If an intruder can gain access to a CA, either physically or by means of the network, he or she might retrieve the CA's private key and then impersonate the CA in order to gain access to valuable network resources. The compromise of even one CA key invalidates the security protection provided by it and any CAs below it in the hierarchy. For this reason, it is important to avoid connecting root CAs to the network.

To ensure the reliability of your CA infrastructure, you should consider specifying that any nonissuing root and intermediate CAs must be kept offline. This minimizes the risk of the CA private keys becoming compromised. Build the CA on a stand-alone (nondomain member) computer running Windows 2000 Server, Windows Server 2003, Windows Server 2008, or Windows Server 2008 R2 by disabling or removing (preferred) its network adapter and then configuring it as a stand-alone CA. Make sure that you keep CAs in a physically secure area with controlled access.

> **IMPORTANT** **THE ROOT CA SHOULD BE A STAND-ALONE, WORKGROUP CA**
>
> Installing an offline CA on a server that is a member of a domain can cause problems with a secure channel when you bring the CA back online after a long offline period. This is because the computer account password changes every 30 days. You can get around this by making offline CA computers members of a workgroup.
>
> Also, installing an offline CA as an enterprise CA can cause Active Directory to have problems updating when you disconnect the server from the network. Therefore, do not use an enterprise CA as a root CA.

When a CA is an offline CA, you publish its certificate and CRL in Active Directory by copying them onto removable media and physically transporting them to a domain controller (sneaker net). You also use sneaker net to process certificate requests for subordinate CA certificates.

Because offline CAs process a small number of certificate requests at infrequent intervals, the administrative costs of maintaining offline CAs are low.

> **✓ Quick Check**
> - Why should a root CA remain offline?
>
> **Quick Check Answer**
> - To protect the entire PKI from becoming compromised in the case of a network attack

Determining the Number of CAs Required

After you have identified your application and user requirements, you can begin to estimate the number of CAs that you need to deploy. If your organization has limited certificate requirements, a small user base, and limited expansion goals, a single CA might be sufficient. By using a single CA, you can still meet a variety of needs by customizing and deploying certificate templates and by using role separation. However, if availability or distributed functionality of Certificate Services is a priority, you must deploy multiple CAs. You also need multiple CAs if you want separate CAs to issue certificates for different purposes.

To determine the number of CAs required, answer the following questions in this order:

- First, do you require only one CA? If security requirements are strict, you are supporting only a single application and location, and 100 percent availability of the CA is not critical, you might be able to use a single root and issuing CA. Otherwise, you probably require one root and one or more subordinate CAs.

- If you need more than one CA, how many root CAs do you require? Although not typical, you might have the need for separate PKI hierarchies. Generally, it is recommended that you have only one root CA as a single source of trust. With multiple root CAs, root maintenance and maintaining an appropriate trust model becomes much more difficult.

- However, organizations with a decentralized security administration model, such as corporations with multiple, largely independent business units and no strong central administrative body, might require more than one root CA.

- How many intermediate or policy CAs do you need? You will need one policy CA for each different set of PKI security requirements. This could be based on different cost centers or divisions within the organization, internal versus external subjects, interfacing with partners' PKI systems, interfacing with government PKI systems, or interfacing with multinational PKI systems.

- How many issuing CAs do you need?

The number of intermediate and issuing CAs that you deploy depends on the following factors:

- **Usage**   Certificates can be issued for a number of purposes (for example, secure email, network authentication, and so on). Each of these uses might involve different issuing policies. Using separate CAs provides a basis for administering each policy separately.

- **Organizational or geographic divisions**   You must have different policies for issuing certificates, depending on the role of an entity or its physical location in the organization. You can create separate subordinate CAs to administer these policies.

- **Distribution of the certificate load**   You can deploy multiple issuing CAs to distribute the certificate load to meet site, network, and server requirements. For example, if network links between sites are slow or discontinuous, you might need to place issuing CAs at each site to meet Certificate Services performance and usability requirements.

- **The need for flexible configuration**   You can tailor the CA environment (key strength, physical protection, protection against network attacks, and so on) to provide a balance between security and usability. For example, you can renew keys and certificates more frequently for the intermediate and issuing CAs that are at high risk for compromise, without requiring a change to established root trust relationships. Also, when you use more than one subordinate CA, you can turn off a subsection of the CA hierarchy without affecting established root trust relationships for the rest of the hierarchy.

- **The need for redundant services**   If one enterprise CA fails, redundancy makes it possible for another issuing CA to provide users with uninterrupted service.

Strive to have only as many CAs as you need to function efficiently. Deploying more CAs than you need creates an unnecessary management burden and introduces additional areas of security vulnerability.

You are an enterprise administrator at Humongous Insurance, Inc., a company that specializes in selling automobile insurance at discount prices. The company consists of a headquarters in New York City and three branch offices in Albany, Binghamton, and Buffalo. The company employs about 800 workers among its four office sites. The Humongous Insurance network consists of a single Active Directory domain, *humongousinsurance.com*.

Humongous Insurance is planning to launch a new version of its website that allows customers to view confidential data. In advance of the new site launch, the company has recently updated its written security policy. The chief security officer has given you the responsibility of designing a PKI to meet the new security needs of the company. Currently, the company does not have any CA deployed.

The company's updated written security policy includes the following requirements:

- The website must require an encrypted Hypertext Transfer Protocol (HTTP) connection when users view account data.
- All email messages and attachments sent among employees must be encrypted.
- All remote server administration must be conducted over an encrypted channel.
- At all of the four company branches, access to the company wireless network must require smart card authentication.

EXERCISE   Planning for a PKI Deployment

In this exercise, you review the business and technical requirements and answer specific questions to help you plan for PKI deployment.

1. Name the specific applications implied by the security policy that require the use of public key cryptography.

    - Web encryption (SSL) for the encrypted HTTP connection when users view account data.
    - Secure email and S/MIME to encrypt email messages and attachments sent among employees.
    - Smart card authentication (with 802.1x) to support the smart card requirement for wireless access.

    (Note that although IPsec is required for the remote server administration over an encrypted channel and can use digital certificates for authentication, IPsec uses Kerberos by default in an Active Directory environment.)

2. Who must obtain the certificates for each of these applications? In particular, specify whether each application requires certificates for users or computers.

    - Web encryption: only the web server (computer) must obtain an SSL server certificate.
    - Secure email and attachments: all users in the organization must obtain certificates.

- Smart card authentication: users needing wireless access must obtain a smart card (which includes a user certificate).

3. For each of the applications, specify whether the certificates required should be assigned by a public CA, an in-house stand-alone CA, or an in-house enterprise CA.

   - Web encryption: the web server should obtain a certificate from a public CA such as VeriSign or Thawte.

   - Secure email: users should obtain certificates from an in-house enterprise CA.

   - Smart card authentication: users should obtain certificates from an in-house enterprise CA.

4. Given the size of the company and the best practices for PKI deployments, design the CA hierarchy for the certificate infrastructure. Specifically, determine how many tiers are needed for the certificate infrastructure; whether a root CA, intermediate CAs, and issuing CAs are needed; and which of these should be kept online and which should be kept offline.

   - Large companies such as Humongous Insurance should include three tiers in the CA hierarchy. The root CA should be kept offline, the intermediate CAs should also be kept offline, and the issuing CAs should be kept online.

Lesson Summary

- To plan a CA infrastructure, you need to determine how many CAs to deploy, the types and roles of CAs to deploy, and the trust relationships among those CAs.

- Within a PKI, the pinnacle of trust is the root CA. The root CA should be kept offline for its entire life. Beneath this root CA, a PKI can include any number of subordinate CAs. A subordinate CA can act as a parent to verify the integrity of another subordinate CA. When a PKI includes three tiers in this way, the higher subordinate is known as an intermediate CA or policy CA. CAs that actively issue certificates are found at the lowest level of the hierarchy and are known as issuing CAs.

- As part of the PKI design process, on a case-by-case basis, you need to determine whether to acquire certificates from an internal CA or an external CA.

- As part of the PKI design process, you need to determine which CAs in your PKI should be enterprise CAs and which should be stand-alone CAs.

Lesson Review

You can use the following questions to test your knowledge of the information in Lesson 2, "Designing the CA Hierarchy." The questions are also available on the companion CD if you prefer to review them in electronic form.

NOTE ANSWERS

Answers to these questions and explanations of why each answer choice is correct or incorrect are located in the "Answers" section at the end of the book.

1. You work as an IT administrator in a large company, City Power and Light. The *cpandl.com* network consists of a single AD DS domain.

   You are a member of a team designing a new in-house PKI for use with EFS. Your goals are to minimize the risk that the entire PKI will be compromised and to minimize the administrative overhead of publishing certificates. Which of the following CAs should you deploy for your PKI hierarchy? (Choose two. Each correct answer represents part of the solution.)

   A. Offline root CA

   B. Online root CA

   C. Enterprise subordinate CA

   D. Stand-alone subordinate CA

2. You work as an IT administrator in a large company, City Power and Light, which operates in an Active Directory environment. The company needs a PKI branch to authenticate its internal users, computers, network devices, and applications. It also plans to develop a relationship with an external business partner that requires an integrated and heightened joint security structure. Following best practices, what PKI systems should you deploy?

   A. One offline root CA, one enterprise issuing CA, one policy CA, and its subordinate enterprise issuing CA

   B. One online root CA, one stand-alone issuing CA, one policy CA, and its subordinate stand-alone issuing CA

   C. One online root and issuing CA

   D. One offline root CA and one policy CA with two subordinate stand-alone issuing CAs

3. Which of the following is used to verify the identity of the end entity before issuing a digital certificate?

   A. CA

   B. CDP

   C. RA

   D. OCSP

Lesson 3: Creating a Certificate Management Plan

Before your CAs issue any certificates, you need to have a plan that describes how certificates will be issued, renewed, and revoked.

This lesson describes the many considerations that go into determining which enrollment, renewal, and revocation methods are most suitable for an organization.

> **After this lesson, you will be able to:**
> - Understand the various certificate enrollment methods and the situations in which each of these methods is most suitable.
> - Understand the difference between using CRLs and OCSP for certification validity checking and the situations in which each of these methods is most suitable.
>
> **Estimated lesson time: 30 minutes**

Selecting a Certificate Enrollment Method

To enable enrollment, you need to specify the enrollment and renewal processes for your certificates. Enrollment involves either configuring permissions to establish which security principals have Enroll permissions for specific templates (in the case of enterprise CAs) or appointing a certificate administrator who reviews each certificate request and issues or denies the request based on the information provided.

AD CS supports the ability to process certificate requests manually, if administrative approval is required, or automatically, if no approval is necessary. The following enrollment and renewal methods are available:

- **Certificate autoenrollment and renewal**   Allows you to automatically issue certificates that enable PKI applications, such as smart card logon, EFS, SSL, and S/MIME, to users and computers within an AD DS environment. Certificate autoenrollment is based on a combination of Group Policy settings and certificate templates, which allows you to enroll computers when they start and to enroll users when they log on to their domain.

  To use autoenrollment, you need a Windows Server 2003, Windows Server 2008, or Windows Server 2008 R2 domain controller; a Windows 7 or Windows Vista client (Business or Ultimate editions), or a Windows XP Professional client; and a Windows Server 2003 Advanced Server enterprise CA or a Windows Server (Standard or Enterprise edition) 2008 or Windows Server 2008 R2 enterprise CA.

- **Certificate Request Wizard and Certificate Renewal Wizard**   Available from the Certificates console, you can use the Certificate Request Wizard to request a certificate from an active enterprise CA on behalf of a user, computer, or service. You can then use the Certificate Renewal Wizard to renew the certificate.

- **Web Enrollment Support pages**   Certificate web enrollment allows users who are not members of the domain to request and obtain new and renewed certificates through a web-based user interface over an Internet or intranet connection. New in Windows Server 2008 R2 is the addition of the Certificate Enrollment Policy Protocol, which allows these users to connect to the CA over a secure HTTPS connection.

- **Network Device Enrollment Service**   The NDES is the Microsoft implementation of SCEP, a PKI communication protocol that enables software running on network devices such as routers and switches, which cannot otherwise be authenticated on the network, to enroll for X.509 certificates from a CA. In Windows Server 2008 R2, SCEP supports device certificate renewal requests.

To select the certificate enrollment and *certificate renewal* processes that are appropriate for your organization, you need to consider the following:

- **The users, computers, devices, and services for which you intend to provide services**   Determine whether they are internal or external to the organization. Identify the operating systems they are running and determine whether they are connected to AD DS.

- **The policies that you establish to manage certificate distribution**   This includes both the procedural policies that you establish for your PKI and the Group Policy settings that you use to implement those policies.

Selecting certificate enrollment and renewal processes involves making decisions about the following:

- Automatic versus manual requests
- Automatic versus manual approval
- An enrollment and renewal user interface
- CA certificate renewal

Selecting Automatic vs. Manual Requests

Whether you choose to generate certificate requests automatically or manually depends on the types of certificates that you intend to use and the number and type of clients that you enroll. For example, if you want all users or computers to use a certain type of certificate, it is not practical for you to require that each certificate be requested individually. Although rolling out a new certificate to all users or computers at one time can generate a large amount of network activity, you can control that activity by deploying the certificate requests one at a time for each OU.

On the other hand, you might want to have users or an administrator request certain high-security certificates, such as those used for digital signing or administrative tasks, only when needed. This can improve administrative control over these certificates, particularly if certificate use is not limited by a user or computer OU or by a security group membership.

You can improve control over your certificates by using one of the following options to limit user certificate requests:

- **Restricted enrollment agent** In Windows Server 2008 Enterprise and Windows Server 2008 Datacenter, organizations can permit an enrollment agent to enroll only a certain group of users. The restricted enrollment agent features allow an enrollment agent to be used for one or many certificate templates. For each certificate template, you can choose the users or security groups on behalf of which the enrollment agent can enroll. The restricted enrollment agent is not available on a Windows Server 2008 Standard–based CA.

- **Restrict access to specific templates** Configure the discretionary access control list (DACL) for each template so that only the required security principals have Enroll and Read permissions for particular templates.

- **Automate the deployment of computer certificates** Configure Group Policy to automatically assign the necessary computer certificates by adding the certificate template to the Automatic Certificate Request Settings option in Group Policy.

Selecting Automatic vs. Manual Approval

Certificate requests on a Windows Server 2008 R2 CA can be configured for either manual or automatic approval. If manual approval is required, the request is held until an administrator approves it or until the verification process is completed. When the certificate request has been approved, the autoenrollment process installs the certificate automatically or automatically renews the certificate on behalf of the user, based on the specifications in the certificate template.

Most of the time, you choose the same method for certificate approval that you choose for certificate requests. However, there are exceptions. For example, if you have the appropriate Group Policy and DACL restrictions on your certificate templates, you might decide to automatically approve a certificate request that was generated manually. Conversely, in some cases it is appropriate to manually approve certificate requests that are automatically generated.

However, in general:

- For routine and high-volume certificates, such as email certificates, automatic approval is the best option for certificate approval as long as the certificate requester has already been authenticated with a valid set of domain credentials.

- When a high degree of administrative oversight is required, such as for software code-signing certificates, consider processing certificate requests manually. By using the Certificate Request Wizard, you can evaluate every certificate request individually or you can delegate this responsibility to another administrator.

Selecting an Enrollment and Renewal User Interface

The user interface that you select for certificate request and approval processing depends on whether you choose automatic or manual certificate request and approval methods. If you decide to use autoenrollment for both certificate requests and certificate approval, you must use a minimal user interface.

However, if all or part of the enrollment process is manual, you must decide whether to use the Web Enrollment Support pages or the Certificate Request Wizard. The Web Enrollment Support pages are the easier interface for users. Users can perform the following tasks from the Web Enrollment Support pages:

- Request and obtain a basic user certificate
- Request and obtain other types of certificates by using advanced options
- Request a certificate by using a certificate request file
- Renew certificates by using a certificate renewal request file
- Save a certificate request to a file
- Save the issued certificate to a file
- Check on pending certificate requests
- Retrieve a CA certificate
- Retrieve the latest CRL from a CA
- Request smart card certificates on behalf of other users (for use by trusted administrators)

However, administrators might prefer to use the Certificate Request Wizard and the Certificate Renewal Wizard. You can start the wizard from the Certificates snap-in. Because the wizard is linked to the Certificates snap-in, you can also create custom snap-ins that you can distribute to CA administrators to whom you have delegated specific roles.

In Windows Server 2008 R2, you can now request certificates using the previously available remote procedure call (RPC)/Distributed Component Object Model (DCOM)-based requests, or you can use the web interface that now runs certificate requests over HTTPS. If a firewall exists between the CA and the requesting client, ensure that port 135 and a dynamic port above 1024 are open for RPC-based Microsoft Management Console (MMC) DCOM communication, or open port 443 for the HTTPS-based requests.

Whether you choose to use the Web Enrollment Support pages or the Certificate Request Wizard and Certificate Renewal Wizard, you might need to prepare documentation that describes how users can request a user certificate, what users can expect after they request the certificate (for example, automatic enrollment or a delay pending administrator approval), and how users can use the certificates after they receive them.

Using CA Certificate Renewal

When the certificate of a CA expires, the CA can no longer provide certificate services. To provide uninterrupted certificate services, use the Certificates console to renew the CA certificate before its expiration date. The interval that is required for CA renewal depends on the certificate lifetime of the CA.

After you renew a CA, the CA continues to issue certificates by using the new CA certificate, and the cycle starts over. Unexpired certificates that were issued by the prerenewal CA continue to be trusted until they expire or are revoked.

You can use the standard enrollment and renewal methods that are available in Windows Server 2008 R2 to renew your CAs and certificates. You can renew certificates with the same private key and public key set or with new private and public keys. However, if you have special needs, you can develop custom certificate enrollment and renewal applications for CAs.

Creating a CA Renewal Strategy

Certificate lifetimes can have an impact on the security of your PKI for the following reasons:

- Over time, encryption keys become more vulnerable to attack. In general, the longer that a key pair is in use, the greater the risk that the key can be compromised. To mitigate this risk, you must establish the maximum allowable key lifetimes and renew certificates with new key pairs before these limits are exceeded.

- When a CA certificate expires, all subordinate certificates that are issued by this CA for validation also expire. This is known as time nesting. When a CA certificate is revoked, all certificates that have been issued by the CA must also be reissued.

- *End entity* certificates expire when the issuing CA certificate reaches the end of its lifetime, unless the end entity certificate is renewed with a new key pair that chains to a CA certificate with a longer lifetime.

- You must plan the CA certificate renewal precisely during the PKI deployment phase. If this important planning step is overlooked, the entire PKI might stop working when the CA certificate expires, because all of the certificates that depend on the CA's certificate are no longer usable for either encryption or signing operations. Remember, however, that a certificate is capable of decrypting data, even if it has expired or been revoked.

Defining a Revocation Policy

You should draw a *certificate revocation* policy to define the circumstances under which certificates should be revoked. This revocation policy should describe the circumstances under which certificates are revoked, the individuals who perform revocation, the method by which certificates are revoked, and the manner in which revocation information is distributed to PKI clients.

The most common means of communicating certificate status is by distributing CRLs. In Windows Server 2008 PKIs, where the use of conventional CRLs is not an optimal solution, an online responder based on OCSP can be used to manage and distribute revocation status information.

Certificate Revocation Lists

In some cases, a CA must revoke a certificate before the certificate's validity period expires. When a certificate is revoked, the CA includes the serial number of the certificate and the reason for the revocation in the *Certificate Revocation List* (CRL).

Windows Server 2008 supports the issuance of two types of CRLs: base CRLs and delta CRLs.

A *base CRL* contains a list of all the revoked certificates associated with a CA, along with the reason(s) for revocation. All time-valid revoked certificates are signed by a CA's specific private key. If a CA's certificate is renewed with a new key pair, a new base CRL is generated that includes only revoked certificates signed with the CA's new private key.

A *delta CRL* is an update to a base CRL and contains only the serial numbers and revocation reasons for certificates revoked since the last base CRL was published. A delta CRL is implemented to provide more timely revocation information from a CA and to decrease the amount of data downloaded when retrieving a CRL. When a new base CRL is published, the revoked certificates in the delta CRL are added to the new base CRL. The next delta CRL will contain only certificates revoked since the new base CRL was published.

The delta CRL is much smaller than the base CRL because only the most recent revocations are included. The base CRL, which contains all revoked certificates, can be downloaded less frequently.

> **IMPORTANT   DELTA CRLS ARE NOT ALWAYS SUPPORTED**
>
> Not all relying parties support delta CRLs. If a relying party does not support delta CRLs, the relying party will inspect only the base CRL to determine a certificate's revocation status.

PROBLEMS WITH CERTIFICATE REVOCATION LISTS

CRLs have historically been the primary method for determining the revocation status of a specific certificate. Although CRLs are widely supported, there are some known issues with using only CRLs to determine a certificate's revocation status.

- **Latency**   The primary issue with CRLs is that there is latency in identifying that a certificate has been revoked. After you have revoked a certificate, relying parties do not recognize the revocation until the next publication of a CRL. The availability is defined by the *CRL publication* schedule. For example, if you publish an updated base CRL at 7:00 A.M. daily, a certificate revoked at 8:00 A.M. will not be recognized as a revoked certificate until the next day's publication takes place.

- **Caching of CRLs**   When a client computer checks the revocation status of a certificate, it first checks for the desired base CRL or delta CRL in the CryptoAPI cache. If it finds the base CRL or delta CRL, the client computer checks the CRL to determine if the CRL is time-valid. Like certificates, a CRL has a validity period defined by the CRL publication interval. If a time-valid CRL is found in the CryptoAPI cache, that version of the CRL is used for revocation checking, even if an updated version of the CRL has been published manually. The use of the cached version of the CRL is done for performance reasons to prevent excess network traffic. In addition, the use of a cached CRL follows the recommendation in RFC 3280, "Internet X.509 Public Key Infrastructure Certificate and Certificate Revocation List (CRL) Profile," to acquire an updated CRL only when the previous CRL expires.

Online Certificate Status Protocol (OCSP)

Windows Server 2008 introduced an alternative to CRLs that allows PKI clients to determine in real time whether a certificate has been revoked: *Online Certificate Status Protocol* (OCSP). Rather than a client downloading a base CRL or delta CRL, the client (OCSP client) sends an HTTP-based certificate status request to a server (referred to as an OCSP responder). The client determines the OCSP responder's URL by inspecting the certificate's Authority Information Access (AIA) extension. If the extension contains an OCSP responder URL and the client supports OCSP, the client can proceed with sending an OCSP request to the OCSP responder.

> **NOTE   OCSP IS NEW TO WINDOWS SERVER 2008**
>
> OCSP was not available in Windows Server 2003. Prior to Windows Server 2008, you had to implement third-party solutions to use OCSP with a Microsoft CA.

Unlike CRLs, which are distributed periodically and contain information about all certificates that have been revoked or suspended, an online responder receives and responds only to client requests for information about the status of a single certificate. The responder communicates with the CA that issued the queried certificate to determine the revocation status and returns a digitally signed response indicating the certificate's status. The OCSP responder can communicate directly with the CA or inspect the CRLs issued by the CA in order to determine the revocation status of the requested certificate.

The advantage of OCSP is that the OCSP responder typically provides more up-to-date revocation information to the OCSP client than a CRL does.

OCSP, however, has disadvantages. One drawback of OCSP is that, for deployments servicing many clients, the OCSP responder can be overwhelmed with requests. For this reason, it is important to deploy your OCSP responder in a Network Load Balancing cluster or other load balancing solution. A second drawback of OCSP is that it is more difficult to implement than CRLs are. A final limitation of OCSP is that it is supported only in Windows Vista, Windows 7, Windows Server 2008, and Windows Server 2008 R2.

When planning for certificate validity checking and revocation, OCSP is preferable to CRLs when the timeliness of revocation information is a high priority and minimized processing of the workload is a low priority. For large deployments used to support many PKI clients across the Internet, CRLs are a more practical solution.

Determining Publication Points

The final technical requirement that your design must meet is determining publication points, either for both CRLs and CA certificates (if you implement CRL checking) or for an OCSP responder (if you implement OCSP).

A PKI client can use the URLs stored in the CDP (if CRL checking is being used) and AIA extensions (if OCSP is being used) to determine a certificate's revocation status.

At each CA in the hierarchy, you must define publication points for certificates issued by that CA. These publication points allow access to *that* CA's certificate and CRL. You can use the following protocols when defining publication points:

- **HTTP URLs**   HTTP URLs are used for both internal and external publication points. The advantage of HTTP URLs is that there is little lag time between publication and availability. After you publish an updated CRL or CA certificate to an HTTP URL, it is immediately available for download by PKI-enabled applications. In addition, HTTP URLs can typically be downloaded by clients behind firewalls and those who are not full Active Directory clients, including those running an operating system earlier than Microsoft Windows 2000 Server and non-Microsoft clients.

- **Lightweight Directory Access Protocol (LDAP) URL**   A CA certificate or CRL that is published to an LDAP URL is, by default, published into the configuration naming context of Active Directory. This means that the CRL or CA certificate is available at all domain controllers in the forest.

> **NOTE   PUBLISHING CERTIFICATES TO LDAP DIRECTORIES**
> Although the default LDAP location references Active Directory, you can publish a CA certificate or CRL to any LDAP directory, such as Active Directory Lightweight Directory Services (AD LDS).

There are two disadvantages to using the default LDAP URL location:

- It can take some time for CRLs or CA certificates to fully replicate to all domain controllers in the forest. The actual time depends on your network's replication latency, especially when the replication must take place between sites and not just between domain controllers in the same site.

- Lack of support for the Active Directory–related LDAP URLs can lead to delays in CRL or CA certificate retrieval. If the default LDAP URL is the first URL in the URL listing, a non–Active Directory enabled client will time out for 10 seconds before it moves on to the next available URL.

The decision about which protocols to implement for CRL or CA certificate publication points depends on the frequency with which you publish CRLs, the protocols allowed to traverse network firewalls, and your network's operating systems. To ensure maximum availability, the URLs should be ordered so that the most common protocol used for CRL or CA certificate retrieval is listed first in the CDP extension. Other protocols are then listed in their order of use.

After you choose the publication protocols, you must choose *where* to publish the CA certificates and CRLs. The location decision includes the physical servers where you publish the files and the location of the servers on the corporate network: intranet or extranet.

Use the following guidelines when choosing publication points:

- If most computers are running Windows 2000 Server or later and are members of the forest, you should include an LDAP URL that references the Active Directory configuration naming context. This location is published to all domain controllers in the forest and ensures availability and fault tolerance.

- If you have several nonforest computers or third-party operating systems, such as UNIX, you should include web server publication points for HTTP URLs.

- If certificates are to be evaluated from the external network, the CA certificate and CDP must be published to an externally accessible location, such as a web server or LDAP server in a perimeter subnet of the network.

- File publication points are typically not used for CA certificate and CRL retrieval. File publication points are more commonly used for publishing CA certificates and CRL information to remote servers.

- The URL order is determined by the types of network clients. The order should be set so that the majority of clients can retrieve the CA certificate or CRL from the first URL in the listing. If a client cannot retrieve the CA certificate or CRL from the first URL, the client times out in an attempt to connect and then proceeds through the next URLs in the listing.

- Delta CRLs are published more frequently than base CRLs. You might not want to publish delta CRLs to LDAP locations because of Active Directory replication latency. Instead, publish delta CRLs to HTTP locations. The Active Directory replication interval must allow the delta CRL to be replicated before the prior delta CRL expires if you plan to publish the delta CRL to Active Directory.

NOTE **PUBLISHING TO AD LDS**
Delta CRLs can be published to a stand-alone LDAP server, such as AD LDS, because replication is not an issue with this form of LDAP server.

- OCSP URLs must be hosted on highly available resources. If the OCSP responder is unavailable when an OCSP client submits a query, revocation checking will fail.

AD CS Best Practices Analyzer

A new tool in Windows Server 2008 R2 Certificate Services to help with configuration and maintenance is the AD CS Best Practices Analyzer. This tool compares your configuration against a database of best practices created and maintained by Microsoft feature teams. The analyzer will check for such issues as trust chaining problems, missing AIA or OCSP pointers, and identifying certificates that are nearing their expiration dates.

> **MORE INFO** **BEST PRACTICES FOR A PKI**
>
> More information on choosing publication points can be found in the "Best Practices for Implementing a Microsoft Windows Server 2003 Public Key Infrastructure" document at *http://technet.microsoft.com/en-us/library/cc772670(WS.10).aspx*. Even though this is a Windows Server 2003 white paper, the concepts hold true for Windows Server 2008 design.

> ✔ **Quick Check**
> - When is it preferable to use web-based CRL publication points?
>
> **Quick Check Answer**
> - When the clients performing certification validity checking are not running Windows operating systems or are not members of an Active Directory forest.

PRACTICE Planning a PKI Management Strategy

You are an enterprise administrator at Fabrikam, Inc., a company based in Buffalo with branch offices in Rochester, Syracuse, Albany, Binghamton, and Elmira. The *fabrikam.com* corporate network consists of a single AD DS domain. The network includes servers that run Windows Server 2003 or Windows Server 2008 and clients that run Windows XP Professional or Windows 7 Professional. All computers and employees have accounts in the *fabrikam.com* domain.

Management has recently decided to add support for SSL connections to its external and internal web servers. Every day, as many as 10,000 independent users from around the world visit the public web server, which is located in a perimeter network outside the corporate AD DS domain. The internal web server is located on a member server in the *fabrikam.com* domain and is used only by employees. You are a member of the team whose job is to define the associated PKI structure along with a certificate enrollment and revocation strategy.

EXERCISE Planning for a PKI Management

In this exercise, you review the business and technical requirements and answer specific questions to help you plan for PKI deployment.

1. You want the external web server to support SSL with server authentication and encryption. Should the certificate used to support SSL on this web server originate from an enterprise CA, a stand-alone CA, or a public CA?

2. You want the internal web server to support SSL with both server and client authentication. Should the certificates used to support SSL on this web server originate from an enterprise CA, a stand-alone CA, or a public CA?

3. If the internal web server will be used by all employees, what is the best method to distribute certificates to support connections to the server—autoenrollment or web enrollment?

4. You want a single technology to support the distribution of revocation information for all clients in your organization. Which revocation technology is best suited to support the CA supporting clients internal to *fabrikam.com*—OCSP or CRLs?

5. Assume that the headquarters site and all branch offices include a domain controller for the *fabrikam.com* domain. If the currency of revocation data is a low priority and the ease of implementation is a high priority, which type of distribution point should you use to publish certificate validity information—HTTP or LDAP?

Lesson Summary

- Part of planning for a PKI involves designing the enrollment, renewal, and revocation processes for certificates.

- AD CS supports the ability to process certificate requests manually if administrative approval is required, or automatically if no administrative approval is necessary.

- Autoenrollment allows you to issue certificates automatically to users and computers in an Active Directory domain. Web enrollment provides an enrollment mechanism for organizations that need to issue and renew certificates for users and computers that are not joined to the domain or are not connected directly to the network and for users of non-Microsoft operating systems. NDES enables software running on network devices to enroll for and renew certificates from a Windows Server 2008 R2 CA.

- A revocation policy should describe the circumstances under which certificates are revoked, the individuals who perform revocation, the method in which certificates are revoked, and the manner in which revocation information is distributed to PKI clients.

- The most common means of communicating certificate status is by distributing CRLs. A base CRL contains a list of all the revoked certificates associated with a CA, along with the reason(s) for revocation. A delta CRL contains only the serial numbers and revocation reasons for certificates revoked since the last base CRL was published. A limitation of CRLs is that there is latency in identifying that a certificate has been revoked.

- OCSP is a new feature of Windows Server 2008 that allows clients to determine the validity of a certificate in real time.

Lesson Review

You can use the following questions to test your knowledge of the information in Lesson 3, "Creating a Certificate Management Plan." The questions are also available on the companion CD if you prefer to review them in electronic form.

> **NOTE** ANSWERS
>
> Answers to these questions and explanations of why each answer choice is correct or incorrect are located in the "Answers" section at the end of the book.

1. You need to design a PKI for your company, Northwind Traders, whose network consists of a single Active Directory domain. You plan to deploy all company CAs on servers running Windows Server 2008 R2. Your goal is to automate the distribution of certificates to users as much as possible. Which of the following represents the best method to issue certificates to users who are not members of an AD DS domain?

    A. Online Certificate Status Protocol (OCSP)

    B. Autoenrollment

    C. Simple Certificate Enrollment Protocol (SCEP)

    D. Web enrollment

2. You run a Windows Server 2008 Service Pack 1 PKI system and have configured the use of digital certificates for your network devices. You wish to configure the PKI environment to automatically renew these device certificates when they approach expiration. What do you need to do to accomplish this?

    A. Install a Windows Server 2008 R2 CA server

    B. Configure OCSP for the environment

    C. Add the Enroll permission to the certificate template

    D. Include this requirement in the certificate practice statements (CPSs) on the policy server

3. You need to design your PKI environment to be able to determine if specific issued certificates are no longer being honored by the organization, such as when an employee who had been issued a user certificate quits. Which of the following could you configure to accomplish this? (Choose two. Each answer provides a complete solution.)

    A. OCSP

    B. Autoenrollment

    C. SCEP

    D. CDP

Chapter Review

To further practice and reinforce the skills you learned in this chapter, you can perform the following tasks:

- Review the chapter summary.
- Review the list of key terms introduced in this chapter.
- Complete the case scenario. This scenario sets up a real-world situation involving the topics of this chapter and asks you to create solutions.
- Complete the suggested practices.
- Take a practice test.

Chapter Summary

- Planning a PKI for a large organization can be summarized in three steps. First, you need to identify the needs of the PKI. Second, you need to design the CA hierarchy. Third, you need to determine how certificates are issued, renewed, and revoked.
- The need for a PKI can be triggered by a company's need to support any number of technologies, including EFS, IPsec, VPNs, SSL, S/MIME, smart cards, and digital signatures.
- A PKI should be designed and deployed as a means to support your company's security policies and overall business strategy.
- Designing the CA hierarchy entails determining how many CAs your organization needs, which CAs will be kept online and which will be kept offline, which CAs should be enterprise CAs and which should be stand-alone CAs, how many tiers your hierarchy should include, and what the trust relationship should be among deployed CAs.
- Designing a certificate management policy for a PKI entails determining whether certificate issuance should occur manually or automatically, the conditions under which certificates should be revoked, and the method by which clients can check the validity of certificates.

Key Terms

Do you know what these key terms mean? You can check your answers by looking up the terms in the glossary at the end of the book.

- CA hierarchy
- Certificate enrollment
- Certificate lifetime
- Certificate practice statement (CPS)
- Certificate renewal

- Certificate repository
- Certificate revocation
- Certificate revocation list (CRL)
- Certificate template
- Certificate verification
- Certification authority (CA)
- CRL Distribution Point (CDP)
- CRL publication
- Cross-certification
- Cryptographic service provider
- Delta CRL
- Digital certificate
- Digital signature
- Enterprise CA
- Federal Information Processing Standards 140-2 (FIPS 140-2)
- Issuing CA
- Online Certificate Status Protocol (OCSP)
- PKI-enabled application/service
- Policy CA
- Private key
- Public CA
- Public key
- Public Key Infrastructure (PKI)
- Qualified subordination
- Registration authority
- Root CA
- Signing
- Stand-alone CA
- Subject/End entity
- Subordinate CA
- X.509 version 3

Case Scenario

In the following case scenario, you apply what you've learned in this chapter. You can find answers to these questions in the "Answers" section at the end of this book.

Case Scenario: Planning a PKI

You are an IT administrator in your organization, Litware, Inc. Litware is a publishing company that partners with many independent writers who contribute articles from around the world. The *litware.com* network consists of a single Active Directory domain. In the network, all servers are running Windows Server 2008 R2, and all clients are running Windows 7 Professional. All employees have user accounts in the domain, but none of the partners do.

Recently, management has determined that the all email attachments sent between Litware employees and partner writers should be encrypted by using the S/MIME standard. In addition, you want all user certificates to be issued by in-house CAs, not by public CAs.

You are a member of the team whose responsibility is to design a PKI to support the new secure email requirement. Your team has already agreed to use a single root CA for the entire PKI.

1. You want all user certificates issued to partners to have a lifetime of one year by default, but you want all user certificates issued to employees to have a lifetime of three years by default. How many CAs should the PKI include, at a minimum?

2. You want to minimize the administrative difficulty of issuing certificates to users. Which certificate enrollment method should you recommend for Litware employees? For partners?

3. It is a high priority to deliver current information to employees about the validity of certificates issued to partners. Which method should you use to enable employee computers to check for revocation status?

   - The PKI should include three CAs, including the root CA. You should have one policy CA for partners and another policy CA for employees.

   - Employees should use autoenrollment. Partners should use web enrollment.

   - OCSP.

Suggested Practices

To help you successfully master the exam objectives presented in this chapter, complete the following tasks.

Watch a Webcast

- **Practice**   Watch the webcast "Best Practices for Public Key Infrastructure: Steps to Build an Offline Root Certification Authority," available at *http://support.microsoft.com /servicedesks/webcasts/seminar/shared/asp/view.asp?url=/servicedesks/webcasts/en /wc042005/manifest.xml*.

Read a White Paper

- **Practice**   Read the white paper "Active Directory Certificate Services." You can access this white paper by searching for its title on the *Microsoft.com* website or by directly visiting *http://technet.microsoft.com/en-us/library/cc770357(WS.10).aspx*.

Take a Practice Test

The practice tests on this book's companion CD offer many options. For example, you can test yourself on just one exam objective, or you can test yourself on all the 70-647 certification exam content. You can set up the test so that it closely simulates the experience of taking a certification exam, or you can set it up in study mode so that you can look at the correct answers and explanations after you answer each question.

> *MORE INFO*   **PRACTICE TESTS**
>
> For details about all the practice test options available, see the "How to Use the Practice Tests" section in this book's introduction.

CHAPTER 11

Designing Software Update Infrastructure and Managing Compliance

When considering the importance of a good software update infrastructure, remember that the most famous worms and viruses have usually exploited weaknesses for which software updates had already been released. The simple fact is that if you apply newly released software updates to the computers in your organization in a timely manner, your organization will be less vulnerable to worms, viruses, trojans, and bugs than organizations that take a more haphazard approach to update management. In this chapter, you learn about several software update solutions that you can deploy in your enterprise environment to ensure that all the computers you are responsible for managing have software that is up to date. You will also learn how to generate and apply baseline security policies, a method of ensuring that the configuration of the computers in your organization is as secure as possible while still performing its assigned functions.

Exam objectives in this chapter:

- Design for software updates and compliance management.

Lessons in this chapter:

Before You Begin

To complete the practices in this chapter, you must have finished the following:

- Installed a server running Microsoft Windows Server 2008 R2 Enterprise configured as a domain controller in the *contoso.internal* domain. Active Directory–integrated Domain Name System (DNS) is installed by default on the first domain controller in a domain.

- Made the following configurations:

  - Named the computer Glasgow.

  - Configured a static IPv4 address of 10.0.0.11 with a subnet mask of 255.255.255.0. The IPv4 address of the DNS server is 10.0.0.11.

  - With the exception of IPv4 configuration and the computer name, accepted all the default installation settings. You can obtain an evaluation version (180 days) of the Windows Server 2008 R2 Enterprise software from the Microsoft download center at *http://www.microsoft.com/windowsserver2008/en/us/trial-software.aspx*.

  - You can obtain the Windows Server Update Services 3.0 SP2 software from the Microsoft download center at *http://www.microsoft.com/Downloads/en/default.aspx*.

> ### 🌐 REAL WORLD
> **Orin Thomas**
>
> The main reason that many organizations do not apply software updates in a timely manner is the fear of causing some conflict with an existing configuration. Although it is true that software updates do, from time to time, cause problems with existing configurations, such problems are the exception rather than the rule. As an enterprise administrator, you need to take a proactive approach to software update deployment. Rather than taking a wait-and-see approach to the deployment of new updates, you need to develop an update management routine so you can test an update to the point where you are satisfied that it will not cause a problem, before rolling it out to all the client computers in your organization. Your routine might involve initially rolling out the update to a set of computers that mirror the configurations deployed in your enterprise, and it might involve deploying the update to a small, select group of test users who can report if the update adversely affects their day-to-day activities. Because Microsoft has a regular schedule for releasing software updates, it is not too difficult for you to make plans to perform *update testing* regularly after the updates are released. Just remember that a big part of planning software update infrastructure is scheduling your own time so that you can confidently test and deploy those updates to the computers in your organization.

Lesson 1: Designing a Software Update Infrastructure .

This lesson examines four software update technologies that are available from Microsoft and informs you about which technology is most appropriate when designing a software update infrastructure for an organization. The lesson begins by examining Microsoft Update and *Windows Server Update Services* (WSUS) 3.0 SP2, solutions used by and appropriate for most small- to medium-sized environments. The lesson then covers System Center Essentials 2010, a technology that works well as a software update platform in small- and medium-sized environments. The lesson finishes by examining System Center Configuration Manager 2007 R3, which is often deployed, among other reasons, as an enterprise software update solution.

After this lesson, you will be able to:

- Design a patch management solution.
- Determine which software update product is appropriate for a given set of circumstances.

Estimated lesson time: 80 minutes

Microsoft Update as a Software Update Solution

Two questions are pertinent when planning the deployment of any software update technology: How are software updates approved for deployment? and Where are the update files stored and retrieved after they have been approved for deployment? How you, as the planner of your organization's software update infrastructure, answer these questions determines the type of solution to incorporate into your designs.

The default configuration of Windows Server 2008 R2, Windows Vista, and Windows 7 uses the *Microsoft Update servers*, hosted by Microsoft and accessible across the Internet, as the source of software update approvals and software update files. When you use this method, the approval of updates is entirely under Microsoft control. Although sole reliance on Microsoft Update reduces an administrator's workload, this method of software update deployment has the following drawbacks in most enterprise environments:

- Each update must be downloaded separately to each client from the Microsoft Update servers over your Internet connection. In enterprise environments where there might be thousands of clients, this can have a significant impact on bandwidth usage and cost.

- This method does not allow for testing updates to determine whether they conflict with any existing applications within the environment. Although Microsoft rigorously tests each update prior to deployment, the company cannot test updates against unique custom software deployed in your enterprise environment.

- There is no provision for centralized reporting. Administrators must use software tools to scan all client computers in order to determine whether an update has installed correctly. These data cannot be extracted directly from the Microsoft Update servers.

There are certain times when you should plan to use Microsoft Update as a complete software update solution in your enterprise environment. These cases are specific and apply to parts of the organization only, rather than to the organization as a whole. Incorporate Microsoft Update into your patch management design when you must plan for the following scenarios:

- Your organization has satellite offices or retail outlets where there are a small number of stand-alone clients. In these circumstances, it is often simpler to enable automatic updates on the clients than to attempt centralized management.

- Your organization's mobile computers rarely connect to the organizational network and a central list of approved updates would rarely be accessed. In this situation, you would also use Network Access Protection (NAP) to ensure that, when these mobile computers do connect to the organizational network, their system health is verified before access to the protected network is granted.

In many cases, it is necessary to separate update approvals from update storage. Taking this approach enables you to manage which updates are installed, although the update files themselves are downloaded from the Microsoft Update servers on the Internet. You would plan this solution for satellite or branch offices where you must exert control over the distribution of updates but where there is not a compelling reason to store updates locally. Remember that update approval traffic has only a small bandwidth footprint, whereas downloading update files can clog a slow wide area network (WAN) link. For example, imagine that your organization has a small satellite office that has fast Internet connectivity and a virtual private network (VPN) WAN link to a branch office. In this situation, you can configure client computers to poll a software update server for a list of approved updates and then to obtain those updates from the Microsoft Update servers on the Internet. A small amount of data is pulled across the VPN WAN link, but the larger amount of update data is pulled across the Internet link.

Windows Server Update Services as a Software Update Solution

Rather than having each update downloaded multiple times to clients on the same network, planning the deployment of WSUS enables you to configure the update server settings so that the update server downloads the update once and clients retrieve the update from the WSUS server. Another feature of WSUS offers administrators the ability to roll back the installation of updates that have already been deployed. WSUS is not limited to updates and can provide a local copy of all content that is published on Microsoft Update. This includes drivers, service packs, feature packs, and security updates.

WSUS 3.0 SP1 was the first version of WSUS compatible with Windows Server 2008, and WSUS 3.0 SP2 is the first version of WSUS compatible with Windows Server 2008 R2. Although not included as a role or feature, the WSUS software itself is freely available, and you can install the software on licensed computers running Windows Server 2008 and Windows Server 2008 R2. WSUS 3.0 SP2 provides support for Windows 7 clients and also for the new BranchCache feature in Windows Server 2008 R2. The WSUS 3.0 SP2 download (less than 85 MB) can be installed on a Windows Server or can be used to upgrade earlier versions of WSUS. You cannot install WSUS 3.0 SP1 or SP2 on computers running a Server Core installation of Windows Server 2008, although this functionality might be available in later versions of the update server software. In the first exercise at the end of this lesson, you will install WSUS 3.0 SP2 on a computer running Windows Server 2008 R2.

Managing WSUS

You can manage a WSUS server locally or remotely by using the Update Services console. WSUS uses administrative roles to assign permissions. Each role can perform a specific set of functions, and you can assign roles to users by adding their user accounts to one of the following local groups:

- **WSUS Administrators**   Users who have accounts that are members of this local group are able to administer the WSUS server. This includes WSUS administration tasks from approving updates and configuring computer groups to configuring automatic approvals and the update source of the server running WSUS. A user who is a member of this group can use the Update Services console to connect remotely to manage WSUS.

- **WSUS Reporters**   Users who have accounts that are members of this local group are able to create reports on the WSUS server. A user who is a member of this group can connect remotely to the server running WSUS using the Update Services console to run these reports. Lesson 2, "Managing Software Update Compliance," covers reporting in more detail.

WSUS Deployment Hierarchies

Each WSUS server is capable of providing software updates to 25,000 client computers. This means that, in theory, a single WSUS server can service the requests of all but the largest enterprise environments. In large organizations, WSUS servers are usually deployed in each Active Directory Domain Services (AD DS) site so that update and approval data can be retrieved from a server on the local network rather than over WAN links. You specify the WSUS server's update source during installation. Updates are stored locally on the WSUS server, or client computers use the WSUS server for a list of approved updates and then download those updates from the Microsoft Update servers on the Internet.

WSUS server hierarchies involve an *upstream server* at the top of the hierarchy and *downstream servers* that retrieve data from the upstream server. It is possible to have multiple layers in the hierarchy, with each downstream server using the server above it as a source of *update approvals* and software update files. In many real-world WSUS deployments, the hierarchy structure is used for the approval of updates only, and the downstream servers retrieve the update files from the Microsoft Update servers. This configuration is popular in organizations that have branch offices connected to a head office by slow WAN links, but where each branch office has a high-speed link to the Internet. In this configuration, approval data travels to the branch office site across the WAN link, and update files are downloaded from the Internet.

EXAM TIP

For the 70-647 exam, remember that in order to reduce bandwidth usage on Internet connections when downloading Windows updates, and for centralized approval of updates, use in-house, WSUS administration servers. Use WSUS servers running in replica mode to distribute updates to different sites for local deployment.

MORE INFO WSUS RESOURCES

For detailed information about WSUS 3.0 SP2, including downloading the WSUS 3.0 SP2 software, a Deployment Guide, Step-by-Step Installation Guide, and an Operations Guide, consult the WSUS TechNet home page at *http://technet.microsoft.com/en-us /windowsserver/bb332157.aspx.*

WSUS Administration Models

The administration model determines how update approvals flow through the organization. There are two options when configuring the administration model for your organization's downstream WSUS servers. The first option, shown in Figure 11-1, is to configure the downstream WSUS server as a replica of the upstream server. When you configure a WSUS server as a replica, all approvals, settings, computers, and groups from the upstream server are used on the downstream server. The downstream server cannot approve updates when configured in replica mode, although you can change a *replica server* to the second mode, called autonomous mode, if you urgently need to deploy an update.

Autonomous mode enables a local WSUS administrator to configure separate update approval settings but still retrieves updates from the upstream WSUS server. Autonomous mode conserves bandwidth for the organization by ensuring that updates are downloaded only once from the Internet but retains the benefit of allowing local administrators discretion over the approval of updates.

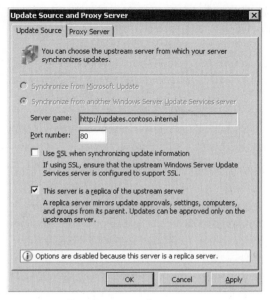

FIGURE 11-1 Downstream replica server

When planning the deployment of WSUS in an enterprise environment, it is likely that you will need to use a mixture of autonomous and replica modes. For example, an organization with two Active Directory forests shares a single Internet connection. The organization wants to minimize the number of updates downloaded from the Internet, but the administrators of each forest want control over which updates are deployed in their organization. To resolve this problem, you can place a WSUS server in the first forest and configure it in autonomous mode. You can place a second WSUS server in the second forest and configure it in autonomous mode, but instead of drawing update files from Microsoft Update, these files can be obtained from the WSUS server in the first forest. All future WSUS servers deployed in each environment can then be configured as replicas of their respective forest's *autonomous WSUS server*.

WSUS Computer Groups

In the most basic form of WSUS deployment, every computer that is a client of the WSUS server receives approved updates at the same time. Although this method works well for many organizations, other organizations prefer to perform staggered rollouts of updates. *Staggered rollouts*, usually to a test group of computers, enable organizations to determine whether a software update has an adverse impact on their client computer's configuration. Various software, especially internally developed custom software, can conflict with an update in an unforeseen manner.

By creating a test group, you can deploy newly released updates to a special group of computers in your organization so you can verify that new updates do not conflict with existing deployed configurations. When you are confident that an update causes no problems, you can roll it out to all clients in the enterprise.

WSUS computer groups have the following properties:

- The two default computer groups are All Computers and Unassigned Computers. Unless a client computer is already assigned to a group, when it contacts the WSUS server for the first time, it will be added to the *Unassigned Computers* group.

- Groups can be organized in a hierarchy. An update deployed to a group at the top of the hierarchy will also be deployed to computers that are in groups lower in the hierarchy. The Unassigned Computers group is a part of the *All Computers* hierarchy.

- Computers can be assigned to multiple groups.

As Figure 11-2 shows, administrators can use two methods to assign computer accounts to WSUS groups. The first method is known as *server-side targeting*. To use this method, open the Update Services console. In the Options section, under Computers, choose the Use The Update Services Console option. A user with WSUS Administrator privileges manually assigns computers in the Unassigned Computers group to specific computer groups using the WSUS console.

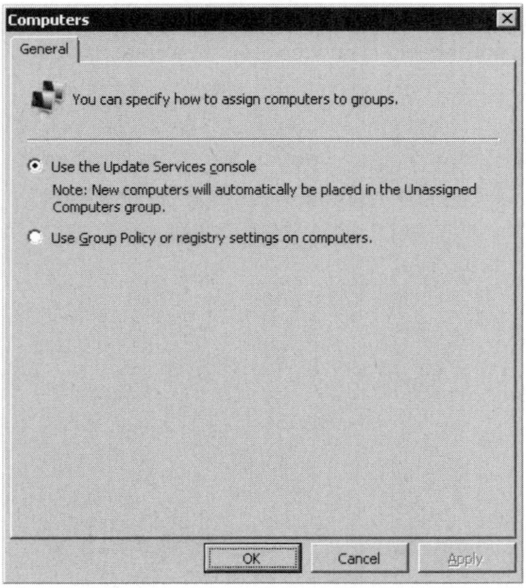

FIGURE 11-2 Computer group option

The other method of assigning computers to groups is to use Group Policy or registry settings on clients of the WSUS server. This method, known as *client-side targeting*, is less time-consuming in enterprise environments and simplifies the group assignment process. Regardless of which method you use to assign computers to groups, you must first create the groups using the WSUS console.

Update Installation Behavior

Other than the policies that determine the assignment of computers to WSUS groups and the location of the local WSUS server, the most important WSUS-related group policies relate to how and when WSUS updates are downloaded and installed. As an administrator, you want to avoid the situation of updates never being installed—either because a user intervenes to cancel update installation or because the update installation is always scheduled for a time when the computer is off. You must balance interrupting a user's work with stopping user intervention. No one will be particularly happy to lose several hours of work on an important spreadsheet because you have configured the update settings to install and reboot the computer without alerting the user in advance.

When scheduling update deployments, consider the following policy settings:

- **Enabling Windows Update Power Management To Automatically Wake Up The System To Install Scheduled Updates** This policy works only with instances of Windows Vista and Windows 7 that are running on compatible hardware and that have an appropriately configured BIOS (*Wake on LAN* feature). Rather than worrying about whether restarts will interrupt users during the update deployment process, use this policy to awaken computers in the middle of the night, deploy the relevant updates, and then return them to sleep. This policy works well in enterprise environments in which hundreds, if not thousands, of computers are deployed, and finding a convenient time during business hours is difficult.

- **Configure Automatic Updates** The Configure Automatic Updates policy enables you to specify whether updates are automatically downloaded and scheduled for installation or whether the user is simply notified that updates (either already downloaded or on the WSUS server) are available.

- **Automatic Updates Detection Frequency** If this policy is not enabled, the default detection frequency is 22 hours. If you want to configure a more frequent interval, use this policy to do so.

- **Allow Automatic Updates Immediate Installation** When enabled, this policy automatically installs all updates that do not require either a service interruption or Microsoft Windows to restart.

- **No Auto-Restart For Scheduled Automatic Updates Installations** When this policy is enabled, the computer will not automatically restart but will wait for the user to restart the computer on his or her own time. The user will be notified that the computer needs to be restarted before the installation of updates is completed. If this policy is not enabled, the computer will automatically restart five minutes after the updates are installed to complete update installation.

- **Delay Restart For Scheduled Installations** This policy enables you to vary the automatic restart period. As mentioned previously, the default period is five minutes. This policy enables you to set a delay period of up to 30 minutes.

- **Reschedule Automatic Updates Scheduled Installations**   This policy ensures that a scheduled installation that did not occur—perhaps because the computer was switched off or disconnected from the network—will occur the specified number of minutes after the next time the computer is started. If this policy is disabled, a missed scheduled installation will occur with the next scheduled installation.

Planning Automatic Approvals

Part of planning a software update infrastructure for an enterprise environment involves determining the level of administrator intervention required during the approval process. *Automatic approval* rules enable you to approve specific categories of updates so that they are deployed without requiring administrator intervention. You can configure updates to apply to specific WSUS computer groups, for a specific classification, or for specific products.

You can have multiple automatic approval rules, and you can enable and disable them as necessary. A new feature in WSUS 3.0 SP2 is the ability to specify an approval deadline (date and time) for all computers or specific computer groups. Configure automatic approval rules through the Automatic Approvals dialog box, shown in Figure 11-3, which is available in the Update Services console under Options. By default, no updates are automatically approved for distribution by WSUS 3.0 SP2.

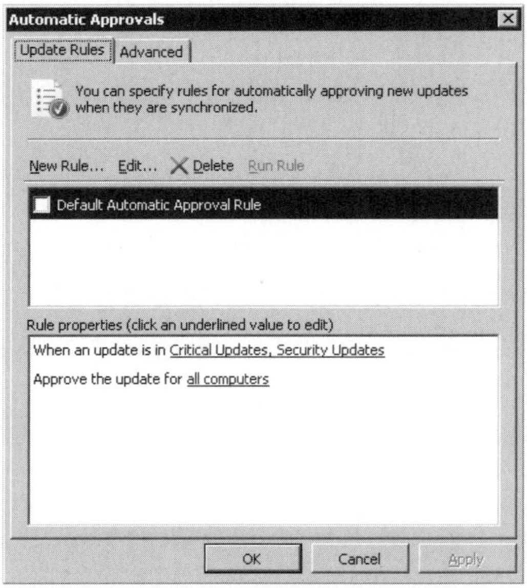

FIGURE 11-3 Configuring automatic approvals

Organizational policy influences planning for automatic approval rules more than technical reasons do. In organizations with highly customized software configurations, a rigorous testing process is likely to be in place for all updates, and automatic approval is unlikely to be enabled. In organizations in which administrators do not test updates prior to deployment, using automatic approval rules can minimize staff workload.

Planning the Deployment of WSUS in Enterprise Environments

The key question that you must address in planning the deployment of WSUS in enterprise environments is who is ultimately responsible for approving updates. In some organizations, it can mean that you have to deploy multiple WSUS servers configured in autonomous mode within the same domain; in other organizations, multiple downstream replica servers deployed throughout multiple forests might use a single *autonomous WSUS server* as an upstream server.

The deployment of WSUS servers themselves in enterprise environments is also dependent on WAN bandwidth configuration. The branch offices of many organizations have a direct connection to the Internet and WAN links, either through a direct link or through a VPN tunnel, to their head office location. In these situations, it makes little sense to pull the software update files over the WAN when they can also be downloaded directly from the Microsoft Update servers on the Internet.

> ✔ **Quick Check**
>
> 1. In what mode should you deploy a downstream WSUS 3.0 SP2 server if you want it to use the approvals and computer group configuration of the designated upstream server?
>
> 2. In what mode should you deploy a downstream WSUS 3.0 SP2 server if the local branch office administrator will be responsible for the approval of software updates?
>
> **Quick Check Answers**
>
> 1. Put the downstream WSUS server into replica mode if you want it to use the approvals and computer group configuration of the designated upstream server.
>
> 2. If a local IT professional is responsible for approving the deployment of updates on a downstream WSUS server, that server needs to be configured to use autonomous, rather than replica, mode.

System Center Essentials 2010

Although limited to managing 500 client computers and 50 servers (up from 30 servers in System Center Essentials 2007), System Center Essentials 2010 provides more features for the deployment of software updates than WSUS 3.0 SP2 does. The primary difference between the products is that you can also use System Center Essentials 2010 to deploy software updates to non-Microsoft products. System Center Essentials 2010 provides advanced update distribution control and scheduling flexibility, as well as basic compliance-checking functionality and inventory management. Although System Center Essentials 2010 functions as much more than a platform for deploying software updates—it also provides health reports and software and hardware inventory—this lesson discusses the update functionality in particular.

Only System Center Essentials 2007 SP1 or later can be installed on a computer running Windows Server 2008.

Unlike WSUS 3.0 SP2, System Center Essentials 2010 is not a free add-on to Windows Server 2008 or Windows Server 2008 R2; a nonevaluation version must be purchased from Microsoft to be permanently deployed in a production environment. System Center Essentials 2010 stores configuration data in a Microsoft SQL Server 2008 database. It can use SQL Server Express with a recommended limit of 150 managed systems, which you can install during the System Center Essentials 2010 installation process, or it can store the System Center Essentials data in a separate SQL Server 2008 database. The SQL Server 2008 database does not need to be hosted on the same server as the other System Center Essentials 2010 components, and all System Center Essentials 2010, including the database, can be installed on a computer hosting the AD DS role.

System Center Essentials offers the following:

- Update management for Microsoft and third-party applications and devices
- Software deployment of MSI and EXE installed software packages, including third-party applications, Microsoft Office 2007, and Microsoft Office 2010
- *Hardware and software inventory* with attributes collected for items such as available disk space, RAM usage, and installed applications with version numbers
- Added *Virtual Machine Manager* 2008 R2 technology to provide support for virtual machines, including server conversions from *physical to virtual* and rapid provisioning of new virtual systems
- New licensing method to aid medium-sized businesses

System Center Essentials 2010 interfaces with client agent software that installs during the System Center Essentials 2010 discovery process. System Center Essentials *computer discovery* involves the System Center Essentials 2010 server detecting all computers on the network. After you run the discovery process, you select which of the detected computers the System Center Essentials 2010 server will manage. The user account you use to perform the System Center Essentials discovery process must have administrative rights on all computers that the System Center Essentials 2010 server will manage. After you select a computer for System Center Essentials 2010 to manage, the *SCE agent* software is automatically deployed to that computer.

System Center Essentials 2010 Software Update Configuration

The System Center Essentials 2010 software update process is similar to the WSUS 3.0 SP2 software update process, and System Center Essentials 2010 is built on top of WSUS. The System Center Essentials 2010 setup process enables you to migrate WSUS settings so that you retain existing computer groups and software update approvals when moving to the new software update platform. As with WSUS 3.0 SP2, you can use computer groups and approval rules with System Center Essentials 2010 to stagger and automate the deployment of updates. The biggest difference between the two platforms is that you can use System Center

Essentials 2010 to deploy updates and service packs to *third-party applications*. This functionality is not available in WSUS 3.0 SP2.

As with WSUS 3.0 SP2, the source of Microsoft-related System Center Essentials 2010 updates can be either the local System Center Essentials 2010 server or Microsoft Update. System Center Essentials 2010 can use a local source to deploy updates only for third-party applications. When deploying updates to third-party applications, you run the New Update Wizard to create an update package. When the update package is created, you select the computer groups to which the update package will be deployed.

> **MORE INFO** **MANAGING UPDATES WITH SYSTEM CENTER ESSENTIALS 2010**
>
> For more information about incorporating System Center Essentials 2010 into your software update design, consult the following links: *http://technet.microsoft.com/en-us/library /bb437260.aspx* and *http://www.microsoft.com/systemcenter/en/us/essentials.aspx*.

System Center Essentials 2010 in the Enterprise

When considering System Center Essentials 2010 as a software update solution in an enterprise environment, remember the following facts:

- System Center Essentials 2010 can provide software updates to a maximum of 50 servers and 500 client computers. Most enterprise environments have more computers than this, which might necessitate multiple System Center Essentials 2010 servers or mean that you will need to deploy System Center Configuration Manager 2010 if your organization requires advanced software update functionality.

- You can install only one System Center Essentials 2010 server in an Active Directory domain. It is possible to have multiple System Center Essentials 2010 servers in an Active Directory forest as long as there is only one System Center Essentials 2010 server per domain. If the domains in your organization all have fewer than 500 clients and 50 servers, System Center Essentials 2010 is a viable software update platform.

- You cannot use System Center Essentials 2010 in a workgroup environment. All System Center Essentials 2010 clients must be members of the same Active Directory forest.

- System Center Essentials 2010 cannot function as part of a WSUS hierarchy. You can deploy WSUS alongside System Center Essentials 2010, but the two software update platforms do not directly interoperate.

- You can use System Center Essentials 2010 to provide software updates to computers in different domains from the System Center Essentials 2010 server as long as these computers are in the same Active Directory forest, and the 500-client, 50-server limit has not been reached.

- You cannot use a single System Center Essentials 2010 server as a software update provider for computers in different Active Directory forests.

System Center Essentials 2010 works very well as a software update solution in an organization that has a single site and fewer than 500 client computers and 50 server computers. System Center Essentials 2010 is not an optimal solution for an organization that has multiple sites connected by WAN links, because pushing software updates across WAN links might flood those links with traffic. As mentioned earlier, you cannot deploy System Center Essentials 2010 as part of a hierarchy, and you cannot deploy multiple System Center Essentials 2010 servers within the same domain.

> **MORE INFO**   **PLANNING THE DEPLOYMENT OF SYSTEM CENTER ESSENTIALS 2010**
>
> For more information about planning the deployment of System Center Essentials 2010 in your enterprise environment, consult the following TechNet link: *http://technet.microsoft.com/en-us/library/bb422980.aspx*.

System Center Configuration Manager 2007

System Center Configuration Manager 2007 R3 provides a software update solution for enterprise-sized environments that exceed the 500-client, 50-server capacity of System Center Essentials 2010. Like System Center Essentials 2010, an organization must purchase System Center Configuration Manager 2007 prior to deploying the product permanently as a software update solution. System Center Configuration Manager 2007 does not ship with its own SQL Server database, and you must deploy and configure SQL Server 2005 SP1 or SQL Server 2008 in your environment prior to deploying System Center Configuration Manager 2007. Only System Center Configuration Manager 2007 SP1 or later can be deployed on a computer running Windows Server 2008. Although you can also use System Center Configuration Manager 2007 to deploy operating systems and distribute software, this lesson concentrates on the software update deployment and management features of the product.

Like System Center Essentials 2010, System Center Configuration Manager 2007 R3 can publish software updates for third-party products. Unlike System Center Essentials 2010, System Center Configuration Manager 2007 can also use hierarchies, with primary sites, secondary sites, parent sites, child sites, and central sites. All sites in a hierarchy must be part of the same Active Directory forest. Each site requires one site server running System Center Configuration Manager 2007. Each site type has the following properties:

- **Primary site**   This is the first System Center Configuration Manager 2007 site. It stores the System Center Configuration Manager 2007 data for itself and for all sites below it in the hierarchy in a SQL Server database.

- **Secondary site**   This site has no local SQL Server database. It is attached to the primary site and administered from the primary site. Secondary sites require no additional System Center Configuration Manager 2007 license. Secondary sites cannot have other sites below them in the hierarchy.

- **Parent site**   This type of site has other sites attached to it in a hierarchy.

- **Child site** A child site is attached to a site above it in the hierarchy. A child site can be either a primary site or a secondary site.
- **Central site** Central sites have no parent sites. These sites are sometimes called standalone sites.

MORE INFO **MORE ON SITES**

To understand more about System Center Configuration Manager 2007 sites, consult the following TechNet article: *http://technet.microsoft.com/en-us/library/bb632547.aspx*.

System Center Configuration Manager 2007 sites host *software update points*, which distribute software updates to computers in the organization. WSUS 3.0 SP2 must be installed on a computer running Windows Server 2008 before it can be configured as a System Center Configuration Manager 2007 software update point. Once it is configured as a software update point, you perform all management tasks using the System Center Configuration Manager 2007 console rather than the original WSUS administration tools.

MORE INFO **PLANNING SOFTWARE UPDATE INFRASTRUCTURE WITH SYSTEM CENTER CONFIGURATION MANAGER 2007**

To learn more about the best practices for planning a software update infrastructure with System Center Configuration Manager 2007, consult the following TechNet article: *http://technet.microsoft.com/en-us/library/bb694244.aspx*.

MORE INFO **SYSTEM CENTER CONFIGURATION MANAGER 2007 VIRTUAL LABS**

To learn more about the functionality of System Center Configuration Manager 2007, visit the following TechNet virtual lab and webcast: *https://msevents.microsoft.com /cui/webcasteventdetails.aspx?eventid=1032343963&eventcategory=3&culture =en-us&countrycode=us&lc=1033* and *http://msevents.microsoft.com/CUI /WebCastEventDetails.aspx?culture=en-US&EventID=1032343569&CountryCode=US*.

<hr>

PRACTICE **Windows Server 2008 Software Update Infrastructure**

In this practice, you install two software update solutions. In the first exercise, you deploy Windows Server Update Services 3.0 SP2 on server Glasgow. In the second exercise, you work with an evaluation virtual hard disk (VHD) of System Center Essentials 2007.

Before beginning Exercise 1, you must perform the following tasks:

- Download Windows Server Update Services 3.0 SP2 from *http://technet.microsoft.com /en-us/wsus/default*.

- Download Microsoft Report Viewer 2008 SP1 Redistributable from *http://www.microsoft.com/downloads/en/details.aspx?FamilyID=bb196d5d-76c2-4a0e-9458-267d22b6aac6*.

In Exercise 2, you configure and use System Center Essentials. However, at the time of this writing, Microsoft has not yet released a VHD for System Center Essentials 2010, so this exercise uses the most recent System Center Essentials VHD, which is System Center Essentials 2007 SP1. This product is a viable update solution for small and medium-sized enterprises. Before beginning Exercise 2, you must perform the following tasks:

- Download the System Center Essentials 2007 SP1 VHD from *http://www.microsoft.com/downloads/en/details.aspx?FamilyID=E6FC3117-48C5-4FD1-A3D2-927EAB397373&displaylang=en*.

- Configure Virtual PC, Virtual Server, Hyper-V, or an alternative solution to host this virtual machine. Instructions included with the VHD explain how to install this computer. Configure the virtual machine so that it has access to the Internet.

EXERCISE 1   Install WSUS 3.0 SP2 on Windows Server 2008 R2

In this exercise, you install WSUS 3.0 SP2 on Windows Server 2008 R2. You configure this installation so that updates are stored on the Microsoft Update servers. This practice should be considered optional because it requires Internet access. You can configure server Glasgow to access the Internet by adding a second network card or by adding a virtual network card and configuring virtual machine network settings appropriately. This practice also assumes that you have not installed Microsoft Internet Information Services (IIS) on server Glasgow. If IIS has been installed, use the Add Role Services functionality to add the additional required components listed in step 4 instead of performing step 3.

1. Log on to server Glasgow using the Kim_Akers user account.

2. Install Report Viewer on server Glasgow.

3. Use the Server Manager console to add the Web Server (IIS) role. Add any required role services. Ensure that the ASP.NET, Windows Authentication, Dynamic Content Compression, and IIS 6 Metabase Compatibility options are selected.

4. Verify that the role services listed in the Confirm Installation Selections dialog box match those shown in Figure 11-4 and then click Install. When the installation process completes, click Close.

5. Double-click the installation file you downloaded to start the WSUS 3.0 SP2 setup process. Install WSUS 3.0 SP2 with the following configurations:

    - Complete a full server installation, including Administration Console.

    - Do not store updates locally.

    - Install the Windows Internal Database locally, as shown in Figure 11-5.

    - Use the existing IIS Default website.

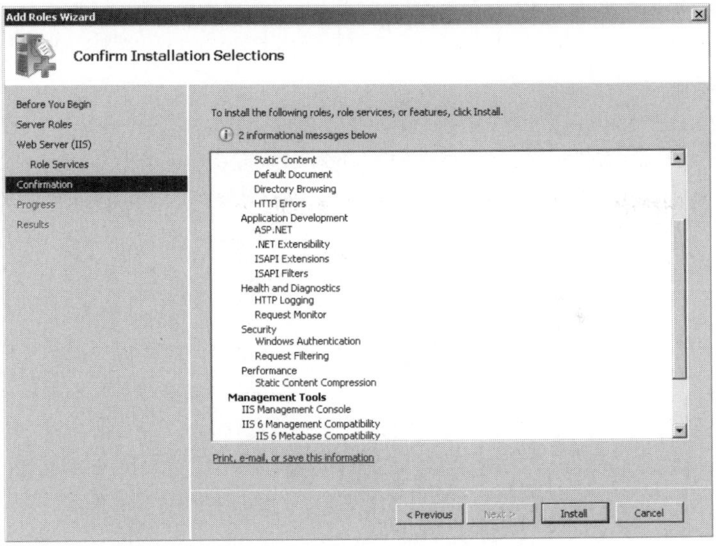

FIGURE 11-4 Preparing IIS for the installation of WSUS

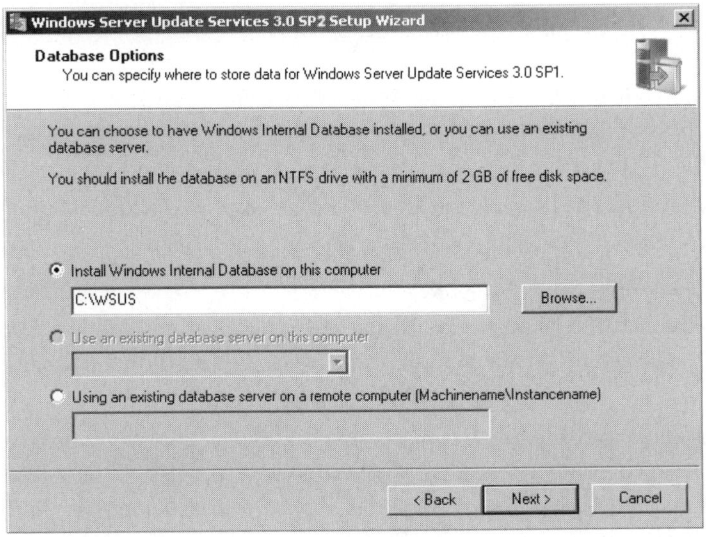

FIGURE 11-5 Configuring WSUS database options

The Windows Server Update Services Configuration Wizard automatically starts when the installation of WSUS 3.0 SP2 is complete.

6. If your Windows Server 2008 computer does not have a connection to the Internet, click Cancel at this point.

7. On the Choose Upstream Server page, shown in Figure 11-6, select Synchronize From Microsoft Update.

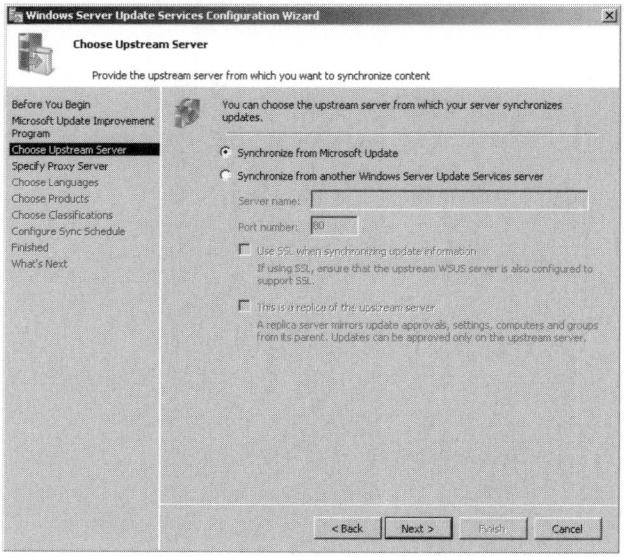

FIGURE 11-6 Configuring synchronization options

8. Unless your organization uses a *proxy server* that requires authentication, you do not need to specify a proxy server.

9. On the Connect To Upstream Server page, click Start Connecting to contact Microsoft Update to determine the type of updates available, the products that can be updated, and the available languages.

10. On the Choose Products page, shown in Figure 11-7, select the All Products check box. On the Choose Classifications page, select the All Classifications check box.

11. On the Set Sync Schedule page, select Synchronize Manually.

12. Ensure that the Launch The Windows Server Update Services Administration Console and the Begin Initial Synchronization check boxes are cleared, and then finish the installation.

13. When the installation completes, you should open the Update Services console and investigate creating computer groups, creating auto-approval rules, and the reporting functionality of WSUS 3.0 SP2. This investigation will help you develop plans to deploy WSUS within your environment.

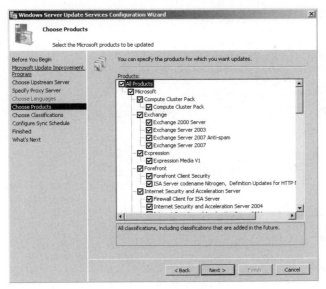

FIGURE 11-7 Choose products that WSUS can update

EXERCISE 2   System Center Essentials 2007 VHD

In this exercise, you configure the System Center Essentials VHD virtual machine and explore the update features available in System Center Essentials 2007. To complete the practice, perform the following steps:

1. Log on to the System Center Essentials 2007 VHD virtual machine using the user name **Administrator** and the password **Evaluation1**.

2. Use DCPROMO to promote the server to a domain controller of the new domain, *fabrikam.internal*, in a new forest, using the default settings.

3. Configure DNS locally on the server. The Windows Installation Files can be located in the C:\WindowsInstallationFiles\i386 folder. Use **Evaluation1** as the restore mode password.

4. When you have finished configuring the computer as a domain controller, double-click the Essentials Setup icon, located on the desktop.

5. Start the installation by clicking Full Setup on the System Center Essentials 2007 Setup page.

6. Complete the installation process, accepting the default settings except on the Installation Location page of the setup wizard, on which you should select the Get Update Files From The Microsoft Update Website option, as shown in Figure 11-8. Use the Administrator account as the computer management account. Finish the installation by choosing not to check for updates at this time.

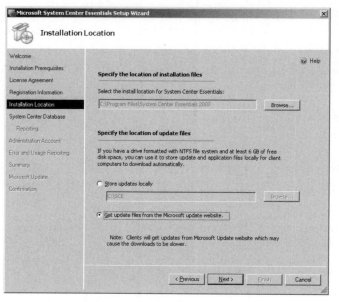

FIGURE 11-8 Location of update files

7. Use the System Center Essentials Console to create computer groups named **Testers**, **Accountants**, and **Research**. Add the computer account for SCEVHDSERVER.fabrikam .internal to each of these groups.

8. From the Updates menu, select Configure Microsoft Update Settings. Navigate through the wizard, synchronizing with Microsoft Update and configuring System Center Essentials 2007 to provide updates to Exchange Server, Microsoft Office, SQL Server, and Windows. Accept all other default settings.

Lesson Summary

- WSUS replicas are downstream servers that inherit the configuration of their upstream server.
- Autonomous-mode WSUS servers are downstream servers that retrieve updates from an upstream server, but their approvals and computer groups are configured by a local administrator.
- Server-side targeting assigns computers to WSUS groups using the WSUS administration console.
- Client-side targeting assigns computers to WSUS groups by using Group Policy or by editing the client computer's registry.
- Deploying updates in a staggered manner or to a test environment enables you to determine whether a particular update has an adverse impact on client computers.

- System Center Essentials 2007 provides greater functionality than WSUS but also requires access to a SQL Server 2005 SP1 or later database. You can install SQL Server Express during the System Center Essentials 2007 setup process.
- System Center Configuration Manager 2007 provides all the extra features of System Center Essentials 2007 without the limitation on the number of clients that can be updated.

Lesson Review

You can use the following questions to test your knowledge of the information in Lesson 1, "Designing a Software Update Infrastructure." The questions are also available on the companion CD if you prefer to review them in electronic form.

> **NOTE   ANSWERS**
>
> Answers to these questions and explanations of why each answer choice is correct or incorrect are located in the "Answers" section at the end of the book.

1. You are planning the deployment of a software update solution to an organization that has 300 computers running Windows Vista, 120 computers running Windows 7, and 20 computers running Windows Server 2008 R2, all hosted at a single site. The organization has a single domain forest, and all computers in the organization are members of the Active Directory domain. Which of the following conditions would require you to plan the deployment by using System Center Essentials 2010 rather than WSUS 3.0 SP2?

    A. The solution must enable you to roll back updates to third-party products.

    B. The solution must enable you to roll back updates to Microsoft products.

    C. The solution must enable you to deploy service packs for Windows Vista, Windows 7, and Windows Server 2008 R2.

    D. The solution must enable you to target the deployment of updates by using computer groups.

2. You are in the process of planning the deployment of WSUS at a university. The university contains five colleges, each of which has its own IT staff and Active Directory forest. The university has a single connection to the Internet through which all traffic passes and wants to minimize the amount of data downloaded from the Microsoft Update servers, but each college's IT staff should have responsibility to approve updates. Which of the following WSUS deployment plans should you use?

    A. Configure one upstream server. Configure a downstream replica server for each college.

    B. Configure a replica server in each college. Configure client computers to retrieve approvals from the WSUS server and updates from Microsoft Update.

C. Configure one upstream server. Configure a WSUS server in each college to use autonomous mode but to retrieve updates from the upstream server.

D. Configure an autonomous server in each college to retrieve updates from Microsoft Update.

3. You want to stagger the rollout of updates from your organization's WSUS 3.0 SP2 server on a departmental basis. The computer accounts for the computers in each department are located in departmental organizational units (OUs). Which of the following should you do? (Choose two. Each answer forms part of the solution.)

A. Create WSUS computer groups for each department.

B. Create Group Policy objects (GPOs) and link them to the domain. In each GPO, specify the name of a departmental WSUS computer group.

C. Create GPOs and link them to each OU. In each GPO, specify the name of a departmental WSUS computer group.

D. Create separate security groups for all the computer accounts in each departmental OU.

E. Create separate security groups for all the user accounts in each departmental OU.

4. Which method can you use to ensure that all *security* and *critical updates* deploy to computers in the PatchTest computer group, using WSUS?

A. Create a scheduled task.

B. Create an Automatic Approval rule that uses the All Computers group as a target.

C. Create an Automatic Approval rule that uses the PatchTest WSUS computer group as a target.

D. Create an Automatic Approval rule that uses the PatchTest security group as a target.

5. You are the enterprise administrator for a large metropolitan university where more than 5,000 computers running Windows Vista, 1,000 computers running Windows 7, and 200 servers running Windows Server 2008 R2 have been deployed. You need to be able to deploy software updates for Microsoft and third-party products and ensure that software updates will still be available in the event that one of the update servers suffers hardware failure. The university forest has five domains, with client and server computers being spread relatively equally across each domain. Which of the following software update server deployment plans meets the university's needs?

A. Two WSUS 3.0 SP2 servers

B. Two System Center Configuration Manager 2007 servers

C. Two System Center Essentials 2010 servers

D. Five System Center Essentials 2010 servers

Lesson 2: Managing Software Update Compliance

Compliance is a term that encompasses all the configurations necessary for ensuring that the computers in your organization are configured to a specific standard. For example, to meet compliance requirements, all client computers running Windows Vista might need Service Pack 1 and a specific set of updates applied, a certain firewall configured, and a specific set of applications installed. In this lesson, you learn about several technologies you can use to assess whether software updates that you have approved have actually been deployed to all the computers in your environment. You also learn how to create a role-based security policy that you can apply to computers in your environment, and you learn about the tools you can use to verify that the applied policy remains active.

After this lesson, you will be able to:

- Monitor software update compliance in complex environments.
- Configure and monitor security baselines.

Estimated lesson time: 40 minutes

Microsoft Baseline Security Analyzer

The *Microsoft Baseline Security Analyzer* (MBSA) is a basic tool that enables system administrators to scan the network to determine which computers are missing updates or are incorrectly configured according to Microsoft best practices recommendations. The best practices scan involves checking Windows Firewall policies, SQL Server—Service Accounts, and other security configuration settings. The MBSA tool can integrate with WSUS, so rather than scanning target systems to see whether any updates are missing from the entire catalog of updates, the MBSA tool only checks whether approved updates are missing from a target computer. You can also use the MBSA tool to detect computers that have not been assigned a software update server. To scan computers with the MBSA tool, your user account must have administrative privileges on the target computer. This enables you to scan computers in your own and trusted forests, assuming your user account has been delegated the appropriate privileges.

MBSA version 2.2, released in 2010, can now assess the latest Windows operating systems including 32-bit and 64-bit operating systems, Windows Vista, Windows 7, and Windows Server 2008 R2. You can use the MBSA tool to scan the Windows systems in enterprise environments for various misconfigurations and vulnerabilities, as shown in Figure 11-9. A drawback to the MBSA tool is that the reports it generates are basic. MBSA is designed for small-to medium-sized businesses. Unlike tools such as System Center Configuration Manager 2007, discussed later in this lesson, you cannot configure the MBSA tool to notify you by email automatically if a server or servers in your environment become noncompliant.

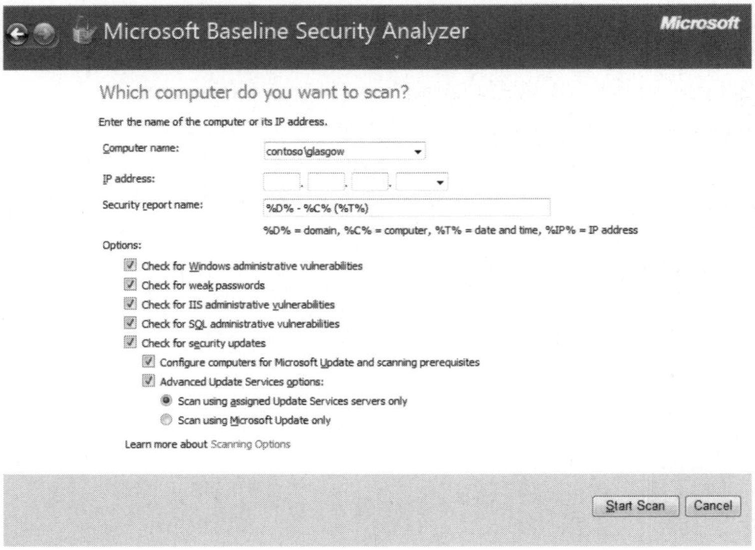

FIGURE 11-9 The MBSA tool

> **MORE INFO**   **MORE ABOUT THE MBSA**
>
> To learn more about the Microsoft Baseline Security Analyzer tool, consult the product website at *http://technet.microsoft.com/en-us/security/cc184924.aspx*.

WSUS Reporting

You can use WSUS 3.0 SP2 to offer basic Microsoft software update compliance reporting functionality in enterprise environments. The reports WSUS generates are based on information communicated with WSUS. WSUS does not scan computers to determine whether updates are missing, but instead records whether updates have been downloaded to target computers and whether the target computers have reported back to the WSUS server that the updates have been successfully installed. Figure 11-10 shows a list of the available WSUS reports.

WSUS reports can be printed or exported to Microsoft Office Excel or in PDF format. If WSUS data are written to a SQL Server database, you can perform your own separate analyses by using your own set of database queries. This enables the generation of more sophisticated reports than are offered by the default WSUS configuration.

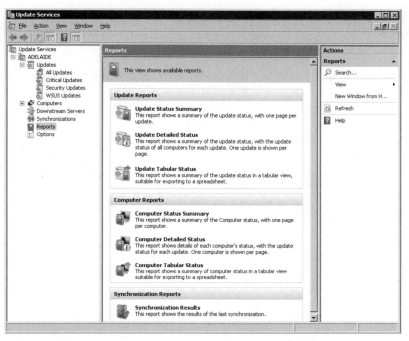

FIGURE 11-10 WSUS reporting options

You can generate the following reports using WSUS 3.0 SP2 if your user account is a member of the WSUS Reporters or WSUS Administrators groups:

- **Update Status Summary**   This report contains basic information about update deployment, including the number of computers on which the update is installed, is needed, or has failed to install, and for which WSUS has no data. One page is available per update. Figure 11-11 shows an Update Status Summary Report.

- **Update Detailed Status**   This report offers significantly more information about the deployment of updates, providing a list of computers and their update status on an update-per-page basis. When you run a detailed update, you can view the report in summary or tabular format.

- **Update Tabular Status**   This report format provides data in a table on a per-update basis. After this report is generated, you can switch the report to Update Status Summary or Update Detailed Status. This form of report is the best to export to Excel because it is already in tabular format, as shown in Figure 11-12.

- **Computer Status Summary**   Similar to the Update Detailed Status report, this report provides update information on a per-computer rather than on a per-update basis. Data are presented in summary form.

- **Computer Detailed Status** This report format provides details about the status of specific updates for a particular computer. After this report is generated, you can switch the report to summary or tabular form.

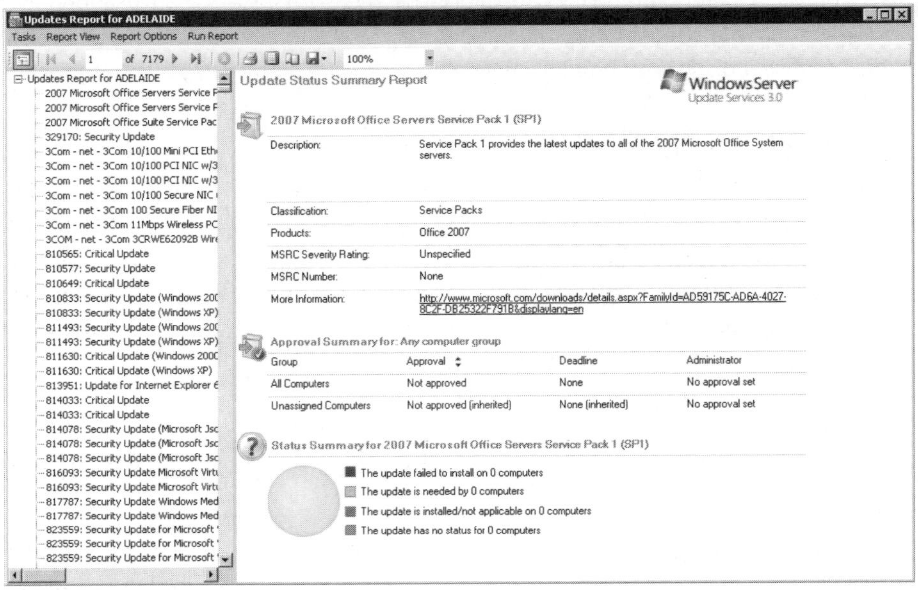

FIGURE 11-11 Update Status Summary Report

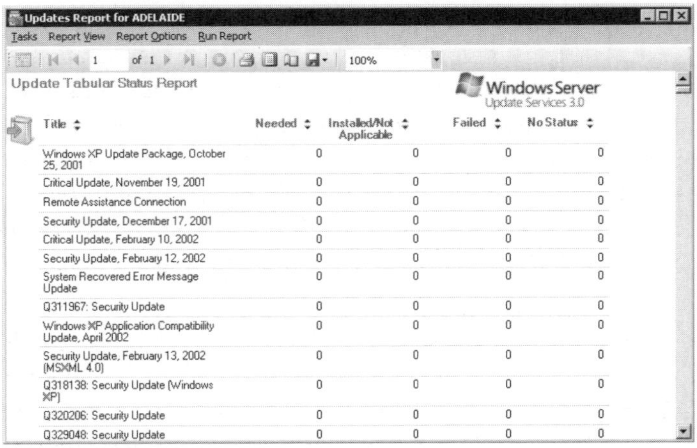

FIGURE 11-12 Update Tabular Status Report

- **Computer Tabular Status** This report provides a table of update status information, with individual computers as rows. After this report is generated, you can switch the report to summary or tabular form.

■ **Synchronization Results**   This report shows the result of the last *synchronization* of the WSUS server.

Enabling the Reporting Rollup For Downstream WSUS Servers option enables update, computer, and synchronization data for replica downstream servers to be included in reports generated on the upstream WSUS server. This is an important option in enterprise environments because it displays a complete view of the software update deployment process.

> *MORE INFO*   **SYSTEM CENTER ESSENTIALS REPORTING**
>
> System Center Essentials 2010 also offers basic reporting features related to the deployment of updates, although these are similar to those available with WSUS 3.0 SP2. You can find out more about the reporting options available in System Center Essentials 2010 by completing Exercise 2, "Use the System Center Essentials VHD to Perform Compliance Tasks," at the end of this lesson or by consulting the following TechNet article: *http://technet.microsoft.com/en-us/library/bb422813.aspx.*

System Center Configuration Manager 2007 Compliance and Reporting

Configuration management is a feature of System Center Configuration Manager 2007 that enables you to assess whether the configuration of computers within your environment matches what is termed a configuration baseline. A configuration baseline can include a specific operating system version, a set of required applications, a set of optional applications, a set of prohibited applications, a set of software updates, and a set of security settings. When you perform a scan against a configuration baseline, you compare the configuration of the computer you are scanning against the baseline configuration. The results of this scan inform you of whether and how the configuration of the scanned computer deviates from that baseline configuration. If the configuration baseline meets all *legal and regulatory requirements*, you can use a configuration baseline scan to determine whether a computer is compliant. A host of legal rules and organizational policies generally dictate compliance, so a computer deemed compliant in one organization might not be considered compliant in another.

You can configure System Center Configuration Manager 2007 to scan the computers regularly deployed in your organization against a set of configuration baselines to determine their level of compliance. System Center Configuration Manager 2007 enables you to go even further, automatically subjecting noncompliant computers to a remediation process by which the noncompliant aspects of the configuration are modified. The remediation process might include installing updates, tightening security, and removing prohibited applications so that the computer can be returned to a compliant configuration.

MORE INFO **MORE ON SYSTEM CENTER CONFIGURATION MANAGER 2007 CONFIGU-RATION MANAGEMENT**

For more information about System Center Configuration Manager 2007 configuration management, consult the following TechNet links: *http://technet.microsoft.com/en-us/library/bb680553.aspx* and *http://technet.microsoft.com/en-us/systemcenter/cm/default.aspx*.

System Center Configuration Manager 2007 can also be used to generate detailed reports about all aspects of computer configuration in your organization's enterprise environment. System Center Configuration Manager 2007 contains a large number of pregenerated reports. Administrators can also create custom reports on the configuration of client computers so they can tailor the reports to specific circumstances. Administrators who are comfortable with writing SQL queries are able to use the System Center Configuration Manager 2007 query designer rather than a wizard to create custom computer configuration reports. Compared to the MBSA tool, WSUS, and System Center Essentials 2007, System Center Configuration Manager 2007 is the most comprehensive reporting and compliance tool available from Microsoft for enterprise administrators.

MORE INFO **MANAGING SYSTEM CENTER CONFIGURATION MANAGER 2007 REPORTS**

For more information about how to manage System Center Configuration Manager 2007 reports, consult the following TechNet article: *http://technet.microsoft.com/en-us/library/bb632699.aspx*.

Planning and Deploying Security Baselines

The concept of an attack surface is that the number of services and applications that a host makes available to the network increases the area that an attacker can target. Hence, a computer hosting a web server, a DNS server, a Simple Mail Transfer Protocol (SMTP) server, and a Dynamic Host Configuration Protocol (DHCP) server has a larger attack surface than a computer hosting only a DHCP server. Reducing a computer's attack surface is part of the general process known as *server hardening.* Part of the process of hardening a server is enforcing *security baseline* configurations, a collection of settings—from service startup status through to firewall rules—that allow only those parts of the server to operate that are necessary for the server to perform its role. In Windows Server 2008 and Windows Server 2008 R2, you harden a computer by applying role-based security policies. You generate, analyze, and apply these policies by using the Security Configuration Wizard and the *Scwcmd* command-line utility.

Security Configuration Wizard

The *Security Configuration Wizard* is a tool used to reduce the attack surface of a computer running Windows Server 2008 or Windows Server 2008 R2. The tool is included in the default installation of Windows Server 2008. You can use this tool to develop security policies that will limit a server to the minimum necessary functionality required for that server to perform its planned role. You can analyze the security policy and then use it to create a GPO that you can apply to all servers that perform the same role across the enterprise.

The first step in deploying role-based security policies in an enterprise environment is to perform *policy prototyping*. Policy prototyping involves creating a security policy on a model server. A model server has a configuration that mirrors the computers in your enterprise environment to which you will be applying the policy. This enables you to test the role-based security policy prior to deploying it in your environment. *Role-based security policies* include settings for the following:

- Services
- Network security, which includes Windows Firewall with Advanced Security rules
- Registry values
- Audit policies

As Figure 11-13 shows, the Security Configuration Wizard enables you to create, edit, apply, and roll back role-based security policies. The Security Configuration Wizard writes security policies in XML format.

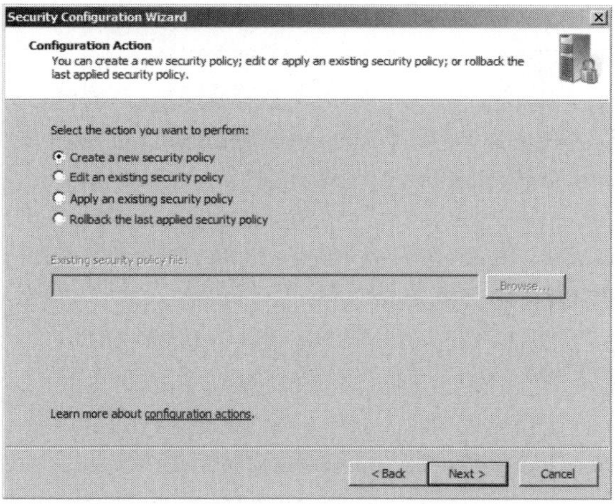

FIGURE 11-13 The Security Configuration Wizard

You can also use the Security Configuration Wizard to apply *security templates*, which are a set of pregenerated security settings located in the *%SystemRoot%\Security\Templates* folder of a computer running Windows Server 2008. You can use security templates to apply some security configuration settings to a computer running Windows Server 2008 that you cannot generate just by running the Security Configuration Wizard. For example, you can use security templates to apply software restriction policies, which are Group Policy settings by which you can restrict the applications that a computer running Windows Server 2008 can execute, using security templates. Apply these extra policies by attaching security template .inf files that include the relevant security settings using the Include Security Templates dialog box. This dialog box also enables you to set the precedence of attached security templates, allowing the settings of one template to override another. These settings remain attached to the XML file and are not directly integrated, although they do become integrated when you use the *Scwcmd* command-line utility to translate a role-based security policy into a GPO.

> **MORE INFO**   **MORE ON SECURITY TEMPLATES**
>
> To learn more about security templates, consult the TechNet blog at *http://blogs.technet .com/b/askds/archive/2008/05/28/default-security-templates-in-windows-2008.aspx*.

The *Scwcmd* Command-Line Tool

The *Scwcmd* command-line tool provides greater functionality than the GUI-based Security Configuration Wizard, although you can launch *Scwcmd* from an elevated command prompt only. Using the *Scwcmd* command-line tool, you can do the following:

- Remotely apply role-based security policy to groups of computers in your organization
- Analyze the configuration of groups of computers against the role-based security policy
- Build GPOs that apply the settings in the role-based security policy

The ability to apply a role-based security policy, using either the *Scwcmd* command-line tool or an applied GPO, enables you to enforce a baseline security configuration across the servers in your organization. The ability to analyze the configuration of computers against the role-based security policy enables you to verify that the computers in your organization remain compliant with that role-based security policy. Because the tool is based on the command line, you can include it in scheduled tasks. The *Scwcmd* command-line tool can output reports in HTML format, so enterprise administrators can use it to script regular reports they can use to assess the security health of the computers in their enterprise environment. To create a GPO from a Security Configuration Wizard policy file, issue the following command from an elevated command prompt on a domain controller:

```
scwcmd transform /p:PathAndPolicyFileName /g:NewGPODisplayName
```

After the command executes, the new GPO will be available under the Group Policy Object node of the Group Policy Management console.

> **NOTE**   **SECURITY CONFIGURATION AND ANALYSIS TOOL**
>
> The Security Configuration and Analysis tool enables you to check the configuration of a computer against a security template. The *Scwcmd* command-line tool enables you to check the configuration of a computer against an XML-formatted security policy file, which includes attached templates. You can find out more about the Security Configuration and Analysis tool by consulting the following link: *http://technet.microsoft.com/en-us/library /bb742512.aspx*.

Because role-based security policies are stored in XML format, it is a relatively simple process to migrate them to other domains or forests if the need arises. Remotely analyzing the security configuration of a computer using the *Scwcmd* command-line utility requires local administrator privileges on the target computer. It is possible to pass alternate credentials to *Scwcmd* so you can use it to analyze the security configuration of computers in separate Active Directory forests, if you have the appropriate credentials for those forests.

It is important to understand the rules of precedence in Windows Server 2008 environments where GPOs, Security Configuration Wizard role-based security policies, and security templates are applied. When planning the deployment of multiple security policies through different methods, remember the following:

- Security policies applied using GPOs have the highest precedence and override policies applied through the Security Configuration Wizard or the *Scwcmd* command-line utility. Standard GPO precedence rules apply.

- XML-based, role-based security policies have higher precedence than security templates attached to the role-based security policy. The priority of templates is configured when you attach them to the XML role-based security policy generated by the Security Configuration Wizard.

> **MORE INFO** **MORE ON SERVER SECURITY POLICIES**
>
> For more information about server security policy management in Windows Server 2008, consult the following TechNet link: *http://technet.microsoft.com/en-us/library /cc754373(WS.10).aspx.*

Role-Based Security Policy Best Practices

When planning and creating role-based security policies, keep the following best practices in mind:

- Ensure that your prototype server properly reflects the configuration of the servers to which the policy will apply. Role-based security policies disable all services that are not present on the prototype server when the policy is created.

- Create separate policies for separate software editions. For example, create a separate policy for 64-bit and 32-bit computers running Windows Server 2008 that host the Web Server (IIS) role.

- When possible, group servers that perform the same role into a single OU in the same domain. When this is not possible, use the same OU name for servers with the same role in different domains and forests. This simplifies the application of policy distribution in complex environments.

- Thoroughly test policies before deploying them on production servers.

PRACTICE   Role-Based Security and System Center Essentials Reporting

In this practice, you perform two common enterprise administrator tasks. The first exercise involves the creation and application of a role-based security policy using the Security Configuration Wizard. The second exercise involves using System Center Essentials 2007 evaluation.

EXERCISE 1   Create and Apply a Role-Based Security Policy

In this exercise, you create a role-based security policy based on the current configuration of server Glasgow and save this policy in XML format. You then transform this XML policy file into a new GPO and apply that GPO to a newly created OU.

1. Log on to server Glasgow using the Kim_Akers user account.

2. Use the Active Directory Users And Computers snap-in to create an OU named **GlasgowClones** in the *contoso.internal* domain. Create a computer account in the GlasgowClones OU named **London**.

3. Use the Security Configuration Wizard to create a new security policy named **GlasgowPolicy.xml**.

4. Use the *Scwcmd* command-line tool to transform the new security policy (located in the %SystemRoot%\Security\Msscw\Policies folder) into a GPO named **GlasgowPolicyGPO**.

5. Use the Group Policy Management console to link GlasgowPolicyGPO to the GlasgowClones OU.

6. Use the Group Policy Modeling Wizard to model the effect that the newly applied GPO has on computer account London.

EXERCISE 2   Use the System Center Essentials VHD to Perform Compliance Tasks

In this exercise, you use the System Center Essentials 2007 evaluation VHD that you downloaded for Exercise 2 in Lesson 1 to perform several reporting and compliance tasks. To complete this exercise, perform the following steps:

1. Log on to the virtual computer using the user name **Administrator** and the password **Evaluation1**.

2. Open the System Center Essentials 2007 management console. Click Required: Configure Product Features. Navigate through the Feature Configuration Wizard. Review and then accept all default settings except the following:

a. On the Agentless Exception Monitoring For Computers page, configure System Center Essentials 2007 so that it does not collect application errors.

b. On the Daily Health Report Settings page, select Do Not Configure The Daily Health Report At This Time. Click Configure to complete the configuration process.

3. Click Reporting to open the Reporting View.

4. Select Microsoft Generic Reports Library.

5. Select the Health report and, from the Actions menu, choose Open.

6. Add the *SCEVHDSERVER.fabrikam.internal* object, set the business hours option as shown in Figure 11-14, and then click Run.

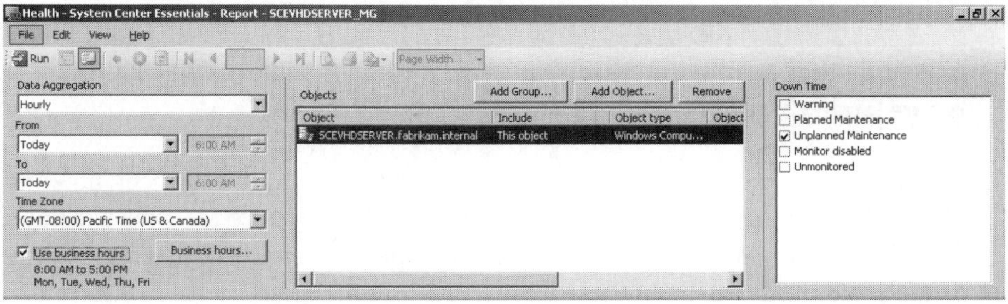

FIGURE 11-14 System Center Essentials Health report

7. Select the Updates view. Under Reports, select the Group Update Deployment Status item.

8. In the Choose The Computer Group For This Report drop-down list, select the All Servers group, and then click Run.

> **MORE INFO** **SYSTEM CENTER ESSENTIALS VIRTUAL LAB**
>
> To learn more about System Center Essentials 2007, complete the virtual labs at *http://technet.microsoft.com/en-us/systemcenter/essentials/bb539977.aspx*.

Lesson Summary

- You can use the MBSA tool to scan computers to determine whether approved updates are installed. The MBSA tool can use a list of updates from an update server or from Microsoft Update. You can also use the MBSA tool to detect a small number of security configuration problems on scanned computers.

- You can use System Center Configuration Manager 2007 to perform compliance scans, comparing the configuration of scanned computers against a configuration baseline. It is possible to configure System Center Configuration Manager 2007 to automatically resolve configuration differences between the configuration of a scanned computer and the configuration baseline.

- You can use the Security Configuration Wizard to create a role-based security policy as well as to capture the entire configuration of a hardened prototype server. You can then apply this policy to other servers, which automatically changes their security configuration to match that of the prototype server.

Lesson Review

You can use the following questions to test your knowledge of the information in Lesson 2, "Managing Software Update Compliance." The questions are also available on the companion CD if you prefer to review them in electronic form.

> **NOTE** ANSWERS
>
> Answers to these questions and explanations of why each answer choice is correct or incorrect are located in the "Answers" section at the end of the book.

1. Tailspin Toys has a single domain forest with 700 client computers running Windows 7 and 24 computers running Windows Server 2008 R2. You are planning the deployment of a product that will be able to perform compliance reporting on all computers in the *tailspintoys.internal* domain to ensure that a specific set of patches is installed and that several security settings have been configured appropriately. Which of the following planned deployments will meet your needs?

   A. A single computer running Windows Server 2008 R2 with System Center Essentials 2010 installed

   B. Two computers running Windows Server 2008 R2 with WSUS 3.0 SP2 installed

   C. Two computers running Windows Server 2008 R2 with System Center Essentials 2010 installed

   D. A single computer running Windows Server 2008 R2 with System Center Configuration Manager 2007 R3 installed

2. Which of the following tools can you use to apply an XML-formatted, role-based security policy remotely to 400 computers running Windows Server 2008 R2 located throughout an Active Directory forest in which your user account has administrative privileges?

   A. Security Configuration and Analysis tool

   B. Microsoft Baseline Security Analyzer 2.2 tool

   C. *Scwcmd* command-line tool

   D. Windows Server Update Services 3.0 SP2

3. Which of the following security settings, when remotely applied to a group of computers running Windows Server 2008 R2 in an Active Directory forest, will take precedence over all the others?

   A. Security settings applied through Group Policy

   B. Security settings applied using the *Scwcmd* command-line tool

   C. Security settings applied using the Security Configuration and Analysis tool

   D. Security settings applied using the Security Configuration Wizard

4. You need a list of computers on which a recent update did not install so that you can send a technician to investigate further. Which of the following WSUS 3.0 SP2 reports should you generate to locate this information quickly?

   A. Update Status Summary

   B. Computer Status Summary

   C. Update Detailed Status

   D. Computer Detailed Status

Chapter Review

To further practice and reinforce the skills you learned in this chapter, you can perform the following tasks:

- Review the chapter summary.
- Review the list of key terms introduced in this chapter.
- Complete the case scenarios. These scenarios set up real-world situations involving the topics of this chapter, and they ask you to create solutions.
- Complete the suggested practices.
- Take a practice test.

Chapter Summary

- You can use WSUS Server to centralize the deployment of updates in a Windows Server 2008 R2 environment. It provides basic compliance reporting functionality.
- System Center Essentials 2010 enables you to provide software updates to third-party applications but is limited to only one server per domain and can be used with only 500 client computers and 50 servers.
- System Center Configuration Manager 2007 has advanced reporting functionality that you can use to verify that computers meet compliance requirements.
- You can use the Security Configuration Wizard and *Scwcmd* command-line utility to generate, analyze, and apply XML-formatted, role-based security policies.

Key Terms

Do you know what these key terms mean? You can check your answers by looking up the terms in the glossary at the end of the book.

- Auto approval
- Autonomous WSUS server
- Branch office
- Central site
- Child site
- Compliance reporting
- Computer discovery
- Critical updates
- Hardware and software inventory
- Legal and regulatory compliance requirements
- Microsoft Baseline Security Manager (MBSA)

- Microsoft Update Server
- No Auto Restart
- Parent site
- Physical to virtual
- Policy prototyping
- Primary site
- Proxy server
- Replica WSUS server
- Role-based policy
- Scwcmd
- Secondary site
- Security baseline
- Security Configuration and Analysis Tool
- Security Configuration Wizard
- Security policy
- Security template
- Security updates
- Server hardening
- Software update point
- Staggered rollout
- Synchronization
- System Center Configuration Manager
- System Center Essentials
- System Center Essentials agent
- Third-party application updates
- Update approval
- Update testing
- Virtual Machine Manager
- Wake on LAN
- Windows Server Update Services (WSUS)
- WSUS Administrator
- WSUS all computers
- WSUS client-side targeting
- WSUS computer groups

- WSUS Configuration Wizard
- WSUS downstream server
- WSUS hierarchy
- WSUS Reporter
- WSUS server-side targeting
- WSUS unassigned computers
- WSUS upstream server/source server

Case Scenarios

In the following case scenarios, you apply what you have learned about patch management and security. You can find answers to these questions in the "Answers" section at the end of this book.

Case Scenario 1: Deploying WSUS 3.0 SP2 at Fabrikam, Inc.

After using an ad hoc approach to patch management over the last few years, the CIO at Fabrikam, Inc., has decided that during the project to upgrade all existing computers running Windows 2000 Server to Windows Server 2008 R2, WSUS 3.0 SP2 should also be deployed. Fabrikam is located in the state of Victoria, Australia. The head office is located in the Melbourne central business district (CBD), and suburban satellite offices are located in Moonee Ponds, Cheltenham, Endeavour Hills, and Glen Waverley.

The current plan is for a WSUS 3.0 SP2 server to be installed on a Windows Server 2008 R2 host at the head office and then for a phased rollout of WSUS servers at the suburban satellite offices. Because all the IT staff work in the Melbourne CBD office, the servers at the satellite offices should use the computer group configuration and the update approvals that are configured on the head office server.

One reason for the ad hoc approach in the past was that Fabrikam uses custom software that sometimes conflicts with updates, causing the installation of those updates to fail. The CIO wants to be able to run reports on updates from her desktop computer to determine when these events occur. The CIO does not require administrative access to the server and never performs hands-on administrative tasks, always delegating this to the systems administrators in her team.

With this information in mind, answer the following questions:

1. To which local group on the computer running Windows Server 2008 R2 hosting WSUS should you add the CIO's user account?

2. How should you configure the update source of downstream WSUS servers at the Fabrikam satellite offices?

3. Which type of report should you instruct the CIO to generate to gain detailed information about the specific computers on which a particular update's installation has failed?

Case Scenario 2: Security Policies at Coho Vineyard and Coho Winery

Coho Vineyard and Coho Winery are two subsidiary companies owned by the same parent. You work for the parent company, and you are responsible for the planning and deployment of security policies for all subsidiary organizations. Coho Vineyard and Coho Winery have their own separate single-domain Active Directory forests. These forests do not share a trust relationship. You have separate user accounts with Enterprise Administrator credentials in both forests but most often use a management server located in the *cohovineyard.internal* domain to perform day-to-day tasks. You are planning the deployment of role-based security policies for intranet servers in each organization's forest.

With this information in mind, answer the following questions:

1. The intranet servers use both the 32-bit and 64-bit versions of Windows Server 2008 as their operating system. How many role-based security policies should you develop for these servers?

2. Which tools can you use to create role-based policies for the intranet servers?

3. You want to perform a daily check of the intranet servers in the *cohowinery.internal* forest to verify that their configuration still conforms to the applied security policy. You want to run this check from your management server in the *cohowinery.internal* forest and have the results output in HTML format. What steps would you take to accomplish this goal?

Suggested Practices

To help you successfully master the exam objectives presented in this chapter, complete the following tasks.

Designing for Software Updates and Compliance Management

Complete the following practice exercises:

- **Practice 1** Install System Center Configuration Manager 2007 in the *contoso.internal* domain by downloading an evaluation version of SQL Server 2008 and System Center Configuration Manager 2007 from the Microsoft website. Deploy a new computer running Windows Server 2008 R2. Install SQL Server 2008 and then System Center Configuration Manager 2007.

- **Practice 2** Prototype and deploy a security policy by installing a new member server in the *contoso.internal* domain and configuring the server with the Web Server (IIS) and DNS Server roles. Use the Security Configuration Wizard to generate a role-based security policy based on the configuration of the newly installed member server. Use the *Scwcmd* command-line utility to create a GPO based on these settings.

Take a Practice Test

The practice tests on this book's companion CD offer many options. For example, you can test yourself on just one exam objective, or you can test yourself on all the 70-647 certification exam content. You can set up the test so that it closely simulates the experience of taking a certification exam, or you can set it up in study mode so that you can look at the correct answers and explanations after you answer each question.

> **MORE INFO** **PRACTICE TESTS**
>
> For details about all the practice test options available, see the "How to Use the Practice Tests" section in this book's introduction.

Answers

Chapter 1: Lesson Review Answers

Lesson 1

1. **Correct Answer: B**

   A. **Incorrect:** Centralized WINS topology uses a single, centralized, high-availability WINS server or WINS server cluster.

   B. **Correct:** Full mesh WINS topology is a distributed WINS design with multiple WINS servers or clusters deployed across the enterprise. Each server or cluster replicates with every other server or cluster.

   C. **Incorrect:** Ring WINS topology is a distributed WINS design created by having each WINS server replicate with only specific neighboring partners, forming a circle.

   D. **Incorrect:** Hub and spoke WINS topology is a distributed WINS design in which a central WINS server is designated as the hub and additional WINS servers only replicate with the hub in the site where they are located.

2. **Correct Answer: A**

   A. **Correct:** You can configure the primary name server, the refresh interval, and the minimum default TTL values for zone resource records in the zone's SOA record.

   B. **Incorrect:** NS records identify the name servers in a DNS zone.

   C. **Incorrect:** SRV records permit AD DS to integrate with DNS and implement dynamic DNS. These records are required for the Locator mechanism to function.

   D. **Incorrect:** Canonical name (CNAME) records map an alias or nickname to the real or canonical name that might lie outside the current zone.

3. **Correct Answer: C**

   A. **Incorrect:** The */createdirectorypartition* switch in the *dnscmd* command is used to create a directory partition and will not enable a DNS server to support GlobalNames zones.

   B. **Incorrect:** The */enlistdirectorypartition* switch in the *dnscmd* command is used to add a DNS server to partition replication scope and will not enable a DNS server to support GlobalNames zones.

   C. **Correct:** The */config* switch in the *dnscmd* command is used to enable a DNS server to support GlobalNames zones.

D. Incorrect: The */createbuiltindirectorypartitions* switch in the *dnscmd* command is used to create the default directory partitions and will not enable a DNS server to support GlobalNames zones.

4. **Correct Answer: A**

   A. Correct: You cannot list DNS records by using *nslookupls–d* unless you have configured the zone to allow zone transfers, even when the records are on the same computer.

   B. Incorrect: You run the command console as an administrator when using configuration commands such as *dnscmd*. You do not need to do so when you are displaying but not changing information.

   C. Incorrect: You can type **nslookupls –d adatum.internal** directly from the command prompt. However you can also type **nslookup** and then type **ls –d adatum.internal** from the nslookup> prompt. In either case, the zone must be configured to allow zone transfers for these commands to function properly.

   D. Incorrect: You can perform most operations on a server, including *nslookup*, by logging on through a Remote Desktop connection. Logging on to servers interactively is bad practice and should be avoided.

5. **Correct Answer: D**

   A. Incorrect: There is no problem with the host record for the web server. Other users can access the internal website.

   B. Incorrect: You do not need to flush the DNS cache on the DNS server. Because others are able to access the website correctly, the problem is at the user's client computer.

   C. Incorrect: Registering the client computer in DNS allows others to find the client computer and does not help the client computer find other systems.

   D. Correct: A DNS cache entry on the client computer has marked the website URL as not resolvable. Flushing the DNS cache on the client computer solves the problem by forcing the client system to query the DNS server, rather than using the cached, negative resolution.

6. **Correct Answer: B**

   A. Incorrect: The NRPT cannot be managed using .inifiles.

   B. Correct: The NRPT is typically managed through GPOs to deploy settings for Active Directory clients. The NRPT can also be managed using Regedit and Regedt32, which is beneficial on non-Active Directory clients.
   Reference: *http://technet.microsoft.com/en-us/library/ee649182(WS.10).aspx*

   C. Incorrect: The *netsh* command cannot be used to configure the NRPT, but it can be used to show the effective NRPT rules on a DNS client.

   D. Incorrect: The *ipconfig* command cannot be used to configure the NRPT.

Lesson 2

1. **Correct Answer: B**

   A. Incorrect: A unique-local unicast IPv6 address identifies a node in a site or intranet. It begins with fc00, and is the equivalent of an IPv4 private address, for example, 10.0.0.1.

   B. Correct: A global unicast address (or aggregatable global unicast address) is the IPv6 equivalent of an IPv4 public unicast address and is globally routable and reachable on the Internet.

   C. Incorrect: A link-local unicast IPv6 address is autoconfigured on a local subnet. It is the equivalent of an IPv4 APIPA address, for example, 169.254.10.123.

   D. Incorrect: Two special IPv6 addresses exist. The unspecified address :: indicates the absence of an address and is equivalent to the IPv4 unspecified address 0.0.0.0. The loopback address ::1 identifies a loopback interface and is equivalent to the IPv4 loopback address 127.0.0.1. Neither is the IPv6 equivalent of an IPv4 public unicast addresses.

2. **Correct Answer: A**

   A. Correct: The solicited node address consists of the 104-bit prefix ff02::1:ff (written ff02::1:ff00:0/104) followed by the last 24 bits of the link-local address, in this case, a7:d43a.

   B. Incorrect: Although the 104-bit prefix is written ff02::1:ff00:0/104, the /104 indicates that only the first 104 bits (ff02::1:ff) are used. Hence, the solicited-node address is ff02::1:ffa7:d43a.

   C. Incorrect: Addresses that start with fec0 are site-local, not solicited-node.

   D. Incorrect: Addresses that start with fec0 are site-local, not solicited-node.

3. **Correct Answer: D**

   A. Incorrect: ARP is a broadcast-based protocol used by IPv4 to resolve MAC addresses to IPv4 addresses. ND uses ICMPv6 messages to manage the interaction of neighboring nodes.

   B. Incorrect: EUI-64 is not a protocol. It is a standard for 64-bit hardware addresses.

   C. Incorrect: DHCPv6 assigns stateful IPv6 configurations. ND uses ICMPv6 messages to manage the interaction of neighboring nodes.

   D. Correct: ND (Neighbor Discovery) protocol uses ICMPv6 messages to manage the inter-action of neighboring nodes.

4. **Correct Answer: A**

   A. Correct: In configured tunneling, data passes through a preconfigured tunnel, using encapsulation. The IPv6 packet is carried inside an IPv4 packet. The encapsulating IPv4 header is created at the tunnel entry point and removed at the tunnel exit point. The tunnel endpoint addresses are determined by configuration information.

B. Incorrect: Dual stack requires that hosts and routers provide support for both protocols and can send and receive both IPv4 and IPv6 packets. Tunneling is not required.

C. Incorrect: ISATAP connects IPv6 hosts and routers over an IPv4 network, using a process that views the IPv4 network as a link layer for IPv6 and other nodes on the network as potential IPv6 hosts or routers. This creates a host-to-host, host-to-router, or router-to-host automatic tunnel. A preconfigured tunnel is not required.

D. Incorrect: Teredo is an enhancement to the 6to4 method. It enables nodes that are located behind an IPv4 NAT device to obtain IPv6 connectivity by using UDP to tunnel packets. Teredo requires the use of server and relay elements to assist with path connectivity. It does not require a preconfigured tunnel.

5. Correct Answer: D

    A. Incorrect: This command displays the IPv6 configuration on all interfaces. It does not configure an IPv6 address.

    B. Incorrect: You can use this command to add the IPv6 address of, for example, a DNS server to an IPv6 configuration. You use *netsh interface ipv6 set address* to configure a static IPv6 address.

    C. Incorrect: This command enables you to change IPv6 interface properties but not an IPv6 address. You use *netsh interface ipv6 set address* to configure a static IPv6 address.

    D. Correct: You use *netsh interface ipv6 set address* to configure a static IPv6 address.

6. Correct Answers: A, D, F, and G

    A. Correct: IPv4 and IPv6 are both supported by Trey's network hardware and service provider. Dual stack is the most straightforward transition strategy.

    B. Incorrect: Trey does not need to encapsulate IPv6 packets inside IPv4 packets. Configured tunneling transition is typically employed if IPv6 is not currently available.

    C. Incorrect: Trey saw no need to configure NAT and use private IPv4 addresses. The organization is unlikely to use unique-local addresses, which are the IPv6 equivalent of private addresses.

    D. Correct: Trey uses public IPv4 addresses throughout its network. It is likely to use global unicast addresses in its IPv6 network.

    E. Incorrect: Trey's clients run Windows Vista Ultimate, and its servers run Windows Server 2008 R2. All Trey's clients and servers support IPv6, and the protocol is installed by default.

    F. Correct: There is no guarantee that Trey's network projectors and network printers support IPv6, although they probably do because the company believes in investing in cutting-edge technology.

    G. Correct: Network management systems need to be checked for IPv6 compatibility.

    H. Incorrect: High-level applications are typically independent of the Internet protocol used.

Chapter 1: Case Scenarios Answers

Case Scenario 1: Configuring DNS

1. You can configure a zone to support only secure dynamic updates. This ensures that only authenticated users and clients can register information in DNS.

2. You can configure zone replication to occur only with DNS servers that have NS records and are listed on the Name Servers tab. Alternatively, you can manually specify a list of servers and configure zone replication so that zone information is replicated only to these servers.

3. When a Windows Server 2008 server is configured as a read-only domain controller (RODC), it replicates a read-only copy of all Active Directory partitions that DNS uses, including the domain partition, ForestDNSZones, and DomainDNSZones. Therefore, DNS zone information on RODCs updates automatically (provided the writable domain controller is configured to allow this).

4. Create an IPv6 reverse lookup zone.

Case Scenario 2: Implementing IPv6 Connectivity

1. Unique-local IPv6 addresses are the direct equivalent of private IPv4 addresses and are routable between VLANs. However, you could also consider configuring every device on your network with an aggregatable global unicast IPv6 address. NAT and CIDR were introduced to address the problem of a lack of IPv4 address space, and this is not a problem in IPv6. You cannot use only link-local IPv6 addresses in this situation because they are not routable.

2. Both IPv4 and IPv6 stacks are available. In this scenario, dual stack is the most straightforward transition strategy.

3. As with DHCP for IPv4, you should configure a dual-scope DHCPv6 server on each subnet. The scope for the local subnet on each server should include 80 percent of the full IPv6 address range for that subnet. The scope for the remote subnet on each server should include the remaining 20 percent of the full IPv6 address range for that subnet.

Chapter 2: Lesson Review Answers

Lesson 1

1. **Correct Answer: B**
   - **A. Incorrect:** Data autonomy does not require a resource forest. Resource forests provide service isolation that is used to protect areas of the network that need to maintain a state of high availability.
   - **B. Correct:** To achieve data autonomy, you can join an existing forest.

C. **Incorrect:** Data autonomy does not require a new organizational forest. An organizational forest provides service autonomy, service isolation, or data isolation.

D. **Incorrect:** Data autonomy does not require a new restricted access forest. A restricted access forest is used for data isolation.

2. **Correct Answer: C**

A. **Incorrect:** A restricted access forest will not provide service autonomy. A restricted access forest is used for data isolation.

B. **Incorrect:** A resource forest will not provide service autonomy. Resource forests provide service isolation that is used to protect areas of the network that need to maintain a state of high availability.

C. **Correct:** An organizational forest will provide service autonomy.

D. **Incorrect:** Joining an existing forest will not provide service autonomy. Joining an existing forest provides data autonomy.

3. **Correct Answers: A, B, C, and D**

A. **Correct:** When deciding whether to upgrade existing domains or deploy new domains, you must determine whether the existing domain model still meets the needs of the organization.

B. **Correct:** The amount of downtime that can be incurred is an important consideration when deciding whether to upgrade existing domains or deploy new domains because the downtime varies between the methods.

C. **Correct:** Time constraints are an important consideration when deciding whether to upgrade existing domains or deploy new domains because the time required varies between the methods.

D. **Correct:** The budget is an important consideration when deciding whether to upgrade existing domains or deploy new domains because the costs vary between the methods.

Lesson 2

1. **Correct Answer: A**

A. **Correct:** The single site model has all domain controllers in the same site and uses intrasite replication.

B. **Incorrect:** The multiple sites model uses intersite replication, not intrasite replication, because domain controllers are distributed across one or more sites.

C. **Incorrect:** The hub and spoke replication topology has multiple sites and uses intersite replication, not intrasite replication.

D. **Incorrect:** The full mesh replication topology has multiple sites and uses intersite replication, not intrasite replication.

2. **Correct Answer: C**

   A. Incorrect: The single site model has all domain controllers in the same site and therefore does not provide efficient replication when the network consists of faster network connections between major computing hubs and slower links connecting branch offices.

   B. Incorrect: There is no replication topology referred to as the ring replication topology in terms of AD DS replication.

   C. Correct: The hub and spoke replication topology provides most efficient replication when the network consists of faster network connections between major computing hubs and slower links connecting branch offices.

   D. Incorrect: The full mesh replication topology is used when each site connects to every other site. With the full mesh replication topology, the propagation of change orders for replicating AD DS can impose a heavy burden on the network and is not efficient when the network consists of faster network connections between major computing hubs and slower links connecting branch offices.

3. **Correct Answer: A**

   A. Correct: The server that holds the PDC emulator operations master role should be placed in the location represented by the hub site because this site would have the largest number of users when the hub and spoke replication topology is used.

   B. Incorrect: The server that holds the PDC emulator operations master role should not be placed in a location represented by a spoke site because the locations represented by spoke sites have fewer users than the location represented by the hub site. The PDC emulator should always be placed in a location where it services the highest number of users.

   C. Incorrect: The server that holds the PDC emulator operations master role cannot be placed in every location represented by a spoke site because there can only be one PDC emulator per domain.

   D. Incorrect: The server that holds the PDC emulator operations master role should not be placed on the server that holds the global catalog server role in a location represented by a spoke site because the locations represented by spoke sites have fewer users than the location represented by the hub site. The PDC emulator should always be placed in a location where it services the highest number of users.

Chapter 2: Case Scenario Answers

Case Scenario 1: Designing the AD DS Forest

1. No. Joining the Wingtip Toys computers to the Tailspin Toys forest will not provide service isolation and will allow the Tailspin Toys administrators to manage the entire forest.

2. Yes. Creating a new organizational forest for Wingtip Toys will meet the service isolation requirements and split the administration capabilities between Tailspin Toys and Wingtip Toys administrators.

Case Scenario 2: Designing AD DS Sites

1. No. Not all locations are connected to a central location. Therefore, the hub and spoke topology will not work.

2. Yes. Using a hybrid topology will work. The U.S., Canada, Mexico, and Italy locations will be using a hub and spoke in this hybrid, with the U.S. location as the hub. The Argentina location will connect directly to the Mexico location, which necessitates a hybrid topology.

Case Scenario 3: Designing the Placement of Domain Controllers

1. No. A global catalog server will also act as a writable domain controller. Therefore, if this server is compromised due to lack of physical security, it can be used to further compromise AD DS and AD DS data.

2. Yes. An RODC in the Argentina location is the best solution because physical security cannot be guaranteed in this location, and RODCs are read-only.

Chapter 3: Lesson Review Answers

Lesson 1

1. **Correct Answer: B**

   A. **Incorrect:** The *adprep /forestprep* command is run to prepare the schema for Windows Server 2008 R2. The domain controller hosting the primary domain controller (PDC) emulator role does not contain a writable copy of the schema.

   B. **Correct:** You must run *adprep /forestprep* on the domain controller hosting the schema master role because this domain controller has a writable copy of the schema.

   C. **Incorrect:** The *adprep /forestprep* command is run to prepare the schema for Windows Server 2008 R2. The domain controller hosting the Relative ID (RID) master role does not contain a writable copy of the schema.

   D. **Incorrect:** The *adprep /forestprep* command is run to prepare the schema for Windows Server 2008 R2. The domain controller hosting the infrastructure master role does not contain a writable copy of the schema.

   E. **Incorrect:** The *adprep /forestprep* command is run to prepare the schema for Windows Server 2008 R2. The domain controller hosting the domain naming master role does not contain a writable copy of the schema.

2. **Correct Answer: D**

    A. **Incorrect:** You should run the *adprep /domainprep /gpprep* command on the computer hosting the infrastructure master role, not on the computer hosting the PDC emulator role.

    B. **Incorrect:** You should run the *adprep /domainprep /gpprep* command on the computer hosting the infrastructure master role, not on the computer running the schema master role.

    C. **Incorrect:** You should run the *adprep /domainprep /gpprep* command on the computer hosting the infrastructure master role, not on the computer hosting the RID master role.

    D. **Correct:** You should run the *adprep /domainprep /gpprep* command on the infrastructure master when preparing a domain for the introduction of a Windows Server 2008 domain controller when the forest has already been prepared.

    E. **Incorrect:** You should run the *adprep /domainprep /gpprep* command on the infrastructure master, not on the domain naming master. Furthermore, there is only one domain naming master per forest.

3. **Correct Answer: A**

    A. **Correct:** Disabling SID filtering enables the *SIDHistory* attribute, allowing SIDs tied to accounts that have been migrated to new domains or forests to access resources in the original domain or forest.

    B. **Incorrect:** SID filtering is enabled by default.

    C. **Incorrect:** Selective Authentication limits which users can access resources across a forest trust.

    D. **Incorrect:** Name suffix routing routes authentication requests to a specific forest.

4. **Correct Answer: A**

    A. **Correct:** When selective authentication is configured for a trust relationship, users from the trusted forest will not automatically be authenticated for resources in the trusting forest. Users from the trusted forest must be explicitly granted access to resources.

    B. **Incorrect:** SID filtering is automatically enabled on Windows Server 2008 trusts as a security measure; it will not ensure that users from a trusted forest are automatically treated as authenticated users by the trusting forest.

    C. **Incorrect:** UPN suffix routing is used to specify where user authentication occurs, not to ensure that users from a trusted forest are automatically treated as authenticated users by the trusting forest.

    D. **Incorrect:** Forest-wide authentication means that users from a trusted forest are automatically treated as authenticated users by the trusting forest.

Lesson 2

1. **Correct Answer: D**

   A. Incorrect: Services for NFS enables you to serve files from a computer running Windows Server 2008 to UNIX-based client computers.

   B. Incorrect: The Password Synchronization component of Identity Management for UNIX enables you to synchronize passwords between AD DS and UNIX-based computers.

   C. Incorrect: Subsystem for UNIX-Based Applications enables you to run POSIX-compliant applications on a computer running Windows Server 2008.

   D. Correct: Active Directory Federation Services enables you to implement a single-sign-on solution for a group of related Web applications.

2. **Correct Answer: B**

   A. Incorrect: AD FS provides a single-sign-on solution for Web applications. It does not synchronize identity data across different products.

   B. Correct: Microsoft Identity Lifecycle Manager Feature Pack 1 can be used as a tool to synchronize user identity data across a heterogeneous environment. This includes synchronizing user identity data stored in a human resources database running on Oracle 9i with a Windows Server 2008 AD DS infrastructure and an Exchange Server 2007 deployment.

   C. Incorrect: Server for NIS does synchronize identity data between NIS and AD DS, but the solution required in this question involves different products. The necessary outcome cannot be achieved by using Server for NIS.

   D. Incorrect: Services for NFS is a file-sharing solution that enables UNIX-based operating systems to access shared files on computers running Windows Server 2008. It cannot be used to synchronize identity data.

3. **Correct Answer: C**

   A. Incorrect: Subsystem for UNIX-Based Applications enables POSIX applications to execute on a computer running Windows Server 2008.

   B. Incorrect: Server for NIS enables a computer running Windows Server 2008 R2 to function as an NIS server for UNIX computers. It is not used to share files between a computer running Windows Server 2008 and UNIX-based client computers.

   C. Correct: Services for NFS enables UNIX-based client computers to access shared files on computers running Windows Server 2008 R2.

   D. Incorrect: Network Policy Server is not related to shared files.

4. **Correct Answers: C, E**

   A. Incorrect: You would not plan to use the Remote Desktop Services role as a method of migrating UNIX-based applications to Windows Server 2008.

B. **Incorrect:** Although it might be possible to virtualize some UNIX-based operating systems using Hyper-V, they cannot all be virtualized because many such operating systems run on architectures other than x64 or x86.

C. **Correct:** The Subsystem for UNIX-Based Applications feature enables POSIX-compliant applications to run on a computer running Windows Server 2008 R2.

D. **Incorrect:** Active Directory Federation Services does not allow POSIX-compliant applications to run on a computer running Windows Server 2008 R2.

E. **Correct:** After SUA has been installed, the POSIX applications still need to be migrated to the new platform.

Chapter 3: Case Scenario Answers

Case Scenario: Phasing Out a UNIX-Based Computer at Tailspin Toys

1. Authentication can be simplified by using Active Directory Federation Services and setting up a federation partnership between Wingtip Toys and Tailspin Toys.

2. Because the application is POSIX-compliant, it probably can be migrated to run under the Windows Server 2008 R2 Subsystem for UNIX-Based Applications environment.

Chapter 4: Lesson Review Answers

Lesson 1

1. **Correct Answer: C**

   A. **Incorrect:** In the centralized model, Group Policy is set at a single central location that is locally administered by a single administration team. This model is best suited to organizations with a single main office and small branch offices.

   B. **Incorrect:** The hybrid model is more commonly known as the mixed model. This model is best suited to medium-sized organizations with a main office and a number of subsidiaries, each of which has a few local administrators. Most Group Policy settings are defined at the central office, but the subsidiaries can configure and administer local configurations.

   C. **Correct:** Northwind Traders is a large multinational organization. Each national office has considerable autonomy and its own administration team. This is the distributed administrative model.

   D. **Incorrect:** The mixed model is best suited to medium-sized organizations with a main office and a number of subsidiaries, each of which has a few local administrators. Most

Group Policy settings are defined at the central office, but the subsidiaries can configure and administer local configurations.

2. **Correct Answers: A, D, E, and F**

   A. **Correct:** Microsoft recommends the Business Unit Administrators management role for delegating data management.

   B. **Incorrect:** Microsoft recommends the Security Policy Administrators management role for delegating service management, not data management.

   C. **Incorrect:** Microsoft recommends the Service Administration Managers management role for delegating service management, not data management.

   D. **Correct:** Microsoft recommends the Resource Administrators management role for delegating data management.

   E. **Correct:** Microsoft recommends the Security Group Administrators management role for delegating data management.

   F. **Correct:** Microsoft recommends the Application-Specific Administrators management role for delegating data management.

   G. **Incorrect:** Microsoft recommends the Replication Management Administrators management role for delegating service management, not data management.

3. **Correct Answer: B**

   A. **Incorrect:** Audit Directory Service Access controls whether auditing for directory service events is enabled or disabled. However, the policy is enabled by default.

   B. **Correct:** Audit Directory Service Access controls whether auditing for directory service events is enabled or disabled. This policy is enabled by default.

   C. **Incorrect:** If Directory Service Changes is enabled, AD DS logs events in the Security event log. This setting does not control whether auditing for directory service events is enabled or disabled.

   D. **Incorrect:** If Directory Service Changes is disabled, AD DS does not log events in the Security event log. This setting does not control whether auditing for directory service events is enabled or disabled.

4. **Correct Answer: D**

   A. **Incorrect:** A forest trust sets up a trust relationship between the domains in two forests. Windows NT 4.0 domains do not use forests.

   B. **Incorrect:** If a UNIX realm uses Kerberos authentication, you can create a realm trust between a Windows domain and the UNIX realm. You cannot create a realm trust between two Windows domains.

   C. **Incorrect:** If users in one child domain in a forest frequently need to access resources in another child domain in another forest, you might decide to create a shortcut trust between the two domains. You cannot create a shortcut trust to a Windows NT 4.0 domain.

D. Correct: You set up an external trust when a domain within your forest requires a trust relationship with a domain that does not belong to a forest. Typically, external trusts are used when migrating resources from Windows NT domains.

5. **Correct Answer: A**

   A. Correct: You should delegate permission to link GPOs. This enables existing GPOs to be linked without allowing those GPOs to be modified.

   B. Incorrect: You should delegate permissions to existing OUs in this scenario, not to GPOs.

   C. Incorrect: The software developers' security group does not need to generate Group Policy modeling data to link GPOs.

   D. Incorrect: The software developers' security group does not need to generate Group Policy results to link GPOs.

Lesson 2

1. **Correct Answer: C**

   A. Incorrect: Although having too many GPOs (often with the same settings) is a common mistake, it is also a bad idea to have too few. However, if a GPO has many policy settings configured in different areas, it can be difficult to understand everything it does or to give it a descriptive name.

   B. Incorrect: Linking GPOs to OUs across sites can slow replication and increase traffic over slow WAN links.

   C. Correct: Both GPOs and OUs should have descriptive names. You might know what GPO06 does right now, but will you remember in three months' time? If you had called it (for example) Kiosk Policy, its function would be much clearer. Similarly, an OU named Human Resources is more helpful than OU23.

   D. Incorrect: Features such as Block Inheritance, Enforced, Security Filtering, and Loopback Policy can be useful in the situations for which they were designed. However, they add complexity and make your Group Policy design more difficult to understand. Use these exceptions only when you can identify a real advantage in doing so.

2. **Correct Answers: B, C, D, and E**

   A. Incorrect: DSA is a service component in the Active Directory data store, not an interface.

   B. Correct: MAPI is an interface in the Active Directory data store.

   C. Correct: SAM is an interface in the Active Directory data store.

   D. Correct: REPL is an interface in the Active Directory data store.

   E. Correct: LDAP is an interface in the Active Directory data store.

   F. Incorrect: ESE is a service component in the Active Directory data store, not an interface.

3. **Correct Answers: A, C, and F**

   A. **Correct:** Enabling Prevent Installation Of Devices Not Described By Other Policy Settings prevents standard users from installing devices except for those devices permitted by other settings.

   B. **Incorrect:** Disabling or not configuring Prevent Installation Of Devices Not Described By Other Policy Settings permits standard users to install any device except those specifically prohibited by other settings.

   C. **Correct:** Enabling Allow Administrators To Override Device Installation Restriction Policies permits administrators to install any device.

   D. **Incorrect:** Disabling or not configuring Allow Administrators To Override Device Installation Restriction Policies results in administrators having the same device installation rights as standard users, which is not what is required.

   E. **Incorrect:** Enabling Prevent Installation Of Devices That Match Any Of These Device IDs and adding the Hardware ID of the approved device to the policy setting would explicitly prohibit the installation of that device.

   F. **Correct:** Enabling Allow Installation Of Devices That Match Any Of These Device IDs and adding the Hardware ID of the approved device to the policy setting would explicitly permit installation of that device and would override the Prevent Installation Of Devices Not Described By Other Policy Settings setting for that device only.

Chapter 4: Case Scenario Answers

Case Scenario 1: Designing a Delegation Strategy

1. Windows Server 2008 provides granular AD DS auditing that enables you to audit the changes made to AD DS configuration and to record what the settings are before they are changed.

2. Advise your team member to use scope filtering. This enables security groups to be defined when the GPO is linked to the OU so that the GPO settings apply only to these groups.

3. The Group Policy Results tool.

Case Scenario 2: Planning Authentication and Authorization

1. Windows Server 2008 introduces fine-grained password policies that enable settings other than the default to be set for specified users or for security groups. You can apply a PSO to a group or an exceptional PSO directly to a user account. In Windows 2003 domains, variations in password policy typically require additional domains.

2. Your team member needs to check domain functional levels and raise them to Windows Server 2008, if necessary.

3. You can use Group Policy to prevent all users except administrators from installing devices on their workstations. This does not affect the Windows ReadyBoost feature, which is a System installation.

Chapter 5: Lesson Review Answers

Lesson 1

1. **Correct Answer: D**

   A. **Incorrect:** The access client would be the VPN client that initiates the connection attempt.

   B. **Incorrect:** The access server is also known as the RADIUS client. In this scenario, it receives the inbound connection attempt from the access client and forwards the authentication request to a remote server through RADIUS.

   C. **Incorrect:** The RADIUS proxy is an intermediary between RADIUS clients and RADIUS servers to facilitate load balancing and forwarding of requests to the appropriate RADIUS server for authentication.

   D. **Correct:** The RADIUS server is the final RADIUS component in the chain of forwarded requests starting from a RADIUS client. It is the endpoint at which a directory server is presented with an authentication request from the RADIUS server.

2. **Correct Answer: B**

   A. **Incorrect:** One of the primary uses of a RADIUS proxy is accepting inbound RADIUS requests from access servers.

   B. **Correct:** The RADIUS client or an access server performs this service.

   C. **Incorrect:** The RADIUS proxy is essential in a RADIUS solution that requires load balancing of requests to back-end RADIUS servers. Normally, access clients can provide load-balanced RADIUS requests by offsetting configurations on the access clients. One access client has a specified primary RADIUS server and a secondary RADIUS server, whereas a second access client has them listed in the opposite order of the first access client.

   D. **Incorrect:** Multiforest environments using RADIUS for authentication of a provided service require a RADIUS proxy to ensure the delivery of a RADIUS request to an appropriate RADIUS server in the same realm as the user account requesting authentication.

3. **Correct Answers: A, C, and D**

   A. **Correct:** The server certificate is first presented to the client and is used to create the encrypted channel between the client and the server.

   B. **Incorrect:** PEAP-TLS uses the server's certificate along with the computer's certificate to create an encrypted tunnel prior to the exchange of certificates for mutual authentication.

C. **Correct:** MS-CHAPv2 uses only the user password for the user's authentication. No other authentication medium is provided for the user.

D. **Correct:** MS-CHAPv2 does provide for mutual authentication of both the client and the server.

Lesson 2

1. **Correct Answers: A, B, and D**

   A. **Correct:** NAP provides a safer internal environment where trusted computers have successfully passed a health validation.

   B. **Correct:** Enforcing a policy that mandates the health level of a computer and requires validation of it prior to entrance into the trusted environment ensures protection.

   C. **Incorrect:** NAP does not provide a firewall block against attackers. NAP does ensure that all computers have an appropriately configured firewall but provides no assurance that computers cannot be attacked.

   D. **Correct:** Enforcing validation of a health policy prior to a computer's entrance into the trusted network enhances the network's ability to fend off an attack.

2. **Correct Answer: D**

   A. **Incorrect:** 802.1x ensures only that a client accessing the trusted environment through an access point has passed a health validation check.

   B. **Incorrect:** DHCP enforcement uses the Classless Static Routes option (Option 249) of DHCP to define the servers in the restricted network for a noncompliant NAP client requiring remediation.

   C. **Incorrect:** VPN enforcement does provide for the confidentiality of the data up to the point at which the access server accepts the inbound connection request. Encryption beyond this point depends on the VPN connection protocols and any other protocol for data confidentiality.

   D. **Correct:** IPsec prevents not only the replay of a communication session but also enables data confidentiality, data integrity, IPsec authentication of the communication channel, and data origin authentication.

Chapter 5: Case Scenario Answers

Case Scenario: Designing a NAP Solution for a Large Enterprise

1. Using the NAP IPsec enforcement requires that all managed computers be trusted. Regardless of the fact that these are branch offices, the users in these locations will be accessing services at the main office. Thus, services accessed by users will require user

authentication at the very least. Access to any resource, including domain controllers, will require IPsec-authenticated access.

2. Again, regardless of the location; how few users; and whether any user requires access to domain services, such as domain controllers, file servers, or email, the user will be required to access those resources from a computer that can provide IPsec-authenticated communication.

Chapter 6: Lesson Review Answers

Lesson 1

1. **Correct Answer: C**

   A. **Incorrect:** The RODC will refer modifications to a writable domain controller.

   B. **Incorrect:** Server Core installs a limited set of services and applications and has a constrained interface, but it does not prohibit an administrator from modifying Active Directory.

   C. **Correct:** Administrator Role Separation allows the branch office administrator the privilege of managing the underlying server operating system but not Active Directory.

   D. **Incorrect:** BitLocker provides encryption of entire volumes on a drive in a system, but it does not stop a logged-on branch office administrator from administering Active Directory.

2. **Correct Answer: D**

   A. **Incorrect:** The RODC provides increased security for Active Directory, but it does not provide user data fault tolerance.

   B. **Incorrect:** Clustering can be used to provide server and application fault tolerance, but it has no built-in mechanism to provide user data fault tolerance.

   C. **Incorrect:** Server Core provides increased security through a reduced attack surface, but it does not provide user data fault tolerance.

   D. **Correct:** DFS replication is used to replicate user data to multiple locations, such as branch offices, making the data fault tolerant.

3. **Correct Answer: C**

   A. **Incorrect:** The relay agent would still need to traverse the WAN link.

   B. **Incorrect:** With the WAN link down, clients in the branch office could not access any scope in the HQ.

   C. **Correct:** The DHCP cluster would provide fault tolerance for IP addressing, even with the failed WAN link.

   D. **Incorrect:** Demand-dial routing, although it might provide redundancy in the WAN link, does not address the DHCP needs of the branch office.

Lesson 2

1. **Correct Answer: B**

   A. **Incorrect:** The full installation of Windows Server 2008 has more features, services, and applications installed by default, making it more vulnerable to attack.

   B. **Correct:** Server Core installs a limited set of services and applications and has a constrained interface, making this the securest installation in the branch office. Installing the read-only version of the domain controller on this Server Core Installation is the most secure combination for a domain controller at a branch office.

   C. **Incorrect:** The full (writable) version of the domain controller can be used to reset or steal additional passwords and to violate the integrity of the data in Active Directory. The full installation of Windows Server 2008 has more features, services, and applications installed by default, making it more vulnerable to attack.

   D. **Incorrect:** The full (writable) version of the domain controller can be used to reset or steal additional passwords and to violate the integrity of the data in Active Directory.

2. **Correct Answer: A**

   A. **Correct:** The RODC requires a writable Windows Server 2008 domain controller in the nearest site, based on site link cost, to the RODC site.

   B. **Incorrect:** RODCs, even on a Windows Server 2008 R2, cannot perform outbound replication and, therefore, cannot be a replication source.

   C. **Incorrect:** Site link costs to the adjacent site should be the lowest to ensure replication.

   D. **Incorrect:** Site link bridging is not a factor of replication to an RODC.

3. **Correct Answer: D**

   A. **Incorrect:** Administrator Role Separation allows the local administrator to maintain the replacement RODC server, but not Active Directory. This will not protect passwords on the stolen RODC.

   B. **Incorrect:** The PSO is used to specify and assign fine-grained password policies to users and groups, not to protect exposed passwords.

   C. **Incorrect:** The IFM disk might be used to perform a remote installation of the replacement RODC, but this should not be the first action taken.

   D. **Correct:** You can use the Deleting Domain Controller Wizard to reset user and computer passwords as well as to export a list of users with passwords on the stolen RODC.

Chapter 6: Case Scenario Answers

Case Scenario 1: Contoso Trucking, Part 1

1. Because these offices will probably be under constant hacker attack by your competitor, these servers should all be Windows Server 2008 Server Core Installations.

2. All domain controllers should be RODCs due to the unskilled administrators and the risk of exposure from the hacker attacks.

3. The junior administrators should be granted local administrator privileges using Administrator Role Separation.

Case Scenario 2: Contoso Trucking, Part 2

1. Initialize BitLocker on the drives in Syracuse. This might require a reinstallation of the operating system to create the proper partition structure to support BitLocker.

2. Raise the domain functional level to Windows Server 2008. Create a global security group named Schenectady Users and add all Schenectady users to the group. Use ADSI Edit or LDIFDE to create a PSO with the following strong password policy settings (for example):

   - Maximum Password Age = 30 days
   - Minimum Password Age = 25 days
   - Minimum Password Length = 12 characters
   - Password History = 24
   - Password Complexity = Enabled
   - Reversible Encryption Enabled = False
   - Account Lockout Threshold = 3
   - Account Lockout Window = 30 minutes
   - Account Lockout Duration = 0 (Only an administrator can unlock the account.)
   - Users or global security groups that the PSO applies to = Schenectady Users

Case Scenario 3: Contoso Trucking, Part 3

1. Precreate the RODC account in Active Directory Users and Computers. Grant the new junior administrator in Saskatchewan the authority to install the RODC. Create IFM media using Ntdsutil and remove the password attribute from all users. Supply the IFM media to the administrator in Saskatchewan.

2. Configure Administrator Role Separation for the administrator in Saskatchewan. Create an OU named Saskatchewan. Place all Saskatchewan users and computers into the Saskatchewan OU. Delegate the appropriate level of privilege to the junior administrator in Saskatchewan.

Chapter 7: Lesson Review Answers

Lesson 1

1. **Correct Answer: D**
   A. **Incorrect:** Automatic license server discovery is no longer supported for RD Session Host servers. Setting a discovery scope is only necessary in deployments involving Windows Server 2003 and Windows Server 2008 Terminal Servers.
   B. **Incorrect:** Automatic license server discovery is no longer supported for RD Session Host servers. Setting a discovery scope is only necessary in deployments involving Windows Server 2003 and Windows Server 2008 Terminal Servers.
   C. **Incorrect:** Automatic license server discovery is no longer supported for RD Session Host servers. Setting a discovery scope is only necessary in deployments involving Windows Server 2003 and Windows Server 2008 Terminal Servers.
   D. **Correct:** Because automatic license server discovery is no longer supported for RD Session Host servers, it is necessary to manually assign the use of a license server for the RD Session Host server. It is necessary to deploy and configure the use of a license server per site because it was stated that Remote Desktop Services CALs would be consumed locally.

2. **Correct Answer: C**
   A. **Incorrect:** It is not necessary to set the forest functional level to Windows Server 2008 prior to deploying an RD Licensing server.
   B. **Incorrect:** It is not necessary to set the domain functional level to Windows Server 2008 to install licenses on an RD Licensing server.
   C. **Correct:** It is necessary to activate the RD Licensing server prior to the installation of Remote Desktop Services CALs.
   D. **Incorrect:** It is not necessary to install IIS on an RD Licensing server.

3. **Correct Answer: D**
   A. **Incorrect:** Using WSRM policies will not enable adding capacity as needed.
   B. **Incorrect:** Hyper-V would not work as a solution because there is an upper limit to processor capacity on the virtual host. This solution requires the ability to add processor capacity as required.
   C. **Incorrect:** Although adding terminal servers would meet emerging capacity needs, it would not meet the requirement that clients need not be reconfigured.
   D. **Correct:** Planning the deployment of an RD Session Host farm enables you to add and remove servers from the farm as necessary without altering client configuration.

4. **Correct Answer: C**

   A. Incorrect: Microsoft Forefront Client Security and other antivirus solutions can check for viruses and malware after a client connection has been made but cannot block unhealthy clients from connecting.

   B. Incorrect: The RD Connection Broker is used to manage sessions that connect to RD Session Host farms. You cannot use it to ensure that connecting clients pass health checks.

   C. Correct: An RD Gateway server can be used in conjunction with NAP to disallow computers that have not passed a health check to connect to the RD Session Host server.

   D. Incorrect: Forefront Threat Management Gateway cannot be used to block clients from connecting to a terminal server if they do not pass a health check. It is possible to use NAP in conjunction with ISA Server 2006 but not specifically to block access to RD clients.

Lesson 2

1. **Correct Answers: A and D**

   A. Correct: You can use Group Policy software deployment in this situation to deploy applications to all clients on the network.

   B. Incorrect: System Center Essentials 2010 is limited to managing 500 clients.

   C. Incorrect: System Center Operations Manager 2007 is not an application deployment tool.

   D. Correct: You can use System Center Configuration Manager 2007 in this situation to deploy applications to all clients on the network.

   E. Incorrect: System Center Virtual Machine Manager 2007 is not an application deployment tool.

2. **Correct Answer: B**

   A. Incorrect: Group Policy Results works only with computers or users who have logged on and is not a suitable tool for simulating an application deployment strategy.

   B. Correct: Group Policy Modeling enables you to simulate an application deployment strategy when using Group Policy software deployment.

   C. Incorrect: You cannot use Active Directory Computers and Users to simulate Group Policy software deployment.

   D. Incorrect: You cannot use Active Directory Sites and Services to simulate a Group Policy software deployment.

3. **Correct Answer: D**

   A. Incorrect: An application can be configured to be uninstalled when it falls out of the scope of management whether it is published or assigned.

   B. Incorrect: The language options will not remove an application if the user account is moved to another OU.

    C. **Incorrect:** The Install This Application At Logon option will not remove an application if the user account is moved to another OU.

    D. **Correct:** Plan to use the Uninstall The Application When It Falls Out Of The Scope Of Management option when an application needs to be removed because a user or computer account is moved from the location in Active Directory that prompted the initial application deployment.

4. **Correct Answer: A**

    A. **Correct:** The System Center Configuration Manager 2007 software metering functionality enables you to determine the frequency with which applications installed on a computer are actually used. You can determine whether the application is necessary by tracking usage patterns.

    B. **Incorrect:** You cannot use Windows Server Update Services 3.0 SP1 to perform software metering.

    C. **Incorrect:** You cannot use the Group Policy Management Console to perform software metering.

    D. **Incorrect:** You cannot use Active Directory Users and Computers to perform software metering.

Chapter 7: Case Scenario Answers

Case Scenario: Planning a Remote Desktop Services Strategy for Wingtip Toys

1. Deploy an RD License server centrally and manually configure each RD Session Host server to use the central license server.

2. Create an RD Connection Broker to manage client access.

3. To access RemoteApp applications through RD Web Access, you must upgrade Windows Vista clients to SP1 and install Remote Desktop Connection 7.0 client.

Chapter 8: Lesson Review Answers

Lesson 1

1. **Correct Answer: B**

    A. **Incorrect:** VSMT is a more appropriate tool to virtualize a small number of existing servers.

    B. **Correct:** You can use SCVMM 2008 to move virtualized servers between virtual hosts over a Fibre Channel SAN. Because you cannot use other types of tools to accomplish this type of migration, this scenario presents the most compelling case for the deployment of SCVMM 2008.

C. **Incorrect:** You can use SCVMM 2008 to manage and monitor thousands of VMs. Although it is possible to manage 10 VMs using this product, the built-in Hyper-V tools are more than adequate for such a task. Because one answer in this set requires SCVMM 2008, this answer is not the most compelling.

D. **Incorrect:** Automating server deployment is accomplished through Windows Deployment Services (WDS) rather than through SCVMM.

2. **Correct Answer: A**

A. **Correct:** It is only possible to install the Hyper-V server role on an x64 version of Windows Server 2008 R2. The Hyper-V server role can be installed on both the full and core installations of Windows Server 2008 R2.

B. **Incorrect:** It is only possible to install the Hyper-V role on an x64 version of Windows Server 2008 R2.

C. **Incorrect:** It only is possible to install the Hyper-V role on an x64 version of Windows Server 2008 R2.

D. **Incorrect:** It is only possible to install the Hyper-V role on an x64 version of Windows Server 2008 R2.

3. **Correct Answers: A and E**

A. **Correct:** A single SCVMM 2008 R2 deployment can be used to manage 8,000 VMs and 400 VM hosts.

B. **Incorrect:** A single SCVMM 2008 R2 deployment can manage only 400 VM hosts.

C. **Incorrect:** A single SCVMM 2008 R2 deployment can manage only 400 VM hosts.

D. **Incorrect:** A single SCVMM 2008 R2 deployment can manage only 8,000 VMs.

E. **Correct:** A single SCVMM 2008 R2 deployment can be used to manage 8,000 VMs and 400 VM hosts.

4. **Correct Answer: D**

A. **Incorrect:** The SCVMM database needs to have good connectivity only to the SCVMM server. An SCVMM library server needs to have good connectivity to a virtual host for the rapid deployment of new VMs.

B. **Incorrect:** The question mentions nothing about SCVMM self-service portals, and these are not required to ensure that rapid VM deployment can occur to branch office VM hosts.

C. **Incorrect:** Only one SCVMM server needs to be deployed in an organization, and this server can be used to manage rapid deployments at a branch office location if a library server is there.

D. **Correct:** You should deploy an SCVMM 2008 R2 library server at a branch office location when you need to use SCVMM 2008 R2 to rapidly deploy new VMs to a branch office virtual host.

5. **Correct Answer: A**

    A. **Correct:** The SCVMM 2008 agent must be installed manually on VM hosts that are configured as stand-alone servers.

    B. **Incorrect:** SCVMM agents are installed on host computers and not on VMs.

    C. **Incorrect:** AD LDS does not need to be installed to allow SCVMM 2008 R2 to manage stand-alone virtual hosts.

    D. **Incorrect:** It is not necessary to install extra instances of SCVMM 2008 R2 because it is possible to manage stand-alone servers if the agent software is manually installed.

Lesson 2

1. **Correct Answer: C**

    A. **Incorrect:** Although DNS round-robin splits load on the basis of request, it is not fault tolerant and will still direct clients to a failed host until manually configured otherwise.

    B. **Incorrect:** Microsoft Application Virtualization Management Server is not a cluster-aware application.

    C. **Correct:** Microsoft recommends that you use Network Load Balancing as a high-availability solution for the Microsoft Application Virtualization Management Server component of an application virtualization solution.

    D. **Incorrect:** A Remote Desktop Session Host server farm does not function as a high-availability solution for the Microsoft Application Virtualization Management Server component of an application virtualization deployment.

2. **Correct Answer: B**

    A. **Incorrect:** The data store is a SQL Server database that holds configuration data.

    B. **Correct:** The App-V sequencer is used to convert traditional applications so that they can be deployed through Microsoft Application Virtualization Management Server to App-V clients.

    C. **Incorrect:** Neither the Remote Desktop Services nor desktop client software is used to perform the App-V sequencing process.

    D. **Incorrect:** Neither the Remote Desktop Services nor desktop client software is used to perform the App-V sequencing process.

3. **Correct Answers: A and D**

    A. **Correct:** This client software is required to ensure that App-V applications can be run on the local computer.

    B. **Incorrect:** Hyper-V is not a component of a Microsoft Application Virtualization Deployment.

    C. **Incorrect:** SCVMM is not a component of a Microsoft Application Virtualization Deployment.

D. Correct: A Microsoft Application Virtualization Management Server needs to be deployed at the local site to ensure that App-V applications can be delivered to local clients.

E. Incorrect: There is no need to deploy Microsoft Application Virtualization for RDS at the branch office site because Remote Desktop Services is not in use.

4. **Correct Answer: D**

A. Incorrect: It is not necessary to deploy Microsoft Application Virtualization in this situation.

B. Incorrect: Although in this situation you should plan to deploy Microsoft Application Virtualization, it is not necessary to use a Remote Desktop Session Host.

C. Incorrect: In this situation it is not necessary to deploy Microsoft Application Virtualization.

D. Correct: Microsoft Application Virtualization for RDS is necessary only when you need to virtualize applications on the Remote Desktop Session Host before serving them to clients.

5. **Correct Answer: C**

A. Incorrect: You should use Microsoft Application Virtualization. RemoteApp will not resolve the problem of applications conflicting when installed on the same Remote Desktop Session Host server.

B. Incorrect: You should use Microsoft Application Virtualization. A Remote Desktop Gateway Server will not resolve the problem of applications conflicting when installed on the same Remote Desktop Session Host server.

C. Correct: Microsoft Application Virtualization allows applications that would normally conflict—including different versions of the same application—to be deployed from the same Remote Desktop Session Host server.

D. Incorrect: You should use Microsoft Application Virtualization. Remote Desktop Web Access will not resolve the problem of applications conflicting when installed on the same Remote Desktop Session Host server.

Chapter 8: Case Scenario Answers

Case Scenario: Tailspin Toys Server Consolidation

1. Install the 64-bit version of Windows Server 2008 R2 Enterprise and deploy Hyper-V. Virtualize the server that hosts the domain controller, DNS, and DHCP services on one virtual server. Virtualize the server that hosts the SQL Server 2000 database and individually virtualize each of the servers hosting the business application. This would require one physical server. It would also be possible to upgrade the existing servers to Windows Server 2008 R2 without requiring extra licenses because the Enterprise edition includes four licenses for virtualized instances of Windows Server 2008 R2.

2. Although it would be possible to virtualize each terminal server, this would not meet the goal of reducing the number of terminal servers (although it would meet the goal of minimizing the amount of server hardware). In this situation, you can reduce the amount of both hardware and terminal servers by deploying Microsoft Application Virtualization, which allows applications to run in virtualized silos so that they do not conflict with each other. Rather than virtualizing the server, this solution virtualizes the applications.

Chapter 9: Lesson Review Answers

Lesson 1

1. **Correct Answer: B**

   A. Incorrect: If you configure the target priority as first among all targets, users in the other four sites will be directed to the New York target even if the local target is available.

   B. Correct: This option achieves the desired effect. By default, users will be directed to the target in their own site, but if the local target is unavailable, they will be directed to the New York site.

   C. Incorrect: You do not want to change the site link cost because this would unintentionally affect other features, such as AD DS replication.

   D. Incorrect: You do not want to change the site link cost because this would unintentionally affect other features, such as AD DS replication.

2. **Correct Answer: D**

   A. Incorrect: Distributed File System is used to group shared folders located on different servers and present them to users as a virtual tree of folders known as a namespace.

   B. Incorrect: Windows SharePoint Services does not include Excel Services, which is required to provide access to real-time, interactive Microsoft Office Excel 2007 spreadsheets from a web browser.

   C. Incorrect: Active Directory Federation Services provides Federated Identity and Access Management.

   D. Correct: Excel Services, which is available through Microsoft Office SharePoint Server 2007, is used to provide access to real-time, interactive Microsoft Office Excel 2007 spreadsheets from a web browser.

3. **Correct Answer: A**

   A. Correct: To create a domain-based namespace in Windows Server 2008 mode, the domain functional level must be Windows Server 2008 or higher.

   B. Incorrect: You cannot raise the domain functional level to Windows Server 2008 R2 because there are domain controllers that have Windows Server 2008 installed. These domain controllers must be upgraded to Windows Server 2008 R2 or replaced with new Windows Server 2008 R2–based domain controllers first.

C. **Incorrect:** The forest functional level cannot be raised because the domain functional level needs to be raised first. Additionally, the forest functional level does not affect the ability to create a domain-based namespace.

D. **Incorrect:** You cannot raise the forest functional level to Windows Server 2008 R2 because there are Windows Server 2008–based domain controllers in the forest.

Lesson 2

1. **Correct Answer: D**

   A. **Incorrect:** You cannot use AD RMS to protect data in a SQL Server database.

   B. **Incorrect:** You need a TPM 1.2 if you want the server to be able to restart without administrator assistance.

   C. **Incorrect:** You cannot use AD RMS to protect data in a SQL Server database.

   D. **Correct:** If your server includes a TPM 1.2 module, you can use BitLocker encryption to protect the data and prevent the disks from being read on another server. In addition, if you choose the TPM-only authentication mode, you can allow the server to restart without requiring an administrator to enter a PIN or provide a USB drive key.

2. **Correct Answer: A**

   A. **Correct:** In this authentication mode, BitLocker uses only a TPM to unlock the VMK and enable a volume to be read. Advantages of this mode are that it requires no user intervention and it protects the data from being read if the drive is stolen.

   B. **Incorrect:** In this mode, both a TPM and a USB flash device are required. To start the computer, a user must insert a USB flash device containing an external key.

   C. **Incorrect:** This authentication mode requires both a TPM and a user to provide a personal identification number (PIN) every time the computer is started.

   D. **Incorrect:** In this mode, the user provides a USB flash device during startup that includes an external key enabling encrypted volumes to be read.

3. **Correct Answer: B**

   A. **Incorrect:** In this authentication mode, BitLocker uses only a TPM to unlock the VMK and enable a volume to be read. Advantages of this mode are that it requires no user intervention and it protects the data from being read if the drive is stolen.

   B. **Correct:** In this mode, both a TPM and a USB flash device are required. To start the computer, a user must insert a USB flash device containing an external key. The advantage of this method is that, in principle, it protects the data even if the entire computer is stolen (because a thief needs access to the USB flash device to read the data).

   C. **Incorrect:** This authentication mode requires both a TPM and a user to provide a personal identification number (PIN) every time the computer is started.

   D. **Incorrect:** In this mode, the user provides a USB flash device during startup that includes an external key enabling encrypted volumes to be read.

Lesson 3

1. **Correct Answer: B**

    A. Incorrect: Node majority is best used for an odd number of nodes.

    B. Correct: This is the quorum configuration used with an even number of nodes and a witness disk.

    C. Incorrect: This is the best quorum configuration to use when you have an even number of nodes and no witness disk. (A file share replaces the witness disk.)

    D. Incorrect: This option is not recommended. It is used when any single node and its storage remains online. It does not use a witness disk.

2. **Correct Answer: A**

    A. Correct: Authoritative restores are required when you need to recover from object deletions.

    B. Incorrect: Nonauthoritative restores will not allow you to recover from object deletions. These will restore the domain controller to the state in the backup file, and thereafter replication will update the domain controller. The deleted objects will not be recovered.

    C. Incorrect: A full server recovery recovers every volume on the server. These are to be used to recover from hard drive failures or file corruption on the same hardware with the same operating system installed.

    D. Incorrect: Critical volume recovery will restore the domain controller to the state of the backup, and thereafter replication will update the domain controller. The deleted objects will not be recovered.

3. **Correct Answer: D**

    A. Incorrect: Whenever you seize operations master roles, you must avoid bringing the server back online to avoid corruption in AD DS. To transfer the role, you must bring it back online.

    B. Incorrect: Authoritative restores are used to recover from object deletions.

    C. Incorrect: Nonauthoritative restores are used to recover a domain controller to the point of the backup. In this case, the role has been seized, so this will cause further issues.

    D. Correct: Whenever you seize operations master roles, you must avoid bringing the server back online to avoid corruption in AD DS. You must remove the server from AD DS and then reinstall the operating system.

Chapter 9: Case Scenario Answers

Case Scenario: Designing Solutions for Sharing, Security, and Availability

1. WSS.
2. DFS and a domain-based namespace. To avoid intersite queries, you should deploy a namespace server at all four sites.
3. AD RMS.
4. Failover clustering.

Chapter 10: Lesson Review Answers

Lesson 1

1. **Correct Answer: C**
   - **A. Incorrect:** EFS encrypts data by using a combination of symmetric and asymmetric methods. EFS requires the use of certificates.
   - **B. Incorrect:** S/MIME uses certificates and public key cryptography to encrypt email.
   - **C. Correct:** IPsec can rely on a certificate infrastructure for authentication, but this is not a requirement. In Windows domains, IPsec usually relies on Kerberos instead.
   - **D. Incorrect:** SSL requires the use of a server certificate.

2. **Correct Answer: D**
   - **A. Incorrect:** Often, business relationships require the use of strong security (confidentiality, integrity, and authenticity). PKI cross-trusts or qualified subordination can be used to satisfy this requirement.
   - **B. Incorrect:** Laws and regulations often require the use of strong security (confidentiality, integrity, and authenticity). Certificates can be used to satisfy this requirement.
   - **C. Incorrect:** Companies typically have valuable information assets they need to protect (confidentiality, integrity, and authenticity). The use of digital certificates can be used to satisfy this requirement.
   - **D. Correct:** The acquisition of a loan for the corporation will often require a strong credit score, but typically does not impose specific security requirements or technologies on the borrower.

3. **Correct Answer: C**
   - **A. Incorrect:** DirectAccess, introduced in Windows 7 and Windows Server 2008 R2, provides secure remote connectivity without requiring users to build a VPN connection.

B. Incorrect: Hyper-V is Microsoft's virtualization platform.

C. Correct: AppLocker is new in Windows 7 and provides control over applications with digital signatures.

D. Incorrect: OCSP is a new service used to verify whether a digital certificate has been revoked.

Lesson 2

1. **Correct Answers: A and C**

   A. Correct: By taking the root CA offline, you can minimize the risk that the entire PKI will be compromised.

   B. Incorrect: Leaving the root CA online leaves that CA open to being compromised. When the root CA is compromised, the entire PKI is compromised.

   C. Correct: In this case, the subordinate CA is an issuing CA. By deploying the CA as an enterprise CA, you can automate the distribution of certificates to domain members.

   D. Incorrect: Using a stand-alone CA does not minimize the administrative overhead of publishing certificates.

2. **Correct Answer: A**

   A. Correct: You need one enterprise issuing CA for your internal uses and a separate PKI branch for the specialized security requirements imposed by the business partner. This branch consists of a policy CA to define the security practices used by the branch and its subordinate issuing CA. This issuing CA will be issuing certificates to your internal users for use when interacting with the partner, who trusts this PKI branch.

   B. Incorrect: The online root CA violates recommended practices, and the stand-alone issuing CAs do not interoperate efficiently with your Active Directory environment.

   C. Incorrect: The online root and issuing CA violates recommended practices.

   D. Incorrect: Because your internal security needs differ from your partner's security needs, the two issuing CAs should not be in the same branch subject to the same security policies and practices.

3. **Correct Answer: C**

   A. Incorrect: The CA issues certificates to end entities.

   B. Incorrect: The CRL distribution point (CDP) is a network location where the CRL is published for certificate verification purposes.

   C. Correct: It is the job of the RA to verify the identity of the end entity who is requesting a digital certificate. Once the identity is verified, the RA submits a certificate request to the CA on behalf of the end entity.

   D. Incorrect: OCSP is a new service used to verify whether a digital certificate has been revoked.

Lesson 3

1. **Correct Answer: D**

    A. Incorrect: OCSP is a protocol that enables real-time certificate validity checking. It doesn't enable certificate enrollment.

    B. Incorrect: Autoenrollment is available as a certificate enrollment method only for enterprise CAs and only to members of the local Active Directory forest.

    C. Incorrect: SCEP is a protocol used to issue certificates to network devices, not to users.

    D. Correct: Web enrollment provides the most automated method to issue certificates to users who are not members of an Active Directory domain.

2. **Correct Answer: A**

    A. Correct: The feature of automatically renewing device certificates is provided with Windows Server 2008 R2. Device certificate renewal can also be provided on Windows Server 2008 by installing Service Pack 2 or hotfix #KB959193.

    B. Incorrect: OCSP is a protocol that enables real-time certificate validity checking. It doesn't enable certificate renewal.

    C. Incorrect: Adding this permission on the template does not enable renewal; it allows a subject the permission to acquire the initial certificate.

    D. Incorrect: The CPS defines the policies and practices in place for a specific branch of the PKI hierarchy. It does not enable certificate renewal.

3. **Correct Answers: A and D**

    A. Correct: OCSP is a protocol that enables real-time certificate validity checking and identifies revoked certificates from the PKI.

    B. Incorrect: Autoenrollment is available as a certificate enrollment method only for enterprise CAs and only to members of the local Active Directory forest. It does not identify revoked certificates.

    C. Incorrect: SCEP is a protocol used to issue certificates to network devices, not to identify revoked certificates.

    D. Correct: The CDP is used to identify revoked certificates. It is often provided through LDAP in Active Directory or as a website available to systems where your certificates are used.

Chapter 10: Case Scenario Answers

Case Scenario: Planning a PKI

1. The PKI should include three CAs, including the root CA. You should have one policy CA for partners and another policy CA for employees.

2. Employees should use autoenrollment. Partners should use web enrollment.

3. OCSP.

Chapter 11: Lesson Review Answers

Lesson 1

1. **Correct Answer: A**

   A. **Correct:** You can use System Center Essentials 2010 to deploy updates to third-party products, and you can roll back the deployment of these updates if necessary.

   B. **Incorrect:** Both WSUS 3.0 SP2 and System Center Essentials 2010 can be used to roll back software updates for Microsoft products.

   C. **Incorrect:** Both WSUS 3.0 SP2 and System Center Essentials 2010 can be used to deploy service packs for Windows Vista, Windows 7, and Windows Server 2008 R2.

   D. **Incorrect:** Both WSUS 3.0 and System Center Essentials 2010 enable the targeted deployment of updates by using computer groups.

2. **Correct Answer: C**

   A. **Incorrect:** Because each college's IT department needs the ability to approve updates, you should not configure downstream servers as replicas.

   B. **Incorrect:** Replica servers do not enable local administrators to approve updates.

   C. **Correct:** Configuring one upstream server to retrieve updates from the Internet and five downstream autonomous servers—one for each college—meets the question's objectives of minimizing bandwidth use and enabling each college's IT department to approve or reject updates.

   D. **Incorrect:** Although five autonomous servers would enable each college's IT department to approve updates, it would not minimize the amount of traffic between the university and Microsoft Update.

3. **Correct Answers: A and C**

   A. **Correct:** You need to create computer groups on the WSUS server and then assign clients to these computer groups using GPOs applied to departmental OUs.

   B. **Incorrect:** You need to assign the GPOs to OUs rather than to the domain.

   C. **Correct:** You need to create computer groups on the WSUS server and then assign clients to these computer groups using GPOs applied to departmental OUs.

   D. **Incorrect:** You do not need to create a security group, but you must create a WSUS computer group.

   E. **Incorrect:** You do not need to create a security group, but you must create a WSUS computer group.

4. **Correct Answer: C**

   A. **Incorrect:** Although it might be possible with a significant amount of effort, creating a scheduled task is not the best way to deploy updates using WSUS. You should create an Automatic Approval rule that uses the PatchTest WSUS computer group as a target.

   B. **Incorrect:** An Automatic Approval rule that deploys updates to the All Computers group will deploy updates to all computers, not to the PatchTest WSUS group as specified in the question.

   C. **Correct:** Automatic Approval rules use WSUS computer groups as targets for update deployment.

   D. **Incorrect:** Automatic Approval rules do not use security groups as targets for update deployment.

5. **Correct Answer: B**

   A. **Incorrect:** You cannot use WSUS 3.0 SP2 to deploy updates for third-party applications.

   B. **Correct:** You can use System Center Configuration Manager 2007 to deploy updates for third-party applications, and a single System Center Configuration Manager 2007 server can service more than 5,000 computers running Windows Vista, 1,000 computers running Windows 7, and 200 computers running Windows Server 2008 R2 if the other System Center Configuration Manager 2007 server fails.

   C. **Incorrect:** A System Center Essentials 2010 server is limited to providing updates to 500 clients and 50 servers. In the event that one System Center Essential 2010 server fails, it will not be able to provide coverage to all the hosts at the university.

   D. **Incorrect:** Five System Center Essentials 2010 servers will not provide adequate coverage for the university environment. At most, five System Center Essentials 2010 servers can cover 2,500 computers running Windows Vista and Windows 7, and 250 computers running Windows Server 2008 R2.

Lesson 2

1. **Correct Answer: D**

   A. **Incorrect:** You cannot use System Center Essentials 2007 SP2 to manage more than 500 client computers or 30 server computers.

   B. **Incorrect:** You cannot use WSUS 3.0 SP2 to generate compliance reports, although it can generate simple patch deployment reports.

   C. **Incorrect:** You can deploy only one System Center Essentials 2010 instance in a domain.

   D. **Correct:** You can use only System Center Configuration Manager 2007 R3 in a single domain environment to provide update and configuration compliance reporting when there are more than 500 client computers or 50 servers.

2. **Correct Answer: C**

   A. **Incorrect:** You use the Security Configuration and Analysis tool to apply template files rather than XML-formatted, role-based security policies.

   B. **Incorrect:** You cannot use the Microsoft Baseline Security Analyzer tool to apply security policies.

   C. **Correct:** You can use the *Scwcmd* command-line tool to apply an XML-formatted, role-based security policy remotely.

   D. **Incorrect:** You cannot use Windows Server Update Services 3.0 SP2 to apply role-based security policies.

3. **Correct Answer: A**

   A. **Correct:** Security settings applied through Group Policy objects override security settings applied using the *Scwcmd* command-line utility, the Security Configuration Wizard, and the Security Configuration and Analysis tool.

   B. **Incorrect:** Security settings applied through the *Scwcmd* command-line tool can be overridden by security settings applied through GPOs.

   C. **Incorrect:** Security settings applied through the Security Configuration and Analysis tool can be overridden by security settings applied through GPOs.

   D. **Incorrect:** Security settings applied through the Security Configuration Wizard tool can be overridden by security settings applied through GPOs.

4. **Correct Answer: C**

   A. **Incorrect:** Update Status Summary will provide information about the number of computers on which the update did not install but will not provide detailed information about specific computers.

   B. **Incorrect:** Computer Status Summary will provide summary information about computers and updates but will not provide detailed information about specific computers.

   C. **Correct:** The Update Detailed Status report provides a per-update report with a list of computers and their update status. Navigating to the page that holds information about the problematic update will enable you to locate the necessary computers quickly.

   D. **Incorrect:** A Computer Detailed Status report will give you one-computer-per-page information about the status of particular updates. Although it would be possible to check every page of such a report to determine which computers did not have the update, this requires significantly more effort than having a single page that lists each computer's status for a particular update.

Chapter 11: Case Scenario Answers

Case Scenario 1: Deploying WSUS 3.0 SP2 at Fabrikam, Inc.

1. Add the CIO's account to the WSUS Reporters local group. This will enable the CIO to run reports without being assigned unnecessary administrative privileges.

2. Configure the downstream WSUS servers at the Fabrikam satellite offices as WSUS replicas. This way, the downstream servers will automatically inherit the update approvals and the computer group configuration at the head office WSUS server.

3. Instruct the CIO to generate an Update Detailed Status report. This will enable her to bring up an update report page that will list the specific computers on which the update failed to install.

Case Scenario 2: Security Policies at Coho Vineyard and Coho Winery

1. Create a role-based security policy for each processor architecture.

2. You can use the Security Configuration Wizard or the *Scwcmd* command-line utility to create role-based security policies for the intranet servers.

3. Create a script that uses *Scwcmd* and your administrative credentials in the *cohowinery .internal* forest to check the configuration of the intranet servers and to output the report in HTML format. Run the script as a scheduled task on your management server in the *cohovineyard.internal* forest.

Glossary

Symbols and Numbers

6to4 An IPv4-to-IPv6 transition technology that allows IPv6 traffic to commute IPv4 networks without requiring the use of a specific tunnel.

A

AAAA forward lookup record A forward lookup resource record mapping a hostname to an IPv6 address.

Active Directory Federation Services (AD FS) Integration of different authentication systems that allows organizations to more securely establish and extend trust with partners and other external groups while reducing the complexity of managing multiple identities.

Active Directory integrated zone A DNS zone that, instead of existing as a file (*domain_name.com.dns*), is stored within Active Directory, providing enhancements including multiple master capability, increased security, and automatic replication.

Active Directory Migration Tool An integrated toolset to facilitate migration and restructuring tasks in an Active Directory infrastructure.

Active Directory Rights Management Services (AD RMS) A technology that allows an organization to control access to and usage of confidential data.

Anycast A network frame that targets one of multiple destination nodes that offer the same service and/or replicated data.

App-V Microsoft's Application Virtualization service.

Attribute store A database or directory service that contains attributes about clients.

Authentication A method to check that users are who they say they are.

Authoritative restore Restores domain controllers to a specific point in time, and marks objects in Active Directory as being authoritative with respect to their replication partners.

Authorization A method to determine whether a user has access to resources through permissions or administrative rights through group membership and delegation.

Auto approval Process to automatically select (approve) updates for deployment without testing. This is usually used on signature and definition updates. Auto approval could introduce some risk into the organization if updates conflict with installed (usually third-party or custom) applications.

Autonomous WSUS server Receives updates from an upstream WSUS server but must be administered locally regarding update approvals and computer groups.

Autonomy The ability to independently manage all or part of service management (service autonomy) and all or part of the data stored in or protected by AD DS (data autonomy).

B

BIND server Berkley Internet Name Domain server. A DNS server service that operates on a Linux or UNIX system, currently on version 9.

BitLocker A data protection feature available in Windows Vista, Windows 7, and Windows Server 2008 R2 that provides data encryption for full volumes and integrity checking for early boot components.

Branch office Remote location within the organization, often with limited technical support or resources.

C

Central site System Center Configuration Manager site that is positioned at the top of the System Center Configuration Manager hierarchy.

Certificate The Federation Service in AD FS 2.0 uses certificates for issuing and receiving tokens, publishing federation metadata, or communicating through Secure Sockets Layer (SSL).

Child site System Center Configuration Manager site that has upstream sites in the System Center Configuration Manager hierarchy; a child site can be a primary or secondary site. Child sites send System Center Configuration Manager client information upstream to parent sites.

Claim rule A rule that is created with a claim rule template or that is written using the claim rule language in AD FS 2.0 that defines how to generate, transform, pass through, or filter claims.

Claim A statement that one subject makes about itself or another subject.

Claims provider A Federation Service that issues claims for a particular transaction.

Compliance reporting Often a necessary component of legal and regulatory compliance requirements to prove and validate compliance.

Computer discovery Scanning process to identify computers, installed software, and system attributes on a network. Performed by using System Center Essentials.

Conditional forwarding A process where a DNS server queries an upstream DNS server that has access to a specific namespace for name resolution.

Critical updates Updates that fix significant problems with the Microsoft operating system or applications. Not all critical updates are related to fixing security vulnerabilities.

D

Data autonomy Involves control over all or part of the data stored in the directory or on member computers (member computers implies they are joined to the directory).

Data isolation Prevents administrators other than those specifically designated to control or view data from controlling or viewing a subset of data in the directory or on member computers.

Data management Administrative operations involved in managing the content stored in or protected by the directory service.

Dedicated forest root domain An AD DS domain created exclusively to function as the forest root domain.

Delegation The transfer of administrative responsibility for a specific task from a higher to a lower authority.

DFS folder targets A location separate from a folder in which data and content are stored.

DFS folder A container in a namespace that redirects clients to a folder target.

DFS namespace root The namespace root is the starting point of the namespace. A domain-based namespace can be hosted on multiple namespace servers to increase the availability of the namespace.

DFS namespace server A namespace server hosts a namespace. A namespace server can be a stand-alone server, a domain member server, or a domain controller.

DFS namespace The virtual view of shared folders in an organization. A namespace is made up of the remaining elements on this list.

DFS Referral An ordered list of targets, transparent to the user, which a client receives from a domain controller or namespace server when the user accesses DFS.

DFS Replication A multimaster replication engine that supports replication scheduling and bandwidth throttling.

Differencing disk Disk file created to maintain the changes of an original VHD file. Can be used to maintain changes for VM snapshots or deployment of VMs using a VHD file as a baseline disk.

DirectAccess A remote access connection established seamlessly by the remote access client on connection to the Internet using multiple IPsec tunnels. Requires use of IPv6 and possible IPv6 transition technologies to connect to resources in the corporate network.

Distributed File System (DFS) A feature in Windows Server 2008 R2 that facilitates access to shared files in a large network.

DNS Cache Locking A function to prohibit DNS cache poisoning.

DNS Devolution A function to walk the namespace tree querying zones during a name resolution process, typically when only a hostname is provided for resolution.

DNS Socket Pool A pool of randomized DNS source ports used to defend against DNS cache poisoning

dnscmd Command-line utility to configure or interrogate a DNS server service.

DNSSEC Domain Name System Security Extensions; a PKI/certificate-based DNS security system that digitally signs DNS-related communications.

Domain restructure migration path Involves copying AD DS objects from the original domain or forest to the new Windows Server 2008 R2 domain or forest.

Domain upgrade migration path Involves upgrading the operating system of a domain controller running Windows Server 2003 or Windows Server 2008 to Windows Server 2008 R2 or installing Windows Server 2008 R2 domain controllers into a Windows 2000 Server or Windows Server 2003 domain.

Dual stack A network node that runs both IPv4 and IPv6 protocol stacks.

E

Encrypting File System (EFS) The file encryption technology built into Windows that is used optionally to encrypt files stored on NTFS volumes.

Endpoints Provide access to the federation server functionality of AD FS 2.0, such as token issuance, and the publishing of federation metadata.

F

Failover cluster A group of two or more computers used to prevent downtime for selected applications and services.

Federation Server proxy A computer running Windows Server 2008 or Windows Server 2008 R2 that has been configured using the AD FS 2.0 Proxy Configuration Wizard to act in the federation server proxy role

Federation Server A computer running Windows Server 2008 or Windows Server 2008 R2 that has been configured using the AD FS 2.0 Federation Server Configuration Wizard to act in the federation server role.

Fine-grained password policies A way to define different password and account lockout policies for different sets of users in a domain.

Forest root domain The first domain deployed in an AD DS forest.

Forwarder An upstream DNS server that has access to additional namespaces for name resolution.

Full mesh replication topology Every site connects to every other site.

G

Global unicast address A public IPv6 address targeting an unambiguous destination. These addresses are reachable in the Internet.

GlobalNames zone Provides hostname resolution without requiring a fully qualified domain name (FQDN) for resolution. Seen as the replacement for WINS NetBIOS name resolution.

Group Policy object (GPO) An AD DS object that contains Group Policy settings. GPOs are typically linked to one or more OUs.

Group Policy setting A configurable setting that determines the security and resource access applied to a user or computer account that is held in an OU.

Group Policy Enables you to systematically apply and enforce security and configuration settings on sets of users and computers.

Guests Term used to refer to the VMs running on a host.

H

Hardware and software inventory Listing of all detected computer systems and the software applications identified on those systems, along with additional operational attributes of the system.

Health Registration Authority (HRA) A service of Network Access Protection that obtains health certificates from a NAP certification authority that are issued to clients that have successfully submitted compliant System Statements of Health (SSoH).

Host Term used to refer to the Hyper-V computer.

Hub and spoke replication topology One site is designated as the hub, and other sites, called spokes, connect to the hub.

Hybrid replication topology A combination of a hub and spoke and a full mesh topology.

Hypervisor Thin management layer that runs on the hardware, providing an abstraction layer between the hardware and VMs. It is also referred to as the virtual machine monitor. Microsoft's hypervisor-based solution is Hyper-V.

I

Identity Management for UNIX A role service that enables you to integrate your Windows users in existing environments that host UNIX-based computers.

Information card Represents a user's digital identity and can be issued by a claims provider.

Interforest migration The migration of Active Directory objects between two separate forests.

Intraforest migration The migration of Active Directory objects within the same forest.

ISATAP Intra-Site Automatic Tunnel Addressing Protocol; used to commute IPv6 packets between dual-stack systems on an IPv4 network.

Isolation The ability to prevent other administrators from controlling or interfering with service management (service isolation) and controlling or viewing a subset of data in AD DS or on member computers that are joined to AD DS (data isolation).

L

Legal and regulatory compliance requirements Industry or government-imposed security and operations requirements aimed at protecting consumers, businesses, and intellectual property.

Link-local address A non-routable IPv4 (APIPA 169.254.0.0 /16) and IPv6 (fe80:: /10) address typically provided by stateless address autoconfiguration.

Loopback address An IPv6 address used to identify the localhost 0:0:0:0:0:0:0:1, which can be reduced to ::1, or an IPv4 address used to identify the localhost 127.0.0.1.

M

Microsoft Baseline Security Manager (MBSA) Security scanning tool used to identify missing updates and other vulnerabilities on local or remote Microsoft systems.

Microsoft Update Server Servers at Microsoft that supply Microsoft updates to Microsoft operating systems and applications over the Internet.

Multicast/broadcast A network frame that targets multiple destination nodes.

Multiple-sites model Consists of domain controllers distributed among two or more site objects, where subnets are associated with sites based on network information and location.

N

NAP enforcement point A logical reference point in a network where certain health criteria and connection requirements are evaluated prior to admitting a connection to a more secure zone of the network.

Network Address Translation An IPv4 technology used to share the limited public addresses among numerous nodes on a private address network. Most often found on network boundary systems, like firewalls.

Network Load Balancing (NLB) Used to support a highly used network service or application.

No Auto Restart Setting to avoid rebooting after the deployment of updates that require a restart. This is used when the system should not be interrupted (shut down) without administrator intervention.

Nonauthoritative restore Returns the domain controller to its state at the time of backup and then allows normal replication to overwrite that state with any changes that occurred after the backup was taken.

NS record A resource record identifying a DNS name server.

nslookup Command-line utility to configure or interrogate zone data on a DNS server service.

O

Organizational forest model User accounts and resources exist in the same forest and are managed separately.

Organizational unit (OU) An AD DS container that can hold user accounts, computer accounts, or both.

Parent site System Center Configuration Manager site that has downstream sites in the System Center Configuration Manager hierarchy. Collections and software distribution objects replicate down to child sites and cannot be modified at the child sites.

P

Password Settings container (PSC) An object class in AD DS that contains PSOs.

Password Settings object (PSO) An AD DS object that contains security settings that can be different from the security settings for the domain.

Physical to virtual Process of converting the operating system and applications running on a physical system into a virtual machine. Referred to as P2V.

Primary site The first site defined in a System Center Configuration Manager hierarchy that stores information about its site and its System Center Configuration Manager downstream sites within the hierarchy. This site hosts a local SQL Server database.

Primary zone The authoritative copy for a DNS zone. For a non–Active Directory–integrated zone, the primary zone is the only writable copy of the zone.

Principle of least privilege Restricts users to only those functions necessary to perform their jobs.

Products and Classifications Selection list of Microsoft applications and operating systems to synchronize updates from Microsoft Update Servers or upstream WSUS servers.

Proxy server Boundary security device in the firewall family used to provide sophisticated (typically Internet) access approvals or denials. Must be considered in the planning and deployment of a WSUS system.

R

RADIUS client Application component that communicates with the RADIUS server across a UDP transport connection. RADIUS clients are usually an application component running on remote access servers, VPN servers, network switches, or network access servers providing the initiation of the authentication request from a remote access client.

RADIUS proxy An application server brokering RADIUS communication from a RADIUS client and a RADIUS server by using a UDP transport connection.

RADIUS server The back-end service of a RADIUS client/server communication providing authentication, authorization, and accounting of usage of network services through the remote access connection.

RD Virtualization Host Role service of Remote Desktop Services utilizing the Hyper-V platform for delivery of RemoteApp and Desktop Connections through virtual machines and virtual desktops.

Read-only domain controller (RODC) A domain controller that holds AD DS information and can authenticate users and resolve DNS inquiries, but does not permit connected users to make any changes to AD DS structure. RODCs contain only a small subset of the domain's user name and password information (if any).

Read-only zone Nonwritable copy of a DNS zone, like a secondary zone or a read-only Active Directory–integrated zone on an RODC.

Regional domain model Consists of a forest root domain and one or more regional domains, which represent the geographic locations within an organization.

Relying party A Federation Service or application that consumes claims in a particular transaction.

Remote Desktop Services Name replacing previously named Terminal Services. RDS provides remote PC access to backend servers for shared applications and data.

RemoteFX New feature included in Windows Server 2008 R2 with SP1 that enables the complete delivery of Windows Experience enhancements using Remote Desktop Protocol.

Replica WSUS server A downstream WSUS server that receives updates, update approvals, and computer groups from its upstream WSUS administration server. Replica servers provide limited WSUS administrative capabilities.

Resource forest model A separate forest is used to manage resources. Resource forests do not contain user accounts other than those required for services.

Restricted access forest model A separate forest is created to contain user accounts and data that must be isolated from the rest of the organization.

Reverse look-up zone A DNS zone that enables an IP address to be resolved to a fully qualified domain name or hostname.

Role-based policy Documentation describing the security posture of a specific type of server fulfilling a specific role in the organization's IT infrastructure.

Root hints Maps IP addresses to root servers for iterative name resolution processes.

S

Scwcmd Command-line utility used to perform many Security Configuration Wizard functions.

Secondary site System Center Configuration Manager site that does not contain a local SQL Server database. Secondary sites are administered from the primary site.

Secondary zone A read-only copy of a DNS zone used to provide increased capacity, geographic distribution, load balancing, and fault tolerance for DNS name resolution.

Security baseline Minimum acceptable security level for a system. A system that drops below this threshold offers too many vulnerabilities or has already been compromised.

Security Configuration and Analysis Tool Tool used to view, compare, configure, and deploy security templates to Microsoft systems.

Security Configuration Wizard Tool to reduce the attack surface of a server by using server roles and then hardening the server to provide those few required services.

Security policy Documentation describing the security posture of an organization.

Security template Preconfigured security settings to be applied to one or more Microsoft systems.

Security updates Updates that mitigate security vulnerabilities in the Microsoft operating system or applications. Some, but not all, security updates are critical.

Server for NIS Enables a Windows Server 2008 R2 domain controller to act as a master server for one or more Network Information Service (NIS) domains.

Server hardening Process of removing vulnerabilities from a server to reduce its attack surface. This often reduces the overall functionality of the server, usually targeting a single specific function.

Service autonomy Involves control over all or part of service management and removing domain controllers as needed.

Service isolation Prevents administrators other than those specifically designated to control service management from controlling or interfering with service management.

Service management Administrative tasks involved in providing secure and reliable delivery of the directory service.

Services for Network File System (NFS) Enables file sharing between Windows-based and UNIX-based computers.

Shadow group A security group that contains all the user accounts in an associated OU. You cannot apply a PSO to an OU, so you apply it to the shadow group instead.

SID History A feature that supports the migration of user and group accounts between domains and allows the user accounts to retain access to resources in their original domain.

Single site model Consists of a single site object, where all domains in the forest belong to the same site object, and all IP subnets are associated with this site object.

Single-domain model A forest with a single domain, where any domain controller can authenticate any user in the forest, and all domain controllers can be global catalog servers.

Site link bridge Connects two or more site links and enables transitivity between site links.

Site links Connect the sites to form the desired replication topology.

Snapshot Capturing the current running configuration of a guest VM stored whereby the original VHD

file is stored as a read-only file. Changes are written to another VHD file.

Software update point Store of software available for client installation via System Center Configuration Manager advertisements or scripts.

SRV record A resource record identifying a directory service server.

Staggered rollout Deployment of updates to selected systems, often used to reduce risk (if the updates might cause problems), manage network bandwidth, assure system availability, or manage issues that might arise from the deployment (help desk support).

Start of Authority (SOA) A resource record for a DNS zone that defines information about the zone. Details include the primary name server, the email address of the domain administrator, and TTLs relating to the zone refresh interval and record expiration.

Starter Group Policy objects (GPOs) Derive from a Group Policy object (GPO), and provide the ability to store a collection of Administrative Template policy settings in a single object.

Statement of Health (SoH) Used by a NAP client to represent the client's claim about its health state.

Stub zone A DNS zone that contains SOA and the NS and associated A records of a zone so the local DNS server can locate name servers for the target zone to provide name resolution. Reduces, but does not eliminate, zone transfer traffic.

Subsystem for UNIX-Based Applications (SUA) A Windows Server 2008 R2 feature that enables enterprises to run UNIX-based applications on computers running Windows Server 2008 R2.

Synchronization Copying computer groups, updates, or approvals from a WSUS source server to a downstream WSUS server.

System Center Configuration Manager Management and deployment system for medium to large-sized businesses. Supports deploying Microsoft updates as well as third-party software deployment. Provides more features than WSUS and System Center Essentials.

System Center Essentials 2010 A systems management application targeted to the small business environment; used to monitor application deployment, patch management, remote control, hardware and software inventory, and alert system for administration of client and server computing systems.

System Center Essentials agent Software deployed to System Center Essentials managed nodes that communicates with the System Center Essentials server(s).

System Center Essentials Management and deployment system for small to medium-sized businesses. Supports deploying Microsoft updates as well as third-party software deployment. Provides more features than WSUS.

System Health Agent (SHA) The client component used to communicate the client health state to the System Health Validator server.

System Health Validator (SHV) The server side of the client/server communication between the SHA and the SHV that verifies the client's declarations of its health state.

Systems Center Configuration Manager 2007 Microsoft's replacement for Systems Management Server (SMS) provides for systems management targeted to medium to large businesses; provides application deployment, patch management, remote control, hardware and software inventory, and alert system for administration of client and server computing systems. It also provides management of multiple sites and locations with hierarchical management integrated into the systems management application.

T

Teredo An IPv4-to-IPv6 transition technology that allows IPv6 traffic to commute IPv4 networks through the use of a tunnel. Specifically targets NAT server passthrough.

Third-party application updates Cannot be deployed using WSUS, but can be deployed using System Center Essentials or System Center Configuration Manager.

U

Unicast A network frame that targets a single, unambiguous destination.

Unique-local address A private network IPv6 (fc00::/7) address. Internet routers block unique-local addresses.

Unspecified address Used to identify the absence of an IPv6 address, 0:0:0:0:0:0:0:0, that can be reduced to ::.

Update approval Configuration setting on each Microsoft update to support the process allowing for the testing of updates and selection for deployment once testing has completed successfully.

Update Languages Updates are supplied in multiple languages. Selection list of languages supported within your organization, used to identify updates required for download to your WSUS servers.

Update testing Process to verify that new updates do not conflict with installed applications and drivers. Usually done before approval and deployment of the updates.

Upgrade-then-restructure migration path Also known as a two-phase migration, involves upgrading the original domain or forest and then migrating AD DS objects to a new Windows Server 2008 R2 domain or forest.

V

Virtual hard disk File used to emulate a hard disk drive of a VM.

Virtual Machine Manager Microsoft application server that provides support for virtual machines (VMs) including rapid provisioning of VMs, physical to virtual conversion, and virtual (VMware) to virtual (Microsoft) conversion. Used in System Center Essentials and System Center Configuration Manager.

VPN Reconnect Newest VPN protocol for remote access using Internet Protocol security (IPsec) Tunnel Mode with Internet Key Encryption version 2 (IKEv2) for the connection.

Vulnerability scanner Specialized system that compares target systems to a database of known vulnerabilities.

W

Wake on LAN Optional feature built into the BIOS on some network adaptors triggering switch on of the computer if it has been shut down and if the adapter receives what is commonly called a "magic" packet. Wake on LAN can be used to deploy updates during nonworking hours, even if the systems have been shut down for the night.

Windows Server Update Services (WSUS) Free add-on service for Windows Server that can provide updates to Microsoft operating systems and applications.

WINS replication partners WINS servers that share NetBIOS name to IP address records.

WSUS Administrator Administrative user with privileges to manage and configure the WSUS update system and process.

WSUS all computers The collection of all WSUS targeted systems.

WSUS client-side targeting Configuring client systems by specifying their WSUS server.

WSUS computer groups Logical groupings of computers to aid in the update management and approval process. Typically, the computers within a computer group have similar applications and security requirements and therefore have similar update requirements. Computers can reside in multiple computer groups.

WSUS Configuration Wizard Utility built into WSUS to simplify the configuration of the update system.

WSUS downstream server WSUS server that receives updates, update approvals. or both from a WSUS server higher in the WSUS hierarchy.

WSUS hierarchy Structured relationships between WSUS servers within an organization for purposes of capacity, geographic distribution, load balancing, the acquisition of updates (bandwidth management), and update approvals.

WSUS Reporter Typically a help desk role to verify patch status, but with no privilege for WSUS system configuration.

WSUS server-side targeting Configuring the WSUS system to deploy updates to specified client systems.

WSUS unassigned computers WSUS targeted systems that do not reside within a WSUS computer group.

WSUS upstream server/source server Upstream WSUS server used to provide updates, update approvals, or both.

Z

Zone transfer Copying or updating DNS records from a master zone to a secondary zone.

Index

Symbols and Numbers

3-leg firewalls, 220
6to4 technology, 50, 72
6to4cfg tool, 47
802.1x standard, 251, 261–265
80-20 rule, 57

A

A (host) records, 6, 9, 22
AAAA records
  about, 9, 72
  IPv6 addresses and, 18
  practice exercises, 28
access control lists (ACLs), 199, 263
access-based enumeration, 406, 410
Account Administrators, 174
Account Operators group, 173
Accounting Configuration Wizard, 241
ACLs (access control lists), 199, 263
Active Directory Certificate Services. *See* AD CS (Active Directory Certificate Services)
Active Directory Domain Services. *See* AD DS (Active Directory Domain Services)
Active Directory Domain Services Installation Wizard. *See* DCPromo utility
Active Directory Federation Services (AD FS), 143, 160
Active Directory integrated zone, 71
Active Directory Lightweight Directory Services (AD LDS), 78, 286, 483
Active Directory Migration Tool (ADMT), 140, 160
Active Directory Rights Management Services. *See* AD RMS (Active Directory Rights Management Services)
Active Directory Rights Management Services console, 428

Active Directory Users and Computers, 307
AD CS (Active Directory Certificate Services), 229, 452, 484
AD DS (Active Directory Domain Services)
  App-V support, 392
  auditing compliance, 180–181
  boundary networks and, 255
  delegating administration, 168–171
  designing domain controller placement, 117–121
  designing domain structure, 85–92
  designing forest structure, 77–84
  designing functional levels, 92–97
  designing printer location policies, 121–124
  designing replication, 112–116
  designing schema, 97–98
  designing site structure, 109–112
  designing trusts, 99–100
  DNS planning recommendations, 5
  identifying role of, 78–79
  integrating with DNS infrastructure, 24–25
  planning maintenance and recovery procedures, 434–438
  practice exercises, 125–130
  restartable, 437–438
  Server Core support, 286
  stopping at command line, 438
  Windows Server integration, 5
AD FS (Active Directory Federation Services), 143, 148–150, 160
AD LDS (Active Directory Lightweight Directory Services), 78, 286, 483
AD RMS (Active Directory Rights Management Services)
  about, 428–429, 448
  applications supported, 431
  creating/viewing rights-protected information, 429–430
  smart card authentication and, 202
  Windows SharePoint Services and, 416

G

H

M

N

About the Authors

DAVID R. MILLER (PCI QSA, SME; MCT; MCITPro; MCSE Windows NT 4.0, Windows 2000, and Windows 2003: Security; CISSP; LPT; ECSA; CEH; CWNA; CCNA; CNE; Security+; A+; N+, etc.) is a consultant in the IT industry who specializes in compliance, security, and network engineering. David is an instructor, an author, and a technical editor of books, curricula, certification exams, and computer-based training videos. He regularly contributes as a Microsoft subject matter expert (SME) on product lines including Microsoft Windows Server 2008, Windows Server 2008 R2, Microsoft Exchange Server 2007, Windows 7, and Windows Vista. He is the lead author on this book, now in its second edition, and on the information systems security book titled *Security Administrator Street Smarts* for Sybex and Wiley Publishing, about to be released in its third edition. David has coauthored two books on Windows Vista for Que Publishing and another book on Exchange Server 2007 for Microsoft Press. In addition, David is working on two new titles for Microsoft Press and a new book for Pearson Education; all three new books are scheduled for publication in 2011.

PAUL MANCUSO (SME, CCSI, DCUCSS, DCNISS, CCNP, CCIP, CCNA, CCDA, VCP, VCAP-DCA, CTT+, CCISP, MCT, MCITP:EA) has offered consulting in the network services area for more than 21 years and has also provided authorized instruction for Cisco, VMware, and Microsoft for more than 18 years.

Paul currently provides extensive training and consulting in data center design and support for Cisco, VMware, and Microsoft technologies. He earned a bachelor of science in zoology and pre-med from Ohio State University, deciding late in his studies to turn his attention toward business services, finance, marketing, and computers. His studies in these areas introduced him to the emerging field of local area networks (LANs), which later spearheaded a revolution in business processes. This early introduction to LANs prompted him to begin a career in network integration upon his graduation. It has become a passion ever since.

He has previously authored books on Windows Vista, Microsoft Exchange Server 2007, and Windows Server 2008. In addition to books, Paul has authored courseware for Microsoft and Cisco courses, and he is currently involved in authoring Cisco labs. Combining his real-world consulting and training experiences, Paul has come to understand the complexities involved in delivering network services in the data center that is rapidly evolving today. His enthusiasm for networking is evident in every lecture he gives and work he authors.

JOHN POLICELLI (MVP for Directory Services) is a solutions-focused IT consultant with Avanade Canada. John has more than a decade of success in architecture, security, strategic planning, and disaster recovery planning. He has designed and implemented dozens of complex directory service, collaboration, web, networking, and enterprise security solutions. John has spent many years focused on identity and access management and has provided thought leadership for some of the largest installations of Active Directory directory service in Canada. He has been involved as an author, technical reviewer, and SME for more than 75 training, certification, and technical white paper projects.

ORIN THOMAS, (MCITP, MCT, MVP) is an author, trainer, and frequent public speaker who has authored more than a dozen books for Microsoft Press. He is the convener of the Melbourne Security and Infrastructure Group and a Microsoft vTSP. His most recent books are on Windows 7 and Exchange Server 2010.

IAN MCLEAN (MCSE, MCITP, MCT) has more than 40 years' experience in industry, commerce, and education. He started his career as an electronics engineer before going into distance learning and then education as a university professor. He currently provides technical support for a government organization and runs his own consultancy company. Ian has written 22 books in addition to many papers and technical articles. Books he has previously coauthored include *MCITP Self-Paced Training Kit (Exam 70-444): Optimizing and Maintaining a Database Administration Solution Using Microsoft SQL Server 2005* and *MCITP Self-Paced Training Kit (Exam 70-646): Windows Server Administration: Windows Server 2008 Administrator*. When not writing, Ian annoys everyone by playing guitar very badly. However, he is forced to play instrumentals because his singing is even worse.

J.C. MACKIN (MCITP, MCTS, MCSE, MCDST, MCT) is a writer, editor, consultant, and trainer who has been working with Microsoft networks for more than a decade. Books he has previously authored or coauthored include *MCSA/MCSE Self-Paced Training Kit (Exam 70-291): Implementing, Managing, and Maintaining a Microsoft Windows Server 2003 Network Infrastructure, MCITP Self-Paced Training Kit (Exam 70-443): Designing a Database Server Infrastructure Using Microsoft SQL Server 2005*, and *MCITP Self-Paced Training Kit (Exam 70-622): Supporting and Troubleshooting Applications on a Windows Vista Client for Enterprise Support Technicians*. He also holds a master's degree in telecommunications and network management. When not working with computers, J.C. can be found with a panoramic camera photographing medieval villages in Italy or France.

What do you think of this book?

We want to hear from you!
To participate in a brief online survey, please visit:

microsoft.com/learning/booksurvey

Tell us how well this book meets your needs—what works effectively, and what we can do better. Your feedback will help us continually improve our books and learning resources for you.

Thank you in advance for your input!